The Price Guide to
AUTOGRAPHS

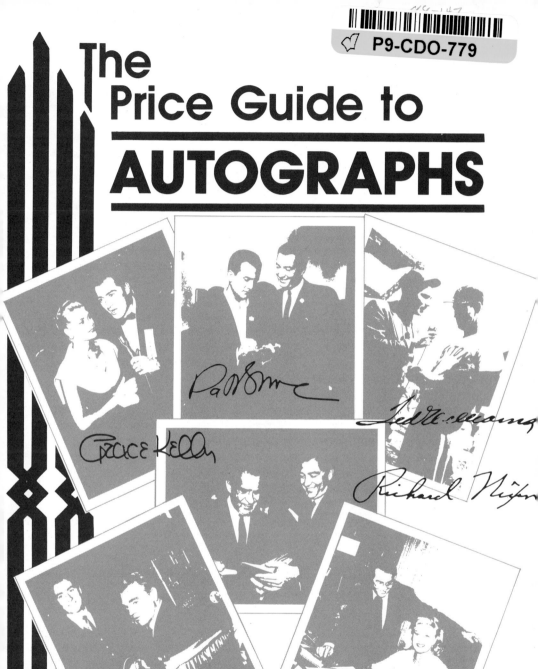

George Sanders • Helen Sanders • Ralph Roberts

Cover design and interior layout: Anthony Jacobson
Editor: Lynne Weatherman

Library of Congress Catalog Card Number 87-51437

ISBN 0-87069-505-3

10 9 8 7 6 5 4 3 2 1

Published by

A Capital Cities/ABC, Inc. Company

Wallace-Homestead Book Company
201 King of Prussia Road
Radnor, Pennsylvania 19089

Contents

Foreword

It was with great excitement that I learned of the plans made by Helen and George Sanders and Ralph Roberts to publish a comprehensive book on autographs, and with great pleasure that I agreed to write a foreword for their book.

As collectors of autograph material in any form, we all contend with two basic difficulties: determining authenticity, and affixing a realistic value to the piece or pieces in question. This is true whether we are buying or selling; whether we are novices or experienced collectors; whether our interest is only in passing, or whether we are scholars or hobbyists or investors, or even dealers deriving our livelihood from the field.

The problem of determining accurate autograph values in any comprehensive fashion is a mammoth undertaking. It is unlike coins or stamps, where condition or variety are the sole determinants of value. An extremely fine 1865 Indian cent will be worth roughly the same no matter which one we examine. An average mint specimen of a 30-cent Colombian commemorative stamp will similarly have no significant fluctuations in value. However, if we attempt to affix a value on a John F. Kennedy letter written in his own hand, the problem of a value becomes infinitely more difficult. Are we talking about a note from Kennedy as Senator, sending best wishes and enclosing his autograph? Or is it a long letter he has written as President, discussing the Cuban missile crisis? The value of one may be ten times the value of the other; yet both can undoubtedly be called *ALSs*.

A second, essential difficulty in an undertaking of this nature concerns the sheer magnitude of the task at hand. A listing of all of the mutual stock funds in the United States involves compiling values for perhaps 2300 entries. A complete series of U.S. cents from 1793 to the present numbers perhaps 300 pieces. Yet, the scope of those who have written letters or signed documents or photographs in the fields of history, politics, literature, sports, art, entertainment, or science can easily number in the tens of thousands.

In the quarter-century that I have been collecting autograph material, I can count on the fingers of one hand the efforts to publish a comprehensive reference on autograph values. Noted autograph dealer Charles Hamilton published the last such book more than ten years ago (*The Book of Autographs*). His reference contained the values of some 5000 pieces. In this book, George Sanders, Helen Sanders, and Ralph Roberts have compiled more than 20,000 entries.

A second and equally important criterion is that of the authenticity of signatures. With the demand for autograph material dating back nearly 200 years in the United States alone, the temptation for forgers dates back nearly as far. Robert Sprint derived a substantial portion of his livelihood by forging George Washington's signature during the mid-nineteenth century, and Joseph Cosey forged Abraham Lincoln's signature 80 years later with such accuracy that many of his pieces remain in collections even to this date. In 1987, one forger reproduced autograph letters of John F. Kennedy which were so accurate that the country's foremost autograph dealers believed their authenticity. Only a 1982 watermark gave the perpetrator away! As long as there is demand, there will be the need to meet the demand illegally.

Over the past several decades, the pressure to meet the tremendous volume of correspondence has caused many celebrities and other notables to retain secretaries who have learned to reproduce the signatures of their bosses with astonishing accuracy. Presidents Wilson, Hoover, Kennedy, and Carter are only a few who have relied on this method.

As technology has advanced, the advent of the Autopen machine has made determination of authentic signatures even more difficult. An ingenious little device which can reproduce identical signatures or even entire passages written by the owner, it is quite a timesaver. Unfortunately, because the original, authentic signatures are reproduced *exactly* by machine, the distinction between real and reproduced is quite difficult to determine. When Dwight D. Eisenhower was President of Columbia University in 1950, he relied upon the autopen machine to handle correspondence for him. To date, no less than 13 different secretarial and 8 different autopen signatures of John F. Kennedy have been discovered.

In an attempt to deal with this problem, Mr. and Mrs. Sanders and Mr. Roberts have reproduced hundreds of signatures in the pages that follow. No autograph reference work to date has so varied and large a number of autograph examples in a single volume.

It can undoubtedly be argued that variations in the condition and content of a piece can significantly affect its value. Yet no one can dispute the inestimable value of a work which provides a basic starting point for us all, as this one does.

As president of the largest autograph club in the world, a private collector, and a very part-time dealer, I have awaited the publication of this work with both interest and anticipation.

I hope that the pages which follow will provide you with as much knowledge and enjoyment as they do me.

Michael Saks, President
Universal Autograph Collector's Club

Acknowledgments

These are the men and women (in alphabetical order) who have made the interesting hobby of autograph collecting one of the most rewarding experiences of our lives. They are all responsible for the happiness and financial gains that made this never-ending pursuit such a truly exciting experience. In most cases this list includes personal friends, acquaintances, competitors, suppliers, and, most importantly, learned authors and advisors.

Robert Adkins
Jeanette and Terry Alford
Raleigh De Geer Amyx
Tim Anderson
Charles Apfelbaum
Pam and Todd M. Axelrod
Conway Barker
Catherine Barnes
Robert F. Batchelder
Leon Becker
Mary A. Benjamin
Bob Bennett
Susan and Patrick Bennett
Marvin B. Blatt
Norman Boas
Bonnie and Edward Bomsey
Harvey Brandwein
Frederic Castaing
Karen and Roger Christensen
Herman Darvick
Roy Deeley
Robert DeShazo
Sophie Dupre
Robert "Bob" Eaton
Gene Elliot
Joan Enders
Frederick M. Evans
Gary Eyler
Joe Fawls
Joseph Fricelli
Roger E. Gilchrist

Phyllis Goldman
Jack B. Good
Chandler Gordon
Jerry Granat
Carl W. Greene
Linda and Bill Hagan
Charles and Diane Hamilton
Don Harman
Doris Harris
Paul Hartunian
Paul Harvey
Sen. Mark O. Hatfield
Celie and Jim Hayes
Dr. Elizabeth Hazelton-Vincent
Raymond Helsel
Jeanne Hoyt
Hudson Rogue Company
Sen. Henry M. Jackson
Christopher C. Jaeckel
Betty and Rod Johnson
Brian Kathenes
Kristin and Michael Kern
Sy Kessler
Stephen Koschal
Ann Krafthofer
Joe Kraus
George H. LaBarre
Neale Lanigan
Robert A. LeGresley
Peggy and Colin Lehmann
Alan Levi

Stephen Levy
William Linehan
James Lowe
David H. Lowenhertz
George S. Lowry
Bill Luetge
Joseph Maddalena
M. Wesley Marans
Peggy and George McGill
Nancy McGlashan
Charles and Pam McKeen
Albert R. McLaughlin
Dennis Means
George Robert Minkoff
Michael Minor
Gil Moody
Howard S. Mott
Alfred "Chip" Muchin
Eugene Muchin
Alain Nicolas
Dr. F. Don Nidiffer
Donn Noble
Karen and James Oleson
Sen. Robert W. Packwood
Jerry E. Patterson
Alice Phillips
Cordelia and Tom Platt
Robert L. Polk
Lynn Pruett
Ray Rawlins
Diana J. Rendell

Kenneth W. Rendell
Sen. Abraham Ribicoff
Paul C. Richards
Stanley J. Richmond
Ibbie and Carl F. Roberts
Hinda Rose
Ranette and Robert Ross
Deirdre and Earle Rowell
Joseph Rubinfine
Sheila and Rhodes T. Rumsey
Joseph R. Sakmyster
Charles Saks
Michael Saks

Donna and Stephen Sanders
George Marston Sanders
David Schulson
Norman Schwab
Pat and Charles Searle
Louis and Gemma Sica
Paul G. Sifton
Kay and Merv Slotnik
Ruth and Dale A. Sorenson
Gerard A. J. Stodolski
George Sullivan
Sy Sussman
Georgia Terry

Bob Tollett
Wallace Turner
Jim Twelmeyer
Cornelius Vanderbilt, Jr.
Larry Vrzalik
Susan and Eliot Wadopian
Dan Weinberg
Dr. B. C. West, Jr.
Geoffrey Whitehead
Evan Williams
John Wilson
William J. Wright
Gary Zimet

In memorial to H. Roger Phillips, Jerry Redlich, and London's Winifred A. Myers.

And to Presidents Herbert Hoover, Harry S. Truman, Dwight D. Eisenhower, John F. Kennedy, Richard M. Nixon, Lyndon B. Johnson, and Ronald Reagan, who made such large and important contributions to our personal collection in person.

And to Malcolm Forbes, Henry Huntington, Adrian H. Joline, and J. P. Morgan, whose collections inspired all those who ever nervously trembled while requesting a celebrity's signature.

1
The Joy and Magic of Autograph Collecting

There are—according to nationally recognized autograph expert and leading author in the field, Charles Hamilton—more than 2,000,000 people who now collect autographs and manuscripts, with more than 20,000 newcomers joining the hobby each year.

Even more than stamps, autographs have a thrill and magic about them. More and more collectors are happily discovering this. Demand for quality reference books on this fascinating and profitable pursuit is widespread.

Stamp collecting, until this book, has had one huge advantage over autograph and manuscript collecting, namely *The Scott Catalogue* (Scott Standard Postage Stamp Catalogue, Amos Press, Sidney, Ohio).

This stamp collectors' bible has gone through close to 150 editions. Each new edition published is guaranteed many tens of thousands of *automatic* sales from collectors and dealers who dare not be without the most current standard pricing information. Overall, Scott's has now sold in the millions of copies. Such a price guide for autographs and manuscripts has long been needed. Wallace-Homestead's *Price Guide to Autographs* is not just a good idea; it is already *wanted* by thousands of autograph and manuscript collectors who would, as stamp collectors do Scott's, automatically order it every year. There is simply no other comprehensive standard pricing guide in the field.

The fact of life for the millions of us who currently collect autographs, and for those newcomers constantly joining this exciting hobby and profession, is that there is now no other guideline to follow except dealers' asking prices.

That needs no amplification as to who has the advantage and the ability to make the superior deal. Digging through auction prices realized on similar material is a bit better, but unfortunately that calls for a lot of time and expense.

So whether you want to buy or sell, *The Price Guide to Autographs* will be invaluable to you. Here, in one handy volume, is more information on the collecting and pricing of autographs than has ever been offered before in one place. We sincerely hope that it will benefit you for years to come.

What's It Worth?

That old document or letter you've just found may be worth thousands of dollars. Or practically nothing.

The first thing to learn about the fascinating field of autograph and manuscript collecting is that age alone means little. Why? Consider the flood of paper that you personally come in contact with weekly—grocery shopping lists, letters from Aunt Sally, canceled checks in your bank statement envelope, memos from the boss, your child's homework, recipes, casually scribbled reminders to yourself, and dozens of other examples. A mountain of handwritten paper—signed and unsigned—towers in all our lives. And, folks, it has always been this way. Millions upon millions of documents have accompanied mankind down through the centuries. So the manuscript has to be really old to be worth much simply because of that one fact.

We may think 1776 was long ago, very ancient times. But as well-known autograph dealer Charles Hamilton states in his widely respected *Collecting Autographs and Manuscripts* (University of Oklahoma Press, 1974), the serious collector and dealer values European documents for their age only if they date from before 1400. In the United States, the dividing line between old and modern, Hamilton states, is 1650. What, then, makes a more recent autograph or manuscript sell for thousands to a dealer or at auction? Two things. The first is the more obvious: a famous person's signature or some kind of association with that person.

An excellent example of association are the letters of James Speed, Attorney General of the United States under Abraham Lincoln in 1864 and 1865. The Civil War and its aftermath overshadowed Speed and he is now lost in the mists of history.

But many of Speed's official letters—written by his clerk and only signed by Speed—are now highly collectible. That clerk was Walt Whitman. Hence, the letters are valuable not for whose autograph is on them, but for the handwriting. Knowing history and being able to prove association for a document can make a casual find, bought for a pittance, into a sought-after collectible worth hundreds or thousands of dollars.

While autographs of celebrities are often cut out of letters and the signature alone sold, they are worth more if left attached to the letter or other manuscript. A note on White House stationery from Franklin D. Roosevelt is worth more, for example, than just his signed name; one of Thomas Wolfe's novels autographed by Wolfe is worth more than just his signed name. Speaking of books, a caution is necessary here. It was common practice during the nineteenth century to include a facsimile of the author's signature in the front of his or her books. These are worthless. You can usually tell a genuine signing from a printed facsimile by holding the page up to the light and examining it from the back. If the ink has not penetrated into the paper, then it was probably printed—which adds no value to the book.

The march of technology has continued to make the collection of celebrity autographs more difficult. Signing machines (Autopens) have relieved busy politicians of the onerous duties of actually signing the many letters they send out. An appeal for political donations from Gerald Ford, Jimmy Carter, or Ronald Reagan may carry what looks like a personal signature, but isn't. These have no real value.

Going a bit further back, many of the notes from Dwight D. Eisenhower were signed for him by other people. Authentication by the collector requires comparison with a known signature by that person. Buying autographs from a reputable dealer who handles a large volume of autographs is one sure way to avoid facsimiles or, worse, forgeries.

The second criterion for collecting manuscripts is historical or topical association. Just as stamp collectors might accumulate only stamps with the pictures of dogs or heads of state, a document collector might specialize only in Presidential autographs or—as J. P. Morgan did in beginning his famous collection—the signatures of Methodist and Episcopal bishops. A collector could, for example, gather letters of Civil War soldiers, or those of World War I doughboys, using a unified and interesting theme to make the whole worth more than the part.

Though a person who holds autographs and manuscripts merely for their investment potential misses out on much of the magic enjoyed by the true collector, prices typically continue to increase. Hamilton, in his book, gives the example of the refugees who left Nazi Germany at the onset of World War II. The lucky few who did manage to escape were stripped of all their jewels, family estates, paintings, and cash. They were allowed by the border guards to pass, in many cases, carrying only a handful of worthless old family papers.

If Marshal Göring, an avid autograph collector, had realized the millions of marks that left the Third Reich in the form of rare letters written by Martin Luther, Voltaire, Beethoven, Napoleon, and others, he might have insisted on personally serving as a customs agent. Those fortunate people who got their assets out in this manner were able to sell them and start afresh in the New World.

The advice that Hamilton and others give in starting an autograph collection of your own is not to specialize too much, but rather to gather five or six different collections at the same time. Experts liken this to the way that a stock investor diversifies his or her portfolio. One example given is what would have happened if you had started collecting 30 years ago in the categories of science, music, World War I, Napoleon, and American Western autographs. Except for the World War I items, in which prices have declined, the collection would have held its value. Plus, because of dramatic increases in values for music and science items, the overall worth would be considerably more than your original outlay.

Another important advantage of diversification is that you can afford to wait on *safe* buys, avoiding premium prices. Since you are collecting in a number of different categories, the opportunities for lower prices will be greater.

Additionally, the wider selection of material will probably be more interesting to your friends. Researching in several fields will also keep each fresher and more exciting to you.

The true rewards of autograph and manuscript collection come not from financial gain, but through the romance of holding true written history. The aura that seems to glow from a paper that George Washington touched and wrote upon, a check signed by Orville Wright, an autographed first edition of Mark Twain's, Napoleon's signature, a letter from Theodore Roosevelt—all these and many others can warm you with the flame of our mutual heritage, as can, equally, the heart-touching letter of a Civil War soldier, little more than a boy, to his sister back home. All these and more are examples of the attraction of owning and having a bit of history.

Practicalities and Tips

One of the best ways we could think of to give an introduction to the true joy and magic of collecting autographs is through the interview included below. Both the beginner and the advanced collector will find helpful tips here.

Being the person *answering* the questions is a somewhat novel experience for the noted autograph collector and coauthor of this book, George Sanders. During more than 40 years of interviewing hundreds of notable people, he has usually been on the receiving side of the microphone.

Harry S. Truman, John F. Kennedy, Martin Luther King, Lyndon Johnson, Jack Nicklaus, Clark Gable, Marilyn Monroe, Bob Hope, Ty Cobb, Ronald Reagan—these are only a few of the movers and shakers who have given him exclusive interviews on his nationally syndicated radio/TV talk-show, "Sanders Meanders."

As a broadcast newsman, a columnist, and an actor himself—in more than 20 motion pictures as well as several TV movies, including *December Bride* and *Wild Bill Hickok*—it was only natural that he start collecting signatures of the celebrities with whom he came in daily contact. His personal collection today totals more than 20,000 pieces, all organized by a home-based computer controlled by his wife, Helen.

Now retired (since 1977), Sanders is a fulltime autograph and manuscript collector. He has earned the respect of dealers and fellow collectors around the world. This interview recently took place in his home.

Sanders: For 40 years I have been tremendously interested in collecting historical documents, letters, manuscripts, signed photographs, and just plain signatures of the men and women who have made and are making history. It has taken years, but I'm now able to buy intelligently and with some expertise. My investment is large and I've learned to protect that investment with considerable research and meaningful study. This is certainly not a hobby for the uninformed.

I've watched autograph material rise in cost from a point where one could acquire choice Presidential letters and documents for $100 to today's market, where the same type of material is priced anywhere from $2,000 to $5,000. That's quite a financial jump in just the past 20 years.

Roberts: How do you find new autograph pieces for your collection?

Sanders: Helen and I have been shopping all over the United States and the world. In 1984 we searched throughout Europe for six weeks and found marvelous letters written by Dr. Sigmund Freud, Charles Darwin, Renoir, Dickens, and some outstanding Winston Churchill material. While walking around London with our dear friend Edward Bomsey, who is a popular American autograph dealer based in Washington, D.C., we visited a stamp shop. We asked if they had any covers (envelopes) with franking signatures on them. The very proper English gentleman pushed some early stamped envelopes across the glass counter, and they just happened to be pieces signed by Charles Dickens.

The stamp dealer was selling them for quite reasonable prices because the old used stamps on them weren't very important to stamp collectors, and that's all he cared about. This sort of thing happens quite frequently. The autograph collector receives a big bargain because stamp dealers or auction houses simply don't grasp the value of autograph items. (This condition, however, is gradually changing.) I once bought a President James Polk free frank at a stamp auction for a mere $35! It is a $750 item, but obviously not in the philatelic world.

Roberts: Do you specialize in anything?

Sanders: Yes, I have the collection divided topically. I'd say the primary portion of my entire collection is in U.S. Presidents, the Arts, Science, Industry, Heads of State, Civil War, Celebrities, and Military Leaders. In 1986, however, a North Carolina collector purchased a sizable portion of the U.S. Presidential material, which I have already replaced. Included in the purchase were association pieces such as assassins, First Ladies, Cabinet members, and advisors. I shall continue to buy good presidential material whenever a really fine value appears.

Those other divisions? The Arts? The artistic side of autographs. Lumped together are artists, composers, and sculptors.

Civil War? Just Civil War material, exclusively, which is separate from Military Leaders, which includes those people from all eras of history. The other categories contain a collection of important heads of state and royalty, men and women of science, plus a general collection of celebrities who do not necessarily fit into a specific category.

Another collection which should be mentioned is Vintage Theatrical and Motion Picture Stars—probably one of the finest in the country today.

My personal collection of modern entertainers is quite extensive because I knew so many film and TV personalities during my 15 years in Hollywood. When I first started as a serious collector, my collection was amassed on the basis of all the notable people I was interviewing on the air. Helen and I kept guest books just as Carol Burnett did, with one page for each celebrity. In my 35 years as a disc jockey, TV host, gossip columnist, commercial announcer, TV news anchorman, and, finally, broadcasting executive, we were able to acquire hundreds of important signatures at no financial cost whatsoever. It also provided us with an excellent collection of authentic in-person autographs—second to none—with which we are able to make truly accurate assessments against the current barrage of Autopens, facsimiles, secretarials, and the ever-dreadful forgeries that so undermine the material of serious collectors.

There was so much of value in that collection of genuine in-person signatures that part of it was sold to a portly entrepreneur for $200,000 in 1983. This same individual owns three posh autograph galleries in the West in which he offers artistically framed museum-mounted pieces of Americana at art gallery prices.

With 20,000 pieces currently in my collection, it is necessary to keep the really expensive autograph pieces in the bank vault. Such items as the personal letters to me from several presidents and the many items John F. Kennedy signed for me in person are, literally, money in the bank.

Roberts: What about the authenticity of a piece, and how do you tell whether it's worth the money?

Sanders: Well, I have probably as fine a library of autograph-related books as anyone for use in private research, where I can carefully check out facsimile or forged material.

Plus, I have the very good fortune to personally know such knowledgeable autograph experts and/or dealers as Mary Benjamin, Paul Richards, Conway Barker, Robert Batchelder, Herman Darvick, Joseph Rubinfine, Neale Lanigan, and the aforementioned Edward Bomsey. I must also include the former autograph auction whiz and authority, Charles Hamilton, who gave our hobby the publicity impetus it needed from the 1950s to the present day. His many books on the subject are oft-consulted tomes and necessary for any serious collector to own.

My mentor for decades has been a lady now in her late seventies—Mary Benjamin—whose gentle persuasion lifted my philographic tastes from the mundane contemporary material I was gathering for free to the valuable historic pieces I now treasure. She's the daughter of Walter R. Benjamin, founder of the oldest autograph-selling firm in America. Miss Benjamin is one of my dearest friends and I'm able to consult with her when I have any questions.

But to more fully answer your question, one way to authenticate material is through personal knowledge of the historically important people one wishes to collect.

Many of the persons I knew and interviewed are now vintage and I have copies of their handwriting in my own collection. I know what their in-person handwriting is really like. Their in-person signatures on photographs, books, and in guest books are extremely worthwhile in comparing with other material of theirs being offered by dealers or private collectors. I have the real thing, so there is little chance that I can't identify nor be unable to know whether an item written in my lifetime is valid or not.

However, it takes years of study to sense what is Autopen and what is not, what is a secretarial signature and what is not.

And the hazards of identification of engraving, woodcuts, or rubber stamps are rather formidable. Naturally, I'm afraid I annoy many trusting souls who offer autographed photos of stars such as Clark Gable, Carole Lombard, Humphrey Bogart, Laurel and Hardy, Charles Chaplin, Fatty Arbuckle, and the like which I frequently (and reluctantly) determine to be bogus.

This is not a hobby for the lazy scholar. Just as you recognize the fact that no two handcrafted antiques are exactly alike, so, too, you have to realize that no two letters are alike. If Jack Kennedy wrote a letter in longhand, he surely didn't write any two alike. His handwriting had many variants, as did his signature, but with careful study and the use of books containing facsimiles of Kennedy's hand, one becomes familiar with these differences.

Roberts: This may be a bad way to phrase it, but what is hot right now?

Sanders: It depends on the age of the collector. If you are an adult with money to invest, I suggest that U.S. Presidents are always a best buy and U.S. Vice Presidents are also a fine investment.

To the young, to teenagers, there's a very good market for rock artists. However, it is a bit on the fad side, and probably such items will not appreciate, let alone hold their present value. Such contemporary show business material is always chancy, but certainly great fun for the youthful collector.

Remember that artist Andy Warhol said we'll all be famous for about 15 minutes, and that's not sufficient time to become a worthwhile autograph item.

For example, what about the big-band leaders of the 1930s, 1940s, and 1950s who were so popular when I was a kid? Let's take the Dorsey Brothers, Russ Morgan, Ted Weems, Stan Kenton, and many, many others. Who remembers?

Glenn Miller, who was killed in a World War II air crash, is still valuable, but most of his contemporaries are selling for very modest prices. Duke Ellington is valuable, but it's his contribution as a composer rather than as a bandleader that placed him on a U.S. postage stamp and into autograph collections.

Returning to my thoughts regarding rock artists, I'd say the Beatles and Elvis Presley will probably retain their good value because they were the first superstars in their musical field. The untimely death of Lennon and of Elvis added value—there are no more signatures of theirs to acquire in person or by mail.

The first of anything is usually valuable. Take inventors. Thomas Edison, Eli Whitney, Cyrus McCormick, Samuel Colt, the Wright Brothers, and Alexander Graham Bell are all expensive items. They have never waned in collectors' interest. In other words, the historic or celebrated people who did something before anyone else thought to do it seem to be forever collectible and increase considerably in value.

Roberts: What about World War I autographs? I have read that they were expensive between the two World Wars, but have dropped in value now. Is that true?

Sanders: I'm pleased you asked about that period of history. For some reason World War I has lost considerable interest. Only General John Pershing, because he was the Commander of the American Expeditionary Force, plus the French field marshals, Foch and Joffre, are sought after. Some of the Germans—Ludendorff, von Hindenburg, Ernst Udet, von Richthofen, and a few others—are worthy of investment. Even theatrical stars of that era, such as Elsie Janis, Douglas Fairbanks, Sr., and most obviously, Sir Harry Lauder, have lost value in recent years.

Colonial and Revolutionary War material is a specialty in itself. Such material has retained its considerable value very well. It's truly American, and if you're wise, you'll collect red, white, and blue American material. However, good colonial pieces are not for an anemic autograph budget.

U.S. presidential items will never be bargain-priced. You can specialize in almost any one president and your investment will grow annually. Most autograph experts, with possibly the exception of Charles Hamilton, try to steer clear of any conversation that deals with the aspects of investment profits.

As for me, I simply wouldn't be interested in nurturing a hobby that didn't show considerable appreciation. Rare autographs are too expensive to be treated as a recreational novelty. These are not toys—they are expensive pieces of world or U.S. history. If there will never be any worthwhile gain financially, then why fool around with them?

What I have just said is adamantly opposed to what a great many autograph dealers want to hear or read. But, I ask you, why should anyone invest $1,000 in a Sigmund Freud letter and learn 20 years later that it's only worth $600? I would like to think that Dr. Freud was important enough in the field of psychiatry and that I had taken good enough care in the area of proper preservation of that letter that it would, in 20 years or even less, be worth far more than my original investment. The 1987 stock market crash seriously diminished many types of investments, but as of this moment, autograph prices have either risen or stablized. Need I say more?

An unwise purchase in autographs is just like an unwise purchase in anything else. Think long and hard before you buy. In other words, autograph collecting is not for the impulse buyer.

Roberts: What about association pieces written by people who are not famous?

Sanders: One of the things that started my interest in the Civil War was that my wife's great-grandfather, Elkanah Doolittle, was an officer, second-in-command, of the 20th Connecticut Volunteers. He was a respected officer who somehow managed to survive four years of combat duty and ultimately die of old age.

His letters had been handed down from generation to generation and no one in the Doolittle family had ever done any research on them. Years ago, at Radio Station KRKD in Los Angeles, I had leisure time between broadcasts to work on his numerous letters written from 1861 to 1865. Doolittle was an educated man and his letters were a joy to read and reread. What was important about his letters was that he had a genuine sense of the history he was living and wrote about important generals he met and served under. He obviously did not like nor vote for Lincoln, but vividly described Lincoln's review of the Connecticut troops and even referred to the great president as that "great ape in the White House," which was the first time I had seen that expression used by a Union officer.

Yes, I find most association pieces extremely important because they preserve the fringe activities surrounding an important historical personage or event.

If someone should discover a letter written by former Secretary of the Interior Albert Fall (in President Harding's Cabinet)—who was proven guilty of accepting bribes in the Teapot Dome scandal of the 1920s—in which he wrote, "Well, I'm an old man now and I don't mind admitting that I was a thief, but I don't know why Harding was covered up. He certainly shared our guilt," suddenly we're talking about a $1,000 or more letter. Few people recall Fall's name at this point in time, but it would be the fact that he was pointing an accusing finger at Harding that would make such a letter highly valuable.

Filed away upstairs I have a letter from an obscure American. I don't know much about its author, but it is a three-page missive written about the Russians from his vantage point as a foreign service officer in Moscow and St. Petersburg in 1850.

It is almost uncanny because you would think it was written a few weeks ago giving an American's view of Russian behavior—their secretiveness, their connivances, their mistrust of outsiders. A letter like this, with that studied description of what was going on inside and out of the Czar's court, is not only exciting to read, but has valuable content for scholars to consider.

Obviously, there are various facets of autograph collecting. That term in itself is a misnomer. Autograph collecting is the act of requesting a celebrity to place his or her signature in your autograph book, or on a menu, or in a book written by or about that celebrity. That's *in-person* autograph collecting.

Many collectors of such signatures mail cards, photographs, typescripts, books, bookplates, and so forth, to the celebrity whose autograph they want. This latter group of collectors, unfortunately, receives secretarial signatures, Autopen junk, or just downright forgeries. Frequently they invest more in postage costs than the signature of the celebrity in question was ever worth. That is the sad, tedious side of autograph collecting.

Manuscript collecting is expensive and worthwhile, with scholars being the prime acquisitors. They know what they want and will all too frequently invest fortunes in their respective collections. It is not an area for the novice.

Whatever your specialty is within this hobby, you must do your homework. If I didn't force myself to go outside and walk in the beautiful North Carolina woods that surround the lovely lake in front of our home, I could happily spend easily eight to ten hours a day with my collections—sometimes without leaving my desk. It is that exciting! I care that much about it and heartily encourage others interested in history, sports, entertainment, science, the arts, or celebrities in general to join with all the world's autograph buffs and share in a hobby that has many benefits both for the soul as well as the pocketbook.

Since this interview, Mrs. George Sanders has made an incredible find in the world of autographs, a *stack* of Greta Garbo letters. These fascinating and exceedingly rare letters are intimate windows into the private life of a public cult goddess also known as a privately mysterious person. Along with extensive other Garbo-related material, they are currently being assembled into book form by George Sanders and Ralph Roberts. At the September 1987 Herman Darvick auction, just one of these Garbo letters sold for $6,600 (including the 10-percent auctioneer's commission).

Recommended Reading and Clubs

We recommend the following reference books:

Axelrod, Todd. *Collecting Historical Documents.* TFH, 1984.
Benjamin, Mary A. *Autographs: A Key to Collecting.* Privately printed, 1963.
Berkley, Edmund, Jr. *Autographs and Manuscripts.* Scribner's.
Darvick, Herman N. *Collecting Autographs.* Julian Messner, 1981.
Hamilton, Charles. *American Autographs.* University of Oklahoma Press, 1983.
Hamilton, Charles. *Signatures of America.* Harper & Row, 1977.
Koschal, Stephen. *Collecting Books and Pamphlets Signed by U.S. Presidents.* Patriotic Publishers, 1982.
Patterson, Jerry E. *Autographs: A Collector's Guide.* Crown, 1973.
Rawlins, Ray. *The Stein and Day Book of World Autographs.* 1978.
Sullivan, George. *Making Money in Autographs.* 1977.
Taylor, John M. *From the White House Inkwell.* Tuttle.

Clubs you should consider joining:

UACC (Universal Autograph Collectors Club)
c/o Robert Erickson
P.O. Box 6181
Washington, DC 20044-6181

Manuscript Society
c/o David R. Smith
350 Niagara St.
Burbank, CA 91505

2
The Autopen

Writing a famous person, especially a politician, and receiving a personally signed letter in return is quite easy. But chances are that the signature was done by a machine called an *Autopen*. These signatures are worth very little indeed compared to actual autographs.

In the case of politicians, the closer to election time it is, the more likely you are to receive a "personally" signed letter. Take President Reagan as an example. The White House mailbag brings in hundreds of letters a day. There is no possible way the President could actually read all his mail, much less dictate and sign all the replies that go out in his name.

Machines do it. The note that comes back to you may appear to have been typed by a secretary and then signed by the Chief Executive, but the technological marvels of a word processor and an Autopen actually generated the letter.

All presidents from John F. Kennedy on have relied extensively on this method to satisfy the enormous demands for their autographs. Congressmen, Senators, Cabinet officers, and (more recently) Supreme Court Justices have taken to this technology with a vengeance.

"Within four or five square blocks (in downtown Washington), you've got more people who need them [Autopens] than anyplace else in the world," Robert DeShazo said in an article by Lynne Cheney published in the *Washingtonian* magazine. DeShazo is president of the International Autopen Company, which is the major manufacturer of automatic signature machines.

Using a mechanical device to duplicate signatures in specific and writing in general goes back many hundreds of years. Those who have had the fortune to visit Thomas Jefferson's home, Monticello (near Charlottesville, Virginia), have seen one of these on display there.

Jefferson's *Polygraph* was the eighteenth-century equivalent of the Xerox machine. He used it to make copies. As he wrote with one pen, another (which was mechanically attached to the first) created an exact copy. It was moderately simple mechanically and works as well today as it did back then. Jefferson, as evidenced by this and the other wondrous devices in his palatial home, was an avid gadgeteer. If he were alive today, his office would no doubt boast a thousand-watt-per-channel state-of-the-art stereo system, every piece of video equiment you could imagine, and a personal computer—all connected into one network that would do everything but brush teeth (and maybe that, too).

That supreme nineteenth-century showman, P. T. Barnum, went even further. He had a machine that could sign his signature in his absence—one of the first true Autopens. With a "sucker" being born every minute, Barnum evidently felt he needed help in corresponding with them.

Still, despite the machines existing, no President felt the need for one until John F. Kennedy took office in 1961. This does not mean that earlier Presidential autographs are all in the actual hand of that President. Many were signed by secretaries and fall under the classification of *secretarial*. More about that later.

President Kennedy and his staff, naturally, did not go around telling autograph collectors that a machine was doing much of his work for him, but certain astute collectors soon became suspicious. The main giveaway was that many of his signatures, when held up to a light, could be *exactly* superimposed on each other. The odds against anyone signing his or her name that precisely every time are astronomic. We humans are simply not that precise.

Noted expert Charles Hamilton, who has meant so much to the world of autograph collecting, warned on the "Today" show during the Kennedy administration of the possible grave consequences of presidential Autopen usage. Pierre Salinger, Kennedy's press secretary, immediately denied that such a device was in the White House.

Hamilton, however, followed his television appearance by demonstrating that not one, but seven patterns were being used by the machine to duplicate JFK signatures. Several of them were *John Kennedy*, but there was also a *Jack Kennedy* to be used on letters to his friends.

Lyndon Johnson took to the Autopen even more enthusiastically. The late Jennifer Casoni (an autograph dealer in Alexandria, Virginia) even maintained that Johnson used the Autopen to sign his vice-presidential oath of office.

Richard Nixon continued the tradition. Casoni, in her book *Best Wishes, Richard Nixon*, identified nine Richard Nixon patterns and three R. N. patterns. The Nixon White House, like previous administrations, was reluctant to admit the use of this automatic signing device.

President Gerald Ford gets credit for honesty in this respect. He was the first president to own up to Autopen usage.

In fact, to the surprise of the autograph collecting world, requests for autographs were often replied to with an Autopen signature *and* a letter stating that it was such. In fact, the combination of these two have some small value just for their historical precedent of presidential honesty.

Jimmy Carter also used the Autopen extensively. These signatures are relatively easy to detect when compared to known patterns. But Carter also made extensive use of the secretarial signature, which irritates collectors a good deal more than the more obvious Autopen.

Herman Darvick, a leading autograph expert and auction gallery owner, says that Susan Clough, a Carter secretary, "forged his name beautifully." While many presidents have encouraged this, Carter's usage of it has been very frustrating to collectors, turning up in places where it shouldn't have.

"I saw a picture," Darvick said, "signed by Begin and Sadat, which was sent to the White House for Carter's signature. Susan Clough signed it for him. The Autopen would have been better—at least it would have been his real signature, even if a machine produced it."

The Reagan White House is also not very anxious to discuss Autopen use. Still, experts agree that approximately a dozen patterns are being used to produce President Reagan's signature. There is a *Ronald Reagan*, a *Ron*, a *Ronnie*, and a *Dutch*. There is also an Autopen pattern of *Ronald Reagan* and *Nancy Reagan* together, given away by the fact that both signatures are on the exact same level, a physical impossibility in a normal signing by two individuals.

Mr. DeShazo has been manufacturing these devices since 1942. We spoke with him in researching this subject recently, and he very kindly gave us some insight into the use of Autopens from the viewpoint of the public figure.

The average person, Mr. DeShazo explained, has no comprehension of the vast amount of mail received by prominent public figures and, thus, little understanding or acceptance of the need for the machines his company provides. Since personal response to each and every letter is physically impossible, it is far better for an Autopen response to be generated than for the correspondent to be simply ignored.

Located in Sterling, Virginia, DeShazo's company ships Autopens all over the world. However, the company's proximity to Washington, D.C., is no accident.

"Almost every member of the Senate has one," he said. The House of Representatives is well stocked with Autopens also, though DeShazo added that sometimes four or five members might share one machine. In all, he estimated that more than 500 Autopens are in use in Washington alone, to the disgust of autograph collectors—but to the relief of public officials facing literal mountains of correspondence.

International Autopen currently has two popular models on the market. The Autopen 80 resembles a small desk with metal arms and springs on the left side of its surface. A pen is screwed into the end of a metal arm. The operator places letters or books or whatever beneath the pen. The machine produces about 300 signatures per hour. Since a standard ink pen is used, the signature looks realistic to the uninitiated.

Inside the desklike structure of the Autopen 80 is the revolving matrix which guides the pen. This matrix looks something like a large boomerang. It is cut according to the sample signature supplied by the customer. The matrix is easily changed to produce another version of the signature, or that of another person. The machine costs about $3,000, with each matrix selling for around $100. A more expensive model of the Autopen (costing around $10,000) adds automatic paper feed and other features to increase productivity.

International Autopen has dominated the automatic signing market for many years. Competition has surfaced from time to time. A complex electronic device called the Signa-Signer is one example, but the simpler Autopen continues to be the machine of choice at the moment.

The new laser printer technology is the latest challenger, being able to produce a signature that looks very close to a handwritten one. With this device attached to a personal computer and a desktop publishing program, letters can be generated that incorporate signatures in a one-step process. In fact, there will very soon come a time when an Autopen signature will be considered a personal touch.

Tips for Detecting Autopen Signatures

Determining whether or not an autograph in your possession, or one under consideration for purchase, is genuine or an Autopen product takes a modicum of detective work. *Comparison* is the hot tip here. That's why so many hundreds of authentic signatures are included in this price guide.

It is also a good idea, in the case of celebrity signatures done since the advent of the Autopen (that is, within the last 30 years, at least), to have some known Autopen examples as a guide.

One reference for this is the book *Seeing Double*, by Marvin B. Blatt and Norman Schwab (1986, La-La Ltd., P.O. Box 2060, North Babylon, New York 11703). Blatt and Schwab's book contains over 250 facsimiles of Autopen signatures, including variants.

A key to using such a reference is to realize that the examples do not have to superimpose exactly 100-percent to be Autopen patterns. If the paper is moved while the Autopen is signing, either deliberately or through mechanical slippage, minor variations can be induced. Still, putting a suspected piece over a known Autopen example and moving them around while holding them up to a strong light will cause parts of the signatures to match.

No one can make two consecutive signatures look exactly alike, so even if just sections of the two signatures match, they are almost certainly done by Autopen.

There are only two ways you can really be sure that a signature was done on the Autopen. The first is to match it to a known Autopen example. The second is if you have two signatures that match exactly. Again, it's a physical impossibility for any person to sign his or her name precisely the same way twice; hence, any two signatures that superimpose exactly are Autopen or some other means of mechanical or electronic reproduction.

The Autopen is a fact of life for the autograph collector. Knowledge is your only real protection. Seeing a current celebrity actually signing the piece in person is the only real guard against its being done by Autopen or a similar device. Dealing with a reputable dealer who can knowledgeably attest to the piece's authenticity by providing provenance (such as a photograph of a book now for sale being signed by a famous author) can also help in guarding against a nonauthentic signature.

3

Inscribed or Uninscribed—That Is the Question!

Edward N. Bomsey

It is fair to say that, in collecting almost anything, there are certain rules which the collector must follow because "That's how it's done." Whether or not these rules are sensible (depending, of course, on who judges what is sensible in the world of collectibles) is unimportant. You follow the rules of the game to protect your investment.

There are certain rules, then, to observe in autograph collecting, and this article's purpose is twofold. It will hopefully convince the collector, first, to take a hard and smart look at a "rule" in one area of autograph collecting and, second, to partially ignore it!

While I do not personally collect film and entertainment autographs, I do buy and sell good, vintage signed photographs of the major film stars from the era beginning with the silent screen and lasting through the 1960s. The Brat Pack, no, but Errol Flynn, yes.

I was exhibiting at a book and paper fair in Baltimore one Sunday a few months ago and a man in his mid-to-late thirties approached my booth and asked me if I had any Buster Crabbe material. (For those too young to remember Buster Crabbe, how about Tarzan, Flash Gordon, Buck Rogers, or Captain Gallant?) This fellow collected only items related to Buster Crabbe and said he had the largest collection anywhere.

Well, I told the collector he was in luck because I had a genuine 1930s vintage photo of Crabbe signed with his real name, Larry Crabbe. It was one of him sitting on a steamer trunk, wearing a lovely coat and hat and reading a newspaper, and I pointed out that it was truly unique. The collector was most interested until he saw the item, but then, while noting how lovely the photo was, and how eminently fair the price, he declined to buy.

Why, you ask, did this number 1 Buster Crabbe fan and collector turn down a fairly priced autographed photo of his hero that he would probably not find anywhere else? A photograph that, he admitted, would have been just perfect for his collection—why? Because it was *inscribed*. Were it not personalized to someone else, this great Buster Crabbe collector would have been delighted to buy the photograph.

This, then, is the central point of this article. Does an inscription on an autograph of a film star or entertainer detract from its value, and if so, should it? To answer my own question, first part first, *yes*. The presence of an inscription may reduce the price and/or value of such an autograph. (I have seen in countless dealer catalogs the notation *inscribed, can be matted out*, or some such comment.)

I have also seen dealers offering two autographed photographs of astronauts, one inscribed and one not inscribed, and have often noted a price differential ranging from 10 to 50 percent. On the other hand, there are dealers who do not charge a premium for an uninscribed item as opposed to what they charge for something inscribed. When material is presented to dealers for sale, often a lower figure is offered for items that are inscribed or personalized. Dealers perhaps assume that, where the autograph is fairly common and inexpensive, they won't be able to sell an inscribed piece as readily as one that is uninscribed.

Should there be a difference? Well, let me waffle a little. Yes and no. I have maintained that an inscription should be important to a collector in the case that the celebrity is alive and his or her signature is fairly common and inexpensive. If the autograph is to be framed and prominently displayed in the home or office, an individual collector simply does not want items originally acquired by someone other than him- or herself in a personal collection.

When should the presence of an inscription *not* make a difference? In the case of the number 1 Buster Crabbe fan, quite frankly, I would say that passing on an opportunity to purchase reasonably a most uncommon, very vintage and interesting photo of a deceased celebrity that the collector greatly admires is folly. Crabbe has been dead for more than 5 years, and the photograph in question was signed more than 50 years ago. To pass it up simply because it was personalized to someone else was a mistake.

Today, a signed and inscribed photograph of a Thomas Edison, Harry S. Truman, Lionel Barrymore, Judy Garland, or other very well known person is not lessened in value because of the inscription. In fact, in many cases, the presence of an interesting inscription, whether a simple signature in an autograph album or on a photograph, will make the item all the more valuable.

An autograph written as *To . . . , with many thanks for all of your help when it was needed* and signed *Henry Ford* would, I believe, certainly be worth more than an item merely signed by that great industrialist. On the other hand, were I collecting astronauts' autographs or those of film/TV/rock stars, I don't think that I would want an item in my collection personalized to someone else—especially if it were something that might be available to me by my own mail efforts, or if I knew that for a slight (or no) price difference I could find it elsewhere.

The difference must be in rarity and in supply and demand. It makes absolutely no sense for a collector to turn down a rare or uncommon item because of the presence of an inscription or personalization of any sort. Can you imagine a collector of film stars' autographs turning down an item autographed by Greta Garbo and inscribed to her grocery delivery boy? Strange as it seems, some collectors would say "No thanks, it's inscribed," and walk away. In doing so, they would pass up the chance to get an extreme rarity and perhaps the seldom-encountered opportunity to buy at a low price a piece worth well over a thousand dollars.

Remember too that in these days of Autopens, secretarial signatures, and printed signatures, a good inscription is sometimes the best way to determine the authenticity of an autograph. The more handwriting there is, the easier the comparisons can be made. To the collector I would say, Use good judgment in determining when to say *no* to an inscribed piece for your collection. You are entitled to your own collecting methods, likes, and dislikes, and I may not convert everyone. Yet I hope you will be able to throw away what often is an artificial barrier to good and smart collecting.

4

Autograph Dealers: Can You Live Without Them?

George R. Sanders

If you seriously desire to own a truly fine collection of legitimate autographs, then you had best become acquainted with an autograph dealer who suits your personality and collectible requirements. I wish it were possible to paraphrase the late humorist Will Rogers with the statement that I had never met a dealer I didn't like, but that would be untrue.

With rare exception, I have found in my 50 years of collecting and 30 years of purchasing autograph material that most dealers are highly knowledgeable, integrity-bound, courteous, interesting, delightfully candid, and tremendously interested in the hobby they represent. Some have become lifelong friends whose personal lives have intertwined with our own. Others are just pleasant voices on the telephone or charming acquaintances with whom we mingle at autograph shows. In short, the dealers I like and the ones with whom I have spent hundreds of thousands of dollars are some of the nicest people I have ever known. I trust them completely.

The bad apples are those fly-by-night, part-time dealers who frequently do not fully guarantee the material they peddle, nor properly investigate or research autograph material before offering it to the unsuspecting collector. They are in this avocation only for the profit they can garner, and have no feeling whatsoever for the hobby or the people who are investing in it.

There are even a few thieves whose light-fingered activities keep honest dealers tensely alert at public autograph shows as well as in the privacy of their respective offices or galleries.

And, last but not least, we have the dealer who buys and knowingly sells forgeries or stolen material. Fortunately, this one is often apprehended and ultimately punished for such transgressions, but usually not before having disillusioned a few innocent collectors.

In other words, you wouldn't purchase a diamond ring or a valuable coin from some little-known dealer or a stranger on the street. If an autograph dealer does not guarantee material and offer to repay your investment in full should the item prove to be bogus, do not deal with that person under any circumstances.

Buying an autograph *as is* is a reckless pursuit and is usually a philographic disaster, particularly with auction houses who insist on such a condition.

If you have read this far, you are now aware that, in most cases, I enjoy buying from dealers and I sincerely relish their good company. Why? Because they sincerely care about what I'm doing and how I spend my money. They offer worthwhile suggestions and search out special items that make my collection more valuable.

Most dealers offer excellent catalogs in which I discover nearly every week some letter, document, or signature that I never dreamt would become available to me. (Even dealers make mistakes and frequently underprice an item that has little interest or value for them, but has been nearly unobtainable for the collector who wants or needs it.)

Don't delude yourself that you can ever have a really valuable collection by only acquiring that which you can get for postage charges and by begging from celebrities in person. I've done both. I have acquired thousands of in-person autographs for free because I was a professional broadcaster with easy access to politicians, sports figures, and celebrities from every walk of public life. However, my contemporary collection of such material certainly does not match the value of my cash investments in this great hobby.

In-person collecting is really great fun, filled with the excitement of the hunt and the ultimate joy of personally contacting one of your favorite celebrities. Alas, you cannot contact the dead, and it is the dead who have become the most sought-after in the autograph world.

This is where dealers become skilled mediums for séances that bring the writings of persons such as Washington, Lincoln, Einstein, Hemingway, Catherine the Great, Horatio Nelson, Thomas Wolfe, Greta Garbo (alive, but practically impossible to obtain), Billy the Kid, Charles Lindbergh, and Marilyn Monroe into your appreciative hands and into your treasured collection of proven historical luminaries. Don't sell your collection short by failing to have the confidence of intelligent investment, and don't try to build a collection without the professional skills of an honest, wise dealer.

Dealers come in all sizes and descriptions. Some have the infectious drawl of the deep South or the comfortable intonations of the Southwest or the prim and proper enunciations of the Northeast or the harsh pronunciations of Manhattan, the Bronx, and Brooklyn. It is an international hobby and everyone in America and the world seems to be represented by competent dealers.

There are scholars, there are truly entertaining humorists, there are always good-friends-to-be. Try not to be captivated by only one dealer, even though you may feel secure in just dealing with that special one.

Catalogs, like their various publishers, have their own personalities, so don't ignore a Xeroxed list because you think it may feature less desirable material. On the other hand, do not ignore a slick, illustrated, luxuriously presented catalog because you assume its autographic ingredients might be too expensive. You'll find great buys in both.

For many years, I dealt only with one dear lady, Ms. Mary Benjamin, who heads the oldest autograph dealership in the nation, and I still buy from her. But she was wise enough to introduce me to others.

Now I have the choice of hundreds of items every month offered by almost 100 dealers. You will find whatever it is you seek if you simply make an effort to acquire every catalog made available—via advertisements in the UACC (Universal Autograph Collectors Club) publication *The Pen and Quill* and the Manuscript Society's *Manuscripts*. The various articles published in the aforementioned publications will also serve as a great source of reference material to enhance your collectibles knowledge.

Over a period of time you will discover that several dealers are just right for you and a marriage of interests will ensue that will be entirely satisfactory to you both.

Good luck, good hunting, and good catalog reading as you collect autographs that make you proud and grateful that the human race—autograph dealers in particular—has preserved written history that you can actually own.

5
Collecting Presidential Books

Stephen Koschal

Serious autograph collecting has never been as popular as it is today. Quite often, local newspapers print articles entitled "Autograph Tips," "Rare Books Gaining As Market Slumps," or "There's Gold in These Autographs." Frequently, television news shows report record prices at auction houses. Autograph clubs such as the Universal Autograph Collectors Club have increased their membership by about one-third in the last year or so and now have members in many other countries. Conventions are held in many states where as many as 20 dealers will display their stock to hundreds of collectors eager to add items to their growing collections.

Among autograph collectors, it is well known that the signatures of our Presidents are highly prized and very desirable. Nothing moves faster from any dealer's stock than documents, letters, and photos autographed by Presidents of the United States.

However, there are many variations in collecting Presidential signatures. Some collectors specialize in signed photographs, whereas others specialize in autographed White House Cards. In both cases, complete collections of the Presidents cannot be formed, since the first President to sign photographs was Millard Fillmore, and President Ulysses S. Grant introduced the Executive Mansion Card, which was later changed to the White House Card by Theodore Roosevelt.

Through the years, I have collected all facets of Presidential autographs, eventually specializing in a relatively obscure aspect of autograph collecting: books owned and/or presented by the Presidents. This specialty is becoming very popular among collectors and dealers alike. Interest in this area is increasing so rapidly that books which were common during the late sixties and early seventies are now somewhat difficult to obtain.

This is also a field that may be completed, if that's the intention. (However, this could take a lifetime, even with luck.) Some Presidents are very difficult to obtain in full handwritten letters, especially many of the Presidents of the twentieth century. On the other hand, I have perused books containing such finds as a three-page inscription by Herbert Hoover and full-page inscriptions, many with astonishing content, by Truman, Nixon, and Ford. It is interesting to note that most collectors with whom I have been associated have little or no intention of completing a set of the Presidents in signed books, but rather their goal is simply to acquire as many signed books as possible to enhance their personal libraries.

While collecting presidential signed books, you can encounter some memorable rarities. It is not unusual to find inscriptions in a book that would normally not be found in a letter, such as unusual quotations and even bits of poetry.

The new enthusiast, if patient, will be able to add many exciting items to a collection. These include books that our Chief Executives considered good enough to own themselves or books that in their opinion were ideal as gifts to friends, associates, and relatives. It is interesting to note that many such books, especially since Theodore Roosevelt's era, were editions limited to small quantities, some as small as 100 copies. Because of the nature of limited editions, existing copies often are inscribed to the President's relatives and close friends, making these volumes interesting association items.

I can assure the collector entering this field that every volume added to his or her library will be a prize to enjoy building on in the future. However, no one should become discouraged should weeks, and even months, pass without a single book being added to the collection. I have observed no recurring pattern in obtaining these books. A copy may turn up in the oddest of places. In my own experience, I found a volume signed by William McKinley in a neighbor's house and a mint copy of Benjamin Harrison's book (containing a beautiful quotation) in an obscure secondhand-book shop in Illinois. The latter was collecting dust on a shelf among the other so-called common items. The dealer was not impressed when I pointed out that the book contained a wonderful inscription by President Harrison, which, in his opinion, did not affect the price of the book.

The best sources for Presidential signed books are the autograph dealers and the rare book dealers. By scanning the various trade publications, you will find many of these dealers advertised. Other excellent sources for acquisitions are the book fairs held throughout the United States. Discuss your interests with the professional dealers and experienced collectors attending.

One of the many benefits I have found while assembling my own library is that, for the most part, you do not encounter the many problems that plague collectors of letters and documents.

For example, several of the Presidents have had secretaries sign countless routine items for them; these signatures are known as *proxy signatures*. Many documents, such as land grants, contain the proxy signatures of Tyler, Fillmore, Pierce, and Buchanan. In my own collection, I presently have 11 books signed by Fillmore and 6 signed by Buchanan, and not one bears a false signature.

In addition to those in my own library, the few books I have encountered by Tyler and Pierce also bear genuine signatures. Franklin Roosevelt had several secretaries during his career, many of whom imitated his signature with some expertise. Of the 13 books I have that are signed by FDR, plus the many I have seen in other collections, not one contained a secretarial signature or inscription.

Another benefit regarding books autographed by modern Presidents is the avoidance of the dreaded Autopen machine. All collectors have encountered countless souvenir items and photographs signed by the Autopen, but to date I have only found one book signed with it: copies of Richard Nixon's *Six Crises* (caveat emptor in dealing with this work). Another advantage in finding a valued presidential inscription in a book is that it is likely to be well preserved. This is in contrast to the many letters and documents I have seen "broken in the folds" through the signature.

Should you have the fortune to meet a President and to spend a few moments with him for an autographing session, you might find him objecting to certain photographs or souvenir items. In my experience, Presidents rarely refuse to sign a book they have authored, or, in many cases, even a book they did not author as long as it is related to them or their career. In the course of several meetings that I have had with President Nixon, he signed at least 50 books, never objecting. He was especially happy to autograph Henry Kissinger's *White House Years*, placing his signature directly above Kissinger's on the limitation page.

6
Women in Collecting

Cordelia Platt

The world of autograph collecting is one of many ways to preserve the past, and I have often wondered why women haven't been more involved in the hobby. As a result I began to realize that, through the ages, the stories handed down have been mostly about the exciting feats of the male in battle, travel, and providing for the family. These tales were told around the fire when the men returned, then enhanced through the years as they were passed on to future generations.

Few women took part in this ritual and their traditional role as home-maker—a role fulfilled because of their natural ability to bear children—went unnoticed and taken for granted.

Early records were kept first through cave drawings and carvings. Most of these dealt with the experiences mentioned above. Very little mention was made of the day-to-day, mundane life of the female. Men wrote of "manly" things, adventures of thought and deed. Then finally someone thought enough of something someone else had written to save it, and the pieces of parchment containing some form of writing and or pictures began to be preserved for future generations.

On through the ages, more thoughts, more deeds, and more information were being protected. One man's work was saved by another man who needed the information to further a thought or project. The keeping of records (births, marriages, and deaths, for instance) created the need for more and larger facilities, and many old storage places for records were abandoned and part of their contents discarded.

Enter the collectors, with their sense of the importance of the past and its records. They have long felt that the destroying of records would destroy the past, and that the future in many ways depends on the past. We all have to leave this Earth sooner or later, but what we write and/or create remains long after we have departed.

Once we begin to realize how much of history has been made by *men*, recorded by *men*, and saved by *men*, it is easy to see why most women have not become involved. The women kept the home fires burning, raised the children, and so forth. Important, yes, but recorded, no. Until recently women were not even allowed or encouraged to participate in historic events. There was no incentive to help preserve the past records and information.

My husband and I sell our material by catalog and at various collectibles shows throughout the country. At many of these shows, at least half of those in attendance are women, but that's not apparent by checking the collectors in the ephemera/autograph booths. Women still seem more involved with other kinds of collectibles.

A few words of advice for women out there, from one of the very few women who have entered this heretofore generally thought "uninteresting" category of collecting: It *is* interesting, exciting, challenging, and rewarding, and usually, much less expensive than collecting those items we traditionally collect.

7
The Pricing of Autographs

Mary A. Benjamin

I am often asked how I know how to price an item. I suppose the only answer to be given is *experience,* but actually there are definite norms. One point, however, must be made clear. Not all autographs have value. The antiquity of a document, for example, may have little to do with its value. Of prime importance is the significance of the individual writing or signing the letter or document. An old legal brief or bill of lading or land deed signed by no one of importance may have no value at all.

The next point to be considered is the likely salability of the item. If it is of interest, I must research it thoroughly. I must first ascertain, of course, whether the letter is handwritten, signed only, or unsigned. What is its condition? And next, what is the letter's date, or if it is undated, is it possible by means of the content to approximate the date? What was the writer doing at the time? Is the addressee of note? If the letter has political contents, did the writer play a significant role at the time? If it is of literary content, does the writer refer to his or her own works? If the letter is musical, the same question applies.

The next step is to check records of prices in both auction and dealers' catalogs. This gives some idea of the current market. Obviously, to determine all these points, the dealer requires an extensive library for research.

Supply and demand are, of course, basic to the pricing of autographs, as in most other fields. However, because of the emphasis stressed by newspapers on high prices of certain types of material, many individuals jump to the conclusion that any old scrap of paper they own must also have value. This is unfortunately not so. A letter, for example, by someone's great-great-great-great-grandmother writing to her daughter on family matters, and dated perhaps in the 1700s, would unquestionably have sentimental value for the family, but not for anyone else.

On the other hand, a letter such as the one we handled some years ago written by Connecticut Senator James Dixon's wife and describing the events of the fatal night when Lincoln was assassinated is of great value. She had been asked by Mrs. Lincoln to stay with her in the room next to that of the dying President. In her letter she gave a detailed account of Mrs. Lincoln's anguish and her conduct on that night. Mrs. Dixon herself was not a woman of political importance, but what she wrote was historically important and had considerable monetary value.

In an incident involving an item of little historical importance, we were recently offered a cigar owned by Battista, Castro's predecessor, signed on the cigar band. The owner believed it might have substantial value. He was soon set straight. As one friend inquired, "Was it smoked or unsmoked?"

The very word *autograph* may be at fault, misleading those who are not collectors. Noncollectors seem to be under the impression that an autograph consists exclusively of a simple signature. This is not so. The word *autograph* may apply to a manuscript, a handwritten letter that is signed or unsigned, or a dictated letter.

Unfortunately, to the young dealers entering the field, every item is new and scarce, and they price their items accordingly. The difference in their list prices and those of the long-established dealers are often confusing to collectors. That some prices have jumped excessively because of inflation is unquestionable.

Collectors who enter the present climbing market in the belief that they will make a killing at a later date may be in for an unpleasant surprise. As is well known to old-timers who have collected over a long period of years, although prices often go up, they also come down. For the past ten years I have warned of the dangers of investment. Only dealers are safe—and even they can lose heavily in a slow period, or in a period in which money is devalued, such as has happened in the past with the German mark, the French franc, and the English pound. Dealers can, in most cases, retrieve their cost, but the customer whose only outlet may be another private collector whom he or she may not know can only turn to the dealer or to the auction house, and auction prices are at best unpredictable.

The use of the Autopen is a modern and more serious problem. Its introduction raised havoc, for it is often impossible to differentiate between an Autopen signature and an authentic signature. Are such Autopen-signed letters or photographs worthless? The answer is normally *yes,* but a secretarially signed letter or photograph may not always be without value. This is a new angle which has developed and must be considered.

A number of years ago I noticed for the first time in a French catalog that a letter of one of the Louis of France was described with a parenthetical note *Secrétaire de la main* (signed by the secretary), immediately following the King's name. The price was not substantial. I soon realized that the price set reflected the significance of the contents of the document and not the value of the signature. This made sense. The item certainly had some historical significance which could not be brushed aside.

The contents, then, of an item signed by a secretary, by Autopen, or by hand stamp must therefore be considered. A military commission signed by President Andrew Johnson with a hand stamp—he had a bad right arm and often resorted to signing in this fashion—should not be simply disregarded as worthless.

The individual who is appointed may give the document some historical value and perhaps some monetary value. Individual letters so signed, if of a routine nature, would be worthless.

For example, a circular letter of appeal signed by Helen Keller by Autopen would have no value, as probably hundreds, if not thousands, of similar ones were mailed out. But a letter with fine contents signed by a secretary or by Autopen should be considered in a different light.

Fads—sudden waves of interest in particular fields as sparked by books or events—have always affected, and still do affect, valuation. I have noticed, for example, a time when opera singers' autographs and signed photographs jumped in value. In the case of photographs it is often the rarity of the photograph which influences value more than the signature does.

Scarcity has a strong influence on prices. One example that can be given is in the field of the American Revolution. Material in past years was plentiful, but this is no longer true of good content letters. Such items today bring very high prices. Documents dated after 1783 that were signed by persons significant to the Revolution still come on the market, but prices for them are markedly lower.

When William Manchester published his first volume of Winston Churchill's biography, the demand for Churchill's letters was overwhelming. Prices actually rose to dramatic heights never approached by the letters of former Prime Ministers in recent times. Similarly, the movie *Gandhi* sparked great interest in that leader, and demand for his letters rose strongly.

The pricing of autographs, then, is not an easy matter. Prices are not just picked out of the sky. Considerable thought and study must be given before an item can be appraised properly.

In the book *Autographs and Manuscripts: A Collector's Manual* (Charles Scribner's Sons), I have written a chapter on values. I urge those who wish to know more about the subject to secure a copy of the book, and I believe their questions on this subject—as well as many others—will be answered.

8
An Overview of Collecting Autographs

Cordelia and Tom Platt

This chapter is based on a guide sheet we made up for new people who come to our booth at the various shows. We get so busy and so many people need to be *educated* that we had the sheets printed to hand out to our booth visitors in order to keep them occupied until we could talk to them individually. An experienced collector may know everything here, but persons new to the field probably do not.

So we offer this simplified overview of autographs and historical material.

Why Should I Collect Autographs?

- The field offers a wide variety of interesting items.
- Items are available to suit every pocketbook.
- Most other adult hobbies cater to the affluent (coins, stamps, art, jewelry, and so forth).
- Collecting autographs can give you the feeling of being close to someone admired, someone you will never know personally.
- Autograph material is easily stored and displayed.
- The hobby can be very profitable and many items are an excellent investment.
- Collecting autographs can increase your knowledge and appreciation of history and culture.

How Much Do Autographs Cost?

- While there are many items available for less than $50, many are also priced in the $100–$500 range. Layaway plans can help collectors purchase the more valuable items.
- The basic rule of supply and demand directly affects the price of autographs.
    - An item in great demand and small supply will bring a high price.
    - An item in good demand and with reasonable supply will bring a moderate price. Most of the highly collected items are in this range.

- Generally speaking, the death of a celebrity will bring an increase in autograph value. The supply has stopped, and demand will begin to increase along with price.
- An autograph in an interesting format will have greater value than a run-of-the-mill item.
- An autograph of a celebrity which relates to that person's trademark is generally more desirable. For example, a photo of Margaret Hamilton as the Wicked Witch would be more valuable than a portrait photograph.
- Condition is very important, and mint condition items are more valuable than those with flaws.

Where Can I Get Autographs?

- *Autograph dealers at shows.* You can learn a great deal about a dealer by the way he or she answers your questions and from the reference materials and facsimile studies the dealer makes available. Generally, a full-time dealer has spent more time studying than has a part-time one.
- *Autograph dealer mailing lists.* Two key concerns are whether there's a guarantee of authenticity with a money-return policy if the buyer is not satisfied, and whether the dealer charges extra for postage and insurance. (If so, how much? and is it reasonable or excessive?)
- *In person.* At least you know the autograph is authentic, but it seems whenever you see a celebrity, all you have is a pencil and a matchbook cover.
- *Writing for autographs.* The price sure is right, and you can certainly build a nice basic collection to be supplemented by dealer purchases of scarce signatures or those of deceased persons. The problem with this approach is the high percentage of nonauthentic autographs by secretaries, rubber stamps, Autopen, and the like.
- *Antique dealers, flea markets, garage sales.* You'll occasionally find some real bargains here, but you face a very high risk of buying nonauthentic material.

How Can I Tell Whether an Autograph Is Authentic?

You probably can't, and that's where a good dealer can help. Most dealers guarantee every signature as authentic for the life of the item, and they have the experience to back up this guarantee.

Here are the most common types of *artificial* signatures:

- *Ghost-written.* Often by a secretary employed for that purpose, used where excessive demand or simple aversion to signing autographs causes a prominent person to pay someone else to handle the task. This was very prevalent in entertainment in the 1920s and 1930s, and in the better political material.
- *Autopen.* This machine can do a large number of signatures per hour and only the experienced collector can tell the difference. It has been used in all categories for many years.

- *Imprinted signatures and lithographs.* Offset printing—either in the item and photographed, then run off by the thousands, or actually on the paper, as seen on official government documents.
- *Stamped.* Stamped signatures can be deceiving to the unknowing. Rudolph Valentino had an exceptional array of different-sized metal stamps.
- *Forgeries.* Usually only found in more expensive items, and can be spotted by the experienced.

Information on Matted Items

Matting a signature with a photograph of the celebrity is a new and interesting concept for your consideration. Since an autograph on a card or piece of paper is the least expensive to purchase, this approach enables the collector to purchase more items for the same number of dollars. Further savings can be achieved if collectors can mat or frame for themselves, buying only the basic autograph.

With matting, more flexibility is offered. The picture can be changed by the collector if desired, while on an autographed photograph, even if it is more valuable, the signature will always be on that photo and that photo only.

Many collectors combine the best of both worlds, buying signed photos, letters, or documents in their price ranges and matting signatures of the more expensive items.

Are Autographs a Good Investment?

Yes! Good autographs are a *good* investment. The previously mentioned supply and demand factors will be very influential. (This is a fast-growing collecting field, and we are seeing increased demands in all areas every year.)

The demand will continue to grow for signatures of people who have made a contribution to their fields, even if theirs are small accomplishments.

There is increased demand for those whose charisma outshines their deeds, and this holds true in all categories.

Generally speaking, the only autographs which will not become more valuable are those of people who are obscure today. They will be forgotten as time goes by.

Chances for speculation abound. All categories offer the opportunity to invest in a future hero who is on his or her way up. Many invest in *Oldies but Goodies*; all categories have famous people who have already made their impact on history and are now in their later years. Others invest in leaders in various fields who are deceased and whose autographs are therefore in very limited supply. For example, the average Presidential item has increased in value about 900 percent in the last 18 years (that's 50 percent per year).

Can You Give Some Good Hints for Beginners?

- Patience is a virtue. You have waited years to start, and you don't have to put together a collection of 1200 Civil War generals in 30 days.
- Know your source. The most expensive autograph is one which is not authentic. Don't take chances. It is discouraging and expensive.
- Read books about autograph collecting. Even if the ones you find in your local library are outdated, the basic principles remain the same.
- Ask questions. If dealers won't give you their time, don't give them your money.
- Protect your collection. Autograph books cover preservation in detail.
- *Never* tape or glue autographs.
- When writing for autographs, always enclose a self-addressed, stamped envelope. If you want pictures signed, send them to the celebrity. Your chances of receiving an authentic reply are greatly enhanced.
- Autographs do not decrease in value just because they are inscribed to another person. Actually, in most instances, the value is increased because of the additional handwriting of the celebrity. Remember that the paper by itself is worth very little. It is the handwriting which gives the item its value, and the more the better.

9
The Universal Autograph Collectors Club

Autograph collecting, or *philography*, is one of the oldest hobbies in the world. The great Roman orator Cicero, who lived more than 2000 years ago, was a collector. One of his most cherished autographs was a handwritten letter from Julius Caesar. There have been other famous philographers. In 1834, former President James Madison sent "an autographic specimen . . . for a collection which the Princess Victoria is making." The future British Queen was only 15 years old at the time.

Financier J. P. Morgan, Sr., began collecting when he was 16, and his son continued adding to the father's collection. As the daughter of the mayor of Boston, Rose Fitzgerald collected autographs, as did her son, John F. Kennedy. William Randolph Hearst and Franklin D. Roosevelt were also autograph collectors.

What Can I Collect?

Letters, documents, manuscripts, checks, notes, quotations, franked envelopes or signatures on album pages, photographs, visiting cards, first-day covers, typescripts, baseballs, menus, programs, books . . . anything ink will adhere to can be collected.

Which Collecting Area Should I Choose?

Whatever interests you. Presidents, authors, scientists, composers, aviators, Supreme Court Justices, royalty, frontiersmen, famous women, actors, actresses, child stars, radio personalities, artists, Revolutionary War leaders, explorers, sports figures, military leaders, Nobel Prize winners, Pulitzer Prize winners, Judaica, world leaders, religious leaders, black leaders, signers of the Declaration of Independence, Vice Presidents, Nazis, criminals, and numerous other areas offer great potential.

Or you can collect autographs relating to certain events (the War of 1812, a Presidential election, Watergate, and so on), institutions (such as the United Nations, the Smithsonian, and the National Geographic Society), your own state (Governors, Senators, famous people born there, and so on), your favorite sports team—again, anything that interests you.

How Can I Start a Collection?

You can write to people for their autographs or you can buy autographs from autograph dealers. Occasionally, you may be able to find an autograph in an antique shop or old bookstore. Once you have a small collection, you can trade with other collectors. By selling some autographs, you'll have extra money to buy others.

How Can Autograph Collecting Be Interesting?

If you want to write to a famous person and you write an interesting letter, the reply you receive may be just as interesting. Here are some examples.

Former Secretary of State Dean Acheson wrote one collector that if Richard Nixon were elected President in 1968, the country "would survive it as we survived General Eisenhower."

African leader Julius K. Nyerere of Tanzania wrote a 19-year-old American that, in general, "the United States puts the interests of her Allies, the rulers or former rulers of Africa, before the interests of Africa, even in questions where the integrity and development of Africa is concerned."

British statesman Clement Attlee commented to another collector that Churchill's greatest service to world peace was in leading the defeat of Hitler, "the Nazi gangster."

Apollo 15 astronaut Jim Irwin admitted in a letter, "On our flight we sighted a good many UFO's but none looked like an extra-terrestrial spacecraft."

Alabama Governor George C. Wallace told a high school student in 1964, "I personally have done more for the Negroes of the State of Alabama than any other individual."

Reading a letter written by Mark Twain in which he tells a friend about his new book or one by Susan B. Anthony giving her views on women's suffrage would certainly be more interesting than reading it in a biography or encyclopedia. And, surprisingly, letters like these are available for collectors to purchase.

So whether you write for autographs or purchase them from dealers, you can assemble an interesting collection without too much trouble.

How Can Autograph Collecting Be Profitable?

If you wrote interesting letters to everyone listed in just one issue of *The Pen and Quill*, the bimonthly journal of the UACC, you probably would receive replies from about half. You could sell these replies to autograph dealers for much, much more than you paid for one year's UACC membership.

A UACC member's 1975 handwritten reply from Jimmy Carter (cost of stationery and postage: less than 15¢) was recently listed in a dealer's catalog for $1500! Another member purchased an important Eisenhower letter from a dealer for $750 and sold it four years later for $3500. Not only is autograph collecting an interesting hobby, but it can be very profitable.

Why Join the UACC?

Once you join the Universal Autograph Collectors Club, you will be listed as a new member in *The Pen and Quill*. Within a few weeks, you'll receive lists and catalogs of autographs for sale from dealer-members. This way, you will get an idea of autograph values. If you do not purchase autographs from a dealer, you'll stop receiving the catalogs after two or three have been sent to you. To keep getting them, write a short note to the dealer indicating your collecting interests. Some dealers charge for their catalogs. In most cases, it's a worthwhile investment.

The Pen and Quill keeps you informed of every topic important to the philographer. Facsimiles are included in every issue.

There are auction reports, information about the authentication of autographs, names and addresses of people who will send their autographs, articles about members' collections, and so forth. With free ads for all members, you can advertise what you would like to buy, trade, or sell. An autograph auction is held every year in New York City; mail bids are accepted.

Frequent UACC Autograph Shows at which dealers buy and sell autographs are held around the world. Atlanta, Chicago, Dallas, Long Island, Los Angeles, Miami/Ft. Lauderdale, Minneapolis, New Orleans, New York, San Francisco, and Washington, D.C., along with the European cities of London and Ultrecht, have had Autograph Shows, and more are in the planning stage for these cities and others. There is never an admission fee charged at a UACC Show.

One aspect of autograph collecting you should be aware of: Facsimiles, signatures done by secretaries, and Autopen machine signatures, as well as forgeries, are all part of this hobby. How can you be sure you are trading for an authentic autograph? Only deal with reputable people who guarantee what they sell.

Reputation is very important in our hobby. *The Pen and Quill* keeps UACC members aware of disreputable dealers and forgers as well as new secretarial and Autopen signatures in use.

News contained in *The Pen and Quill* has made headlines in newspapers throughout the world. The fact that former President Nixon had resumed signing autographs was picked up by more than 40 papers coast to coast, including Canada, and even by an English-language daily in India. Information concerning a change in Jimmy Carter's signature during his second year in office was noted in a New York newspaper and a British weekly with *The Pen and Quill* listed as the source of the story.

UACC members include men, women, and children of all ages in every state and on six continents. Students, teachers, housewives, farmers, politicians, businesspeople, doctors, dentists, military men and women, factory workers, undertakers, scientists, barbers, musicians, athletes, entertainers, religious leaders, authors, judges, retired men and women, and book, antique, stamp, coin, and autograph dealers—everybody is represented in the UACC.

How Do I Join the UACC?

Simply write for an application:

UACC
c/o Robert Erickson
P.O. Box 6181
Washington, DC 20044-6181

10
The Care and Feeding of Your Collection

Collecting autographs is an exciting and profitable hobby.

Autographs, as shown in Wallace-Homestead's *Price Guide to Autographs*, continue to rise in value at a faster rate than do most other collectibles. Autograph items, normally being just pieces of paper such as letters and photographs, are also easy to store. A collection worth many thousands of dollars fits easily within an album, a safety deposit box, or, for that matter, a plain old shoe box.

The potential for "buying low, selling high" is no less than astonishing in autographs. For example, if you were so incredibly lucky as to meet Greta Garbo on a New York City street and got this notoriously signature-shy lady to sign her autograph, you would have an instant rarity. You could then take that slip of paper to Herman Darvick's autograph auction, also in the Big Apple, and realistically expect about $1,000.

To a lesser degree, the same instant profit is true of most celebrities. Any of the living Presidents and ex-Presidents, Frank Sinatra, Pope John Paul II, Nobel Prize winners, Norman Mailer, the Prime Minister of Canada, Clint Eastwood—all these and thousands of other celebrities give you immediate assets just by signing their name. Whether you get a signature in person or an authentic one through the mail, the value is there.

Look at baseball players for a more mundane example. Go to any major league game and, with a little luck, $200 or $300 worth of autographs are yours merely for politely asking. A very few years of perseverance on your part and the worth of your autograph collection is awesome in light of the effort expended.

Add in the meticulous study of autograph dealers' catalogs and the snatching up of the many bargains you will find in signatures of people living or dead, and then trade judiciously with fellow collectors—and even more profit accrues.

Which brings us to the point of this chapter. A collector of sterling silver would not leave Paul Revere pieces out in the rain to tarnish, nor where light-fingered persons could make their own instant profit.

There are a number of considerations the autograph collector should keep in mind. These fall into two major areas:

• Preservation, safeguarding, and display

and

• Record Keeping

The latter, in these days of complicated taxes, can be extremely important, especially if you decide to sell, insure, or donate items. As in any business, in the case of an IRS audit or a theft, proper record keeping is a necessity.

Record Keeping

Paper can deteriorate or be defaced easily if care is not taken. In past years, collectors often would take a pencil and write the source and purchase price of a letter or other document directly on the letter or document. Many thousands of pieces now have such markings on them, or dealers' prices and comments such as *very rare.*

Whatever you do, *do not* attempt to erase these penciled notes. They don't injure the paper and may be of considerable importance in establishing provenance. The handwriting of many old-time dealers and collectors is recognizable by many current dealers and collectors who have handled large numbers of manuscripts, thus helping to prove authenticity.

Now, however, *nothing* should be written on an autograph item. Nor, for reasons we will discuss shortly, should other paper (unless absolutely known to be acid-free) come in contact with it. So records for your collection need to be kept separately in some manner.

The simplest way is by the use of index cards, which may be alphabetized by category and easily filed. On the card for a specific autograph, the following minimum information should be recorded: author, source of the autograph, date obtained, cost, and exact measurements as well as other identifying characteristics. (This is important in identifying your piece in case of loss or theft.)

If you store autographs in plastic sleeves placed in a three-ring binder (an excellent way of storing), a good practice for more important pieces is to type up a page with yet more information that you can then place in a facing sleeve. This page can include a complete transcript of the document or letter (increasing your facility in learning how to decipher handwriting of all types). Other facts about the autograph should also be recorded.

Some of these facts are public exhibitions, other existing copies, repairs, known publications, and the address of the dealer (if you bought the piece). Having this data with the autograph can save you a lot of fumbling about to find it later.

Including biographical information and a picture of the person also enhances the display of your collection, its value, and (most importantly) *your* enjoyment of it.

If the autograph was purchased from a dealer, save the correspondence relating to it along with the bill of sale.

42

Reputable dealers will provide a sales slip on which they list the piece and include a description. A statement to the effect that *All autographs are guaranteed genuine* is usually included. If not, ask for it. There is no logical reason for a dealer to refuse to guarantee authenticity, so don't be shy in demanding it. Otherwise, take your money elsewhere.

If you've purchased a packet of letters from the same person, or a group of documents that are all related in some manner, record keeping can become a bit more complicated. In such cases, you should break the collection down and assign a pro rata value to each piece. This holds true also for unrelated items which you may have purchased for one lump sum. Record keeping may seem onerous, but doing it at the time of purchase is a lot easier than trying to reconstruct it years later.

The Computer Age. There are other ways to keep records for an autograph collection. Ledger books and loose-leaf notebooks are only two.

The advent of the Computer Age is proving a boon to many collectors. Autograph collecting, being in essence the management of large amounts of data, lends itself well to record keeping via a personal computer.

The fact that a good IBM-compatible system, including printer and monitor, can now be had for a relatively small investment makes this option more and more attractive. Whether a hobby or a business, autograph collection should be and can be fun. A computer eliminates much of the bookkeeping drudgery.

A full explanation of the myriad of computerization benefits for collectors is beyond the scope of this article, but the basic two programs needed are a database manager and a word processing program.

Any large group of related facts, such as facts about autographs, is called a database. A database manager program allows you to enter and retrieve these facts quickly and easily.

It will alphabetize and generate reports for you, giving a total of your holdings and telling what each individual piece is worth, either for a category such as Artists, or for the collection in its entirety.

Going to an autograph show? Print out a list of what you have and avoid buying duplications. Found a listing in a dealer's catalog for a football player you may or may not have? Don't thumb through your albums or card index looking when all you have to do is key it into the computer and have all the pertinent information pop up on the screen.

The other program you need, a word processor, speeds up correspondence and allows neatly formatted descriptions to be included in autograph albums. As already detailed, this enhances the value of your collection and increases enjoyment.

A computer is just a tool, like a hammer. Properly used, it can enhance your hobby and make it even more profitable.

Preservation

No matter how precise your record keeping may be, computerized or not, the actual autograph itself must be kept in the very best condition possible. Proper preservation will ensure that your collection not only retains its value, but increases in value as well.

There are several good books on this subject, with two of the better sources being the material included in *Autographs: A Collector's Guide*, by Jerry E. Patterson (Crown, 1973), and *Collecting Historical Documents*, by Todd Axelrod (TFH Publications, 1984).

Older documents suffer from being folded. Before the invention of the file cabinet, papers were usually tied up in bundles with string or ribbon for storage. (The English government often used red tape instead of string, thus coining the term *red tape* as applied to bureaucracy.)

It is not uncommon to find such bundles still tied and folded in this manner. Should you acquire one of these, immediately unfold each piece and place it between two pieces of acid-free paper and onto a flat surface for gradual unwrinkling. A weight, such as a book, may be placed on top as long as it does not come in contact with the document. All items such as paper clips, pins, and ribbons should be removed. Wax seals, if intact (which is rare), should be left in place.

Many pieces of paper carry the seeds of their own destruction deep within: *acid*. Dealers and librarians can tell horror stories of autograph collections, preserved in folders or framed, in which the paper degenerated or was left with stains and other unsightly damage.

Acid occurs naturally in wood. One look at an old pulp magazine from the 1930s—pages yellowed, tattered, and crumbling—can immediately show you how this internal destructive process works. Or last year's newspaper, for that matter. Older paper, from the nineteenth century and earlier, usually had a higher rag content than modern papers and, thus, less acid content.

As a rule of thumb, the higher the pulp content of the paper, the greater the acid content. Newsprint, the cheapest kind of paper, has the most pulp content. Even newspapers, pulp magazines, and old comic books (also with a high pulp content) can be preserved, though. In fact, a good collectible-comic-book store can be of great benefit to the autograph collector. The better ones carry such preservation materials as acetate bags and de-acidification sashes. The latter actually remove acid from paper, dramatically increasing its life. For valuable pieces on cheap paper, these can be a very worthwhile investment.

The mistake some collectors make is to put a newspaper clipping in the same folder with an autograph piece. Even though the autograph might be on good paper, the acid in the newsprint can quickly stain, even ruin, the autograph document. So put autograph items in an acetate folder, and protect them from contact with other paper.

Acetate folders are also available at most stationers' stores, as well as those specializing in stamp or photography supplies. Even if designed for holding comic books, stamps, or photographs, these are just fine for autographs, too. Always ask for *acid-free* material.

We autograph collectors can learn a lot about preservation from stamp collectors. Stamps are usually more delicate and likely to fade than autograph documents. Pages sold for philatelists are just as useful to us.

Buying acetate folders already punched for a three-ring binder makes your storage problems a lot easier. You can have notebooks for each category of your collection: Civil War, Presidential, Sports, Vintage Movie Stars, and so forth.

If you have a manuscript of several pages, remove all paper clips and staples, since these will rust and discolor the paper. The general rule here is to let nothing but the protective acetate come in contact with the piece. Engravings, newspaper clippings, even photographs (which are sometimes still coated with chemicals) should be stored in a separate sleeve or folder.

Acid is not the only enemy of paper; so, too, is humidity. Excessive humidity, such as that risked by storing papers in a basement or garage, can lead to mold. Some areas, such as the Southeastern U.S., are especially hazardous to the collectors of books, stamps, and autographs. If you have this problem, the purchase of a dehumidifier for the room the autographs are stored in is a very wise investment.

You may also place small packets of silica gel (the stuff that is packed with new cameras and radios) inside binders. These soak up water vapor from the air, but must be replaced after a period of time. The relative humidity should never be more than 70 percent, and about 50 is the best. Cold is no problem.

Another enemy is light, especially the ultraviolet-laden destructiveness of direct sunlight. If you display an autograph in a frame, ultraviolet shields are available which will protect them, both from the sun and artificial sources.

Dust can also be harmful. The shelves where you keep your collection should be kept clean. The same applies for filing cabinets, if those are used. Dust can carry particles of various chemicals that deteriorate paper.

In general, there is nothing wrong with taking an autograph out of its storage place for an occasional airing, just as stamp collectors air stamps. In fact, air circulating around paper is usually beneficial. No autograph should be sealed up too tightly.

Framing, matting, and display. As we've just seen, light is an enemy of autographs. The simple fact of life is that light causes ink on paper to fade.

Ultraviolet shields, nonreflective glass, and the like can decrease this fading action, but nothing except total darkness forever will completely guard against light's harm.

So a really valuable autograph, such as a George Washington letter, should not be framed and displayed. A better choice might be a favorite actor, actress, baseball player, or whatever reflects your interest in current celebrities.

If you do frame and hang a piece (and such a display can look quite awesome in your living room), *never* place it where direct sunlight has a chance of hitting it. Reflected daylight is also dangerous, since it causes fading, as does fluorescent lighting. The plastic ultraviolet shields already mentioned will help protect against the worst of light damage.

Framing or matting (placing the autograph between two pieces of cardboardlike material with a cut-out in the top one to thus frame the item) takes a modicum of skill, tools, and materials. This craft, if you collect and/or sell a lot of autographs, is well worth learning and will quickly pay for itself. Professional framers charge professional prices.

Still, for the occasional piece, most people go to a framing shop. When you entrust an autograph document or letter or signed photograph to a framer, some precautions are in order. First, you must insist that the matting board used be *museum board*—that is, acid-free. The thickness of board chosen should be one which will keep the autograph from touching the glass of the frame and also allow for some air circulation.

Explain vigorously to the framer that Scotch tape, masking tape, or any other kind of tape should *never* be used, nor should the autograph be pasted down in any manner, not even to prevent wrinkling or buckling. Also, the framer must not be allowed to cut or trim the piece in any way. Engravings or photographs framed with the autograph must not be allowed to touch it, either.

In conclusion, autograph collecting is a wondrously exciting and potentially profitable hobby. Proper record keeping and care of your autographs greatly enhance this fascinating pursuit.

11
It's a Bull Market in Sports Autographs

Charles "Chuck" McKeen

Charles McKeen has been a play-by-play sports announcer, a syndicated sports commentator, an editor, and, for 30 years, a collector of fine memorabilia.

Somewhere in every family history there's a black sheep, and that's as true in autograph collecting as it is elsewhere.

In the gathering of hobbyists and dealers who make up the family of philographers, the black sheep designation has fallen over the heads of those collecting signatures of sports heroes. (Oh, there are exceptions to that rule. Certainly if your whim has been to accumulate the bold strokings of Babe Ruth, or the neat penmanship of Lou Gehrig, or the angry tangled lines of Ty Cobb ... well, that has been pronounced as acceptable by virtually everyone in the hobby.)

So today it might come as a surprise to find that not only have sports autographs suddenly found themselves highly sought after, but that items signed by even some recently deceased sports heroes have zoomed skyward in price at a rate unmatched anywhere in the hobby. That trend holds true for everything from signed 3 × 5 cards to baseball and football cards and more limited collector issues.

The growth in sports autographs has been stunningly quick, and has been led by the 1980s trend toward paying sports figures goodly amounts of money to sign their autographs. This all came about through the so-called *superstar collector shows* where such greats as Mickey Mantle or Joe DiMaggio, and even lesser lights such as Mike Shannon (in case you don't know, a former journeyman baseball player for the St. Louis Cardinals), are paid to sit and sign autographs for two to four hours.

Those autographs cost the collector anything in the $2–$8 range. These prices are for each item signed.

In addition, it costs another $2–$3 to get into the show, and then there is the cost of the item to be signed. What it all adds up to is that these shows are hot business, and they have shown the athletes that they can make money signing autographs. The fact that fans and collectors will happily stand in line for anywhere from 30 minutes to several hours to get the signatures has helped make some tremendous changes in the hobby. One of the results has been that many sports figures who have always been willing to sign items for free now ask a fee for autographs through the mail.

At the same time this influx of new sports-autograph collectors has meant a rejuvenation of the entire field. Signatures of athletes who died 10–15 years ago have zoomed up in price. In the 1970s, collectors could have purchased signatures of Baseball Hall of Famer Max Carey for literally 25¢–50¢. Today you hardly ever find signatures of Carey, and if you do, be prepared to pay. That 25¢ signature is now going to cost you $10, or maybe more.

There have definitely been changes. In the 1970s there were something like 100 actual collectors of sports autographs in the entire United States! Today there are thousands—possibly even tens of thousands. In the 1970s, too, anyone who collected autographed baseball cards was literally laughed at and certainly scorned by those involved in the more *serious* pursuits of *meaningful* autographs.

Today, those collecting baseball or football cards signed by the athletes are still mocked by some people, but there is a difference. Ten years ago, most signed baseball cards were worth 10¢–50¢, with a few exceptions. Now there are many cards signed by active players that go in the $5–$10 range. Cards of even the most common of players now sell for prices ranging from 50¢ to $1 and higher.

A collector who puts together a complete set of signed baseball cards—sets of cards issued by such companies as Topps, Donruss, or Fleer—well, what used to be a $50–$100 set is now likely in the range of $500–$1,000 in value. It's difficult to put meaningful dollar values on such compilations; the hobby is changing so rapidly and growing so swiftly that prices acceptable two months ago are laughed at today. Assuming nothing drastically changes the situation, it might take months or years for prices to settle into a truly universally acceptable range.

It has all been complicated by many factors, including these:

• The increasing popularity of sports, mainly baseball.
• The escalating numbers of baseball card collectors, many of whom have turned to autographs as a sideline.
• Increasing numbers of athletes who are no longer willing to sign autographs, at least not for free.

- Superstar collector shows where sometimes even athletes who have refused to sign autographs for years have been induced to show up and accept nice sums of money—$5,000 to $25,000 is the price range one hears for such stars—to sign autographs.
- The willingness of collectors to pay for what previously they had always gotten for free—autographs.

It's been a changing world for those involved in sports autographs. There have been good points and bad points to it all.

The collector has to have a sense of humor. Otherwise, how can you accept such things as a rookie baseball player answering your mail with a rubber stamp? It's true—ask those who wrote Terry Steinbach, who had a fine 1987 season as a rookie with the Oakland Athletics. If you wrote early in the season you were likely to receive authentic autographs. If you wrote after the first two months it was probably answered with a stamped signature.

Even more disheartening is to pay a pretty good price—say, a total of $10—and stand in line for an hour or two waiting to get an item signed by your particular sports hero, and then find an uncommunicative person who hurriedly scrawls a name across a photo and pushes it back at you. That has happened much too often with some of the biggest names in sports.

There have been many bright spots in the surge. Those who have for years enjoyed collecting autographs of football figures have found that field showing some very significant increases in both interest and price. Football cards, especially, used to be almost ignored. Today there is a lot of interest in that area. Nothing like baseball, but still enough to demand attention.

As for the biggest names in sports history, demand for their autographs has never been higher, and the prices continue to go up unbelievably. A Babe Ruth signature that could have been purchased for $50 just ten years ago is likely in the $300–$400 range today. A Babe Ruth signed baseball might have been picked up for $150–$200 ten years ago. Today, you might be looking at a range of $400–$800, depending on the condition of the ball and signature.

Of course, Babe Ruth is the epitome of the sports autograph. His signature has always been sought by virtually all collectors, even those who didn't specialize in this area. And there are many other names that non-sport collectors are looking for. Some are not that long removed from the playing fields. Two of the toughest are basketball greats Bill Russell and Kareem Abdul-Jabbar.

Russell has refused to sign autographs for years. Abdul-Jabbar has taken a similar stance. One of Abdul-Jabbar's signatures under his original name of Lew Alcindor is just as rare as a Bill Russell—maybe rarer.

Muhammad Ali is another of the legendary stars of the recent past who is regarded as a likely target for collectors. Ali, the former heavyweight boxing champion of the world, is spotty at signing for fans, although he has been known to be extremely cooperative through the mail. Most scarce, of course, is his signature as Cassius Clay, the name under which he originally rose to fame before accepting the Muslim faith.

There are other great names out there to collect. In baseball, the list starts with Ruth, Gehrig, and Cobb, and then runs through the history of more than 100 years of stars. The names, for the most part, are well known.

The list continues to expand rapidly, too. In 1987 there was a great influx of baseball players who are highly popular with collectors. The names include rookie home-run king Mark McGwire, World Series hero Frank Viola, and such new names as Kevin Seitzer, Bobby Whitt, Juan Nieves, Ruben Sierra, Jim Lindeman, and so on. In that short list alone could be Hall of Famers of the Class of 2005.

That, after all, is perhaps the primary interest of sports autograph collectors: to figure out who will make the Hall of Fame. There are many former baseball stars who will someday make the Hall. Unfortunately, they, like the late Ernie Lombardi, won't be around to enjoy the honor and the adulation.

Already some are gone. If you have or can find autographs of such players as Gil Hodges, Nelson Fox, Wes Ferrell, Carl Mays, Joe Gordon, Vic Willis, or Thurman Munson, you will have signatures from deceased players who have every chance to be eventually voted into the Hall. Most of those were never common to begin with. All of them died before sports autographs really caught on, so there aren't that many autographs of them around.

That is one of the interesting challenges of collecting in this field today. Unlike celebrities in other autograph categories such as movie stars or politics or authors, sports heroes were not haunted for autographs by true autograph collectors. Not until the last few years, anyway. So there is a scarcity in this field.

This scarcity is more dramatic for other sports. In football, only a few of the great heroes of the golden years are left. For the 1920s, there are only two major stars around, and they're beauts: Red Grange and Bronko Nagurski.

Still sought are the autographs of such greats as Sammy Baugh, Don Hutson, Glenn Davis, Felix "Doc" Blanchard, Doak Walker, Sid Luckman, Tom Harmon, Bill Dudley, George McAfee, Charlie Trippi, Howard Cassady, and on and on, right to the more modern era of O. J. Simpson, Johnny Unitas, and Raymond Berry. All of these great players belong in any sports autograph collection, and most are extremely cooperative about autographs.

But look through the ranks of the missing—those who have gone home for their final awards and, hopefully, applause. The list is long and filled with great names. Norm van Brocklin and Bob Waterfield, Bill George, Ricky Bell, George Halas—all were free with their autographs, but all are gone now and, as football autographs grow in popularity, theirs are going to be difficult to find.

Still, they are going to be common compared to some names that are either ardently sought today or else will be. Find something signed by Niles Kinnick, the Iowa All-American who died early in World War II. Or how about University of Minnesota All-American Bruce Smith, like Kinnick a Heisman Trophy winner? To say nothing of John Heisman himself, the great player/coach/ innovator who died in 1936. Then there's the legendary Bert Bell, any of Notre Dame's Four Horsemen, blonde Ernie Nevers, Wilber "Fats" Henry, Big Daddy Lipscomb, Eddie Price, or Amos Alonzo Stagg.

Of course, the want list of most collectors, when it comes to football, is headed by Jim Thorpe and Knute Rockne. They're tough to find, and will only get tougher.

Football and baseball are obviously the main sports that furnish collectible autographs. There are, however, many great names from other sports that are highly sought. Bill Vukovich won the Indianapolis 500 two years in a row, and then died in the race the next year. He's incredibly difficult to find. John L. Sullivan used to walk into a bar and holler that he could beat any man in the house. Such a statement signed by him would be worth a lot of money today.

Howie Morenz was a legend in hockey and is virtually impossible to get in autograph form. James Naismith invented basketball. He's to be found on most want lists.

That's one of the fun things about collecting sports autographs: The list goes on and on and is awesomely varied. There are so many sports, and so many people have participated.

For example, some collectors try to get something signed by every modern Olympic gold medalist. Some are even trying for every Olympic medalist, which would seem to be an absolutely impossible task, but fun to attempt.

Collectors try to put together complete compilations of every player who appeared for certain teams; others look for players from specific years or with certain names. You pick the specialty; the list is infinite, limited only by the imagination of the hobbyist.

The hobby of collecting sports autographs can be shaped to fit the needs and desires of each individual collector. It can be a relatively cheap pursuit if you choose to make it that way, getting sports cards signed in person by the athletes or, where possible, signed through the mail. Or it can be an expensive hobby, zeroing in exclusively on the rare and the costly signatures.

Either way, you'll find no lack of subjects. As the hobby becomes more competitive, with more and more collectors seeking sports autographs, the challenge to put together a nice collection will become more complex. Of course, that's all part of the fun.

It's interesting to note that now there are probably more sports autograph collectors than any other kind of collector.

For the 100 or so avid and true sports collectors of a decade ago, that thought is almost incomprehensible: to be in the majority in the vast philographic hobby. It's certainly a different feeling. It has brought problems to the field; no one can argue that. At the same time, it is the same exciting hobby it always was. There are simply a few more obstacles to clear.

12

Autograph Collecting in the Nineteenth Century

The hobby, avocation, and passion of collecting autographs is hundreds of years old—far older, for example, than stamp collecting. To those who might think the hobby a recent invention, we offer the excerpt below from the *American Cyclopedia* (D. Appleton and Company, 1858). Edited by those nineteenth-century men of letters George Ripley and Charles Dana, this article on autographs shows how widespread the hobby was more than 100 years ago.

A numerous and generally very intelligent body, scattered all over the civilized portions of the world, bear the name, from what they apply themselves to, of autograph collectors. . . .

It may be stated that those who ride the hobby of collecting autographs generally do it with higher purpose than mere curiosity. Whatever the original inducement, whenever the pursuit ripens into a passion, augmented knowledge, historical as well as biographic, is the result. A genuine collector is not satisfied with an autograph until he obtains as much information as possible concerning the writers. Very frequently the letter or document itself contains something which illustrates a doubtful point of history, or throws light upon an obscure passage of biography.

The largest private collection of modern times (the 1850's), in England, was that formed by the late William Upcott, of London. Upon his death it was sold by auction and dispersed. Sir Richard Phillips was a great collector, and claimed to be the first of the tribe.

"It is certain," says Catharine Hutton, "that he was in possession of these precious relics, each arranged by the alphabetical name of the writer. He was so well aware of their value, at a time when they were little thought of by others, that he has been heard to say he would as soon part with a tooth as a letter of Colley Cibber's; and that he expected a grant of land in America for a manuscript of Washington's."

There is another good collection in London, the property of Mr. Donnedieu, a Frenchman. Mr. Robert Dole, also of London, has a splendid collection—probably the largest in England, though he may be challenged by Mr. Dawson Turner of Great Yarmouth (surviving brother of the later Sharon Turner, the Anglo-Saxon historian), and the Rev. Dr. Raffles of Liverpool. These gentlemen have collections, each worth many thousands of pounds, and the arrangement of their treasures is at once simple and complete.

In Scotland, where autograph collectors are numerous, an Edinburgh bookseller, Mr. W. F. Watson, is confessedly the most successful and enterprising. Though a great portion of his treasures were obtained by exchange and gift, he has expended £15,000 on the purchase of rare autographs and costly portraits, views, maps, and title-pages to illustrate them.

In the United States, perhaps the most extensive collection has been formed by the Rev. Dr. William B. Sprague of Albany. In 1828, he commenced his collection, and much about the same time, Mr. Gilmor, of Baltimore, entered upon the same field. Mr. Gilmor's collection, which was very fine, has been much increased by Mr. Dreer, of Philadelphia, who purchased it.

Other eminent autograph collectors are Mr. Tefft of Savannah, Mr. Cist of Cincinnati (believed to reside now in St. Louis), Mr. Keeler of Mississippi, Mrs. Zachariah Allen of Providence, Mrs. T. A. Green and Miss Arnold of New Bedford, the Rev. Mr. Waterman of Boston, and Dr. Shelton Mackenzie (chiefly of modern European celebrities), now of Philadelphia. Mr. Charles B. Norton of New York has probably the largest public collection of autographed letters in this country.

For the information of collectors, who abound in the United States, we may mention that Dr. Sprague's mode of arrangement is twofold—one alphabetical, the other according to subjects, and one being to a great extent a duplicate of the other. He possesses (what is extremely rare) complete sets of the signers of the American Declaration of Independence, framers of the Constitution, generals of the revolution and, with a very few exceptions, of the members of the old congress.

Autograph collectors ought to be held in esteem, as often saving from oblivion or destruction many documents of great value. The original of the Magna Carta, now in London, was actually in a tailor's hands, for the purpose of being cut up into parchment measures, when it was rescued by an antiquary who fortunately knew its value and preserved it as an object of national interest and importance.

13
In-Person Autographs: The Ultimate Authenticity

George R. Sanders

To the inveterate autograph seeker there can be no more genuine thrill than to acquire a favorite personality's signature *in person*. As a professional broadcaster, interviewer, columnist, actor, master-of-ceremonies, radio and TV news commentator, and ultimately, a long-time broadcasting executive in the U.S. and abroad, I had the very good fortune of meeting the famous and infamous from every walk of life.

On motion picture sets, in radio and television studios, in sports arenas, in public auditoriums, in their homes, in their offices and mine, in foreign lands, and even in the White House, I've had my pen always at hand so that the celebrity of the moment could accommodate my request. I have never been refused or embarrassed by a star of stage, screen, or TV—nor by a sports figure. Nor by a political giant, a pygmy, or a President. Nor by a king or a prime minister.

On the next pages, we give you some samples of *photo opportunities* that clearly illustrate how most famous people are delighted to oblige with their coveted signatures. Our thanks to some of the world's greatest photographers, who opened their respective lenses to capture so many exciting moments in a thrill-packed life.

These photo artists include Julius "Bud" Claus, Charles Allegrina, Helen Doolittle Sanders, Al Boyer, Hal Jann, Carl Vermilya, Bruce Luzader, Hollywood's Mac Julian (Warner's), Academy Award–winning cinematographer William "Bill" Fraker (Paramount), Alex Jessen, O'Brien Photos, Photo-Art Commercial Studios, Earl Leaf (Republic, Eagle-Lion, Universal), Lucretia, and Floyd McCarty (Warner Brothers). Also included are staff photographers of MGM, RKO, and 20th-Century Fox, including J. Allen Hawkins, Ken Whitmore, Irving L. Antler of Columbia Pictures—plus actress Elizabeth Taylor, who, as a teenager, took our only honeymoon pictures in Hollywood.

You will find examples or facsimiles of the signatures of the celebrities pictured elsewhere in this book.

Jockey Eddie Arcaro

Left to right: George Sanders, Louis Armstrong, John Salisbury

56

Sanders with Lauren Bacall and Humphrey Bogart in 1954

Sanders interviews Lucille Ball and Desi Arnaz at their Beverly Hills home.

Richard M. Nixon, Patrick Buchanan *(at left)*

Helen and George with the Duke and Duchess of Bedford

Pat Boone

Dr. Ralph Bunche

Raymond Burr

James Cagney

Pearl S. Buck with the authors

Sanders with Groucho Marx and baseball's immortal Ty Cobb

Johnny Cash

Ronald Colman

Dr. Howard De Bakey

Cecil B. DeMille

Joan Crawford

Press conference with Secretary Fred Seaton. Can you find Sanders and Walter Cronkite?

Bing Crosby

Sanders with Terry Moore and James Dean

Thomas E. Dewey

Patty Duke

Astronaut Charlie Duke

Duke Ellington

Bob Feller with George and his son, George III

Joan Fontaine

Henry Fonda

Clark Gable

Associate Justice Arthur Goldberg

1964 Presidential candidate Sen. Barry
Goldwater

Sonja Henie

Dr. Billy Graham

Sanders gossiping with Susan Hayward on RKO set.

Sir Edmund Hillary

Ann Miller, Sanders, and Conrad Hilton

Jimmy Hoffa

Sir Keith Holyoake, Prime Minister of New Zealand, 1977

Captain Bob Hope gives Sanders some last-minute baseball instructions during a 1950 Hollywood charity softball game. Sanders was a participant in these star-studded events for five years.

Vice President Hubert H. Humphrey

Lyndon Johnson

Sanders joins singers Barbara Mandrell, Sonny James, and Susan Wadopian during a concert he emceed.

Sen. Jacob Javits

Grace Kelly

John F. Kennedy

Robert Kennedy; Ed Guthman points to camera.

Dr. Martin Luther King

At right, Gov. and Mrs. Goodwin Knight of California

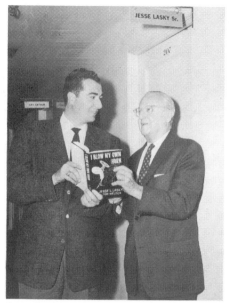

Juscelino Kubitschek, President of Brazil

Jesse Lasky

Notre Dame's Frank Leahy

Astronaut Ken Mattingly

Helen and George relax with Jerry Lewis in his Palm Springs home, 1955.

Sanders fishing with baseball stars Johnny Lindell, Ralph Kiner, and Ewell Blackwell (1947)

In this 1957 photograph, Sanders visits Shirley MacLaine in her dressing room at Paramount Pictures during the filming of *The Matchmaker*, which costarred Shirley Booth.

King Mahendra and Queen Ratna of Nepal are welcomed to the U.S. (Sanders at far right).

Presidential candidate George McGovern

Noted author/playwright Arthur Miller autographs the "Sanders Meanders" guest book as George's oldest son, G. M. "Sandy" Sanders, looks on in 1970.

Roger Miller

Paul Newman

Rocky Marciano

Sixteen-year-old Sanders with bandleader
Glenn Miller

Bronko Nagurski

Ferenc Nagy, Prime Minister of Hungary

Jack Nicklaus

1947 photo of a 23-year-old Sanders with his dad and Dick Nixon

LeRoy "Satchel" Paige

Jesse Owens

Dolly Parton

Dr. Linus Pauling and wife

Nancy and Ronald Reagan

Ronald Reagan

Yitzhak Rabin, premier of Israel

Eddie Rickenbacker and Bruce Luzader

Jackie Robinson

Nelson Rockefeller

83

David Rockefeller

Dr. Albert Sabin

Col. Harlan Sanders

Frank Sinatra

Ginger Rogers signs books in George's office.

Dr. Benjamin Spock

85

Astronaut Alan Shepard

Jean Simmons

Adlai Stevenson

Author William Styron

Jacqueline Susann

Sen. John Tower

Elizabeth Taylor admires Sanders' national trophy

President Harry S. Truman signs George's copy of his autobiography.

Director King Vidor in Hollywood during the 1950s

Lex Barker and Lana Turner with Sanders
at Hollywood premiere

Raquel Welch

Associate Justice Byron White

Charlton Heston, Frank Lloyd Wright, and author Tom Tryon with Sanders at Wright's Taliesen West in Arizona.

Tammy Wynette

Ted Williams

14
Finally—A Price Guide for Autograph Collectors

An immense number of hours have gone into preparing this price guide. We have journeyed to exceptional lengths to be as accurate as possible and to set up our computer databases so that market changes will be realistically reflected in future editions.

There are certain things you should keep in mind, though. This volume has the words *price guide* in its title, not *price bible*. A letter written by Abraham Lincoln to his grocer, deploring the condition of the last slab of bacon or barrel of flour delivered, is *not* going to be worth the same as a letter to a prominent Senator about the Emancipation Proclamation. Yet both are Autograph Letters Signed (ALS).

Content and condition, then, affect the true price of a particular piece. Each price given in this book is a medium price, a *guide* as to the price at which you could expect to buy or sell a particular autograph item.

The following are some of the special factors which should be emphasized with regard to autograph values.

Condition. Condition—as in the collecting of coins, stamps, comic books, and so forth—is the all-important consideration in autograph collecting. The prices quoted in this guide are for autographs in good to fine condition. Extra-fine letters, documents, cut signatures, and so forth are worth more. Tattered paper, creased or crinkled signed photographs, smudged or light signatures, and the like decrease the value of an autograph.

Pricing. As already stated, a great deal of effort has gone into estimating the prices that appear in this guide. Careful study was made of all available retail and wholesale offerings, auction prices, and realized reports, and of discussions with many dealers and collectors in the field. These and other factors were weighed in determining the prices given here for each piece and for each category. The prices in this guide represent the figures which we have calculated to be the average for a fine item offered by an informed dealer to an informed buyer.

Sales, of course, are often made at lower prices because of bargaining, overstock, changes in popularity, and lack of local interest. Conversely, prices can be higher if the celebrity whose signature is being offered has a local connection (like Thomas Wolfe in his birthplace of Asheville, N.C.), or if the piece is in excellent condition or has exceptional content. A letter by Lincoln about slavery and written while he was President would naturally be worth more than one by a young Lincoln concerning some more mundane matter. Also, a collector in need of a particular item to complete a topical collection might be willing to go higher than book value just to obtain a rare autograph.

The prices given in this book are retail prices—that is, the ones you would *pay* to a dealer or at an auction. If you sell to a dealer, a legitimate offer to you would be about half of the retail price. Since the dealer may have to hold the piece for years before selling it, this is a fair markup. You may always, however, bargain and haggle.

For those interested, the incredible mass of data necessary to determine pricing was compiled on three IBM-compatible computers using Borland's *Reflex* database and a very extensive customized program, written especially for this purpose by coauthor Ralph Roberts, which allows the easy updating of following editions. This special program—named *HELEN* in honor of coauthor Helen Sanders—was written in *Turbo Basic* (also from Borland).

While every effort is made to ensure the accuracy of the material contained in this book, the authors and publisher will in no event be liable for any loss of profit or any other damage—including, but not limited to, special, incidental, consequential, or other damages.

Pricing Categories

While there are more than four pricing categories in autographs, we have chosen the four most important ones for this guide. These are the ones which will cover the vast majority of autograph items, and exceptions may be interpolated from these prices. Here are the definitions of our categories:

• *Signature.* This is the price that a *cut* signature is worth—that is, just the actual signature itself on a card, or cut out of a letter, or in an autograph album.
• *Letter Signed* or *Document Signed*. An example of more recent pieces might be a typed letter or document signed by the celebrity. During the nineteenth century, before typewriters, it was common for secretaries to prepare handwritten letters or documents for their bosses' signature. These also fall within the LS/DS category.
• *Autograph Letter Signed* is generally the most important category. This is a letter (or document) completely written in the hand of the celebrity. As a rule of thumb, the greater the quantity of the handwriting of the important personage, the more valuable the piece.

- *Signed Photograph* (or engraving, painting, woodcut, and so on). Obviously, this category will usually only have a price for items dating since the invention of photography—that is, from about 1840 on. But there are exceptions for signed paintings predating the photography era.

Major Autograph Categories

The prices in this guide are broken down into major alphabetical categories such as Artists, Authors, Military Leaders, Presidents, and so forth. There are few duplications of names between categories. If a person was famous in several fields, you will usually find him or her listed in the one in which the most significant career success was achieved.

Dwight Eisenhower, for example, was a renowned military leader, but you will find him in the Presidents category—that being his ultimate achievement. Lew Wallace was both a military leader (a general in the Civil War) and the territorial governor of New Mexico, yet his greatest achievement was as the author of *Ben Hur* and other novels. He is, thus, listed in the Authors category.

Each category is alphabetized. If you are not sure about which one is most appropriate for a certain celebrity, simply refer to the complete index at the back of this book.

Photographs and Facsimiles

The next section is comprised of photographs of signatures. (Other autograph facsimiles are displayed in each category.) Great care has been expended to make sure that all facsimiles in this book are of authentic signatures, so you may compare your own pieces to these with confidence. Prices for the person whose facsimile signature is depicted below will be found under the appropriate category, or, again, you may find his or her name in the index, which will tell you the category to consult.

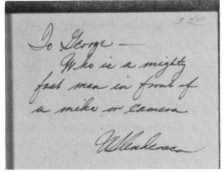

U. S. Andersen

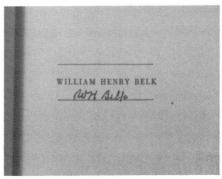

W. H. Belk

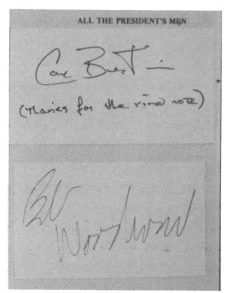

Carl Bernstein and Bob Woodward

Bismarck

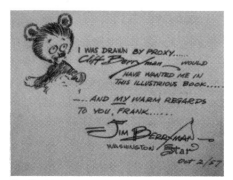

Jim Berryman

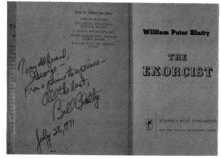

William Peter Blatty

Marlon Brando

A. Whitten Brown

Mountbatten of Burma

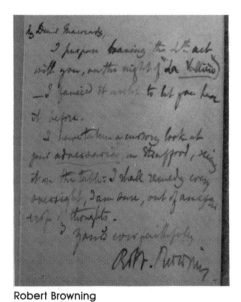

Robert Browning

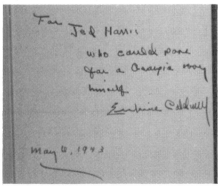

Erskine Caldwell

Pearl S. Buck

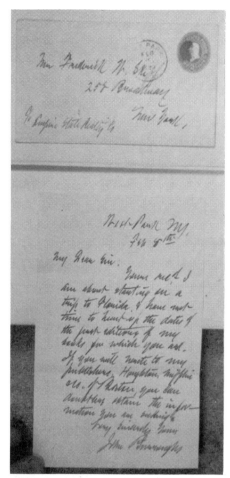

John Burroughs (Naturalist)

Louis Charbonneau

Prince Charles

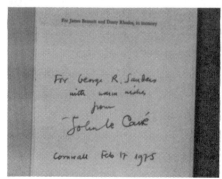

John Le Carré

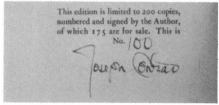

Joseph Conrad

Winston Churchill

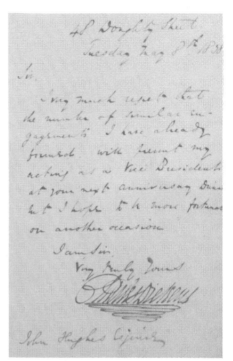

Charles Dickens

Samuel Clemens (Mark Twain)

Elizabeth II

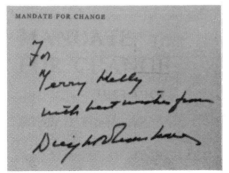

Dwight D. Eisenhower

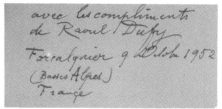

Raoul Dufy

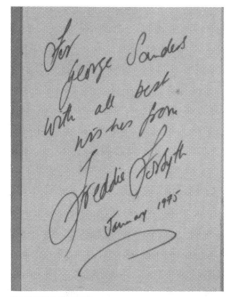

Frederick Forsyth

Generalissimo Francisco Franco

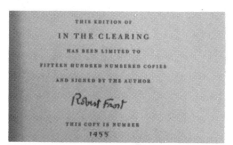

Robert Frost

Y. Frank Freeman, Cecil B. DeMille, Samuel Goldwin, Jesse L. Lasky, Henry Wilcoxon, Jane Darwell, and Leo Carrillo.

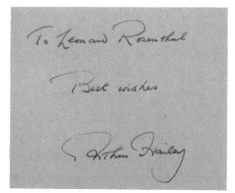

Arthur Hailey

Harry Golden

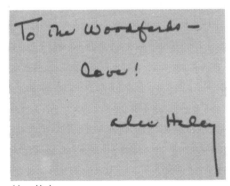

Alex Haley

Moss Hart

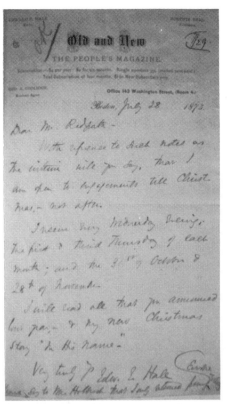

Edward Everett Hale

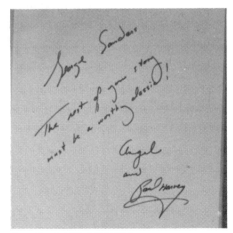

Angel and Paul Harvey

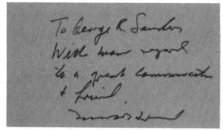

Sen. Mark O. Hatfield of Oregon

Patrick Henry

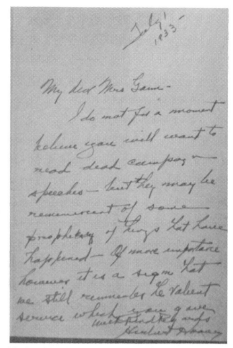

Herbert Hoover

Katherine Hepburn

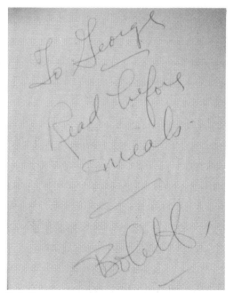

Bob Hope

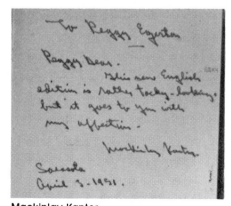

Mackinlay Kantor

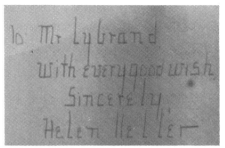

Helen Keller

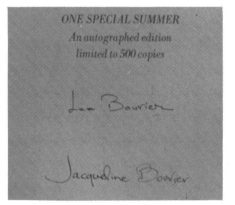

Jacqueline Bouvier Kennedy

Robert F. Kennedy

John F. Kennedy

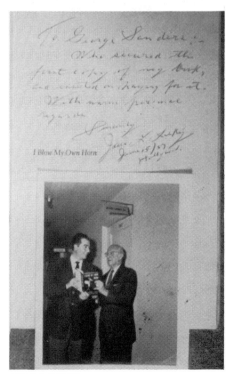

Jesse L. Lasky

Robert E. Lee

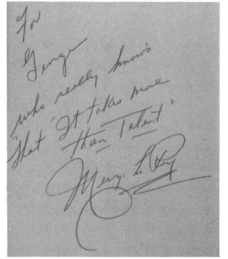

Mervyn LeRoy

Robert Ludlum

Douglas MacArthur

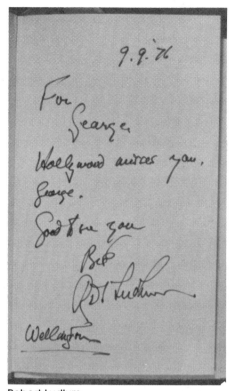

Shirley MacLaine

Rod McKuen

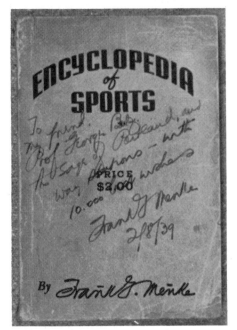

Frank G. Menke

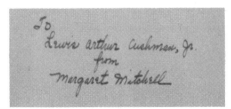

Margaret Mitchell

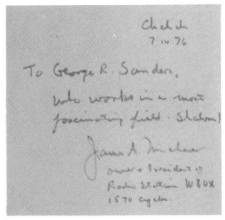

James A. Michener

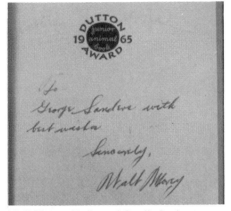

Walt Morey (Author of *Gentle Ben*)

Benito Mussolini

Admiral C. W. Nimitz

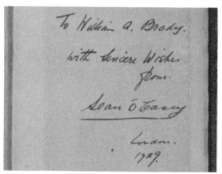

Sean O'Casey (rare)

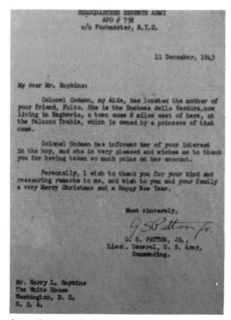

Gen. George Patton

Picasso

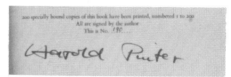

Harold Pinter

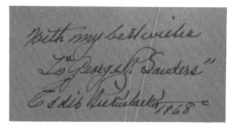

Eddie Rickenbacker

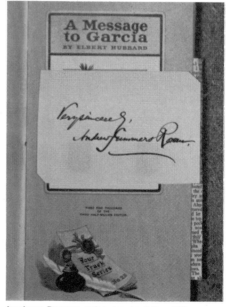

Andrew Rowan, who carried the "Message to Garcia"

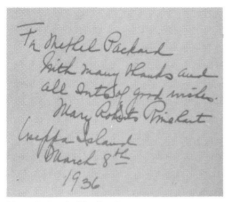

Mary Roberts Rinehart

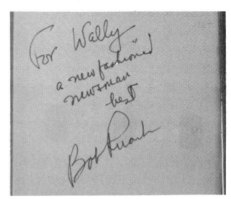

Robert Ruark

Robert Ripley

William Saroyan

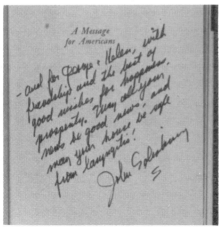

John Salisbury

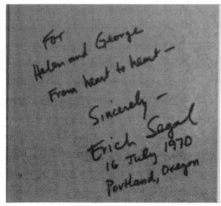

Erich Segal

107

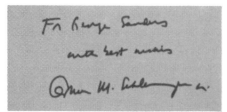

Arthur M. Schlesinger, Jr.

Haile Selassi

Dr. Seuss

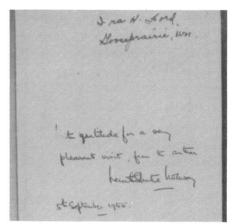

Nevil Shute

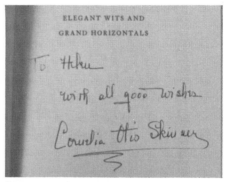

Cornelia Otis Skinner

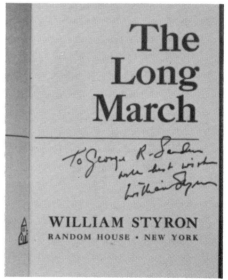

William Styron

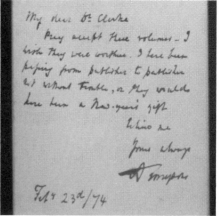

Irving Stone

Alfred Lord Tennyson

Jacqueline Susann

Gary Trudeau

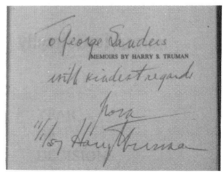

Harry Truman

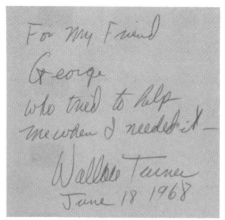

Wallace Turner, *New York Times*

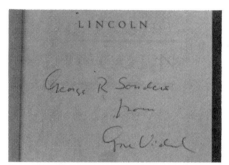

Gore Vidal

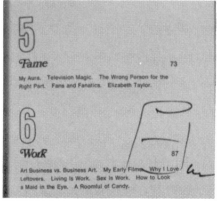

Andy Warhol

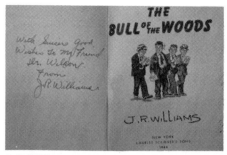

J. R. Williams

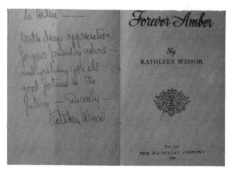

Kathleen Winsor

Natalie Wood

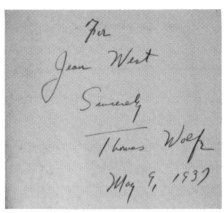

Thomas Wolfe

Air Aces

The United States has fought four "modern" wars in this century, each of which featured the progressively more sophisticated military art of aerial combat. For those wars, some 100,000 men were trained by the U.S. as fighter pilots. Of that number, just over 1 percent—some 1300—achieved the ranking of *ace*, which comes with the confirmed total of five victories over the enemy. A victory, of course, means the *other* plane was shot down.

For the autograph collector, that has meant a very exclusive hall of fame and a roster that is probably impossible to complete, since so many aces themselves subsequently lost their lives in combat or in other air crashes, usually in test-pilot jobs.

Because of the changes in the way future wars are likely to be fought, it is probable that there will never be another air ace. In fact, in Vietnam, the United States only had two aces for the entire tenure of the war, and they are probably the last two aces this country will ever see.

The collecting of aces has become an increasingly popular hobby over the past few years. The following is a look at some of the United States' fighter pilots who reached that coveted status (the first price is for a signature; the second, for a signed photo).

American Aces

Col. C. E. Anderson. WWII ace with 16.25 kills to his credit. Wingman to Chuck Yeager. $12.00, $25.00.

Rex T. Barber. WWII ace with 5 kills and 3 probables. He was a principal in the shooting down of Japanese Admiral Yamamoto, getting credit for one of the 3 planes shot down that day. $20.00, $40.00.

Maj. Gen. Charles Bond. Flying Tiger ace with 9 kills; he was shot down twice in combat. $15.00, $30.00.

Col. Gregory "Pappy" Boyington. Legendary leader of the Black Sheep Squadron. Claimed 6 victories as Flying Tigers ace, 28 victories total. $30.00, $65.00.

Capt. David S. Campbell. Navy legend, Medal of Honor winner—he downed 9 Japanese planes in one day, an all-time record for an American pilot. He had 34 total victories in the air, and destroyed 20 on the ground. $15.00, $40.00.

Randy Cunningham. One of only two U.S. aces in Vietnam. $17.00, $35.00.

Col. Jeff DeBlanc. Congressional Medal of Honor winner for action near Guadalcanal. Had 9 kills, 3 probables. $15.00, $30.00.

Archie Donahue. Fourteen confirmed WWI victories; one of only two to have twice reached *ace in a day* status, with five or more kills in a single day. $15.00, $30.00.

William R. Dunn. First American fighter ace of WWII as a member of the RAF in August, 1941. $15.00, $30.00.

Col. Glenn T. Eagleston. USAF ace with 18.5 German aircraft destroyed in WWII; added two MiG kills in Korea. $15.00, $20.00.

Joe Foss. Great Marine pilot with 26 WWII kills; Medal of Honor winner; also, first president of the American Football League. $15.00, $35.00.

Col. Francis S. Gabreski. Third-ranking American ace of all time with 34.5 total victories, of which 28 were in WWII and 6.5 in Korea. $15.00, $30.00.

David Lee "Tex" Hill. Served with the American Volunteer Group—the Flying Tigers—and was credited with 12.25 kills there; got 6 more later with the 14th Air Force for a total of 18.25. $17.00, $35.00.

Robert S. Johnson. 28 kills in WWI, tied for fifth highest total ever for an American pilot. $15.00, $30.00.

Thomas Lanphier, Jr. Seven aerial victories in WWII, including being credited with shooting down the Betty bomber which bore Admiral Isoroku Yamamoto, architect of the Pearl Harbor victory for the Japanese, and commander in chief of the Japanese Navy. $25.00, $55.00.

Charles H. MacDonald. His 27 victories rank his total as seventh highest ever for an American. $17.00, $35.00.

Col. Walker M. Mahurin. Had 21 German aircraft destroyed credited to him in WWII, plus one Japanese, and added 3.5 kills in Korea. $15.00, $30.00.

Bob Neale. Leading ace of the Flying Tigers. $20.00, $40.00.

Gen. Robin Olds. Only WWII ace also to have kills in Vietnam, with 17 total kills. $15.00, $30.00.

Steve Richie. One of only two U.S. aces in Vietnam. $17.00, $35.00.

Gen. Robert L. Scott, Jr. Flew "guest missions" with the Flying Tigers, then headed the 23rd fighter group when the Tigers were disbanded and the U.S. took over the area. Wrote the book *God Is My Co-Pilot*, which was made into a movie. His kill total was probably 22, although several of those were officially credited as probables. $17.00, $35.00.

Witold A. Urbanowicz. Flew with the USAF in WWII, although he became an ace with his native Polish forces and furthered that with the RAF. His career total was 28 German and Japanese planes. $20.00, $50.00.

Lt. Col. George Vaughn, Jr. WWI ace with 13 official victories. $25.00, $65.00.

Lt. Col. Kenneth A. Walsh. Marine ace, won Medal of Honor, had 21 victories in WWII. $15.00, $30.00.

Col. Hubert Zemke. Hub Zemke was a legendary flight leader credited with 17.75 aerial victories. Great tactical leader. $20.00, $40.00.

Gen. Adolf Galland. One of the top Luftwaffe pilots in WWII with 104 victories. At one time he headed the German fighter corps. $30.00, $75.00.

Maj. Erich Hartmann. All-time leading ace of aces with the Luftwaffe. He was credited with 352 kills in WWII. $25.00, $50.00.

There are fewer than 400 American aces still alive, and an unknown total in other countries. Foreign aces are difficult to find, and many American aces have likewise become rare. Under the urging of the U.S. Fighter Pilot Aces Association, many of these pilots will not sign autographs. This has further reduced the number of aces you can find for a collection.

Autographs of aces who died during combat are extremely hard to find. The all-time leading American scorer, Richard Bong, is exceedingly rare, for instance.

Photos signed by aces are less common than signatures, and in many cases command a larger premium than the normal doubling of signature prices.

The most common American aces are priced at $10 for a signature and $20 for a photograph, although really top-notch combat-era photos could go for a 50-percent premium above that. The same is true for the higher-priced aces.

Artists and Photographers

It's a pity that we cannot correspond just with artists who could write to us in the manner of James M. Whistler, Charles M. Russell, Howard Pyle, Maxfield Parrish, Salvador Dali, or Frederic Remington—all of whom embellished their correspondence with individual artistic trademarks. Some of these autographic souvenirs include butterflies, pirates, steer's skulls, and bucking broncos as well as graceful calligraphic signatures.

However, many of our most artisic and highly sought-after contributors to the world of art wrote in a most unattractive and illegible fashion, leaving us thinking that we could certainly make no judgment as to artistic ability were we to use penmanship as a criteria.

The following represents many artists of the world. There are, of course, hundreds more. The fact that an artist is not included on the list is in no way a reflection of the ability of that artist. It means only that data on a philographic item of his or hers was not accessible at the time of publishing.

* = Data incomplete, estimate only. ** = Last published price.

Name	Signature Only	Letter or Document Signed	Autograph Letter Signed	Signed Photograph
Abbey, Edwin Austin	$ 10.00	$ 21.00	$ 35.00	
Adams, Ansel	40.00	75.00	122.50	$ 60.00
Addams, Charles	17.50	35.00	55.00	
Aitken, Robert	25.00	75.00	190.00	
Alma Tadema, Lawrence	7.00	20.00	50.00	
Armstead, Henry Hugh	5.00	15.00	30.00	
Audubon, John J.	750.00	975.00	2,400.00	
Avedon, Richard	10.00	20.00	35.00	25.00
Bacharach, Fabian	18.00	40.00	45.00	30.00
Bartholdi, Auguste	65.00	175.00	331.25	
Bartlett, Paul Wayland	5.00	10.00	20.00	
Beardsley, Aubrey	175.00	375.00	675.00	
Beaton, Cecil	20.00	60.00	150.00	75.00
Bellows, George	80.00	175.00	275.00	
Benton, Thomas Hart	46.67	125.00	375.00	
Biddle, George	25.00	60.00	125.00	
Bierstadt, Albert	63.57	175.00	291.67	
Bitter, Karl	10.00	25.00	75.00	
Block, Herb	10.00	20.00	30.00	15.00
Bonheur, Rosa	95.00	147.50	287.50	
Borglum, Gutzon	115.00	300.00	450.00	
Borglum, Lincoln	15.00	35.00	60.00	
Bourke-White, Margaret	55.00	80.00	150.00	
Bouton, Charles Marie	102.50	120.00	400.00	
Boyle, John J.	5.00	10.00	20.00	
Brady, Mathew B.	250.00	925.00	2,200.00	
Braque, Georges	138.00	425.00	810.00	
Brook, Alexander	25.00	40.00	75.00	
Burke, Selma	10.00	20.00	75.00	10.00
Burne-Jones, Sir Edward	25.00	50.00	135.00	
Cadmus, Paul	30.00	55.00	95.00	
Calder, Alexander	100.00	190.00	385.00	150.00
Caniff, Milton	10.00	15.00	25.00	19.25
Capp, Al	40.00	60.00	125.00	40.00
Cassatt, Mary	225.00	475.00	850.00	
Cellini, Benvenuto	1,000.00	4,800.00	15,000.00	
Cézanne, Paul	650.00	1,450.00	5,500.00	
Chabas, Paul Emile	35.00	60.00	135.00	
Chagall, Marc	122.00	255.00	525.00	
Christy, Howard Chandler	40.00	75.00	110.00	
Church, Frederick E.	35.00	105.00	265.00	
Clovio, Giorgio Guilio	650.00	1,400.00	2,000.00	

California 1948
Photographed by ANSEL ADAMS

Ansel Adams

Charles Dana Gibson

Grandma Moses

Joan Miro

August Rodin

Georgia O'Keeffe

Norman Rockwell

Andrew Wyeth

Name	Signature Only	Letter or Document Signed	Autograph Letter Signed	Signed Photograph
Coombs, Patricia	10.00	20.00	35.00	10.00
Cooper, Thomas Sidney	10.00	20.00	32.00	
Copley, John Singleton	325.00	675.00	1,250.00	
Cornell, Joseph	125.00	375.00	507.50	
Corot, J. B. Camile	140.00	325.00	500.00	
Courbet, Gustave	200.00	475.00	750.00	
Crane, Walter	35.00	50.00	100.00	
Cruikshank, George	65.00	125.00	216.67	
D'Orsay, Count A. G.	20.00	55.00	130.00	
Dali, Salvador	46.67	125.00	375.00	100.00
Daubigny, Charles F.	80.00	200.00	306.00	
Daumier, Honoré	240.00	575.00	1,187.50	
Davenport, Homer C.	15.00	40.00	100.00	
David, Jacques Louis	160.00	300.00	575.00	
Davidson, Jo	35.00	75.00	102.50	
da Vinci, Leonardo*	5,100.00	13,000.00	34,000.00	
De Kooning, Willem	60.00	150.00	275.00	60.00
Dégas, Edgar	200.00	375.00	1,100.00	
Delacroix, F. V. Eugene	150.00	275.00	445.00	
Didier-Pouget, W.	20.00	45.00	75.00	
Doré, Paul Gustave	40.00	88.00	180.00	900.00
Dufy, Raoul	287.50	325.00	475.00	350.00
Durer, Albrecht	2,500.00	7,500.00	21,000.00	
Eastlake, Sir Charles L.	15.00	35.00	90.00	
Eilshemius, Louis	25.00	50.00	110.00	
Epstein, Sir Jacob	60.00	125.00	250.00	
Ernst, Max	175.00	310.00	805.00	
Fantin-Latour, Henri	30.00	75.00	160.00	
Flagg, James Montgomery	30.00	100.00	225.00	
Foster, Myles B.	15.00	35.00	60.00	
French, Daniel Chester	60.00	83.00	150.00	75.00

Name	Signature Only	Letter or Document Signed	Autograph Letter Signed	Signed Photograph
Gainsborough, Thomas	225.00	575.00	987.50	
Galle, Emile	85.00	275.00	575.00	
Gaugin, Paul	500.00	1,100.00	4,050.00	
Gibson, Charles Dana	35.00	75.00	138.33	
Goldberg, Rube	25.00	45.00	100.00	
Goya, Francisco	1,200.00	7,500.00	16,500.00	
Greenaway, Kate	125.00	220.00	395.20	
Gropper, William	20.00	45.00	125.00	
Gross, Chaim	42.50	65.00	150.00	
Hassam, Childe	140.00	225.00	325.00	
Hawes, Elizabeth	10.00	20.00	35.00	
Henri, Robert	50.00	110.00	250.00	
Herkomer, Hubert Von	10.00	25.00	45.00	
Hogarth, William	303.00	1,200.00	2,600.00	
Homer, Winslow	200.00	450.00	1,000.00	
Hunt, William Holman	30.00	60.00	190.00	180.00
Hurd, Peter	80.00	175.00	250.00	
Indiana, Robert	40.00	85.00	150.00	100.00
Ingres, Jean A. D.	125.00	245.00	550.00	
James, Will	60.00	150.00	210.00	
John, Augustus	30.00	65.00	130.00	
Jongkind, Johan	200.00	450.00	912.50	
Kandinsky, Wassily	150.00	325.00	575.00	
Karsh, Yousuf	25.00	45.00	125.00	40.00
Kent, Rockwell	30.00	115.00	167.50	40.00
Kingman, Dong	10.00	25.00	50.00	30.00
LaFarge, John	35.00	80.00	150.00	
Landseer, Sir Edwin H.	30.00	35.00	85.00	
Lawrence, Sir Thomas	95.00	225.00	400.00	
Leech, John	60.00	100.00	140.00	
Leighton, Frederic	9.00	15.00	35.00	
Lichtenstein, Roy	30.00	65.00	95.00	40.00
Lipchitz, Jacques	100.00	195.00	408.00	
Lossing, Benson J.	15.00	35.00	75.00	
Magritte, René	150.00	350.00	765.00	
Maillol, Aristide	138.00	395.00	750.00	
Manet, Edouard	200.00	497.00	671.67	
Martiny, Philip	20.00	35.00	70.00	25.00
Masson, André	35.00	50.00	85.00	
Matisse, Henri	200.00	325.00	600.00	
McManus, George	51.00	100.00	185.00	
McPherson, Craig	10.00	15.00	20.00	
Michelangelo Buonarroti*	2,250.00	10,000.00	25,000.00	
Millais, Sir John E.	30.00	60.00	80.67	
Milles, Carl	25.00	50.00	75.00	
Millet, Francis D.	25.00	40.00	113.00	
Millet, Jean François	147.50	370.00	925.00	
Miro, Joan	137.50	245.00	485.00	
Modigliani, A.	275.00	800.00	1,750.00	
Mondrian, Piet	200.00	575.00	1,105.00	
Monet, Claude	150.00	440.00	1,038.71	
Moore, Henry	50.00	125.00	210.00	56.20

Name	Signature Only	Letter or Document Signed	Autograph Letter Signed	Signed Photograph
Morse, Samuel F. B.	90.00	200.00	550.00	
Moses, A. M. R. (Grandma)	95.00	200.00	350.00	150.00
Nadar (F. Tournachon)	80.00	175.00	298.33	
Nast, Thomas	115.00	175.00	250.00	495.00
Neiman, LeRoy	16.33	45.00	95.00	35.00
Nevelson, Louise	30.00	50.00	90.00	50.00
O'Keeffe, Georgia	170.00	225.00	400.00	175.00
Oberhardt, William	30.00	65.00	135.00	
Parrish, Maxfield	150.00	195.00	400.00	
Peale, Charles Willson	225.00	495.00	850.00	
Peale, Rembrandt	150.00	275.00	540.00	
Picasso, Pablo	333.33	600.00	1,175.00	1,166.67
Pincus, Harry	10.00	30.00	60.00	
Pissarro, Camille	117.50	275.00	880.00	
Pope, Alexander	100.00	175.00	350.00	
Powers, Hiram	10.00	30.00	75.00	
Powers, Preston	25.00	65.00	162.50	
Poynter, Edward John	10.00	15.00	20.00	
Pyle, Howard	60.00	152.50	275.00	
Rapaport, Lester	10.00	15.00	30.00	15.00
Raphael*	2,125.00	6,000.00	21,000.00	
Read, T. Buchanan	15.00	25.00	35.00	
Rembrandt van Rijn	2,500.00	13,000.00	36,000.00	
Remington, Frederic	175.00	325.00	1,100.00	700.00
Renoir, Pierre Auguste	200.00	450.00	800.00	
Reynolds, Sir Joshua	200.00	336.00	550.00	
Rivera, Diego	195.00	360.00	700.00	
Rivers, Larry	40.00	75.00	125.00	
Rockwell, Norman	62.50	130.00	350.00	185.00
Rodin, Auguste	85.00	190.00	290.00	
Romney, George	130.00	225.00	450.00	
Rossetti, Dante Gabriel	135.00	180.00	290.00	
Roualt, Georges	125.00	425.00	690.00	350.00
Rousseau, Theodore	75.00	175.00	350.00	
Rowlandson, Thomas	200.00	520.00	800.00	
Rubens, Peter Paul*	1,500.00	8,000.00	25,000.00	
Russell, Charles M.	175.00	525.00	1,150.00	
Ryder, Albert P.	80.00	250.00	500.00	
Saint-Gaudens, Augustus	45.00	112.50	152.50	
Sargent, John Singer	50.00	125.00	210.00	
Sartain, John	15.00	30.00	125.00	
Savoia, Attilio	17.50	40.00	75.00	
Schary, Emanuel	10.00	20.00	30.00	
Schulz, Charles M.	25.00	75.00	100.00	65.00
Searle, Ronald	10.00	20.00	30.00	
Shahn, Ben	50.00	125.00	210.00	120.00
Shapiro, Harry	10.00	25.00	45.00	
Shoumatoff, Elizabeth	20.00	35.00	50.00	
Signac, Paul	70.00	150.00	306.25	
Sisley, Alfred	110.00	320.00	800.00	
Skinner, Stella	25.00	40.00	75.00	
Smith, Francis Hopkins	10.00	15.00	25.00	

Guion Bluford, Jr.

Dan Brandenstein

Apollo 15 Astronaut

James B. Irwin

HIGH

Frank Borman

Scott Carpenter—Second U.S. Astronaut to Orbit Earth

Pilot: Fitz Fulton

Fitz Fulton

John A. Glenn, Jr.

"Gus" Grissom

Gurraycha—First Mongolian Cosmonaut

Hank Hartsfield

Ivanov—Cosmonaut

Sigmund Jahn—East German Cosmonaut

Christopher Kraft—Houston Mission Control

Kizim—Cosmonaut

Sir Bernard Lovell

Maguari—First Hungarian Cosmonaut

T. McMurtry

Tom McMurtry

Eugene Kranz—Apollo Flight Director

121

Name	Signature Only	Letter or Document Signed	Autograph Letter Signed	Signed Photograph
Covey, Richard O.				15.00
Creighton, John O.				15.00
Crippen, Robert L.				20.00
Culbertson, Frank L., Jr.				20.00
Cunningham, R. Walter				20.00
Duffy, Brian				15.00
Duke, Charles M., Jr.	40.00			20.00
Dunbar, Bonnie J.				15.00
Eisele, Donn F.				20.00
England, Anthony W.				15.00
Engle, Joe Henry				15.00
Evans, Ronald E.				20.00
Fabian, John M.				15.00
Fisher, Anna L.				25.00
Fisher, William F.				20.00
Freeman, Ted	40.00			25.00
Fullerton, Charles Gordon				20.00
Fulton, Fitz	15.00		$15.00	15.00
Gagarin, Yuri	100.00			550.00
Gardner, Dale A.				25.00
Gardner, Guy S.				25.00
Garriott, Owen I.				20.00
Gentry, Jerauld R.				15.00
Gibson, Edward G.				20.00
Gibson, Robert L.				20.00
Gilruth, Robert R.				20.00
Givens, Edward G., Jr.				25.00
Glenn, John	25.00			27.50
Gordon, Richard F., Jr.				20.00
Grabe, Ronald J.				20.00
Graveline, Duane E., M.D.				20.00
Gregory, Frederick D.				15.00
Grissom, Virgil I. "Gus"		250.00		125.00
Gutierrez, Sid				15.00
Haise, Fred W., Jr.				15.00
Hammond, L. Blaine				15.00
Hart, Terry J.				20.00
Hartsfield, Henry W., Jr				15.00
Hauck, Frederick H.				25.00
Hawley, Steven A.				20.00
Henize, Charles G.				15.00
Hilmers, David C.				20.00
Hock, Robert C. (SKYLAB)				15.00
Hoffman, Jeffrey A.				15.00
Holmquest, Donald L.				20.00
Irwin, James B.	10.00			35.00
Ivins, Marsha S.				15.00
Jahn, Sigmund				35.00
Jarvis, Gregory B.				150.00
Jernigan, Tamara E.				15.00
Kerwin, Joseph P.				20.00
Kraft, Chris	10.00			20.00

Ed Mitchell

Story Musgrove

Andryen Grigoryevich Nikolayev

R. Nebel

Ellison Onizuka—*Challenger* Crew Member

Remek

Judith Resnick—*Challenger* Crew Member

David Scott

Dick Scobee—*Challenger* Crew Member

Stu Roosa

Alan B. Shepard, Jr.—*Apollo 15*

Valentina Vladimirovna Tereskova—
First Woman in Space

Ed White

Charles E. "Chuck" Yeager

Name	Signature Only	Letter or Document Signed	Autograph Letter Signed	Signed Photograph
Lee, Mark C.				15.00
Leestma, David C.				15.00
Lenoir, William B.				15.00
Leonov, Aleksei	100.00			200.00
Lind, Don L.				20.00
Llewellyn, Anthony				25.00
Lounge, John M.				15.00
Lousma, Jack F.	25.00			25.00
Lovell, James A., Jr.	15.00			30.00
Low, G. David				15.00
Lucid, Shannon W.				15.00
Lunney, G.				15.00
Mattingly, Thomas Ken	15.00			35.00
McAuliffe, Christa				250.00
McBride, Jon A.				15.00
McCandless, Bruce, II				22.50
McCulley, Michael J.				15.00
McDivitt, James A.				25.00
McDonald, A. J. (Al)	30.00			20.00
McNair, Ronald E.				150.00
Michel, Frank Curtis				15.00
Mitchell, Edgar D.				30.00
Mullane, Richard M.				15.00
Musgrove, Dr. Story			16.25	15.00
Nagel, Steven R.				15.00
Nelson, George D.				15.00
Nikolayev, Andryen	150.00			150.00
O'Connor, Bryan D.				15.00
O'Leary, Brian				15.00
Onizuka, Ellison S.	125.00			175.00
Oswald, Steve				15.00
Overmyer, Robert				15.00
Parker, Robert A.				20.00
Peterson, Bruce A.				15.00
Peterson, Donald H.				15.00
Peterson, Forrest (RADM)				15.00
Pogue, William R.				20.00
Popovich, Pavel				150.00
Resnik, Judith	80.00			150.00
Richards, Richard N.				15.00
Ride, Sally K.	40.00			35.00
Roosa, Stuart R.				25.00
Ross, Jerry L.				15.00
Schirra, Walter M.				35.00
Schmitt, Harrison H.				25.00
Schneider, William C. (SKYLAB)				20.00
Schweickart, Russell L.				25.00
Scobee, Dick				175.00
Scott, David R.	20.00			30.00
Seddon, Margaret R.				20.00
See, Elliot M., Jr.				100.00
Shaw, Brewster H.				20.00

Name	Signature Only	Letter or Document Signed	Autograph Letter Signed	Signed Photograph
Shepard, Alan B.	30.00			50.00
Shepherd, William M.				15.00
Shriver, Loren J.				15.00
Shulman, Ellen L.				20.00
Slayton, Donald K.	15.00			25.00
Smith, Michael				150.00
Spring, Sherwood C.				20.00
Springer, Robert C.				15.00
Stafford, Thomas P.				50.00
Stewart, Robert L.				15.00
Sullivan, Kathryn D.				30.00
Swigert, John L., Jr.				25.00
Thagard, Norman E.				15.00
Thornton, Kathryn C.				20.00
Thornton, Dr. William E.				15.00
Truly, Richard H.				25.00
Van Hoften, James D.				20.00
Veach, Charles L.				15.00
Walker, David M.				15.00
Webb, James E. (ADM)				25.00
Weitz, Paul J.				25.00
Wetherbee, James D.				15.00
White, Edward H., II	200.00			250.00
Williams, Clifton C.				25.00
Williams, Donald E.				15.00
Worden, Al M.				25.00
Young, John	30.00			70.00

Authors

The following list represents many authors. There are, of course, hundreds more. The fact that a writer is not included on the list is in no way a reflection of the ability of that writer. It means only that data on a philographic item of his or hers was not accessible at the time of publishing.

These prices are only for autograph material. If you have a signed book by the author which also has collectible value (such as a first edition), the value of the book should be added. Since many book dealers often do not realize the values of autographs, some very good acquisitions may be obtained by the collector who finds a signed book that is of little value to a book collector but contains a valuable signature.

Name	Signature Only	Letter or Document Signed	Autograph Letter Signed	Signed Photograph
Abbott, Lyman	$ 20.00	$ 35.00	$ 70.00	$ 25.00
Adamic, Louis	15.00	45.00	110.00	20.00
Adams, Henry	100.00	220.00	650.00	
Adams, William T.	10.00	15.00	40.00	10.00
Addison, Joseph	65.00	170.00	315.00	
Ade, George	15.00	38.00	85.00	30.00
Aiken, Conrad	25.00	67.50	145.00	
Albee, Edward	20.00	86.00	95.00	22.50
Alcott, A. Bronson	25.00	55.00	115.00	
Alcott, Louisa May	80.00	200.00	400.00	
Aldrich, Thomas Bailey	20.00	30.00	40.00	
Alger, Horatio	80.00	160.00	319.00	
Allen, Grant	5.00	15.00	30.00	10.00
Amis, Kingsley	15.00	30.00	65.00	25.00
Andersen, Hans Christian	200.00	330.00	660.00	1,165.00
Anderson, Jack	3.00	5.00	6.50	10.00
Anderson, Maxwell	20.00	50.00	101.67	35.00
Anderson, Robert	5.00	15.00	30.00	10.00
Anderson, Sherwood	30.00	75.00	116.67	35.00
Angell, Sir Norman	20.00	50.00	80.00	65.00
Anouilh, Jean	20.00	60.00	150.00	25.00
Apollinaire, Guillaume	60.00	150.00	325.00	
Armstrong, Martin	5.00	10.00	15.00	5.00
Arnold, Matthew	30.00	40.00	87.50	
Arnold, Sir Edwin	52.50	30.00	57.50	20.00
Arvin, Newton	16.00	40.00	85.00	
Asimov, Isaac	11.50	21.67	70.00	95.00
Asturias, Miquel Angel	50.00	135.00	285.00	
Atherton, Gertrude	10.00	20.00	60.00	20.00
Auchincloss, Louis	15.00	35.00	75.00	25.00
Auden, W. H. (Wystan)	40.00	75.00	185.00	
Auel, Jean M.	6.00	10.00	25.00	10.00
Austen, Jane	625.00	2,250.00	7,500.00	
Bacon, Francis	1,150.00	4,225.00	10,347.00	
Bailey, Temple	30.00	45.00	110.00	
Baillie, Joanne	5.00	10.00	25.00	5.00
Baldwin, Faith	10.00	25.00	45.00	15.00
Baldwin, James	25.00	70.00	145.00	50.00
Balzac, Honoré de	600.00	2,000.00	2,500.00	
Bancroft, George	15.00	40.00	62.50	
Banks, Michael A.	10.00	20.00	40.00	5.00
Banning, Margaret C.	5.00	12.00	25.00	5.00
Baraka, Imanu Amiri	35.00	50.00	75.00	40.00
Baretti, Giuseppe	5.00	10.00	20.00	
Baring-Gould, Sabine	5.00	15.00	30.00	10.00
Barlow, Jane	3.00	5.00	10.00	5.00
Barnes, Djuna	45.00	110.00	260.00	85.00
Barrie, Sir James M.	25.00	70.00	164.17	75.00
Barth, John	20.00	40.00	85.00	30.00
Barzun, Jacques	5.00	10.00	20.00	10.00

Richard Adler

Edward Albee

Horatio Alger

Jack Anderson

Maxwell Anderson

Norman Angell

Isaac Asimov

James Baldwin

Michael A. Banks

J. M. Barrie

S. N. Behrman

Saul Bellow

Josh Billings

Ray Bradbury

Peter Benchley

Bertolt Brecht

Robert Browning

Ned Buntline

James Branch Cabell

Name	Signature Only	Letter or Document Signed	Autograph Letter Signed	Signed Photograph
Bates, Katharine Lee	25.00	70.00	145.00	50.00
Baum, L. Frank	75.00	132.50	300.00	
Baxter, James P., III	5.00	15.00	30.00	10.00
Beach, Rex	15.00	28.33	85.00	30.00
Baudelaire, Charles	1,055.00	2,785.00	6,000.00	
Beckett, Samuel	50.00	120.00	300.00	
Beecher, Henry Ward	40.00	60.00	105.00	
Beerbohm, Max	55.00	115.00	168.00	55.00
Behan, Brendan F.	150.00	295.00	440.00	
Behrman, S. N.	10.00	20.00	60.00	20.00
Beith, Ian Hay	10.00	30.00	60.00	20.00
Bellamy, Edward	10.00	30.00	60.00	
Bellamy, Elizabeth W.	3.00	5.00	10.00	
Belloc, Hilaire	15.00	64.00	68.33	20.00
Belloc-Lowndes, Marie	15.00	35.00	110.00	20.00
Bellow, Saul	15.00	30.00	85.00	30.00
Bemelmans, Ludwig	10.00	18.00	60.00	20.00
Benchley, Peter	7.50	13.50	27.50	15.00
Benchley, Robert	15.00	30.00	50.00	40.00
Benét, Stephen Vincent	20.00	47.50	67.50	125.00
Benét, William Rose	10.00	30.00	45.00	
Bergson, Henri	25.00	55.00	110.00	
Besant, Annie	35.00	125.00	195.00	
Betham-Edwards, M.	3.00	5.00	10.00	5.00
Betjeman, Sir John	35.00	80.00	106.67	50.00
Bialik, Chaim	45.00	175.00	300.00	70.00
Bierce, Ambrose	150.00	425.00	850.00	
Biggers, Earl Derr	75.00	190.00	295.00	
Billings, Josh	21.75	65.00	145.00	35.00
Bishop, Jim	15.00	35.00	45.00	15.00
Bjornsen, Bjornstierne	20.00	40.00	65.00	
Black, Alexander	5.00	10.00	20.00	5.00
Blanc, Louis	10.00	20.00	40.00	
Blasco-Ibanez, Vicente	15.00	55.00	110.00	
Blatty, William Peter	10.00	15.00	20.00	10.00
Bok, Edward	25.00	55.00	135.00	40.00
Boll, Heinrich	15.00	30.00	95.00	20.00
Bombeck, Erma	5.00	15.00	25.00	10.00
Bosanquet, Helen D.	5.00	10.00	15.00	5.00
Bottome, Margaret	15.00	45.00	100.00	20.00
Boulle, Pierre	5.00	10.00	20.00	5.00
Boyesen, Hjalmar H.	10.00	30.00	70.00	15.00
Boyle, Kay	7.50	55.00	130.00	15.00
Bradbury, Ray	15.00	35.00	100.00	25.00
Braithwaite, William Stanley	25.00	75.00	170.00	40.00
Brecht, Bertolt	200.00	500.00	1,100.00	
Breton, André	40.00	115.00	250.00	
Brisbane, Arthur	15.00	35.00	100.00	25.00
Bromfield, Louis	15.00	30.00	108.33	20.00
Brooke, Rupert	400.00	540.00	1,200.00	
Brooks, Gwendolyn	7.50	15.00	27.00	25.00
Brooks, Phillips	20.00	25.00	40.00	

Name	Signature Only	Letter or Document Signed	Autograph Letter Signed	Signed Photograph
Broun, Heywood	10.00	30.00	70.00	15.00
Brown, Helen Gurley	5.00	10.00	15.00	10.00
Browne, Charles F.	10.00	25.00	50.00	15.00
Browning, Elizabeth Barrett	400.00	1,085.00	1,580.00	2,500.00
Browning, Robert	175.00	325.00	700.00	685.00
Bryant, William Cullen	27.00	108.75	139.29	
Buchwald, Art	10.00	15.00	25.00	15.00
Buck, Paul H.	2.00	10.00	15.00	5.00
Buck, Pearl S.	15.00	40.50	95.00	40.00
Buckle, Henry Thomas	5.00	10.00	20.00	5.00
Bullock, Walter	2.00	4.00	6.50	5.00
Buntline, Ned	140.00	170.00	250.00	55.00
Burdette, Robert J.	10.00	20.00	35.00	15.00
Burnett, Frances H.	20.00	40.00	70.00	
Burns, Robert	500.00	1,430.00	3,640.00	
Burroughs, Edgar Rice	90.00	275.00	475.00	
Burroughs, John	20.00	50.00	140.00	40.00
Burrows, Abe	10.00	15.00	25.00	5.00
Burton, Lady Isabel	24.00	85.00	181.00	
Butler, Samuel	20.00	60.00	165.00	
Byers, Samuel Hawkins	12.50	19.00	30.00	10.00
Byron, George Gordon Lord	950.00	2,350.00	6,100.00	
Cable, George	10.00	30.00	65.00	15.00
Caine, Sir Thomas Hall	7.00	15.00	39.00	
Caldwell, Erskine	15.00	50.00	85.00	50.00
Cameron, Betsy	5.00	10.00	20.00	10.00
Cammaerts, Emile	5.00	15.00	35.00	10.00
Camus, Albert	55.00	260.00	355.00	
Canetti, Elia	60.00	225.00	350.00	
Capote, Truman	50.00	195.00	425.00	65.00
Carleton, Will	15.00	50.00	100.00	25.00
Carlyle, Thomas	60.00	195.00	325.00	60.00
Carryl, Guy Wetmore	3.00	5.00	6.50	
Carson, Rachel	25.00	70.00	150.00	35.00
Cartland, Barbara	15.00	50.00	70.00	75.00
Casanovo, Giacomo*	135.00	580.00	915.00	
Cather, Willa	50.00	125.00	225.00	60.00
Catherwood, Mary	10.00	15.00	20.00	
Catton, Bruce	15.00	45.00	100.00	25.00
Cerf, Bennett	15.00	20.00	30.00	10.00
Cervantes, Miguel de*		10,000.00	15,000.00	
Chambers, Robert William	5.00	10.00	20.00	
Chandler, Raymond	190.00	540.00	975.00	
Channing, William E.	5.00	15.00	25.00	
Charteris, Leslie	20.00	55.00		80.00
Chase, Mary Ellen	25.00	70.00	150.00	35.00
Chateaubriand, Count F. R.	60.00	200.00	370.00	
Chayefsky, Paddy	30.00	85.00	153.00	35.00
Cheever, John	25.00	50.00	170.00	40.00
Chekhov, Anton*	525.00	1,535.00	4,300.00	
Chesterton, G. K.	15.00	70.00	150.00	
Christie, Agatha	110.00	294.29	550.00	

Name	Signature Only	Letter or Document Signed	Autograph Letter Signed	Signed Photograph
Churchill, Winston	10.00	20.00	40.00	30.00
Clarke, Arthur C.	15.00	35.00	75.00	25.00
Clavell, James	10.00	25.00	55.00	15.00
Clemens, Samuel L. (Mark Twain)	374.00	867.50	1,600.00	1,615.00
Cobb, Irvin S.	30.00	40.00	50.00	25.00
Cocteau, Jean	30.00	108.33	189.00	400.00
Cohen, Octavus Roy	15.00	30.00	45.00	25.00
Coleridge, Samuel Taylor	190.00	600.00	1,110.00	
Collette, Sidonie G.	45.00	140.00	300.00	210.00
Collins, Jackie	7.00	10.00	15.00	12.00
Collins, Wilkie	80.00	187.50	503.00	
Condon, Richard	5.00	15.00	35.00	10.00
Connelly, Marc	15.00	40.00	60.00	25.00
Conrad, William	115.00	350.00	765.00	
Cooke, Alistair	7.00	15.00	35.00	15.00
Cooper, James Fenimore	65.00	130.00	437.50	
Corelli, Marie	10.00	40.00	55.00	35.00
Cousins, Norman	10.00	17.00	25.00	5.00
Coward, Noel	70.00	165.00	325.00	200.00
Crane, Hart	130.00	600.00	1,500.00	
Crane, Stephen	210.00	737.50	1,650.00	
Crawford, Christina	8.00	12.00	17.00	15.00
Crichton, Michael	6.00	15.00	35.00	10.00
Crockett, Samuel R.	5.00	15.00	30.00	
Crompton, Richmal	15.00	40.00	80.00	30.00
Cronin, A. J.	20.00	55.00	120.00	25.00
Crothers, Rachel	5.00	20.00	42.50	10.00
Crouse, Russell	5.00	15.00	35.00	5.00
Cullen, Countee	35.00	100.00	250.00	
Cummings, E. E.	150.00	325.00	500.00	
Curtis, George William	10.00	15.00	25.00	
Cuyler, Theodore L.	8.00	15.00	30.00	
Dahl, Roald	9.00	20.00	35.00	5.00
Dahlberg, Edward	15.00	30.00	35.00	20.00
Dana, Richard Henry	25.00	70.00	187.50	
Dangerfield, George	5.00	10.00	25.00	5.00
D'Annunzio, Gabriele	50.00	100.00	375.00	
Davies, Rhys	5.00	20.00	35.00	5.00
Davis, Richard Harding	5.00	10.00	20.00	5.00
De Acosta, Mercedes	5.00	15.00	30.00	
DeCasseres, Benjamin	2.00	4.00	10.00	
Defoe, Daniel	1,500.00	7,500.00		
de la Mare, Walter	15.00	50.00	75.00	25.00
Descartes, René*	895.00	3,880.00	9,700.00	
Dewey, John	55.00	140.00	250.00	
Dickens, Charles	225.00	459.00	1,116.71	400.00
Dickey, James	10.00	20.00	45.00	15.00
Dickinson, Anna Elizabeth	20.00	45.00	70.00	
Dickinson, Emily	300.00	1,500.00	2,500.00	
Dinesen, Isak	30.00	125.00	212.50	35.00
Dix, Dorothy	5.00	13.00	40.00	10.00

Erskine Caldwell

Albert Camus

T. Capote
Truman Capote

Dale Carnegie

Bruce Catton

G. K. Chesterton

Irvin S. Cobb

Michael Crichton

Dr. A. J. Cronin

E. E. Cummings

Sincerely yours,
Paddy Chayefsky

John Dos Passos

Lloyd C. Douglas

Arthur Conan Doyle

T. S. Eliot

Ralph Waldo Emerson

Edna Ferber

Eugene Field

E. M. Forster

John Fowles

John Galsworthy

Sincerely yours,
Erle Stanley Gardner

Henry George

Zane Grey

131

Name	Signature Only	Letter or Document Signed	Autograph Letter Signed	Signed Photograph
Dixon, Thomas	5.00	20.00	40.00	
Dobie, Charles Caldwell	5.00	10.00	15.00	5.00
Doctorow, E. L.	10.00	25.00	75.00	30.00
Dodge, Mary Mapes	10.00	25.00	60.00	10.00
Dodgson, C. L. (Lewis Carroll)	180.00	500.00	1,200.00	
Doolittle, Hilda	60.00	175.00	445.00	
Dorr, Julia C. R.	3.00	5.00	15.00	
Dos Passos, John	17.00	35.00	80.00	15.00
Dostoevsky, Fyodor*	450.00	2,300.00	5,300.00	
Douglas, Lloyd C.	20.00	40.00	50.00	10.00
Dowden, Edward	4.00	10.00	15.00	
Doyle, Arthur Conan	200.00	525.00	1,000.00	
Dreiser, Theodore	55.00	117.50	235.00	
Drinkwater, John	20.00	41.50	70.00	25.00
Drury, Allen	5.00	10.00	22.00	12.00
Du Chaillu, Paul B.	10.00	15.00	87.50	
Dumas, Alexandre (Fils)	38.00	72.00	120.00	425.00
Dumas, Alexandre (Père)	55.00	95.00	156.71	
Du Maurier, Daphne	10.00	20.00	50.00	10.00
Du Maurier, George	10.00	40.00	65.00	
Dunne, Phillip	4.00	15.00	30.00	10.00
Durant, Ariel	20.00	35.00	90.00	30.00
Durant, Will	20.00	45.00	150.00	40.00
Durrell, Lawrence	20.00	55.00	187.00	40.00
Eastman, Max	20.00	40.00	60.00	
Eberhart, Richard	5.00	15.00	40.00	12.00
Edmonds, Walter Dumanx	5.00	25.00	40.00	20.00
Eliot, T. S.	95.00	295.00	610.00	
Ellis, Havelock	15.00	40.00	145.00	
Emerson, Ralph Waldo	95.00	197.50	387.50	
Erskine, John	25.00	51.50	145.00	
Fairchild, David	3.00	5.00	10.00	5.00
Fast, Howard	10.00	25.00	75.00	15.00
Faulkner, William	150.00	750.00	1,500.00	
Ferber, Edna	25.00	100.00	150.00	
Ferlinghetti, Lawrence	10.00	15.00	35.00	21.00
Field, Eugene	65.00	100.00	210.00	200.00
Field, Mary French	5.00	10.00	20.00	15.00
Fitgerald, Edward	45.00	120.00	300.00	
Fitzgerald, F. Scott	175.00	502.50	1,400.00	2,010.00
Flaubert, Gustave	150.00	325.00	683.57	
Fleming, Ian	70.00	355.00	575.00	250.00
Forester, C. S.	30.00	135.00	200.00	
Forster, Edward Morgan	70.00	160.00	253.00	
Forster, John	15.00	25.00	45.00	
Foss, Sam Walter	5.00	10.00	20.00	10.00
Fowles, John	25.00	35.00	50.00	30.00
France, Anatole	45.00	85.00	130.00	
Frith, William Powell	5.00	15.00	. 35.00	
Frost, Robert	105.00	275.00	1,415.00	500.00
Fry, Christopher	15.00	40.00	95.00	

Name	Signature Only	Letter or Document Signed	Autograph Letter Signed	Signed Photograph
Gale, Zona	10.00	15.00	25.00	5.00
Gallico, Paul W.	10.00	25.00	40.00	35.00
Galsworthy, John	27.50	65.00	115.00	
Gardner, Erle Stanley	40.00	80.00	175.00	50.00
Garland, Hamlin	15.00	25.00	35.00	10.00
Garnett, Francis H.	20.00	60.00	125.00	
Gaskell, Elizabeth Cleghorn	55.00	165.00	405.00	
Gay, Sydney Howard	3.00	7.00	10.00	5.00
Genêt, Jean	125.00	175.00	290.00	
George, Henry	20.00	72.50	90.00	15.00
Gibbon, Edward	250.00	740.00	1,805.00	
Gibran, Kahlil	105.00	295.00	750.00	115.00
Gide, André	140.00	275.00	500.00	
Gilder, Jeannette L.	2.00	4.00	6.50	4.00
Ginsberg, Allen	18.33	45.00	100.00	35.00
Gladden, Washington	5.00	10.00	15.00	
Glyn, Elinor	20.00	60.00	150.00	
Goethe, Johann W. von	1,200.00	1,875.00	4,475.00	
Gogol, Nikolai*	450.00	3,000.00	6,000.00	
Golding, Louis	10.00	15.00	25.00	10.00
Golding, William	30.00	45.00	65.00	25.00
Goldman, Michael	5.00	10.00	15.00	5.00
Gorki, Maxim	365.00	925.00	1,250.00	
Gosse, Sir Edmund	5.00	15.00	30.00	10.00
Grahame, Kenneth				150.00
Grass, Gunter	20.00	60.00	150.00	25.00
Graves, Robert	60.00	160.00	340.00	110.00
Gray, Thomas	675.00	2,005.00	4,150.00	
Greeley, Horace	25.00	90.00	122.50	
Green, Anna Katherine	10.00	15.00	25.00	
Greene, Graham	70.00	275.00	475.00	80.00
Greenwood, G. (Lippincott)	10.00	30.00	75.00	15.00
Grey, Zane	35.00	187.50	255.00	112.50
Grimm, Jacob	500.00	1,425.00	3050.00	
Grimm, Wilhelm	500.00	1,425.00	3,050.00	
Guest, Edgar A.	7.50	20.00	40.00	25.00
Habberton, John	10.00	15.00	25.00	
Haggard, Sir H. Rider	40.00	110.00	125.00	
Hailey, Arthur	25.00	40.00	65.00	35.00
Hale, Edward Everett	25.00	50.00	110.00	200.00
Halevy, Ludivic	20.00	60.00	150.00	
Haley, Alex	15.00	25.00	40.00	20.00
Halpine, Charles G.	20.00	35.00	90.00	
Hamilton, Donald	7.00	15.00	30.00	10.00
Hammett, Dashiell	450.00	1,058.33	1,750.00	575.00
Hardy, Thomas	140.00	365.00	715.00	567.50
Harland, Marion	5.00	10.00	20.00	
Harris, Joel Chandler	25.00	203.33	399.17	
Hart, Moss	15.00	39.00	70.00	
Harte, Francis Bret	60.00	120.00	190.00	
Hauptmann, Gerhart				375.00

Name	Signature Only	Letter or Document Signed	Autograph Letter Signed	Signed Photograph
Hawkins, Anthony Hope	5.00	10.00	26.50	5.00
Hawthorne, Nathaniel	287.50	500.00	1,900.00	
Healey, Robert C.	10.00	14.00	25.00	5.00
Hefner, Christie	5.00	10.00	15.00	10.00
Heine, Heinrich*	300.00	650.00	1,150.00	
Heller, Joseph	5.00	25.00	40.00	10.00
Hellinger, Mark	35.00	90.00	225.00	40.00
Hellman, Lillian	27.50	65.63	95.00	90.00
Helps, Sir Arthur	5.00	10.00	20.00	5.00
Hemingway, Ernest	520.00	965.50	2,150.00	900.00
Hemingway, Mary	15.00	35.00	60.00	
Herbert, F. Hugh	10.00	15.00	25.00	15.00
Herbert, Frank	10.00	15.00	25.00	5.00
Hergesheimer, Joseph	20.00	48.00	125.00	25.00
Hersey, John	15.00	40.00	115.00	20.00
Hesse, Herman	85.00	175.00	612.50	175.00
Heyman, Edward "Eddie"	5.00	10.00	25.00	5.00
Heyse, Paul	45.00	125.00	335.00	
Heyward, DuBose	20.00	50.00	110.00	25.00
Higginson, Thomas W.	10.00	20.00	50.00	
Hillis, Marjorie	5.00	10.00	15.00	
Hilton, Sir James	30.00	70.00	150.00	25.00
Holland, Josiah Gilbert	5.00	10.00	25.00	
Holley, Marietta	8.00	15.00	30.00	
Holmes, Burton	10.00	15.33	40.00	20.00
Holmes, Oliver Wendell	40.00	140.00	235.00	
Hood, Thomas (Elder)	15.00	40.00	100.00	
Hood, Thomas (Younger)	10.00	25.00	68.33	
Hornberger, Richard H.	20.00	30.00	45.00	25.00
Howard, Sidney	20.00	50.00	125.00	25.00
Howe, Julia Ward	40.00	130.00	183.00	
Howes, Barbara	7.00	10.00	20.00	10.00
Hoyle, Edmund	90.00	250.00	625.00	
Hubbard, Elbert	35.00	100.00	220.00	
Hughes, Langston	213.00	148.57	275.00	60.00
Hughes, Rupert	10.00	25.00	75.00	
Hugo, Victor	65.00	120.00	467.31	525.00
Hurst, Fannie	13.33	38.13	45.00	40.00
Huxley, Aldous	67.50	170.00	218.00	
Ibsen, Henrik	175.00	371.00	550.00	500.00
Inge, William	30.00	60.00	125.00	
Irving, John	5.00	12.00	20.00	5.00
Irving, Washington	85.00	225.00	316.67	
Isherwood, Christopher	30.00	87.50	170.00	42.50
Jabotinsky, Vladimir	40.00	120.00	300.00	50.00
Jackson, Helen Hunt	5.00	10.00	20.00	5.00
James, Henry	70.00	195.00	451.43	
Jerome, Jerome K.	15.00	50.00	92.67	
Johnson, James Weldon	20.00	65.00	155.00	
Johnston, Richard M.	5.00	10.00	20.00	
Jones, James	40.00	95.00	225.00	
Jong, Erica	7.00	10.00	20.00	15.00

Allen Ginsberg

William Golding

Edgar Guest

Thomas Hardy

H. Rider Haggard

Joel Chandler Harris

Joseph Heller

Paul Harvey

Lillian Hellman

Frank Herbert

Victor Herbert

John Hersey

Oliver Wendell Holmes

Julia Ward Howe

Victor Hugo

Henrik Ibsen

Aldous Huxley

Carolyn Keene

Ring Lardner

Erica Jong

John LeCarré

James Russell Lowell

Sincerely,

Clare Boothe Luce

135

Name	Signature Only	Letter or Document Signed	Autograph Letter Signed	Signed Photograph
Kafka, Franz			16,400.00	
Kanin, Garson	5.00	15.00	35.00	20.00
Kant, Immanuel	675.00	2,765.00	4,850.00	
Kantor, MacKinlay	10.00	20.00	45.00	20.00
Kaufman, George S.	30.00	125.00	175.00	35.00
Keeble, John	10.00	30.00	75.00	
Keene, Carolyn	4.00	8.00	13.00	5.00
Keillor, Garrison	15.00	20.00	35.00	15.00
Kelland, C. Buddington	20.00	55.00	150.00	25.00
Keller, Helen	70.00	225.00	442.50	250.00
Kesey, Ken	15.00	25.00	40.00	10.00
Key, Francis Scott	160.00	450.00	841.67	
Kilmer, Joyce	150.00	325.00	535.00	
Kimbrough, Emily	10.00	20.00	45.00	15.00
King, Stephen	25.00	55.00	135.00	55.00
Kingsley, Charles	25.00	55.00	106.00	
Kipling, Rudyard	118.00	290.00	466.11	
Knowles, James S.	10.00	20.00	47.50	
Krock, Arthur	5.00	15.00	40.00	10.00
Krylov, Ivan A.	10.00	30.00	75.00	15.00
Kyne, Peter B.	5.00	15.00	30.00	5.00
Lagerkvist, Pär F.				100.00
Lagerlöf, Selma	60.00	90.00	185.00	60.00
L'Amour, Louis	8.00	20.00	35.00	25.00
Lamb, Charles	100.00	225.00	525.00	
Lanier, Sidney	175.00	450.00	825.00	
Lardner, Ring	35.00	105.00	260.00	45.00
Lardner, Ring, Jr.	5.00	15.00	35.00	10.00
Lathrop, George P.	5.00	10.00	15.00	
Lattimore, Richard	10.00	14.00	20.00	5.00
Lawrence, D. H.	195.00	512.50	1,280.00	
Lawrence, T. E.	340.00	830.00	1,576.00	550.00
Lease, Mary Elizabeth	5.50	10.00	14.00	
LeCarré, John	20.00	40.00	75.00	30.00
Lee, Harper	15.00	30.00	75.00	25.00
Lefevre, Edwin	2.00	4.00	6.50	
Leopardi, Giacomo*	80.00	350.00	475.00	
Lermontov, Mikhail	540.00	2,300.00	4,625.00	
Lerner, Max	5.00	25.00	40.00	10.00
Lewis, Sinclair	50.00	200.00	525.00	90.00
Lindbergh, Anne Morrow	10.00	20.00	50.00	25.00
Lindsay, Howard	5.00	25.00	30.00	15.00
Lindsey, Vachel	30.00	65.00	160.00	65.00
Lippman, Walter	15.00	25.00	40.00	20.00
Locke, John	660.00	1,880.00	4,750.00	
Locke, William John	20.00	35.00	70.00	30.00
Logan, Josh	5.00	15.00	35.00	10.00
London, Jack	140.00	350.00	855.00	270.00
Longfellow, Henry Wadsworth	87.50	275.00	560.00	350.00
Loos, Anita	15.00	22.50	55.00	25.00
Lorca, Garcia	435.00	1,240.00	3,125.00	
Lord, Walter	3.00	5.00	10.00	5.00

Name	Signature Only	Letter or Document Signed	Autograph Letter Signed	Signed Photograph
Lovecraft, H. P.	150.00	275.00	1,100.00	180.00
Low, Sir David	15.00	45.00	110.00	
Lowell, Amy	35.00	120.00	250.00	
Lowell, James Russell	37.50	117.50	130.00	
Lucas, Edward Verrall	3.00	5.00	15.00	5.00
Luce, Clare Boothe	10.00	25.00	75.00	15.00
Ludlum, Robert	7.50	15.00	30.00	10.00
Ludwig, Emil	35.00	75.00	110.00	
Lytton, E. George Earle Bulwer-	10.00	25.00	53.00	
MacArthur, Charles	15.00	25.00	40.00	20.00
Macaulay, Lord Thomas B.	40.00	55.00	111.00	
Machiavelli, Niccolò*	450.00	2,325.00	7,825.00	
MacLeish, Archibald	18.00	50.00	125.00	35.00
Maeterlinck, Maurice	33.00	100.00	245.00	
Maiakovski, Vladimir V.	275.00	795.00	2,000.00	
Mailer, Norman	35.00	100.00	175.00	45.00
Malamud, Bernard	20.00	40.00	95.00	25.00
Malone, Dumas	10.00	30.00	75.00	15.00
Mann, Thomas	67.00	395.00	810.00	290.00
Markham, Edwin	20.00	35.00	55.00	40.00
Marquand, John P.	20.00	66.67	130.00	35.00
Marryat, Frederick	15.00	40.00	95.00	
Marsh, Dame Ngaio	15.00	25.00	45.00	30.00
Marshall, Catherine	20.00	60.00	150.00	25.00
Martin, Sir Theodore	5.00	10.00	20.00	5.00
Marx, Karl*	540.00	1,500.00	3,850.00	
Masefield, John	15.00	44.00	70.00	30.00
Mason, Alfred Edward W.	5.00	25.00	30.00	5.00
Masters, Edgar Lee	35.00	80.00	155.00	40.00
Maugham, W. Somerset	54.67	122.50	190.00	150.00
Maupassant, Guy de	225.00	400.00	975.00	
Maurois, André	28.00	60.00	100.00	
McBain, Ed	10.00	20.00	50.00	15.00
McCormick, Anne O'Hare	30.00	45.00	110.00	35.00
McCullers, Carson	55.00	180.00	375.00	70.00
McCullough, Colleen	30.00	90.00	190.00	25.00
McGinley, Phyllis	10.00	30.00	45.00	20.00
McIntyre, O. O.	15.00	20.00	30.00	10.00
McKuen, Rod	7.00	20.00	30.00	15.00
Melville, Herman	335.00	740.00	3,950.00	
Mencken, H. L.	25.00	135.00	210.00	35.00
Michener, James A.	10.00	30.00	75.00	15.00
Miles, Josephine	7.00	15.00	25.00	8.00
Mill, James	15.00	40.00	100.00	
Millay, Edna St. Vincent	107.50	287.50	625.00	100.00
Miller, Arthur	17.50	40.00	65.00	30.00
Miller, Henry	46.00	160.00	262.50	100.00
Miller, Joaquin	5.00	10.00	13.00	
Milne, A. A.	49.00	125.00	225.00	
Milosz, Czeslaw	20.00	45.00	110.00	25.00
Mistral, Frederic	15.00	60.00	100.00	25.00
Mistral, Gabriela	10.00	35.00	60.00	15.00

Name	Signature Only	Letter or Document Signed	Autograph Letter Signed	Signed Photograph
Mitchell, Margaret	500.00	900.00	1,785.00	
Mitford, Jessica	10.00	15.00	20.00	15.00
Molnar, Ferenc	40.00	112.50	160.00	
Momaday, N. Scott	10.00	15.00	25.00	15.00
Moore, Clement C.	85.00	240.00	600.00	
Moore, Marianne	32.00	95.00	150.00	40.00
Moore, Thomas	25.00	60.00	127.00	45.00
Morgan, Charles L.	10.00	20.00	45.00	
Morley, Christopher	20.00	70.00	107.50	
Morris, Sir Lewis	5.00	10.00	15.00	
Mosel, Tad	3.00	5.00	10.00	5.00
Motley, John Lothrop	20.00	30.00	67.00	
Moulton, Louise C.	15.00	25.00	40.00	
Nasby, Petroleum V.	20.00	60.00	145.00	
Nash, Ogden	20.00	25.00	68.00	15.00
Nathan, George Jean	10.00	15.00	25.00	10.00
Nicholson, Meredith	20.00	50.00	125.00	30.00
Niebuhr, Reinhold	15.00	35.00	85.00	
Nietzsche, Friedrich*	470.00	775.00	6,300.00	
Nin, Anais	10.00	30.00	65.00	20.00
Nordhoff, Charles	15.00	25.00	50.00	
Norris, Frank	113.33	250.00	523.33	
Norris, Kathleen	15.00	30.00	50.00	20.00
Noyes, Alfred	15.00	39.00	50.00	30.00
Nye, Bill	10.00	18.00	30.00	
Oates, Joyce Carol	10.00	25.00	60.00	15.00
O'Casey, Sean	65.00	140.00	280.00	75.00
Odets, Clifford	30.00	73.00	114.00	135.00
O'Higgins, Harvey	10.00	20.00	75.00	15.00
Oliphant, Laurence	5.00	20.00	40.00	
O'Neill, Eugene	140.00	334.00	763.00	250.00
Orczy, Baroness E.	30.00	40.00	71.50	
Osborne, John	5.00	15.00	26.00	10.00
Ouida	20.00	40.00	90.00	
Packard, Vance	6.00	20.00	45.00	10.00
Page, Thomas Nelson	5.00	15.00	35.00	
Parker, Dorothy	20.00	35.00	80.00	25.00
Parkman, Francis	25.00	65.00	158.25	
Pasternak, Boris	340.00	610.00	1,200.00	
Patten, Gilbert	20.00	60.00	145.00	95.00
Pegler, Westbrook	15.00	20.00	35.00	20.00
Phillpotts, Eden	5.00	15.00	38.33	
Pinero, Arthur Wing	10.00	30.00	60.00	56.67
Plimpton, George	5.00	15.00	25.00	10.00
Poe, Edgar Allan			29,700.00	
Pollock, Channing	20.00	50.00	145.00	25.00
Pope, Alexander	557.50	1,556.67	4,333.33	
Porter, Gene Stratton	50.00	130.00	295.00	60.00
Porter, Katherine A.	56.67	200.00	325.00	125.00
Porter, William Sydney (O. Henry)	210.00	425.00	891.67	
Post, Emily	12.50	35.00	75.00	20.00

Robert Ludlum

Archibald MacLeish

Norman Mailer

Bernard Malamud

Thomas Mann

W. Somerset Maugham

E. L. Masters

Arthur Miller

Christopher Morley

John Lothrop Motley

Henry Miller

Alfred Noyes

Ogden Nash

Clifford Odets

Eugene O'Neill

Baroness Emmuska Orczy

George Plimpton

Katherine Anne Porter

Howard Pyle

Ezra Pound

Eugene M. Prevost

Emily Post

Mario Puzo

Ernie Pyle

Name	Signature Only	Letter or Document Signed	Autograph Letter Signed	Signed Photograph
Potter, Beatrix	90.00	255.00	638.00	125.00
Pound, Ezra	120.00	326.43	781.00	
Powell, Talmage	10.00	20.00	40.00	10.00
Prevost, Eugene M.	5.00	10.00	15.00	
Priestley, J. B.	30.00	71.50	170.00	75.00
Proctor, Edna Dean	5.00	10.00	20.00	5.00
Proust, Marcel	450.00	1,325.00	3,285.00	
Pushkin, Alexander*	775.00	3,075.00	5,400.00	
Puzo, Mario	7.00	10.00	20.00	10.00
Pyle, Ernie	150.00	175.00	200.00	175.00
Pepys, Samuel	295.00	788.00	2,140.00	
Queen, Ellery (Dannay)	20.00	27.00	40.00	
Reed, John	175.00	650.00	1,270.00	205.00
Remarque, Erich Maria	35.00	90.00	225.00	45.00
Repplier, Agnes	5.00	10.00	16.25	
Resnick, Mike	10.00	20.00	40.00	10.00
Reston, John "Scotty"	10.00	20.00	35.00	10.00
Rexroth, Kenneth	10.00	30.00	65.00	15.00
Rice, Elmer	20.00	35.00	45.00	30.00
Riis, Jacob A.	10.00	37.50	30.00	
Riley, James Whitcomb	100.00	125.00	311.00	200.00
Rilke, Rainer Maria	132.50	345.00	555.00	
Rinehart, Mary Roberts	15.00	40.00	80.00	20.00
Robbins, Harold	7.50	30.00	70.00	15.00
Roberts, Kenneth	16.00	68.00	100.00	15.00
Roberts, Ralph	10.00	20.00	40.00	10.00
Robinson, Edwin Arlington	25.00	60.00	135.00	
Roethke, Theodore	30.00	85.00	200.00	35.00
Rogers, Samuel	10.00	25.00	55.00	
Roget, Dr. Peter M.	20.00	55.00	112.50	
Rohmer, Sax (A. S. Ward)	60.00	200.00	375.00	85.00
Rolfe, William James	5.00	10.00	20.00	5.00
Rolland, Romain	10.00	20.00	35.00	10.00
Ross, Robert	5.00	10.00	20.00	5.00
Rossetti, Christina	40.00	90.00	200.00	
Roth, Philip	10.00	30.00	55.00	15.00
Rousseau, Jean J.	65.00	180.00	450.00	
Runyon, Damon	60.00	150.00	275.00	75.00
Ruskin, John	50.00	107.50	168.88	40.00
Russell, Bertrand	50.00	140.00	185.00	220.00
Sabatini, Rafael	20.00	45.00	75.00	
Sacher-Masoch, Leopold von	30.00	90.00	215.00	
Sackler, Howard	5.00	15.00	25.00	7.00
Sade, Marquis de	185.00	375.00	1,625.00	
Sagan, Dr. Carl	5.00	10.00	15.00	8.00
Salinger, J. D.	20.00	60.00	145.00	25.00
Salinger, Pierre	3.00	8.00	10.00	7.00
Salten, Felix	35.00	100.00	235.00	
Sanborn, Franklin B.	5.00	15.00	35.00	10.00
Sanborn, Katherine A.	5.00	10.00	19.00	5.00
Sand, George	80.00	152.50	382.14	
Sandburg, Carl	41.00	86.25	155.00	245.00

Ellery Queen

James B. Reston

Robert Reud

James Whitcomb Riley

Kenneth Roberts

Sigmund Romberg

Bertrand Russell

Damon Runyon

Rafael Sabatini

George Sand

Carl Sandburg

Arthur Schlesinger, Jr.

Sir Walter Scott

Dr. Seuss

George Bernard Shaw

Georges Simenon

Neil Simon

Upton Sinclair

Isaac Bashevis Singer

B. T. Skinner

Mickey Spillane

Sincerely,

Rex Stout

Name	Signature Only	Letter or Document Signed	Autograph Letter Signed	Signed Photograph
Sandoz, Marie	25.00	68.00	170.00	40.00
Santayana, George	28.00	125.00	275.00	
Saroyan, William	50.00	126.00	225.00	50.00
Sartre, Jean-Paul	45.00	135.00	290.00	65.00
Sassoon, Siegfried	120.00	200.00	342.33	
Saxe, John G.	10.00	20.00	40.00	10.00
Sayers, Dorothy	85.00	175.00	540.00	120.00
Schanberg, Sydney H.	10.00	20.00	70.00	15.00
Schlesinger, Arthur, Jr.	10.00	15.00	25.00	10.00
Schliemann, Heinrich	75.00	210.00	270.00	
Schopenhauer, Arthur*	650.00	1,750.00	4,400.00	
Schulberg, Budd	3.00	4.00	6.50	5.00
Scott, Sir Walter	100.00	275.00	515.00	
Scudder, Horace E.	10.00	20.00	50.00	
Seawell, Molly Elliot	5.00	7.50	35.00	10.00
Sedgwick, Catherine M.	10.00	20.00	40.00	10.00
Seignolle, Claude	120.00	150.00	204.00	160.00
Serling, Rod	45.00	150.00	225.00	55.00
Seton, Ernest Thompson	50.00	86.00	240.00	45.00
Seuss, Dr.	10.00	20.00	35.00	26.00
Shaffer, Peter L.	7.00	15.00	30.00	10.00
Shapiro, Karl	10.00	30.00	70.00	15.00
Shaw, George Bernard	125.00	390.00	828.57	635.00
Shaw, Irwin	25.00	60.00	170.00	40.00
Sheldon, Sidney	5.00	10.00	25.00	10.00
Shelley, Percy Bysshe	1,060.00	2,285.00	14,625.00	
Sheridan, Richard Brinsley	60.00	110.00	258.33	
Sherwood, Martha	5.00	10.00	20.00	5.00
Sherwood, Robert E.	30.00	80.00	190.00	45.00
Shirer, William L.	5.00	18.00	25.00	5.00
Shoemaker, William L.	5.00	8.00	15.00	
Simenon, Georges	35.00	100.00	235.00	125.00
Simms, William G.	35.00	100.00	250.00	
Simon, Neil	15.00	25.00	35.00	17.50
Sinclair, Upton	20.00	64.38	105.00	25.00
Singer, Isaac B.	10.00	30.00	70.00	15.00
Sitwell, Dame Edith	60.00	120.00	214.17	
Sitwell, Sir Osbert	20.00	40.00	110.00	
Skinner, B. F.	15.00	25.00	40.00	20.00
Skinner, Cornelia Otis	15.00	30.00	45.00	10.00
Slaughter, Frank G.	5.00	10.00	35.33	10.00
Smith, Samuel Francis	10.00	30.00	61.67	
Snow, C. P.	25.00	75.00	170.00	60.00
Solzhenitsyn, Alexandr	85.00	250.00	495.00	
Sontag, Susan	10.00	20.00	45.00	16.00
Southey, Robert	20.00	50.00	133.20	30.00
Speed, John Gilmer	5.00	10.00	15.00	
Spender, Stephen	30.00	80.00	170.00	55.00
Spillane, Mickey	15.00	35.00	50.00	20.00
Spofford, Harriet P.	3.00	5.00	10.00	5.00
Squier, Emma	5.00	10.00	15.00	
St. Johns, Adela Rogers	7.00	20.00	35.00	10.00

Name	Signature Only	Letter or Document Signed	Autograph Letter Signed	Signed Photograph
Stacpoole, Henry	15.00	45.00	100.00	
Stanhope, Philip H.	5.00	15.00	25.00	5.00
Stead, William Thomas	3.00	5.00	8.00	
Steele, Richard	200.00	600.00	1,320.00	
Steffens, Lincoln	20.00	100.00	175.00	
Stein, Gertrude	120.00	300.00	650.00	795.00
Steinbeck, John	162.50	725.00	1,125.00	280.00
Stendhal (Marie H. Beyle)*	340.00	895.00	4,335.00	
Stevenson, Robert Louis	300.00	566.50	1,045.00	
Stockton, Frank R.	20.00	60.00	135.00	30.00
Stoker, Bram	30.00	60.00	120.00	186.00
Stone, Irving	12.00	20.00	40.00	20.00
Stoppard, Tom	10.00	36.00	70.00	15.00
Stout, Rex	20.00	60.00	135.00	30.00
Stowe, Harriet Beecher	73.75	130.00	300.08	
Stribling, T. S.	15.00	45.00	100.00	
Styron, William	10.00	30.00	70.00	15.00
Susann, Jacqueline	20.00	35.00	45.00	40.00
Swinburne, Algernon C.	185.00	235.00	395.00	
Swope, Herbert Bayard	10.00	30.00	75.00	15.00
Tagore, Rabindranath	70.00	195.00	395.00	145.00
Taine, John (Eric T. Bell)	12.50	20.00	35.00	15.00
Tarbell, Ida	15.00	40.00	88.00	25.00
Tarkington, Booth	29.00	105.67	161.67	108.75
Taylor, Bayard	15.00	40.00	72.00	20.00
Tennyson, Alfred Lord	72.50	175.38	324.20	410.00
Terhune, Albert Payson	20.00	39.00	85.00	40.00
Terkel, Studs	8.00	15.00	25.00	12.00
Thackeray, William Makepeace	88.00	138.75	345.20	
Thaxter, Celia	10.00	15.00	25.00	5.00
Thomas, Dylan	350.00	525.00	1,093.75	
Thompson, Dorothy	15.00	45.00	90.00	25.00
Thoreau, Henry David	300.00	750.00	2,250.00	
Thorpe, Rose Hartwick	3.00	7.50	15.00	
Thurber, James	75.00	185.00	370.00	95.00
Toklas, Alice B.	25.00	75.00	250.00	
Tolkien, John R. R.	140.00	475.00	916.67	
Tolstoy, Leo	425.00	1,065.00	2,100.00	1,425.00
Torrence, Ridgely	5.00	15.00	35.00	10.00
Tourgee, Albion W.	15.00	20.00	25.00	
Toynbee, Arnold	10.00	30.00	70.00	15.00
Train, Arthur	5.00	10.00	26.00	5.00
Traven, B. (H. Croves)	265.00	800.00	1,765.00	
Trollope, Anthony	87.50	225.00	325.00	
Tryon, Thomas	5.00	15.00	25.00	10.00
Turgenev, Ivan	130.00	390.00	850.00	
Untermeyer, Louis	15.00	51.67	80.00	10.00
Updike, John	25.00	40.00	105.00	40.00
Uris, Leon	10.00	75.00	115.00	20.00
Vance, Louis Joseph	15.00	35.00	90.00	
Van Dine, S. S. (W. H. Wright)	30.00	90.00	200.00	225.00
Van Doren, Carl	10.00	30.00	50.00	15.00

Name	Signature Only	Letter or Document Signed	Autograph Letter Signed	Signed Photograph
Van Doren, Mark	10.00	20.00	45.00	10.00
Van Druten, John W.	5.00	20.00	30.00	10.00
Van Loon, Hendrik	10.00	20.00	45.00	40.00
Van Vechten, Carl	30.00	75.00	220.00	35.00
Verlaine, Paul	75.00	136.00	386.50	
Verne, Jules	125.00	265.00	538.00	
Vidal, Gore	10.00	20.00	30.00	15.00
Voelker, John D.	5.00	10.00	15.00	5.00
Voltaire, Francois	330.00	1,125.00	1,900.00	
Von Däniken, Erich	10.00	30.00	70.00	12.00
Vonnegut, Kurt	8.00	25.00	55.00	35.00
Wallace, Dillon	5.00	15.00	30.00	10.00
Wallace, Edgar	45.00	129.00	260.00	300.00
Wallace, Irving	7.50	25.00	50.00	30.00
Wallmann, Jeff	5.00	7.00	15.00	5.00
Walpole, Horace	150.00	450.00	982.50	
Walpole, Sir Hugh	13.00	30.00	72.50	
Wambaugh, Joseph	7.00	20.00	35.00	13.33
Warner, Charles Dudley	10.00	20.00	30.00	
Warren, Charles Marquis	5.00	15.00	25.00	5.00
Warren, Robert Penn	10.00	25.00	45.00	20.00
Waterston, Robert C.	5.00	10.00	15.00	
Waugh, Evelyn	35.00	177.50	225.00	50.00
Webb, Charles Henry	4.00	7.00	13.00	
Webster, Noah	125.00	365.00	700.00	
Weidman, Jerome	5.00	10.00	20.00	5.00
Welles, H. G.	125.00	129.00	302.00	175.00
Wells, Carolyn	5.00	20.00	40.00	10.00
Wells, Carveth	20.00	45.00	110.00	25.00
Welty, Eudora	25.00	75.00	170.00	100.00
West, Jessamyn	5.00	10.00	15.00	5.00
West, Morris L.	15.00	40.00	75.00	25.00
West, Dame Rebecca	10.00	20.00	65.00	
Weyman, Stanley J.	10.00	20.00	48.00	
Wharton, Edith	35.00	125.00	235.00	55.00
White, Stewart E.	5.00	10.00	35.00	10.00
White, Theodore	7.50	15.00	25.00	10.00
White, William Allen	10.00	35.00	70.00	15.00
Whitman, Walt	330.00	625.00	1,600.00	
Whittier, John Greenleaf	35.00	154.17	310.71	400.00
Wiggin, Kate Douglas	10.00	20.00	40.00	50.00
Wilbur, Richard	5.00	10.00	35.00	10.00
Wilde, Oscar	325.00	580.00	2,500.00	445.00
Wilde, Percival	18.00	55.00	120.00	
Wilder, Thornton	35.00	62.50	162.50	40.00
Williams, Ben Ames	7.00	15.00	25.00	10.00
Williams, Jonathan	5.00	15.00	25.00	
Williams, Tennessee	127.50	250.00	650.00	245.00
Winchell, Walter	15.00	30.00	45.00	35.00
Winsor, Kathleen	15.00	35.00	85.00	20.00
Wister, Owen	25.00	60.00	140.00	60.00

Booth Tarkington

Studs Terkel

Leon Uris

S. S. Van Dine

Carl Van Doren

Mark Van Doren

Jules Verne

Erich Von Däniken

Irving Wallace

Robert Penn Warren

Jessamyn West

Theodore H. White

Walt Whitman

Oscar Wilde

Thornton Wilder

Ben Ames Williams

Tennessee Williams

Walter Winchell

Owen Wister

Thomas Wolfe

Grant Wood

John Greenleaf Whittier

Frank Yerby

Name	Signature Only	Letter or Document Signed	Autograph Letter Signed	Signed Photograph
Wolfe, Thomas	260.00	1,175.00	1,866.67	
Wolfe, Tom	7.50	17.50	30.00	10.00
Woodward, Bob	10.00	20.00	35.00	20.00
Woolf, Virginia	215.00	495.00	750.00	750.00
Wordsworth, William	135.00	425.00	665.00	
Wouk, Herman	15.00	30.00	45.00	75.00
Wright, Harold Bell	5.00	15.00	31.42	10.00
Wright, Richard	20.00	50.00	125.00	
Wylie, Philip	10.00	25.00	58.00	10.00
Yeats, Jack Butler	20.00	60.00	150.00	
Yeats, William Butler	190.00	306.67	492.56	165.00
Yerby, Frank	30.00	50.00	100.00	25.00
Zangwill, Israel	30.00	50.00	93.75	55.00
Zola, Emile	95.00	161.00	443.00	195.00
Zweig, Stefan	25.00	70.00	150.00	

Aviation

While the history of aviation is relatively short, the mark made by the men and women in this field has been remarkably vivid. The participants are primarily military, but they have been singled out in a category of their own in order to take their places among the pioneers of this relatively young and exciting specialty of autograph collecting.

Those who collect signed photographs are discovering that they welcome a signed photo or postcard of the pilot's plane as readily as one of the person him- or herself, but that they must pay a premium because of the scarcity of any of these pictorial items.

Name	Signature Only	Letter or Document Signed	Autograph Letter Signed	Signed Photograph
Acosta, Bert	$ 30.00	$ 60.00	$ 120.00	$ 80.00
Alcock, John W.	225.00	450.00	600.00	475.00
Auriol, Jacqueline	10.00	25.00	40.00	25.00
Bader, Douglas	45.00	65.00	185.00	65.00
Balbo, Italo	70.00	150.00	200.00	125.00
Balchen, Bernt	25.00	40.00	75.00	45.00

Name	Signature Only	Letter or Document Signed	Autograph Letter Signed	Signed Photograph
Barber, Rex T.	20.00	35.00	60.00	40.00
Baucus, Bob	8.00	18.00	32.00	21.00
Baur, Hans	18.00	35.00	80.00	50.00
Bellanca, Giuseppe M.	35.00	75.00	145.00	85.00
Bellonte, Maurice	67.50	130.00	245.00	174.50
Bennett, Floyd	250.00	370.00	695.00	405.00
Bishop, William "Billy"	25.00	70.00	115.00	50.00
Bleriot, Louis	230.00	365.00	595.00	343.33
Boardman, Russell	25.00	55.00	100.00	70.00
Bodenschatz, Karl	8.00	17.00	30.00	20.00
Borchers, Adolf	6.00	14.00	24.00	18.00
Boyington, Gregory "Pappy"	30.00	45.00	70.00	65.00
Brown, Arthur W.	225.00	350.00	575.00	475.00
Bryant, Alys McKey	35.00	60.00	140.00	75.00
Byrd, Richard E.	50.00	106.25	205.00	147.50
Callahan, Laurence K.	9.00	18.50	35.00	23.00
Campbell, Douglas	25.00	40.00	55.00	42.00
Carl, Marion	15.00	35.00	60.00	40.00
Chamberlin, Clarence	27.50	120.00	230.00	125.00
Chavez, George A.	40.00	55.00	165.00	60.00
Chenault, Claire L.	120.00	250.00	575.00	275.00
Cobham, Alan J.	15.00	30.00	50.00	45.00
Cochran, Jacqueline	25.00	45.00	75.00	35.00
Connor, Harry P.	15.00	30.00	45.00	40.00
Conrad, Gerhard	10.00	22.00	40.00	17.00
Corrigan, Douglas	23.00	33.00	50.00	45.00
Coste, Dieudonne	85.00	200.00	385.00	225.00
Crossfield, A. Scott	10.00	15.00	25.00	20.00
Curtis, Wilfred A.	10.00	25.00	40.00	25.00
Curtiss, Glenn	150.00	250.00	365.00	575.00
De Havilland, Geoffrey	50.00	125.00	175.00	100.00
Doering, Arnold	6.00	15.00	25.00	20.00
Doolittle, James H.	20.00	58.00	85.00	39.00
Douglas, Donald W., Sr.	45.00	250.00	400.00	250.00
Drexel, J. A.	40.00	55.00	95.00	60.00
Eaker, Ira	13.50	43.00	65.00	32.50
Earhart, Amelia	175.00	350.00	600.00	712.50
Eckener, Hugo	110.00	253.00	395.00	285.00
Elder, Ruth	70.00	150.00	275.00	175.00
Everest, F. K. "Pete"	10.00	25.00	40.00	30.00
Falch, Wolfgang	15.00	35.00	60.00	25.00
Farman, Henri	35.00	65.00	145.00	150.00
Ferebee, Thomas	30.00	65.00	120.00	70.00
Fieseler, Gerhard	20.00	50.00	80.00	80.00
Fischer, Siegfried	4.00	8.00	15.00	10.00
Flint, Lawrence	7.00	15.00	30.00	20.00
Fokker, Anthony	110.00	240.00	435.00	275.00
Foss, Joe	15.00	30.00	50.00	35.00
Galland, Adolf	30.00	85.00	140.00	75.00
Gatty, Harold	46.00	100.00	185.00	115.00
Gerland, Alfred	15.00	35.00	60.00	40.00
Gibbons, Floyd	50.00	150.00	225.00	140.00

Name	Signature Only	Letter or Document Signed	Autograph Letter Signed	Signed Photograph
Goard, Nona	5.00	10.00	20.00	7.00
Godfrey, A. Earl	25.00	55.00	100.00	70.00
Goodwin, E. S.	2.00	5.00	10.00	
Graf, Herman	20.00	35.00	50.00	42.00
Grahame-White, Claude	52.50	95.00	217.50	110.00
Grange, E. R.	10.00	20.00	40.00	30.00
Grasser, Hartmann	8.00	17.00	30.00	20.00
Gronau, Wolfgang von	50.00	110.00	205.00	175.00
Groom, Victor	20.00	45.00	80.00	55.00
Haldeman, George W.	25.00	50.00	100.00	70.00
Hartmann, Erich	18.00	40.00	73.00	50.00
Haught, Helmut	5.00	10.00	20.00	12.00
Havens, Beckwith	15.00	35.00	45.00	40.00
Hawks, Frank	45.00	80.00	210.00	100.00
Helbig, Joachim	7.00	16.00	29.00	20.00
Hiller, Frank, Jr.	70.00	150.00	275.00	125.00
Hillig, Otto	40.00	85.00	150.00	115.00
Hinton, Walter	35.00	70.00	110.00	80.00
Hoiriis, Holger	40.00	85.00	165.00	95.00
Hulshoff, Karl	4.00	10.00	18.00	12.00
Jacobs, Josef	25.00	35.00	75.00	50.00
Jacobsen, Fritz	7.00	16.00	29.00	20.00
Jaehnert, Erhard	4.00	10.00	18.00	12.00
James, Daniel, Jr.	15.00	30.00	75.00	40.00
Johnson, Amy (Mollison)	60.00	75.00	125.00	177.86
Johnson, J. A.	30.00	65.00	120.00	75.00
Johnson, Richard L.	10.00	14.00	25.00	15.00
Jones, Casey	45.00	90.00	175.00	150.00
Jope, Berhard	10.00	20.00	37.00	25.00
Kammhuber, Josef	15.00	25.00	60.00	20.00
Kindermann, K. B.	3.00	8.00	14.00	9.00
Kingsford-Smith, Charles	35.00	105.00	195.00	125.00
Koehler, Armin	7.00	15.00	27.00	18.00
Krupinski, Walter	13.00	28.00	52.00	35.00
Lahm, Frank	35.00	75.00	140.00	90.00
Langley, Samuel P.	100.00	213.00	395.00	250.00
Lanphier, Tom, Jr.	20.00	45.00	80.00	55.00
Latham, Hubert	25.00	40.00	100.00	75.00
Law, Ruth	27.00	55.00	85.00	55.00
Lee, E. Hamilton	10.00	22.00	45.00	30.00
Lewis, David "Duffy"	13.00	28.00	50.00	35.00
Lewis, Gwilym H.	20.00	45.00	80.00	55.00
Lindbergh, Charles A.	325.00	640.00	1,290.00	700.00
Litjens, Stefan	6.00	12.00	22.00	15.00
Lockheed, Alan	35.00	75.00	145.00	85.00
Loos, Walter	8.00	17.00	30.00	20.00
Losigkeit, Fritz	6.00	15.00	25.00	17.00
Machado, Anesia Pinheiro	35.00	50.00	75.00	60.00
Magg, Alois	4.00	8.00	15.00	10.00
Martin, Glenn L.	45.00	162.50	225.00	155.33
Mattern, Jimmie	15.00	25.00	60.00	35.00
Merrill, Henry T.	25.00	45.00	100.00	60.00

Bernt Balchen

Jacqueline Auriol

Jacqueline Cochran

"Wrong Way" Corrigan

Sir Geoffrey De Havilland

Cordially yours,

Donald W. Douglas

Amelia Earhart

Hugo Eckner

Anthony Fokker

Samuel Pierpont Langley

Glenn L. Martin

J. S. McDonnell

Herb Morrison

Wiley Post

Capt. Eddie Rickenbacker

Francis Gary Powers

Dick Rutan

Kingford Smith

Most cordially,

Alexander P. de Seversky

Roscoe Turner

Jeana Yeager

Sir Thomas Sopwith

Ferdinand Von Zeppelin

149

Name	Signature Only	Letter or Document Signed	Autograph Letter Signed	Signed Photograph
Merrill, Richard	23.00	50.00	90.00	60.00
Messerschmitt, Willy	45.00	110.00	250.00	295.00
Mitchell, Billy	125.00	437.50	600.00	387.50
Monteverde, Alfred de	20.00	45.00	80.00	50.00
Monteverde, George de	20.00	45.00	80.00	50.00
Morrison, Herb	40.00	80.00	160.00	100.00
Nobile, Umberto	45.00	100.00	200.00	175.00
Nungesser, Charles	100.00	175.00	225.00	250.00
O'Donald, Emmett	15.00	30.00	50.00	35.00
Osterkamp, Theo	30.00	55.00	120.00	65.00
Ovington, Earle	40.00	56.25	147.50	125.00
Pangborn, Clyde	55.00	125.00	220.00	150.00
Paulham, Louis	35.00	70.00	125.00	75.00
Pierson, Roland	10.00	20.00	35.00	25.00
Pingel, Rolf	7.00	14.00	26.00	18.00
Polando, John	25.00	55.00	100.00	67.00
Portal, Charles	20.00	45.00	80.00	50.00
Post, Augustus	20.00	37.50	50.00	45.00
Post, Wiley	237.50	325.00	550.00	400.00
Povey, Len	5.00	10.00	20.00	15.00
Powers, Gary Francis	62.50	60.00	75.00	50.00
Preddy, George E.	10.00	25.00	40.00	25.00
Quesada, Elwood R.	15.00	25.00	40.00	25.00
Read, A. C.	40.00	80.00	160.00	110.00
Reichers, Lou	25.00	40.00	55.00	60.00
Reitsch, Hanna	60.00	150.00	240.00	175.00
Richthofen, Manfred von	600.00	2,400.00	5,000.00	2,500.00
Rickenbacker, Edward	50.00	170.00	375.00	136.67
Rodgers, John	50.00	125.00	240.00	125.00
Rogers, Joseph W.	12.00	27.00	49.00	33.00
Rosendahl, Charles	50.00	90.00	175.00	110.00
Rossman, Edmond	10.00	25.00	40.00	20.00
Rudel, Hans Ulrich	40.00	100.00	150.00	75.00
Rumpler, Edward	16.00	36.00	65.00	44.00
Rutan, Dick	20.00	25.00	30.00	35.00
Ryan, T. Claude	75.00	125.00	225.00	140.00
Santos-Dumont, A.	250.00	325.00	500.00	720.00
Saunders, Hugh W.	4.00	8.00	15.00	10.00
Schoenert, Rudolf	6.00	14.00	25.00	17.00
Schoepfel, Gerhard	5.00	11.00	20.00	13.00
Scott, C. W. A.	20.00	45.00	80.00	50.00
Scott, Robert, Jr.	12.00	25.00	40.00	20.00
Seversky, Alexander de	33.33	75.00	135.00	90.00
Sikorsky, Igor	40.00	105.00	150.00	141.67
Smith, Elinor	45.00	95.00	150.00	125.00
Sopwith, Thomas O. M.	20.00	45.00	120.00	75.00
Spaatz, Carl	20.00	45.00	80.00	45.00
Stadlman, Anthony	7.00	15.00	28.00	19.00
Steinhoff, J. "Mickey"	12.00	25.00	47.00	31.50
Stepp, Hans	4.00	10.00	18.00	12.00
Stolle, Bruno	5.00	11.00	20.00	13.00
Sullivan, Kathryn D.	10.00	25.00	40.00	25.00

Name	Signature Only	Letter or Document Signed	Autograph Letter Signed	Signed Photograph
Tetard, J.	40.00	55.00	160.00	95.00
Tibbetts, Paul W.	22.50	30.00	37.50	29.00
Todd, Robert	10.00	25.00	40.00	20.00
Turner, Roscoe	30.00	42.50	120.00	107.50
Twining, Nathan	20.00	95.00	150.00	48.50
Twiss, Peter	7.00	15.00	27.00	18.00
Udet, Ernst	175.00	380.00	690.00	435.00
Urbanowicz, Witold A.	20.00	45.00	80.00	50.00
Vaughn, George, Jr.	25.00	40.00	100.00	65.00
Vedrines, Jules	155.00	335.00	610.00	255.00
Vermehren, Werner	15.00	35.00	60.00	30.00
Voisin, Gabriel	55.00	120.00	225.00	125.00
Wade, Leigh	25.00	35.00	50.00	38.00
Warsitz, Erich	18.00	40.00	72.00	48.00
Watson, Harold F.	10.00	30.00	45.00	25.00
Wedell, Jimmie	10.00	25.00	37.00	30.00
Wellman, Walter	10.00	25.00	35.00	
Williams, Alford J., Jr.	25.00	40.00	90.00	117.50
Wittber, Bill	20.00	50.00	75.00	80.00
Woidick, Franz	11.00	24.00	44.00	30.00
Wright, Orville	250.00	450.00	575.00	950.00
Wright, Wilbur	300.00	575.00	1,675.00	1,050.00
Yeager, Chuck	15.00	30.00	35.00	40.00
Yeager, Jeana	16.00	30.00	35.00	30.00
Zeppelin, Ferdinand von	225.00	700.00	950.00	523.00

Baseball

We've grouped all our baseball categories into one chapter. Below you'll find sections on baseball 3 × 5 index cards, promotional (or *trading*) cards, Hall of Fame plaques, postcards, and general signatures and signed photographs, as well as one section dealing with signed baseballs.

3 × 5 Cards

A distinct subcategory in baseball autograph collecting is the 3 × 5 index card. These are simply standard index cards—the kind you can buy in any office supply store—that are sent via mail to various players and (hopefully) returned signed. Also, at personal appearance events, many collectors hand a stack of cards to the ball player for signing.

Such a card signed by an average living baseball player is worth $1–$3. Regional variances have some effect on price. An Atlanta Braves player's signature, for example, is normally worth more in Georgia than in California, while the converse is true of cards signed by Angels or Dodgers.

The list in this section contains names of players whose signed 3 × 5 index card usually falls within this $1–$3 range.

Abernathy, Woody
Abrams, Cal
Ackley, Fritz
Adair, Jimmy
Adams, Charles "Babe"
Adams, Dwight "Red"
Adlish, Dave
Agee, Tommie
Agromonde, Ken
Ainsmith, Eddie
Albright, Jack
Alderson, Dale L.
Alexander, Bob
Allen, Ethan
Alou, Jesus
Amalfitano, Joe
Amaro, Reuben
Anderson, Alf
Anderson, Craig
Anderson, George "Sparky"
Andrews, "Hub"
Andrus, William "Bill"
Antonelli, Bill
Appling, Luke
Arrigo, Gerry
Arroyo, Luis
Auker, Eldon
Austin, Rick
Averill, Earl
Azcue, Joe
Babich, John
Baczewski, Fred

Bahnsen, Stan
Baker, Tom
Bamberger, George
Barlick, Al
Bancroft, Dave
Bando, Sal
Barkowski, Bob
Barnes, Frank
Barnes, John F.
Barney, Rex
Barrett, "Red"
Bartell, Dick
Bartirome, Tony
Basgall, Monty
Bauman, Frank
Baumholtz, Frank
Beck, Walter "Boom Boom"
Becker, Joe
Berardino, John
Berger, Bosey
Berger, Wally
Berra, Yogi
Bertrand, Roman "Lefty"
Betts, Huck
Blackwell, Ewell
Blair, L. N. "Buddy"
Blake, Eddie
Blanchard, Johnny
Bluege, Ossie
Blyleven, Bert
Bolling, Milt
Bollo, Greg

Bonura, Zeke
Boone, Bob
Boone, Lute J. "Danny"
Boone, Ray
Borgmann, Glenn
Borowy, Hank
Bouchee, Ed
Boudreau, Lou
Bouton, Jim
Bowa, Larry
Bowman, Bob
Branca, Ralph
Breeden, Hal
Brewer, Jim
Brewer, Maurie
Bridges, Rocky
Brinkman, Chuck
Bristol, Dave
Brock, Lou
Broglio, Ernie
Brosnan, Jim
Brown, Bobby
Brown, Mace
Brown, Ollie
Bruce, Bob
Bucha, Johnny
Bucher, Jimmy
Buford, Johnny
Bumbry, Al
Bunning, Jim
Burgess, Smoky
Burkhart, Ken
Burton, Eddie
Busby, Jim
Bush, Guy
Buzhardt, Jim
Byrd, Sam
Caballero, Ralph
Calderone, Sammy
Caldwell, Don
Callison, Johnny
Camilli, Dolph
Camilli, Doug
Carpenter, Bob
Castiglione, Pete
Castleman, Clyde
Castner, Paul

Cavaretta, Phil
Chandler, "Spud"
Chapman, Sam
Chase, Ken
Chozen, Harry
Cipriani, Frank
Clary, Ellis
Cleveland, Reggie
Clendenon, Donn
Coan, Gil
Coleman, Joe
Coleman, Ray
Collins, Joe
Consuegra, Sandy
Coogan, Dale
Coombs, Bobby
Cooney, Johnny
Cooper, Walker
Covaleski, Stanley
Craft, Harry
Cramer, Roger "Doc"
Crone, Ray
Cronin, Jim
Cronin, Joe
Crosetti, Frank
Cuccinello, Tony
Dahlgren, "Babe"
Danning, Harry
Dark, Al
Davenport, Jim
Davis, George
Davis, Red
Davis, Tom
Delsing, Jim
DeMaestri, Joe
DeMerit, John
DeMola, Don
Dempsey, Con
Dente, Sam
DeShong, Jimmy
DeViveiros, Bernie
Dickerson, Murry
Dickman, Emerson
Diering, Chuck
Dillinger, Bob
DiMaggio, Vince
DiPietro, Bob

Donald, Atley
Donovan, Dick
Downing, Al
Doyle, Denny
Drabowski, Moe
Drake, Tom
Dropo, Walt
Drott, Dick
Duliba, Bob
Dunning, Steve
Earnshaw, George
Ehrhardt, "Rube"
Elder, George
Embree, "Red"
Endicott, Bill
English, Woody
Epperly, Al
Erautt, Eddie
Ermer, Cal
Erskine, Carl
Esegian, Chuck
Etten, Nick
Evers, Hoot
Faber, "Red"
Fairly, Ron
Falk, Bibb
Fallon, George
Feeney, Charles "Chub"
Feller, Bob
Ferrell, Rick
Ferris, Dave "Boo"
Fine, Tommy
Fischer, Bill
Fisher, Ray L.
Fitzsimmons, "Fat Freddy"
Flaherty, John
Fletcher, Elbie
Fondy, Dee
Fonseca, Lew
Ford, "Whitey"
Forsch, Ken
Fox, Charlie
Francona, Tito
Franks, Herman
Freehan, Bill
French, Ray
Frick, Ford

Friend, Bob
Friend, Owen
Frisch, Frankie
Fuentes, Tito
Gaffke, "Fabe"
Galan, Augie
Galehouse, Denny
Gallagher, Alan
Garagiola, Joe
Garbark, Bob
Garcia, Mike
Gardner, Rob
Garmes, Deb
Garr, Ralph
Garver, Ned
Gaston, "Milt"
Gearhart, Lloyd
Gehringer, Charles
Gentry, Gary
Gernert, Dick
Gettel, Allen
Gibbs, Jake
Gilbert, Andy
Gill, Edward
Gilligan, John
Giuliani, Tony
Glaviano, Tommy
Glenn, Joe
Glynn, Bill
Goldsberry, Gordon
Goldsmith, Harold E.
Gomez, "Lefty"
Gonder, Jesse L.
Gorman, Tom
Goryl, Johnny
Grabarkewitz, Billy
Grace, Earl
Grammas, Alex
Grasso, Mickey
Green, Dick
Green, Fred
Greenberg, "Hank"
Greengrass, Jim
Greenwade, Tom
Grim, Bob
Grimes, Burleigh
Grimm, Charlie

Grissom, Lee "Lefty"
Grissom, Marv
Grodzicki, Johnny
Groh, "Connie"
Gromek, Steve
Gross, Don
Groth, Johnny
Gryska, Sig
Gumbert, Harry
Gumpert, Randy
Gustine, Frank
Gutteridge, Don
Hacker, Warren
Haeffner, Billy
Hall, Dick
Harder, Mel
Hartung, Clint
Hassett, "Buddy"
Hatten, Joe
Hatton, Grady
Hayworth, Ray
Heffner, Don
Helf, "Hank"
Henrich, Tommy
Hernandez, Rudy
Hicks, Jim
Higby, Kirby
Hitchcock, Billy
Hogsett, Elon "Chief"
Hogue, Bobby
Howard, Bruce
Howerton, Bill
Hutchinson, Ed
Jansen, Larry
Javier, Julian
Johnson, Billy
Johnson, Ken
Johnson, "Si"
Johnson, Syl
Johnstone, Jay
Jolley, Smead
Joost, Eddie
Jordan, Baxter "Buck"
Jordan, Tom
Jorgens, Arndt
Jorgensen, "Spider"
Judson, Howie

Jurges, Billy
Kamm, Willie
Kanehl, Rod
Kazak, Eddie
Keller, Charlie "King Kong"
Keltner, Ken
Kennedy, Vernon
Kenney, Art
Kerr, J. Mel
Kimball, Newell
King, Clyde
King, Jim
Klimchock, Lou
Kluszewski, Ted
Kluttz, Clyde
Knott, Jack
Koenig, Mark
Kralick, Jack
Kravitz, Danny
Kretlow, Lou
Krist, Howard
Krsnicki, Mike
Kubek, Tony
Kuenn, Harvey
Kuhel, Joe
Kuiper, Duane
Kunkel, Bill
Laabs, Chet
Labine, Clem
Lacy, Lee
Lake, Eddie
Landrum, Don
Lanier, Max
Larsen, Don
Lasorda, Tom
Law, Vernon
Leach, Fred
Lee, Thornton
Lefebvre, Jim
Lehman, Ken
Leiber, Hank
LeJohn, Don
Lemon, Bob
Lenhardt, Don
Lennon, Robert
Leonard, Emil "Dutch"
Leslie, Sam

Lewis, Buddy
Lindblad, Paul
Lindell, Johnny
Linke, Ed
Linzy, Frank
Lipon, Johnny
Litwhiler, Danny
Lockman, Whitey
Logan, Bob
Lohrman, Bill
Lonborg, Jim
Lonnett, Joe
Lucadello, Johnny
Lumpe, Jerry
Lund, Don
Lupien, Tony
Lopat, Ed
Lopez, Hector
Lowenstein, John
Luby, Hugh
Madison, Dave
Maglie, Sal
Maguire, Jack
Mahoney, Jim
Majeski, Hank
Makosky, Frank
Malinoski, "Tony"
Malzone, Frank
Mancuso, Gus
Mapes, Cliff
Marion, Marty
Marquard, Rube
Marshall, Jim
Marshall, Willard
Martin, Fred
Martin, Morrie
Masi, Phil
Masterson, Walt
Mathias, Carl
Mauch, Gene
Maxvill, Dal
Maxwell, Charlie
Mayo, Eddie
Mazeroski, Bill
McCabe, Joe
McCarver, Tim
McCullough, Clyde

McDaniel, Lindy
McDaniel, Von
McDougal, Gil
McDowell, Sam
McHale, Johnny
McMillan, Roy
McNally, Dave
McQuillan, Glenn "Red"
Mele, Sam
Melton, Bill
Melton, Cliff
Menke, Denis
Merritt, Jim
Merson, Johnny "Jack"
Mesner, Steve
Messersmith, Andy
Metkovich, George
Metro, Charles
Meyer, Don
Michael, Gene
Michaels, Cass
Michaels, Ralph J.
Miksis, Eddie
Millan, Felix
Miller, Bob
Mincher, Don
Miranda, Willy
Mitchell, Dale
Mize, Johnny
Mizell, "Vinegar Bend"
Monbouquette, Bill
Moore, Jim
Moore, Joe
Moore, Terry
Morehart, Ray
Morgan, Bobby
Morgan, Tom
Morton, Carl
Moryn, Walt
Moses, Wally
Moss, Howie
Moss, Les
Mota, Manny
Mueller, Ray
Mulleavy, Greg
Muller, Ron
Mullin, Pat

Munger, George
Mungo, Van Lingle
Munzel, Edgar
Murff, Red
Murphy, Danny
Musser, Bobby
Naragon, Hal
Narleski, Ray
Narron, Sam
Negray, Ron
Nelson, Rocky
Neun, Johnny
Newcombe, Don
Newman, Fred
Newsome, Lamar "Skeeter"
Nicholson, Bill
Niekro, Phil
Noren, Irv
Nottebart, Don
O'Connor, Andrew J.
O'Connor, Dick
O'Dea, Ken
O'Farrell, Bob
Oldis, Bob
Oliva, Tony
Olmo, Luis
Olson, Karl
Oravetz, Ernie
Osteen, Claude
Owen, Marv
Pafko, Andy
Palica, Erv
Pappas, Milt
Parker, Wes
Parsons, Tom
Patek, Fred
Peacock, John
Perry, Gaylord
Perry, Jim
Pesky, Johnny
Peterson, Cap
Peterson, Fritz
Petrocelli, Rico
Philley, Dave
Phillips, Taylor
Piet, Tony
Pignatano, Joe

Pilarcik, Al
Pizarro, Juan
Plews, Herb
Poholski, Tom
Porto, Al
Posedel, Bill
Portocarrero, Arnie
Post, Ray
Presko, Joe
Qualters, Tom
Quilici, Frank
Raffensberger, Ken
Rapp, Earl
Raschi, Vic
Reese, Jimmy
Regalado, Rudy
Reichardt, Rick
Reiser, Pete
Renna, Bill
Rensa, George
Repulski, "Rip"
Reynolds, Allie
Rhodes, Dusty
Richards, Paul
Richardson, Bobby
Riddle, Johnny
Rigney, Bill
Ripplemeyer, Ray
Rivera, Jim
Roach, Mel
Robertson, Bob
Robinson, Craig
Robinson, Earl
Robinson, Eddie
Rodgers, Bobby
Roebuck, Ed
Rojas, "Cookie"
Roof, Phil
Roselli, Bob
Rosen, Al
Rosenthal, Larry
Runnels, Pete
Russell, Bill
Russell, Jim
Russell, John
Russo, Marius
Rutherford, Dr. Johnny

Ryan, Connie
Saltzgaver, Jack
Sanders, Ray
Sanford, Fred
Sanford, Jack
Sanguillen, Manny
Santo, Ron
Sauer, Eddie
Sauer, Hank
Sawatski, Carl
Sawyer, Eddie
Scalzi, Frank "Skeeter"
Scarborough, Ray
Schacht, Al
Schaffernoth, Joe
Schayes, Dolph
Scheib, Carl
Schmidt, Bob
Schmidt, Fred
Schofield, Dick
Schott, Gene
Schuble, "Heinie"
Schult, Art
Schultz, Joe
Schumacher, Hal
Schuster, Bill
Secory, Frank
Seeds, Bob
Seerey, Pat
Seibert, Dick
Selkirk, George
Semproch, Ray
Serena, Bill
Sessi, Walt
Shea, Pat
Shea, "Spec"
Sherry, Larry
Sievers, Roy
Silvestri, Ken
Sipek, Dick
Sisler, Dick
Sisti, Sibbi
Smith, Hal
Snyder, Gene
Snyder, Jerry
Speake, Bob
Spangler, Al

Stainback, "Tuck"
St. Claire, Ebba
Steen, Bill
Stephenson, Jerry
Stephenson, Riggs
Stewart, Ed
Stoddard, Tim
Stone, George
Storti, Lin
Stottlemeyer, Mel
Stripp, "Jersey Joe"
Stromme, Floyd
Suarez, Ken
Suhr, Gus
Sullivan, John
Surkont, Max
Taylor, C. L. "Chink"
Tebbetts, "Birdie"
Tenace, Gene
Terry, Zeb A.
Thompson, Charley
Thompson, Gene
Thompson, Jocko
Thurman, Bob
Torborg, Jeff
Torre, Joe
Todd, Al
Travis, Cecil
Treadway, Leon "Red"
Tresh, Tom
Turchin, Eddie
Turner, Jim
Turner, Tom
Valdivielso, Jose
Valentine, "Corky"
Vance, Sandy
Van Cuyk, Chris
Vandenberg, "Hy"
VanderMeer, Johnny
Vaughn, Charlie
Vaughn, Porter
Verban, Emil
Vergez, Johnny
Vernon, Mickey
Versalles, Zoilo
Virdon, Bill
Virgil, Ozzie

Voiselle, Bill
Wade, Ben
Wagner, Charlie
Wagner, Hal
Walker, Gerald "Gee"
Walker, Harry "The Hat"
Walters, Bucky
Ward, Preston
Wasdell, Jimmy
Weaver, Monte
Weintraub, Phil
Welaj, Johnny
Werber, Billy
Werlas, Johnny
West, Sam
Westlake, Wally
Westrum, "Wes"
White, "Jo Jo"

White, Roy
Whitehead, Burgess
Whitney, Pinky
Wight, Bill
Wilber, Del
Wilkie, Aldon J.
Will, Bob
Windhorn, Gordie
Wise, Rick
Wisner, Jack
Wood, Wilbur
Wright, Ed
Wyatt, Whitlow
Wynn, Jimmy
Wyrostek, Johnny
Zarilla, Al
Zimmerman, Jerry
Zinn, Jimmy

Cards

The following list consists of baseball cards personally signed by various players. Prices are based on the age of the card and the visibility of the signature. These are cards signed by common-to-good players who are not superstars or Hall-of-Famers. The cards were issued by such companies as Bowman, Donruss, Fleer, and Topps. There were also various promotional and collector issues.

One important consideration is regional variance in prices. Obviously, cards are worth more in the team's hometown—Atlanta Braves cards in Atlanta, Indians cards in Cleveland, and so forth—than elsewhere because of heightened interest. Generally, however, you can expect to buy or sell signed baseball cards based on the following criteria:

• Signed cards in good condition and issued sometime between 1948 and 1955: $7–$10.
• Signed cards in good condition and issued between 1956 and 1959: $5–$8.
• Signed cards in good condition and issued between 1960 and 1969: $4–$7.
• Signed cards in good condition and issued between 1970 and 1979: $2–$5.
• Signed cards in good condition and issued during the 1980s: $1.50–$2.

Players listed below usually go for more than indicated by the guidelines above. This list represents many players, coaches, and other baseball notables. There are, of course, hundreds more. The fact that someone is not included on the list is in no way a reflection of that person's ability. It means only that data on a philographic item of his was not accessible at the time of publishing.

Name	Signed Card	Name	Signed Card
Abrams, Cal	$ 4	Bowa, Larry	2
Adcock, Joe	3	Bowens, Sam	2
Agee, Tommie	3	Boyer, Clete	4
Albury, Vic	2	Breeden, Hal	2
Allen, Bernie	3	Brewer, Jim	5
Allen, Richie	6	Brideweser, Jim	3
Allison, Bob	3	Bridges, Rocky	3
Alomar, Sandy	2	Bright, Harry	3
Alou, Jesus	3	Brock, Lou	6
Alston, Walt	7	Broglio, Ernie	4
Alusik, George	2	Brown, Gates	3
Anderson, George	6	Brown, Ike	3
Anderson, Sparky	3	Bruton, Bill	6
Antonelli, Johnny	4	Bucha, Johnny	4
Armbrister, Ed	2	Buhl, Bob	4
Arroyo, Luis	3	Bumbry, Al	3
Aspromonte, Bob	3	Bunker, Wally	3
Auerbach, Rick	2	Burgess, Smoky	3
Augustine, Jerry	2	Burgmeier, Tom	3
Babich, Johnny	4	Burnette, Wally	3
Baily, Ed	3	Burroughs, Jeff	2
Baker, Dusty	3	Burtschy, Ed	2
Baker, Gene	4	Busby, Jim	2
Bando, Sal	3	Busby, Steve	2
Banks, Ernie	7	Buzhardt, John	2
Barbee, Dave	4	Byrd, Harry	4
Barr, Jim	2	Calderone, Sam	3
Bauer, Hank	4	Callison, Johnny	3
Beard, Ted	3	Cambria, Fred	2
Beckert, Glenn	2	Campaneris, Bert	4
Bell, Buddy	4	Campbell, Bill	2
Bennett, Dennis	3	Campbell, Bruce	4
Bartell, Dick	3	Cardenas, Leo	3
Bibby, Jim	3	Cardwell, Don	2
Billingham, Jack	2	Carew, Rod	8
Birrer, Bave	3	Carreon, Camilo	4
Bishop, Charlie	4	Castiglione, Pete	3
Blackaby, Ethan	4	Castro, Bill	2
Blackwell, Ewell	5	Caudill, Bill	2
Blair, Paul	4	Causey, James	2
Blanchard, John	4	Cavarretta, Phil	5
Bolger, Jim	3	Chambers, Cliff	3
Bolling, Frank	3	Chambliss, Chris	3
Bolling, Milt	3	Chance, Bob	3
Bonds, Bobby	5	Chapman, Sam	3
Boone, Bob	4	Chase, Ken	3
Boone, Ray	3	Clarke, Mel	2
Boozer, John	2	Cline, Ty	2
Borbon, Pedro	2	Clines, Gene	2
Borgmann, Glenn	2	Coan, Gil	2
Borland, Tom	2	Colavito, Rocky	3
Bosman, Dick	2	Colbert, Nate	3
Boudreau, Lou	5	Cole, Dick	3
Bouton, Jim	5	Coleman, Jerry	3

Name	Signed Card	Name	Signed Card
Collins, Joe	3	Ford, Dan	2
Combs, Earle	20	Ford, Whitey	10
Consolo, Billy	3	Forster, Terry	2
Cooney, Johnny	4	Fosse, Ray	2
Craig, Roger	2	Fowler, Art	2
Crandell, Del	3	Fox, Terry	3
Crawford, Willie	3	Francis, Earl	3
Crone, Ray	3	Francona, Tito	3
Cronin, Joe	12	Franks, Herman	3
Crowe, George	6	Freehan, Bill	3
Culp, Ray	3	Freese, Gene	3
Cunningham, Joe	3	Fregosi, Jim	2
Dailey, Bud	3	Frias, Pepe	2
Dark, Al	3	Fricano, Marion	6
Darwin, Bobby	3	Friend, Bob	3
Davalillo, Vic	4	Fuentes, Tito	2
Davenport, Jim	3	Gagliano, Phil	2
Davis, Tommy	4	Galehouse, Dennis	2
Davis, Willie	5	Gamble, Oscar	2
DeBusschere, Dave	4	Garagiola, Joe	7
Delsing, Jim	3	Garcia, Mike	6
Demeter, Don	3	Gardner, Billy	3
DeMola, Don	2	Garr, Ralph	3
Dempsey, Rick	2	Garver, Ned	3
Dickson, Murry	4	Gehringer, Charlie	12
Diering, Chuck	3	Gentile, Jim	4
Dillard, Ron	3	Geronimo, Cesar	3
DiMaggio, Dom	6	Gibbs, Jake	3
Dittmer, Jack	3	Giel, Paul	3
Dobbek, Dan	3	Gladding, Fred	3
Dobson, Joe	3	Glynn, Bill	3
Doby, Larry	5	Goldsberry, Gordon	4
Drabowski, Moe	3	Goltz, David	2
Dressler, Bob	2	Gonder, Jesse	3
Driessen, Dan	3	Goodman, Billy	6
Dropo, Walt	5	Goodson, Ed	2
Drysdale, Don	7	Gorman, Tom	5
Duffy, Frank	2	Gossage, Rich	3
Duren, Ryne	4	Grammas, Alex	2
Durocher, Leo	5	Grant, Jim	4
Ellis, Sammy	2	Gray, Ted	4
Elston, Don	2	Greenberg, Hank	15
Ennis, Del	4	Greengrass, Jim	5
Epstein, Mike	2	Grich, Bobby	2
Erautt, Ed	3	Grieve, Tom	2
Ermer, Cal	3	Grim, Bob	3
Evers, Walter	4	Grimes, Burleigh	15
Face, Roy	4	Groat, Dick	5
Fairey, Jim	3	Gromek, Steve	3
Fairly, Ron	4	Groth, Johnny	3
Feller, Bob	10	Guidry, Ron	4
Fingers, Rollie	5	Gullett, Don	4
Fitzgerald, Eddie	3	Gura, Larry	3
Fondy, Dee	3	Hacker, Warren	3

Name	Signed Card	Name	Signed Card
Haddix, Harvey	3	James, Charley	3
Hale, Arvel	3	Jarvis, Pat	3
Haller, Tom	3	Jay, Joe	4
Handy, Fred	3	Jenkins, Fergie	4
Hansen, Ron	3	Jensen, Larry	3
Hargrove, Mike	3	John, Tommy	3
Harmon, Chuck	3	Johnson, Billy	4
Harper, Tommy	3	Johnson, Bob	2
Harrah, Toby	3	Johnson, Darrell	3
Harrelson, Bud	2	Johnson, Deron	3
Hart, Jim	4	Johnson, Ernie	3
Hartman, Bob	3	Johnson, Ken	2
Hatfield, Fred	4	Johnson, Robert	2
Hatton, Grady	3	Johnstone, Jay	2
Hauser, Joe	4	Jones, Cleon	2
Hearns, Jim	5	Jones, Dalton	2
Hebner, Rich	4	Jones, Mack	2
Hegan, Mike	2	Jones, Randy	2
Held, Woodie	2	Joost, Eddie	5
Herbel, Ron	2	Judson, Howie	4
Herman, Billy	8	Kaat, Jim	4
Herman, Floyd	10	Kaiser, Don	3
Hermanski, Gene	3	Katt, Ray	3
Herzog, Whitey	4	Keegan, Bob	3
Hetki, John	3	Kekich, Mike	2
Hickman, Jim	3	Kell, George	6
Hiller, Chuck	3	Kellner, Alex	3
Hiller, John	3	Kelly, Pat	3
Hillman, Dave	3	Kessinger, Don	3
Hinton, Chuck	3	Kiely, Leo	3
Hisle, Larry	3	Killebrew, Harmon	8
Hitchcock, Billy	4	Kindall, Jerry	3
Hobbie, Glen	3	Kiner, Ralph	8
Hoderlein, Mel	3	King, Jim	3
Hofman, Bob	3	Klimchock, Lou	3
Hogue, Bobby	3	Kline, Ron	3
Hooton, Burt	2	Klippstein, Johnny	4
Hough, Charlie	2	Kluszewski, Theodore	4
Houk, Ralph	3	Knox, John	3
House, Tom	2	Kokos, Dick	3
Howard, Frank	4	Koosman, Jerry	3
Hrabosky, Al	2	Koppe, Joe	3
Hubbell, Carl	12	Kubek, Tony	4
Hughes, James	3	Kuenn, Harvey	4
Hughes, Terry	2	Kunkel, Bill	3
Hunt, Ron	2	LaCock, Pete	2
Hunter, Billy	5	Lacy, Lee	3
Hunter, Jim	4	Lamabe, Jack	3
Irwin, Monte	5	Landrith, Hobie	3
Jackson, Bob	2	LaPalme, Paul	4
Jackson, Larry	3	Lary, Frank	3
Jackson, Randy	3	Lasorda, Tom	2
Jackson, Reggie	8	Latman, Barry	3
Jackson, Travis	15	Law, Vern	3

Hank Aaron

Cal Abrams

Hank Aguirre

Bernie Allen

Sparky Anderson

Ruben Amaro

Luke Appling

Dusty Baker

Sal Bando

Red Barber

Dick Bartell

James "Cool Papa" Bell

Chief Bender

Yogi Berra

Bill Bevens

Jim Bibby

Ewell Blackwell

Johnny Blanchard

Vida Blue

Jimmy Bloodworth

Ossie Bluege

Bert Blyleven

163

Name	Signed Card	Name	Signed Card
Lee, Bill	3	Metcalf, Tom	3
Lefebvre, Jeff	3	Michaels, Cass	4
LeFlore, Ron	4	Micher, Don	3
Lemaster, Denver	3	Miksis, Eddie	3
LeMaster, Johnnie	3	Milbourne, Larry	2
Lemon, Chet	3	Miller, John	2
Lemon, Jim	3	Miller, Stu	3
Lenhardt, Don	3	Minner, Paul	4
Lepcio, Ted	3	Mize, Johnny	8
Liddle, Don	3	Mizell, Wilmer	4
Lillis, Bob	3	Monday, Rick	4
Limmer, Lou	3	Money, Don	3
Lindell, Johnny	5	Moon, Wally	3
Lockman, Whitey	3	Morgan, Bob	3
Logan, Johnny	3	Morgan, Tom	3
Lonborg, Jim	3	Moses, Wally	4
Long, Richard	3	Moss, Les	4
Lopat, Ed	4	Mossi, Don	3
Lopata, Stan	4	Mota, Manny	3
Lopes, Davey	3	Mueller, Don	4
Lopez, Al	8	Mullin, Pat	4
Lowenstein, John	3	Murray, Ray	4
Lown, Turk	3	Musial, Stan	12
Lund, Don	3	Naragon, Hal	3
Lynch, Jerry	3	Nash, Cotton	3
MacDaniel, Lindy	3	Neeman, Cal	3
Mackanin, Pete	2	Nelson, Dave	3
MacKenzie, Ken	3	Nelson, Rock	3
Maglie, Sal	4	Nettles, Craig	4
Malzone, Frank	3	Newcombe, Don	3
Mapes, Cliff	3	Nicholson, Dave	3
Marshall, Willard	4	Niekro, Phil	4
Masterton, Walt	4	Nieman, Bob	3
Mathews, Ed	7	Nixon, Willard	3
Mauch, Gene	3	Nolan, Gary	3
May, Dave	3	Noren, Irv	3
Mayberry, John	3	Norris, Mike	3
Mazeroski, Bill	4	Northup, Jim	3
McAnally, Ernie	3	Nuxhall, Joe	3
McCarver, Tim	3	O'Dell, Bill	3
McDaniel, Von	3	Odom, John	4
McDougald, Gil	3	Oldis, Bob	3
McDowell, Sam	4	Oliva, Tony	3
McGhee, Ed	3	Olson, Karl	3
McGraw, Tug	3	Osteen, Claude	2
McKeon, Jack	2	O'Toole, Jim	3
McMillan, Roy	4	Owen, Mickey	4
McMullen, Ken	2	Paciorek, Tom	2
McNally, Dave	3	Pafko, Andy	4
McRae, Hal	4	Palmer, Jim	6
Medich, George	2	Pappas, Milt	3
Mele, Sam	3	Parker, Wes	4
Melton, Bill	3	Parnell, Mel	4
Messersmith, Andy	3	Parrish, Larry	2

Jim Bolger

Don Bollweg

John Boozer

Lou Boudreau

George Brett

Lou Brock

Ron Cey

Mordecai Brown

Jim Busby

Roy Campanella

Steve Carlton

Happy Chandler

Chris Chambliss

Rocky Colavito

Earle Combs

James "Ripper" Collins

Jocko Conlan

Stanley Coveleski

Bob Cox

Name	Signed Card	Name	Signed Card
Patek, Freddie	2	Roush, Edd	12
Peden, Les	2	Rudi, Joe	3
Perez, Tony	4	Ruffing, Red	15
Perkowski, Harry	3	Runnels, Pete	4
Perranoski, Ron	3	Rush, Bob	4
Perry, Jim	3	Russell, Bill	2
Pesky, Johnny	3	Salmon, Chico	5
Peters, Gary	3	Sanguillen, Manny	4
Peterson, Fred	3	Santo, Ron	4
Petrocelli, Rico	3	Sauer, Hank	3
Philley, Dave	3	Saverine, Bob	2
Phillips, Bubba	3	Schaffer, Jimmie	2
Phillips, Taylor	3	Scheffing, Bob	3
Phoebus, Tom	3	Scheib, Carl	3
Pierce, Billy	3	Schilling, Chuck	3
Pignatano, Joe	3	Schoendienst, Al	3
Pillette, Duane	3	Schoendienst, Red	4
Piniella, Lou	3	Schroll, Al	3
Podres, Johnny	4	Schult, Art	3
Poholsky, Tom	3	Scoiscia, Mike	2
Powell, Boog	4	Score, Herb	3
Pramesa, John	3	Seaver, Tom	8
Presko, Joe	3	Segui, Diego	3
Qualters, Tom	3	Sembera, Carroll	3
Radatz, Dick	3	Seminick, Andy	3
Raffensberger, Ken	3	Sewell, Joe	8
Rakow, Ed	3	Sewell, Luke	8
Randle, Len	2	Sexton, Jim	2
Raschi, Vic	4	Seyfried, Gordon	3
Renick, Rick	2	Shamsky, Art	3
Reniff, Hal	3	Shantz, Bobby	3
Renna, Bill	3	Shaw, Bob	3
Repulski, Rip	3	Shea, Frank	3
Reuschel, Paul	2	Shearer, Ray	3
Reuschel, Rick	3	Siebern, Norm	3
Reynolds, Allie	4	Sievers, Roy	3
Rhodes, Jim	4	Simmons, Curt	3
Richardson, Bobby	3	Simmons, Ted	3
Riddle, John	4	Simpson, Harry	6
Righetti, Dave	3	Singer, Bill	3
Rivera, Jim	4	Sisler, Dave	4
Rizzuto, Phil	4	Sisler, Dick	3
Roach, Mel	3	Sisler, George	20
Roberts, Dave	2	Skinner, Bob	3
Roberts, Robin	8	Skowron, Bill	3
Robinson, Bill	3	Slaughter, Enos	7
Robinson, Brooks	6	Sleater, Lou	3
Robinson, Eddie	4	Sluder, Pete	3
Roebuck, Ed	3	Smalley, Roy	2
Rogers, Steve	2	Smith, Al	4
Rollins, Rich	2	Smith, Dick	3
Rose, Pete	10	Smith, Hal	3
Roseboro, John	5	Smith, Mayo	5
Rosen, Al	4	Smith, Reggie	4

Best Wishes
Jim Davenport

"Daffy" Dean

Dizzy Dean

Eric Davis

Bobby Del Greco

Rick Dempsey

Bill Dickey

Joe DiMaggio

Abner Doubleday

Al Downing

Don Drysdale

Leo Durocher

Bob Feller

Rick Ferrell—Hall of Fame

Rollie Fingers

Elmer Flick—Hall of Fame

Curt Flood

Jimmie Foxx

George Foster

Bob Friend

167

Name	Signed Card	Name	Signed Card
Soderholm, Eric	2	Versalles, Zoillo	5
Spahn, Warren	8	Veryzer, Tom	3
Spangler, Al	2	Virdon, William	3
Spencer, Daryl	3	Vollmer, Clyde	3
Spencer, Jim	2	Walker, Dixie	6
Spenser, James	2	Walters, Bucky	4
Splittorff, Paul	2	Waner, Lloyd	15
Stange, Lee	3	Ward, Jay	3
Stanhouse, Don	2	Ward, Pete	3
Stanley, Mickey	3	Ward, Preston	3
Stargell, Willie	6	Watson, Bob	3
St. Clair, Ebba	4	Watt, Eddie	3
Stengel, Casey	25	Weaver, Earl	3
Stigman, Dick	3	Weaver, Floyd	3
Stinson, Bob	3	Werhas, John	3
Stock, Wes	3	Westlake, Wally	3
Stone, George	2	Westrum, Wes	3
Stottlemyre, Mel	3	Whitaker, Lou	2
Strickland, George	3	White, Bill	3
Stuart, Dick	5	White, Frank	2
Sullivan, Frank	3	White, Sammy	3
Surkont, Max	3	Whitman, Dick	3
Tanana, Frank	3	Wietelmann, Whitey	3
Tappe, Elvin	3	Wilcox, Milt	3
Taylor, Antonio	3	Wilhelm, Hoyt	8
Taylor, Bob	3	Williams, Davey	4
Taylor, Ron	3	Williams, Dick	3
Tenace, Gene	3	Williams, Earl	3
Terrell, Jerry	3	Williams, Stan	3
Terry, Bill	15	Williams, Steve	3
Terwilliger, Wayne	3	Wilson, Earl	3
Thompson, Bobby	4	Wilson, Red	3
Thorton, Andy	3	Winkles, Bobby	3
Tiant, Luis	4	Wise, Rick	2
Tillman, Bob	3	Wohlford, Jim	2
Tolan, Bob	3	Wolf, Wally	2
Torgeson, Earl	3	Wood, Wilbur	3
Torre, Joe	3	Woodling, Gene	3
Tovar, Cesar	4	Wynn, Early	8
Tremel, Bill	3	Wynn, Jim	3
Tresh, Tom	3	Wyrostek, Johnny	3
Trucks, Virgil	3	Yeager, Steve	2
Turley, Bob	3	Yost, Eddie	3
Uhlaender, Ted	3	Yount, Robin	4
Valo, Elmer	3	Yvars, Sal	3
Van Cuyk, Chris	3	Zanni, Dom	3
VanderMeer, Johnny	3	Zernial, Gus	3
Veale, Bob	3	Zimmer, Don	2
Vernon, Mickey	3	Zimmerman, Jerry	3

Ned Garver

Charles Gehringer

Bob Gibson

Steve Garvey

Fred Goldsmith—Inventor of Curve Ball

Lefty Grove

Lefty Gomez—Hall of Fame

Goose Goslin

Hank Greenberg

Clark Griffith
President

Burleigh A. Grimes

"Chick" Hafey

Jesse Haines

Ron Hansen

Jim Hearn

Babe Herman

Keith Hernandez

Harry Hooper

Gil Hodges

Ralph Houk

Joel Horlen

169

Hall of Fame Plaques
(Gold and Black-and-White Cards)

The Baseball Hall of Fame sells postcard-sized reproductions of the plaques honoring its various members. The cards were originally issued in black and white, but now feature a gold color. These cards have been popular with collectors for many years. The list below covers the value of those cards which have been signed by the player they honor, and some have very respectable values.

Name	Gold	B & W	Name	Gold	B & W
Aaron, Henry "Hank"	$ 5		Gehringer, Charlie	10	
Alexander, Grover		$200	Gibson, Bob	10	
Alston, Walter	25		Gomez, Lefty	10	
Aparicio, Luis	12		Goslin, Goose	190	
Appling, Luke	12		Greenberg, Hank	15	35
Averill, Earl	10		Griffith, Clark		175
Baker, Frank		175	Grimes, Burleigh	10	
Bancroft, Dave	150		Grove, Lefty	40	
Banks, Ernie	5		Hafey, Chick	20	
Bell, James	10		Haines, Jess	22	
Bench, Johnny	6		Harris, Bucky	65	
Bender, Chief		325	Hartnett, Gabby	45	80
Berra, Yogi	6		Herman, Billy	6	
Boudreau, Lou	6		Hooper, Harry	14	
Brock, Lou	6		Hornsby, Rogers		165
Burkett, Jessie		200	Hoyt, Waite	15	
Carey, Max	10		Hubbard, Cal	125	
Chandler, Happy	5		Hubbell, Carl	10	
Clarke, Fred		125	Irvin, Monte	6	
Cobb, Ty		200	Jackson, Travis	10	
Cochrane, Mickey		90	Johnson, Jim "Judy"	6	
Collins, Eddie		175	Johnson, Walter		400
Combs, Earl	20		Kaline, Al	5	
Conlan, Jocko	6		Kell, George	6	
Connolly, Tommy		190	Kelly, George	10	
Coveleski, Stan	10		Killebrew, Harmon	6	
Crawford, Sam	35	55	Kiner, Ralph	6	
Cronin, Joe	12	45	Koufax, Sandy	10	
Dean, Dizzy	25	60	Lajoie, Nap		160
Dickey, Bill	10	35	Lemon, Bob	6	
DiMaggio, Joe	25	45	Leonard, Buck	6	
Doerr, Bobby	5		Lindstrom, Fred	10	
Drysdale, Don	5		Lopez, Al	6	
Duffy, Hugh		150	Lyons, Ted	6	
Evers, John		250	Mack, Connie		140
Faber, Red	22		Mantle, Mickey	15	
Feller, Bob	6		Manush, "Heinie"	40	
Ferrell, Rick	5		Marichal, Juan	5	
Flick, Elmer	35	50	Marquard, Rube	12	
Ford, Whitey	10		Mathews, Eddie	6	
Foxx, Jimmie	200	175	Mays, Willie	10	
Frick, Ford	22		McCarthy, Joe	15	30
Frisch, Frankie	25	45	McCovey, Willie	5	

Elston Howard

Carl Hubbell

Jim "Catfish" Hunter

Travis Jackson

Monte Irvin

Joe Judge

Al Kaline

Willie Kamm

Reggie Jackson

George Kell

Charlie Keller

George L. Kelly

Herman Killebrew

Ralph Kiner

Dave Kingman

Mark Koenig

Sandy Koufax

Bowie Kuhn

Larry Lajoie

Don Larsen

Best of
Tommy Lasorda

Bob Lemon

Name	Gold	B & W		Name	Gold	B & W
McKetchnie, Bill		85		Sisler, George	30	45
Medwick, Joe	20			Slaughter, Enos	6	
Mize, Johnny	6			Snider, Duke	6	
Musial, Stan	6			Spahn, Warren	6	
Nichols, Kid		175		Speaker, Thris		180
Ott, Mel		175		Stengel, Casey	30	
Paige, Satchel	25			Terry, Bill	14	
Reese, PeeWee	6			Tinker, Joe		200
Rice, Sam	25	40		Traynor, Pie	100	100
Roberts, Robin	6			Vance, Dizzy		150
Robinson, Brooks	6			Wagner, Honus		175
Robinson, Frank	8			Waner, Lloyd	12	25
Robinson, Jackie	175	175		Waner, Paul		90
Roush, Edd	6			Wheat, Zack	45	90
Ruffing, Red	15			Wilhelm, Hoyt	6	
Ruth, Babe		500		Williams, Ted	15	
Schalk, Ray	35	55		Wynn, Early	6	
Sewell, Joe	6			Young, Cy		175
Simmons, Al		200				

Signatures and Signed Photographs

Below is a representative cross-section of major league baseball players. These are basically ball players of the twentieth century, and the prices given are for signatures or signed photographs in reasonable-to-average condition—that is, not creased or smeared. Most photographs are priced for black and white, but the more recent prices are based on 8 × 10 color photos.

Name	Signature	Signed Photograph
Aaron, Henry "Hank"	$ 10	$ 20
Abbott, Glenn	2	4
Abrams, Cal	2	5
Adams, Red	2	5
Adcock, Joe	4	10
Aguilera, Rick	3	12
Aguirre, Hank	2	5
Ainge, Dan	3	10
Allen, Bernie	2	5
Allen, Mel	5	7
Allison, Bob	2	5
Aloma, Luis	1	5
Alston, Walt	7	20
Amalfitano, Joe	2	5
Amaro, Ruben	2	5
Anderson, George "Sparky"	5	10
Andujar, Joaquin	3	15
Aparicio, Luis	6	16
Appling, Luke	5	15
Armas, Tony	4	10
Ashburn, Richie	4	12
Averill, Earl	5	15

"Dutch" Leonard

Walter Buck Leonard

Johnny Logan

Alfonso Lopez

Ted Lyons

Connie Mack

Roger Maris

"Rube" Marquard

Billy Martin

Pepper Martin

Gary Matthews

Joe McCarthy

You gotta believe

Tug McGraw

Scott McGregor

Johnny Mize

Wally Moon

Dale Murphy

Eddie Murray

Stan Musial

Don Newcombe

Phil Niekro

173

Name	Signature	Signed Photograph
Auerbach, Rick	3	5
Auker, Elden	4	10
Backman, Wally	3	12
Bagby, Jim, Jr.	4	7
Baker, Del	3	5
Baker, Franklin "Home Run"	30	150
Baker, John "Dusty"	2	5
Ballenfant, Lee	2	5
Bamberger, Hal	2	5
Bancroft, Dave	15	80
Bando, Sal	3	7
Banks, Ernie	5	16
Barber, Red	3	5
Barlick, Al	3	5
Barney, Rex	2	5
Barrett, Marty	5	10
Bartell, Dick	3	7
Bass, Richard "Dick"	2	5
Bauer, Hank	3	10
Baumholtz, Frank	3	7
Baylor, Don	3	12
Belanger, Mark	3	10
Bell, Buddy	3	15
Bell, James "Cool Papa"	5	20
Bench, Johnny	5	15
Bender, Chief	35	150
Benedict, Bruce	3	9
Berardino, Johnny	3	5
Berg, Moe	35	50
Berra, Yogi	5	12
Bevacqua, Kurt	2	5
Bevans, Bill	2	5
Bibby, Jim	2	4
Biittner, Larry	2	5
Black, Joe	3	10
Blackwell, Ewell	5	12
Blair, Paul	2	5
Blalock, Jim	2	4
Blanchard, John	2	5
Blass, Steve	2	4
Blasingame, Don	2	4
Blaylock, Gary	2	4
Blaylock, Marv	2	4
Bloodworth, Jimmy	2	5
Blue, Vida	5	15
Bluege, Ossie	4	10
Blyleven, Bert	5	10
Boddicker, Mike	4	10
Boggs, Wade	5	25
Bolger, Jim	2	4
Bolling, Milt	2	4
Bollweg, Don	2	5
Bonham, Bill	3	6
Bonura, Zeke	3	10
Boone, Bob	3	5

Al Oliver

Jim Palmer

Roger Peckinpaugh

Jeff Rearden

Pee Wee Reese

Dusty Rhodes

Cal Ripkin, Jr.

Bobby Richardson

Phil Rizzuto

Robin Roberts

Brooks Robinson

Jackie Robinson

Red Rolfe

Edd J. Roush

Red Ruffing

Babe Ruth

Ray Schalk

Herb Score

Tom Seaver

Joe Sewell

175

Name	Signature	Signed Photograph
Boone, Lute "Danny"	4	15
Boozer, John	3	5
Borowy, Hank	3	5
Boudreau, Lou	5	10
Bouton, Jim	3	8
Bowa, Larry	3	10
Boyer, Ken	6	20
Bragan, Bobby	3	5
Braggs, Glenn	3	10
Brahanski, Tom	3	5
Branca, Ralph	3	7
Brecheen, Harry	3	5
Breeding, Marv	3	5
Bressoud, Ed	3	5
Brett, George	5	10
Breuer, Marv	2	4
Bridges, Rocky	3	5
Bridges, Tommy	3	10
Briles, Nelson	2	4
Brock, Greg	3	7
Brock, Lou	5	10
Brown, Bobby	3	7
Brown, Dick	5	15
Brown, Joe L.	3	7
Brown, Mace	3	5
Brown, Mordecai	50	300
Browning, Tom	3	15
Bouton, Bill	3	5
Brunansky, Tom	4	12
Bucher, Jim	2	4
Buckner, Bill	4	10
Bumbry, Al	3	5
Bunning, Jim	3	7
Burda, Bob	2	4
Burdette, Lew	4	10
Burgess, Smoky	3	5
Burkhart, Ken	3	5
Burleson, Rick	3	8
Burroughs, Jeff	3	6
Busby, Jim	3	5
Busby, Steve	2	4
Bush, Guy	5	20
Byrd, Harry	3	6
Byrd, Sam	4	8
Byrne, Tommy	3	6
Cain, Bob	2	5
Camilli, Dolph	3	8
Campanella, Roy	100	175
Campaneris, Bert	4	12
Campanis, Al	12.50	25
Candini, Milo	2	4
Canseco, Jose	4	12
Cardenal, Jose	2	4
Cardwell, Don	2	5

Roy Sievers

Ken Singleton

George Sisler

Duke Snider

Dick Starr

Warren Spahn

George Steinbrenner

Casey Stengel

Sammy Stewart

Mel Stottlemyre

Bill Terry

Joe Tinker

Joe Torre

Bob Uecker

Johnny VanderMeer

Harry Walker

Ted Williams

Bucky Walters

Lloyd Waner
"Little Poison"

Maury Wills

Rick Wise

177

Name	Signature	Signed Photograph
Carew, Rod	4	15
Carey, Andy	3	10
Carey, Max	6	25
Carlton, Steve	3	8
Carter, Gary	3	8
Carter, Joe	3	10
Carty, Rico	3	5
Cash, Norm	5	25
Castleman, Clydell	2	4
Cavaretta, Phil	3	7
Caudill, Bill	3	12
Cedeno, Cesar	3	12
Cepeda, Orlando	4	12
Cey, Ron "Penguin"	3	7
Chambliss, Chris	3	7
Chase, Hal	25	75
Chance, Dean	4	12
Chandler, A. B. "Happy"	5	10
Chandler, "Spud"	3	6
Chapman, Ben	5	10
Chapman, Sam	4	8
Chiti, Harry	3	5
Chylak, Nestor	3	5
Cicotte, Eddie	50	200
Clark, Jack	3	12
Clarke, Fred C.	50	175
Clemens, Roger	8	25
Clemente, Roberto	75	125
Clift, Harland	3	7
Clifton, "Flea"	4	8
Cline, Ty	3	5
Cobb, Ty	75	200
Cochrane, Gordon "Mickey"	50	125
Coleman, Vince	3	15
Colavito, Rocky	3	5
Coleman, Gerry	3	7
Coleman, Gordon	3	6
Collins, "Eddie"	70	150
Collins, Eddie, Jr.	4	8
Collins, James "Rip"	10	30
Collins, Jimmy	200	375
Collins, Joe	3	6
Colosi, Nick	3	6
Colton, Joe	3	5
Combs, Earle	10	30
Combs, Merrill	3	6
Comiskey, Charles	25	350
Conatser, Clint	3	6
Concepcion, Dave	3	15
Cone, Dave	3	10
Conigliaro, Tony	8	20
Conlan, John B. "Jocko"	5	10
Conley, Gene	3	5
Connors, Chuck	5	30
Consolo, Billy	2	4

Name	Signature	Signed Photograph
Consuegra, Sandy	5	20
Cook, Cliff	2	5
Cooper, Cecil	4	10
Cooper, Walker	5	10
Cooper, Wilbur	10	35
Coscarart, Pete	3	5
Coveleski, Stan	5	15
Cowens, Al	3	6
Cox, Billy	5	20
Cox, Bob	2	4
Craft, Harry	3	5
Crandall, Del	3	7
Crawford, "Shag"	5	10
Crawford, "Wahoo" Sam	40	95
Crespi, Frank "Creepy"	3	6
Cresse, Mark	3	7
Cronin, Joe	6	25
Crosetti, Frankie	5	12
Cross, Jeff	2	4
Crowley, Terry	2	4
Cuccinello, Tony	5	15
Cullenbine, Roy	3	6
Cuyler, Hazen "KiKi"	80	175
Dahlgren, Babe	5	15
Dallessandro, Dom	2	5
Dalrymple, Clay	2	4
Danning, Harry "The Horse"	2	5
Dark, Al	3	7
Darling, Ron	4	12
Darwin, Danny	2	4
Dascoli, Frank	2	4
Davalillo, Vic	2	4
Davenport, Jim	2	5
Davis, Alvin	3	10
Davis, Chili	3	10
Davis, Eric	4	10
Davis, George	2	4
Davis, Jody	4	8
Davis, Storm	4	10
Davis, Tommy	3	7
Davis, Willie	4	10
Dawson, Andre	4	12
Dean, Jay "Dizzy"	12	60
Dean, Paul "Daffy"	5	20
DeCinces, Doug	3	5
Decker, Joe	2	4
de la Hoz, Mike	2	4
Del Greco, Bobby	2	5
Delsing, Jim	2	4
DeMaestri, Joe	2	4
Demeter, Don	3	5
Dempsey, Rick	3	10
Denkinger, Don	6	10
Dente, Sam	4	15
Dickey, Bill	5	10

Name	Signature	Signed Photograph
DiMaggio, Dom	4	10
DiMaggio, Joe	15	35
DiMaggio, Vince	6	20
Dobson, Joe	3	5
Doby, Larry	5	10
Doerr, Bobby	5	10
Donald, Atley	3	5
Donatelli, Augie	3	5
Dorish, Harry	2	4
Downing, Al	3	5
Downing, Brian	3	5
Dravecky, Dave	4	10
Dreesen, Tom	3	12
Dressen, Chuck	12	35
Dropo, Walt	3	5
Drysdale, Don	4	10
Dugan, "Joe"	6	20
Duren, Ryne	3	5
Durham, Leon	4	15
Durocher, Leo	5	12
Dyer, Eddie	6	20
Dykstra, Lenny	3	10
Early, Jake	2	4
Earnshaw, George	4	25
Easler, Mike	4	10
Eckert, Gen. William D.	10	30
Eisenreich, Jim	5	10
Elliott, Glenn	3	5
Ennis, Del	3	5
Erskine, Carl	4	7
Etchebarren, Andy	3	5
Etten, Nick	3	5
Evans, Darrell	4	15
Evans, Dwight	4	12
Evers, Walter "Hoot"	3	7
Faber, Urban "Red"	15	30
Face, El Roy	3	7
Fain, Ferris	4	10
Fanzone, Carmen	3	5
Feeney, Charles S. "Chub"	4	7
Feller, Bob	5	12
Fernandez, Sid	4	10
Ferrell, Rick	5	12
Ferrick, Tom	3	5
Fidrych, Mark "The Bird"	4	8
Fingers, Rollie	3	6
Finley, Charles O.	7	25
Fisk, Carlton	3	7
Fitzsimmons, "Fat Freddie"	5	30
Flanagan, Mike	3	10
Flick, Elmer	14	40
Flood, Curt	10	20
Fonseca, Lew	3	7
Ford, Walter Clay	3	5
Ford, Whitey	5	12

Name	Signature	Signed Photograph
Foster, George	5	10
Fosse, Ray	3	6
Fox, Nelson	10	40
Foxx, Jimmie	70	150
Franco, John	4	10
Freehan, Bill	3	6
Freese, Gene	3	5
Freese, George	3	5
French, Larry	5	15
Frey, Lonny	3	5
Frick, Ford	12	35
Friend, Bob	3	5
Frisch, Frank	15	65
Furillo, Carl	5	10
Gabrielson, Len	3	5
Gaetti, Gary	3	8
Gaffke, Fabian	2	4
Gaines, Joe	3	5
Galan, Augie	3	7
Garagiola, Joe	3	5
Garver, Ned	3	5
Garvey, Steve	3	7
Gehrig, Lou	400	650
Gehringer, Charley	5	20
Gibson, Bob	5	15
Gibson, Kirk	5	15
Giles, Warren C.	15	35
Gilliam, Jim "Junior"	7	25
Gionfriddo, Al	4	7
Glaviano, Tommy	3	5
Goldsmith, Fred E.	40	125
Gomez, Vernon "Lefty"	5	10
Gonder, Jesse	2	4
Gooden, Dwight	4	20
Gordon, Joe	4	25
Gordon, Sid	6	20
Gore, Artie	3	7
Goslin, Leon "Goose"	20	80
Gossage, Rich "Goose"	5	15
Gowdy, Curt	3	5
Grant, Jim "Mudcat"	5	10
Gray, Pete	5	15
Green, Dick	3	5
Green, George "Dallas"	3	5
Greenberg, Hank	7	25
Griffith, Calvin	4	7
Griffith, Clark C.	90	150
Grimes, Burleigh	5	20
Grimm, Charlie	5	20
Grote, Jerry	2	4
Groth, Johnny	3	5
Grove, Robert "Lefty"	25	40
Guerrero, Pedro	3	10
Guidry, Ron	5	10
Gullickson, Bill	5	10

Name	Signature	Signed Photograph
Gumpert, Randy	3	6
Gwynn, Chris	3	8
Gwynn, Tony	5	15
Hack, Stan	5	20
Haddix, Harvey	4	15
Hafey, Charles "Chick"	18	45
Haines, Jesse	10	40
Hale, John	2	5
Hall, Dick	3	5
Haller, Tom	2	4
Hamilton, Milo	2	4
Hamlin, Luke	3	5
Hancock, Fred	2	4
Hands, Bill	2	4
Haney, Fred	5	20
Hannan, Jim	2	4
Hansen, Ron	2	5
Hardy, Carroll	2	4
Harmon, Chuck	2	4
Harrelson, Bud	3	5
Harridge, William	30	75
Harris, Spencer	5	20
Harris, Stanley "Bucky"	12	35
Harstad, Oscar	4	6
Hartman, Bob	2	4
Hartnett, Leo "Gabby"	15	80
Hartung, Clint	3	5
Hassett, "Bud"	3	5
Hatfield, Fred	3	5
Hauser, Joe	2	4
Hayes, Von	4	15
Hayworth, Ray	3	6
Hearn, Jim	3	6
Heath, Tommy	2	4
Heffner, Don	3	6
Hegan, Jim	5	20
Held, Woody	3	6
Helf, "Hank"	2	4
Hemus, Solly	3	5
Henderson, Ricky	3	10
Henrich, Tommy	4	15
Herman, Billy	5	10
Herman, Floyd "Babe"	5	20
Hernandez, Keith	4	20
Hernandez, Willie	4	15
Herndon, Larry	4	10
Herr, Tom	4	10
Hersheiser, Orel	4	15
Herzog, Whitey	4	8
Higbe, Kirby	3	5
Hobaugh, Ed	2	4
Hoderlein, Mel	2	4
Hodges, Gil	20	70
Hoerner, Joe	2	4
Hofman, Bobby	2	4

Name	Signature	Signed Photograph
Holmes, Tommy	5	10
Holtzman, Ken	2	4
Honeycutt, Rick	3	12
Hooper, Harry	12	35
Hopp, Johnny	3	7
Horlen, Joe	4	10
Horner, Bob	4	10
Hornsby, Rogers	50	150
Houk, Ralph	3	7
House, Frank	2	4
House, Tom	2	4
Howard, Elston	5	25
Howe, Art	3	5
Howe, Steve	3	7
Howell, Millard "Dixie"	10	25
Howser, Dick	7	25
Hoyt, LaMarr	4	8
Hoyt, Waite	6	15
Hrbek, Kent	3	8
Hubbard, Cal	25	50
Hubbard, Glenn	3	10
Hubbell, Carl	10	20
Huffman, Bennie	2	4
Hughes, Jim	2	4
Hunt, Ron	3	5
Hunter, Bill	2	4
Hunter, Jim "Catfish"	3	8
Hurdle, Clint	2	4
Incaviglia, Pete	3	10
Irvin, Monte	3	8
Jablonski, Ray	3	6
Jackson, Larry	2	4
Jackson, Reggie	4	20
Jackson, Ron	2	4
Jackson, Ron H.	2	5
Jackson, Travis	10	15
Jansen, Larry	3	7
Jeffcoat, Hal	3	5
Jenkins, Ferguson	3	8
Jensen, Jackie	5	20
John, Tommy	4	10
Johnson, Alex	4	10
Johnson, Billy	3	5
Johnson, Cliff	2	4
Johnson, Dave	3	5
Johnson, Howard "Hujo"	4	10
Johnson, Judy	5	10
Johnson, Walter "Big Train"	50	350
Johnstone, Jay	3	6
Jones, Davy	5	10
Jones, Randy	4	8
Jones, Tracy	3	9
Joost, Eddie	3	5
Jordan, Tom	2	4
Jorgens, Art	2	4

Name	Signature	Signed Photograph
Joshua, Von	3	6
Joyner, Wally	3	12
Judge, Joe	10	35
Kaat, Jim	3	6
Kaline, Al	5	10
Kamm, "Willie"	3	6
Kampouris, Alex	2	4
Keely, Bob	2	4
Kell, George	5	10
Keller, Charlie "King Kong"	5	10
Kelly, George L.	6	15
Kemp, Steve	3	6
Kennedy, John	2	4
Kennedy, Terry	3	10
Kenworthy, Dick	2	4
Kerr, Johnny	3	5
Killebrew, Harmon	3	10
Kiner, Ralph	5	10
Kingman, Dave	3	6
Kison, Bruce	3	6
Kittle, Ron	4	12
Kline, Ron	2	4
Kluszewski, Ted	5	10
Knight, Ray	4	10
Knott, Jack	3	5
Koenig, Mark A.	5	10
Koosman, Jerry	5	10
Koufax, Sanford "Sandy"	6	20
Krausse, Lew	2	4
Kreevich, Mike	3	6
Kress, Ralph "Red"	3	6
Kubek, Tony	4	8
Kuenn, Harvey	5	10
Kuhn, Bowie	4	8
Kunkel, Bill	4	8
Laabs, Chet	3	6
Labine, Clem	4	8
Lacy, Lee	3	6
Lajoie, Napoleon "Larry"	65	140
Landis, Kenesaw Mountain	90	200
Landreaux, Ken	4	8
Landrum, Don	3	5
Landrum, Joe	2	4
Langford, Rick	4	6
Langston, Mark	4	12
Larker, Norm	3	5
Larsen, Don	4	8
LaRussa, Tony	3	5
Lary, Frank	3	8
Lasorda, Tommy	4	8
Lavagetto, Cookie	5	15
Law, Vernon	4	8
Lefebvre, Jim	2	4
Lemon, Bob	4	10

Name	Signature	Signed Photograph
Leonard, Emil "Dutch"	4	15
Leonard, Walter "Buck"	5	10
Liddle, Don	4	15
Lindell, Johnny	4	15
Lindstrom, Fred	8	25
Liska, Ad	2	5
Lockman, Whitey	4	7
Logan, Johnny	3	5
Lombardi, Vic	3	6
Lonborg, Jim	3	5
Lopat, Ed	4	8
Lopes, Davey	3	6
Lopez, Al	5	10
Lopez, Aurelio	3	7
Lowrey, Harry "Peanuts"	3	15
Luzinski, Greg	4	8
Lyle, "Sparky"	4	9
Lynn, Fred	5	10
Lyons, Ted	5	20
Mack, Connie	50	125
MacPhail, Larry	50	100
MacPhail, Lee	3	6
Madlock, Bill	4	15
Maglie, Sal "The Barber"	4	8
Majeski, Hank	3	6
Maloney, Jim	3	6
Malzone, Frank	3	6
Mancuso, Gus	3	6
Mantilla, Felix	3	5
Mantle, Mickey	10	20
Manush, Henry "Heinie"	20	75
Maranville, Walter "Rabbit"	75	140
Marichal, Juan	4	15
Marion, Marty	5	10
Maris, Roger	5	15
Marquard, Rube	7	20
Marshall, Mike	4	10
Marshall, Willard	4	8
Martin, Billy	5	10
Martin, Fred	2	4
Martin, "Pepper"	10	40
Martin, Renie	2	4
Martinez, Carmelo	4	10
Mathews, Ed	5	10
Matthews, Gary	4	10
Mattingly, Don	5	25
Matlock, Jon	2	4
Mauch, Gene	3	6
May, Lee	3	5
Mays, Carl	10	35
Mays, Willie	6	15
Mazeroski, Bill	3	6
Mazzilli, Lee	4	8
McCarthy, Joe	12	30

Name	Signature	Signed Photograph
McCormick, Mike	3	6
McCoskey, Barney	4	8
McCovey, Willie	4	10
McDaniel, Lindy	3	5
McDougal, Gil	3	6
McDowell, "Sudden Sam"	4	15
McGraw, John J.	350	475
McGraw, Tug	4	8
McGregor, Scott	3	7
McGwire, Mark	5	25
McKechnie, Bill	35	85
McLain, Denny	4	10
McMillan, Roy	4	6
McNally, Dave	3	6
McNamara, John	3	5
McReynolds, Kevin	4	10
Medwick, Joe "Ducky"	15	40
Melton, Bill	4	8
Merullo, Lennie	3	5
Messersmith, Andy	3	6
Meusel, Bob	5	25
Meusel, Emil	10	40
Michael, Gene	4	8
Miksis, Eddie	4	8
Miller, Ralph	15	50
Mills, Buster	3	8
Minoso, Minnie	4	8
Miranda, Willy	3	6
Mitchell, Kevin	4	12
Mize, Johnny	5	12
Mizell, "Vinegar Bend"	5	10
Molitor, Paul	5	10
Money, Don	3	5
Moon, Wally	4	8
Moore, Charlie	3	5
Moore, Joe	3	5
Moore, Terry	4	8
Moreland, Keith	4	10
Morgan, Joe	4	10
Morgan, Tom	3	7
Moriarty, George	4	8
Morris, Jack	5	12
Mota, Manny	4	8
Mulleavy, Greg	5	15
Mullin, Pat	3	6
Mungo, Van Lingle	4	20
Murphy, Dale	5	20
Murray, Eddie	5	10
Murray, Jim	5	20
Murtaugh, Danny	5	25
Musial, Stan "The Man"	5	12
Navin, Charles F.	25	45
Nettles, Graig	5	10
Neun, Johnny	3	6
Newcombe, Don	4	12

Name	Signature	Signed Photograph
Newhouser, Hal	5	10
Newsom, Bobo	5	10
Nichols, Charles A. "Kid"	75	100
Nicholson, Bill	5	10
Niedenfuer, Tom	4	12
Niekro, Joe	4	8
Niekro, Phil	5	15
Noren, Irv	4	6
Nuxhall, Joe	4	6
Oakes, Rehal	4	8
Oates, Johnny	2	5
O'Dell, Billy	2	4
O'Dea, Ken	2	4
O'Doul, Lefty	12	50
Oeschger, Joe	9	20
Oglivie, Ben	3	7
Oh, Sadaharu	21	35
Ojeda, Bob	5	10
Oliva, Tony	4	10
Oliver, Al	3	6
Olmo, Luis	7	25
O'Malley, Peter	3	5
O'Malley, Walter	10	35
O'Neill, Steve	15	35
Orosco, Jesse	4	9
Osteen, Claude	3	6
Otero, Reggie	3	5
Otis, Amos	4	7
Ott, Mel	50	130
Owen, Marvin	3	6
Owen, Mickey	3	6
Paciorek, Tom	3	5
Pafko, Andy	4	8
Page, Joe	15	50
Pagliaroni, Jim	3	4
Pagliarulo, Mike	4	10
Paige, Leroy "Satchel"	20	55
Palica, Erv	5	20
Palmer, Jim	5	10
Pappas, Milt	3	6
Parker, Dave	5	14
Parker, Wes	3	7
Parnell, Mel	3	6
Parrish, Lance	5	15
Partee, Roy	2	5
Pascual, Camilo	3	6
Pasqua, Dan	4	10
Patek, Fred	2	4
Patkin, Max	4	8
Paul, Gabe	4	8
Pearson, Albie	4	6
Pearson, Monte	10	15
Peckinpaugh, Roger	4	15
Pena, Tony	4	12
Pennock, Herb	75	150

Name	Signature	Signed Photograph
Perez, Tony	4	8
Perry, Gaylord	4	12
Perry, Jim	3	6
Pesky, Johnny	4	9
Peters, Gary	3	5
Phillips, Bubba	3	5
Pierce, Billy	3	5
Piersall, Jimmy	4	15
Pignatano, Joe	3	6
Pilney, Andy	4	15
Pinelli, Babe	5	25
Piniella, Lou	4	8
Pipgrass, George W.	3	20
Plesac, Dan	3	6
Podres, Johnny	3	6
Porter, Darrell	3	5
Power, Ted	3	6
Puckett, Kirby	5	15
Puhl, Terry	4	8
Quisenberry, Dan	5	10
Raines, Tim	5	10
Ramirez, Rafael	4	8
Randolph, Willie	4	12
Raschi, Vic	4	10
Ray, Johnny	4	10
Reardon, "Beans"	10	35
Reardon, Jeff	4	12
Reese, "Pee Wee"	5	10
Reiser, Pete	10	30
Repulski, Rip	3	6
Reuss, Jerry	4	10
Reuschel, Rick	4	12
Reynolds, Allie	5	10
Rhodes, Dusty	5	10
Rice, Edgar "Sam"	17	35
Rice, Jim	5	10
Richard, J. R.	4	8
Richards, Paul	4	15
Richardson, Bobby	4	8
Rickey, Branch	50	90
Rigney, Bill	4	8
Ripken, Bill	3	5
Ripken, Cal, Sr.	4	6
Ripken, Cal, Jr.	5	9
Rixey, Eppa, Jr.	30	65
Rizzuto, Phil	5	10
Roberts, Robin	5	10
Robidoux, Billie Joe	4	10
Robinson, Brooks	5	10
Robinson, Eddie	3	5
Robinson, Frank	6	12
Robinson, Jackie	75	150
Robinson, Wilbert	25	450
Roe, Preacher	4	8
Rogell, Billy	4	10

Name	Signature	Signed Photograph
Rogers, Steve	4	10
Rojas, Cookie	3	5
Rolfe, Red	7	25
Romano, John	3	5
Root, Charlie	5	30
Rose, Pete	5	15
Rosen, Al	4	8
Roush, Edd J.	5	10
Rowe, Lynwood "Schoolboy"	6	25
Ruel, Harold "Muddy"	10	25
Ruffing, Charles "Red"	5	20
Ruppert, Col. Jacob	25	50
Russell, Bill	5	10
Ruth, George Herman "Babe"	550	900
Ruth, Mrs. "Babe"	10	20
Ryan, Nolan	5	15
Saberhagen, Bret	5	10
Saffell, Tom	2	4
Samuel, Juan	5	10
Sandberg, Ryne	5	15
Sanders, Ben	2	4
Sanders, John	2	4
Sanders, Ray	4	8
Sanders, Reggie	2	4
Sanderson, Scott	5	10
Sanford, Jack	4	5
Santiago, Benito	7	12
Santo, Ron	3	6
Sax, Steve	4	8
Schacht, Al	5	10
Schalk, Ray	20	65
Schmidt, Mike	5	15
Schmitz, Johnny	2	5
Schoendienst, "Red"	4	8
Schreiber, Paul	4	15
Schumacher, Hal	4	8
Score, Herb	4	8
Scully, Vin	4	8
Seaver, Tom	5	10
Seitzer, Kevin	5	10
Selkirk, George	5	10
Seminick, Andy	3	6
Sessi, Walt	2	4
Sewell, Joe	5	9
Shantz, Bobby	4	8
Shawkey, "Bob"	5	20
Shea, "Spec"	4	6
Sherry, Larry	3	5
Shuba, George "Shotgun"	4	6
Sieburn, Norm	4	8
Sierra, Ruben	4	10
Sievers, Roy	4	8
Simmons, Al	75	100
Simmons, Curt	4	7
Simmons, Ted	3	5

Name	Signature	Signed Photograph
Sims, Duke	3	6
Singer, Bill	3	6
Singleton, Ken	3	6
Sisk, Tom	2	4
Sisler, Dick	3	6
Sisler, George	25	50
Sisti, Sibbi	3	5
Skowron, Bill "Moose"	4	10
Slaughter, Enos	5	10
Smalley, Roy	4	8
Smith, Dave	3	5
Snider, Edwin "Duke"	5	12
Snyder, Cory	5	14
Soar, "Hank"	3	5
Soto, Mario	4	10
Souchock, Steve	3	5
Spahn, Warren	5	10
Spalding, Albert G.	200	500
Speake, Bob	2	4
Speaker, Tris	65	130
Spink, J. G. Taylor	15	40
Splittorff, Paul	2	4
Spooner, Karl	4	8
Stainback, George "Tuck"	5	10
Staley, Gerry	4	8
Stanley, Gerry	4	8
Stargell, Willie	5	12
Starr, Dick	2	4
Steib, Dave	5	10
Steinbach, Terry	5	7
Steinbrenner, George M.	4	8
Stengel, Casey	22	35
Stephenson, Riggs	5	25
Stevens, Johnny	2	4
Stewart, Sammy	3	6
Stoneham, Horace C.	7	25
Stottlemyre, Mel	4	8
Stratton, Monty	10	30
Strawberry, Darryl	5	25
Sundberg, Jim	4	8
Surhoff, B. J.	5	10
Sutcliffe, Rick	5	16
Sutter, Bruce	5	12
Sutton, Don	5	12
Swain, Dale	4	10
Swindell, Greg	5	10
Tabler, Pat	5	9
Tanana, Frank	5	10
Tanner, Chuck	3	6
Taylor, Tony	3	6
Tebbetts, "Birdie"	4	8
Templeton, Garry	4	8
Tenace, Gene	3	5
Terry, Bill	25	45
Terry, Ralph	4	8

190

Name	Signature	Signed Photograph
Terwilliger, Wayne	3	5
Tewksbury, Bob	4	12
Thompson, Jason	5	8
Thompson, Shag	15	30
Thomson, Bobby	10	20
Tiant, Luis	5	10
Tinker, Joe	175	300
Tolan, Bobby	4	8
Torborg, Jeff	2	5
Torre, Frank	4	8
Torre, Joe	4	9
Torrez, Mike	2	4
Trammell, Alan	4	10
Traynor, Pie	35	100
Treblehorn, Tom	3	5
Tresh, Tom	3	6
Trosky, Hal	5	25
Trotter, Bill	4	8
Trout, Steve	4	8
Trucks, Virgil	4	9
Turley, Bob	3	6
Turner, Ted	4	8
Uecker, Bob	4	8
Ueberroth, Peter	6	15
Valenzuela, Fernando	5	15
Valo, Elmer .	4	8
Vance, Dazzy	45	150
VanderMeer, Johnny	5	12
Vaughn, Arky	100	250
Veeck, Bill, Jr.	7	30
Veeck, William, Sr.	25	50
Vernon, James "Mickey"	5	10
Viola, Frank	5	8
Virdon, Bill	4	8
Voiselle, Bill	3	5
Wagner, Honus	85	200
Walker, Fred "Dixie"	5	20
Walker, Gerald "Gee"	5	20
Walker, Harry "The Hat"	5	10
Wallach, Tim	4	12
Wallaesa, Jack	2	5
Walsh, Edward "Big Ed"	100	300
Walters, "Bucky"	5	20
Waner, Lloyd	10	20
Waner, Paul	40	90
Ward, Pete	4	8
Warneke, Lon	5	20
Wasdell, Jimmy	3	5
Washington, U. L.	3	5
Watlan, Johnny	2	4
Weaver, Earl	5	10
Weiss, George	40	100
Welch, Bob	4	12
Werber, Bill	4	8
Westlake, Wally	5	10

Name	Signature	Signed Photograph
Wheat, Zack	30	75
Whitaker, Lou	5	12
White, Frank	3	5
White, Joyner "Jo-Jo"	10	20
Whitehead, Burgess "Whitey"	3	5
Whitehead, Johnny	10	35
Wilhelm, Hoyt	7	15
Will, Bob	2	5
Williams, Billy	10	20
Williams, Dick	4	8
Williams, Fred	7	30
Williams, Ted	10	30
Wills, Maury	5	10
Wilson, Don	5	20
Wilson, Lewis "Hack"	75	325
Wilson, Mookie	5	10
Winfield, Dave	5	15
Wise, Rick	4	8
Wisner, Jack	4	8
Witt, Bobby	5	10
Witt, Mike	5	12
Wood, Joseph "Smokey Joe"	10	30
Woodling, Gene	4	8
Woods, Gary	2	5
Worrell, Todd	5	12
Wyatt, Whitlow	4	8
Wynn, Early	7	12
Yastrzemski, Carl	5	12
Yawkey, Tom	50	100
Yawkey, Mrs. Jean	5	10
Yeager, Steve	4	8
York, Rudy	10	35
Yost, Eddie	4	8
Youmans, Floyd	4	10
Young, Cy	75	150
Yount, Robin	5	15
Zahn, Geoff	4	8
Zernial, Gus	4	8
Zisk, Richie	2	4

Signed Baseballs

For those who collect autographs of major league baseball players, what could be more natural than having some of them signed on baseballs? That aspect of the hobby has grown dramatically over the past decade, and now there are few hobbyists who haven't picked up some for display, among them a rapidly increasing number who are specializing in this field.

Because of this rise in interest, there has been a steady hike in values, with team balls—those signed by all the members and usually the manager of a particular team in a year—or those of Hall-of-Famers leading the way.

Since it has always been natural to get baseball players to sign baseballs, there is a good supply available, even from the great teams and the great players such as the 1927 Yankees, and the main draw of the game, Babe Ruth.

Thanks here to Chuck McKeen, who was of great assistance in finding and evaluating the values given below.

General Guidelines

First, here are some general guidelines for team-signed balls. A 1938 New York Yankees–signed baseball including the signatures of Joe DiMaggio, Lou Gehrig, Vernon "Lefty" Gomez, Bill Dickey, and John "Red" Ruffing sells for $1250–$1500.

An American League All-Star team ball of 1946—including the autographs of Luke Appling, Bobby Doerr, and Ted Williams—would go for $400.

A National League All-Star team ball of the same year—including signatures by Enos Slaughter and Johnny Mize—sells at $350. Single team balls in the 1946–47 era should be priced in the $175 range. A 1955 Brooklyn Dodgers ball—with the signatures of Jackie Robinson, Roy Campanella, Walt Austin, Pee Wee Reese, Gil Hodges, Carl Furillo, and Duke Snyder—is worth $750.

There are decent numbers of the above available on the market. Usually (during the All-Star games, for example), players got as many as 25 of these signed balls each. It must have taken them longer to sign all the balls than to play the actual game, but, regardless, this is a boon to those who collect signed balls today.

Baseballs Signed by Single Members

For Hall-of-Famers, here is a rundown on the value of a ball signed by a single member.

Player	Price	Player	Price
Aaron, Henry "Hank"	$ 15	Campanella, Roy	325
Alexander, Grover	450	Carey, Max	40
Alston, Walter	75	Chance, Frank	650
Aparicio, Luis	20	Chandler, Happy	5
Appling, Luke	15	Charleston, Oscar	650
Averill, Earl	35	Chesbro, Jack	700
Baker, Frank	175	Clarke, Fred	200
Bancroft, Dave	150	Clemente, Roberto	250
Banks, Ernie	20	Cobb, Ty	350
Barrow, Ed	135	Cochrane, Mickey	150
Bell, James "Cool Papa"	30	Collins, Eddie	275
Bender, Chief	200	Collins, Jimmy	700
Besnahan, Roger	525	Combs, Earl	75
Bottomley, Jim	200	Comiskey, Charles	400
Boudreau, Lou	15	Connolly, Tommy	325
Brock, Lou	15	Connor, Roger	1,200
Burkett, Jessie	400	Coveleski, Stan	40

Player	Price	Player	Price
Crawford, Sam	200	Kelly, Joe	1,400
Cronin, Joe	40	Killebrew, Harmon	20
Cuyler, KiKi	250	Kiner, Ralph	20
Dean, Dizzy	125	Klein, Chuck	300
Dickey, Bill	40	Klem, Bill	300
Dihigo, Martin	400	Koufax, Sandy	25
DiMaggio, Joe	35	Lajoie, Nap	350
Drysdale, Don	20	Landis, K. M.	550
Duffy, Hugh	350	Lemon, Bob	15
Evans, Billy	200	Leonard, Buck	30
Ewing, Buck	700	Lindstrom, Fred	40
Faber, Red	45	Lombardi, Eddie	85
Feller, Bob	15	Lopez, Al	25
Ferrell, Rick	20	Lyons, Ted	50
Flick, Elmer	200	Mack, Connie	250
Ford, Whitey	20	MacPhail, Larry	150
Foxx, Jimmie	250	Mantle, Mickey	25
Frick, Ford	80	Manush, "Heinie"	125
Frisch, Frankie	85	Marichal, Juan	20
Gehrig, Lou	750	Marquard, Rube	65
Gehringer, Charlie	20	Mathews, Eddie	20
Gibson, Bob	20	Mathewson, Christy	1,000
Gibson, Josh	800	Mays, Willie	20
Giles, Warren	65	McCarthy, Joe	80
Gomez, Lefty	20	McCovey, Willie	15
Goslin, Goose	150	McGinnity, Joe	1,200
Greenberg, Hank	40	McGraw, John	550
Griffith, Clark	250	McKetchnie, Bill	150
Grimes, Burleigh	40	Medwick, Joe	85
Grove, Lefty	85	Mize, Johnny	20
Hafey, Chick	125	Musial, Stan	20
Haines, Jesse	85	Nichols, Kid	350
Hamilton, Billy	1,000	Ott, Mel	275
Harridge, Will	125	Paige, Satchel	85
Harris, Bucky	85	Reese, Pee Wee	20
Hartnett, Gabby	95	Rice, Sam	95
Heilmann, Harry	350	Rickey, Branch	250
Herman, Billy	15	Rixey, Eppa	175
Hooper, Harry	70	Roberts, Robin	15
Hornsby, Rogers	300	Robinson, Brooks	15
Hoyt, Waite	40	Robinson, Frank	20
Hubbard, Cal	175	Robinson, Jackie	300
Hubbell, Carl	25	Robinson, Wilbert	600
Huggins, Miller	850	Roush, Edd	25
Hunter, Jim	15	Ruffing, Red	45
Irvin, Monte	20	Rusie, Amos	1,250
Jackson, Travis	40	Ruth, Babe	600
Jennings, Hugh	1,000	Schalk, Ray	125
Johnson, Ban	750	Sewell, Joe	20
Johnson, "Judy"	25	Simmons, Al	250
Johnson, Walter	650	Sisler, George	125
Joss, Addie	1,250	Slaughter, Enos	15
Kaline, Al	20	Snider, Duke	20
Kell, George	15	Spahn, Warren	15
Keller, Willie	1,500	Speaker, Thris	350
Kelly, George	40	Stengel, Casey	150

Player	Price	Player	Price
Terry, Bill	40	Wheat, Zack	150
Tinker, Joe	450	Wilhelm, Hoyt	20
Traynor, Pie	200	Williams, Billy	20
Vance, Dizzy	250	Williams, Ted	30
Wagner, Honus	300	Wilson, Hack	500
Walsh, Ed	200	Wynn, Early	20
Waner, Lloyd	60	Yawkey, Tom	150
Waner, Paul	225	Young, Cy	450
Weiss, George	200	Youngs, Ross	800

Baseball Postcards

Postcard-sized pictures of ball players have been printed by a number of companies during the past 30 or 40 years. The teams themselves are the main publishers of this collectible. The following list gives prices for these cards when autographed by the player depicted on them.

Player	Price	Player	Price
Abernathy, Ted	$ 2	Budnick, Mike	2
Aker, Tom	2	Buford, Don	2
Allison, Bob	3	Bumbry, Al	2
Appling, Luke	8	Burnside, Pete	2
Aspomonte, Bob	3	Byrd, Harry	3
Averill, Earl	12	Cain, Bob	2
Baker, Dusty	3	Camilli, Lou	2
Baker, Gene	2	Carey, Max	20
Bamberger, George	2	Carpin, Frank	2
Barber, Steve	2	Carty, Rico	3
Barnes, Frank	2	Castiglione, Pete	3
Baylor, Don	3	Cepeda, Orlando	5
Bearnarth, Larry	2	Chapman, Ben	3
Berra, Yogi	6	Clinton, Lou	3
Birrer, Babe	3	Clyde, David	2
Blackburn, Ron	3	Colavito, Rocky	3
Blanchard, Johnny	3	Coleman, Jerry	3
Block, Cy	3	Coleman, Joe	3
Bolling, Milt	3	Coleman, Ray	2
Bond, Walter	12	Collins, Joe	3
Bonura, Zeke	3	Conley, Gene	3
Boone, Ray	3	Cooper, Walker	4
Bordagaray, "Frenchy"	12	Coveleski, Stanley	12
Borowy, Hank	4	Cox, Bobby	2
Bosman, Dick	2	Craig, Roger	2
Boudreau, Lou	6	Cramer, Roger "Doc"	4
Brand, Ron	2	Crandell, Del	2
Brando, Sal	2	Critz, Hughie	18
Brewer, Jim	5	Crone, Ray	3
Brideweser, Jim	2	Cronin, Joe	15
Brown, Hal	2	Crosetti, Frankie	4
Brown, Larry	2	Cuccinello, Tony	10
Bryan, Bill	2	Cunningham, Joe	2
		Dailey, Bill	2

Player	Price	Player	Price
DalCanton, Bruce	2	Green, Fred	3
Dalrymple, Clay	2	Greenberg, Hank	15
Davalillo, Vic	4	Grimes, Burleigh	15
Davidson, Ted	2	Grimm, Charlie	10
Davis, Bob	2	Grissom, "Lefty"	3
Davis, Jim	2	Grisson, Marv	3
Davis, Tommy	3	Groat, Dick	3
DeCinces, Doug	2	Groh, Connie	3
Delsing, Jim	2	Gumpert, Randy	3
DeMola, Don	2	Gutteridge, Don	3
Dickey, Bill	15	Haas, Eddie	3
DiMaggio, Dom	4	Hacker, Warren	3
DiMaggio, Joe	15	Haddix, Harvey	3
Downing, Brian	2	Haefner, Mickey	2
Drebowsky, Moe	2	Hall, Dick	2
Dropo, Walt	3	Haney, Fred	8
Dunning, Steve	2	Harder, Mel	4
Durocher, Leo	3	Harmon, Chuck	4
Ennis, Del	3	Harrah, Toby	2
Erskine, Carl	3	Harrell, Billy	2
Etten, Nick	3	Harris, Bucky	20
Evers, Hoot	3	Harris, Luman	3
Faber, U. C. "Red"	15	Harrison, Chuck	2
Fairly, Ron	4	Hatten, Joe	3
Feller, Bob	5	Hatton, Grady	3
Fernandez, Chico	2	Hegan, Jim	8
Ferrell, Wes	15	Henderson, Ken	2
Ferrick, Tom	3	Hendricks, Elrod	2
Ferris, Dave "Boo"	3	Herman, Babe	8
Fitzsimmons, Freddie	15	Herman, Billy	6
Fondy, Dee	3	Hiller, Chuck	2
Ford, Whitey	15	Hiller, Frank	3
Forster, Terry	2	Hillman, Dave	2
Fosse, Ray	2	Hinton, Chuck	2
Franks, Herman	3	Hitchcock, Billy	3
French, Larry	6	Hobbie, Glen	2
Frencona, Tito	2	Hooper, Harry	20
Friend, Bob	3	Hopp, Johnny	3
Fuentes, Tito	2	Horland, Joel	2
Funk, Frank	2	House, Frank	2
Garagiola, Joe	4	House, Tom	2
Garbark, Bob	2	Howard, Bruce	2
Garcia, Mike	8	Hoyt, Waite	15
Garr, Ralph	3	Hrabosky, Hal	3
Garver, Ned	3	Hubbell, Carl	12
Garvey, Steve	4	Hudson, Sid	2
Gehringer, Charles	12	Huffman, Ben	2
Giles, Warren	20	Hunter, Billy	6
Glaviano, Tom	3	Irvin, Monte	7
Gomez, Lefty	5	Jackson, Grant	2
Gomez, Preston	3	Jackson, Randy	2
Goodman, Bill	8	Johnson, Alex	4
Gorman, Tom	8	Johnson, Art	2
Grant, "Mudcat"	5	Johnson, Bill	2

Player	Price	Player	Price
Johnson, Bob	2	Lyons, Ted	18
Johnson, Earl	2	MacKenzie, Ken	2
Johnson, Ken	2	Maglie, Sal	3
Jones, Dalton	2	Majeski, Hank	3
Jones, Mack	2	Malzone, Frank	3
Jorgensen, Spider	3	Mantilla, Felix	3
Katt, Jim	3	Marchildon, Phil	4
Katt, Ray	3	Marquard, Rube	15
Keegan, Bob	3	Marshall, Willard	14
Keely, Bob	4	Marty, Joe	3
Kell, George	6	Maxvill, Dal	3
Keller, Charlie	4	May, Dave	3
Kellner, Alex	3	Mays, Willie	9
Kelly, George L.	12	McAnally, Ernie	3
Keltner, Ken	3	McCarthy, Joe	20
Killebrew, Harmon	6	McCormick, Mike	3
Kirkland, Willie	3	McCosky, Barney	3
Klaus, Billy	3	McCovey, Willie	4
Klimchock, Lou	3	McDaniel, Lindy	3
Klippstein, Johnny	3	McDougal, Gil	3
Kluszewski, Ted	3	McDowell, "Sudden Sam"	3
Kokos, Dick	3	Melton, Bill	3
Kolloway, Don	3	Mercer, Bobby	3
Koufax, Sandy	7	Merritt, Jim	3
Kryhoski, Dick	3	Messersmith, Andy	3
Kubek, Tony	3	Miller, Bob	3
Kuenn, Harvey	3	Miller, Stu	3
Kuiper, Duane	3	Minoso, Minnie	4
Kuzava, Bob	3	Mitchell, Dale	8
Labine, Clem	3	Mitterwald, George	3
Lamb, Ray	3	Mize, Johnny	7
Lang, Chip	2	Moore, Terry	3
LaPalme, Paul	3	Morgan, Bobby	3
Latman, Barry	4	Morgan, Joe	3
Lau, Charley	8	Morgan, Tom	3
Law, Vernon	3	Moryn, Walt	3
Lee, Thornton	3	Moses, Wally	3
Lemon, Bob	6	Mueller, Ron	3
Leonard, Buck	10	Muffett, Billy	2
Leonard, "Dutch"	10	Mullin, Pat	3
Leonhard, Dave	3	Murtaugh, Danny	12
Lillis, Bob	3	Musial, Stan	9
Lindell, Johnny	8	Nagelson, Russ	3
Lindstrom, Fred	15	Negray, Ron	3
Linzy, Frank	2	Neiger, Al	3
Littlefield, Dick	3	Neun, Johnny	4
Long, Dale	3	Newhouser, Hal	3
Lonnett, Joe	3	Nichols, Chet	3
Lopat, Ed	3	Nieman, Bob	5
Lopata, Stan	3	Nixon, Willard	3
Lopez, Al	10	Oates, Johnny	3
Lown, Turk	3	Odom, John	4
Lucadello, Johnny	3	Oldis, Bob	3
Lynch, Gerry	3	Oliva, Tony	4

Player	Price	Player	Price
Osteen, Claude	2	Shawkey, Bob	10
Ostrowski, Joe	3	Sherry, Larry	3
Otis, Amos	3	Shopay, Tom	3
Palmer, Jim	5	Sievers, Roy	3
Partee, Roy	4	Silvera, Charlie	3
Pavletich, Don	3	Sipek, Dick	3
Pepitone, Joe	5	Sisler, Dick	3
Pesky, Johnny	3	Skowron, "Moose"	3
Philley, Dave	3	Slaughter, Enos	3
Piche, Ron	3	Sleater, Lou	3
Piechota, Al	3	Smith, Al	3
Piersall, Jim	10	Smith, Mayo	4
Piet, Tony	8	Soderholm, Eric	2
Pizarro, Juan	5	Spahn, Warren	7
Post, Wally	8	Speake, Bob	3
Powers, Johnny	3	Spenser, Jim	3
Ragland, Tom	3	Staller, George	3
Ramos, Pedro	8	Stephens, Gene	3
Raschi, Vic	3	Stevenson, John	3
Rau, Doug	2	Stinson, Bob	2
Reese, Jimmie	3	Stock, Wes	2
Reese, "Pee Wee"	8	Striker, Jake	3
Rettenmund, Merv	2	Strom, Brent	2
Reynolds, Allie	3	Sunkel, Tom	2
Reynolds, Bob	2	Taylor, Tony	2
Ripplemeyer, Ray	3	Tebbetts, George "Birdie"	4
Rizzuto, Phil	6	Tenace, Gene	3
Roberts, Paul	2	Terry, Bill	15
Roberts, Robin	7	Terry, Ralph	3
Robinson, Brooks	7	Thomas, Valmy	5
Robinson, Eddie	3	Thompson, Tim	4
Roe, Preacher	4	Thomson, Bobby	4
Roselli, Bob	3	Thurman, Bob	3
Rosen, Al	3	Tiant, Luis	5
Roush, Edd	10	Tillman, Bob	3
Ruffing, "Red"	15	Torborg, Jeff	3
Runnels, Pete	3	Trucks, Virgil	3
Rush, Bob	3	Turner, Jim	4
Russell, Bill	2	Uhle, George	5
Russell, Jim	5	Verban, Emile	3
Ryan, Connie	3	Vernon, Mickey	3
Ryan, Nolan	5	Voss, Bill	3
Santo, Ron	4	Wade, Ben	3
Sauer, Hank	3	Wagner, Leon	6
Saverine, Bob	2	Wahl, Kermit	3
Sawyer, Eddie	4	Walker, Gerald "Gee"	10
Schmidt, Bob	2	Walker, Harry "The Hat"	3
Schoendienst, Red	3	Waner, Lloyd	15
Schofield, Dick	2	Ward, Pete	3
Score, Herb	3	Watson, Bob	3
Seaver, Tom	7	Watt, Ed	3
Seminick, Andy	3	Weaver, Earl	3
Sewell, Joe	7	Weaver, Monte	4
Shantz, Bobby	3	Werber, Billy	3

Player	Price	Player	Price
Werhas, Johnny	3	Wood, Wilbur	4
Wert, Don	3	Woodling, Gene	3
Westrum, Wes	3	Wright, Tom	3
Wietelmann, Whitey	3	Wynn, Early	8
Williams, Dick	2	Zimmer, Don	2
Wood, "Smokey" Joe	10	Zuber, Bill	4

Basketball Hall of Fame Members

This section contains prices for members of the Basketball Hall of Fame. Prices for other basketball players, including those still active, are in the General Sports category.

Players	Signature	Signed Photograph
Arizin, Paul	$ 4	$ 10
Barlow, Thomas	10	20
Baylor, Elgin	5	12
Beckman, John	10	20
Borgmann, Bennie	10	20
Bradley, Bill	6	15
Brennan, Joseph	10	20
Cervi, Al "Digger"	4	12
Chamberlain, Wilt	15	40
Cooper, Charles "Tarzan"	10	20
Cousy, Bob	5	12
Davies, Bob	4	10
DeBernardi, Forrest	10	20
DeBusschere, Dave	4	12
Dehnert, H. G. "Dutch"	10	20
Endacott, Paul	10	20
Foster, Harold "Bud"	5	15
Friedman, Max "Marty"	15	30
Fulks, Joe	15	40
Gale, Lauren "Laddie"	10	30
Gola, Tom	4	12
Greer, Hal	4	10
Gruenig, Robert "Ace"	10	20

Players	Signature	Signed Photograph
Hagan, Cliff	4	12
Hanson, Victor	10	20
Havlicek, John	5	15
Holman, Nat	10	25
Hyatt, Chuck	10	20
Johnson, William	10	20
Jones, Sam	5	12
Krause, Edward "Moose"	5	20
Kurland, Bob	10	20
Lapchick, Joe	20	50
Lucas, Jerry	5	15
Luisetti, Angelo "Hank"	10	40
Macaulay, Ed "Easy Ed"	5	15
Martin, Slater	5	12
McCracken, Branch	20	40
McCracken, Jack	15	30
Mikan, George	10	22
Murphy, Charles "Stretch"	5	15
Page, H. O. "Pat"	10	20
Pettit, Bob	15	40
Phillip, Andy	4	12
Pollard, Jim	5	12
Ramsey, Frank	4	12
Reed, Willis	5	15
Robertson, Oscar	10	20
Roosma, John S.	10	20
Russell, Bill	150	300
Russell, John "Honey"	10	20
Schayes, Adolph "Dolph"	5	12
Schmidt, Ernest	10	20
Schommer, John	10	20
Sedran, Barney	10	20
Sharman, Bill	5	12
Steinmetz, Christian	10	20
Thompson, John "Cat"	10	20
Thurmond, Nate	5	12
Twyman, Jack	4	12
Vandivier, Robert "Fuzzy"	10	20
Wachter, Edward	10	20
West, Jerry	10	20
Wooden, John	10	20

Coaches	Signature	Signed Photograph
Anderson, Harold	$10	$20
Auerbach, Arnold J. "Red"	5	12
Barry, Sam	10	20
Blood, Ernest	10	20
Cann, Howard	5	12
Carlson, Dr. H. Clifford	10	20
Carnevale, Ben	10	20
Case, Everett	10	20
Dean, Everett	10	20
Diddle, Edgar	10	20

Red Auerbach   Bob Davies

Players	Signature	Signed Photograph
Drake, Bruce	10	20
Gaines, Clarence	25	50
Gardner, Jack	10	20
Gill, Amory "Slats"	5	15
Harshman, Marv	4	12
Hickey, Edgar "Ed"	10	20
Hobson, Howard	5	15
Iba, Hank	5	15
Julian, Alvin F. "Doggie"	10	20
Keaney, Frank	10	20
Keogan, George	10	20
Lambert, Ward	10	20
Litwack, Harry	10	20
Loeffler, Kenneth "Ken"	10	20
Lonborg, A. C. "Dutch"	10	20
McCutchan, Arad	15	30
McGuire, Frank	4	12
McLendon, John	10	20
Meanwell, Dr. Walter E.	10	20
Meyer, Ray	5	15
Newell, Pete	4	12
Rupp, Adolph	25	75
Sacks, Leonard	10	20
Shelton, Everett	10	20
Smith, Dean	5	15
Teague, Bertha F.	10	20
Wade, Margaret	10	20
Wooden, John	5	15

Referees	Signature	Signed Photograph
Enright, James	$10	$20
Hepbron, George	10	20
Hoyt, George	10	20
Kennedy, Matthew	10	20
Leith, Lloyd	10	20
Nucatola, John	10	20
Quigley, Ernest	10	20
Shirley, J. Dallas	10	20
Tobey, David	5	15
Walsh, David	10	20

Contributors	Signature	Signed Photograph
Abbott, Senda (Berenson)	$ 10	$ 20
Allen, Phog	20	50
Bee, Clair	20	40
Brown, Walter	25	50
Bunn, John	10	20

Contributors	Signature	Signed Photograph
Douglas, Bob	10	20
Duer, Al O.	10	20
Fagan, Clifford B.	10	20
Fisher, Harry	10	20
Gottlieb, Edward	10	20
Gulick, Dr. Luther H.	10	20
Harrison, Lester	10	20
Hepp, Dr. Ferenc	10	20
Hickox, Edward	10	20
Hinkle, Tony	10	20
Irish, Ned	35	100
Jones, R. W.	10	20
Kennedy, Walter	25	50
Liston, Emil	10	20
Mokray, Bill	10	20
Morgan, Ralph	10	20
Morgenweck, Frank	10	20
Naismith, Dr. James	100	250
O'Brien, John	10	20
Olsen, Harold	10	20
Podoloff, Maurice	30	75
Porter, H. V.	10	20
Reid, William	10	20
Ripley, Elmer	10	20
Saperstein, Abe	30	75
Schabinger, Arthur	10	20
Seitz, Edward S.	10	20
Stagg, Amos Alonzo	30	75
St. John, Lynn	10	20
Taylor, Chuck	10	20
Tower, Oswald	10	20
Trester, Arthur	10	20
Wells, Clifford	10	20
Wilke, Lou	10	20

Boxing

Below is a small cross-section of world champions, major contenders, and other well-known names in boxing. Recently such material has gained in popularity and value.

Charles "Chuck" Adkins

Mushy Callahan

Tony Canzoneri

Primo Carnera

Jimmy Carter

Ezzard Charles

James J. Corbett

Jack Dempsey

Rocky Graziano

Larry Holmes

Beau Jack

Jim Jeffries

Joe Louis

Rocky Marciano

Floyd Patterson

Aaron Pryor

Sugar Ray Robinson

Earnie Shavers

Ken Norton

Name	Signature	Signed Photograph
Adkins, Charles "Chuck"	$ 4	$ 8
Akins, Virgil "Honey Bear"	4	8
Ali, Muhammad	10	20
Ambers, Lou	5	15
Andrade, Cisco	4	8
Apostoli, Fred	5	10
Aragon, Art "Golden Boy"	4	12
Armstrong, Henry	12	30
Attell, Abe	25	50
Baer, Buddy	10	30
Baer, Max	30	75
Basilio, Carmen	5	20
Battalino, Battling	10	20
Bettina, Melio	10	20
Braddock, James J.	15	40
Breland, Mark	4	8
Burns, Tommy	40	80
Callahan, Mushy	5	10
Canzoneri, Tony	20	40
Carnera, Primo	20	50
Carpentier, Georges	40	80
Carter, Jimmy	10	30
Castellani, Rocky	5	15
Charles, Ezzard	25	50
Chuvalo, George	5	10
Clay, Cassius M.	100	200
Conn, Billy	10	25
Cooney, Gerry	5	10
Corbett, James J.	25	75
Coulon, Johnny	5	10
Davey, Chuck	4	8
Dempsey, Jack	20	40
Dixon, George	5	10
Duran, Roberto	5	15
Farr, Tommy	10	20
Fields, Jackie	5	10
Fleischer, Nat	5	15
Foreman, George	10	20
Frazier, "Smokin' " Joe	5	15
Fullmer, Gene	5	15
Fusari, Charlie	5	10
Garcia, Ceferino	5	10
Giambra, Joey	5	10
Giardello, Joey	5	10
Graziano, Rocky	10	20
Griffith, Emile	10	20
Hagler, Marvin	10	20
Hearns, Thomas	10	20
Holmes, Larry	10	20
Hostak, Al	25	50
Jack, Beau	20	40
Jeffries, James J.	25	50
Jenkins, Lew	5	10
Johansson, Ingemar	15	30

Name	Signature	Signed Photograph
Johnson, Jack	290	550
Jones, Ralph "Tiger"	7	20
Kearns, Jack	5	10
King, Don	4	8
King, Rafiu	5	10
LaBarba, Fidel	5	10
LaMotta, Jake	10	20
Layne, Rex	4	8
Leonard, Benny	20	40
Leonard, "Sugar Ray"	10	20
Lesnevich, Gus	10	20
Lewis, John Henry	5	10
Liston, Sonny	50	100
Loughran, Tommy	20	40
Louis, Joe	20	50
Mancini, Ray "Boom Boom"	10	20
Mandell, Sammy	10	20
Marciano, Rocky	30	75
McGovern, Terry	10	25
McLarnin, Jimmy	10	20
McLean, Stewart	5	10
Mills, Freddie	5	10
Mitchell, Charles W.	20	40
Moore, Archie	10	20
Moyer, Denny	5	10
Moyer, Phil	5	10
Muniz, Armando	5	10
Norton, Ken	5	10
Olson, Carl "BoBo"	10	20
Patterson, Floyd	10	20
Pep, Willie	10	20
Pryor, Aaron	5	10
Quarry, Jerry	4	8
Risko, Eddie "Babe"	10	20
Ritchie, Willie	20	40
Robinson, Sugar Ray	15	35
Rosenbloom, "Slapsie Maxie"	10	20
Ross, Barney	16	30
Schmeling, Max	20	40
Servo, Marty	5	10
Sharkey, Jack	10	20
Shavers, Earnie	5	20
Spinks, Leon	10	20
Sullivan, John L.	250	450
Taylor, Bernard	5	10
Tunney, Gene	20	40
Turpin, Randy	10	20
Tyson, Mike	10	20
Walcott, Jersey Joe	10	20
Walker, Mickey "The Toy Bulldog"	25	50
Whitaker, Pernell	5	10
Wilde, James	5	10
Willard, Jess	60	125

Players	Signature	Signed Photograph
Williams, "Ike"	10	25
Zale, Tony	10	20
Zarate, Carlos	5	10
Zivic, Fritzie	10	20

Business

This chapter contains prices for business leaders, financiers, philanthropists, major executives, and people whose names became trademarks.

Name	Signature Only	Letter or Document Signed	Autograph Letter Signed	Signed Photograph
Adler, Max	$ 7.00	$ 20.00	$ 30.00	$ 15.00
Albertson, Joseph A.	3.00	7.00	15.00	16.00
Alexander, Henry	3.00	7.00	15.00	10.00
Allen, William M.	5.00	12.00	22.00	20.00
Amos, Wally "Famous"	5.00	10.00	25.00	20.00
Anderson, Roy A.	5.00	14.00	22.00	7.00
Annenberg, Walter H.	7.00	25.00	40.00	30.00
Arden, Elizabeth	20.00	50.00	120.00	35.00
Arkell, Bartlett	5.00	30.00	45.00	10.00
Arkell, W. J.	3.00	10.00	30.00	5.00
Ash, Roy L.	7.00	20.00	55.00	30.00
Astor, John Jacob	95.00	250.00	415.00	
Astor, John Jacob, Jr.	10.00	30.00	100.00	30.00
Astor, Mrs. John J.	40.00	100.00	195.00	
Astor, Waldorf	10.00	32.00	80.00	48.00
Astor, William B.	60.00	125.00	200.00	
Atlas, Charles	10.00	19.00	30.00	20.00
Auchincloss, Janet L.	3.00	5.00	10.00	5.00
Avery, Sewell	23.00	36.00	70.00	25.00
Bache, Harold L.	15.00	45.00	110.00	65.00
Baekeland, Dr. L. H.	7.00	20.00	50.00	
Baer, George F.	7.00	25.00	45.00	30.00
Barton, Bruce	5.00	30.00	40.00	10.00
Beatty, Clyde	20.00	65.00	185.00	85.00
Belmont, August	30.00	50.00	133.00	100.00
Benton, William	8.00	30.00	65.00	20.00
Bessemer, Sir Henry	30.00	55.00	138.33	80.00
Biddle, Nicholas	101.67	300.00	550.00	

Wally "Famous" Amos

Walter H. Annenberg

Waldorf Astor

Leo Hendrik Baekeland

Clarence Birdseye

Sincerely your friend,

W. E. Brock

William John Burns

David D. Buick

David Burpee

Andrew Carnegie

Dale Carnegie

Peter Cooper

"Coco" Gabrielle Chanel

Chairman of the Board.

Walter P. Chrysler

P. F. Collier

André Citroën

Ezra Cornell

Charles Crocker

John Deere

Sir Samuel Cunard

Pierre S. duPont.

Pierre S. duPont

James D. Dole

207

Name	Signature Only	Letter or Document Signed	Autograph Letter Signed	Signed Photograph
Bigelow, Erastus B.	95.00	250.00	510.00	
Birdseye, Clarence	95.00	250.00	575.00	
Black, Eugene R.	5.00	12.00	30.00	
Blass, Bill	5.00	15.00		20.00
Bloch, Richard	16.00	35.00	90.00	20.00
Block, Joseph L.	3.00	5.00	9.00	6.00
Blough, Roger	3.00	10.00	20.00	15.00
Bok, Edward W.	6.00	15.00	40.00	
Brady, "Diamond Jim"	135.00	275.00	550.00	330.00
Brock, Sen. William G.	20.00	70.00	125.00	25.00
Brown, Nicholas	25.00	65.00	150.00	
Buick, David D.	125.00	300.00	750.00	250.00
Burnett, Leo	5.00	10.00	25.00	5.00
Burns, W. J.	30.00	70.00	175.00	
Burpee, David	8.00	25.00	55.00	15.00
Burpee, Jonathan	7.00	15.00	40.00	10.00
Busch, August A.	10.00	25.00	50.00	20.00
Cadbury, Richard	20.00	40.00	136.00	50.00
Candler, Asa Griggs	65.00	150.00	380.00	125.00
Carnegie, Andrew	80.00	200.00	333.33	500.00
Carnegie, Dale	10.00	20.00	55.00	25.00
Cassini, Oleg	10.00	20.00	55.00	10.00
Cello, Aldo	3.00	9.00	20.00	10.00
Chandler, Dorothy "Buff"	8.00	20.00	45.00	25.00
Chandler, Norman	15.00	30.00	75.00	20.00
Chandler, Otis	10.00	20.00	50.00	15.00
Chanel, Coco	40.00	95.00	235.00	85.00
Chrysler, Walter P.	76.75	400.00	637.50	313.00
Citroën, André	95.00	290.00	541.67	195.00
Cole, Edward N.	5.00	12.00	30.00	10.00
Colgate, James C.	8.00	20.00	50.00	
Collier, Peter F.	12.00	30.00	65.00	
Cone, Fairfax M.	8.00	36.00	45.00	15.00
Conover, Harry	10.00	15.00	20.00	10.00
Cooke, Jay	60.00	175.00	250.00	125.00
Cooper, Peter	34.00	115.00	260.00	161.00
Coors, W. K.	5.00	15.00	35.00	28.00
Copeland, L. du Pont				50.00
Cornell, Ezra		80.00	150.00	65.00
Cornfeld, Bernard	10.00	25.00	60.00	40.00
Corning, Erastas	45.00	125.00	310.00	
Crawford-Frost, William A.	15.00	25.00	55.00	
Cresap, Mark	3.00	6.00	15.00	5.00
Crocker, Charles	15.00	40.00	90.00	
Crosley, Powel, Jr.	20.00	70.00	95.00	
Cudahy, Michael F.	15.00	60.00	90.00	50.00
Cunard, Sir Samuel	75.00	95.00	150.00	
Currie, Sir Donald	40.00	10.00	24.00	
Curtis, Cyrus H. K.	18.00	45.00	108.00	65.00
Dart, Justin	50.00	100.00	250.00	75.00
De La Renta, Oscar	6.00	15.00	35.00	12.00
Disney, Walter E.	600.00	800.00	1,400.00	1,050.00

	Signature Only	Letter or Document Signed	Autograph Letter Signed	Signed Photograph
nson, Leonard H.	10.00	20.00	35.00	15.00
ear, Charles	175.00	475.00	1,062.50	
ear, Charles, Jr.	20.00	50.00	130.00	25.00
n, John F.	2.00	5.00	15.00	3.00
George	7.00	15.00	20.00	10.00
Jay	100.00	375.00	435.00	
E. G.	20.00	50.00	125.00	40.00
Donald	10.00	25.00	40.00	15.00
Katherine	10.00	26.00	58.00	10.00
W. T.	15.00	60.00	100.00	
Bowman	5.00	10.00	35.00	10.00
ll, Moses H.	5.00	15.00	40.00	
Courtlandt	3.00	8.00	15.00	10.00
nor, Gilbert H.	25.00	100.00	175.00	
Mrs. Winston	5.00	10.00	15.00	10.00
nheim, Daniel	10.00	25.00	65.00	35.00
nheim, Peggy	10.00	20.00	55.00	15.00
ss, Edward C.	4.00	10.00	25.00	15.00
oyce C.	12.00	40.00	55.00	15.00
er, Armand	25.00			35.00
an, Edward Henry	30.00	48.00	75.00	40.00
an, W. Averell	20.00	35.00	55.00	30.00
rd, George L.	35.00	125.00	250.00	75.00
rd, Huntington	10.00	25.00	45.00	20.00
Phoebe	12.00	35.00	80.00	
William Randolph	45.00	150.00	338.00	150.00
William Randolph, Jr.	5.00	15.00	37.00	15.00
Christie	3.00	10.00	20.00	15.00
Henry John	90.00	375.00	750.00	300.00
t, William R.	20.00	50.00	130.00	25.00
mes J.	30.00	85.00	115.00	75.00
Barron	5.00	15.00	20.00	10.00
Conrad	30.00	75.00	190.00	37.50
Duncan	25.50	65.00	165.00	50.00
an, Paul G.	10.00	15.00	25.00	20.00
ay, Ben	130.00	400.00	750.00	
Howard	1,000.00	2,200.00	5,900.00	2,500.00
H. L.	90.00	260.00	580.00	175.00
ames Bunker	5.00	15.00	35.00	10.00
gton, Henry E.	40.00	90.00	153.00	
Lee A.	5.00	20.00	45.00	20.00
ll, Robert H.	50.00	120.00	150.00	125.00
Samuel	25.00	75.00	165.00	
n, Howard	40.00	55.00	115.00	50.00
Thomas V.	3.00	7.00	17.00	10.00
Otto H.	25.00	50.00	90.00	30.00
Henry J.	40.00	70.00	155.00	50.00
Frederick R.	3.00	6.00	15.00	5.00
ary	3.00	8.00	15.00	10.00
John Harvey	10.00	25.00	55.00	
W. K.	50.00	120.00	265.00	100.00
y, Joseph P.	35.00	90.00	200.00	75.00

George Eastman

John Eberhard Faber

James A. Farley

Cyrus Field

Marshall Field, Jr.

Benson Ford

Edsel Ford

Henry Ford

Malcolm Forbes

Henry Ford, II

Frank Gannett

J. Paul Getty

President

A. C. Gilbert

Charles Goodyear, Jr.

E. G. Grace

Gimbel Brothers

Very sincerely yours,

Gilbert Grosvenor

Daniel Guggenheim

Peggy Guggenheim

Sincerely

Joyce Hall

Name	Signature Only	Letter or Document Signed	Autograph Letter Signed	Signed Photograph
Dodge, Joseph M.	4.00	10.00	25.00	
Dodge, William Earl	5.00	10.00	25.00	
Dole, James D.	35.00	85.00	200.00	50.00
Dole, Sanford B.	30.00	75.00	185.00	50.00
Dollar, Robert	15.00	35.00	90.00	40.00
Douglas, Donald W., Jr.		60.00		
Duesenberg, Frederick S.	85.00	350.00	515.00	
Du Pont, Elizabeth H.	15.00	65.00	90.00	25.00
duPont, Pierre S.	30.00	90.00	195.00	55.00
Duryea, Charles E.	38.00	90.00	205.00	
Eastman, George	75.00	307.50	575.00	250.00
Egbert, Sherwood	3.00	12.00	30.00	12.00
Faber, J. Eberhard	125.00	500.00	750.00	
Factor, Max, Jr.	7.00	16.00	40.00	18.00
Fairchild, Sherman	6.00	15.00	35.00	20.00
Fairless, Benjamin F.	35.00	95.00	190.00	68.00
Fargo, J. C.	15.00	40.00	100.00	
Fargo, William G.	140.00	450.00	950.00	
Feldman, Charles K.	3.00	10.00	20.00	5.00
Ferkauf, Eugene	3.00	5.00	10.00	10.00
Ferrari, Enzo	60.00	90.00	200.00	150.00
Field, Cyrus W.	21.67	122.22	222.50	
Field, Marshall, Jr.	15.00	35.00	85.00	30.00
Firestone, Harvey S.	102.50	250.00	375.00	145.00
Firestone, Leonard K.	10.00	25.00	65.00	15.00
Fisher, Lawrence P.	50.00	130.00	350.00	
Fisk, James	40.00	100.00	150.00	75.00
Fitzhugh, Gilbert	2.00	5.00	12.00	5.00
Forbes, Bertie Charles	15.00	40.00	100.00	25.00
Forbes, Malcolm	10.00	30.00	85.00	25.00
Ford, Benson	3.00	10.00	25.00	5.00
Ford, Edsel	95.00	350.00	500.00	200.00
Ford, Edsel B., II	3.00	10.00	20.00	5.00
Ford, Henry	900.00	1,350.00	3,750.00	1,500.00
Ford, Henry, II	5.00	10.00	25.00	40.00
Ford, John Anson	5.00	10.00	20.00	10.00
Funk, Isaac K.	16.00	75.00	125.00	
Gallo, Ernest and Julio				35.00
Gallup, George	5.00	20.00		20.00
Galvin, Robert	12.25	17.00	25.00	15.00
Gannett, Frank E.	15.00	50.00	125.00	25.00
Gary, Elbert H.	20.00	80.00	175.00	25.00
Geneen, Harold S.	5.00	10.00	25.00	10.00
Gernreich, Rudi	5.00	15.00	35.00	20.00
Getty, J. Paul	80.00	200.00	375.00	120.00
Giannini, A. P.	45.00	95.00	235.00	
Gifford, Walter S.	2.00	7.00	15.00	5.00
Gilbert, A. C.	50.00	75.00	175.00	
Gimbel Brothers		300.00		
Gimbel, Bernard F.	15.00	60.00	95.00	75.00
Girard, Stephen	100.00	220.00	370.00	
Givenchy, Hubert de	40.00	75.00	100.00	80.00

Dr. Armand Hammer

William Randolph Hearst

Lee Iacocca

Sincerely,
W. K. Kellogg

Henry J. Kaiser

J. L. Kraft

Joseph P. Kennedy

Sincerely yours
Edwin Land

Allan H. Lockheed

Henry R. Luce

Bernarr Macfadden

Thomas Lipton

Frederick L. Mc

C. H. McCormick
Cyrus McCormick

Rupert

W. Averell

Christie

Robert

Ca

Kathryn and Arthur Murray

John Ringling North

Random E. Olds

William S. Paley

David Packard

J. C. Penney

Eugene Peugeot

J. S. Pillsbury—Governor and Flour Miller

Joseph Pulitzer

Richard S. Reynolds

David Rockefeller

Happy Rockefeller

John D. Rockefeller, Jr.

Charles S. Rolls

Helena Rubinstein

Yves Saint Laurent

David Sarnoff

Charles M. Schwab

Vidal Sassoon

Harry F. Sinclair

213

Name	Signature Only	Letter or Document Signed	Autograph Letter Signed	Signed Photograph
Kettering, C. F.	35.00	70.00	155.00	50.00
Kintner, Robert	5.00	10.00	30.00	10.00
Klein, Calvin	5.00	15.00	35.00	22.00
Knight, Phil	5.00	20.00	35.00	25.00
Knopf, Alfred A.	5.00	15.00	35.00	
Knudsen, William S.	20.00	40.00	90.00	30.00
Kraft, James L.	20.00	50.00	120.00	
Kragen, Ken	5.00	10.00	20.00	15.00
Kresge, S. S.	30.00	163.00	250.00	75.00
Kroc, Mrs. Ray (Joan)	5.00	15.00	35.00	16.00
Kroc, Ray	7.00	20.00	50.00	20.00
Krupp, Alfred	165.00	310.00	430.00	
Lamont, Thomas S.	8.00	22.50	40.00	38.00
Land, Edwin H.	15.00	40.00	100.00	
Lasker, Mary	5.00	7.00	15.00	5.00
Lauren, Ralph	6.00	15.00	37.00	27.50
Lay, Herman W.	7.00	20.00	45.00	30.00
Lazarus, Ralph	3.00	7.00	10.00	5.00
Lear, Norman	8.00	15.00	43.00	18.00
Lear, William P., Sr.	20.00	45.00	115.00	35.00
Leland, W. C.	20.00	55.00	140.00	40.00
Lever, William Hesketh	30.00	100.00	190.00	55.00
Lewisohn, Adolph	18.00	40.00	65.00	25.00
Liggett, Louis Kroh	50.00	115.00	265.00	
Lipton, Sir Thomas	30.00	105.00	260.00	
Loew, Marcus	30.00	40.00	65.00	35.00
Loper, Don	5.00	15.00	30.00	7.00
Lorillard, Peter	75.00	225.00	450.00	
Luce, Henry R.	35.00	83.00	205.00	40.00
Lyons, William	40.00	80.00	175.00	
Macfadden, Bernarr	10.00	48.00	105.00	35.00
Mackie, Bob	5.00	10.00	25.00	12.00
Mahen, Robert A.	12.00	30.00	70.00	40.00
Marcus, Stanley	20.00	65.00	120.00	40.00
Marriott, J.	18.00	30.00	70.00	25.00
Matsushita, Konosuke	25.00	65.00	145.00	40.00
Maytag, Frederick L.	40.00	245.00	540.00	150.00
McCarthy, Michael W.	3.00	5.00	10.00	5.00
McCormick, Robert R.	15.00	25.00	35.00	15.00
McDonald, Richard J.	75.00	186.25	410.00	155.00
McDonnell, James S.	12.00	30.00	65.00	25.00
Mellon, Andrew	40.00	78.00	340.00	130.00
Mesta, Perle	12.00	30.00	70.00	25.00
Miller, Arjay R.	3.00	10.00	22.00	5.00
Mohler, A. L.	3.00	10.00	15.00	5.00
Morgan, J. P., Jr.	45.00	100.00	198.00	50.00
Morgan, J. P., Sr.	200.00	440.00	875.00	700.00
Mortimer, Charles	4.00	12.00	26.00	10.00
Muntz, Earl "Madman"	13.00	18.00	25.00	20.00
Murchison, Clint	10.00	15.00	25.00	20.00
Murchison, Clint, Jr.	5.00	10.00	20.00	12.00
Murdock, Rupert	6.00	16.00	40.00	18.00

Chairman

Alfred P. Sloan, Jr.

L. C. Smith

Edward Robinson Squibb

Frank Stanton

Harold H. Swift

Donald J. Trump

Ted Turner

Cornelius Vanderbilt

George W. Vanderbilt

George Westinghouse

Thomas J. Watson

Eli Whitney

Name	Signature Only	Letter or Document Signed	Autograph Letter Signed	Signed Photograph
Murray, Arthur	5.00	10.00	18.00	7.00
Newhouse, Samuel	5.00	15.00	35.00	20.00
Niarchos, Stavro	40.00	110.00	190.00	70.00
North, John Ringling	20.00	50.00	110.00	45.00
Northrup, John K.	12.00	30.00	65.00	20.00
Ochs, Adolph S.	30.00	65.00	130.00	50.00
O'Connell, Charles	10.00	14.00	30.00	15.00
Olin, John M.	5.00	10.00	15.00	10.00
Onassis, Aristotle	62.00	160.00	312.00	200.00
Packard, David	15.00	40.00	85.00	
Paley, William S.	12.00	30.00	65.00	20.00
Park, Roy H.	8.00	25.00	55.00	15.00
Patterson, William Allan	3.00	7.00	12.00	5.00
Paulucci, Jeno F.	15.00	25.00	35.00	20.00
Peabody, George F.	25.00	60.00	120.00	150.00
Penney, J. C.	22.50	45.00	100.00	40.00

Name	Signature Only	Letter or Document Signed	Autograph Letter Signed	Signed Photograph
Peterson, Rudolph A.	3.00	5.00	15.00	10.00
Peugeot, Eugene	35.00	90.00	200.00	
Pillsbury, John S.	13.00	25.00	55.00	20.00
Pinkerton, Allan	165.00	435.00	950.00	
Pinkerton, Robert A.	35.00	95.00	205.00	75.00
Post, Marjorie Meriwether	10.00	30.00	65.00	20.00
Powers, John Robert	5.00	15.00	20.00	15.00
Pulitzer, Joseph	75.00	250.00	435.00	
Pullman, George M.	150.00	220.00	435.00	165.00
Putnam, George Palmer	14.00	37.00	75.00	30.00
Quant, Mary	3.00	7.00	15.00	10.00
Rathbone, Monroe J.	3.00	8.00	12.00	5.00
Redenbacker, Orville	3.00	7.00	15.00	12.50
Reynolds, Richard S.	40.00	100.00	220.00	55.00
Ringling, Henry	15.00	35.00	80.00	40.00
Ringling, John	50.00	130.00	295.00	140.00
Roberts, Xavier	13.00	20.00	35.00	25.00
Robinson, Dwight P.	4.00	10.00	22.00	8.00
Roche, James M.	3.00	12.00	25.00	10.00
Rockefeller, Abby A.	10.00	25.00	60.00	15.00
Rockefeller, David	5.00	15.00	40.00	25.00
Rockefeller, Happy	4.00	15.00	25.00	10.00
Rockefeller, John D.	190.00	496.25	1,272.50	505.00
Rockefeller, John D., Jr.	15.00	50.00	195.00	75.00
Rockefeller, Laurance	5.00	10.00	20.00	10.00
Rolls, Charles S.	90.00	225.00	525.00	
Romanoff, Michael	40.00	65.00	145.00	55.00
Rosenwald, Julius	15.00	40.00	80.00	35.00
Rothschild, Alix de	70.00	190.00	375.00	
Rothschild, Guy de	15.00	40.00	80.00	85.00
Rothschild, Lionel	10.00	30.00	55.00	25.00
Rothschild, Nathan Meyer	285.00	750.00	1,525.00	
Rotia, Rocky	5.00	15.00	30.00	25.00
Rubinstein, Helena	25.00	90.00	200.00	55.00
Runkel, Louis	4.00	10.00	15.00	5.00
Ruppert, Jacob	30.00	80.00	165.00	65.00
Russell, Donald J. M.	4.00	9.00	20.00	10.00
Rutgers, Henry	25.00	40.00	100.00	
Sage, Russell	35.00	90.00	220.00	130.00
Saint Laurent, Yves	20.00	30.00	75.00	45.00
Salt, Sir Titus	5.00	14.00	30.00	
Sanders, Harlan	8.00	22.00	50.00	20.00
Sardi, Vincent	4.00	10.00	25.00	10.00
Sarnoff, David	12.00	55.00	89.00	35.00
Sassoon, Vidal	12.50	18.00	25.00	15.00
Saunders, Stuart J.	3.00	7.00	15.00	10.00
Schacht, Hjalmar	40.00	175.00	275.00	125.00
Schram, Emil	3.00	10.00	17.00	5.00
Schwab, Charles M.	15.00	53.75	95.00	100.00
Seawell, William T.	3.00	7.00	15.00	20.00
Selfridge, Harry G.	7.00	20.00	45.00	27.00

Name	Signature Only	Letter or Document Signed	Autograph Letter Signed	Signed Photograph
Shea, William A.	5.00	20.00	40.00	10.00
Shoen, Sam	5.00	15.00	35.00	25.00
Shuster, W. Morgan	10.00	15.00	35.00	15.00
Silverman, Fred	3.00	9.00	20.00	10.00
Simon, Norton	12.00	35.00	65.00	25.00
Sinclair, Harry	50.00	130.00	270.00	105.00
Sloan, Alfred P., Jr.	15.00	35.00	80.00	35.00
Smith, Frederick W.	15.00	30.00	55.00	20.00
Smith, Harsen	3.00	10.00	25.00	7.00
Smith, L. C.	40.00	100.00	215.00	
Squibb, Edward R.	25.00	60.00	135.00	
Stanford, Leland	43.33	115.00	235.00	90.00
Stanton, Dr. Frank	15.00	35.00	80.00	30.00
Statler, Ellsworth M.	75.00	180.00	370.00	145.00
Steinway, Henry	5.00	15.00	30.00	20.00
Stewart, Alexander T.	5.00	15.00	25.00	
Stewart, John A.	3.00	8.00	20.00	
Straus, Jack	4.00	10.00	22.00	10.00
Sturge, Joseph	5.00	15.00	25.00	
Sulzberger, Art Ochs	3.00	10.00	18.00	10.00
Swearingen, John	5.00	14.00	30.00	10.00
Tattersall, Richard	15.00	40.00	80.00	
Thaw, Harry K.	35.00	95.00	190.00	75.00
Thomas, Philip Evan	5.00	15.00	25.00	
Thompson, John P.	16.00	45.00	90.00	30.00
Thomson, James	5.00	15.00	30.00	10.00
Thornton, Charles Tex	5.00	12.00	20.00	10.00
Tiffany, Charles L.	35.00	85.00	170.00	
Tillinghast, Charles	5.00	20.00	30.00	10.00
Topping, Dan	5.00	12.00	27.00	10.00
Townsend, Lynn	7.00	15.00	30.00	10.00
Trump, Donald J.	10.00	28.00	65.00	25.00
Turner, Ted	8.00	20.00	50.00	20.00
Vanderbilt, Cornelius	110.00	416.67	825.00	
Vanderbilt, Cornelius, Jr.	10.00	30.00	65.00	25.00
Vanderbilt, George W.	20.00	60.00	100.00	
Vanderbilt, Gloria	13.00	35.00	75.00	30.00
Vanderbilt, William H.	8.00	20.00	35.00	15.00
Vassar, Matthew	27.00	70.00	160.00	60.00
Wallace, Lila Acheson	10.00	17.00	35.00	15.00
Wanamaker, John	25.00	40.00	90.00	100.00
Warner, Harry M.	40.00	110.00	245.00	95.00
Warner, Jack L.	25.00	65.00	150.00	60.00
Watson, Thomas J.	15.00	45.00	75.00	30.00
Watson, Thomas J., Jr.	10.00	18.00	40.00	20.00
Webb, Del	4.00	10.00	20.00	10.00
Welch, Robert	25.00	38.00	85.00	30.00
Wells, H., and Fargo, William G.		800.00		
Wells, Henry	115.00	305.00	615.00	
Westinghouse, George	80.00	300.00	690.00	300.00

Name	Signature Only	Letter or Document Signed	Autograph Letter Signed	Signed Photograph
Wilder, Marshall P.	5.00	13.00	30.00	10.00
Willys, John North	50.00	90.00	204.00	75.00
Wilson, Charles E.	14.00	26.67	55.00	20.00
Wilson, Kemmons	15.00	30.00	80.00	35.00
Woolworth, Frank W.	120.00	260.00	600.00	
Wrigley, William, Jr.	50.00	100.00	225.00	85.00
Young, Owen D.	8.00	25.00	45.00	20.00
Zellerbach, J. D.	15.00	30.00	80.00	35.00

Cartoonists and Illustrators

The prices for sketches in this section refer to those done for collectors, not for published work. These may be on anything from a 3 × 5 inch index card to a much larger piece (Milton Caniff, for example, has done impromptu sketches as large as 11 × 17). The actual price of a piece (as opposed to the median guidelines below) depends on its age, complexity, level of execution, and the character drawn. For example, a drawing of a cow by Chester Gould would not be worth as much as one of Dick Tracy. Era can also be important. A drawing of Maggie and Jiggs from the 1940s is more desirable from the collector's standpoint than one from the 1930s or a more recent period (since the 1940s was the "Golden Age" of the strip).

Other influences on price include whether it is in pencil or ink. Here you need to know something about the artist. Some only work in pencil; therefore you will never be able to acquire an ink sketch from them. Rarity is sometimes an extreme factor, also. Take the $3,500 price listed below for a Walt Disney sketch. This is the one price here at which we admit to taking an educated guess. Actual sketches by Disney himself are scarcer than Donald Duck's teeth. The owner of an authenticated one can pretty well write his or her own ticket.

Charles Addams

Bud Blake

Herb Block—"Herblock"

Dik Browne

Milton Caniff

Al Capp

Ed Dodd

Jim Davis

Fred Fredericks

Dave Graue

Chester Gould

Johnny Hart

Bil Keane

Hank Ketcham

Walter Lantz

George McManus

Russell Myers

Dick Moores

Charles Schulz

Gary Trudeau

Robert Ripley

Name	Signature	Sketch
Addams, Charles (Addams Family)	$17.50	$ 50
Anderson, Brad (Marmaduke)	5	20
Anderson, Carl (Henry)	15	60
Andriola, Alfred (Kerry Drake)	5	20
Arriola, Gus (Gordo)	5	20
Avery, Tex (animator)	25	400
Baker, George (Sad Sack)	30	150
Barks, Carl (Donald Duck comic-book art)	20	150
Batiuk, Tom (Funky Winkerbean)	5	20
Berndt, Walter (Smitty)	10	50
Bess, Gordon (Redeye)	5	20
Blake, Bud (Tiger)	5	20
Block, Herb ("Herblock," political cartoonist)	10	75
Breathed, Berke (Bloom County)	5	35
Briggs, Claire (Mr. and Mrs.)	15	40
Brown, Bo (magazine cartoonist)	5	20
Browne, Dik (Hi and Lois, Hagar)	15	30
Bushmiller, Ernie (Nancy)	15	40
Calkin, Dick (Buck Rogers)	25	350
Campbell, E. Simms (magazine—first Black cartoon)	20	150
Caniff, Milton (Terry, Steve Canyon)	10	100
Capp, Al (Li'l Abner)	40	100
Cox, Palmer (Brownies)	30	125
Crane, Roy (Wash Tubs)	20	100
Crosby, Percy (Skippy)	30	150
Crumb, Robert (underground cartoons)	25	260
Davis, Jim (Garfield)	15	150
Day, Chon (Brother Sebastian)	5	20
Debeck, Billy (Barney Google)	20	165
Demslow, W. W. (Illustrator of *Wizard of OZ*)	50	175
Ding, J. N. Darling (political cartoonist)	20	200
Dirks, Rudolph (Katzenjammer Kids)	50	300
Disney, Walt (Mickey and Donald)	600	3,500
Drayton, Gracie (created Campbell Soup Kids)	20	125
Dr. Seuss (Cat in the Hat—early)	25	450
Dumas, Jerry (Sam)	5	20
Dunagin, Raply (The Middletons)	5	20
Ed, Carl (Harold Teen)	10	30
Feiffer, Jules (magazine cartoonist)	10	50
Fisher, Bud (Mutt and Jeff)	30	200
Fisher, Ham (Joe Palooka)	40	155
Fleischer, Max (animator)	50	400
Foster, Hal (Tarzan, Prince Valiant)	25	250
Fox, Fontaine (Toonerville Folks)	25	150
Fredericks, Fred (Mandrake)	5	20
Frost, A. B. (illustrator)	40	250
Gately, George (Heathcliff)	5	20
Goldberg, Rube (Contraptions)	25	125
Gottfrederson, Floyd (Mickey Mouse strip art)	10	150
Gould, Chester (Dick Tracy)	20	125
Graue, Dave (Alley Oop)	5	20
Gray, Harold (Little Orphan Annie)	50	300
Gross, Milt (Nize Baby)	20	100

Name	Signature	Sketch
Gruelle, Johnny (Raggedy Ann and Andy)	30	200
Guisewite, Cathy (Cathy)	5	20
Hanna and Barbera (Bill and Joe—animators)	10	100
Harman, Fred (Red Ryder)	20	125
Hart, Johnny (B.C. and Wizard of Id)	10	50
Hasen, Irwin (Dondi)	5	20
Hatlo, Jimmy (Little Iodine)	20	100
Hawple, Stu (Wood Allen)	5	20
Held, John, Jr. (magazine illustrator)	35	250
Hergi (Tin Tin)	20	200
Herriman, George (Krazy Kat)	50	400
Hirschfeld, Al (*New York Times* caricaturist)	10	150
Hirshfield, Harry (caricaturist)	10	200
Hoest, Bill (The Lockhorns)	5	20
Hogarth, Burne (Tarzan—second artist)	10	100
Hokinson, Helen (magazine cartoonist)	20	100
Johnson, Crockett (Barnaby)	20	300
Johnson, Lynn (For Better or for Worse)	5	20
Jones, Chuck (animator)	15	75
Keane, Bil (The Family Circus)	5	20
Kelly, Walt (Pogo)	25	250
Kent, Jack (King Aroo)	15	50
Ketcham, Hank (Dennis the Menace)	10	30
Key, Ted (Hazel)	5	20
King, Frank (Gasoline Alley)	15	125
Kinstler, E. R. (illustrator)	10	25
Kirby, Jack (Captain America)	15	100
Kliban, B. (Cat Cart for *New Yorker*)	10	100
Koren, Edward (*New Yorker* cartoonist)	10	75
Kotzky, Alex (Apt. 3-G)	5	20
Lantz, Walter (Woody Woodpecker)	10	20
Lazarus, Mell (Miss Peach, Momma)	10	20
Ledoux, Harold (Judge Parker)	5	20
Levine, David (caricaturist)	15	150
MacNelly, Jeff (Shoe)	5	100
Mamlin, V. T. (Alley Oop)	20	100
Margie (Little Lulu)	20	200
Mauldin, Bill (Willie and Joe)	25	250
McCay, Winsor (Little Nemo and animation)	50	400
McManus, George (Bringing Up Father)	51	95
Messick, Dale (Brenda Starr)	5	20
Messmer, Otto (Felix the Cat)	30	300
Montana, Bob (Archie)	20	125
Moores, Dick (Gasoline Alley)	5	20
Mosley, Zack (Smilin' Jack)	10	35
Mullin, Willard (sports cartoonist)	10	30
Murphy, John Cullen (Big Ben Bolt)	5	20
Myers, Russell (Broom Hilda)	10	35
Nast, Thomas (political cartoonist)	115	400
Opper, F. B. (Happy Hooligan)	25	100
Outcault, Richard (Yellow Kid, Buster Brown)	50	300
Peters, Mike (Mother Grimm)	5	25
Raymond, Alex (Flash Gordon)	35	350
Ripley, Robert (Believe It or Not)	25	200

Name	Signature	Sketch
Sansom, Art (Born Loser)	5	20
Schulz, Charles (Peanuts)	25	175
Segar, Elzie C. (Popeye)	100	400
Sickles, Noel (Scorchy)	20	175
Siegel and Shuster (Jerry and Joe—Superman)	50	500
Smith, Al (Mutt and Jeff)	5	20
Smith, George and Virginia (The Smiths)	5	20
Smith, Sydney (The Gumps)	30	150
Smythe, Reg (Andy Capp)	5	20
Soglow, Otto (Little King)	20	75
Steig, William (*New Yorker* cartoonist)	20	100
Sterrett, Cliff (Polly and Her Pals)	20	175
Sullivan, Pat (Felix)	35	400
Swinnerton, James (Little Jimmy)	20	150
Templeton, Ben (Motley's Crew)	5	20
Terry, Paul (Mighty Mouse animator)	50	250
Thaves, Bob (Frank and Ernest)	5	20
Thurber, James (magazine cartoonist)	75	500
Trudeau, Garry (Doonesbury)	30	200
Turner, Morrie (Wee Pals)	5	20
Walker, Mort (Beetle Bailey)	10	30
Watterson, Bill (Calvin and Hobbes)	5	20
Webster, H. T. (The Timid Soul)	20	100
Westover, Russ (Tillie the Toiler)	15	75
Willard, Frank (Moon Mullins)	20	125
Williams, Gluyas (*New Yorker* cartoonist)	10	75
Williams, J. R. (Out Our Way)	20	60
Wilson, Gahan (magazine cartoonist)	40	60
Wilson, Tom (Ziggy)	10	30
Woggon, Elmer (Big Chief Wahoo)	5	20
Young, Art (political cartoonist)	20	125
Young, Chic (Blondie)	20	75
Young, Lyman (Tim Tyler's Luck)	10	35

Celebrities

Celebrities are famous people who, for one reason or another, do not fit properly within one of the other categories in this price guide. (Remember, if you are having trouble finding a particular name, to consult the index. Persons who gained fame in several fields are usually only listed in this book in the area in which they achieved the greatest success.) Explorers, Supreme Court (SC) Justices, architects, politicians, outlaws, reformers, theologians, revolutionaries, and more fall in this category.

Name	Signature Only	Letter or Document Signed	Autograph Letter Signed	Signed Photograph
Abernathy, Ralph	$ 5.00	$ 15.00	$ 52.00	$ 10.00
Abzug, Bella	6.00	19.00	65.00	10.00
Adams, Abigail	465.00	1,950.00	4,037.50	
Adams, Louisa C.	150.00			
Addams, Jane	47.00	70.00	225.00	250.00
Akin, Susan	4.00	7.00	12.00	10.00
Alphand, Nicole H.				10.00
Alsop, Joseph	5.00	10.00	30.00	5.00
Alsop, Stewart	7.00	26.00	35.00	5.00
Altieri, Albert				10.00
Ammundsen, Roald	75.00	125.00	300.00	386.67
Anthony, Susan B.	75.00	175.00	478.57	
Astor, Nancy (Viscountess)	15.00	55.00	90.00	20.00
Auckland, Baron	5.00	15.00	40.00	
Austin, Stephen F.	835.00	1,900.00	7,500.00	
Back, Sir George	5.00	20.00	50.00	
Bacon, Edmund	4.00			10.00
Bailey, F. Lee	10.50	22.00	45.00	15.00
Bairnsfather, Bruce	10.00	25.00	110.00	20.00
Baker, Sir Samuel	17.50	30.00	45.00	
Baldwin, Henry (SC)	10.00	30.00	95.00	
Ballard, Dr. Robert	10.00	30.00	80.00	20.00
Banks, Joseph	25.00	85.00	215.00	
Barbe-Marbois, F.	8.00	25.00	60.00	
Baring, Sir Francis	15.00	25.00	67.00	
Barnard, F. A. P.	10.00	25.00	75.00	
Barne, Michael	10.00	35.00	90.00	40.00
Barnum, Phineas T.	101.25	300.00	660.83	
Barry, Marion	5.00	8.00	15.00	15.00
Barry, Sir John Wolfe	5.00	10.00	30.00	12.00
Barth, Dr. Karl	3.00	6.00	15.00	15.00
Barton, Clara	50.00	237.50	395.00	295.00
Baruch, Bernard M.	25.00	55.00	105.00	175.00
Beaverbrook, Lord William	25.00	75.00	190.00	30.00
Beck, Dave	20.00	35.00	50.00	25.00
Beebe, William	10.00	25.00	67.00	30.00
Beecher, Henry Ward	10.00	32.50	75.00	
Beke, Charles Tilstone	15.00	40.00	100.00	
Belcher, Sir Edward	10.00	30.00	75.00	
Bel Geddes, Norman	15.00	50.00	155.00	25.00
Belli, Melvin	5.00	15.00	35.00	20.00
Bent, James Theodore	5.00	10.00	25.00	5.00
Berkowitz, David		250.00	97.00	
Bernard, Sir Francis		40.00	95.00	
Berrigan, Father Daniel	10.00	30.00	70.00	10.00
Berry, Jim	10.00			
Bethune, Dr. Mary M.	65.00	192.50	360.00	

Name	Signature Only	Letter or Document Signed	Autograph Letter Signed	Signed Photograph
Bevin, Ernest	20.00	53.00	122.50	38.00
Black, Hugo (SC)	27.83	81.67	215.00	65.00
Blackmun, Harry A. (SC)	18.00	80.00	212.50	35.00
Blackwell, Alice Stone	10.00	25.00	75.00	
Blair, John (SC)			925.00	
Blake, Eugene Carson	15.00	35.00	90.00	25.00
Blatchford, Samuel (SC)	18.00	40.00	125.00	
Bloch, Ernst	20.00	45.00	105.00	30.00
Bloustein, Edward J.	5.00	12.00	20.00	5.00
Boland, Frederick	5.00	15.00	25.00	10.00
Bolingbroke, Henry	25.00	75.00	225.00	40.00
Bonaparte, Caroline	35.00	95.00	268.67	
Bond, Julian	6.00	18.00	48.00	12.00
Bonvalot, Gabriel				155.00
Booth, Ballington	10.00	65.00	90.00	
Booth, Evangeline	35.00	115.00	360.00	60.00
Booth, Maude	30.00	78.00	205.00	
Booth, William	55.00			122.67
Boyd, Belle	800.00			
Bradley, Ed	3.00	7.00	22.00	10.00
Bradley, Joseph P. (SC)	29.40	50.00	150.00	
Bradley, Tom	6.00	20.00	42.00	20.00
Brandeis, Louis D. (SC)	72.50	350.00	457.78	
Braun, Eva			1,050.00	
Breger, Dave		15.00		
Brennan, William J. (SC)	16.00	30.00	95.00	28.33
Breslin, Jimmy	4.00	15.00	40.00	10.00
Breuer, Marcel				125.00
Brewer, David J. (SC)	30.00		118.33	
Brewster, Kingman, Jr.	3.00	5.00	10.00	10.00
Bridges, Harry	25.00			100.00
Bridgman, Laura D.	10.00	45.00	85.00	
Bright, John	3.00		13.00	
Brokaw, Tom	5.00	12.00	25.00	12.00
Brothers, Joyce	4.00	10.00	24.00	10.00
Brougham, Henry	25.00	85.00	220.00	
Browder, Earl	10.00	30.00	65.00	15.00
Brown, Henry B. (SC)	25.00	55.00	150.00	
Brown, Moses	27.00			
Brummel, George B. "Beau"	60.00	185.00	575.00	
Buber, Martin	45.00	150.00		
Buckley, William F.	5.00	15.00	40.00	10.00
Bulwer, Henry	15.00	50.00	135.00	
Bunche, Ralph	28.00	56.00	175.00	65.00
Bundy, McGeorge	20.00	33.00	45.00	25.00
Bunsen, Baron C. J.	10.00	35.00	100.00	
Bunting, Mary	10.00			15.00
Burdette, Robert J.	3.00	5.00	10.00	5.00
Burger, Warren E. (SC)	21.25	70.00	108.00	45.00
Burton, Harold H. (SC)	25.00	95.78	220.00	83.00
Butler, Nicholas M.	10.00	26.67	80.00	25.00
Butler, Pierce (SC)	25.00	85.00	273.00	45.00

Red Adair

Joseph Alsop

Lady Astor

Jane Addams

F. Lee Bailey

P. T. Barnum

Roald Ammundsen

Clara Barton

Bernard M. Baruch

Ezra Taft Benson

Dan Berrigan

Hugo Black

Harry A. Blackmun

Karl Branting

Julian Bond

Evangeline Booth

Louis D. Brandeis

Justice William J. Brennan, Jr.

Ralph Bunche

Warren E. Burger

Kellye Cash

Whittaker Chambers

Cesar Chavez

Lady Clementine Churchill

225

Name	Signature Only	Letter or Document Signed	Autograph Letter Signed	Signed Photograph
Byrne, Jane	5.00	10.00	28.00	10.00
Byrnes, James F. (SC)	20.00	50.00	173.00	35.00
Cadwalader, Lambert	10.00	20.00	62.00	
Campbell, George J. D.	25.00	60.00	130.00	
Campbell, John A. (SC)	60.00		175.00	
Caplin, Mortimer	3.00	5.00	10.00	8.00
Cardozo, Benjamin N. (SC)	55.00	230.00	441.83	85.50
Carlisle, Earl of	5.00	10.00	20.00	
Carnarvon, Henry, 4th Earl of	5.00	15.00	36.00	
Carter, Billy	4.00	10.00	15.00	10.00
Carter, Boake	5.00	20.00	50.00	10.00
Carter, Lillian	12.00	17.00		15.00
Carter, Rosalynn	15.00	43.00	130.00	35.00
Cassin, René	24.00	65.00	175.00	30.00
Catron, John (SC)	*Rare—No price available*			
Catt, Carrie Chapman	50.00	130.00	250.00	
Cecil, Lord Algernon	10.00	20.00	90.00	
Chabot, Phillipe (Brion)		1,750.00		
Chamberlain, Austen	10.00	30.00	100.00	50.00
Chambers, Whittaker	15.00	50.00	150.00	25.00
Charcot, Jean	25.00	98.00	204.00	375.00
Chase, Salmon P. (SC)	75.00	126.67	290.00	150.00
Chateaubriand, F. René de	75.00	305.00	650.00	
Chavez, Cesar E.	9.00	13.00	20.00	10.00
Chennault, Anna	5.00	20.00	50.00	10.00
Chichester, Sir Francis	15.00	100.00	147.00	60.00
Child, Julia	4.00	11.00	16.00	10.00
Childs, George William	10.00	15.00	25.00	
Choate, Joseph H.	10.00	25.00	88.00	20.00
Christopher, Warren	5.00	10.00	17.00	13.00
Chung, Connie	5.00	10.00	18.00	8.00
Churchill, Clementine S.	50.00	150.00	145.00	120.00
Churchill, Jennie (Jerome)	15.00	75.00	90.00	50.00
Churchill, Lord Randolph	30.00	88.00	270.00	
Churchill, Sarah	20.00	70.00	145.00	40.00
Clark, Tom C. (SC)	16.57	30.00	95.00	25.00
Clark, William	217.50	1,328.57	2,500.00	
Cleveland, Frances F.	30.00	64.00	110.44	
Clifford, Nathan (SC)	48.00	88.00	158.67	50.00
Cobo, Albert E.	10.00	15.00	44.00	12.00
Cody, John Cardinal	5.00	25.00	36.00	30.00
Cody, William F.	355.83	600.00	835.00	853.33
Cohn, Roy	18.00	25.00	40.00	20.00
Coleridge, John Duke	5.00	10.00	25.00	
Colson, Charles	20.00			
Conant, James Bryant	3.00	5.00	10.00	20.00
Cook, Capt. James	3,000.00	8,835.00	25,245.00	
Cook, Dr. Frederick A.	20.00	65.00	172.50	150.00
Cook, Joseph	3.00	7.00	15.00	
Cook, Thomas	30.00	95.00	275.00	
Cooke, Terence Cardinal	10.00	25.00	65.00	30.00
Coolidge, Grace	45.56	125.00	179.00	125.00

Dewitt Clinton

Roy Cohn

William F. "Buffalo Bill" Cody

Richard Cardinal Cushing

Richard J. Daley
Mayor

Richard Harding Davis

Thomas Dewey

William O. Douglas

Abba Eban

William Du Bois

Mary Baker Eddy

Julie Nixon Eisenhower

Charles Evers

James A. Farley
Chairman

Mayor Diane Feinstein

Bobby Fischer

Father Edward Flanagan

Justice Felix Frankfurter

R. Buckminster Fuller

Milton Friedman

William Lloyd Garrison

Gary Gabelich

George W. Goethals

227

Name	Signature Only	Letter or Document Signed	Autograph Letter Signed	Signed Photograph
Coolidge, William D.	15.00		75.00	
Cooper, Alfred Duff	10.00	20.00	60.00	15.00
Corrigan, M./B. Williams				45.00
Couch, Virgil	3.00		7.00	5.00
Coughlin, Charles E.	15.00	40.00		30.00
Couve de Murville, M.	5.00	12.00	20.00	15.00
Cox, Archibald	5.00	28.00	50.00	10.00
Cox, James M.	10.00	56.67	75.00	25.00
Coxey, Jacob S.	15.00	40.00	135.00	
Cripps, Sir Stafford	30.00	80.00	192.50	
Croker, Richard	15.00	25.00		
Cronkite, Walter	8.00	12.00	20.00	10.00
Curtis, Benjamin R. (SC)	20.00	70.00	139.33	
Cushing, Richard Cardinal	10.00	15.00	37.38	10.00
Daley, Richard J.	10.00	16.25	50.00	13.00
Dalton, Emmett	570.00	1,866.67	5,015.00	977.50
Dana, Charles A.	10.00	20.00	62.00	35.00
Daniel, Peter Vivian (SC)	25.00	100.00	195.00	
Daniloff, Nick	20.00			25.00
Darrow, Clarence	62.50	350.00	611.67	150.00
Davies, Mandy Rice	5.00	10.00	25.00	25.00
Davies, Ronald N.	25.00			30.00
Davis, Angela	5.00	10.00	25.00	20.00
Davis, David (SC)	25.00	112.83	230.00	
Davis, John W.	5.00	25.00	35.00	
Davis, Nancy (Reagan)				200.00
Davis, Noah	10.00	25.00	58.00	
Day, William R. (SC)	20.00	44.00	135.00	25.00
Dean, John	4.00	10.00	15.00	10.00
Debs, Eugene	22.00	45.00	75.13	110.00
Deems, Charles Force	5.00	10.00	20.00	
Denver, James W.	60.00	130.00	350.00	
Depew, Chauncey M.	10.00	25.00	50.00	
Dewey, John	25.00	66.67	118.00	30.00
Dewey, Thomas E.	19.00	34.50	60.00	35.00
De Windt, Harry	5.00	15.00	40.00	25.00
Dilke, Charles W.	5.00	15.00	30.25	5.00
Dizengoff, Meir	40.00	150.00		
Dodd, Ed	5.00	15.00	27.50	10.00
Donovan, Hedley	4.00	6.00	15.00	10.00
D'Orsay, Count Alfred	10.00	15.00	35.00	
Douglas, Stephen A.	45.00	135.00	265.00	215.00
Douglas, William O. (SC)	25.00	40.00	65.00	38.67
Douglass, Frederick	88.00	171.00	400.00	
Dow, Neal	10.00	35.00	70.00	
Du Bois, W. E. B.	25.00	175.00	225.00	50.00
Duke, Clarence	4.00	10.00	25.00	5.00
Dulles, Allen W.	20.00	110.00	175.00	25.00
Dummar, Melvin E.	20.00	30.00	40.00	
Duncan, Charles T.	4.00	10.00	25.00	10.00
Duval, Gabriel (SC)	25.00	95.00	175.00	
Eads, James B.	45.00	145.00	425.00	

Samuel Gompers

Horace Greeley

Oliver Wendell Holmes

Sir Edmund Hillary

Thor Heyerdahl

Jimmy Hoffa

John Edgar Hoover

Charles E. Hughes

Aimee McPherson Hutton

Jesse Jackson

Leon Jouhau

Helen Keller

Coretta Scott King

Ethel Kennedy

Rufus King

Lane Kirkland

Edward I. Koch

Evel Knievel

Fiorello LaGuardia

Simon Lake

Bert Lance

Ann Landers

Alf Landon

Irving R. Levine

229

Name	Signature Only	Letter or Document Signed	Autograph Letter Signed	Signed Photograph
Earp, Virgil	475.00	1,525.00	4,675.00	
Eban, Abba	15.00	35.00	75.00	30.00
Eddy, Mary Baker	600.00	1,500.00	2,185.00	
Eiffel, Gustave	45.00	135.00	378.67	500.00
Eisenhower, Julie Nixon	5.00	10.00	25.00	25.00
Eisenhower, Mamie Doud	43.75	86.43	123.50	54.17
Eisenstaedt, Alfred	10.00	25.00	35.00	30.00
Eliot, Charles W.	15.00	45.00	79.25	
Ellsberg, Daniel	18.00	25.00	55.00	20.00
Ellsworth, Oliver (SC)	40.00	219.07	372.29	
Estes, Billy Sol	5.00	20.00	45.00	10.00
Everett, Edward	10.00	20.00	60.00	
Evers, Charles	5.00	10.00	40.00	10.00
Faithfull, Emily	15.00	35.00	40.00	
Falwell, Jerry	15.00	25.00		22.50
Fawcett, Dame Millicent	10.00	30.00	88.00	
Feinstein, Diane	4.00	10.00	22.00	18.00
Felder, Dr. Rodney	5.00	8.00	17.00	5.00
Ferraro, Geraldine	25.00	40.00	60.00	38.00
Field, Stephen J. (SC)	38.00	150.00	185.00	250.00
Fillmore, Caroline	650.00			
Fischer, Bobby	15.00	50.00	150.00	60.00
Fitzsimmons, Frank E.	3.00	8.00	25.00	10.00
Flanagan, Father Edward	10.00	50.50	75.50	25.00
Flower, Sir William Henry	5.00	25.00	45.00	
Flynn, Edward J.	3.00	10.00	20.00	5.00
Flynt, Larry	3.00			5.00
Ford, John T.		190.00	425.00	
Fortas, Abe (SC)	13.43	42.00	105.00	
Fosdick, Harry E.	7.00	15.00	35.00	
Foxworth, P. E.	5.00	15.00	35.00	
Frankfurter, Felix (SC)	75.71	232.86	283.50	415.00
Franklin, Sir John	60.00	115.00	466.67	
Friedman, Milton	5.00	10.00	15.00	15.00
Fritchie, Barbara		8,800.00		
Fromme, Lynette	15.00	50.00	125.00	20.00
Fry, Elizabeth	33.00	125.00	178.33	
Fuchs, Sir Vivian E.	19.67	70.00	113.00	
Fuller, Buckminster	7.00	15.00	38.00	25.00
Fuller, John G.	4.00	10.00		
Fuller, Melville W. (SC)	22.00	71.00	180.00	100.00
Galard, Geneviève de	40.00			50.00
Galbraith, John Kenneth	10.00			20.00
Garfield, Lucretia R.	63.33	150.00	250.00	
Garrison, William Lloyd	55.00	68.00	125.00	
Gavin, John	5.00	15.00	35.00	12.00
Gaynor, William J.	20.00	55.00	115.00	30.00
Gerlache, Adrien de				300.00
Giesler, Jerry	7.00	20.00	35.00	10.00
Gilbert, Cass	5.00	10.00	26.00	5.00
Gilbert, H. E.	3.00	4.00	9.00	5.00

Sincerely yours,

John L. Lewis

Dr. David Livingstone

Alice Roosevelt Longworth

Horace Mann

Clare Booth Luce

Justice Thurgood Marshall

Newton Minow

Sincerely,
President

George Meany

Martha Mitchell

Sincerely yours,

Edward R. Murrow

Edwin Newman

Sandra D. O'Connor

Thomas T. Noguchi, M.D.

Svetlana Peters—Stalin's daughter

Marina Oswald Porter

Hubert A. Philbrick

Lewis F. Powell, Jr.

Dith Pran

Jackie Presser

John Profumo

Vidkun Quisling

Melvin Purvis

James Earl Ray

William Rehnquist

Oral Roberts

Walter Reuther

231

Name	Signature Only	Letter or Document Signed	Autograph Letter Signed	Signed Photograph
Gilmore, Gary	15.00	27.00		
Gloucester (William Frederick)	5.00	15.00	40.00	
Glueck, Nelson	5.00	20.00	45.00	10.00
Godoy, Manuel de		295.00		
Gody, Louis A.	15.00	45.00	135.00	
Goldberg, Arthur J. (SC)	17.00	37.33	135.00	36.25
Goldman, Emma	50.00	236.67	425.00	60.00
Gompers, Samuel	225.00	208.00	265.00	
Gough, John B.	5.00	10.00	28.00	5.00
Gould, Samuel B.	3.00	5.00	8.00	4.00
Graham, Dr. Billy	10.00	25.00	60.00	15.00
Grandi, Count Dino	12.50	30.00	65.00	35.00
Grant, Julia D.		375.00		
Gray, Horace (SC)	20.00	45.00	125.00	25.00
Green, William	40.00	95.00	295.00	125.00
Grenfell, Sir Wilfred	10.00	15.00	32.50	
Gropius, Walter	40.00	162.50	360.00	
Gross, Calvin	2.00	3.00	5.00	4.00
Grossinger, Jennie	25.00	75.00	195.00	40.00
Guilford, Lord	5.00	10.00	25.00	
Guinan, Texas	15.00	40.00	55.00	35.00
Guiteau, Charles	325.00		2,000.00	
Guy, Thomas	10.00	35.00	95.00	
Hague, Frank	5.00	30.00	37.00	5.00
Halaby, Najeeb	10.00	30.00		
Haldeman, H. R.	5.00	15.00	45.00	10.00
Hall, Abraham O.	2.33	3.00	15.00	5.00
Hall, Alvin W.	5.00	10.00		35.00
Hall, Gus	30.00	55.00	150.00	20.00
Halliburton, Richard	25.00	30.00	151.00	35.00
Hamilton, Alexander, Jr.	5.00	15.00	35.00	
Hancock, John, Jr.	5.00	15.00	40.00	
Hanna, Marcus A.	15.00	40.00	90.00	25.00
Hardin, John Wesley	2,600.00			
Harding, Florence Kling	55.00	160.00		70.00
Harlan, John M. (SC)	35.00	60.00	165.00	
Harlan, John Marshall (SC)	20.00	50.00	105.00	35.00
Harper, Joseph W.	10.00	30.00	80.00	
Harris, Jean	35.00	55.00	160.00	25.00
Harrison, Mary Lord	25.00	48.75	135.00	
Hartman, David	4.00	8.00	12.00	10.00
Harvey, Paul	5.00	20.00	45.00	10.00
Hastings, Warren	45.00	110.00	168.00	
Hatcher, Richard G.	3.00	7.00	15.00	10.00
Hayden, Tom	4.00	10.00	25.00	20.00
Hayes, Isaac Israel	15.00	25.00	57.50	
Hearst, Patricia	10.00	51.00	75.00	30.00
Hedin, Sven				100.00
Helen, Princess H. R. H.	5.00	15.00	30.00	20.00
Heller, Walter	5.00	10.00	20.00	10.00
Helms, Richard	5.00	15.00	45.00	15.00
Henson, Matthew A.	90.00	250.00		

Jerry Rubin

Sir Ernest Shackleton

Pierre Salinger

Maria Shriver

Alfred E. Smith

Francis Cardinal Spellman

Sir Henry Stanley—who found Dr. Livingston

Harold Stassen

God bless you

Mother Teresa

Adlai E. Stevenson

Lowell Thomas

Norman Thomas

Arnold J. Toynbee

Maria Von Trapp

Jeremy Thorpe

Amy Vanderbilt

Harold Washington

Lech Walesa

Daniel Webster

Terry Waite

Byron R. White

Charles E. Whittaker

Benjamin M. Weir

233

Name	Signature Only	Letter or Document Signed	Autograph Letter Signed	Signed Photograph
Herbert, George E. (Carnarvon)	5.00	10.00	30.00	
Herzog, Chaim	15.00			
Hesburgh, Theodore M.	4.00	10.00	30.00	10.00
Heyerdahl, Thor	15.00	35.00	80.00	20.00
Hill, Sir Rowland	20.00	60.00	157.00	
Hillary, Sir Edmund	20.00	70.00	95.00	42.00
Hinchingbrooke, Alex	5.00	16.00	45.00	10.00
Hiss, Alger	20.00	35.00	60.00	40.00
Hitz, John	10.00	35.00	90.00	
Hoffa, James R.	250.00			
Hoffer, Eric	5.00	10.00	25.00	10.00
Holmes, D. Brainerd	10.00			25.00
Holmes, Oliver W. (SC)	65.00	225.00	625.83	220.00
Hooks, Benjamin L.	5.00	12.00	25.00	10.00
Hoover, J. Edgar	35.00	66.25	130.00	75.00
Hoover, Lou Henry	60.00	123.33		75.00
Hopkins, Mark	25.00	80.00	220.00	
Horowitz, David	3.00	7.00	16.00	5.00
House, Edward M. "Colonel"	35.00	100.00	310.00	45.00
Howe, Samuel	5.00	10.00	30.00	
Hubbard, Gardiner	20.00	55.00	150.00	
Hughes, Charles E. (SC)	25.63	87.31	185.00	125.00
Hume, Joseph	9.00	30.00	80.00	15.00
Hunt, E. Howard	10.00	20.00	90.00	23.00
Hunt, Sir John	5.00	20.00	50.00	
Hunt, Ward (SC)	55.00		170.00	
Impellitteri, Vincent	3.00	10.00	23.00	5.00
Ingersoll, Robert Green	15.00	25.00	45.00	
Irwin, David	5.00	18.00	45.00	10.00
Jackson, Howell E. (SC)				100.00
Jackson, Rev. Jesse	10.00	20.00	40.00	48.00
Jackson, Maynard	4.00	9.00	20.00	10.00
Jackson, Robert H. (SC)	30.00	70.00	145.00	
James, Frank	783.33	1,875.00	4,212.50	
James, William	45.00	135.00	400.00	
Jarriel, Tom	3.00	10.00	15.00	10.00
Jarvis, Howard	4.00	12.00	25.00	8.00
Jaworski, Leon	5.00	15.00	45.00	10.00
Jay, John (SC)	320.00	1,066.67	2,458.33	
Jennings, Al				165.00
Johnson, Hugh S.	20.00	90.00	150.00	25.00
Johnson, Lady Bird	22.75	68.33		65.00
Johnson, Oliver	5.00	10.00	20.00	
Jones, Anson	220.00		1,100.00	
Jones, Bob	10.00	20.00	55.00	15.00
Jones, Mary H. "Mother"	50.00	195.00	400.00	
Jordan, Hamilton	4.00	10.00	20.00	10.00
Jorgensen, Christine	3.00	10.00	30.00	15.00
Jowett, Benjamin	5.00	10.00	25.00	
Kaltenborn, H. V.	5.00	15.00	30.00	10.00
Karman, Theodore von	20.00	45.00	95.00	25.00
Karpis, Alvin	60.00	183.00		75.00

Sincerely yours,

Walter Winchell

Wendell L. Wilkie

Walter Winchell

Brigham Young Pres.

Brigham Young

Name	Signature Only	Letter or Document Signed	Autograph Letter Signed	Signed Photograph
Katz, Alvin S.		5.00	10.63	
Keble, John	30.00	90.00	248.67	
Keller, Helen	45.00	100.00	200.33	225.00
Kelley, Clarence M.	3.00	5.00	10.00	5.00
Kemper, John M.	3.00	7.00	15.00	10.00
Kennedy, Edward M.	35.00	49.00	135.00	45.00
Kennedy, Ethel	25.00	50.00	75.00	40.00
Kennedy, Gerald Bishop	3.00	5.00	10.00	7.00
Kennedy, Jacqueline	150.00	375.00	862.50	
Kennedy, Rose	20.00	150.00	185.00	50.00
Kenny, Sister Elizabeth	100.00			125.00
Kent, James	35.00	120.00	275.00	
Keppel, Francis	3.00	5.00	15.00	10.00
Kerr, Clark	5.00	10.00	20.00	10.00
Ketcham, Henry K.		25.00		
Keynes, John Maynard	65.00	325.00	550.00	165.00
King, Coretta Scott	10.00	35.00	90.00	10.00
King, Martin Luther	395.00	645.00	1,800.00	500.00
Kirkland, Lane	8.00	12.00	20.00	10.00
Kittinger, Joe	10.50	25.00		
Knievel, Evel	5.00	15.00	35.00	27.50
Koch, Edward I.	10.00	20.00	35.00	10.00
Koppel, Ted	5.00	10.00	25.00	12.00
Kropotkin, Peter	20.00	55.00	161.25	
Kuralt, Charles	10.00	20.00	35.00	15.00
LaGuardia, Fiorello	14.00	40.00		25.00
Lake, Simon	50.00		185.00	
Lamar, Joseph R. (SC)	34.00	95.00		
Lamar, Lucius Q. C. (SC)	25.00	70.00		
Lambert, Ray	4.00			
LaMotta, Vikki	3.00			10.00
Lance, Bert	5.00	10.00	15.00	10.00
Land, E. S.		20.00	30.00	5.00
Lander, Frederick West		180.00	430.00	
Landers, Ann	4.00	10.00	25.00	7.00
Landon, Alf	9.00	50.00	80.00	12.50
Lawes, Lewis E.	15.00	40.00	97.50	20.00
Layard, Austin Henry	9.00	20.00	48.00	
Le Corbusier	40.00		250.00	50.00
LeHand, M. A. "Missy"	15.00	40.00	95.00	15.00
Lehman, Herbert H.	10.00	41.67		15.00

Name	Signature Only	Letter or Document Signed	Autograph Letter Signed	Signed Photograph
Leopold, Nathan F.	65.00	200.00	555.00	150.00
Levine, Irving R.	3.00	10.00		5.00
Lewis, John L.	27.50	58.00		40.00
Lewis, Meriwether		4,500.00		
Liberman, Evsei Prof	15.00			20.00
Liddy, G. Gordon	5.00	20.00	50.00	10.00
Lilienthal, David E.	15.00	30.00		20.00
Lillie, G. A. "Pawnee Bill"	60.00	200.00		
Liman, Arthur	4.00	12.00		18.00
Lincoln, Evelyn	15.00	20.00		20.00
Lincoln, Mary Todd	275.00	850.00	2,332.50	
Lindsay, John	4.00	8.00		10.00
Lisa, Manuel		762.50		
Livermore, Daniel P.	15.00	20.00	45.00	
Livermore, Mary A.	35.00	65.00	91.67	
Livingston, Henry B. (SC)	100.00	310.00		
Livingstone, David	95.00	325.00	778.00	
Lockwood, Belva A.	175.00			
Lodge, Henry Cabot, Jr.	13.00	53.33	80.00	15.00
Longworth, Alice Roosevelt	13.33	20.00		
Lossing, Benson	15.00	35.00	95.00	15.00
Luce, Clare Boothe	10.00	25.00	40.00	25.00
Lumiere, Louis		250.00		205.00
Luther, Martin			37,250.00	
MacChesney, Nathan William	10.00	20.00	85.00	
MacMillian, Donald B.	15.00	47.00	115.00	
Madison, Dolley Payne	687.50	905.00	1,108.33	
Malcolm X	110.00	340.00	930.00	
Malmesbury, 1st Earl of	5.00	10.00	20.00	
Malthus, Thomas Robert	200.00		2,500.00	
Mann, Horace	15.00	45.00	125.00	
Mann, Thomas Clifton	3.00			4.00
Manning, Henry E.		30.00	70.00	
Manning, William T.	10.00	25.00	55.00	15.00
Manson, Charles	30.00	175.00	262.50	
Markham, Sir Albert H.	5.00	20.00	45.00	
Markham, Sir Clements	10.00	20.00	55.00	
Marshall, John (SC)	350.00	1,281.25	2,333.33	
Marshall, Thurgood (SC)	16.00	113.00	140.00	20.00
Masterson, Bat			3,850.00	
Mata Hari (G. M. Zelle)	205.00	950.00	1,750.00	
Matthews, Stanley (SC)	15.00	30.00	60.00	
Maxwell, Elsa	7.50	20.00	35.00	10.00
Mazzini, Joseph	10.00	30.00	75.00	
McGuffy, William H.	20.00	65.00	170.00	
McGuigan, James Cardinal	3.00	5.00	15.00	5.00
McKenna, Joseph (SC)	15.00	25.00	65.00	20.00
McLean, John (SC)	20.00	88.00	158.33	
McLintock, Sir Francis	10.00	30.00	75.00	
McPherson, Aimee S.	55.00	170.00	385.00	70.00
McReynolds, James C. (SC)	20.50	75.00	130.50	

Name	Signature Only	Letter or Document Signed	Autograph Letter Signed	Signed Photograph
Meany, George	11.00	15.00	40.00	25.00
Medina, Harold R.	10.00	25.00		15.00
Michelson, Charles	15.00			25.00
Mill, John Stuart	115.00	350.00	950.00	
Miller, Samuel F. (SC)	38.00	65.00	175.00	45.00
Milnes, Richard M.	5.00	10.00	25.00	10.00
Minow, Newton N.	3.50	5.00	15.00	4.00
Minton, Sherman (SC)	28.00	75.00	160.00	35.00
Mirabehin (M. Slade)	20.00			30.00
Mitchell, Martha	35.00	100.00		45.00
Mitchelson, Marvin	5.00	7.00	15.00	7.00
Moody, William H. (SC)	10.00	30.00	75.00	25.00
Mooney, Tom	15.00	40.00	130.00	20.00
Moore, Alfred (SC)	Rare—No price available			
Moore, Sara Jane	15.00	45.00	125.00	
Moscone, George R.	75.00			90.00
Moses, Robert	3.00	7.00	15.00	10.00
Mosley, Sir Oswald	25.00	65.00	180.00	140.00
Mossadegh, Muhammad				150.00
Mott, Lucretia	45.00	140.00	375.00	
Mountevens, Baron (E. Evans)	14.00	40.00		
Moyers, Bill	5.00	15.00	45.00	10.00
Moynihan, Pat	10.00	20.00	55.00	18.00
Mudd, Roger	5.00	10.00	30.00	10.00
Muhammed, Elijah	40.00	117.50	345.00	
Murphy, Frank (SC)	25.00	87.00	197.50	61.67
Murray, John C. (Society of Jesus)	3.00	5.00	10.00	5.00
Murray, Philip	35.00	45.00		40.00
Murrow, Edward R.	20.00	60.00		25.00
Myerson, Bess	10.00	20.00		25.00
Nansen, Fridtjof	85.00	110.00	225.00	510.00
Napier, McVey	5.00	10.00	20.00	
Nation, Carrie	50.00	150.00	208.33	
Nelson, Samuel (SC)	45.00	135.00	190.00	
Neumann, Theresa	45.00	130.00	350.00	105.00
Newman, Edwin	4.00	10.00	20.00	5.00
Newman, John Cardinal	56.00	160.00	342.93	250.00
Nicolay, John G.	15.00	45.00	125.00	
Niemoller, Dr. Martin	25.00	90.00	220.50	45.00
Nixon, Patricia	25.00	113.33	175.00	350.00
Nizer, Louis	25.00	78.00	215.00	30.00
Noel-Baker, Philip	15.00	40.00	130.00	20.00
Noguchi, Thomas T.	10.00			
Nordenskjold, Adolf E.	200.00			340.00
Nordenskjold, Otto	185.00			300.00
Norgay, Tenzing	30.00	95.00	255.00	40.00
Norris, Dr. J. Frank	3.00	10.00	25.00	5.00
Oakley, Annie	1,366.67			3,000.00
O'Brien, Lawrence	10.00	20.00		15.00
O'Connor, Basil	10.00	25.00		35.00
O'Connor, Sandra Day (SC)	20.00	63.33	145.00	45.00

Name	Signature Only	Letter or Document Signed	Autograph Letter Signed	Signed Photograph
O'Connor, Thomas Power	60.00	108.00		
Ogle, William	5.00	10.00	15.00	8.00
Olmstead, Frederick Law	40.00	110.00	300.00	
Ono, Yoko	35.00	70.00	195.00	60.00
Oswald, Marina	20.00	45.00	125.00	50.00
Pankhurst, Christabel	15.00			
Pankhurst, Emmeline	25.00	78.00	175.00	330.00
Pankhurst, E. Sylvia	50.00	143.00		65.00
Parker, Alton B.	5.00	20.00	35.00	10.00
Parks, Rosa	15.00		25.00	40.00
Parnell, Charles Stewart	35.00	100.00	290.00	
Parry, Sir William E.	26.00	35.00	96.25	
Paul, Arthur	3.00	7.00	12.00	15.00
Pauley, Jane	4.00	10.00	15.00	10.00
Pavie, Auguste	30.00	135.00	228.00	
Payer, Julius von				285.00
Payne, Cril	3.00	8.00	15.00	10.00
Peabody, Francis	10.00	25.00	85.00	
Peale, Norman Vincent	10.00	45.00	110.00	20.00
Peckham, Rufus W. (SC)	22.50	50.00	137.50	100.00
Pendergast, Thomas J.	15.00	45.00	105.00	35.00
Pereira, William L.	4.00	20.00	30.00	10.00
Petrie, Flinders (M. Matthews)	79.50		105.00	
Philbrick, Herbert A.	5.00	25.00	45.00	15.00
Phillips, Wendell	5.00	20.00	35.00	25.00
Pierce, Jane M.	100.00	300.00	831.67	
Pike, Bishop James A.	53.00	140.00		
Pike, Zebulon M.	50.00	140.00	384.25	
Pinchot, Gifford	10.00	25.00	62.50	20.00
Pire, Father Dominique Georges	45.00			60.00
Pitney, Mahlon (SC)	22.50	45.00	135.00	20.00
Poling, Daniel A.	5.00	15.00	45.00	10.00
Polk, Sarah	175.00	360.00	1,000.00	
Ponting, Herbert George	20.00	55.00	165.00	
Powderly, Terence V.	20.00	30.00	45.00	25.00
Powell, Adam Clayton	30.00			45.00
Powell, Lewis F., Jr. (SC)	13.67	40.00	105.00	15.00
Powers, Bert	3.00	4.00	10.00	4.00
Pran, Dith	10.00	20.00	42.00	10.00
Presser, Jackie	10.00	25.00		25.00
Profumo, John	50.00			
Profumo, Valerie (Hobson)	5.00			20.00
Pulitzer, Joseph, Jr.	5.00	15.00	45.00	10.00
Pulitzer, Roxanne	5.00	15.00	45.00	20.00
Purvis, Melvin	20.00	62.67	150.00	25.00
Pusey, Edward B.	10.00	30.00	73.00	15.00
Pusey, Nathan M.	15.00	40.00	100.00	25.00
Putney, Mahlon	20.00			
Queensberry, William Douglas	10.00	30.00	75.00	
Ramsey, Arthur M.	10.00	20.00		25.00
Rasmussen, Knute	200.00			305.00
Rasputin, Gregori E.		2,000.00	3,500.00	

Name	Signature Only	Letter or Document Signed	Autograph Letter Signed	Signed Photograph
Ray, James Earl	25.00	100.00	211.00	285.00
Raymond, Henry J.	10.00	15.00	30.00	
Reagan, Maureen	5.00	12.00	30.00	10.00
Reasoner, Harry	4.00	10.00	20.00	10.00
Redmond, John E.	5.00	15.00	40.00	10.00
Reed, Stanley (SC)	17.50	30.00	80.00	25.00
Rehnquist, William H. (SC)	27.50	45.00	110.00	
Reid, Whitelaw	26.00	55.00	69.17	
Reischauer, Edwin O.	3.00	5.00	10.00	5.00
Reuther, Walter	20.00	38.00	92.50	25.00
Rice-Davies, Mandy	5.00	10.00	25.00	20.00
Richardson, Sir John	15.00	40.00	100.00	
Riefenstahl, Leni	20.00	35.00	50.00	40.00
Roberts, Oral	10.00	20.00	50.00	15.00
Roberts, Owen J. (SC)	20.00	60.00	190.00	30.00
Robertson, Pat	10.00	25.00	40.00	15.00
Robinson, C. Roosevelt	5.00	15.00	20.00	5.00
Roehm, Ernest	170.00			
Romulo, Carlos P.	5.00	10.00	24.00	20.00
Roosevelt, Edith K.	31.67	60.00	130.00	
Roosevelt, Eleanor	58.33	114.20	291.25	250.00
Roosevelt, James	5.00	15.00	45.00	10.00
Roosevelt, Sarah D.	15.00	75.00	35.00	
Rose, Billy	25.00	40.00	80.00	35.00
Rosenman, Samuel I.	4.00	20.00	48.50	5.00
Ross, John (Coowescoowe)			1,500.00	
Ross, Sir John	25.00	125.00	178.33	
Rubin, Jerry	15.00		40.00	20.00
Ruby, Jack	155.00	450.00		
Rukeyser, Louis	5.00	10.00	20.00	10.00
Rustin, Bayard	10.00	25.00	60.00	20.00
Rutledge, John (SC)	190.00	575.00	1,500.00	
Rutledge, Wiley B. (SC)	20.00	108.00	245.00	35.00
Saarinen, G. Eliel	16.00	45.00	125.00	25.00
Sacco, Nicola			3,700.00	
Salinger, Pierre	3.00	5.00	10.00	5.00
Sandwich, 4th Earl of	50.00	150.00	415.00	
Sanger, Margaret	30.00	70.00		45.00
Sawyer, Diane	5.00	12.00	20.00	15.00
Schaff, Philip	3.00	5.00	12.00	10.00
Schlafly, Phyllis	10.00	15.00	35.00	15.00
Schumann, Clara	50.00	140.00	266.67	170.00
Schwatka, Frederick	10.00	20.00	55.00	
Scopes, John T.	50.00	150.00		65.00
Scott, Robert Falcon	60.00	245.00	471.43	175.00
Sergeant, John	5.00	10.00	20.00	5.00
Serpico, Frank	5.00	15.00	45.00	10.00
Seymour, Horatio	15.00	52.50	73.57	
Shackleton, Ernest	63.00	120.00	331.25	351.00
Shaftesbury (A. A. Cooper)	20.00	50.00	165.00	
Shaw, Anna Howard	5.00	21.25	45.00	10.00
Sheen, Fulton J.	30.00	50.00		28.00

Name	Signature Only	Letter or Document Signed	Autograph Letter Signed	Signed Photograph
Shiras, George, Jr. (SC)	35.33	110.00		45.00
Shriver, Maria	3.00	5.00	10.00	7.00
Shriver, Sargent	5.00	15.00		10.00
Shuman, Charles B.	3.00	7.00	15.00	5.00
Sliwa, Lisa	6.00			10.00
Smith, Alfred E.	46.50	93.13	414.00	85.00
Smith, F. E.	36.00			
Smith, Gerrit	15.00	40.00	100.00	
Smith, Ida B. Wise	3.00	5.00	8.00	4.00
Smith, Joseph	515.00	1,533.33		
Southampton, 1st Earl of		187.50		
Southcott, Joanna	15.00	40.00	100.00	
Spellman, Francis Cardinal	15.00	38.67	87.50	30.50
Stalin, Svetlana	30.00	90.00	250.00	40.00
Stanhope, Lady Hester	10.00	20.00	30.00	
Stanhope, Philip D., 4th Earl of Chesterfield	5.00	10.00	20.00	
Stanley, Henry Morton	81.67	140.00	379.92	135.00
Stanton, Elizabeth Cady	35.00	105.00	283.33	
Stassen, Harold	5.00	15.00	30.00	10.00
Stefensson, Vilhjalmur	15.00	100.00	202.50	
Steinem, Gloria	10.00	20.00	45.00	25.00
Stevens, John Paul (SC)	18.33	35.00	97.50	25.00
Stewart, Potter (SC)	18.00	45.00	140.00	45.00
Stokes, Carl Burton	5.00	15.00	35.00	10.00
Stone, Harlan Fiske (SC)	25.00	114.60	188.00	150.00
Stone, Lucy	35.00	100.00	195.00	
Story, Joseph (SC)	65.00	125.00	250.00	
Strauss, Franz Josef	15.00	45.00	125.00	20.00
Stritch, Samuel Cardinal	10.00	25.00	55.00	15.00
Strong, William (SC)	50.00			
Sunday, William A. "Billy"	30.00	95.00	232.50	375.00
Sutherland, George (SC)	25.00	75.00	100.00	125.00
Sutro, Adolph H. J.	25.00	63.00	152.50	
Sutter, John A.	500.00	3,412.50	15,000.00	
Swayne, Noah H. (SC)	41.67	75.00	195.00	
Szold, Henrietta	95.00	298.00	430.00	
Taft, Charles P.	10.00	15.00	25.00	10.00
Taft, Helen Manning	55.00		114.50	
Taft, Henry W.	2.00	5.00	10.00	5.00
Taney, Roger B. (SC)	50.00	152.14	276.25	
Tarnower, Dr. Herman	15.00	45.00	120.00	20.00
Tate, Sir Henry	40.00	120.00	325.00	
Teresa, Mother	40.00	85.33	205.00	100.00
Terry, Dr. Luther	3.00	5.00	10.00	5.00
Thomas, Lowell	32.50	30.00		23.75
Thomas, Norman	10.00	108.00	245.00	55.00
Thompson, Smith (SC)	25.00	85.00	125.00	
T Hooft, Visser	3.00	5.00	10.00	5.00
Thorpe, Jeremy	5.00	16.00	40.00	10.00
Thorson, Ralph "Papa"	5.00	20.00	35.00	10.00

Name	Signature Only	Letter or Document Signed	Autograph Letter Signed	Signed Photograph
Tilden, Samuel J.	10.00	60.00	85.00	40.00
Tilghman, William M.	150.00	750.00	1,200.00	
Todd, Charles Scott	5.00	15.00	40.00	
Toynbee, Arnold J.	15.00	40.00	120.00	20.00
Truman, Bess V. W.	35.00	68.67	195.00	150.00
Truman, Harry (Mt. St. Helens)	3.00			25.00
Truman, Margaret (Daniels)	10.00	34.00	80.00	15.00
Tully, Alice	16.00	30.00		20.00
Tutu, Bishop Desmond	35.00	95.00		100.00
Tweed, William M. "Boss"	110.00	198.75	350.00	300.00
Tyler, Julia Gardiner	150.00	445.00		
Unger, Jim		10.00		
Unruh, Howard	80.00			
Van Buren, Abigail	5.00	12.00	30.00	10.00
Vanderbilt, Amy	10.00	25.00	40.00	35.00
Van Devanter, Willis (SC)	24.67	75.00	200.00	40.00
Vanzetti, Bartolomeo	470.00	1,375.00	3,750.00	
Varga, Francis	30.00			
Viljoen, Benjamin	5.00	15.00	40.00	10.00
Vincent de Paul	420.00	1,200.00	3,750.00	
Vinson, Frederick M. (SC)	40.00	150.00	345.00	185.00
Von Bulow, Claus	18.00	25.00		20.00
Von Trapp, Baroness Maria	15.00	65.00	120.00	25.00
Wagner, Robert F.	10.00	15.00	25.00	10.00
Waite, Morrison R. (SC)	35.00	60.00	163.33	50.00
Waite, Terry	30.00			40.00
Wald, Lillian D.	30.00	87.50	175.00	40.00
Waldheim, Kurt	25.00	65.00	150.00	35.00
Walesa, Lech	20.00	62.50		100.00
Walker, James J.	15.00	50.00	125.00	30.00
Wallace, Mike	5.00	12.00	20.00	10.00
Walpole, Spencer H.	3.00	7.00	15.00	
Walters, Barbara	5.00	10.00	25.00	10.00
Warren, Earl (SC)	30.00	80.00		67.50
Washington, Booker T.	75.00	158.50	287.50	
Washington, Bushrod (SC)	60.00	180.00	485.00	
Washington, Harold	5.00	20.00	45.00	20.00
Waterston, Robert C.	5.00	10.00	25.00	
Wayne, James M. (SC)	30.00	45.00	70.00	
Weed, Thurlow	4.00	7.00	10.00	5.00
Weir, Benjamin M.	12.00	15.00	22.00	20.00
Wesley, John	90.00	260.00	699.33	
Westheimer, Dr. Ruth	4.00	15.00	23.00	16.00
Weston, Agnes Dame	5.00	10.00	25.00	8.00
White, Andrew D.	14.00	41.67	61.67	25.00
White, Byron R. (SC)	21.00	40.00	85.00	32.00
White, Edward D. (SC)	45.00	158.00	338.00	135.00
White, Sanford	45.00	135.00	363.00	60.00
Whittaker, Charles E.(SC)	23.40	50.00	138.00	35.00
Wiesenthal, Simon	17.00	40.00	85.00	20.00
Wilberforce, William	40.00	136.67	328.00	

Name	Signature Only	Letter or Document Signed	Autograph Letter Signed	Signed Photograph
Wilentz, David T.	25.00	40.00	75.00	
Wilkes, Charles	15.00	45.00	113.00	
Wilkins, Sir Hubert	12.00	25.00	40.00	
Wilkins, Roy	12.50	25.00	81.67	15.00
Willard, Frances	30.00	45.00	60.00	75.00
Williams, Edward B.	5.00	15.00	40.00	10.00
Williams, Eleazer	35.00	95.00	250.00	
Willkie, Wendell	20.00	45.00	45.00	33.00
Wilson, Earl	5.00	10.00	30.00	10.00
Wilson, Edith Bolling	50.00	110.00	177.50	150.00
Wilson, Ellen Louise	75.00	220.00	600.00	
Wilson, Lt. George W.	15.00	35.00	120.00	
Wilson, Rev. James (SC)	150.00	325.00	475.00	
Winchell, Walter	5.00	15.00	40.00	10.00
Wise, Stephen S.	10.00	40.50	60.00	30.00
Wolfe-Barry, John	5.00	10.00	25.00	5.00
Woll, Matthew	10.00	30.00	80.00	
Wood, Fernando	10.00	25.00	70.00	
Woodbury, Levi (SP)	20.00	70.00	185.00	
Woodcock, Walter	5.00			10.00
Woodhull, Victorio C.	85.00	175.00	475.00	
Woodruff, Wilford	20.00	45.00	100.00	
Woods, Rose Mary	20.00			15.00
Woods, William B. (SC)	30.00	60.00	165.00	110.00
Wooley, Mary E.	30.00	90.00	215.00	
Wren, Christopher	1,100.00	3,525.00		
Wright, Frank Lloyd	130.00	887.50	1,030.00	350.00
Wunder, George		20.00	42.00	
Yamaer, George	10.00	20.00	80.00	15.00
Yamasaki, Minoru	5.00	15.00	40.00	10.00
Yorty, Sam	4.00	10.00	30.00	10.00
Young, Andrew	10.00	20.00	35.00	25.00
Young, Brigham	375.00	1,242.50	3,766.67	
Young, Coleman	4.00	12.00	20.00	10.00
Young, Whitney	4.00	10.00	15.00	10.00
Younger, Bob	2,000.00			
Younger, Cole	1,250.00	2,250.00	4,200.00	
Zapata, Emiliano	275.00	805.00		

Civil War

The following represents persons of note related to the American Civil War. There are, of course, many hundreds more. If a name was excluded, it means only that data on a philographic item of his or hers was not accessible at the time of publishing.

Name	Signature Only	Letter or Document Signed	Autograph Letter Signed	Signed Photograph
Alvord, Benjamin	$ 10.00	$ 20.00	$ 30.00	
Ammen, Daniel	15.00	25.00	25.00	$ 95.00
Anderson, Robert	75.00	170.00	225.00	
Anderson, S. R.	65.00	140.00	350.00	
Auger, Christopher C.	15.00	20.00	50.00	
Ayres, R. B.	15.00	35.00	45.00	
Babcock, Orville	5.00	10.00	20.00	
Badeau, Adam	15.00	20.00	25.00	
Bailey, Theodorus	30.00	70.00	85.00	
Baker, Alpheus	90.00	175.00	350.00	
Baker, Edward D.	10.00	17.50	25.00	
Banks, Nathaniel P.	25.00	45.00	72.50	
Barlow, Francis C.	15.00	25.00	50.00	
Beauregard, P. G. T.	65.00	275.00	400.00	375.00
Bee, Barnard E.	75.00	260.00	390.00	
Belknap, William W.	30.00	40.00	82.50	
Benjamin, Judah P.	115.00	350.00	785.00	
Benning, Henry Lewis	100.00	180.00	250.00	
Benteen, F. W.	175.00	450.00	530.00	
Birney, William	25.00	55.00	72.50	
Bliss, George, Jr.	5.00	10.00	20.00	
Bliss, J. S.	5.00	10.00	20.00	
Bliss, Zenas R.	20.00	30.00	45.00	
Bonham, M. L.	45.00	90.00	125.00	
Booth, John Wilkes	1,200.00	1,780.00	2,050.00	
Bowen, John S.	10.00	15.00	20.00	
Bragg, Braxton	175.00	285.00	325.00	900.00
Bragg, Edward S.	5.00	7.00	13.00	
Branch, Lawrence O.	142.50	295.00	375.00	
Breckinridge, William C.	60.00	125.00	171.67	
Brent, J. L.	75.00	100.00	150.00	
Brooke, John R.	20.00	30.00	35.00	
Brown, John	220.00	465.00	1,010.00	
Buckner, Simon B.	75.00	125.00	200.00	150.00
Buell, Don Carlos	25.00	40.00	47.50	120.00
Burns, William W.	25.00	40.00	45.00	135.00
Burnside, Ambrose E.	35.00	100.00	400.00	
Butler, Benjamin F.	25.00	60.00	111.25	

Name	Signature Only	Letter or Document Signed	Autograph Letter Signed	Signed Photograph
Butler, M. Calbraith	40.00	75.00	117.50	
Butterfield, Daniel	47.50	90.00	150.00	
Cadwalader, George	35.00	75.00	105.00	
Cameron, Simon	22.50	50.00	115.00	
Campbell, Charles Thomas	16.00	35.00	50.00	
Canby, Edward	38.33	110.00	175.00	
Casey, Silas	25.00	65.00	112.50	
Chamberlain, Joshua	17.50	40.00	50.00	
Clark, Charles	75.00	150.00	220.00	
Clingman, T. L.	30.00	50.00	60.00	
Cobb, Howell	50.00	88.00	184.00	
Colquitt, Alfred H.	50.00	105.00	150.00	
Connor, James	28.00	105.00	150.00	
Cooper, Samuel	70.00	150.00	213.00	
Corse, John M.	10.00	20.00	35.00	
Cosby, George B.	35.00	70.00	95.00	
Couch, Darius Nash	20.00	35.00	40.00	
Coulter, Richard	25.00	45.00	50.00	
Craig, James	20.00	40.00	55.00	
Crawford, Samuel W.	15.00	40.00	75.00	
Crook, George	45.00	80.00	143.00	400.00
Custer, Elizabeth	30.00	92.50	150.00	
Custer, George A.	1,650.00	2,700.50	5,650.00	
Dahlgren, John A.	40.00	110.00	150.00	
Davis, Charles Henry	10.00	20.00	25.00	
Davis, Jefferson	300.00	725.00	900.00	
Davis, Jefferson C.	35.00	60.00	75.00	
Davis, Nelson H.	15.00	20.00	30.00	
Davis, Varina	100.00	170.00	200.00	
Delafield, Richard	25.00	40.00	65.00	
Dibrell, G. G.	90.00	250.00	300.00	
Dix, Dorothea	75.00	185.00	225.00	
Dix, John Adams	30.00	70.00	165.00	125.00
Dodge, William G.	15.00	25.00	30.00	
Doubleday, Abner	125.00	215.00	250.00	
Dow, Neal	30.00	45.00	55.00	
Dribrell, George G.	95.00	250.00	300.00	
Drum, Richard C.	15.00	20.00	25.00	
Duke, Basil W.	15.00	50.00	120.00	
Early, Jubal	120.00	150.00	175.00	
Eaton, Amos B.	15.00	30.00	55.00	
Echols, John	45.00	110.00	195.00	
Ellsworth, Elmer			1,000.00	
Emory, W. H.	45.00	125.00	200.00	
Ericsson, John	45.00	80.00	158.33	
Evans, Lt. Col. D. M.	15.00	25.00	40.00	
Fairchild, Lucius	13.00	20.00	25.00	
Farragut, David	75.00	162.50	225.00	
Ferguson, S. W.	95.00	200.00	280.00	
Ferry, Orris S.	18.00	30.00	40.00	
Fessenden, Francis	15.00	30.00	35.00	
Finley, Jesse J.	20.00	40.00	50.00	

Union Gen. Robert Anderson

Theodorus Bailey

Maj. Gen. Zenas Bliss

Pierre Gustave Tounant Beauregard

Gen. D. C. Buell

Ambrose E. Burnside

Maj. Gen. Benjamin F. Butler

Maj. Gen. Howell Cobb, C.S.A.

General Samuel Cooper—Highest-Ranking Confederate Officer

Jefferson Davis

Lt. Gen. Jubal Early, C.S.A.

Maj. Gen. Abner Doubleday

John Charles Fremont

Maj. Gen. John White Geary, U.S.A.

Brig. Gen. Joseph Hawley, U.S.A.

Maj. Gen. Oliver Otis Howard, U.S.A.

Robert Edward Lee

General George McClellan

Maj. Gen. Philip Kearny

Maj. Gen. George Meade, U.S.A

Nelson Appleton Miles

Maj. John S. Mosby, C.S.A.—"The Gray Ghost"

Adm. David D. Porter

Gen. William S. Rosecrans

Gen. Philip Sheridan

Winfield Scott

Alfred H. Terry

Name	Signature Only	Letter or Document Signed	Autograph Letter Signed	Signed Photograph
Fisk, Clinton B.	15.00	25.00	50.00	
Floyd, John B.	65.00	150.00	250.00	450.00
Forrest, Nathan Bedford	262.50	550.00	1,420.00	
Foster, John Gray	20.00	32.00	55.00	
Franklin, William Buell	30.00	50.00	75.00	170.00
Fremont, Jessie B.	20.00	32.00	50.00	
Fremont, John C.	75.00	225.00	540.00	
French, Samuel Gibbs	130.00	250.00	315.00	
French, William H.	22.50	45.00	55.00	
Frost, D. M.	105.00	150.00	250.00	
Fry, James Barnet	25.00	36.00	70.00	
Gaines, Edmund P.	90.00	175.00	220.00	
Garnett, R. B.	55.00	130.00	200.00	
Geary, John W.	25.00	70.00	125.00	
Gillmore, Quincy A.	30.00	95.00	120.00	
Gordon, George H.	20.00	40.00	50.00	
Gordon, George W.	145.00	280.00	350.00	
Gordon, John Brown	35.00	60.00	125.00	
Gorgas, Josiah	105.00	200.00	250.00	
Granger, Gordon	35.00	70.00	85.00	
Green, Thomas	65.00	120.00	150.00	
Gregory, F. H.	15.00	30.00	40.00	
Grierson, Benjamin	75.00	145.00	185.00	
Grover, Cuvier	15.00	22.00	35.00	
Halleck, Henry W.	50.00	120.00	262.50	150.00
Hampton, Wade	100.00	150.00	233.33	
Hancock, Winfield S.	40.00	60.00	113.33	
Hardee, William J.	60.00	130.00	175.00	
Hardee, W. L.	55.00	100.00	150.00	
Hartranft, John F.	18.00	40.00	55.00	
Hartsuff, George L.	30.00	55.00	70.00	
Hartwell, Alfred S.	15.00	40.00	80.00	
Haswell, Charles H.	10.00	18.00	25.00	
Hatch, John Porter	15.00	30.00	45.00	
Hatton, Robert	125.00	265.00	365.00	
Hawley, Joseph R.	20.00	25.00	30.00	
Hawthorn, Alex T.	130.00	250.00	315.00	
Hayes, Joseph	50.00	95.00	125.00	150.00
Hazen, William Babcock	20.00	45.00	87.50	
Hebert, Paul O.	65.00	125.00	160.00	
Heintzelman, Samuel P.	25.00	55.00	70.00	
Herron, Francis J.	25.00	50.00	60.00	
Heth, Henry	75.00	160.00	200.00	
Higginson, Thomas W.	25.00	50.00	60.00	
Hill, D. H.	40.00	90.00	150.00	
Hilliard, Henry W.	20.00	45.00	60.00	
Hitchcock, Ethan Allen	25.00	45.00	55.00	
Hollins, George Nichols		450.00		
Hood, John Bell	65.00	225.00	365.00	225.00
Hooker, Joseph M.	75.00	120.00	150.00	
Howard, Oliver O.	25.00	75.00	185.00	150.00
Howe, Albion P.	15.00	30.00	40.00	

Gen. W. T. Sherman

George A. Trenholm—Secretary of the Confederate Treasury

Name	Signature Only	Letter or Document Signed	Autograph Letter Signed	Signed Photograph
Humes, William Y. C.	50.00	150.00	190.00	
Humphreys, A. A.	25.00	40.00	55.00	
Hunter, David	35.00	70.00	90.00	150.00
Hunter, R. M. T.	55.00	115.00	140.00	
Imboden, John Daniel	70.00	175.00	225.00	
Jackson, T. J. "Stonewall"	766.67	2,615.00	2,920.00	
Johnson, Bradley T.		130.00	200.00	
Johnston, Albert S.	75.00	150.00	210.00	435.00
Johnston, Joseph E.	80.00	165.00	225.00	
Jones, Edward F.	20.00	45.00	60.00	125.00
Jones, William E.	25.00	50.00	75.00	
Kane, Thomas L.	35.00	75.00	100.00	
Kearny, Philip	260.00	350.00	600.00	
Keifer, Joseph W.	15.00	25.00	45.00	
Kelly, John H.	355.00	750.00		
Keyes, Erasmus	40.00	75.00	125.00	
Kimberly, Lewis	10.00	20.00	22.75	
Lardner, James L.	25.00	55.00	75.00	
Lawton, A. R.	95.00	187.50	275.00	
Lee, Fitzhugh	71.67	150.00	466.67	
Lee, George Washington Custis	127.50	265.00	365.00	
Lee, Robert E.	600.00	2,000.00	3,100.00	2,000.00
Lee, Samuel P.	30.00	60.00	90.00	
Lee, William R.	10.00	25.00	35.00	
Lockwood, Capt. Charles W.	5.00	15.00	30.00	
Logan, John A.	28.33	180.00	250.00	
Lomax, L. L.	75.00	155.00	215.00	
Longstreet, James	92.50	185.00	300.00	
Loomis, Gustavus	20.00	45.00	95.00	
Loring, William Wing	75.00	150.00	230.00	
Lowe, Thaddeus S. C.	140.00	250.00	400.00	
Lubbock, Francis R.	85.00	175.00	245.00	
MacPherson, James B.	100.00	205.00	285.00	
Magruder, John B.	250.00	450.00		
Manning, Stephen H.	20.00	40.00	80.00	
Mansfield, Joseph K. F.	125.00	250.00	350.00	
Martin, W. S.	105.00	215.00	300.00	
Mason, James M.	30.00	60.00	80.00	
Maury, Dabney H.	75.00	155.00	215.00	1,000.00
Maxey, Samuel Bell	40.00	85.00	115.00	
McClellan, George B.	66.67	107.50	165.00	
McClernand, John A.	50.00	70.00	125.00	
McCook, Alexander, M. D.	8.00	20.00	25.00	

Name	Signature Only	Letter or Document Signed	Autograph Letter Signed	Signed Photograph
McCullock, Ben	110.00	225.00	315.00	
McLaws, Lafayette	70.00	145.00	212.50	
McQuade, James	8.00	14.00	25.00	
Meade, George Gordon	50.00	100.00	275.00	200.00
Meigs, Montgomery C.	20.00	75.00	150.00	250.00
Memminger, Christopher G.	25.00	75.00	138.00	
Miles, Nelson A.	36.67	125.00	160.00	
Miller, John F.	10.00	20.00	30.00	
Morgan, John Tyler	70.00	105.00	191.67	112.50
Morgan, Thomas Jefferson	25.00	50.00	75.00	
Mosby, John S.	113.00	212.50	450.00	
Mower, Joseph A.	25.00	48.33	75.00	
Newton, John	15.00	30.00	45.00	
Nichols, F. T.	40.00	75.00	115.00	
Ord, E. H. C.	20.00	50.00	205.00	
Paulding, Hiram	20.00	40.00	60.00	
Paxton, Elisha		750.00		
Pegram, John	112.50	210.00	275.00	
Pemberton, John C.	60.00	125.00	175.00	
Pettus, Edmund W.	50.00	90.00	265.00	
Phelps, John S.	15.00	35.00	45.00	
Pickett, G. E.	250.00	515.00	720.00	
Pierce, N. B.	30.00	60.00	90.00	
Pike, Albert	125.00	200.00	275.00	
Pillow, Gideon J.	115.00	240.00	352.50	
Polk, Leonidas	250.00	575.00	1,350.00	
Pope, John	75.00	90.00	113.33	350.00
Porter, David D.	45.00	106.07	225.00	
Porter, Fitz-John	25.00	65.00	112.50	
Porter, Horace	30.00	70.00	135.00	90.00
Preble, George H.	15.00	43.00	55.00	
Pryor, Roger Atkinson	50.00	110.00	250.00	
Randolph, George Wythe	170.00	350.00	490.00	
Reagan, John H.	75.00	175.00	215.00	
Reynolds, Joseph J.	15.00	35.00	45.00	
Rhett, R. Barnwell	100.00	205.00	290.00	
Ringgold, George H.	7.50	15.00	20.00	
Robinson, John C.	25.00	65.00	90.00	
Roddy, Philip Dale	55.00	115.00	160.00	
Roden, George	30.00	55.00	81.25	
Rodgers, John	65.00	130.00	180.00	
Rogers, William F.	5.00	10.00	15.00	
Rosecrans, W. S.	125.00	175.00	245.00	
Rosser, Thomas L.	90.00	185.00	260.00	
Rowan, Stephen C.	20.00	45.00	60.00	
Rucker, Daniel H.	20.00	45.00	60.00	120.00
Ruger, Thomas H.	20.00	35.00	50.00	
Ruggles, Daniel	50.00	130.00	170.00	
Rusling, James F.	10.00	20.00	25.00	
Rust, Albert	50.00	110.00	145.00	
Sanders, Horace T.	15.00	25.00	45.00	

Name	Signature Only	Letter or Document Signed	Autograph Letter Signed	Signed Photograph
Saxon, Rufus, Jr.	18.00	40.00	55.00	
Schenk, Robert C.	15.00	25.00	45.00	
Schofield, J. A.	45.00	95.00	130.00	
Schofield, John M.	17.00	49.00	85.00	
Schurz, Carl	26.67	35.00	98.58	
Scott, Winfield	56.67	166.67	300.00	
Selfridge, Thomas O.	35.00	70.00	100.00	
Semmes, Raphael	150.00	750.00		1,500.00
Shafter, William R.	20.00	40.00	75.00	40.00
Shaler, Alexander	25.00	45.00	75.00	
Sheridan, Philip H.	75.00	160.00	325.00	400.00
Sherman, William T.	53.33	100.00	239.44	200.00
Sibley, Henry H.	90.00	180.00	250.00	
Sickles, Daniel E.	25.00	58.00	115.00	150.00
Sigel, Franz	30.00	65.00	90.00	
Slidel, John	55.00	110.00	150.00	
Sloat, John Drake	35.00	70.00	100.00	
Slocum, Henry Warner	30.00	60.00	80.00	
Smith, E. Kirby	100.00	205.00	290.00	
Smith, G. W.	90.00	180.00	250.00	
Smith, William	55.00	137.50	175.00	
Sorrel, G. M.	170.00	350.00	483.33	
Stephens, Alexander Hamilton	100.00	240.00	595.00	
Stevenson, R. H.	10.00	17.50	30.00	
Stoneman, George	35.00	85.00	137.50	
Stuart, J. E. B.	850.00	1,428.67	2,000.00	
Sullivan, Peter	40.00	75.00	115.00	
Sully, Alfred	25.00	55.00	80.00	120.00
Swanson, J.	55.00	110.00	150.00	
Swayne, Wager	5.00	10.00	75.00	
Swift, Frederick W.	15.00	50.00	100.00	
Tappan, James C.	25.00	50.00	75.00	
Taylor, Richard	145.00	300.00	425.00	
Taylor, Thomas H.	7.50	15.00	25.00	
Terry, Alfred Howe	25.00	45.00	97.50	
Terry, Henry D.	20.00	55.00	90.00	
Terry, William Richard	55.00	110.00	150.00	
Thatcher, Henry Knox	40.00	75.00	115.00	
Thomas, George Henry	25.00	180.00	250.00	
Thomas, Lorenzo	18.00	40.00	55.00	
Thompson, M. Jeff	112.50	235.00	325.00	
Thruston, Gates P.	10.00	15.00	20.00	
Tidball, John C.	45.00	95.00	130.00	
Toombs, Robert	35.00	50.00	107.08	
Totten, Joseph G.	10.00	30.00	55.00	
Tower, Zealous B.	10.00	25.00	30.00	
Townsend, Edward D.	12.50	22.00	35.00	
Townsend, Frederick	10.00	15.00	20.00	
Trenholm, George A.	50.00	100.00	150.00	
Truxton, W. T.	20.00	45.00	60.00	
Turner, Ashby	100.00	265.00	350.00	
Tyndale, Hector	20.00	35.00	60.00	100.00

Name	Signature Only	Letter or Document Signed	Autograph Letter Signed	Signed Photograph
Vance, Robert B.	55.00	85.00	150.00	
Van Dorn, Earl	170.00	300.00	490.00	
Van Wyck, Charles Henry	20.00	45.00	60.00	
Viele, Egbert L.	15.00	25.00	35.00	70.00
Vincent, Thomas M.	20.00	35.00	60.00	
Wadsworth, James	40.00	85.00	115.00	
Walcutt, Charles C.	20.00	40.00	60.00	
Walker, Mary E.	100.00	175.00	385.00	
Wallace, Lew	21.25	165.00	200.00	
Ward, J. H. Hobart	10.00	20.00	35.00	
Warren, Gouverneur K.	25.00	50.00	70.00	
Washburn, C. C.	20.00	45.00	60.00	
Wayne, Henry C.	70.00	145.00	200.00	250.00
Webb, Alexander S.	15.00	30.00	40.00	
Weitzel, Godfrey	15.00	30.00	40.00	
Wheeler, Joseph	35.00	81.67	108.00	
Whipple, Amiel Weeks	10.00	20.00	25.00	
Whipple, William D.	10.00	15.00	17.50	
Wilcox, O. B.	20.00	60.00	125.00	
Wild, Edward A.	60.00	125.00	175.00	
Wilkes, Charles	35.00	75.00	100.00	
Williams, Seth	20.00	43.00	60.00	
Wilson, James H.	35.00	75.00	110.00	
Winder, J. H.	60.00	150.00	175.00	
Wise, Henry A.	45.00	110.00	126.67	
Woods, Charles Robert	20.00	35.00	60.00	
Wool, John E.	27.00	50.00	90.00	
Worden, John	35.00	75.00	100.00	
Wright, Henry C.	5.00	7.50	15.00	
Wright, Horatio G.	30.00	40.00	140.00	
Wright, Marcus J.	35.00	65.00	90.00	
Young, Henry E.	15.00	32.00	50.00	
Ziegler, George M.	5.00	10.00	15.00	30.00
Zollicoffer, Felix K.	60.00	200.00	250.00	

Composers

The following represents persons of note in the composing of music (yes, pun intended). If the name of a composer has been excluded, it means only that data on a philographic item of his or hers was not accessible at the time of publishing.

Name	Signature Only	Letter or Document Signed	Autograph Letter Signed	Signed Photograph
Addinsell, Richard	$ 5.00	$ 20.00	$ 50.00	$ 15.00
Adler, Richard	10.00	20.00	40.00	15.00
Allen, Peter	5.00	10.00	17.50	10.00
Anderson, Leroy	25.00	80.00	180.00	40.00
Anka, Paul	5.00	10.00	17.50	10.00
Arlen, Harold	30.00	35.00	50.00	35.00
Bach, Johann Sebastian	2,500.00	18,750.00	35,000.00	
Bacharach, Burt	12.50	22.50	35.00	25.00
Barber, Samuel	35.00	125.00	235.00	50.00
Bartok, Bela	200.00	500.00	825.00	550.00
Beethoven, Ludwig van	1,600.00	4,500.00	17,833.33	
Berg, Alban	135.00	485.00	1,425.00	
Berlin, Irving	108.75	274.29	695.00	275.00
Berlioz, Hector	105.00	375.00	960.00	
Bernstein, Elmer	5.00	20.00	40.00	15.00
Bernstein, Leonard	10.00	70.00	100.00	50.00
Bizet, Georges	200.00	775.00	1,750.00	
Blackwell, Otis	25.00	85.00	175.00	
Blake, Eubie	30.00	57.50	125.00	63.00
Bloch, Raymond	5.00	20.00	35.00	5.00
Bond, Carrie Jacobs	15.00	45.00	105.00	40.00
Borodin, Alexander	175.00	400.00	900.00	
Boulez, Pierre	10.00	35.00	70.00	16.00
Brahms, Johannes	475.00	950.00	1,675.00	
Britten, Benjamin	25.00	224.40	313.00	167.25
Bruch, Max	30.00	195.00	250.00	70.00
Bruckner, Anton	740.00	2,500.00	5,110.00	2,500.00
Cadman, Charles Wakefield	25.00	80.00	240.00	70.00
Caesar, Irving	16.25	45.00	70.00	35.00
Cage, John	10.00	30.00	43.25	
Cahn, Sammy	10.00	21.25	30.00	25.00
Carmichael, Hoagy	20.00	45.00	110.00	40.00
Casals, Pablo	70.00	90.00	150.00	125.00
Casella, Alfredo	30.00	100.00	200.00	
Chabrier, Emmanuel	60.00	205.00	415.00	
Chaminade, Cecile	25.00	40.00	67.50	
Chapin, Harry	47.50	90.00	180.00	30.00

Name	Signature Only	Letter or Document Signed	Autograph Letter Signed	Signed Photograph
Charpentier, Gustave	60.00	110.00	225.00	135.00
Chavez, Carlos	10.00	35.00	70.00	20.00
Cherubini, Luigi	150.00	285.00	550.00	
Chevalier, Albert	5.00	20.00	35.00	
Chopin, Frédéric	1,200.00	2,250.00	4,250.00	
Coates, Eric	21.50	45.00	75.00	50.00
Cohan, George M.	85.00	187.50	266.67	192.50
Coleridge-Taylor, Samuel	25.00	75.00	145.00	30.00
Comden, Betty	5.00	25.00	35.00	25.00
Conti, Bill	60.00	85.00	100.00	25.00
Coots, J. Fred	25.00	45.00	90.00	20.00
Copland, Aaron	34.00	100.00	175.00	52.50
Cross, Christopher	3.00	5.00	7.00	4.50
Czerny, Carl	40.00	135.00	275.00	
Damrosch, Walter	15.00	50.00	105.00	25.00
David, Hal	5.00	20.00	35.00	30.00
Debussy, Claude	340.00	635.00	960.00	
DeKoven, Reginald	15.00	35.00	50.00	25.00
Delibes, Leo	35.00	60.00	108.50	
Delius, Frederick	105.00	345.00	700.00	
Dello Joio, Norman	30.00	105.00	210.00	45.00
D'Indy, Vincent	20.00	65.00	135.00	105.00
Donizetti, Gaetano	400.00	700.00	1,300.00	
Dukas, Paul	30.00	100.00	283.33	
Dussek, Jan L.	20.00	65.00	125.00	
Dvorak, Antonin	365.00	825.00	1,450.00	
Elgar, Edward	85.00	255.00	504.00	525.00
Ellington, Duke	70.00	155.00	423.33	135.00
Elliott, Carter	40.00	125.00	280.00	
Emmett, Daniel D.	250.00	425.00	500.00	
Evans, Ray	15.00	30.00	45.00	40.00
Falla, Manuel de	45.00	225.00	300.00	65.00
Fauré, Gabriel	65.00	220.00	450.00	
Flotow, Frederich von	55.00	185.00	375.00	
Foster, Stephen	1,000.00	3,200.00	9,000.00	
Franck, Cesar	250.00	500.00	700.00	
Friml, Rudolf	82.50	106.67	216.67	150.00
German, Sir Edward	27.50	95.00	190.00	75.00
Gershwin, George	375.00	670.00	1,500.00	1,150.00
Gershwin, Ira	47.50	95.00	150.00	75.00
Gilbert, Sir William S.	130.00	283.33	400.00	325.00
Goosens, Eugene	10.00	35.00	70.00	15.00
Gordon, Mack	30.00	60.00	130.00	40.00
Gould, Morton	10.00	20.00	50.00	
Gounod, Charles	90.00	165.00	224.29	
Grainger, Percy	40.00	75.00	130.00	95.00
Green, Adolph	5.00	10.00	17.50	10.00
Green, John(ny)	10.00	20.00	80.00	20.00
Grieg, Edvard	250.00	340.00	676.00	525.00
Grofe, Ferde	50.00	70.00	175.00	60.00
Halevy, Jacques	40.00	70.00	122.00	
Hamlisch, Marvin	7.50	15.00	25.00	20.00

Irving Berlin

Hoagy Carmichael

Pablo Casals

Sammy Cahn

Aaron Copland

Ira Gershwin

Edvard Grieg

John Green

Moss Hart

Marvin Hamlisch

Sincerely,

Oscar Hammerstein

E. Y. "Yip" Harburg

Franz Liszt

Quincy Jones

Henry "Moon River" Mancini

Johnny Marks

Cole Porter

PHOTO:

Richard Rodgers

André Previn

Name	Signature Only	Letter or Document Signed	Autograph Letter Signed	Signed Photograph
Hammerstein, Oscar	55.00	175.00	325.00	100.00
Hancock, Herbie	8.00	15.00	45.00	15.00
Handel, George Frederick	800.00	5,800.00	21,000.00	
Handy, W. C.	150.00	263.33	400.00	300.00
Harburg, E. Y. "Yip"	30.00	137.50	210.00	45.00
Haydn, Joseph	650.00	3,675.00	19,833.33	
Hefti, Neal	5.00	20.00	30.00	15.00
Herbert, Victor	75.00	113.00	165.00	150.00
Herman, Jerry	5.00	10.00	20.00	15.00
Holst, Gustav	25.00	75.00	145.00	
Honnegger, Arthur	25.00	65.00	130.00	45.00
Hummel, Johann Nepomuk	50.00	175.00	350.00	
Humperdinck, Engelbert	45.00	110.00	225.00	200.00
Ives, Charles E.	200.00	462.50	825.00	375.00
Joachim, Joseph		75.00	137.50	140.00
Jones, Quincy	5.00	20.00	35.00	10.00
Joplin, Scott	650.00	980.00	2,000.00	
Kander, John	5.00	20.00	35.00	10.00
Kaper, Bronislaw	10.00	30.00	55.00	15.00
Karas, Anton	25.00	40.00	85.00	100.00
Kent, Walter	5.00	10.00	20.00	5.00
Kern, Jerome	117.50	225.00	375.00	250.00
Khchaturian, Aram	110.00	175.00	480.00	420.00
Kodaly, Zoltan	45.00	140.00	285.00	60.00
Korngold, Erich W.	30.00	100.00	200.00	45.00
Kreisler, Fritz	40.00	85.00	125.00	100.00
Legrand, Michel	4.00	10.00	15.00	12.50
Lehar, Franz	60.00	110.00	185.00	269.38
Leoncavallo, Ruggiero	120.00	265.00	320.00	375.00
Lerner, Alan Jay	15.00	40.00	85.00	50.00
Liszt, Franz	225.00	475.00	975.00	1,275.00
Livingston, Jay	15.00	30.00	45.00	40.00
Loewe, Frederick	15.00	40.00	85.00	50.00
MacDowell, Edward	125.00	250.00	380.00	400.00
Mahler, Gustav	500.00	1,465.50	2,183.33	2,000.00
Mancini, Henry	17.50	22.00	35.00	26.25
Marks, Johnny	30.00	40.00	55.00	45.00
Mascagni, Pietro	110.00	280.00	350.00	308.33
Massenet, Jules	40.00	65.00	150.00	295.00
Mendelssohn-Bartholdy, Felix	450.00	1,250.00	2,266.67	
Menotti, Gian Carlo	130.00	300.00	500.00	350.00
Mercer, Johnny	40.00	55.00	125.00	60.00
Meyerbeer, Giacomo	65.00	140.00	190.00	275.00
Milhaud, Darius	50.00	150.00	275.00	250.00
Mitropoulous, Dimitri	10.00	45.00	45.00	10.00
Mozart, Wolfgang A.	2,500.00	8,000.00	30,000.00	
Nevin, Ethelbert	30.00	45.00	110.00	40.00
Nielsen, Carl	100.00	200.00	300.00	
Offenbach, Jacques	115.00	195.00	263.33	275.00
Olcott, Chauncey	40.00	75.00	150.00	60.00
Paderewski, Ignace J.	65.00	140.00	300.00	265.00
Paganini, Nicolo	200.00	450.00	912.50	

Pete Seeger

Sir Arthur Sullivan (of Gilbert and Sullivan)

John Williams

Meredith Willson

Igor Stravinsky

Mason Williams

Paul Williams

Name	Signature Only	Letter or Document Signed	Autograph Letter Signed	Signed Photograph
Parsons, Albert Ross	5.00	10.00	15.00	5.00
Piston, Walter	35.00	110.00	245.00	50.00
Porter, Cole	135.00	235.00	300.00	475.00
Previn, André	10.00	25.00	35.00	20.00
Previn, Dorey	5.00	10.00	17.00	5.00
Prokofiev, Sergei	330.00	700.00	1,500.00	500.00
Puccini, Giacomo	250.00	500.00	902.78	1,175.00
Rachmaninoff, Sergei	150.00	220.00	550.00	398.00
Ravel, Maurice	350.00	625.00	1,135.00	
Respighi, Ottorino	45.00	155.00	312.50	
Rice, Tim	10.00	30.00	58.50	15.00
Richie, Lionel	10.00	20.00	35.00	40.00
Riegger, Wallingford	20.00	65.00	125.00	30.00
Rimsky-Korsakov, Nicolai	230.00	565.00	825.00	590.00
Rodgers, Richard	41.67	60.00	150.00	86.25
Romberg, Sigmund	115.00	160.00	295.00	185.00
Rome, Harold	10.00	30.00	70.00	15.00
Rose, David	10.00	15.00	25.00	10.00
Rossini, Gioachino	350.00	600.00	1,065.00	1,325.00
Rubinstein, Anton	60.00	185.00	425.00	405.00
Ruby, Harry	20.00	35.00	70.00	25.00
Sager, Carole Bayer	5.00	15.00	20.00	7.50
Saint-Saëns, Camille	80.00	170.00	273.00	225.00
Satie, Erik	210.00	825.00	1,500.00	
Scarlatti, Alessandro	725.00	4,150.00	11,000.00	
Scharwenka, Xaver	5.00	15.00	25.00	
Schifrin, Lalo	5.00	10.00	20.00	10.00
Schoenberg, Arnold	165.00	412.50	572.50	610.00

Name	Signature Only	Letter or Document Signed	Autograph Letter Signed	Signed Photograph
Schubert, Franz	1,800.00	5,400.00	9,100.00	
Schumann, Robert	420.00	950.00	2,500.00	
Scott, Cyril Meir	15.00	50.00	105.00	20.00
Scott, Raymond	5.00	15.00	20.00	10.00
Scriabin, Alexander	520.00	3,500.00	5,000.00	
Sedaka, Neil	5.00	20.00	35.00	10.00
Seeger, Pete	40.00	50.00	95.00	20.00
Sessions, Roger	10.00	15.00	22.00	15.00
Shostakovich, Dmitri	185.00	450.00	680.00	462.50
Sibelius, Jean	250.00	475.00	812.50	750.00
Siegmeister, Elie	25.00	85.00	175.00	40.00
Simon, Paul	3.00	5.00	10.00	12.00
Sinding, Christian	40.00	100.00	175.00	
Sondheim, Stephen	15.00	30.00	75.00	70.00
Sousa, John Philip	120.00	221.67	350.00	298.00
Sterling, Andrew B.	15.00	50.00	100.00	
Still, William Grant	60.00	125.00	225.00	165.00
Straus, Oscar	70.00	240.00	485.00	100.00
Strause, Charles	7.50	15.00	27.50	25.00
Strauss, Johann	250.00	420.00	675.00	
Strauss, Johann, Jr.	300.00	500.00	825.00	875.00
Strauss, Richard	158.75	360.00	687.50	540.00
Stravinsky, Igor	235.00	505.00	1,225.00	815.00
Styne, Julie	10.00	15.00	25.00	20.00
Sullivan, Sir Arthur	125.00	264.00	455.90	380.00
Suppe, Franz von	110.00	225.00	362.50	395.00
Tansman, Alexandre	40.00	125.00	280.00	
Taylor, Deems	12.00	30.00	55.00	50.00
Tchaikovsky, Pëtr I.	1,800.00	3,000.00	4,833.33	5,000.00
Thomas, Ambroise	65.00	90.00	195.00	
Thompson, Virgil	35.00	41.67	55.00	35.00
Tosti, Paolo	15.00	40.00	100.00	
Van Heusen, James	25.00	50.00	100.00	57.50
Vaughn-Williams, Ralph	55.00	195.00	375.00	80.00
Verdi, Giuseppe	625.00	1,250.00	2,150.00	1,875.00
Villa-Lobos, Heitor	75.00	225.00	525.00	110.00
Von Tilzer, Albert	30.00	90.00	200.00	45.00
Wagner, Richard	795.00	1,175.00	2,011.25	1,950.00
Warren, Harry	15.00	40.00	55.00	25.00
Weber, Karl Maria von	375.00	1,037.50	1,350.00	
Webster, Paul Francis	15.00	35.00	50.00	40.00
Weill, Kurt	200.00	450.00	825.00	375.00
Weingartner, Felix von	20.00	60.00	117.50	25.00
Williams, John	5.00	15.00	30.00	27.50
Williams, Mason	7.50	10.00	15.00	10.00
Williams, Paul	5.00	7.00	15.00	15.00
Willson, Meredith	10.00	45.00	70.00	35.00
Wood, Haydn	15.00	25.00	35.00	10.00

Country Music Stars

Just as country music has become more popular with the general public, so has the collecting of country music stars' autographs. There are some real values here, such as a signed photograph of the late Patsy Cline at $795.

Name	Signature	Signed Photograph
Acuff, Roy	$ 6	$ 18
Alabama (signed by all four)	35	75
Allan, Buddy	5	12
Anderson, Bill	4	12
Anderson, Les "Carrot-Top"	10	20
Anderson, Lynn	4	12
Arnold, Eddie	10	20
Ashworth, Ernie	10	20
Atkins, Chet	4	20
Austin, Bobby	10	20
Axton, Hoyt	4	12
Bee, Molly	6	20
Bird, Jerry	10	20
Bond, Johnny	10	20
Brown, Jim Ed	5	15
Butler, Carl and Pearl	15	30
Campbell, Archie	8	25
Carman, Tex J.	10	20
Carter, Helen	10	20
Carter, Mother Maybelle	40	80
Carter, Wilf	10	20
Cash, Johnny	8	20
Cash, June Carter	6	15
Cash, Tommy	5	10
Chaparral, John and Paul	20	40
Clark, "Cottonseed"	15	30
Clark, Roy	6	12
Cline, Patsy	350	795
Cooley, Spade	10	30
Copas, Cowboy	50	100
Cotton, Carolina	15	30
Coulter, Jessie	6	15
Craddock, Crash	5	12
Cramer, Floyd	5	12
Crystal Gayle	5	15
Curless, Dick	10	20
Curtis, Ken	6	15
Daniels, Charlie	6	20
Darrell, Johnny	10	20
Davis, Governor Jimmie	30	60
Davis, Mack	10	20

Name	Signature	Signed Photograph
Dean, Eddie	5	12
Dean, Jimmy	5	12
Dickens, Jimmy	5	10
Dillard, Herb, Dean, Rodney, and Merle	25	60
Douglas, Leon	10	20
Draper, Rusty	5	12
Dudley, Dave	6	15
Duncan, Johnny	10	20
Durham, Bobby	10	20
Erwin, Durward	10	20
Fargo, Donna	6	15
Flatt, Lester, and Earl Scruggs	50	125
Foley, Red	30	85
Ford, Tennessee Ernie	5	10
Fricke, Janie	2	8
Frizzell, Lefty	25	65
The Frontiersmen	25	50
Geezinslaw, Sam and Dewayne	15	30
Gentry, Bobbie	5	12
Glazer, Tom Paul	15	30
Guitar, Bonnie	20	40
Guthrie, Arlo	4	10
Haggard, Merle	6	18
Hall, Tom T.	5	12
Hamblen, Stewart	10	20
Homer and Jethro	30	125
The Homesteaders	25	50
Houston, David	5	10
Husky, Ferlin	5	10
Hutton, Gunilla	5	10
Inman, Jerry	10	20
Jackson, Wanda	10	20
James, Sonny	10	30
Jean, Norma	10	20
Jennings, Waylon	15	35
Jones, Anne	10	20
Jones, Anthony Armstrong	10	20
Jones, George	10	25
Jones, Grandpa	5	12
Kilgore, Merle	10	20
King, Pee Wee	5	12
Kirk, Eddie	10	20
Lee, Brenda	5	12
LeGarde, Tom and Ted	10	20
Lewis, Jerry Lee	15	40
Luse, Harley	10	20
Lynn, Loretta	6	15
Mandrell, Barbara	6	15
Maphis, Joe and Rose Lee	10	20
McDonald, Skeets	10	20
The McLains	25	50
Medley, Bill	6	20

Name	Signature	Signed Photograph
Miller, Roger	7	20
Montgomery, Melba	10	20
Morgan, George	25	75
Morrison, Harold	10	20
Mullican, Moon	10	20
Nelson, Willie	12	25
Nutter, Mayf	10	20
Orbison, Roy	20	40
Owens, Buck	5	15
Owens, Tex	10	20
Paduca, Duke of	20	40
Parton, Dolly	5	15
Paycheck, Johnny	8	25
Pearl, Minnie	5	12
Perkins, Carl	15	30
Perryman, Lloyd	10	20
Phillips, Bill	10	20
Pierce, Web	4	10
The Plainsmen	25	50
Powell, Max	10	20
Pride, Charley	5	12
Rainwater, Marvin	15	30
Ray, Susan	5	12
Red River Dave	10	20
Reynolds, Donn	10	20
Riddle, George	10	20
Riley, Jeannie C.	5	12
Ritter, Tex	75	150
Robbins, Marty	25	50
Roberts, Jack	10	20
Rogers, Marianne and Kenny	8	30
Ronstadt, Linda	15	40
Rose, Fred	30	60
Rose, Juanita	10	20
Rusk, Johnny	4	12
Seeley, Jeannie	10	20
Shannon, Del	6	20
Sledd, Patsy	4	12
Smiley, Delores	10	20
Smith, Carl	5	12
Smith, Connie	5	12
Snow, Hank	5	12
Sons of the Pioneers	100	300
Sooter, Rudy	10	20
Sovine, Red	12	35
Spenser, Tim	10	20
The Statlers	25	50
Stevens, Ray	5	12
Stewart, Wynn	10	20
Stoney Mountain Cloggers	30	60
Taylor, Mary	10	20
Thompson, Hank	6	15
Thompson, Orlo and Marvis	20	40
Thompson, Sue	10	25

Name	Signature	Signed Photograph
Tillis, Mel	5	12
Tillman, Floyd	10	20
Tillotson, Johnny	6	20
Tiny, Texas	10	20
Trask, Diana	10	20
Travis, Merle	20	40
Tubb, Ernest	12	35
Tubb, Justin	5	10
Tuttle, Wes and Marilyn	15	30
Twitty, Conway	7	25
Tyler, T. Texas	15	30
Van Dyke, Leroy	5	15
Wagner, Porter	5	12
Wakely, Jimmy	20	45
Wells, Kitty	5	15
West, Dottie	5	15
Whitley, Ray	10	35
Whitman, Slim	5	15
Williams, Hank	400	800
Williams, Hank, Jr.	6	20
Williams, Tex	10	20
Willing, Foy	10	20
Wills, Bob	75	200
Wooley, Sheb	5	15
Wright, Bobby	7	15
Wynette, Tammy	5	15
Yorgesson, Yogi	10	20
Young, Faron	5	12

Dynamic Duos and Other Groups

Lucy and Desi, Doc Blanchard and Glenn Davis, Martin and Lewis, the Honeymooners, Mickey Mantle and Roger Maris—these are only a few of the famous pairs and groups that make up an exciting subclass of autograph collecting.

Any baseball fan would love to have something signed by Babe Ruth, but to have an item signed by Ruth together with longtime teammate Lou Gehrig would be really exciting. For TV fans, a photo signed by Sally Struthers is nice, but one signed by her with her "All in the Family" costars—Jean Stapleton, Carroll O'Connor, and Rob Reiner—would be a lot nicer.

It can be argued that it isn't as exciting to have Sonny and not Cher; Laurel and not Hardy; Donny and not Marie; Farrah without Jaclyn and Kate. So here's a look at some combination signatures that could prove fun to add to your collection.

Lucy and Desi. The death in 1987 of Desi Arnaz does not end the more than 40-year name association of these two TV pioneers. Since the "I Love Lucy" series is as funny today as when it was first aired more than 30 years ago, the duo will forever be hailed as the stars they were. It is rare to find anything signed with a complete name by either one. Most items autographed by the two are signed *Lucy and Desi,* in each's hand. A card signed by the two would be in the area of $25; a photo, around $55.

Donny and Marie. These two Osmonds have both had success beyond that of their late-1970s TV show. Donny has had several hits as a rock-and-roll singer; Marie, several as a country star. Marie's has been the more difficult autograph to find. A card signed by the two should bring $15; a photo, $30.

Karen and Richard Carpenter. The Carpenters were the most popular pop singing duo of the 1970s. Karen's death as a young woman has made their autographs very valuable. A card signed by both is around $50; a photo starts at $100.

Charlie's Angels. A card signed by Farrah Fawcett, Kate Jackson, and Jaclyn Smith would be around $20, and a photo, $40. Adding Cheryl Ladd to the group would take the card to $25 and the photo to $50. The most difficult Angel to find has long been Shelley Hack. A trio of her, Cheryl Ladd, and Jaclyn Smith would see a card at around $25 and a photo at $45. The last Angel, Tanya Roberts, has been a relatively cooperative signer. Combining her with Cheryl and Jaclyn would put the prices at $15 and $35.

Richie and the Fonz. Ron Howard and Henry Winkler made these characters famous in "Happy Days." Both have been relatively easy autographs at times, but have become more difficult to obtain. A card signed by the two would be around $17; a photo, $35.

The Andy Griffith Show. A card signed by Andy Griffith, Ron Howard, and Don Knotts should go for $25, and a photo for $100.

Other Combinations

Note: The first price reflects that of a signature, the second, that of a signed photograph.

Television

The Avengers. Diana Rigg, Patrick McNee. $20.00, $50.00.

Batman. Adam West, Burt Ward, Yvonne Craig. $22.00, $50.00.

Beverly Hillbillies. Buddy Ebsen, Donna Douglas, Nancy Kulp. $20.00, $40.00.

Bonanza. Lorne Green, Dan Blocker, Michael Landon. $85.00, $250.00.

Cagney and Lacey. Sharon Gless, Tyne Daly. $12.00, $25.00.

Dukes of Hazzard. Catherine Bach, John Schneider, Tom Wopat, Denver Pyle. $25.00, $50.00.

The FBI. Efrem Zimbalist, Jr., Roger Moore, and Edd Barnes. $20.00, $50.00.

Gilligan's Island. Bob Denver, Tina Louise, Jim Backus, Dawn Wells, Natalie Schaefer, Russell Johnson. $30.00, $60.00.

The Honeymooners. Jackie Gleason, Art Carney, Joyce Randolph, and Audrey Meadows. $80.00, $150.00.

I Dream of Jeannie. Larry Hagman, Barbara Eden, Hayden Rourke, Bill Daily. $25.00, $55.00.

Laugh-In. Dan Rowan, Dick Martin. $18.00, $35.00.

Leave It to Beaver. Jerry Mathers, Tony Dow, Barbara Billingsley. $20.00, $40.00.

Lost in Space. Guy Williams, Angela Cartwright, June Lockhart, Bill Mumy. $40.00, $90.00.

Man from U.N.C.L.E. Robert Vaughan, David McCallum. $22.00, $50.00.

M*A*S*H. Alan Alda, Wayne Rogers, McLean Stevenson, Larry Linville, Loretta Switt, Gary Burghoff, Bill Christopher, Jamie Farr. $115.00, $250.00.

Moonlighting. Cybill Shepherd, Bruce Willis. $25.00, $60.00.

The Munsters. Fred Gwynne, Yvonne DeCarlo, Al Lewis. $30.00, $60.00.

Star Trek. William Shatner, Leonard Nimoy, DeForrest Kelly. $50.00, $100.00.

Movies

China Syndrome. Jane Fonda, Jack Lemmon, Michael Douglas. $25.00, $50.00.

Gone with the Wind. Olivia de Havilland, Butterfly McQueen, Rand Brooks, Cammie King. $40.00, $90.00.

Grease. John Travolta, Olivia Newton-John. $20.00, $40.00.

Prizzi's Honor. Jack Nicholson, Anjelica Huston, Kathleen Turner. $30.00, $60.00.

Psycho. Anthony Perkins, Janet Leigh. $20.00, $45.00.

"Road" Movies. Bob Hope, Dorothy Lamour. $16.00, $30.00.

Thin Man. William Powell, Myrna Loy. $30.00, $70.00.

Time After Time. Mary Steenburgen, Malcolm McDowell. $20.00, $40.00.

Other Movie Couples

Clint Eastwood and Sondra Locke. $20.00, $40.00
Jane and Henry Fonda. $30.00, $60.00
Dean Martin and Jerry Lewis. $15.00, $35.00
Ginger Rogers and Fred Astaire. $75.00, $150.00
Roy Rogers and Dale Evans. $15.00, $30.00
Jimmy Stewart and Marlene Dietrich. $25.00, $60.00

Sports

Henry Aaron and Ed Mathews. $15.00, $30.00
Doc Blanchard and Glenn Davis. $15.00, $30.00
Joe DiMaggio and Mickey Mantle. $25.00, $50.00
Frank Gifford, Don Meredith, and Howard Cosell. $20.00, $40.00
George Halas and Bronko Nagurski. $25.00, $60.00
Gordon Howe and Bobby Hull. $17.00, $35.00
Mickey Mantle and Roger Maris. $35.00, $75.00
Willie Mays and Duke Snider. $20.00, $40.00
John Unitas and Raymond Berry. $15.00, $30.00

Miscellaneous

Ernest and Julio Gallo. $15.00, $35.00
Dr. Albert Sabin and Dr. Jonas Salk. $30.00, $60.00
Bob Woodward and Carl Bernstein. $25.00, $50.00

These are just a few of the thousands of potential multiple-signed items. They are limited mainly to celebrities and noted achievers who are still alive and many of whom can be found for autographs. There are some exceptions to this, such as the "Bonanza" cast photo, from which both Lorne Greene and Dan Blocker are deceased. If more combinations of deceased persons were included, some of the outstanding items to look for would include anything signed by Abbott and Costello, Laurel and Hardy, Grace Kelly and Cary Grant, and so on.

In each case above, the items being priced were signatures on a 3 × 5 card or the equivalent, and on a black-and-white 8 × 10 photograph. An outstanding photograph, or one in color, would see the prices rise—smaller photos, of course, meaning lower prices.

Entertainers (Current)

The signed photographs of entertainers such as screen actors, television personalities, and so forth is a very popular category of collecting. There are so very many collectible people in this area that it is broken up into Current (generally, persons still alive) and Vintage (persons either deceased or whose fame derives from an earlier period). This section contains the prices for Current entertainers.

Unlike the situation for most other categories, the emphasis here and in the Vintage section is on signed photographs, with little pricing information on signatures and signed documents generally available. However, we have interpolated from whatever data was available to give you complete pricing here.

Name	Signature Only	Letter or Document Signed	Autograph Letter Signed	Signed Photograph
Abraham, F. Murray	$11.00	$ 21.00	$ 36.00	$ 27.00
Adams, Brooke	7.00	14.00	24.00	20.00
Adams, Don	5.00	11.00	18.00	15.00
Adams, Edie	2.00	4.00	6.00	5.00
Adams, Julie	3.00	6.00	10.00	8.00
Adams, Maude	6.00	19.00	32.00	20.00
Agutter, Jenny	4.00	7.00	12.00	10.00
Akins, Claude	2.00	4.00	7.00	6.00
Alberghetti, Anna Maria	2.00	4.00	6.00	5.00
Albert, Eddie	6.00	7.00	12.00	10.00
Albertson, Jack	12.00	18.00	30.00	25.00
Alda, Alan	10.00	18.00	30.00	25.00
Alda, Robert	5.00	11.00	18.00	15.00
Alexander, Jane	5.00	7.00	12.00	10.00
Alicia, Ana	4.00	7.00	12.00	10.00
Allen, Debbie	5.00	6.00	10.00	8.00
Allen, Karen	6.50	9.00	15.00	18.00
Allen, Marty	2.00	4.00	6.00	5.00
Allen, Rex	4.00	7.00	12.00	10.00
Allen, Steve	3.00	6.00	10.00	8.00
Allen, Woody	18.00	35.00	60.00	33.00
Ally, Kirstie	13.00	25.00	42.00	35.00
Allyn, Kirk	10.00	20.00	33.00	28.00
Allyson, June	4.00	7.00	12.00	10.00
Alpert, Herb	2.00	4.00	6.00	5.00
Alt, Carol	8.00	14.00	24.00	21.00
Altman, Robert	4.00	8.00	14.00	12.00

Ralph Bellamy

Ken Berry

Pat Boone

David Brinkley

David Frost

Sessue Hayakawa

Charles Kuralt

David Lean

Norman Lear

Gina Lollobrigida

Marlee Matlin

Brigitte Nielsen

Frank Sinatra

Ann Sothern

Barbara Walters

Name	Signature Only	Letter or Document Signed	Autograph Letter Signed	Signed Photograph
Alvarez, Roma	2.00	4.00	6.00	5.00
Ameche, Don	7.00	18.00	30.00	25.00
Anderson, Harry	4.00	7.00	12.00	10.00
Anderson, Judith	8.00	15.00	26.00	22.00
Anderson, Lonnie	7.00	13.00	22.00	18.00
Anderson, Richard	2.00	4.00	6.00	5.00
Andress, Ursula	5.00	11.00	18.00	15.00

Name	Signature Only	Letter or Document Signed	Autograph Letter Signed	Signed Photograph
Andrews, Dana	4.00	7.00	12.00	10.00
Andrews, Julie	7.00	14.00	24.00	20.00
Anka, Paul	2.00	4.00	6.00	5.00
Ann-Margaret	5.00	11.00	18.00	20.00
Ansara, Michael	5.00	10.00	17.00	14.00
Anton, Susan	2.00	4.00	6.00	5.00
Antonelli, Laura	14.00	27.00	46.00	39.00
Archer, Anne	5.00	11.00	18.00	15.00
Arden, Eve	4.00	7.00	12.00	10.00
Arkin, Alan	4.00	8.00	13.00	11.00
Arms, Russ	2.00	4.00	6.00	5.00
Arnaz, Desi	4.00	7.00	12.00	10.00
Arnaz, Lucie	5.00	7.00	12.00	10.00
Arness, James	4.00	7.00	12.00	10.00
Arngrim, Alison	5.00	6.00	10.00	8.00
Arquette, Rosanna	10.00	20.00	33.00	24.00
Arthur, Beatrice	10.00	11.00	18.00	15.00
Ashby, Hal	3.00	5.00	8.00	7.00
Ashcroft, Dame Peggie	7.00	14.00	24.00	20.00
Ashley, Elizabeth	5.00	9.00	15.00	13.00
Asner, Ed	2.00	4.00	6.00	5.00
Assante, Armand	5.00	11.00	18.00	20.00
Astin, John	2.00	4.00	6.00	5.00
Atkins, Christopher	5.00	11.00	18.00	15.00
Auberjonois, René	2.00	4.00	6.00	5.00
Austin, Karen	4.00	7.00	12.00	10.00
Autry, Gene	9.00	18.00	30.00	25.00
Avalon, Frankie	5.00	11.00	18.00	15.00
Avery, Margaret	2.00	4.00	6.00	5.00
Aykroyd, Dan	4.00	7.00	12.00	15.00
Ayres, Lew	6.00	9.00	15.00	14.00
Babcock, Barbara	3.00	6.00	10.00	8.00
Bacall, Lauren	7.00	8.00	14.00	18.00
Bach, Barbara	5.00	11.00	18.00	15.00
Bach, Catherine	5.00	10.00	17.00	16.00
Backus, Jim	4.00	7.00	12.00	10.00
Bacon, Kevin	7.00	14.00	24.00	22.00
Badler, Jane	7.00	11.00	18.00	20.00
Baer, John	4.00	7.00	12.00	10.00
Baez, Joan	3.00	6.00	10.00	8.00
Bailey, Pearl	2.00	4.00	6.00	5.00
Bain, Barbara	4.00	8.00	13.00	11.00
Baio, Scott	4.00	7.00	12.00	10.00
Baker, Blanche	2.00	4.00	6.00	5.00
Baker, Carroll	9.00	18.00	30.00	27.50
Baker, Dame Janet	2.00	4.00	6.00	5.00
Baker, Diane	2.00	4.00	6.00	5.00
Baldwin, Judy	2.00	4.00	6.00	5.00
Ball, Lucille	60.00	116.00	198.00	166.00
Ballard, Kaye	2.00	4.00	6.00	5.00
Balsam, Martin	7.00	14.00	24.00	20.00
Bancroft, Anne	5.00	11.00	18.00	15.00
Barbeau, Adrienne	5.00	11.00	18.00	15.00

Name	Signature Only	Letter or Document Signed	Autograph Letter Signed	Signed Photograph
Bardot, Brigitte	14.00	28.00	48.00	33.00
Barker, Bob	2.00	3.00	5.00	4.50
Barnes, Joanna	4.00	7.00	12.00	10.00
Barnes, Priscilla	6.00	11.00	19.00	18.00
Barr, Doug	2.00	4.00	6.00	5.00
Barrie, Barbara	2.00	4.00	6.00	5.00
Barry, Gene	2.00	4.00	6.00	5.00
Barrymore, Drew	4.00	7.00	12.00	10.00
Bartle, Joyce	4.00	7.00	12.00	10.00
Bartlett, Bonnie	4.00	7.00	12.00	10.00
Barty, Billy	3.00	5.00	8.00	7.00
Baryshnikov, Mikhail	32.50	63.00	107.00	90.00
Basinger, Kim	7.00	14.00	24.00	22.00
Bateman, Justine	9.00	18.00	30.00	25.00
Bauer, Jaime Lyn	5.00	7.00	12.00	13.00
Bauer, Steven	5.00	11.00	18.00	22.00
Baumer, Steven	9.00	18.00	30.00	25.00
Baxley, Barbara	3.00	4.00	6.00	5.00
Baxter, Keith	2.00	4.00	6.00	5.00
Baxter-Birney, Meredith	5.00	11.00	18.00	15.00
Beacham, Stephanie	4.00	7.00	12.00	10.00
Beals, Jennifer	13.00	25.00	42.00	35.00
Beatty, Warren	15.00	25.00	42.00	35.00
Beaty, Ned	2.00	4.00	6.00	5.00
Beck, John	2.00	4.00	6.00	5.00
Bedelia, Bonnie	2.00	4.00	6.00	5.00
Beery, Noah, Jr.	5.00	7.00	12.00	10.00
Begley, Ed, Jr.	3.00	6.00	11.00	12.00
Belafonte, Shari	4.00	8.00	14.00	15.00
Bellamy, Ralph	6.00	11.00	19.00	16.00
Beller, Kathleen	5.00	11.00	18.00	15.00
Bellwood, Pamela	5.00	11.00	18.00	15.00
Belushi, James	4.00	7.00	12.00	10.00
Benedict, Dirk	7.00	14.00	24.00	23.00
Bennett, Bruce	5.00	11.00	18.00	17.00
Bennett, Joan	5.00	11.00	18.00	16.00
Bennett, Julie	2.00	4.00	6.00	5.00
Bennett, Tony	3.00	6.00	10.00	8.00
Benson, Robbie	4.00	8.00	14.00	12.00
Benton, Barbi	4.00	8.00	13.00	11.00
Berenson, Marisa	7.00	14.00	24.00	20.00
Bergen, Candice	4.00	7.00	12.00	10.00
Bergen, Polly	5.00	7.00	12.00	10.00
Bergere, Lee	3.00	6.00	11.00	9.00
Bergman, Ingmar	15.00	21.00	36.00	30.00
Bergman, Sandahl	5.00	11.00	15.00	15.00
Berle, Milton	8.00	11.00	18.00	15.00
Berman, Shelley	2.00	4.00	6.00	5.00
Bernsen, Corbin	14.00	28.00	48.00	31.00
Bernstein, Leonard	15.00	29.00	50.00	42.00
Bertinelli, Valerie	5.00	11.00	18.00	15.00
Best, James	4.00	7.00	12.00	10.00
Beswick, Martine	4.00	7.00	12.00	10.00

Name	Signature Only	Letter or Document Signed	Autograph Letter Signed	Signed Photograph
Biehn, Michael	7.00	14.00	24.00	20.00
Bieri, Ramon	2.00	4.00	6.00	5.00
Billingsley, Barbara	2.00	4.00	6.00	5.00
Binns, Edward	3.00	4.00	6.00	5.00
Birney, David	4.00	8.00	14.00	12.00
Bishop, Joey	2.00	4.00	6.00	5.00
Bisset, Jacqueline	5.00	11.00	18.00	17.00
Bixby, Bill	2.00	4.00	6.00	13.00
Black, Karen	5.00	10.00	17.00	14.00
Blackman, Honor	5.00	11.00	18.00	18.50
Blackstone, Harry, Jr.	3.00	4.00	6.00	5.00
Blaine, Vivian	4.00	7.00	12.00	10.00
Blair, Frank	2.00	4.00	6.00	5.00
Blair, Linda	9.00	18.00	30.00	26.00
Blake, Robert	2.00	4.00	7.00	6.00
Blakely, Susan	5.00	11.00	18.00	15.00
Blanc, Mel	3.00	5.00	8.00	7.00
Blanks, Mary Lynn	2.00	4.00	6.00	5.00
Bloom, Claire	5.00	11.00	18.00	15.00
Bloom, Lindsay	6.00	11.00	18.00	15.00
Blyden, Larry	2.00	4.00	5.00	5.00
Blyth, Ann	4.00	7.00	12.00	11.00
Bochner, Lloyd	3.00	5.00	8.00	7.00
Bogdonavich, Peter	4.00	8.00	14.00	12.00
Bohay, Heidi	4.00	7.00	12.00	10.00
Bolling, Tiffany	2.00	4.00	6.00	10.00
Bonerz, Peter	2.00	4.00	6.00	5.00
Book, Sorrell	2.00	4.00	6.00	5.00
Boone, Pat	2.00	4.00	6.00	5.00
Booth, Shirley	5.00	11.00	18.00	18.00
Boothe, Powers	4.00	7.00	12.00	10.00
Boozer, Brenda	2.00	4.00	6.00	5.00
Borge, Victor	2.00	4.00	6.00	5.00
Borgnine, Ernest	1.00	3.00	5.00	4.00
Bosson, Barbara	3.00	5.00	8.00	7.00
Bostwick, Barry	5.00	11.00	18.00	15.00
Bottoms, Joseph	3.00	5.00	8.00	7.00
Bottoms, Sam	5.00	11.00	18.00	15.00
Bowden, Doris	2.00	4.00	6.00	5.00
Bower, Antoinette	2.00	4.00	7.00	6.00
Bowker, Judy	5.00	11.00	18.00	15.00
Boxleitner, Bruce	6.00	11.00	19.00	17.00
Boyle, Peter	5.00	11.00	18.00	15.00
Brady, Scott	2.00	4.00	6.00	5.00
Braga, Sonia	9.00	18.00	30.00	25.00
Brandauer, Klaus Maria	10.00	20.00	33.00	28.00
Brando, Marlon				125.00
Brazzi, Rossano	6.00	11.00	19.00	16.00
Brennan, Eileen	3.00	6.00	11.00	9.00
Brewer, Teresa	2.00	4.00	6.00	5.00
Bridges, Beau	4.00	7.00	12.00	10.00
Bridges, Jeff	4.00	8.00	14.00	12.00
Bridges, Lloyd	4.00	7.00	12.00	12.50

Name	Signature Only	Letter or Document Signed	Autograph Letter Signed	Signed Photograph
Brinegar, Paul	2.00	4.00	6.00	5.00
Brinkley, Christie	8.00	15.00	26.00	23.00
Brisebois, Danielle	2.00	4.00	6.00	5.00
Brittany, Morgan	9.00	18.00	30.00	25.00
Broccli, Cubby	2.00	4.00	6.00	5.00
Broderick, Matthew	7.00	14.00	24.00	18.00
Brodhead, James E.	4.00	7.00	12.00	10.00
Brolin, James	10.00	13.00	21.00	18.00
Bromfield, John	2.00	4.00	6.00	5.00
Bronson, Charles	8.00	15.00	26.00	22.00
Brooks, Foster	4.00	7.00	12.00	10.00
Brooks, Mel	2.00	4.00	6.00	5.00
Brooks, Randi	5.00	10.00	17.00	14.00
Brophy, Kevin	2.00	5.00	8.00	6.50
Brosnan, Pierce	5.00	11.00	18.00	15.00
Brough, Candi and Randi	2.00	4.00	6.00	5.00
Brown, Blair	5.00	10.00	17.00	14.00
Browne, Coral	3.00	5.00	8.00	7.00
Browne, Leslie	4.00	7.00	12.00	10.00
Brubeck, Dave	2.00	4.00	6.00	5.00
Bry, Ellen	2.00	4.00	6.00	5.00
Bryant, Anita	4.00	7.00	12.00	10.00
Budd, Julie	2.00	4.00	6.00	5.00
Bujold, Geneviève	5.00	11.00	18.00	15.00
Bumbry, Grace	2.00	4.00	6.00	5.00
Burke, Delta	8.00	14.00	24.00	22.00
Burke, Paul	4.00	7.00	12.00	10.00
Burnett, Carol	4.00	7.00	12.00	15.00
Burns, George	7.00	13.00	21.00	19.00
Burr, Raymond	7.00	14.00	24.00	20.00
Burstyn, Ellen	5.00	7.00	12.00	10.00
Burton, LeVar	5.00	11.00	18.00	15.00
Busey, Gary	5.00	11.00	18.00	15.00
Butler, Daws	2.00	4.00	7.00	6.00
Buttons, Red	2.00	4.00	6.00	5.00
Buzzi, Ruth	2.00	4.00	6.00	5.00
Byner, John	2.00	4.00	7.00	6.00
Caan, James	5.00	11.00	18.00	15.00
Caesar, Sid	4.00	7.00	12.00	10.00
Cage, Nicholas	9.00	18.00	30.00	25.00
Caine, Michael	8.00	15.00	26.00	22.00
Caldwell, Zoe	4.00	7.00	12.00	10.00
Calhoun, Rory	2.00	4.00	6.00	5.25
Callas, Charlie	2.00	4.00	6.00	5.00
Calloway, Cab	30.00	35.00	60.00	50.00
Calvet, Corinne	7.00	13.00	21.00	18.50
Camp, Colleen	7.00	13.00	23.00	19.00
Campanella, Joseph	2.00	4.00	6.00	5.00
Campbell, Glen	4.00	7.00	12.00	10.00
Candy, John	3.00	6.00	10.00	12.00
Cannon, Dyan	5.00	11.00	18.00	15.00
Canova, Diana	2.00	4.00	6.00	5.00
Cantrell, Lana	2.00	4.00	6.00	5.00
Capers, Virginia	2.00	4.00	6.00	5.00

Name	Signature Only	Letter or Document Signed	Autograph Letter Signed	Signed Photograph
Capka, Carol	2.00	4.00	6.00	5.00
Capra, Frank	5.00	14.00	24.00	20.00
Capshaw, Kate	5.00	11.00	18.00	15.00
Captain and Tennile	4.00	8.00	14.00	12.00
Capucine	4.00	7.00	12.00	10.00
Carey, Harry, Jr.	5.00	11.00	18.00	15.00
Carey, Macdonald	2.00	4.00	6.00	5.00
Carey, Michele	4.00	14.00	24.00	20.00
Carey, Ron	4.00	7.00	12.00	10.00
Carlin, George	3.00	5.00	8.00	7.00
Carlin, Lynn	2.00	4.00	6.00	5.00
Carlisle, Kitty	3.00	5.00	9.00	7.50
Carne, Judy	5.00	11.00	18.00	15.00
Carney, Art	4.00	7.00	12.00	10.00
Caron, Leslie	10.00	20.00	35.00	24.00
Carpenter, Richard	3.00	6.00	10.00	8.00
Carr, Darleen	2.00	4.00	6.00	5.00
Carr, Vicki	2.00	4.00	6.00	5.00
Carradine, Keith	5.00	7.00	12.00	10.00
Carrera, Barbara	5.00	11.00	18.00	15.00
Carroll, Diahann	5.00	11.00	18.00	15.00
Carroll, Lisa Hart	5.00	11.00	18.00	15.00
Carson, Johnny	9.00	14.00	24.00	20.00
Carter, Lynda	5.00	10.00	17.00	14.00
Carter, Tony	3.00	6.00	11.00	9.00
Cartwright, Angela	4.00	7.00	12.00	10.00
Cash, Rosanne	4.00	7.00	12.00	10.00
Cassavetes, John	5.00	7.00	12.00	10.00
Cassidy, Joanna	4.00	7.00	12.00	10.00
Castle, Peggy	2.00	4.00	6.00	5.00
Cates, Phoebe	5.00	11.00	18.00	19.00
Chakiris, George	8.00	14.00	24.00	20.00
Chamberlain, Richard	10.00	14.00	24.00	22.00
Chambers, Marilyn	9.00	18.00	30.00	25.00
Champion, Marge	3.00	5.00	9.00	7.50
Chandler, George	2.00	4.00	6.00	5.00
Channing, Carol	3.00	6.00	11.00	9.00
Channing, Stockard	3.00	5.00	8.00	7.00
Chaplin, Geraldine	9.00	18.00	30.00	25.00
Charisse, Cyd	4.00	7.00	12.00	12.00
Charles, Ray	9.00	18.00	30.00	25.00
Charles, Suzette	4.00	7.00	12.00	10.00
Charo	2.00	4.00	6.00	5.00
Chase, Chevy	4.00	7.00	12.00	10.00
Chayefski, Paddy	5.00	7.00	12.00	10.00
Checkers, Chubby	14.00	28.00	48.00	40.00
Cher	9.00	18.00	30.00	25.00
Chiles, Lois	4.00	7.00	12.00	10.00
Chong, Rae Dawn	5.00	11.00	18.00	15.00
Christie, Julie	9.00	14.00	24.00	20.00
Christine, Virginia	3.00	6.00	10.00	8.00
Christopher, Dennis	2.00	4.00	6.00	5.00
Christopher, William	4.00	7.00	12.00	10.00

Name	Signature Only	Letter or Document Signed	Autograph Letter Signed	Signed Photograph
Cimino, Michael	5.00	11.00	18.00	15.00
Clanton, Jimmy	2.00	4.00	6.00	5.00
Clark, Candy	2.00	4.00	6.00	5.00
Clark, Dick	5.00	11.00	18.00	15.00
Clark, Petula	2.00	4.00	6.00	5.00
Clark, Susan	8.00	7.00	12.00	10.00
Clary, Robert	3.00	5.00	8.00	7.00
Clayburgh, Jill	4.00	7.00	12.00	13.00
Cleese, John	4.00	8.00	14.00	12.00
Cliburn, Van	18.00	35.00	60.00	50.00
Clooney, Rosemary	4.00	8.00	14.00	12.00
Close, Glenn	7.00	14.00	24.00	20.00
Coburn, James	8.00	15.00	26.00	23.50
Coker, Jack	5.00	10.00	17.00	14.00
Colbert, Claudette	14.00	27.00	46.00	35.50
Cole, Michael	2.00	4.00	6.00	5.00
Coleman, Dabney	4.00	7.00	15.00	10.00
Coleman, Gary	7.00	14.00	24.00	20.00
Collins, Joan	10.00	20.00	33.00	26.00
Collins, Judy	4.00	7.00	12.00	10.00
Como, Perry	2.00	4.00	6.00	5.00
Conforti, Gino	2.00	4.00	6.00	5.00
Conley, Joe	2.00	4.00	6.00	5.00
Connery, Sean	13.00	25.00	42.00	33.00
Conniff, Ray	4.00	7.00	12.00	10.00
Connors, Chuck	3.00	6.00	11.00	9.00
Connors, Mike	2.00	4.00	6.00	5.00
Connors, Patti	2.00	4.00	6.00	5.00
Conrad, William	4.00	7.00	12.00	10.00
Conroy, Kevin	2.00	4.00	6.00	5.00
Conte, Richard	2.00	4.00	6.00	5.00
Conway, Tim	4.00	8.00	14.00	12.00
Cook, Elisha, Jr.	7.00	14.00	24.00	20.00
Cooper, Alice	10.00	11.00	18.00	15.00
Cooper, Jackie	4.00	7.00	12.00	19.00
Copperfield, David	5.00	11.00	18.00	17.00
Coppola, Francis	5.00	10.00	17.00	14.00
Cornell, Lydia	2.00	4.00	6.00	5.00
Cosby, Bill	7.00	14.00	24.00	20.00
Cotten, Joseph	5.00	11.00	18.00	21.00
Craig, Yvonne	2.00	4.00	6.00	10.00
Crain, Jeanne	13.00	25.00	42.00	35.00
Cramer, Grant	5.00	11.00	18.00	15.00
Crawford, Johnny	3.00	6.00	10.00	8.00
Crawford, Michael	10.00	20.00	35.00	29.00
Crenna, Richard	4.00	8.00	14.00	12.00
Cristal, Linda	10.00	11.00	19.00	16.00
Cronyn, Hume	8.00	15.00	25.00	21.00
Crosby, Gary	2.00	4.00	6.00	5.00
Crosby, Kathryn	8.00	15.00	25.00	21.00
Crosby, Kathy Lee	7.00	14.00	24.00	20.00
Crosby, Mary	2.00	4.00	6.00	5.00
Crosby, Norm	4.00	8.00	13.00	11.00

Name	Signature Only	Letter or Document Signed	Autograph Letter Signed	Signed Photograph
Crothers, Scat Man	4.00	8.00	14.00	12.00
Crouse, Lindsay	10.00	18.00	30.00	25.00
Crowley, Pat				10.00
Cruise, Tom	16.00	31.00	52.00	44.00
Culp, Robert	7.00	14.00	24.00	20.00
Curtis, Jamie Lee	7.00	14.00	24.00	20.00
Curtis, Ken	7.00	13.00	21.00	18.00
Curtis, Robin	5.00	10.00	17.00	14.00
Curtis, Tony	6.00	11.00	19.00	16.00
Cushing, Peter	12.00	23.00	39.00	33.00
Dahl, Arlene	4.00	8.00	13.00	11.00
Dalton, Abby	4.00	7.00	12.00	10.00
Daly, James	4.00	7.00	12.00	10.00
Daly, John				5.00
Daly, Tyne	7.00	14.00	24.00	20.00
Damon, Cathryn	4.00	7.00	12.00	10.00
Dangerfield, Rodney	8.00	15.00	25.00	21.00
Danner, Blythe	4.00	7.00	12.00	10.00
Dannihill, Albert	2.00	4.00	6.00	5.00
Danning, Sybil	7.00	14.00	24.00	20.00
Dano, Royal	7.00	13.00	21.00	18.00
Danova, Cesare	5.00	10.00	17.00	14.00
Danson, Ted	8.00	15.00	26.00	22.00
Danza, Tony	9.00	18.00	30.00	25.00
Daval, Danny	4.00	7.00	12.00	10.00
Davidson, John	2.00	4.00	6.00	5.00
Davis, Bette	11.00	21.00	36.00	30.00
Davis, Brad	8.00	15.00	26.00	21.50
Davis, Clifton	2.00	4.00	6.00	5.00
Davis, Geena	8.00	15.00	26.00	22.00
Davis, Nancy (as Actress)				75.00
Davis, Patti	4.00	7.00	12.00	10.00
Davis, Phyllis	2.00	4.00	6.00	5.00
Davis, Sammy, Jr.	7.00	13.00	23.00	19.00
Dawber, Pam	7.00	13.00	21.00	18.00
Day, Dennis	2.00	4.00	6.00	5.00
Day, Doris	5.00	10.00	17.00	14.00
Day, Linda (George)	5.00	11.00	18.00	15.00
DeCarlo, Yvonne	6.00	11.00	19.00	16.00
DeCordova, Fred	4.00	7.00	12.00	10.00
Dee, Francis	4.00	7.00	12.00	10.00
Dee, Ruby	4.00	8.00	14.00	12.00
Dee, Sandra	5.00	11.00	18.00	15.00
Deering, Olive	3.00	6.00	10.00	8.00
DeHaven, Gloria	5.00	9.00	15.00	13.00
DeHavilland, Olivia	10.00	17.00	29.00	24.00
Dehner, John	3.00	5.00	8.00	7.00
DeLaCroix, Raven	2.00	4.00	6.00	5.00
Delaney, Kim	2.00	4.00	6.00	5.00
DeLaPena, George	2.00	4.00	6.00	5.00
Dell, Gabriel	7.00	14.00	24.00	20.00
DeLorean, Cristina	4.00	7.00	12.00	10.00
DeLuise, Dom	4.00	7.00	12.00	10.00

Name	Signature Only	Letter or Document Signed	Autograph Letter Signed	Signed Photograph
DeMornay, Rebecca	9.00	17.00	29.00	24.00
Deneuve, Catherine	8.00	15.00	26.00	22.00
DeNiro, Robert	7.00	14.00	24.00	20.00
Dennehy, Brian	5.00	11.00	18.00	15.00
Dennis, Sandy	9.00	18.00	30.00	25.00
Dennison, Jo Carroll	4.00	7.00	12.00	10.00
Denver, Bob	2.00	4.00	6.00	5.00
Denver, John	4.00	8.00	13.00	11.00
Derek, Bo	8.00	16.00	27.00	23.00
Derek, John	5.00	11.00	18.00	15.00
Dern, Bruce	5.00	11.00	18.00	15.00
Deutsch, Patti	2.00	4.00	6.00	5.00
DeVane, William	3.00	6.00	11.00	9.00
DeVito, Danny	6.00	12.00	20.00	17.00
DeWitt, Joyce	2.00	4.00	6.00	5.00
Dey, Susan	7.00	14.00	24.00	20.00
Diamond, Neil	4.00	7.00	12.00	10.00
Dickinson, Angie	5.00	9.00	15.00	12.50
Dietrich, Marlene	11.00	21.00	36.00	30.00
Diller, Phyllis	6.00	12.00	20.00	17.00
Dillman, Bradford	6.00	7.00	12.00	10.00
Dillon, Matt	12.00	24.00	40.00	34.00
Dixon, Donna	7.00	14.00	24.00	20.00
Dobson, Kevin	4.00	7.00	12.00	10.00
Dodge, Jerry	2.00	4.00	6.00	5.00
Dodson, Jack	5.00	10.00	17.00	14.00
Domingo, Placido	11.00	21.00	36.00	30.00
Domino, Fats	9.00	18.00	30.00	25.00
Donahue, Elinor	4.00	7.00	12.00	10.00
Donahue, Troy	4.00	7.00	12.00	10.00
Donat, Peter	4.00	7.00	12.00	10.00
Donnell, Jeff	4.00	7.00	12.00	10.00
Donnelly, Ruth	4.00	8.00	13.00	11.00
Doohan, James "Scotty"	5.00	10.00	17.00	14.00
Dooley, Paul	4.00	8.00	14.00	12.00
Doran, Ann	2.00	4.00	6.00	5.00
Doucette, John	5.00	9.00	15.00	13.00
Douglas, Donna	5.00	11.00	18.00	15.00
Douglas, Kirk	5.00	11.00	18.00	15.00
Douglas, Michael	7.00	14.00	24.00	20.00
Douglas, Mike	3.00	5.00	8.00	7.00
Douglass, Robyn	3.00	6.00	10.00	8.00
Dow, Tony	3.00	5.00	8.00	7.00
Down, Lesley-Anne	4.00	7.00	12.00	10.00
Downing, "Big" Al	2.00	4.00	6.00	5.00
Downs, Hugh	4.00	7.00	12.00	10.00
Dreyfus, Richard	8.00	15.00	25.00	21.00
Duchin, Peter	4.00	7.00	12.00	10.00
Duff, Howard	4.00	8.00	13.00	11.00
Duffy, Julia	7.00	14.00	24.00	20.00
Duggan, Andrew	5.00	11.00	18.00	15.00
Duke, Patty (Astin)	6.00	11.00	19.00	16.00
Dullea, Keir	6.00	12.00	20.00	17.00

Name	Signature Only	Letter or Document Signed	Autograph Letter Signed	Signed Photograph
Dunaway, Faye	9.00	18.00	30.00	25.00
Duncan, Sandy	3.00	7.00	12.00	10.00
Dunne, Irene	10.00	20.00	33.00	28.00
Durning, Charles	4.00	7.00	12.00	10.00
Dussault, Nancy	2.00	4.00	6.00	5.00
Duvall, Robert	8.00	16.00	27.00	23.00
Duvall, Shelley	5.00	10.00	15.00	14.00
Dysart, Richard	8.00	10.00	17.00	14.00
Eastwood, Clint	9.00	18.00	30.00	25.00
Eberly, Bob	2.00	4.00	6.00	5.00
Ebsen, Buddy	4.00	11.00	18.00	15.00
Eden, Barbara	9.00	18.00	30.00	25.00
Edwards, Anthony	7.00	14.00	24.00	20.00
Edwards, Blake	4.00	7.00	12.00	10.00
Edwards, Douglas	2.00	4.00	6.00	5.00
Edwards, Gail J.	4.00	7.00	12.00	10.00
Edwards, Ralph	3.00	5.00	8.00	7.00
Eggar, Samantha	5.00	11.00	18.00	15.00
Eisenman, Robin G.	3.00	6.00	11.00	9.00
Ekberg, Anita	5.00	9.00	15.00	13.00
Ekland, Britt	5.00	11.00	18.00	15.00
Elam, Jack	4.00	8.00	14.00	12.00
Elliott, Bob	2.00	4.00	6.00	5.00
Elliott, Sam	7.00	13.00	21.00	18.00
Elman, Mischa	10.00	20.00	33.00	28.00
Elvira	6.00	11.00	19.00	16.00
Ely, Ron	4.00	7.00	12.00	10.00
Engel, Georgia	4.00	8.00	14.00	12.00
Enriquez, Rene	4.00	8.00	14.00	12.00
Erickson, Leif	5.00	10.00	17.00	14.00
Estevez, Emilio	8.00	16.00	27.00	23.00
Estrada, Erik	3.00	5.00	8.00	7.00
Eubanks, Bob	3.00	6.00	11.00	9.00
Evans, Dale	4.00	11.00	18.00	15.00
Evans, Gene	4.00	7.00	12.00	10.00
Evans, Linda	7.00	13.00	23.00	19.00
Everett, Chad	4.00	7.00	12.00	10.00
Evigan, Greg	2.00	4.00	6.00	5.00
Ewell, Tom	5.00	11.00	18.00	15.00
Fabares, Shelley	8.00	15.00	26.00	22.00
Fabray, Nanette	4.00	7.00	12.00	10.00
Fairbanks, Douglas, Jr.	4.00	8.00	13.00	11.00
Fairchild, Morgan	9.00	17.00	20.00	23.75
Falk, Peter	4.00	7.00	12.00	10.00
Falkenburg, Jinx	4.00	7.00	12.00	10.00
Farnsworth, Richard	6.00	11.00	19.00	16.00
Farr, Jamie	5.00	8.00	14.00	12.00
Farrell, Mike	4.00	7.00	12.00	10.00
Farrow, Mia	8.00	15.00	25.00	21.00
Fawcett, Farrah	7.00	14.00	24.00	20.00
Faye, Alice	5.00	7.00	12.00	10.00
Feldon, Barbara	4.00	7.00	12.00	10.00
Feldshuh, Tovah	4.00	8.00	13.00	11.00

Name	Signature Only	Letter or Document Signed	Autograph Letter Signed	Signed Photograph
Feliciano, José	4.00	8.00	13.00	11.00
Fellini, Frederico	15.00	20.00	33.00	28.00
Fenneman, George	2.00	4.00	6.00	5.00
Ferrare, Cristina	5.00	10.00	16.25	14.00
Ferrer, José	8.00	15.00	26.00	22.00
Ferrigno, Lou	5.00	9.00	15.00	13.00
Fetchit, Stepin	9.00	18.00	30.00	25.00
Fiedler, John	2.00	4.00	6.00	5.00
Field, Sally	9.00	17.00	29.00	24.00
Finlay, Frank	4.00	7.00	12.00	10.00
Finney, Albert	7.00	13.00	23.00	19.00
Fisher, Carrie	7.00	13.00	23.00	19.00
Fisher, Cindy	4.00	7.00	12.00	10.00
Fisher, Eddie	7.00	14.00	24.00	20.00
Fitzgerald, Ella	20.00	39.00	65.00	55.00
Fitzgerald, Geraldine	5.00	11.00	18.00	15.00
Fix, Paul	4.00	7.00	12.00	10.00
Flagg, Fannie	2.00	4.00	6.00	5.00
Flavin, James	3.00	6.00	10.00	8.00
Fleischer, Richard	3.00	6.00	10.00	8.00
Fleming, Rhonda	5.00	9.00	15.00	12.50
Fletcher, Louise	5.00	11.00	18.00	15.00
Flowers, Wayland	4.00	8.00	14.00	12.00
Flynn, James	3.00	5.00	8.00	7.00
Foch, Nina	2.00	4.00	7.00	6.00
Fonda, Jane	5.00	12.00	20.00	17.00
Fonda, Peter	5.00	11.00	18.00	15.00
Fontaine, Joan	5.00	12.00	21.00	17.50
Fonteyn, Margot	30.00	58.00	99.00	83.00
Ford, Glenn	8.00	15.00	25.00	21.00
Ford, Harrison	13.00	25.00	42.00	35.00
Ford, Tennessee Ernie	2.00	4.00	6.00	5.00
Forslund, Constance	4.00	8.00	13.00	11.00
Forsythe, John	7.00	13.00	21.00	18.00
Fosse, Bob	5.00	11.00	18.00	15.00
Foster, Jodie	9.00	14.00	24.00	20.00
Fountain, Pete	5.00	10.00	17.00	14.00
Fox, Michael J.	9.00	18.00	30.00	25.00
Foxworth, Robert	3.00	6.00	11.00	9.00
Foxx, Redd	4.00	8.00	14.00	12.00
Frakes, Jonathan	6.00	12.00	20.00	17.00
Franchi, Sergio	2.00	4.00	6.00	10.00
Franciosa, Anthony	3.00	6.00	10.00	8.00
Francis, Anne	4.00	8.00	13.00	11.00
Francis, Connie	2.00	4.00	6.00	5.00
Francis, Genie	4.00	8.00	14.00	12.00
Franciscus, James	3.00	5.00	8.00	7.00
Franklin, Bonnie	3.00	6.00	11.00	9.00
Frann, Mary	4.00	7.00	12.00	10.00
Freed, Bert	4.00	7.00	12.00	10.00
Freeman, Mona	5.00	10.00	17.00	14.00
Freleng, Friz	11.00	14.00	24.00	20.00
French, Victor	4.00	7.00	12.00	10.00
Fuller, Robert	3.00	5.00	8.00	7.00

Name	Signature Only	Letter or Document Signed	Autograph Letter Signed	Signed Photograph
Funicello, Annette	4.00	8.00	14.00	12.00
Gabet, Sharon	4.00	7.00	12.00	10.00
Gabor, Zsa Zsa	4.00	8.00	14.00	12.00
Gail, Max	2.00	4.00	7.00	6.00
Gardenia, Vince	3.00	6.00	10.00	8.00
Gardner, Ava	8.00	16.00	27.00	23.00
Garner, James	4.00	7.00	12.00	10.00
Garr, Terri	8.00	16.00	27.00	23.00
Garrett, Betty	4.00	7.00	12.00	10.00
Garson, Greer	7.00	13.00	23.00	19.00
Gatlin Brothers	5.00	11.00	18.00	15.00
Gaynor, Mitzi	5.00	9.00	15.00	13.00
Geary, Anthony "Tony"	5.00	7.00	12.00	10.00
Geer, Ellen	3.00	5.00	8.00	7.00
George, Phyllis	3.00	6.00	11.00	9.00
George, Susan	5.00	9.00	15.00	13.00
Gerard, Gil	7.00	13.00	21.00	18.00
Gere, Richard	13.00	25.00	42.00	35.00
Ghostley, Alice	2.00	4.00	6.00	5.00
Gibb, Cynthia	4.00	8.00	13.00	11.00
Gibbs, Marla	5.00	11.00	18.00	15.00
Gibson, Mel	13.00	25.00	42.00	35.00
Gielgud, John	4.00	7.00	12.00	10.00
Gillespie, Dizzy	7.00	14.00	24.00	20.00
Gillette, Anita	2.00	4.00	6.00	5.00
Gilliland, Richard	3.00	5.00	8.00	7.00
Gless, Sharon	6.00	12.00	20.00	17.00
Glover, Danny	4.00	7.00	12.00	10.00
Gobel, George	2.00	4.00	7.00	6.00
Goddard, Paulette	5.00	9.00	15.00	13.00
Golan, Menahem	4.00	7.00	12.00	10.00
Goldberg, Whoopi	9.00	18.00	30.00	25.00
Goldblum, Jeff	5.00	9.00	15.00	13.00
Golonka, Arlene	3.00	7.00	12.00	10.00
Goodman, Dody	3.00	5.00	8.00	7.00
Goodson, Mark	2.00	4.00	6.00	5.00
Gordon, Gale	3.00	6.00	10.00	8.00
Gormé, Eydie	3.00	6.00	11.00	9.00
Gorney, Karen Lynn	2.00	4.00	6.00	5.00
Gorshin, Frank	3.00	6.00	10.00	8.00
Gould, Elliott	4.00	8.00	14.00	12.00
Gould, Harold	4.00	7.00	12.00	10.00
Goulding, Ray	2.00	4.00	6.00	5.00
Goz, Harry	5.00	10.00	17.00	14.00
Graham, Martha	8.00	15.00	25.00	21.00
Grandy, Fred	4.00	7.00	12.00	10.00
Granger, Stewart	11.00	21.00	36.00	30.00
Grant, Amy	4.00	7.00	12.00	10.00
Grant, Gogi	4.00	7.00	12.00	10.00
Grant, Kirby	7.00	13.00	21.00	18.00
Grant, Lee	5.00	9.00	15.00	13.00
Grassle, Karen	3.00	6.00	10.00	8.00
Gravatte, Marianne	3.00	6.00	10.00	8.00

Name	Signature Only	Letter or Document Signed	Autograph Letter Signed	Signed Photograph
Graves, Peter	7.00	13.00	21.00	18.00
Gray, Colleen	4.00	7.00	12.00	10.00
Gray, Erin	7.00	14.00	24.00	20.00
Gray, Linda	5.00	13.00	21.00	18.00
Grayco, Helen	2.00	4.00	6.00	5.00
Grayson, Kathryn	3.00	8.00	14.00	12.00
Greco, José	5.00	11.00	18.00	15.00
Greene, Shecky	4.00	7.00	12.00	10.00
Greer, Jane	4.00	8.00	13.00	11.00
Gregg, Virginia	4.00	7.00	12.00	10.00
Gregory, Dick	6.00	12.00	20.00	16.50
Gregory, James	4.00	7.00	12.00	10.00
Grey, Joel	5.00	11.00	18.00	15.00
Grier, Pam	4.00	8.00	13.00	11.00
Griffith, Andy	7.00	11.00	18.00	15.00
Griffith, Melanie	8.00	15.00	26.00	22.00
Grizzard, George	4.00	7.00	12.00	10.00
Grodin, Charles	5.00	9.00	15.00	12.50
Guardino, Harry	5.00	11.00	18.00	15.00
Gudunov, Alexander	8.00	15.00	26.00	22.00
Guest, Lance	5.00	11.00	18.00	15.00
Guillaume, Robert	9.00	18.00	30.00	25.00
Guinness, Alec	7.00	14.00	24.00	20.00
Gulager, Clu	3.00	6.00	10.00	8.50
Guthrie, Arlo	4.00	7.00	12.00	10.00
Guttenberg, Steve	10.00	20.00	33.00	28.00
Gwynn, Fred	5.00	11.00	18.00	15.00
Hack, Shelley	3.00	6.00	11.00	9.00
Hackett, Buddy	4.00	7.00	12.00	10.00
Hackman, Gene	7.00	14.00	24.00	20.00
Haggerty, Dan	4.00	8.00	13.00	11.00
Hagman, Larry	5.00	9.00	15.00	12.50
Hale, Alan, Jr.	4.00	7.00	12.00	10.00
Hale, Barbara	3.00	5.00	9.00	7.50
Hale, Monte	5.00	11.00	18.00	15.00
Hall, Harry	2.00	4.00	6.00	5.00
Hall, Monty	2.00	4.00	6.00	5.00
Hamel, Veronica	7.00	14.00	24.00	20.00
Hamill, Mark	6.00	11.00	19.00	16.00
Hamilton, Margaret	14.00	28.00	48.00	40.00
Hamlin, Harry	9.00	17.00	29.00	24.50
Hamlisch, Marvin	4.00	8.00	14.00	12.00
Hampton, Lionel	5.00	11.00	18.00	15.00
Handelman, Stanley M.	2.00	4.00	6.00	5.00
Hardin, Ty	5.00	11.00	18.00	15.00
Harmon, Mark	7.00	14.00	24.00	20.00
Harper, Tess	7.00	14.00	24.00	20.00
Harper, Valerie	4.00	7.00	12.00	10.00
Harrington, Pat	3.00	6.00	10.00	8.50
Harris, Ed	4.00	7.00	12.00	10.00
Harris, Julie	5.00	9.00	15.00	12.50
Harris, Richard	8.00	15.00	26.00	22.00
Harris, Robert H.	2.00	4.00	6.00	5.00

Name	Signature Only	Letter or Document Signed	Autograph Letter Signed	Signed Photograph
Harrison, Gregory	7.00	13.00	21.00	18.00
Harrison, Jenilee	3.00	5.00	8.00	7.00
Harrison, Rex	12.00	15.00	26.00	22.00
Harrold, Kathryn	6.00	12.00	20.00	17.00
Hart, Corey	5.00	11.00	18.00	15.00
Hart, Mary	4.00	7.00	12.00	10.00
Hartley, Mariette	4.00	7.00	12.00	10.00
Hartman, David	4.00	7.00	12.00	10.00
Hartman, Lisa	8.00	15.00	26.00	22.00
Harvey, Paul	5.00	10.00	17.00	14.00
Hasselhoff, David	5.00	11.00	18.00	15.00
Hausner, Jerry	3.00	5.00	8.00	7.00
Haven, Annette	7.00	14.00	24.00	20.00
Hawn, Goldie	6.00	12.00	20.00	17.00
Haworth, Jill	3.00	6.00	10.00	8.00
Hayes, Helen	7.00	16.00	40.00	16.00
Hayes, Isaac	5.00	10.00	17.00	14.00
Haynes, Linda	3.00	5.00	8.00	7.00
Hays, Robert	2.00	4.00	6.00	5.00
Hayworth, Rita	72.00	140.00	238.00	200.00
Heatherton, Joey	7.00	13.00	23.00	19.00
Heckart, Eileen	4.00	7.00	12.00	10.00
Heckerling, Amy	4.00	7.00	12.00	10.00
Hedison, David	3.00	6.00	11.00	9.00
Hedren, Tippi	4.00	8.00	14.00	12.00
Helmond, Katherine	4.00	7.00	12.00	10.00
Hemingway, Margaux	7.00	13.00	21.00	18.00
Hemingway, Mariel	4.00	7.00	12.00	10.00
Hemsley, Sherman	5.00	11.00	18.00	15.00
Henderson, Florence	2.00	4.00	6.00	5.00
Hendry, Gloria	2.00	4.00	7.00	6.00
Henner, Marilu	5.00	11.00	18.00	15.00
Henreid, Paul	4.00	7.00	12.00	10.00
Henry, Buck	2.00	4.00	6.00	5.00
Henson, Jim	8.00	16.00	27.00	23.00
Hepburn, Audrey	29.00	56.00	95.00	80.00
Herman, Pee Wee	7.00	14.00	24.00	20.00
Herman, Woody	7.00	14.00	24.00	20.00
Hesseman, Howard	4.00	7.00	12.00	10.00
Heston, Charlton	8.00	15.00	26.00	22.00
Hickman, Dwayne	4.00	7.00	12.00	10.00
Hill, Arthur	4.00	7.00	12.00	10.00
Hill, Dana	5.00	11.00	18.00	15.00
Hill, William	2.00	4.00	6.00	5.00
Hillerman, John	7.00	14.00	24.00	20.00
Hilliard, Harriet	2.00	4.00	6.00	5.00
Hines, Gregory	7.00	14.00	24.00	20.00
Hingle, Pat	4.00	7.00	12.00	10.00
Ho, Don	4.00	7.00	12.00	10.00
Hoffman, Dustin	8.00	15.00	26.00	22.00
Hogan, Paul	10.00	20.00	33.00	28.00
Holbrook, Hal	5.00	7.00	12.00	10.00
Hole, Jonathan	2.00	4.00	6.00	5.00

Name	Signature Only	Letter or Document Signed	Autograph Letter Signed	Signed Photograph
Holliday, Polly	4.00	7.00	12.00	10.00
Holliman, Earl	3.00	5.00	8.00	7.00
Holm, Celeste	4.00	25.00	14.00	12.00
Hope, Bob	8.00	16.00	27.00	22.50
Hopkins, Anthony	5.00	9.00	15.00	13.00
Hopkins, Bo	4.00	7.00	12.00	10.00
Horne, Lena	7.00	14.00	24.00	20.00
Horne, Marilyn	4.00	8.00	13.00	11.00
Horsley, Lee	5.00	11.00	18.00	15.00
Horton, Robert	2.00	4.00	6.00	5.00
Houseman, John	5.00	11.00	18.00	15.00
Hovis, Larry	3.00	5.00	8.00	7.00
Howard, Ken	5.00	9.00	15.00	13.00
Howard, Ron	4.00	7.00	12.00	10.00
Howell, C. Thomas	9.00	18.00	30.00	25.00
Howland, Beth	4.00	7.00	12.00	10.00
Hulce, Tom	7.00	14.00	24.00	20.00
Hunt, Helen	8.00	15.00	25.00	21.00
Hunt, Linda	9.00	18.00	30.00	25.00
Hunter, Kim	4.00	7.00	12.00	10.00
Hunter, Tab	6.00	12.00	21.00	17.50
Hurt, John	7.00	14.00	24.00	20.00
Hurt, Mary Beth	5.00	11.00	18.00	15.00
Hurt, William	20.00	39.00	65.00	55.00
Hussey, Olivia	5.00	11.00	18.00	15.00
Hussey, Ruth	2.00	4.00	6.00	5.00
Huston, Anjelica	9.00	18.00	30.00	25.00
Hutton, Lauren	7.00	14.00	24.00	20.00
Hutton, Timothy	7.00	14.00	24.00	20.00
Hyer, Martha	5.00	4.00	6.00	5.00
Ireland, Jill	4.00	7.00	12.00	10.00
Irons, Jeremy	8.00	15.00	25.00	21.00
Irving, Amy	7.00	14.00	24.00	20.00
Ives, Burl	5.00	11.00	18.00	15.00
Jackson, Anna	5.00	11.00	18.00	15.00
Jackson, Glenda	5.00	11.00	18.00	15.00
Jackson, Kate	8.00	15.00	25.00	21.00
Jackson, Michael	72.00	140.00	238.00	200.00
Jacobi, Lou	2.00	4.00	6.00	5.00
Jaeckel, Richard	3.00	6.00	10.00	8.00
Jagger, Dean	5.00	11.00	18.00	15.00
Jagger, Mick	29.00	56.00	95.00	80.00
Jeffreys, Anne	4.00	7.00	12.00	10.00
Jenner, Bruce	2.00	4.00	6.00	5.00
Jenrette, Rita	7.00	14.00	24.00	20.00
Jensen, Karen	3.00	6.00	10.00	8.00
Jett, Joan	4.00	7.00	12.00	10.00
Jewison, Norman	4.00	7.00	12.00	10.00
Jillian, Ann	5.00	11.00	18.00	15.00
Joel, Billy	5.00	11.00	18.00	15.00
Johns, Glynis	9.00	18.00	30.00	25.00
Johnson, Ben	6.00	12.00	20.00	17.00
Johnson, Don	18.00	35.00	60.00	50.00

Name	Signature Only	Letter or Document Signed	Autograph Letter Signed	Signed Photograph
Johnson, Lynn-Holly	2.00	4.00	6.00	5.00
Johnson, Russ	2.00	4.00	6.00	5.00
Jones, Dean	7.00	14.00	24.00	20.00
Jones, Grace	9.00	18.00	30.00	25.00
Jones, James Earl	4.00	8.00	14.00	12.00
Jones, Janet	9.00	18.00	30.00	25.00
Jones, Jennifer	16.00	32.00	54.00	45.00
Jones, Marcia Mae	4.00	7.00	12.00	10.00
Jones, Shirley	4.00	7.00	12.00	10.00
Jones, Tom	6.00	11.00	19.00	16.00
Jones, Tommy Lee	4.00	8.00	14.00	12.00
Jordon, Richard	4.00	7.00	12.00	10.00
Jorgensen, Christine	5.00	11.00	18.00	15.00
Jourdan, Louis	7.00	14.00	24.00	20.00
Joyce, Elain	3.00	5.00	8.00	7.00
Jump, Gordon	4.00	7.00	12.00	10.00
Kahn, Madeline	4.00	7.00	12.00	10.00
Kanaly, Steve	5.00	11.00	18.00	15.00
Kane, Carol	3.00	6.00	10.00	8.00
Kangaroo, Captain	4.00	7.00	12.00	10.00
Karras, Alex	4.00	7.00	12.00	10.00
Kasem, Casey	2.00	4.00	6.00	5.00
Kashfi, Anna	4.00	8.00	14.00	12.00
Kay, Dianne	2.00	4.00	6.00	5.00
Kaye, Celia	3.00	5.00	8.00	7.00
Kazan, Elia	5.00	8.00	14.00	12.00
Keach, Stacy	6.00	12.00	20.00	17.00
Keaton, Diane	9.00	17.00	29.00	24.00
Keel, Howard	4.00	7.00	12.00	10.00
Keith, Brian	3.00	6.00	10.00	8.00
Keith, David	4.00	7.00	12.00	10.00
Kellerman, Sally	4.00	7.00	12.00	10.00
Kelley, Deforest	8.00	15.00	25.00	21.00
Kelly, Gene	11.00	21.00	36.00	30.00
Kelly, Paula	2.00	4.00	6.00	5.00
Kelsey, Linda	4.00	8.00	13.00	11.00
Kennedy, George	4.00	7.00	12.00	10.00
Kennedy, Jayne	5.00	9.00	15.00	13.00
Kercheval, Ken	3.00	6.00	10.00	8.00
Kerr, Deborah	6.00	12.00	21.00	17.50
Keyes, Evelyn	5.00	14.00	24.00	20.00
Khambatta, Persis	3.00	5.00	8.00	7.00
Kidder, Margot	5.00	11.00	18.00	15.00
Kiley, Richard	5.00	11.00	18.00	15.00
King, Alan	4.00	7.00	12.00	10.00
King, Perry	5.00	10.00	17.00	14.00
Kingsley, Ben	7.00	13.00	21.00	18.00
Kinski, Nastassia	5.00	11.00	18.00	15.00
Kirkconnell, Clare	3.00	6.00	11.00	9.00
Kirsten, Dorothy	4.00	8.00	14.00	12.00
Kitt, Eartha	2.00	4.00	6.00	5.00
Kline, Kevin	5.00	11.00	18.00	16.00
Klugman, Jack	3.00	6.00	11.00	9.00

Name	Signature Only	Letter or Document Signed	Autograph Letter Signed	Signed Photograph
Knight, Gladys	11.00	21.00	36.00	30.00
Knight, Shirley	7.00	13.00	23.00	19.00
Knotts, Don	5.00	11.00	18.00	15.00
Knox, Alexander	9.00	18.00	30.00	25.00
Kohner, Susan	2.00	4.00	7.00	6.00
Korman, Harvey	4.00	7.00	12.00	10.00
Kovack, Nancy (Mehta)	3.00	6.00	10.00	8.00
Kove, Martin	5.00	11.00	18.00	15.00
Kragen, Ken	7.00	13.00	21.00	18.00
Kramer, Stanley	5.00	10.00	16.25	14.00
Krige, Alice	3.00	6.00	10.00	8.00
Kristel, Sylvia	4.00	7.00	12.00	10.00
Kristofferson, Kris	5.00	11.00	18.00	15.00
Kubrick, Sidney	3.00	5.00	8.00	7.00
Kwan, Nancy	5.00	11.00	18.00	15.00
Kyser, Kay	4.00	8.00	14.00	12.00
Ladd, Cheryl	6.00	12.00	20.00	16.50
Ladd, Diane	4.00	7.00	12.00	10.00
LaDelle, Jack	2.00	4.00	6.00	5.00
Lahti, Christine	5.00	8.00	14.00	12.00
LaLanne, Jack	3.00	6.00	10.00	8.00
Lamarr, Hedy	7.00	14.00	24.00	20.00
Lamas, Lorenzo	7.00	13.00	23.00	19.00
Lamour, Dorothy	7.00	13.00	21.00	18.00
Lancaster, Burt	7.00	14.00	24.00	20.00
Lanchester, Elsa	13.00	25.00	42.00	35.00
Landau, Martin	2.00	4.00	6.00	5.00
Landers, Audrey	5.00	11.00	18.00	15.00
Landers, Judy	4.00	7.00	12.00	10.00
Landis, John	10.00	11.00	18.00	15.00
Landon, Michael	5.00	11.00	18.00	15.00
Lane, Abbe	2.00	4.00	6.00	5.00
Lane, Christy	4.00	8.00	13.00	11.00
Lane, Diane	5.00	9.00	15.00	13.00
Lange, Hope	4.00	7.00	12.00	10.00
Lange, Jessica	7.00	14.00	24.00	20.00
Lansbury, Angela	4.00	11.00	19.00	16.00
Lantz, Walter	5.00	11.00	18.00	15.00
Larch, John	5.00	11.00	18.00	15.00
Laredo, Ruth	10.00	20.00	33.00	28.00
Larmouth, Kathy	3.00	5.00	8.00	7.00
Larroquette, John	4.00	11.00	18.00	15.00
LaRue, Lash	2.50	7.00	12.00	10.00
Lauper, Cyndi	11.00	21.00	36.00	22.50
Laurie, Piper	5.00	11.00	18.00	15.00
Lavin, Linda	4.00	7.00	12.00	10.00
Law, John Phillip	5.00	11.00	18.00	15.00
Lawrence, Barbara	2.00	4.00	6.00	5.00
Lawrence, Carol	4.00	7.00	12.00	10.00
Lawrence, Steve	5.00	10.00	17.00	14.00
Lawrence, Vicki	4.00	5.00	12.00	10.00
Lazenby, George	9.00	17.00	29.00	24.00
Leachman, Cloris	5.00	10.00	17.00	14.00

Name	Signature Only	Letter or Document Signed	Autograph Letter Signed	Signed Photograph
Lean, Sir David	4.00	7.00	12.00	10.00
Lear, Norman	5.00	11.00	18.00	15.00
Learned, Michael	7.00	13.00	23.00	19.00
LeBrock, Kelly	9.00	17.00	29.00	24.00
Lederer, Francis	5.00	11.00	18.00	15.00
Lee, Michele	4.00	7.00	12.00	10.00
Lee, Pinkie	2.00	4.00	6.00	5.00
Lee, Ruta	3.00	6.00	10.00	8.00
LeGallienne, Eva	4.00	7.00	12.00	10.00
Leibman, Ron	4.00	7.00	12.00	10.00
Leigh, Janet	6.00	12.00	20.00	17.00
Lelouch, Claude	7.00	14.00	24.00	20.00
Lembeck, Michael	2.00	4.00	6.00	5.00
Lemmon, Jack	5.00	10.00	17.00	14.00
Lenske, Rula	3.00	5.00	8.00	7.00
Leonard, Gloria	4.00	8.00	13.00	11.00
Leonard, Sheldon	4.00	7.00	12.00	10.00
LeRoy, Mervyn	4.00	8.00	13.00	11.00
Leslie, Joan	5.00	11.00	18.00	15.00
Lester, Buddy	2.00	4.00	6.00	5.00
Letterman, David	6.00	11.00	19.00	16.00
Levine, James	5.00	11.00	18.00	15.00
Lewis, Emmanuele	5.00	11.00	18.00	15.00
Lewis, Huey	9.00	18.00	30.00	25.00
Lewis, Jerry	4.00	7.00	12.00	10.00
Lewis, Ramsey	5.00	10.00	17.00	14.00
Lewis, Shari	5.00	10.00	17.00	14.00
Light, Judith	8.00	16.00	27.00	22.50
Linden, Hal	2.00	4.00	6.00	5.00
Lindfors, Viveca	7.00	14.00	24.00	20.00
Lindsey, George	5.00	11.00	18.00	15.00
Linkletter, Art	2.00	4.00	6.00	5.00
Linville, Larry	2.00	4.00	6.00	5.00
Lipton, Peggy	3.00	6.00	10.00	8.00
Lithgow, John	4.00	7.00	12.00	10.00
Little, Cleavon	2.00	4.00	6.00	5.00
Little Richard	14.00	27.00	46.00	39.00
Lloyd, Christopher	9.00	18.00	30.00	25.00
Lloyd, Kathleen	3.00	6.00	11.00	9.00
Lloyd, Norman	3.00	6.00	10.00	8.00
LoBianco, Tony	5.00	11.00	18.00	15.00
Locke, Sandra	7.00	13.00	21.00	18.00
Lockhart, June	4.00	8.00	13.00	11.00
Locklear, Heather	8.00	15.00	26.00	22.00
Loggia, Robert	5.00	10.00	17.00	14.00
Lollobrigida, Gina	8.00	16.00	27.00	23.00
Long, Shelley	7.00	14.00	24.00	20.00
Longet, Claudine	11.00	21.00	36.00	30.00
Lord, Jack	5.00	11.00	18.00	15.00
Loren, Sophia	9.00	17.00	29.00	24.00
Loring, Gloria	5.00	10.00	17.00	14.00
Loughlin, Lori	2.00	4.00	6.00	5.00
Louise, Tina	7.00	13.00	21.00	18.00

Name	Signature Only	Letter or Document Signed	Autograph Letter Signed	Signed Photograph
Loy, Myrna	5.00	11.00	18.00	15.00
Lucas, George	16.00	32.00	54.00	45.00
Lucci, Susan	5.00	11.00	18.00	15.00
Luke, Keye	6.00	12.00	20.00	17.00
Lumley, Joanna	4.00	7.00	12.00	10.00
Lupino, Ida	5.00	9.00	15.00	13.00
Lynley, Carol	11.00	21.00	36.00	30.00
Lyon, Sue	7.00	13.00	21.00	18.00
MacArthur, James	5.00	11.00	18.00	15.00
MacGraw, Ali	6.00	11.00	19.00	16.00
MacKenzie, Gisele	2.00	4.00	6.00	5.00
MacLaine, Shirley	10.00	18.00	30.00	25.00
MacLeod, Gavin	5.00	11.00	18.00	15.00
MacMurray, Fred	4.00	8.00	14.00	12.00
MacRae, Gordon	6.00	12.00	20.00	17.00
Macy, Bill	3.00	5.00	9.00	7.50
Madigan, Amy	7.00	13.00	21.00	18.00
Madison, Guy	5.00	11.00	22.00	17.00
Madsen, Virginia	5.00	11.00	18.00	15.00
Maffett, Debbie Sue	3.00	5.00	8.00	7.00
Maharis, George	9.00	18.00	30.00	25.00
Majors, Lee	4.00	7.00	12.00	10.00
Malden, Karl	7.00	13.00	21.00	18.00
Malone, Dorothy	12.00	22.00	38.00	32.00
Mancini, Henry	4.00	8.00	14.00	12.00
Mandel, Howie	5.00	11.00	18.00	15.00
Mangione, Chuck	4.00	8.00	13.00	11.00
Mankiewicz, Joseph	12.00	30.00	40.00	25.00
Manning, Irene	5.00	10.00	17.00	14.00
Marceau, Marcel	7.00	13.00	32.50	19.00
Marinaro, Ed	5.00	11.00	18.00	15.00
Marsalis, Wynton	5.00	7.00	12.00	10.00
Marshall, E. G.	4.00	7.00	12.00	10.00
Martin, Dean	4.00	7.00	12.00	10.00
Martin, Dick	5.00	11.00	18.00	15.00
Martin, Mary	5.00	13.00	21.00	18.00
Martin, Pamela Sue	5.00	11.00	18.00	15.00
Martin, Ross	3.00	6.00	10.00	8.00
Martin, Steve	8.00	16.00	27.00	22.50
Martino, Al	2.00	4.00	6.00	5.00
Mason, Marsha	7.00	14.00	24.00	20.00
Massie, Paul	4.00	5.00	8.00	7.00
Mastrantonio, Mary	8.00	15.00	26.00	22.00
Mathers, Jerry ("Beaver")	4.00	7.00	12.00	10.00
Matheson, Tim	9.00	18.00	30.00	25.00
Mathis, Johnny	7.00	13.00	21.00	18.00
Matlin, Marlee	16.00	32.00	54.00	45.00
Matthau, Walter	4.00	11.00	18.00	15.00
Mature, Victor	7.00	13.00	21.00	18.00
Maye, Carolyn	2.00	4.00	6.00	5.00
Mayo, Virginia	5.00	11.00	18.00	15.00
McArdle, Andrea	4.00	7.00	12.00	10.00
McBain, Diane	4.00	7.00	12.00	10.00

Name	Signature Only	Letter or Document Signed	Autograph Letter Signed	Signed Photograph
McCalla, Irish	8.00	16.00	27.00	23.00
McCallum, David	4.00	7.00	12.00	10.00
McClanahan, Rue	7.00	14.00	24.00	20.00
McCloskey, Lee	4.00	7.00	12.00	10.00
McCoo, Marilyn	4.00	7.00	12.00	10.00
McCormack, Patty	5.00	11.00	18.00	15.00
McCrea, Joel	11.00	21.00	36.00	30.00
McDowell, Malcolm	4.00	8.00	14.00	12.00
McDowell, Roddy	7.00	13.00	21.00	18.00
McGillis, Kelly	9.00	18.00	30.00	25.00
McGovern, Elizabeth	8.00	16.00	27.00	22.50
McGuire, Barry	4.00	8.00	13.00	11.00
McGuire, Dorothy	5.00	11.00	18.00	15.00
McKay, Gardner	5.00	10.00	17.00	14.00
McKenna, Siobhan	6.00	11.00	19.00	16.00
McKeon, Nancy	3.00	5.00	8.00	7.00
McMahon, Ed	4.00	7.00	12.00	10.00
McMillan, Kenneth	4.00	8.00	14.00	12.00
McNee, Patrick	4.00	8.00	14.00	12.00
McNichols, Kristy	4.00	7.00	12.00	10.00
McQueen, Butterfly	11.00	21.00	36.00	30.00
McShane, Ian	7.00	14.00	24.00	20.00
McWilliams, Caroline	3.00	5.00	8.00	7.00
Meara, Anne	3.00	6.00	10.00	8.00
Meeker, Ralph	4.00	8.00	14.00	12.00
Mehta, Zubin	5.00	11.00	18.00	15.00
Menuhin, Yehudi	11.00	21.00	36.00	30.00
Mercouri, Melina	5.00	11.00	18.00	15.00
Meredith, Burgess	8.00	15.00	26.00	22.00
Meriwether, Lee	4.00	7.00	12.00	10.00
Merrick, David	14.00	28.00	48.00	40.00
Merrill, Dina	5.00	9.00	15.00	12.50
Merrill, Gary	5.00	12.00	20.00	17.00
Michele, Denise	2.00	4.00	7.00	6.00
Midler, Bette	7.00	14.00	24.00	20.00
Miles, Sarah	7.00	13.00	21.00	18.00
Miles, Sylvia	4.00	7.00	12.00	10.00
Miles, Vera	5.00	11.00	18.00	15.00
Miller, Denny	2.00	4.00	6.00	5.00
Miller, Marvin	3.00	5.00	8.00	7.00
Miller, Mitch	2.00	4.00	6.00	5.00
Miller, Taylor	3.00	6.00	10.00	8.00
Mills, Donna	7.00	13.00	21.00	18.00
Mills, Hayley	8.00	15.00	26.00	22.00
Mills, John	6.00	12.00	20.00	17.00
Mills, Juliette	5.00	11.00	18.00	15.00
Milner, Martin	3.00	6.00	10.00	8.00
Milsap, Ronnie	4.00	7.00	12.00	10.00
Mimieux, Yvette	4.00	8.00	14.00	12.00
Miner, Jan	4.00	7.00	12.00	10.00
Minnelli, Liza	7.00	14.00	24.00	20.00
Minnelli, Vincent	4.00	7.00	12.00	10.00
Mirisch, Walter	5.00	10.00	17.00	14.00

Name	Signature Only	Letter or Document Signed	Autograph Letter Signed	Signed Photograph
Mitchum, Robert	4.00	7.00	12.00	10.00
Mobley, Mary Ann	5.00	11.00	18.00	15.00
Moffo, Anna	5.00	10.00	17.00	14.00
Moll, Richard	5.00	11.00	18.00	15.00
Montalban, Ricardo	8.00	15.00	26.00	22.00
Montana, Monte	2.00	4.00	6.00	5.00
Montand, Yves	5.00	11.00	18.00	15.00
Montgomery, Elizabeth	5.00	11.00	18.00	15.00
Montgomery, George	5.00	11.00	18.00	15.00
Moore, Clayton	4.00	7.00	12.00	10.00
Moore, Dudley	6.00	12.00	20.00	17.00
Moore, Joanna	4.00	7.00	12.00	10.00
Moore, Mary Tyler	9.00	18.00	30.00	25.00
Moore, Roger	7.00	13.00	23.00	19.00
Moore, Terry	4.00	7.00	12.00	10.00
Moranis, Rick	10.00	19.00	32.00	27.00
Moreno, Rita	7.00	13.00	23.00	19.00
Morgan, Dennis	4.00	7.00	12.00	10.00
Morgan, Harry	4.00	8.00	14.00	12.00
Morgan, Jaye P.	2.00	4.00	7.00	6.00
Morita, Pat	9.00	18.00	30.00	25.00
Morris, Anita	5.00	11.00	18.00	15.00
Muldaur, Diana	5.00	11.00	18.00	15.00
Muldaur, Maria	2.00	4.00	6.00	5.00
Mulgrew, Kate	4.00	7.00	12.00	10.00
Mull, Martin	4.00	8.00	14.00	12.00
Mulligan, Richard	3.00	6.00	11.00	9.00
Mullowney, Deborah	3.00	5.00	8.00	7.00
Mumy, Bill	4.00	7.00	12.00	10.00
Munro, Caroline	4.00	7.00	12.00	10.00
Murphy, Ben	4.00	7.00	12.00	10.00
Murphy, Eddie	27.00	53.00	89.00	75.00
Murray, Anne	3.00	6.00	11.00	9.00
Murray, Jan	1.00	3.00	5.00	4.00
Murray, Ken	4.00	7.00	12.00	10.00
Musante, Tony	3.00	6.00	10.00	8.00
Nabors, Jim	4.00	7.00	12.00	10.00
Nader, George	11.00	21.00	36.00	30.00
Napier, Charles	3.00	5.00	8.00	7.00
Nash, Clarence	4.00	7.00	12.00	10.00
Natwick, Mildred	4.00	7.00	12.00	10.00
Neal, Patricia	5.00	14.00	24.00	20.00
Needham, Hal	3.00	6.00	11.00	9.00
Neill, Noel	3.00	6.00	10.00	8.00
Nelson, Jimmy	2.00	4.00	6.00	5.00
Nelson, Lori	4.00	7.00	12.00	10.00
Nero, Peter	5.00	9.00	15.00	13.00
Nettleton, Lois	4.00	7.00	12.00	10.00
Newhart, Bob	5.00	11.00	18.00	15.00
Newley, Anthony	4.00	7.00	12.00	10.00
Newman, Barry	3.00	6.00	10.00	8.00
Newman, Paul	9.00	18.00	30.00	25.00
Newmar, Julie	7.00	13.00	21.00	18.00

Name	Signature Only	Letter or Document Signed	Autograph Letter Signed	Signed Photograph
Newton, Juice	5.00	11.00	18.00	15.00
Newton, Wayne	7.00	14.00	24.00	20.00
Newton-John, Olivia	9.00	18.00	30.00	25.00
Nicholas, Denise	2.00	4.00	7.00	6.00
Nichols, Michelle	5.00	11.00	18.00	15.00
Nicholson, Jack	8.00	15.00	25.00	21.00
Nielsen, Brigitte	9.00	18.00	30.00	25.00
Nielson, Leslie	2.00	4.00	6.00	5.00
Nimoy, Leonard	5.00	11.00	18.00	15.00
Nixon, Marion	3.00	6.00	10.00	8.00
Noble, James	4.00	7.00	12.00	10.00
Nolan, Jeanette	4.00	7.00	12.00	10.00
Nolte, Nick	8.00	15.00	25.00	21.00
Norris, Chuck	6.00	12.00	20.00	17.00
North, Sheree	4.00	8.00	13.00	11.00
Norton-Taylor, Judy	6.00	11.00	18.00	15.50
Novak, Kim	5.00	11.00	18.00	15.00
Nureyev, Rudolf	31.00	61.00	104.00	87.00
Nuyen, France	5.00	11.00	18.00	15.00
Oakes, Randi	3.00	6.00	10.00	8.00
O'Brian, Hugh	4.00	7.00	12.00	10.00
O'Brien, Cubby	2.00	4.00	6.00	5.00
O'Brien, Margaret	5.00	11.00	18.00	15.00
O'Connor, Carroll	5.00	11.00	18.00	15.00
O'Connor, Donald	4.00	7.00	12.00	10.00
Oh, Soon-Teck	3.00	5.00	8.00	7.00
O'Hara, Maureen	5.00	10.00	17.00	14.00
O'Laughlin, Gerald S.	2.00	4.00	6.00	5.00
Olivier, Laurence	15.00	29.00	49.00	41.00
Olmos, Edward James	4.00	7.00	12.00	10.00
Olson, Merlin	7.00	13.00	23.00	19.00
O'Neal, Ryan	7.00	11.00	18.00	15.00
O'Neal, Tatum	4.00	11.00	18.00	15.00
O'Neill, Jennifer	4.00	8.00	14.00	12.00
Ono, Yoko	11.00	21.00	36.00	30.00
Ontkean, Michael	4.00	7.00	12.00	10.00
Opatoshu, David	5.00	11.00	18.00	15.00
Ormandy, Eugene	7.00	14.00	24.00	20.00
Osmond, Donny	5.00	10.00	17.00	14.00
Osmond, Marie	11.00	21.00	36.00	30.00
O'Sullivan, Maureen	8.00	15.00	26.00	22.00
O'Toole, Peter	16.00	31.00	52.00	44.00
Oxenberg, Catherine	11.00	21.00	36.00	30.00
Oz, Frank	4.00	7.00	12.00	10.00
Paar, Jack	5.00	11.00	18.00	15.00
Pacino, Al	5.00	11.00	18.00	15.00
Pacula, Joanna	7.00	13.00	21.00	18.00
Page, Geraldine	11.00	21.00	36.00	30.00
Paige, Janice	5.00	9.00	15.00	12.50
Palance, Jack	4.00	14.00	24.00	20.00
Palmer, Betsy	3.00	5.00	8.00	7.00
Parker, Fess	8.00	15.00	26.00	22.00

Name	Signature Only	Letter or Document Signed	Autograph Letter Signed	Signed Photograph
Parker, , Ray, Jr.	4.00	7.00	12.00	10.00
Parker, Sarah Jessica	7.00	14.00	24.00	20.00
Parkins, Barbara	5.00	11.00	18.00	15.00
Parrish, Julie	3.00	6.00	11.00	9.00
Parsons, Estelle	4.00	7.00	12.00	10.00
Paulsson, Pat	4.00	7.00	12.00	10.00
Pavarotti, Luciano	9.00	18.00	30.00	25.00
Peck, Gregory	9.00	18.00	30.00	25.00
Penn, Arthur	3.00	6.00	10.00	8.00
Penn, Sean	15.00	29.00	50.00	42.00
Peppard, George	5.00	11.00	18.00	15.00
Perkins, Tony	7.00	13.00	23.00	19.00
Perlman, Itzhak	5.00	11.00	18.00	15.00
Perlman, Rhea	4.00	7.00	12.00	10.00
Perrine, Valerie	4.00	7.00	12.00	10.00
Persoff, Nehemiah	4.00	7.00	12.00	10.00
Peters, Bernadette	4.00	8.00	14.00	12.00
Peters, Brock	4.00	7.00	12.00	10.00
Peters, Roberta	4.00	7.00	12.00	10.00
Pettet, Joanna	4.00	7.00	12.00	10.00
Pfeiffer, Michelle	8.00	15.00	26.00	22.00
Pflug, Jo Ann	2.00	4.00	7.00	6.00
Phillips, Julianne	6.00	12.00	20.00	17.00
Phillips, Michelle	7.00	13.00	23.00	19.00
Pickett, Cindy	2.00	4.00	6.00	5.00
Pine, Phillip	2.00	4.00	7.00	6.00
Pitney, Gene	3.00	6.00	10.00	8.00
Pleasence, Donald	5.00	11.00	18.00	15.00
Pleshette, Suzanne	5.00	11.00	18.00	15.00
Plowright, Joan	5.00	9.00	15.00	13.00
Plummer, Christopher	5.00	11.00	18.00	15.00
Poitier, Sidney	5.00	10.00	17.00	20.00
Pollack, Sydney	5.00	9.00	15.00	13.00
Ponti, Carlo	6.00	11.00	18.00	15.00
Porizkova, Paulina	7.00	14.00	24.00	20.00
Porter, Don	2.00	4.00	6.00	5.00
Post, Markie	5.00	11.00	18.00	15.00
Powell, Jane	7.00	13.00	21.00	18.00
Powers, Mala	2.00	8.00	20.00	5.00
Powers, Stephanie	7.00	13.00	23.00	19.00
Prentiss, Paula	5.00	11.00	18.00	15.00
Presley, Priscilla	7.00	14.00	24.00	20.00
Price, Leontyne	7.00	14.00	24.00	20.00
Price, Vincent	7.00	14.00	24.00	20.00
Principal, Victoria	7.00	13.00	21.00	18.00
Prinz, Rosemary	2.00	4.00	6.00	5.00
Prosky, Robert	4.00	7.00	12.00	10.00
Prouse, Juliet	5.00	11.00	18.00	15.00
Provine, Dorothy	4.00	7.00	12.00	10.00
Pryor, Richard	7.00	14.00	24.00	20.00
Purcell, Lee	3.00	5.00	8.00	7.00
Purcell, Sarah	4.00	7.00	12.00	10.00

Name	Signature Only	Letter or Document Signed	Autograph Letter Signed	Signed Photograph
Purl, Linda	5.00	11.00	18.00	15.00
Pyle, Denver	3.00	6.00	11.00	9.00
Quaid, Dennis	5.00	11.00	18.00	15.00
Quaid, Randy	5.00	11.00	18.00	15.00
Quale, Anthony	4.00	8.00	14.00	12.00
Quinn, Anthony	5.00	11.00	18.00	15.00
Quinn, Carmel	2.00	4.00	6.00	5.00
Raffin, Deborah	5.00	9.00	15.00	12.50
Rainey, Ford	2.00	4.00	7.00	6.00
Rambo, Dack	7.00	14.00	24.00	20.00
Rampling, Charlotte	7.00	13.00	23.00	19.00
Randall, Tony	4.00	7.00	12.00	10.00
Randolph, Boots	2.00	4.00	7.00	6.00
Randolph, Joyce	3.00	6.00	10.00	8.00
Ray, Aldo	3.00	5.00	8.00	7.00
Raye, Martha	7.00	13.00	23.00	14.00
Read, Dolly	4.00	7.00	12.00	10.00
Reddy, Helen	7.00	14.00	24.00	20.00
Redford, Robert	5.00	11.00	18.00	15.00
Redgrave, Lynn	5.00	11.00	18.00	15.00
Redgrave, Vanessa	10.00	18.00	30.00	25.00
Reed, Jerry	2.00	4.00	6.00	5.00
Reed, Rex	4.00	7.00	12.00	10.00
Reed, Robert	3.00	6.00	11.00	9.00
Reese, Della	2.00	4.00	6.00	5.00
Reeve, Christopher	9.00	17.00	29.00	24.00
Reeves, Steve	3.00	6.00	10.00	8.00
Reid, Tim	4.00	7.00	12.00	10.00
Reiner, Carl	3.00	6.00	11.00	9.00
Reiner, Rob	4.00	7.00	12.00	10.00
Reinking, Ann	7.00	14.00	24.00	20.00
Remick, Lee	8.00	15.00	26.00	22.00
Reynolds, Burt	6.00	12.00	20.00	17.00
Reynolds, Debbie	5.00	10.00	17.00	14.00
Richie, Lionel	4.00	7.00	12.00	10.00
Rickles, Don	4.00	7.00	12.00	10.00
Rigg, Diana	9.00	17.00	29.00	24.00
Ringwald, Molly	18.00	35.00	60.00	50.00
Ritt, Martin	4.00	8.00	13.00	11.00
Ritter, John	4.00	7.00	12.00	10.00
Rivera, Geraldo	4.00	7.00	12.00	10.00
Rivers, Joan	5.00	11.00	18.00	15.00
Roach, Hal, Sr.	13.00	25.00	42.00	35.00
Roarke, Hayden	3.00	7.00	12.00	10.00
Robards, Jason	6.00	11.00	19.00	16.00
Roberts, Doris	6.00	12.00	20.00	17.00
Roberts, Eric	5.00	11.00	18.00	15.00
Roberts, Roy	5.00	10.00	17.00	14.00
Roberts, Tanya	7.00	13.00	23.00	19.00
Roberts, Tony	4.00	7.00	12.00	10.00
Robertson, Cliff	4.00	7.00	12.00	10.00
Rockwell, Robert	7.00	14.00	24.00	20.00
Rodman, Judy	4.00	7.00	12.00	10.00

Name	Signature Only	Letter or Document Signed	Autograph Letter Signed	Signed Photograph
Rogers, Fred	4.00	8.00	14.00	12.00
Rogers, Ginger	14.00	28.00	48.00	40.00
Rogers, Roy	7.00	14.00	24.00	20.00
Roland, Gilbert	7.00	14.00	24.00	20.00
Rolle, Esther	2.00	4.00	6.00	5.00
Roman, Ruth	4.00	8.00	13.00	11.00
Rome, Sydney	4.00	7.00	12.00	10.00
Romero, Cesar	5.00	10.00	17.00	14.00
Ronstadt, Linda	9.00	21.00	36.00	23.00
Rooney, Mickey	6.00	11.00	19.00	16.00
Rorke, Hayden	3.00	4.00	6.00	5.00
Ross, Diana	5.00	11.00	18.00	15.00
Ross, Katharine	3.00	6.00	11.00	9.00
Ross, Marion	3.00	6.00	11.00	9.00
Rountree, Richard	4.00	7.00	12.00	10.00
Rowan, Dan	5.00	11.00	18.00	15.00
Rowland, Gena	4.00	7.00	12.00	10.00
Roylance, Pamela	2.00	4.00	6.00	5.00
Rubinstein, John	4.00	7.00	12.00	10.00
Rush, Barbara	4.00	8.00	14.00	12.00
Russell, Harold	7.00	14.00	24.00	20.00
Russell, Jane	7.00	13.00	21.00	18.00
Russell, Kurt	8.00	14.00	24.00	20.00
Russell, Theresa	9.00	18.00	30.00	25.00
Rutherford, Ann	9.00	17.00	29.00	32.00
Ryan, Sheila	4.00	7.00	12.00	10.00
Sahl, Mort	4.00	8.00	14.00	12.00
Saint, Eva Marie	5.00	9.00	15.00	12.50
Sales, Soupy	3.00	6.00	10.00	8.00
Salmi, Albert	4.00	7.00	12.00	10.00
Salt, Jennifer	2.00	4.00	6.00	5.00
Samms, Emma	5.00	11.00	18.00	15.00
Sanford, Isabel	4.00	7.00	12.00	10.00
Santos, Joe	4.00	7.00	12.00	10.00
Sarandon, Susan	7.00	14.00	24.00	20.00
Sargent, Dick	2.00	4.00	6.00	5.00
Sassoon, Beverly	2.00	4.00	6.00	5.00
Saunders, Lori	2.00	4.00	7.00	6.00
Savalas, Telly	4.00	7.00	12.00	10.00
Scalia, Jack	7.00	13.00	23.00	19.00
Scarwid, Diana	3.00	5.00	8.00	7.00
Schaal, Richard	2.00	4.00	7.00	6.00
Schaal, Wendy	2.00	4.00	6.00	5.00
Schallert, William	4.00	7.00	12.00	10.00
Schary, Dore	5.00	11.00	18.00	15.00
Scheider, Roy	5.00	11.00	18.00	15.00
Schneider, John	3.00	6.00	10.00	8.00
Schreiber, Avery	2.00	4.00	6.00	5.00
Schwarzenegger, Arnold	13.00	25.00	42.00	35.00
Scofield, Paul	14.00	28.00	48.00	40.00
Scott, Eric	3.00	5.00	9.00	7.50
Scott, George C.	11.00	21.00	36.00	30.00
Scott, Lizbeth	6.00	11.00	19.00	16.00

Name	Signature Only	Letter or Document Signed	Autograph Letter Signed	Signed Photograph
Scott, Willard	3.00	6.00	11.00	9.00
Sedaka, Neil	3.00	6.00	11.00	9.00
Seeger, Pete	4.00	7.00	12.00	10.00
Segal, George	5.00	11.00	18.00	15.00
Seka	7.00	14.00	24.00	20.00
Sellecca, Connie	5.00	11.00	18.00	15.00
Selleck, Tom	9.00	18.00	30.00	25.00
Severinson, Doc	5.00	10.00	18.00	15.00
Seymour, Jane	8.00	15.00	26.00	22.00
Shannon, Del	3.00	6.00	10.00	8.00
Sharif, Omar	16.00	32.00	54.00	45.00
Shatner, William	10.00	19.00	32.00	27.00
Shaunessy, Charles	4.00	8.00	14.00	12.00
Shawn, Ted	7.00	13.00	23.00	19.00
Shear, Rhonda	2.00	4.00	7.00	6.00
Sheedy, Ally	9.00	18.00	30.00	25.00
Sheen, Charles	13.00	25.00	42.00	35.00
Sheen, Martin	7.00	13.00	21.00	18.00
Sheffer, Chris	5.00	11.00	18.00	15.00
Shelton, Deborah	6.00	11.00	19.00	16.00
Shepherd, Cybill	10.00	20.00	33.00	28.00
Shera, Mark	2.00	4.00	6.00	5.00
Shields, Brooke	7.00	13.00	15.00	19.00
Shigeta, James	5.00	10.00	17.00	14.00
Shoop, Pamela Susan	4.00	8.00	14.00	12.00
Shore, Dinah	5.00	9.00	16.00	13.50
Showalter, Max	3.00	6.00	11.00	9.00
Shrimpton, Jean	4.00	7.00	12.00	10.00
Sidney, Sylvia	6.00	12.00	20.00	17.00
Sierra, Gregory	3.00	5.00	8.00	7.00
Sierra, Margarita	2.00	4.00	6.00	5.00
Signoret, Simone	20.00	28.00	48.00	40.00
Sikking, James B.	5.00	9.00	15.00	13.00
Sills, Beverly	5.00	11.00	18.00	15.00
Simmons, Jean	6.00	12.00	20.00	17.00
Simmons, Richard	2.00	4.00	6.00	5.00
Simon, Carly	8.00	15.00	25.00	21.00
Sinatra, Frank	45.00	87.00	148.00	124.00
Sinatra, Nancy	7.00	14.00	24.00	20.00
Singleton, Penny	3.00	6.00	10.00	8.00
Sixty Minutes (all)	11.00	21.00	36.00	30.00
Skala, Lilia	8.00	15.00	26.00	22.00
Skelton, Red	12.00	22.00	38.00	32.00
Skerrit, Tom	6.00	12.00	20.00	17.00
Smedley, Richard	2.00	4.00	7.00	6.00
Smirnoff, Yakov	6.00	12.00	20.00	16.50
Smith, Alexis	4.00	7.00	12.00	10.00
Smith, Bernie	5.00	9.00	15.00	13.00
Smith, Charles M.	2.00	4.00	6.00	5.00
Smith, Jaclyn	5.00	11.00	18.00	15.00
Smith, Maggie	10.00	15.00	26.00	22.00
Smith, Martha	3.00	5.00	8.00	7.00
Smithers, Jan	5.00	11.00	18.00	15.00

Name	Signature Only	Letter or Document Signed	Autograph Letter Signed	Signed Photograph
Smothers Brothers (both)	8.00	15.00	25.00	21.00
Soarez, Alana	2.00	4.00	6.00	5.00
Soles, P. J.	2.00	4.00	6.00	5.00
Somers, Suzanne	5.00	11.00	18.00	15.00
Sommer, Elke	7.00	14.00	24.00	20.00
Sommers, Joanne	2.00	4.00	6.00	5.00
Sothern, Ann	7.00	13.00	21.00	18.00
Soul, David	7.00	14.00	24.00	20.00
Sparv, Camilla	6.00	12.00	20.00	17.00
Spelling, Aaron	5.00	7.00	12.00	10.00
Spielberg, David	4.00	7.00	12.00	10.00
Spielberg, Steven	11.00	21.00	36.00	30.00
Stack, Robert	5.00	11.00	18.00	15.00
Stack, Rose Marie B.	3.00	5.00	8.00	7.00
Stafford, Jo	2.00	4.00	6.00	5.00
Stallone, Sylvester	12.00	24.00	40.00	34.00
Stamp, Terence	6.00	12.00	20.00	17.00
Stanton, Harry Dean	5.00	11.00	18.00	15.00
Stanwyck, Barbara	7.00	15.00	25.00	21.00
Stapleton, Jean	3.00	5.00	8.00	7.00
Stapleton, Maureen	6.00	12.00	20.00	17.00
Starker, Janos	5.00	10.00	17.00	14.00
St. Cyr, Lili	9.00	17.00	29.00	24.00
Steele, Karen	3.00	5.00	8.00	7.00
Steenburgen, Mary	8.00	15.00	25.00	21.00
Steiger, Rod	5.00	14.00	24.00	20.00
Stern, Isaac	5.00	11.00	18.00	15.00
Stevens, Andrew	6.00	12.00	20.00	17.00
Stevens, Connie	5.00	9.00	15.00	12.50
Stevens, Craig	6.00	11.00	19.00	16.00
Stevens, Stella	5.00	11.00	18.00	15.00
Stevens, Warren	3.00	6.00	11.00	9.00
Stewart, James	16.00	53.00	125.00	30.00
Stewart, Rod	9.00	18.00	30.00	25.00
St. Jacques, Ramond	5.00	11.00	18.00	15.00
St. John, Jill	6.00	12.00	20.00	17.00
Stoltz, Eric	7.00	13.00	21.00	18.00
Storch, Larry	2.00	4.00	6.00	5.00
Straight, Beatrice	4.00	10.00	14.00	12.00
Strasberg, Lee	9.00	18.00	30.00	25.00
Strasberg, Susan	11.00	21.00	36.00	30.00
Streep, Meryl	11.00	21.00	36.00	30.00
Streisand, Barbra	18.00	35.00	60.00	50.00
Struthers, Sally	2.00	4.00	6.00	5.00
Sturges, John	4.00	7.00	12.00	10.00
Sullivan, Barry	3.00	5.00	8.00	7.00
Sullivan, Susan	4.00	7.00	12.00	10.00
Sutherland, Donald	4.00	7.00	12.00	10.00
Sutherland, Joan	5.00	11.00	18.00	15.00
Svenson, Bo	3.00	6.00	11.00	9.00
Swayze, John Cameron	2.00	4.00	6.00	5.00
Swit, Loretta	5.00	11.00	18.00	15.00
Sylvia	4.00	7.00	12.00	10.00

Name	Signature Only	Letter or Document Signed	Autograph Letter Signed	Signed Photograph
Szell, George	4.00	8.00	14.00	12.00
Talbot, Nita	3.00	5.00	8.00	7.00
Tamblyn, Russ	5.00	11.00	18.00	15.00
Tambor, Jeffrey	5.00	7.00	12.00	10.00
Tandy, Jessica	4.00	7.00	12.00	10.00
Tayback, Vic	3.00	5.00	8.00	7.00
Taylor, Elizabeth	18.00	35.00	60.00	50.00
Taylor, Rod	3.00	6.00	11.00	9.00
Taylor-Young, Leigh	5.00	11.00	18.00	15.00
Tedrow, Irene	2.00	4.00	6.00	5.00
Te Kanawa, Dame Kiri	7.00	14.00	24.00	20.00
Temple, Shirley (Black)	5.00	7.00	12.00	10.00
Thinnis, Roy	4.00	7.00	12.00	10.00
Thomas, Betty	4.00	7.00	12.00	10.00
Thomas, Danny	2.00	4.00	6.00	5.00
Thomas, Heather	7.00	14.00	24.00	20.00
Thomas, Kurt	4.00	7.00	12.00	10.00
Thomas, Marlo	2.00	4.00	6.00	5.00
Thomas, Richard	4.00	7.00	12.00	10.00
Thompson, Gordon	6.00	11.00	19.00	16.00
Thompson, Lea	9.00	18.00	30.00	25.00
Thompson, Marshall	4.00	7.00	12.00	10.00
Tiegs, Cheryl	6.00	12.00	20.00	17.00
Tierney, Gene	7.00	14.00	24.00	20.00
Tiffin, Pamela	5.00	11.00	18.00	15.00
Tilly, Jennifer	2.00	4.00	7.00	6.00
Tilly, Meg	6.00	12.00	20.00	17.00
Tilton, Charlene	5.00	11.00	18.00	15.00
Tinker, Grant C.	6.00	11.00	18.00	15.00
Tiny Tim	8.00	10.00	17.00	14.00
Tobey, Ken	2.00	4.00	6.00	5.00
Tomlin, Lily	4.00	7.00	12.00	10.00
Tompkins, Angel	7.00	13.00	21.00	18.00
Towers, Constance	4.00	7.00	12.00	10.00
Travalena, Fred	4.00	7.00	12.00	10.00
Travanti, Daniel J.	5.00	11.00	18.00	15.00
Travolta, John	7.00	14.00	24.00	20.00
Treas, Terri	2.00	4.00	6.00	5.00
Trebek, Alex	7.00	14.00	24.00	20.00
Treen, Mary	3.00	5.00	8.00	7.00
Trevor, Claire	8.00	15.00	25.00	21.00
Tryon, Tom	5.00	11.00	18.00	15.00
Tucker, Forest	5.00	11.00	18.00	15.00
Tucker, Tanya	5.00	11.00	18.00	15.00
Tune, Tommy	5.00	11.00	18.00	15.00
Turkel, Ann	2.00	4.00	6.00	5.00
Turner, Kathleen	8.00	16.00	28.00	23.50
Turner, Lana	7.00	14.00	24.00	20.00
Turner, Tina	13.00	25.00	42.00	35.00
Tweed, Shannon	7.00	14.00	24.00	20.00
Twiggy	5.00	11.00	18.00	15.00
Tyson, Cicely	7.00	7.00	12.00	10.00
Uggams, Leslie	2.50	4.00	6.00	5.00

Name	Signature Only	Letter or Document Signed	Autograph Letter Signed	Signed Photograph
Ullman, Liv	5.00	11.00	18.00	15.00
Umeki, Miyoshi	250.00			600.00
Urich, Robert	8.00	16.00	27.00	23.00
Ustinov, Peter	9.00	18.00	30.00	25.00
Vaccaro, Brenda	4.00	8.00	14.00	12.00
Vacio, Natividad	2.00	4.00	6.00	5.00
Valenti, Jack	3.00	5.00	8.00	7.00
Valentine, Karen	3.00	5.00	8.00	7.00
Vallone, Raf	4.00	8.00	14.00	12.00
Van Ark, Joan	5.00	11.00	18.00	15.00
Van Cleef, Lee	3.00	6.00	10.00	8.00
Van Doren, Mamie	8.00	15.00	25.00	21.00
Van Dyke, Dick	4.00	7.00	12.00	10.00
Van Fleet, Jo	5.00	14.00	24.00	20.00
Van Patten, Dick	4.00	5.00	8.00	7.00
Van Patten, Joyce	3.00	5.00	8.00	7.00
Van Valkenburgh, Debbie	5.00	10.00	17.00	14.00
Vee, Bobby	3.00	4.00	6.00	5.00
Verdon, Gwen	4.00	7.00	12.00	10.00
Vigran, Herb	2.00	4.00	6.00	5.00
Vincent, Jan-Michael	5.00	9.00	16.00	13.50
Vincent, Romo	4.00	8.00	13.00	11.00
Voight, Jon	4.00	7.00	12.00	10.00
Waggin, Patti	2.00	4.00	6.00	5.00
Wagner, Lindsay	5.00	11.00	18.00	15.00
Wagner, Robert	8.00	15.00	26.00	22.00
Waite, Ralph	4.00	7.00	12.00	10.00
Walken, Christopher	11.00	21.00	36.00	30.00
Walker, Clint	6.00	11.00	19.00	16.00
Walker, Jerry Jeff	5.00	10.00	17.00	14.00
Walker, Jimmy	2.00	4.00	6.00	5.00
Wallace, Dee	4.00	7.00	12.00	10.00
Wallace, Mike	4.00	7.00	12.00	10.00
Wallach, Eli	4.00	8.00	13.00	11.00
Walley, Deborah	4.00	7.00	12.00	10.00
Wallis, Shani	3.00	4.00	7.00	6.00
Walsh, M. Emmet	4.00	7.00	12.00	10.00
Walsh, Raoul	4.00	7.00	12.00	10.00
Walter, Jessica	5.00	11.00	18.00	15.00
Walters, Julie	4.00	7.00	12.00	10.00
Ward, Rachel	7.00	14.00	24.00	20.00
Warden, Jack	5.00	9.00	15.00	13.00
Warfield, William	5.00	11.00	18.00	15.00
Warner, Jack	25.00	80.00	110.00	45.00
Warren, Jennifer	2.00	4.00	6.00	5.00
Warren, Leslie Ann	4.00	7.00	12.00	10.00
Warren, Michael	2.00	4.00	6.00	5.00
Warrick, Ruth	7.00	14.00	24.00	20.00
Washington, Denzel	5.00	11.00	18.00	15.00
Watanabe, Gedde	7.00	13.00	21.00	18.00
Waterston, Sam	5.00	11.00	19.00	16.00
Wayne, David	4.00	7.00	12.00	10.00
Weathers, Carl	5.00	11.00	18.00	15.00

Name	Signature Only	Letter or Document Signed	Autograph Letter Signed	Signed Photograph
Weaver, Dennis	5.00	11.00	18.00	15.00
Weaver, Sigourney	7.00	14.00	24.00	20.00
Webber, Robert	4.00	8.00	14.00	12.00
Welch, Raquel	5.00	11.00	18.00	15.00
Weld, Tuesday	9.00	18.00	30.00	25.00
Welk, Lawrence	4.00	7.00	12.00	10.00
Weller, Peter	8.00	15.00	25.00	21.00
Wells, Dawn	4.00	7.00	12.00	10.00
West, Adam	3.00	5.00	8.00	7.00
Whelan, Arleen	2.00	4.00	6.00	5.00
White, Betty	7.00	14.00	24.00	20.00
White, Jesse	2.00	4.00	6.00	5.00
White, Vanna	7.00	13.00	23.00	19.00
Whitmore, James	2.00	4.00	6.00	5.00
Wickes, Mary	3.00	4.00	7.00	6.00
Widmark, Richard	7.00	14.00	24.00	20.00
Wilde, Cornel	4.00	7.00	12.00	10.00
Wilder, Gene	5.00	11.00	18.00	15.00
Wilke, Robert J.	5.00	11.00	18.00	15.00
Wilkinson, June	5.00	11.00	18.00	15.00
Willard, Fred	2.00	4.00	6.00	5.00
Williams, Barry	3.00	6.00	11.00	9.00
Williams, Bill	5.00	10.00	17.00	14.00
Williams, Billy Dee	5.00	10.00	17.00	14.00
Williams, Cindy	2.00	4.00	6.00	5.00
Williams, Esther	6.00	12.00	20.00	17.00
Williams, Robin	9.00	18.00	30.00	25.00
Williams, Roger	2.00	4.00	6.00	5.00
Williams, Treat	8.00	15.00	26.00	22.00
Williams, Vanessa	10.00	16.00	27.00	23.00
Windom, William	3.00	6.00	11.00	9.00
Windsor, Marie	4.00	7.00	12.00	10.00
Winfield, Paul	4.00	7.00	12.00	10.00
Winfrey, Oprah	9.00	18.00	30.00	25.00
Winger, Debra	8.00	15.00	26.00	22.00
Winkler, Henry	4.00	7.00	12.00	10.00
Winters, Jonathan	7.00	14.00	24.00	20.00
Winters, Shelley	5.00	9.00	15.00	12.50
Winwood, Estelle	4.00	7.00	12.00	10.00
Wise, Robert	4.00	8.00	13.00	11.00
Wolper, David	4.00	7.00	12.00	10.00
Wonder, Stevie	4.00	8.00	14.00	12.00
Wood, Lana	3.00	5.00	8.00	7.00
Woods, James	9.00	18.00	30.00	25.00
Woodward, Edward	8.00	17.00	29.00	26.00
Woodward, Joanne	10.00	12.00	20.00	17.00
Wopat, Tom	5.00	10.00	17.00	14.00
Worth, Irene	2.00	4.00	6.00	5.00
Wray, Fay	4.00	7.00	12.00	10.00
Wright, Theresa	13.00	25.00	42.00	35.00
Wyatt, Jane	2.00	4.00	6.00	5.00
Wyler, Gretchen	4.00	7.00	12.00	10.00
Wyman, Jane	6.00	12.00	20.00	17.00

Name	Signature Only	Letter or Document Signed	Autograph Letter Signed	Signed Photograph
Wynn, Keenan	2.00	4.00	6.00	5.00
Wynter, Dana	2.00	4.00	6.00	5.00
Yarnell, Lorine	2.00	4.00	6.00	5.00
York, Michael	6.00	12.00	20.00	17.00
York, Susanna	5.00	11.00	18.00	15.00
Young, Burt	3.00	5.00	8.00	7.00
Young, Loretta	7.00	14.00	24.00	20.00
Young, Robert	4.00	8.00	14.00	12.00
Youngman, Henny	2.00	4.00	6.00	5.00
Zabach, Florian	2.00	4.00	6.00	5.00
Zadora, Pia	7.00	14.00	24.00	20.00
Zanuck, Richard Darryl	5.00	7.00	12.00	10.00
Zeman, Jacklyn	5.00	9.00	15.00	12.50
Zerbe, Anthony	4.00	7.00	12.00	10.00
Zimbalist, Efrem, Jr.	5.00	11.00	18.00	15.00
Zimbalist, Stephanie	5.00	11.00	18.00	15.00
Zimmer, Norma	2.00	4.00	6.00	5.00
Zmed, Adrian	4.00	7.00	12.00	10.00

Entertainers (Vintage)

As mentioned in the previous section, the Entertainers category has been broken into two parts. This section contains the prices for those persons classified as *Vintage*—either people who are deceased, or those whose fame and fortune derives from an earlier period.

Name	Signature Only	Letter or Document Signed	Autograph Letter Signed	Signed Photograph
Aadland, Beverly	$ 2.00	$ 4.00	$ 8.00	$ 10.00
Abbado, Claudio	1.00	4.00	7.00	9.00
Abbott, Bud	80.00	93.00	174.00	200.00
Abbott, George	21.00	25.00	46.00	58.00
Abel, Walter	10.00	12.00	21.00	27.00
Adams, Joey	2.00	5.00	10.00	12.00
Adams, Maude	50.00	64.00	119.00	150.00
Adams, Nick	35.00	41.00	76.00	95.00
Adler, Luther	9.00	11.00	20.00	25.00

Name	Signature Only	Letter or Document Signed	Autograph Letter Signed	Signed Photograph
Adler, Stella	5.00	9.00	16.00	20.00
Adoree, Renee	25.00	29.00	54.00	68.00
Adrian, Iris	6.00	6.00	12.00	15.00
Agar, John	4.00	6.00	12.00	15.00
Aherne, Brian	11.00	13.00	24.00	30.00
Albanese, Licia	15.00	17.00	32.00	40.00
Albright, Lola	6.00	7.00	13.00	16.00
Albritton, Louise	20.00	24.00	44.00	55.00
Alexander, George	5.00	6.00	11.00	14.00
Allen, Elizabeth	11.00	13.00	24.00	30.00
Allen, Fred	30.00	35.00	65.00	82.00
Allen, Gracie	22.00	26.00	48.00	60.00
Allen, Valerie	4.00	5.00	10.00	12.00
Allen, Viola	7.50	9.00	16.00	20.00
Ames, Leon	7.00	9.00	16.00	20.00
Ames, Nancy	4.00	5.00	9.00	11.00
Amos & Andy	50.00	60.00	111.00	140.00
Ancerl, Karel	2.00	4.00	8.00	10.00
Anderson, "Bronco Billy"	30.00	34.00	64.00	80.00
Anderson, Marian	24.00	28.00	52.00	65.00
Anderson, Mary (1859-1940)	12.00	15.00	27.00	34.00
Andrews, Maxine	6.00	7.00	13.00	18.00
Andrews Sisters (3)	35.00			100.00
Angel, Heather	10.00	12.00	21.00	30.00
Ankers, Evelyn	13.00	15.00	28.00	35.00
Annabella	20.00	24.00	44.00	55.00
Anthony, Ray	4.00	5.00	10.00	12.00
Appleby, Ray	2.00	3.00	6.00	8.00
Arbuckle, Maclyn	5.00	7.50	15.00	14.00
Arbuckle, Roscoe	225.00	375.00	500.00	600.00
Arden, Nicke	1.00	3.00	6.00	7.00
Arlen, Richard	20.00	24.00	44.00	55.00
Arliss, George	40.00	47.00	87.00	110.00
Armetta, Henry	11.00	13.00	25.00	40.00
Armstrong, Louis	73.00	64.00	119.00	175.00
Armstrong, Robert	78.00	91.00	170.00	210.00
Arnaz, Desi	10.00	12.00	22.00	28.00
Arnold, Edward	24.00	28.00	52.00	65.00
Arquette, Cliff	10.00	12.00	21.00	30.00
Arthur, Jean	55.00	64.00	119.00	150.00
Astaire, Fred	68.00		80.00	100.00
Asther, Nils	13.00	15.00	28.00	35.00
Astor, Mary	18.00	21.00	40.00	50.00
Auer, Mischa	28.00	32.00	60.00	75.00
Auld, Georgie	4.00	5.00	9.00	11.00
Aumont, Jean Pierre	9.00	11.00	20.00	25.00
Ayres, Agnes	50.00	58.00	108.00	136.00
Baby Peggy	3.00	4.00	8.00	10.00
Bacon, Frank	5.00	6.00	11.00	14.00
Baddeley, Hermione	7.00	8.00	15.00	19.00
Bailey, Jack	2.00	4.00	8.00	10.00
Bainter, Fay	40.00	47.00	88.00	110.00
Baker, Josephine	95.00	110.00	205.00	250.00

Bud Abbott

Maude Adams

Jack Albertson

Fred Allen

Marian Anderson

Nils Asther

Maxine and Patty Andrews

Roscoe "Fatty" Arbuckle

Gene Autry

Tallulah Bankhead

Mona Barrie

Ethel Barrymore

Lionel Barrymore

Freddie Bartholomew

Noah Beery

Joan Bennett

Most sincerely,

Gertrude Berg

Elisabeth Bergner

Sarah Bernhardt

Eubie Blake

Yussi Bjorling

"P-P-P- Porky Pig"

Mel Blanc

Eleanor Boardman

Ray Bolger

Edwin Booth

Major Edward Bowes

Bill "Hopalong Cassidy" Boyd

Clive Brook

297

Name	Signature Only	Letter or Document Signed	Autograph Letter Signed	Signed Photograph
Baker, Kenny	5.00	6.00	11.00	15.00
Baker, "Wee" Bonnie	8.00	9.00	18.00	25.00
Balanchine, George	15.00	18.00	33.00	40.00
Ballew, Smith	6.00	6.00	12.00	15.00
Bancroft, George	15.00	17.00	32.00	40.00
Bankhead, Tallulah	50.00	58.00	107.00	135.00
Banky, Vilma	29.00	34.00	64.00	80.00
Bara, Theda	70.00	83.00	155.00	195.00
Barbejacque, Prince	2.00	3.00	6.00	8.00
Barbier, George	9.00	11.00	20.00	25.00
Bari, Lynn	5.00	6.00	10.00	15.00
Barker, Lex (SP as Tarzan)	55.00	64.00	119.00	150.00
Barnabee, Henry Clay	5.00	6.00	11.00	14.00
Barnes, Binnie	11.00	13.00	24.00	30.00
Barrie, Mona	11.00	13.00	24.00	30.00
Barrie, Wendy	13.00	15.00	28.00	35.00
Barry, Don "Red"	17.00	19.00	36.00	45.00
Barry, Wesley	6.00	7.00	14.00	17.00
Barrymore, Diana	25.00	35.00	50.00	70.00
Barrymore, Ethel	48.00	64.00	119.00	150.00
Barrymore, John	140.00	200.00	304.00	385.00
Barrymore, Lionel	40.00	47.00	87.00	110.00
Barthelmess, Richard	35.00	41.00	76.00	95.00
Bartholomew, Freddie	10.00	12.00	21.00	30.00
Basehart, Richard	10.00	12.00	20.00	25.00
Basie, Count	50.00			75.00
Bates, Blanche	10.00	12.00	21.00	27.00
Baxter, Anne	15.00	18.00	33.00	35.00
Baxter, Warner	25.00	29.00	54.00	60.00
Bayne, Beverly	15.00	8.00	20.00	23.00
Beal, John	7.00	9.00	16.00	20.00
Beane, Hilary	9.00	11.00	20.00	25.00
Beatty, Clyde	11.00	13.00	24.00	30.00
Becker, Barbara	2.00	4.00	8.00	10.00
Beems, Patricia	2.00	4.00	8.00	10.00
Beery, Noah	40.00	48.00	80.00	100.00
Beery, Wallace	85.00	100.00	185.00	225.00
Begley, Ed, Sr.	30.00	35.00	66.00	83.00
Belasco, David	40.00	55.00	103.00	129.00
Belita	15.00	18.00	33.00	41.00
Bellamy, Madge	12.00	14.00	26.00	33.00
Bellson, Louis	5.00	6.00	11.00	14.00
Bendix, William	25.00	47.00	88.00	110.00
Bennett, Bruce	9.00	11.00	20.00	25.00
Bennett, Constance	25.00	32.00	44.00	55.00
Bennett, Joan	8.00	9.00	18.00	22.00
Benny, Jack	24.00	43.00	80.00	100.00
Benson, Frank Robert	4.00	5.00	8.00	10.00
Berg, Gertrude	20.00	23.00	43.00	54.00
Bergen, Edgar	30.00	37.50	75.00	125.00
Bergen, Frances	2.00	4.00	8.00	10.00
Berger, Senta	9.00	11.00	20.00	25.00
Bergman, Ingrid	40.00	47.00	125.00	110.00

Rand Brooks

Joe E. Brown

Johnny Mack Brown

Billie Burke

Francis Bushman

James Cagney

Rod Cameron

Yakima Canutt

Mary Carlisle

Hoagy Carmichael

Sunset Carson

Enrico Caruso

Mae Clark

Ronald Coleman

Lee J. Cobb

Jerry Colonna

Jackie Coogan

Ann Corio

Joan Crawford

Marion Davies

Dolores Del Rio

Bing Crosby

Cecil B. DeMille

Howard da Silva

Diane Dors

Selma Diamond

Love 'n kisses,

JIMMY DURANTE

JD/lt

Jimmy Durante

299

Name	Signature Only	Letter or Document Signed	Autograph Letter Signed	Signed Photograph
Bergner, Elizabeth	11.00	13.00	33.00	30.00
Berkeley, Busby	50.00	60.00	111.00	140.00
Bernhardt, Sarah	74.00	86.00	160.00	200.00
Bernie, Ben	10.00	14.00	21.00	27.00
Berosini, Josephine	4.00	5.00	10.00	12.00
Berry, Ken	4.00	6.00	12.00	15.00
Besser, Joe	6.00	11.00	20.00	25.00
Best, Edna	10.00	15.00	28.00	35.00
Betz, Carl	28.00	32.00	60.00	75.00
Bey, Turhan	17.00	19.00	36.00	45.00
Bickford, Charles	18.00	21.00	40.00	50.00
Bing, Rudolph	7.00	9.00	16.00	20.00
Bingham, Amelia	5.00	6.00	11.00	14.00
Bishop, Julie	6.00	7.00	13.00	16.00
Bjoerling, Jussi	100.00			
Blackmer, Sidney	10.00	18.00	21.00	27.00
Blair, Janet	6.00	7.00	14.00	17.00
Blake, Eubie	20.00	24.00	44.00	55.00
Blanc, Mel	5.00	6.00	11.00	14.00
Blane, Sally	7.00	8.00	14.00	18.00
Blondell, Joan	29.00	34.00	64.00	80.00
Blore, Eric	18.00	21.00	40.00	50.00
Blue, Ben	20.00	24.00	44.00	55.00
Blue, Monte	18.00	21.00	40.00	50.00
Boardman, Eleanor	15.00	17.00	32.00	40.00
Bogart, Humphrey	600.00	700.00	1,375.00	1,650.00
Boland, Mary	20.00	24.00	44.00	55.00
Boles, John	12.00	14.00	26.00	33.00
Bolger, Ray	15.00	15.00	17.50	35.00
Bondi, Beulah	10.00	13.00	24.00	30.00
Boone, Richard	7.00	9.00	16.00	20.00
Booth, Edwin	18.00	21.00	39.00	49.00
Borden, Olive	28.00	50.00	60.00	75.00
Bordoni, Irene	11.00	13.00	24.00	30.00
Boshell, Louise	5.00	6.00	11.00	14.00
Boswell, Connie	5.00	6.00	10.00	15.00
Bosworth, Hobart	15.00	18.00	33.00	40.00
Boucicault, Dion	10.00	19.00	32.50	45.00
Bow, Clara	92.00	107.00	199.00	250.00
Bowe, Rosemarie	4.00	5.00	10.00	12.00
Bowes, Major Edward	21.00	25.00	46.00	58.00
Bowman, Lee	2.00	4.00	8.00	10.00
Boyd, Bill	50.00	64.00	120.00	150.00
Boyd, Steven	28.00	32.00	60.00	75.00
Boyer, Charles	35.00	45.00	60.00	75.00
Bracken, Eddie	7.00	9.00	16.00	20.00
Bradna, Olympe	5.00	6.00	11.00	14.00
Brady, Alice	50.00	60.00	108.00	140.00
Brady, William A.	13.00	15.00	28.00	35.00
Breen, Bobby	10.00	11.00	21.00	26.00
Brendel, El	15.00	17.00	25.00	40.00
Breneman, Tom	10.00	12.00	21.00	25.00
Brennan, Walter	40.00	86.00	159.00	200.00

Sam Jaffe

Lois January

Jim "Fibber McGee" Jordan

Andy Kaufman

Buster Keaton

Emmett Kelly

Arthur Kennedy

Grace Kelly

Cammie King

Werner Klemperer

Wayne King

Ted Knight

Alan Ladd

Veronica Lake

Arthur Lake

Dorothy Lamour

Carole Landis

Lillie Langtry

Stan Laurel

Lash LaRue

Gertrude Lawrence

Love,

Anna Lee

Beatrice Lillie

Gypsy Rose Lee

Lila Lee

Jenny Lind

Name	Signature Only	Letter or Document Signed	Autograph Letter Signed	Signed Photograph
Carey, Harry	25.00	29.00	54.00	70.00
Carlisle, Mary	9.00	11.00	20.00	25.00
Carmen, Jean	4.00	5.00	9.00	11.00
Carnovsky, Morris	15.00	17.00	32.00	40.00
Carol, Sue (Ladd)	3.00	4.00	8.00	10.00
Carpenter, Carleton	5.00	6.00	10.00	13.00
Carradine, John	50.00	58.00	108.00	125.00
Carrillo, Leo	11.00	13.00	24.00	30.00
Carroll, Earl	17.00	20.00	36.00	45.00
Carroll, John	10.00	12.00	21.00	27.00
Carroll, Madeleine	35.00	41.00	68.00	85.00
Carson, Sunset	3.00	5.00	10.00	12.50
Carter, Benny	28.00	32.00	60.00	75.00
Carter, Janis	4.00	5.00	10.00	12.00
Carter, Leslie, Mrs.	15.00	18.00	33.00	45.00
Caruso, Anthony	17.00	19.00	36.00	45.00
Caruso, Enrico	90.00	105.00	250.00	305.00
Cassidy, Jack	17.00	20.00	37.00	45.00
Castle, Irene	47.00	55.00	103.00	129.00
Castle, Lee	5.00	6.00	10.00	13.00
Catlett, Walter	9.00	11.00	20.00	25.00
Caulfield, Joan	9.00	11.00	20.00	25.00
Cavanaugh, Hobart	4.00	6.00	12.00	15.00
Cayvan, Georgia	5.00	6.00	11.00	14.00
Chaliapin, Fyodor	80.00	92.00	170.00	215.00
Chandler, Jeff	50.00	58.00	80.00	100.00
Chaney, Lon, Jr.(the Wolfman)	85.00	99.00	185.00	232.00
Chaney, Lon, Sr.	500.00	650.00	1,085.00	1,200.00
Chaplin, Charles	175.00			350.00
Chaplin, Lita Grey	10.00	12.00	21.00	27.00
Chaplin, Sydney	9.00	11.00	20.00	25.00
Chase, Ilka	10.00	13.00	16.00	20.00
Chatterton, Ruth	15.00	26.00	48.00	60.00
Chevalier, Maurice	35.00	41.00	75.00	95.00
Christians, Mady	20.00	25.00	32.00	40.00
Churchill, Sarah	9.00	10.00	19.00	24.00
Claire, Ina	11.00	45.00	24.00	30.00
Clanton, Jimmy	40.00	47.00	88.00	110.00
Clark, Bobby	10.00	12.00	21.00	25.00
Clark, Dane	9.00	11.00	20.00	25.00
Clark, Marguerite	2.50	4.00	8.00	10.00
Clarke, Annie	10.00	12.00	21.00	27.00
Clarke, Mae	15.00	17.00	32.00	40.00
Clayton, Jan	3.00	4.00	8.00	10.00
Clift, Montgomery	185.00	215.00	500.00	450.00
Clyde, June	6.00	7.00	14.00	17.00
Cobb, Lee J.	25.00	51.00	96.00	120.00
Coburn, Charles	40.00	47.00	87.00	95.00
Coca, Imogene	10.00	11.00	21.00	26.00
Cochran, Steve	35.00	41.00	76.00	95.00
Coco, James	4.00	6.00	12.00	15.00
Cody, Buck	4.00	5.00	10.00	12.00
Cody, Iron Eyes	11.00	13.00	24.00	30.00

Liberace

Harold Lloyd

Jeanette MacDonald

Marion Mack

Ted Mack

Sheila MacRae

Mantovani

Harpo Marx

Groucho Marx

Zeppo Marx

Colonel Tim McCoy

Raymond Massey

Adolphe Menjou

Ethel Merman

Burgess Meredith

With every good wish,
Marvin Miller

Marvin Miller

Ray Milland

Tom Mix

Jack Oakie

Pola Negri

Edmond O'Brien

Pat O'Brien

Sincerely yours,
Louella O. Parsons

Slim Pickens

Mary Pickford

305

Name	Signature Only	Letter or Document Signed	Autograph Letter Signed	Signed Photograph
Cody, Lew	7.00	8.00	15.00	19.00
Cole, Nat King	138.00	170.00	250.00	325.00
Coleman, Nancy	5.00	6.00	11.00	14.00
Collinge, Patricia	5.00	6.00	12.00	15.00
Collins, Lottie	10.00	12.00	21.00	27.00
Colman, Ronald	90.00	105.00	140.00	175.00
Colonna, Jerry	6.00	7.00	13.00	16.00
Columbo, Russ	62.00	73.00	135.00	170.00
Compson, Betty	20.00	24.00	44.00	55.00
Compton, Joyce	6.00	7.00	13.00	16.00
Conklin, Chester	28.00	32.00	60.00	75.00
Conniff, Ray	12.00	14.00	26.00	33.00
Connolly, Walter	30.00	35.00	65.00	82.00
Conquest, Ida	10.00	12.00	21.00	27.00
Conrad, Michael	11.00	13.00	24.00	30.00
Conried, Hans	11.00	13.00	24.00	30.00
Conte, John	4.00	6.00	12.00	15.00
Coogan, Jackie	10.00	15.00	28.00	35.00
Coogan, Richard	2.50	4.00	8.00	10.00
Cool, Harry	2.50	3.00	6.00	7.00
Cooper, Gary	170.00	190.00	314.00	395.00
Cooper, Gladys Dame	18.00	21.00	40.00	50.00
Cooper, Jackie	9.00	11.00	20.00	25.00
Corey, Wendell	24.00	28.00	52.00	65.00
Corio, Ann	5.00	9.00	16.00	20.00
Corlett, Irene	3.00	4.00	8.00	10.00
Cornell, Katharine	10.00	12.00	21.00	27.00
Cortez, Ricardo	11.00	13.00	24.00	30.00
Cossart, Ernest	15.00	18.00	33.00	40.00
Costello, Delores	18.00	21.00	40.00	50.00
Costello, Lou	110.00	128.00	239.00	300.00
Cowl, Jane	10.00	13.00	24.00	30.00
Crabbe, Buster	20.00	24.00	44.00	55.00
Crabtree, Lotta	11.00	13.00	25.00	36.00
Crane, Bob	9.00	11.00	20.00	25.00
Crane, William H.	30.00	35.00	65.00	82.00
Crawford, Broderick	11.00	13.00	24.00	30.00
Crawford, Joan	35.00	40.00	75.00	95.00
Cregar, Laird	84.00	98.00	183.00	230.00
Crews, Laura Hope	25.00	29.00	54.00	68.00
Crisp, Donald	50.00	75.00	139.00	175.00
Crooks, Richard	15.00	18.00	33.00	41.00
Crosby, Bing	39.00	45.00	84.00	105.00
Crosby, Bob	2.50	3.00	6.00	7.00
Cugat, Xavier	6.00	7.00	13.00	16.00
Culver, Roland	7.00	9.00	16.00	20.00
Curtis, Alan	11.00	13.00	24.00	30.00
Cushman, Charlotte S.	23.00	27.00	50.00	65.00
Dailey, Dan	13.00	15.00	28.00	35.00
Dailey, Peter F.	5.00	6.00	11.00	14.00
Dalton, Charles	4.00	4.00	8.00	10.00
Dalton, Dorothy	15.00	17.00	32.00	40.00
Daly, John Charles	4.00	5.00	9.00	11.00

Zasu Pitts

Lily Pons

Dick Powell

Eleanor Powell

Sincerely,

Tyrone Power

Robert Preston

Otto Preminger

Freddie Prinze

Rags Ragland

Sally Rand

Duncan Renaldo

Leni Riefenstahl

Jason Robards

Ginger Rogers

Arthur Rubinstein

CHARLIE RUGGLES

Charlie Ruggles

Lillian Russell

Ann Rutherford

Randolph Scott

Jean Seberg

David O. Selznick

Rod Serling

Mack Sennett

Norma Shearer

307

Name	Signature Only	Letter or Document Signed	Autograph Letter Signed	Signed Photograph
Damita, Lily	22.00	26.00	48.00	60.00
Daniels, Bebe	22.00	26.00	48.00	60.00
Dantine, Helmut	10.00	12.00	21.00	25.00
Darnell, Linda	18.00	82.50	40.00	50.00
Darro, Frankie	7.00	8.00	15.00	19.00
Darwell, Jane	24.00	28.00	52.00	65.00
da Silva, Howard	5.00	6.00	11.00	14.00
Dauvray, Helen	2.00			5.00
Davenport, Fanny	12.00	14.00	26.00	35.00
Davies, Marion	25.00	30.00	56.00	70.00
Davis, Fay	2.00	3.00	6.00	7.00
Davis, Jim	17.00	19.00	36.00	45.00
Davis, Jo	2.50	4.00	8.00	10.00
Davis, Johnny "Scat"	5.00	6.00	10.00	13.00
Davis, Nancy	18.00	21.00	40.00	50.00
Day, Laraine	5.00	6.00	12.00	15.00
Dean, James	550.00	641.00	1,195.00	1,500.00
Dean, Julia	5.00	6.00	11.00	14.00
Dekker, Albert	55.00	64.00	119.00	150.00
Dell, Myrna	2.50	4.00	8.00	10.00
Della Chiesa, Vivian	8.00	10.00	18.00	23.00
Del Rio, Dolores	30.00	35.00	65.00	82.00
Demarest, William	9.00	11.00	20.00	25.00
DeMille, Agnes	23.00	27.00	50.00	65.00
DeMille, Cecil B.	40.00	64.00	119.00	150.00
DeMille, Katherine	5.00	6.00	12.00	15.00
Denning, Richard	5.00	6.00	11.00	14.00
Devine, Andy	20.00	24.00	44.00	55.00
DeWolf, Billy	22.00	26.00	48.00	60.00
Diamond, Selma	7.00	8.00	15.00	19.00
Dix, Richard	18.00	21.00	40.00	50.00
Dixey, Henry E.	1.00	2.00	4.00	5.00
Donat, Robert	37.00	43.00	80.00	100.00
Donnelly, Ruth	9.00	11.00	20.00	25.00
Doran, Ann	10.00	12.00	21.00	27.00
Dors, Diana	28.00	32.00	60.00	75.00
D'Orsay, Fifi	7.00	9.00	16.00	25.00
Dorsey, Jimmie	8.00	9.00	18.00	22.00
Dorsey, Tommy	20.00	24.00	44.00	55.00
Douglas, Helen G.	40.00	47.00	87.00	109.00
Douglas, Melvyn	20.00	24.00	44.00	55.00
Douglas, Paul	15.00	17.00	32.00	40.00
Dove, Billie	17.00	19.00	36.00	45.00
Dowling, Eddie	15.00	18.00	33.00	41.00
Downey, Morton	10.00	12.00	21.00	27.00
D'Oyly Carte	23.00	27.00	50.00	63.00
Dragonette, Jessica	8.00	9.00	18.00	22.00
Drake, Frances	6.00	6.00	12.00	15.00
Drake, Tom	4.00	5.00	10.00	12.00
Draper, Ruth	26.00	30.00	56.00	70.00
Dresser, Louise	18.00	21.00	40.00	50.00
Drew, Ellen	2.00	3.00	6.00	7.50
Drew, John	50.00	58.00	108.00	136.00

Ann Sheridan

Phil Silvers

Andres Segovia

Lili St. Cyr

Tempest Storm

Jimmy Stewart

Howard Thurston

John Wayne

Forrest Tucker

Charlie Weaver (Cliff Arquette)

Esther Williams

Name	Signature Only	Letter or Document Signed	Autograph Letter Signed	Signed Photograph
Driscoll, Bobby	44.00	51.00	96.00	120.00
Drouet, Robert	20.00	24.00	44.00	55.00
Dru, Joanne	4.00	5.00	10.00	12.00
Duchin, Eddie	25.00	29.00	54.00	68.00
Duna, Steffi	4.00	5.00	10.00	12.00
Dunbar, Dixie	5.00	6.00	11.00	14.00
Dunn, James	47.00	55.00	102.00	128.00
Durante, Jimmy	28.00	37.50	60.00	75.00
Durbin, Deanna	9.00	11.00	20.00	25.00
Duryea, Dan	10.00	20.00	21.00	27.00
Duse, Eleanora	138.00	161.00	300.00	375.00
Dvorak, Ann	4.00	5.00	10.00	12.00
Earle, Virginia	5.00	6.00	11.00	14.00
Eddy, Nelson	35.00	44.00	64.00	80.00
Egan, Richard	9.00	11.00	20.00	25.00
Eilers, Sally	10.00	13.00	24.00	30.00
Ekberg, Anita	9.00	11.00	20.00	25.00
Elliott, Maxine	25.00	29.00	54.00	68.00
Elliott, Wild Bill	55.00	64.00	119.00	150.00
Ellison, James	2.50	4.00	8.00	10.00
Eltinge, Julian	15.00	17.00	32.00	40.00
Emerson, Faye	12.50	15.00	27.00	34.00
Emery, John	10.00	12.00	21.00	30.00
Evans, Joan	7.00	9.00	16.00	20.00
Evans, Madge	9.00	11.00	20.00	25.00
Eythe, William	9.00	11.00	20.00	25.00

Name	Signature Only	Letter or Document Signed	Autograph Letter Signed	Signed Photograph
Eytinge, Rose	5.00	6.00	11.00	14.00
Fairbanks, Douglas	75.00	80.00	96.00	120.00
Farmer, Frances	50.00	58.00	108.00	136.00
Farnum, Dustin	30.00	35.00	65.00	82.00
Farrar, Geraldine	30.00	35.00	60.00	75.00
Farrell, Charles	5.00	7.00	14.00	17.50
Farrell, Glenda	13.00	15.00	28.00	35.00
Fay, Frank	15.00	18.00	33.00	41.00
Faye, Alice	7.00	9.00	16.00	20.00
Faye, Julia	3.00	4.00	8.00	10.00
Faylen, Frank	11.00	13.00	24.00	30.00
Fazenda, Louise	14.00	16.00	22.00	37.50
Feld, Fritz	11.00	13.00	24.00	30.00
Feldany, Eric	1.50	2.00	4.00	5.00
Fellows, Edith	11.00	13.00	24.00	30.00
Fernandel	28.00	32.00	60.00	75.00
Fidler, Jimmie	8.00	9.00	18.00	22.00
Fiedler, Arthur	25.00	29.00	54.00	68.00
Field, Virginia	7.00	8.00	15.00	19.00
Fields, Gracie	15.00	11.00	20.00	25.00
Fields, Stanley	9.00	11.00	20.00	25.00
Fields, W. C.	250.00	300.00	550.00	680.00
Finch, Peter	40.00	53.00	100.00	125.00
Fisk, Minnie Maddern	18.00	21.00	40.00	50.00
Fitzgerald, Geraldine	5.00	6.00	11.00	14.00
Florence, W. J., Mrs.	4.00	5.00	9.00	11.00
Flowers, Bess	5.00	6.00	11.00	14.00
Flunger, Anna	5.00	6.00	11.00	14.00
Flynn, Errol	150.00	190.00	285.00	375.00
Foch, Nina	5.00	9.00	16.00	20.00
Fonda, Henry	13.00	15.00	28.00	35.00
Fontaine, Joan	20.00	24.00	44.00	55.00
Forbes, Ralph	10.00	12.00	21.00	27.00
Forbes-Robertson, J.	15.00	18.00	33.00	41.00
Ford, John		95.00		
Ford, Paul	15.00	18.00	33.00	40.00
Ford, Wallace	18.50	21.00	40.00	50.00
Formes, Karl	18.00	21.00	40.00	50.00
Forrest, Edwin	23.00	27.00	50.00	63.00
Forrest, Sally	7.00	9.00	16.00	20.00
Fosse, Bob	9.00	11.00	20.00	25.00
Foster, Norman	12.00	14.00	26.00	35.00
Foster, Preston	10.00	12.00	21.00	30.00
Foster, Susanna	10.00	12.00	21.00	27.00
Foy, Eddie, Jr.	11.00	13.00	24.00	30.00
Francis, Arlene	7.00	9.00	16.00	20.00
Francis, Kay	18.00	21.00	39.00	49.00
Friganza, Trixie	16.00	19.00	35.00	44.00
Frohman, Daniel	15.00	17.00	32.00	40.00
Froman, Jane	12.00	14.00	26.00	33.00
Furness, Betty	7.00	9.00	16.00	20.00
Furstenberg, Betsy von	4.00	5.00	10.00	12.00
Gable, Clark	150.00	225.00	325.00	400.00

Name	Signature Only	Letter or Document Signed	Autograph Letter Signed	Signed Photograph
Gable, Kay	7.00	9.00	16.00	20.00
Gadski, Johanna	11.00	13.00	24.00	30.00
Gallian, Ketti	8.00	10.00	18.00	23.00
Galli-Curci, Amelita	37.00	43.00	80.00	100.00
Gam, Rita	4.00	6.00	12.00	15.00
Garbo, Greta	1,000.00	3,500.00	10,000.00	9,800.00
Garden, Mary	23.00	27.00	50.00	65.00
Garfield, John	95.00	115.00	200.00	250.00
Gargan, William	9.00	11.00	20.00	25.00
Garland, Judy	195.00	225.00	420.00	525.00
Garner, Peggy Ann	22.50	26.00	49.00	55.00
Garroway, Dave	6.00	6.00	12.00	15.00
Gaxton, William	7.00	9.00	16.00	20.00
Gaynor, Janet	15.00	18.00	33.00	40.00
Genn, Leo	7.00	9.00	16.00	20.00
George, Christopher	17.00	19.00	36.00	45.00
George, Gladys	18.00	21.00	40.00	50.00
George, Grace	5.00	6.00	11.00	14.00
Gerri, Toni	4.00	5.00	10.00	12.00
Gibson, Hoot	75.00	86.00	159.00	200.00
Gilbert, Billy	13.00	15.00	28.00	35.00
Gilbert, John	65.00	75.00	139.00	175.00
Gilbert, Lynn	3.00	4.50	6.00	8.00
Gillette, William	20.00	24.00	44.00	55.00
Gilmore, Virginia	10.00	12.00	21.00	27.00
Gingold, Hermione	4.00	5.00	10.00	12.00
Gish, Lillian	20.00	25.00	28.00	35.00
Glad, Gladys	9.00	11.00	20.00	25.00
Glaser, Lulu	10.00	12.00	21.00	27.00
Gleason, Jackie	17.00	19.00	36.00	45.00
Godfrey, Arthur	18.00	21.00	40.00	50.00
Goldwyn, Sam	70.00	80.00	150.00	175.00
Gombell, Minna	24.00	28.00	52.00	65.00
Gomez, Thomas	10.00	12.00	21.00	27.00
Goodman, Benny	30.00	40.00	49.00	60.00
Goodman, Dody	3.00	4.00	8.00	10.00
Goodwin, Nat	5.00	6.00	11.00	14.00
Gordon, Huntley	6.00	7.00	14.00	17.50
Gordon, Ruth	8.00	11.00	16.00	25.00
Goudal, Jetta	7.00	8.00	14.00	18.00
Grable, Betty	28.00	32.00	50.00	75.00
Grahame, Gloria	35.00	53.00	100.00	125.00
Grant, Cary	100.00	118.00	219.00	275.00
Granville, Bonita	15.00	18.00	33.00	40.00
Grauman, Sid	25.00	30.00	54.00	65.00
Gray, Gilda	32.50	40.00	70.00	90.00
Greco, José	5.00	6.00	11.00	14.00
Green, Dorothy	2.50	4.00	8.00	10.00
Green, Mitzi	8.00	9.00	18.00	22.00
Greene, Lorne	20.00	24.00	44.00	55.00
Greenstreet, Sydney	150.00	175.00	326.00	375.00
Greenwood, Charlotte	15.00	18.00	33.00	41.00
Gregg, Virginia	4.00	5.00	10.00	12.00

Name	Signature Only	Letter or Document Signed	Autograph Letter Signed	Signed Photograph
Grey, Nan	10.00	12.00	21.00	27.00
Grey, Virginia	8.00	10.00	18.00	22.50
Griffith, Corinne	24.00	28.00	52.00	65.00
Griffith, David W.	250.00	300.00	550.00	695.00
Griffith, Hugh	200.00	233.00	434.00	545.00
Grimes, Tammy	4.00	5.00	9.00	11.00
Grossmith, George	9.00	11.00	20.00	25.00
Guilbert, Yvette	28.00	32.00	60.00	75.00
Guild, Nancy	5.00	6.00	11.00	14.00
Gurie, Sigrid	7.00	8.00	14.00	18.00
Gwenn, Edmund	75.00	87.00	162.00	197.00
Gwynne, Anne	5.00	6.00	10.00	13.00
Gye, Albani	6.00	7.00	13.00	16.00
Hackett, Bobby	4.00	5.00	9.00	11.00
Hackett, J. K.	5.00	6.00	11.00	14.00
Hackett, Joan	11.00	13.00	24.00	30.00
Haenschen, Gus	2.00	4.00	8.00	10.00
Haines, William	9.00	11.00	20.00	25.00
Hale, Richard	5.00	6.00	11.00	14.00
Haley, Jack	22.00	26.00	48.00	60.00
Hall, Huntz	7.00	9.00	16.00	20.00
Hall, Jon	28.00	32.00	40.00	50.00
Hall, Josephine	5.00	6.00	11.00	14.00
Hall, Pauline	4.00	4.00	8.00	10.00
Halle, Wilhelmine	5.00	6.00	11.00	14.00
Halop, Billy	33.00	38.00	72.00	90.00
Hamilton, Neil	9.00	11.00	20.00	25.00
Hampden, Walter	15.00	18.00	33.00	40.00
Hampton, Hope	15.00	18.00	32.50	40.00
Hansen, William	5.00	6.00	11.00	14.00
Hardie, Russell	7.00	9.00	16.00	20.00
Harding, Ann	9.00	11.00	20.00	25.00
Hardwicke, Cedric	33.00	38.00	72.00	90.00
Harlow, Jean	550.00	640.00	1,195.00	1,500.00
Hart, Dolores	15.00	25.00	55.00	75.00
Hart, Dorothy	3.00	4.00	8.00	10.00
Hart, William S.	100.00	120.00	179.00	225.00
Hartman, Paul and Grace	5.00	6.00	11.00	15.00
Harvey, Lawrence	28.00	32.00	60.00	75.00
Harvey, Lilian	2.00	4.00	8.00	10.00
Haskell, James K.	10.00	12.00	21.00	27.00
Hatfield, Hurd	5.00	6.00	11.00	15.00
Haver, June	5.00	6.00	10.00	13.00
Havoc, June	7.00	8.00	15.00	19.00
Hawkins, Jack	11.00	13.00	24.00	30.00
Hayakawa, Sessue	60.00	75.00	139.00	175.00
Hayden, Mellisa	3.00	4.00	8.00	10.00
Hayes, Helen	7.00	16.00	40.00	16.00
Hayes, Margaret	7.00	8.00	15.00	19.00
Hays, Will H.	34.00	40.00	75.00	50.00
Hayward, Louis	7.00	9.00	16.00	20.00
Hayward, Susan	110.00	128.00	239.00	300.00
Hayworth, Rita	72.00	140.00	238.00	200.00

Name	Signature Only	Letter or Document Signed	Autograph Letter Signed	Signed Photograph
Healy, Ted	9.00	11.00	20.00	25.00
Heflin, Van	45.00	53.00	98.00	123.00
Heidt, Horace	9.00	11.00	20.00	25.00
Heifetz, Jascha	21.00	24.00	45.50	57.00
Held, Anna	40.00	47.00	87.00	110.00
Heming, Violet	10.00	12.00	21.00	30.00
Hendrix, Wanda	11.00	13.00	24.00	30.00
Henry, Bill	9.00	11.00	20.00	25.00
Henry, Gloria	2.00	3.00	6.00	7.00
Hepburn, Katharine	70.00	100.00	152.00	200.00
Herbert, Hugh	15.00	18.00	33.00	40.00
Herbert, Sidney	10.00	12.00	21.00	27.00
Herman, Woody	10.00	12.00	21.00	27.00
Hern, James A.	10.00	12.00	21.00	27.00
Hersholt, Jean	25.00	29.00	54.00	65.00
Hervey, Irene	4.50	5.00	10.00	12.00
Hess, Myra Dame	11.00	13.00	24.00	30.00
Hexum, Jon-Erik	90.00	107.00	199.00	250.00
Heyman, Edward	2.00	3.00	4.00	5.00
Hildegarde	5.00	6.00	10.00	13.00
Hill, Annie	5.00	6.00	11.00	14.00
Hill, Tiny	5.00	6.00	11.00	14.00
Hiller, Wendy	15.00	18.00	33.00	40.00
Hitchcock, Alfred	150.00	175.00	220.00	275.00
Hobart, Rose	5.00	5.00	10.00	12.50
Hodiak, John	13.00	15.00	28.00	35.00
Hoffman, Maud	4.00	5.00	9.75	12.00
Hofmann, Josef	30.00	35.00	65.00	80.00
Holden, William	30.00	35.00	65.00	85.00
Holliday, Judy	70.00	83.00	155.00	195.00
Holloway, Stanley	28.00	32.00	60.00	75.00
Holloway, Sterling	8.00	9.00	18.00	22.00
Holt, Jack	29.00	34.00	64.00	80.00
Holt, Tim	46.00	53.00	100.00	125.00
Homolka, Oscar	11.00	13.00	24.00	35.00
Hopkins, Miriam	10.00	32.00	60.00	75.00
Hopper, DeWolf	10.00	12.00	21.00	27.00
Hopper, Hedda	12.00	20.00	26.00	33.00
Horowitz, Vladimir	13.00	15.00	28.00	35.00
Horton, Edward Everett	15.00	17.00	32.00	40.00
Houdini, Harry	202.00	355.00	585.00	550.00
Houghton, Katharine	6.00	10.00	12.00	15.00
Howard, John	11.00	13.00	24.00	30.00
Howard, Leslie	100.00	120.00	220.00	275.00
Howard, Moe	55.00	65.00	120.00	150.00
Howard, Willie	20.00	25.00	46.00	58.00
Hudson, Rochelle	10.00	30.00	56.00	70.00
Hudson, Rock	18.00	21.00	40.00	50.00
Hughes, Mary Beth	7.00	8.00	15.00	19.00
Hull, Henry	11.00	13.00	20.00	30.00
Hull, Josephine	75.00	86.00	160.00	200.00
Hull, Warren	9.00	11.00	20.00	25.00
Hunt, Marsha	6.00	7.00	12.00	15.00

Name	Signature Only	Letter or Document Signed	Autograph Letter Signed	Signed Photograph
Hunter, Jeff	18.00	21.00	40.00	50.00
Huston, John	11.00	13.00	24.00	30.00
Huston, Walter	25.00	40.00	54.00	68.00
Hutchins, Will	5.00	7.00	10.00	12.00
Hutchinson, Josephine	7.00	9.00	16.00	20.00
Hutton, Betty	5.00	6.00	11.00	14.00
Hutton, Jim	35.00	41.00	76.00	95.00
Hyams, Leila	17.00	19.00	36.00	45.00
Hyde-White, Wilfrid	13.00	15.00	28.00	35.00
Ingle, Red	4.00	5.00	9.00	11.00
Irving, Sir Henry	30.00	35.00	65.00	82.00
Irwin, May	10.00	12.00	21.00	27.00
Jaffe, Sam	10.00	19.00	36.00	45.00
James, Harry	7.00	9.00	16.00	20.00
Janis, Elsie	20.00	24.00	44.00	55.00
Jannings, Emile	200.00	233.00	434.00	545.00
Janssen, David	15.00	17.00	32.00	40.00
January, Lois	2.00	3.00	6.00	8.00
Jaroff, Serge	4.00	5.00	10.00	12.00
Jarrett, Art	3.00	4.00	6.00	8.00
Jason, Sybil	3.00	4.00	8.00	10.00
Jean, Gloria	9.00	11.00	20.00	25.00
Jefferson, Joe	15.00	18.00	33.00	40.00
Jepson, Helen	7.00	9.00	16.00	20.00
Jessel, George	13.00	15.00	28.00	35.00
Johnson, Betty	2.00	3.00	6.00	7.00
Johnson, Osa	9.00	11.00	20.00	25.00
Jolson, Al	72.00	83.00	155.00	195.00
Jones, Allan	10.00	12.00	21.00	27.00
Jones, Buck	60.00	70.00	130.00	165.00
Jones, Carolyn	22.00	26.00	48.00	60.00
Jones, Isham	5.00	6.00	11.00	14.00
Jordan, Dorothy	9.00	11.00	20.00	25.00
Jordan, Jim (Fibber)	5.00	6.00	11.00	14.00
Jory, Victor	18.00	21.00	40.00	50.00
Joy, Leatrice	6.00	6.00	12.00	15.00
Joyce, Alice	9.00	11.00	20.00	25.00
Judge, Arline	11.00	13.00	24.00	30.00
Karloff, Boris	105.00	120.00	300.00	275.00
Kaufman, Andy	18.00	21.00	40.00	50.00
Kay, Beatrice	5.00	6.00	11.00	14.00
Kaye, Danny	26.00	30.00	56.00	40.00
Kean, Jane	3.00	4.00	8.00	10.00
Keane, Edward	9.00	11.00	20.00	25.00
Keaton, Buster	150.00	180.00	239.00	300.00
Kedrova, Lila	9.00	11.00	20.00	25.00
Keeler, Ruby	9.00	11.00	20.00	25.00
Keene, Charles S.	11.00	13.00	25.00	35.00
Kelcey, Herbert	5.00	6.00	11.00	14.00
Kellard, Ralph	4.00	5.00	10.00	12.00
Kellerman, Annette	46.00	53.00	100.00	125.00
Kelly, Emmett, Sr.	13.00	15.00	28.00	35.00
Kelly, Gene	11.00	21.00	36.00	30.00

Name	Signature Only	Letter or Document Signed	Autograph Letter Signed	Signed Photograph
Kelly, Grace	50.00			75.00
Kelly, Nancy	15.00	17.00	32.00	40.00
Kelly, Patsy	18.00	21.00	40.00	50.00
Kelly, Paul	25.00	29.00	54.00	68.00
Kelton, Pert	11.00	13.00	25.00	31.00
Kemp, Hal	17.00	20.00	37.00	40.00
Kendal, Madge	9.00	11.00	20.00	25.00
Kennedy, Arthur	5.00	6.00	11.00	14.00
Kennedy, Edgar	55.00	64.00	119.00	150.00
Kenton, Stan	4.00	5.00	10.00	12.00
Kenyon, Doris	13.00	15.00	28.00	35.00
Keyes, Evelyn	5.00	14.00	24.00	20.00
Kilian, Victor	6.00	6.00	12.00	15.00
King, Cammie	5.00	6.00	11.00	14.00
King, Walter Woolf	10.00	12.00	21.00	27.00
King, Wayne	3.00	4.00	8.00	10.00
Kirk, Phyllis	5.00	6.00	11.00	14.00
Kirkwood, Joe	50.00			
Klemperer, Werner	7.00	8.00	14.00	18.00
Knight, June	8.00	9.00	18.00	22.00
Knight, Ted	6.00	7.00	13.00	16.00
Knox, Elyse	11.00	13.00	24.00	30.00
Korda, Alexander	30.00	35.00	65.00	75.00
Korvin, Charles	3.00	4.00	7.00	9.00
Kruger, Kurt	4.00	6.00	12.00	15.00
Kruger, Otto	15.00	18.00	33.00	43.00
Krupa, Gene	30.00	35.00	65.00	80.00
Kubelik, Jan	14.00	16.00	30.00	38.00
Ladd, Alan	29.00	34.00	64.00	80.00
Ladd, Sue Carol	7.00	9.00	16.00	20.00
Laemmle, Carl	26.00	100.00	225.00	60.00
Lake, Arthur	10.00	12.00	21.00	25.00
Lake, Veronica	95.00	111.00	206.00	260.00
Lamas, Fernando	13.00	15.00	28.00	35.00
Landi, Elissa	20.00	24.00	44.00	45.00
Landis, Carole	80.00	90.00	111.00	140.00
Lane, Lola	10.00	12.00	21.00	27.00
Lane, Priscilla	7.00	9.00	16.00	20.00
Lane, Rosemary	9.00	11.00	21.00	26.00
Lang, Anton	7.00	8.00	15.00	19.00
Lang, Rosa	13.00	15.00	28.00	35.00
Lang, Sebastian	9.00	11.00	20.00	25.00
Langan, Glenn	9.00	11.00	20.00	25.00
Langdon, Harry	40.00	47.00	87.00	95.00
Langford, Frances	5.00	6.00	10.00	13.00
Langtry, Lillie	69.00	80.00	150.00	195.00
Lanza, Mario	250.00	295.00	549.00	690.00
La Rocque, Rod	9.00	11.00	20.00	25.00
LaRue, Lash	2.50	7.00	12.00	10.00
Lauder, Harry	40.00	47.00	50.00	110.00
Laughton, Charles	65.00	75.00	139.00	175.00
Laurel and Hardy	300.00			650.00
Laurette, Taylor	10.00	12.00	21.00	27.00

Name	Signature Only	Letter or Document Signed	Autograph Letter Signed	Signed Photograph
Lawford, Peter	30.00	35.00	65.00	74.00
Lawrence, Gertrude	25.00	29.00	54.00	60.00
Lawrence, Marc	7.00	9.00	16.00	20.00
Lederer, Francis	8.00	9.00	18.00	22.00
Lee, Anna	4.00	5.00	10.00	12.00
Lee, Dixie (Mrs. Bing Crosby)	9.00	11.00	20.00	25.00
Lee, Gypsy Rose	22.00	40.00	48.00	60.00
Lee, Lila	6.00	6.00	12.00	15.00
Leeds, Andrea	13.00	15.00	28.00	35.00
Le Gallienne, Eva	8.00	9.00	18.00	22.00
Lehmann, Lotte	30.00	35.00	65.00	75.00
Lehr, Lew	13.00	15.00	28.00	35.00
Leigh, Vivien	225.00			475.00
Leinsdorf, Erich	3.00	4.00	8.00	10.00
Leontovich, Eugenie	30.00	40.00	75.00	45.00
LeRoy, Mervyn	7.00	9.00	16.00	20.00
Leslie, Joan	3.00	4.00	7.00	9.00
Levene, Sam	9.00	11.00	20.00	25.00
Lewis, James	5.00	6.00	11.00	14.00
Lewis, Joe E.	15.00	18.00	33.00	35.00
Lewis, Ted	11.00	13.00	24.00	30.00
Liberace	28.00	32.00	60.00	75.00
Liberace, George	5.00	6.00	11.00	14.00
Lightner, Winnie	13.00	15.00	28.00	35.00
Lillie, Beatrice	11.00		24.00	30.00
Lind, Jenny	75.00	91.00	170.00	215.00
Lindsay, Howard	7.00	9.00	16.00	20.00
Lindsay, Margaret	15.00	18.00	25.00	32.00
Litel, John	9.00	11.00	20.00	25.00
Livingston, Margaret	3.00	4.00	8.00	10.00
Lloyd, Harold	88.00	103.00	191.00	240.00
Lockwood, Margaret	11.00	13.00	24.00	30.00
Logan, Ella	10.00	12.00	21.00	27.00
Logan, Joshua	5.00	6.00	11.00	14.00
Lombard, Carole	195.00	227.00	423.00	525.00
Lombardo, Guy	7.00	9.00	16.00	20.00
London, Julie	3.00	4.00	8.00	10.00
Long, Johnny	4.00	5.00	9.00	11.00
Louise, Anita	10.00	12.00	21.00	25.00
Lowe, Edmund	15.00	15.00	28.00	35.00
Lubitsch, Ernst	37.00	43.00	80.00	100.00
Lugosi, Bela	175.00	192.00	358.00	450.00
Lukas, Paul	28.00	32.00	60.00	75.00
Luke, Keye	11.00	13.00	24.00	30.00
Lum and Abner	17.00	19.00	36.00	45.00
Lumiere, Louis	175.00	250.00	466.00	585.00
Lund, John	4.00	5.00	8.00	10.00
Lunt and Fontanne	45.00			90.00
Lupino, Ida	5.00	9.00	16.00	20.00
Lynde, Paul	7.00	9.00	16.00	20.00
Lynn, Diana	9.00	11.00	20.00	25.00
Lynn, Jeffrey	7.00	8.00	14.00	18.00
Lytell, Bert	15.00	17.00	32.00	40.00

Name	Signature Only	Letter or Document Signed	Autograph Letter Signed	Signed Photograph
MacDonald, Jeanette	29.00	34.00	64.00	80.00
Mack, Helen	18.00	21.00	39.00	50.00
Mack, Marion	7.00	9.00	15.00	20.00
Mack, Ted	3.00	4.00	8.00	10.00
MacKaill, Dorothy	15.00	19.00	36.00	45.00
MacMurray, Fred	9.00	10.00	19.00	24.00
MacRae, Sheila	3.00	4.00	7.00	9.00
Mahoney, Jock	3.00	4.00	8.00	10.00
Makarova, Natalia	7.00	9.00	16.00	20.00
Malo, Gina	3.00	4.00	7.00	9.00
Mandel, John	4.00	5.00	9.00	11.00
Mannering, Mary	5.00	6.00	11.00	14.00
Mansfield, Jayne	73.00	100.00	159.00	200.00
Mantell, Robert B.	5.00	6.00	11.00	14.00
Mantovani	4.00	6.00	12.00	15.00
Mara, Adele	5.00	6.00	11.00	14.00
Marcellino, Muzzy	7.00	9.00	16.00	20.00
March, Fredric	18.00	21.00	39.00	45.00
Margo (Mrs. Ed Albert)	9.00	11.00	20.00	25.00
Maritza, Sari	8.00	9.00	17.00	21.00
Marlow, Lucy (Mrs. A. Carey)	3.00	4.00	8.00	10.00
Marlowe, Hugh	10.00	12.00	21.00	25.00
Marlowe, Julia	15.00	18.00	33.00	41.00
Marly, Florence	2.00	3.00	6.00	7.00
Marsh, Joan	12.00	14.00	26.00	30.00
Marsh, Mae	25.00	30.00	48.00	60.00
Marshall, Herbert	13.00	15.00	31.00	35.00
Martin, Dean Vincent	3.00	4.00	8.00	10.00
Marvin, Lee	30.00	32.00	40.00	45.00
Marx, Chico	90.00	86.00	159.00	200.00
Marx, Groucho	75.00	100.00		120.00
Marx, Harpo	100.00			200.00
Marx, Zeppo	100.00			200.00
Marx Brothers (all four)	550.00			
Mason, James	30.00	35.00	65.00	75.00
Mason, Sully	4.00	5.00	9.00	11.00
Massen, Osa	10.00	12.00	21.00	27.00
Massey, Illona	10.00	9.00	16.00	25.00
Massey, Raymond	17.00	20.00	37.00	46.00
Masters, Frankie	3.00	5.00	9.00	11.00
Mauch, Billy	8.00	9.00	18.00	22.00
Maxwell, Marilyn	4.00	6.00	12.00	15.00
May, Edna	10.00	12.00	21.00	27.00
Mayer, Louis B.	35.00	125.00	200.00	90.00
Mayfair, Mitzi	1.00	2.00	3.00	4.00
Maynard, Ken	43.00	50.00	94.00	118.00
Mazurki, Mike	3.00	4.00	8.00	10.00
Mcaffee, Johnny	3.00	4.00	7.00	9.00
McCallister, Lon	9.00	11.00	20.00	25.00
McCambridge, Mercedes	15.00	18.00	33.00	39.00
McCormack, John	50.00	85.00	150.00	120.00
McCormick, Myron	13.00	15.00	28.00	35.00
McCoy, Clyde	5.00	6.00	11.00	14.00

Name	Signature Only	Letter or Document Signed	Autograph Letter Signed	Signed Photograph
McCoy, Tim	15.00	45.00	54.00	41.00
McDaniel, Hattie	185.00	215.00	401.00	500.00
McDonald, Marie	26.00	30.00	56.00	70.00
McHugh, Frank	15.00	17.00	32.00	40.00
McKenzie, Fay	4.00	5.00	10.00	12.00
McLaglen, Victor	70.00	85.00	147.00	185.00
McLeod, Catherine	6.00	6.00	12.00	15.00
McMahon, Horace	12.50	15.00	27.00	34.00
McNally, W.	3.00	4.00	8.00	10.00
McNeill, Don	5.00	6.00	11.00	14.00
McQueen, Butterfly	11.00	21.00	36.00	30.00
McQueen, Steve	100.00	120.00	220.00	275.00
Meadowlarks (all)	3.50	5.00	10.00	12.50
Medina, Patricia	5.00	6.00	11.00	14.00
Meighan, Tom	15.00	36.00	55.00	40.00
Melba, Nellie	55.00	64.00	119.00	150.00
Melton, James	12.50	15.00	27.00	34.00
Menjou, Adolphe	15.00	17.00	32.00	40.00
Menken, Helen	10.00	12.00	21.00	27.00
Mercer, Frances	7.00	8.00	15.00	19.00
Mercer, Marian	9.00	11.00	20.00	25.00
Merkel, Una	10.00	12.00	21.00	25.00
Merman, Ethel	7.00	9.00	16.00	20.00
Merrill, Robert	4.00	5.00	9.00	11.00
Mielziner, Jo	20.00	35.00	44.00	40.00
Mifune, Toshiro	15.00	17.00	32.00	40.00
Milestone, Lewis	9.00	11.00	20.00	25.00
Milland, Ray	12.00	40.00	50.00	35.00
Miller, Glen	73.00	86.00	159.00	200.00
Miller, Henry	25.00	29.00	54.00	60.00
Miller, Marilyn	80.00	90.00	111.00	140.00
Miller, Marvin	6.00	7.00	13.00	16.00
Miller, Patsy Ruth	4.00	6.00	12.00	15.00
Minnelli, Vincent	6.00	7.00	13.00	16.00
Minter, Mary Miles	60.00	75.00	139.00	175.00
Miranda, Carmen	100.00	115.00	159.00	200.00
Miroslava	19.00	22.00	41.00	45.00
Mitchell, Maggie	6.00	7.00	13.00	21.00
Mitchell, Thomas	64.00	75.00	139.00	175.00
Mitropoulos, Dimitri	15.00	18.00	33.00	36.00
Mix, Tom	100.00	117.00	199.00	250.00
Mix, Victoria	4.00	6.00	12.00	15.00
Modjeske, Helena	15.00	18.00	33.00	40.00
Mojica, José	3.00	4.00	8.00	10.00
Monk, Thelonious	20.00	24.00	44.00	55.00
Monroe, Marilyn	800.00			2,000.00
Monroe, Vaughn	4.00	5.00	9.00	11.00
Montenegro, Conchita	7.00	9.00	16.00	20.00
Montez, Maria	23.00	27.00	50.00	62.50
Montgomery, Douglass	7.00	9.00	16.00	20.00
Montgomery, George	7.50	9.00	16.00	20.00
Montgomery, Robert	20.00	25.00	32.00	30.00
Montoya, Carlos	7.00	8.00	14.00	18.00

Name	Signature Only	Letter or Document Signed	Autograph Letter Signed	Signed Photograph
Moore, Colleen	7.00	9.00	16.00	20.00
Moore, Dick	4.00	6.00	12.00	15.00
Moore, Grace	55.00	64.00	120.00	150.00
Moore, Tom	20.00	24.00	44.00	55.00
Moore, Victor	10.00	12.00	21.00	30.00
Moran, Lois	5.00	6.00	10.00	13.00
Moran, Polly	30.00	35.00	65.00	75.00
Moreland, Mantan	65.00	76.00	141.00	175.00
Moreno, Anthony	9.00	15.00	20.00	25.00
Morgan, Dennis	4.00	6.00	12.00	15.00
Morgan, Edward J.	10.00	12.00	21.00	27.00
Morgan, Frank	37.00	43.00	80.00	100.00
Morgan, Helen	25.00	43.00	80.00	100.00
Morgan, Michele	5.00	6.00	12.00	14.50
Morgan, Ralph	23.00	27.00	50.00	120.00
Morris, Chester	22.00	26.00	48.00	60.00
Morris, Wayne	18.00	21.00	39.00	49.00
Morrison, Patricia	10.00	12.00	21.00	27.00
Morrow, Jeff	3.00	4.00	8.00	10.00
Morrow, Vic	18.00	21.00	40.00	50.00
Mostel, Zero	11.00	13.00	24.00	30.00
Muir, Jean	7.00	9.00	16.00	20.00
Muni, Paul	40.00	47.00	87.00	110.00
Munsel, Patrice	7.00	8.00	15.00	19.00
Munson, Ona	29.00	34.00	64.00	80.00
Murphy, George	9.00	11.00	20.00	25.00
Murray, Mae	18.00	21.00	40.00	50.00
Nagel, Conrad	13.00	15.00	28.00	35.00
Naish, J. Carroll	10.00	12.00	21.00	30.00
Naldi, Nita	20.00	24.00	44.00	55.00
Napier, Alan	8.00	9.00	18.00	22.00
Navarro, Ramon	28.00	32.00	60.00	75.00
Nazimova, Alla	35.00	41.00	76.00	95.00
Neagle, Anna Dame	7.00	9.00	16.00	20.00
Neal, Tom	17.50	21.00	38.00	40.00
Negri, Pola	33.00	38.00	72.00	90.00
Nelson, Ozzie	30.00	35.00	65.00	70.00
Nelson, Rick	40.00	46.50	76.00	95.00
Nesbit, Cathleen	12.50	15.00	27.00	35.00
Neville, Henry	3.00	4.00	7.00	9.00
Nielsen, Alice	20.00	24.00	44.00	55.00
Nielsen, Terry	5.00	6.00	11.00	14.00
Nilssen, Anna Q.	22.00	26.00	48.00	60.00
Niven, David	20.00	25.00	36.00	45.00
Noble, Ray	31.00	36.00	68.00	85.00
Nolan, Kathleen	4.00	6.00	12.00	15.00
Nolan, Lloyd	15.00	18.00	33.00	30.00
Normand, Mabel	119.00	150.00	279.00	350.00
Novello, Ivor	13.00	15.00	28.00	35.00
Nugent, Elliott	7.00	8.00	15.00	19.00
Oakie, Jack	15.00	18.00	33.00	41.00
Oberon, Merle	20.00	24.00	44.00	55.00
Oboler, Arch	21.00	25.00	46.00	35.00

Name	Signature Only	Letter or Document Signed	Autograph Letter Signed	Signed Photograph
O'Brien, Edmond	18.00	21.00	40.00	50.00
O'Brien, George	11.00	15.00	18.00	20.00
O'Brien, Margaret	5.00	11.00	18.00	15.00
O'Brien, Pat	10.00	17.00	32.00	40.00
O'Connell, Helen	5.00	6.00	11.00	14.00
O'Connor, Donald	4.00	7.00	12.00	10.00
O'Keefe, Dennis	7.50	9.00	16.00	20.00
Oland, Warner	29.00	34.00	64.00	80.00
Oliver, Edna May	30.00	35.00	65.00	75.00
Olsen and Johnson	15.00			40.00
Olson, Nancy	4.00	5.00	10.00	12.00
O'Neill, Henry	6.00	7.00	13.00	16.00
O'Neill, James	15.00	18.00	33.00	30.00
O'Neill, Peggy	4.00	6.00	12.00	15.00
Osborne, Baby Marie	4.00	6.00	12.00	15.00
O'Sullivan, Maureen	8.00	15.00	26.00	25.00
Otis, Elita Proctor	7.00	9.00	16.00	20.00
Ouspenskaya, Maria	100.00	128.00	239.00	300.00
Page, Anita	3.00	4.00	8.00	10.00
Paige, Janis	5.00	6.00	11.00	14.00
Pallette, Eugene	13.00	15.00	28.00	35.00
Palmer, Lilli	10.00	17.00	32.00	40.00
Parker, Colonel Tom	3.00	4.00	8.00	10.00
Parker, Eleanor	9.00	11.00	20.00	25.00
Parker, Jean	15.00	18.00	33.00	40.00
Parker, Suzy	5.00	6.00	11.00	15.00
Parrish, Helen	4.00	6.00	12.00	15.00
Parsons, Louella O.	30.00	65.00	100.00	45.00
Pasternak, Joe	34.00	40.00	75.00	35.00
Pastor, Tony	5.00	6.00	11.00	14.00
Patrick, Gail	7.00	8.00	15.00	19.00
Patti, Adelina	15.00	18.00	33.00	41.00
Paul, Les	10.00	12.00	21.00	27.00
Paulton, Harry	11.00	13.00	25.00	31.00
Pavlova, Anna	128.00	150.00	279.00	350.00
Paxinou, Katina	120.00	140.00	260.00	325.00
Payne, John	15.00	18.00	33.00	40.00
Peabody, Eddie	9.00	11.00	20.00	25.00
Peckinpah, Sam	17.00	20.00	37.00	45.00
Peerce, Jan	7.00	9.00	16.00	20.00
Pendleton, Nat	9.00	11.00	20.00	25.00
Penner, Joe	13.00	15.00	28.00	35.00
Pennington, Ann	17.00	19.00	36.00	45.00
Perkins, Millie	22.00	26.00	48.00	60.00
Perkins, Osgood	13.00	15.00	28.00	35.00
Peters, Susan	18.00	21.00	39.00	45.00
Philbin, Mary	10.00	12.00	21.00	25.00
Piaf, Edith	50.00	58.00	108.00	135.00
Piatigorsky, Gregor	40.00	47.00	87.00	110.00
Pickens, Slim	12.00	14.00	26.00	33.00
Pickford, Mary	45.00	49.00	64.00	80.00
Picon, Molly	13.00	15.00	28.00	35.00
Pidgeon, Walter	11.00	13.00	24.00	30.00

Name	Signature Only	Letter or Document Signed	Autograph Letter Signed	Signed Photograph
Pinza, Ezio	25.00	29.00	54.00	68.00
Pitts, ZaSu	8.00	10.00	18.00	23.00
Pometti, Vincenzo	3.00	4.00	8.00	10.00
Pons, Lily	25.00	29.00	54.00	60.00
Ponty, Jean-Luc	5.00	6.00	11.00	14.00
Potter, Cora	10.00	12.00	21.00	20.00
Powell, Dick	40.00	47.00	87.00	95.00
Powell, Eleanor	5.00	6.00	10.00	13.00
Powell, William	17.00	20.00	38.00	50.00
Power, Tyrone	95.00	107.00	199.00	250.00
Preminger, Otto	10.00	15.00	28.00	35.00
Presley, Elvis	110.00	128.00	239.00	300.00
Preston, Robert	7.00	9.00	16.00	20.00
Preston the Magician	2.00	4.00	7.00	9.00
Prince, William	10.00	12.00	21.00	30.00
Pringle, Aileen	9.00	11.00	20.00	25.00
Prinze, Freddie	30.00	35.00	65.00	45.00
Pryor, Roger	11.00	13.00	24.00	30.00
Puelo, Johnny	4.00	6.00	12.00	15.00
Raft, George	10.00	19.00	36.00	45.00
Ragsland, Rags	6.00	7.00	13.00	16.00
Rainer, Luise	11.00	13.00	24.00	30.00
Raines, Ella	5.00	6.00	8.00	10.00
Rains, Claude	50.00	55.00	92.00	115.00
Raitt, John	5.00	6.00	11.00	14.00
Raleigh, Cecil	5.00	6.00	11.00	14.00
Raleigh, Sara	5.00	6.00	11.00	14.00
Ralston, Esther	7.00	9.00	16.00	20.00
Ralston, Jobyna	18.00	21.00	40.00	50.00
Ralston, Vera Hruba	7.00	9.00	16.00	20.00
Rambeau, Marjorie	15.00	18.00	33.00	40.00
Rand, Sally	29.00	34.00	64.00	80.00
Rank, J. Arthur	17.00	20.00	37.00	40.00
Rathbone, Basil	110.00	128.00	239.00	300.00
Ratoff, Gregory	15.00	17.00	32.00	40.00
Rawlinson, Herbert	11.00	13.00	24.00	30.00
Ray, Charles	18.00	21.00	40.00	50.00
Ray, Leah	4.00	5.00	10.00	12.00
Raye, Martha	7.00	13.00	23.00	14.00
Raymond, Gene	7.00	9.00	16.00	20.00
Redgrave, Sir Michael	13.00	15.00	28.00	35.00
Reed, Donna	20.00	24.00	44.00	55.00
Reed, Phillip	9.00	11.00	20.00	25.00
Reeves-Smith, Olive	3.00	4.00	8.00	10.00
Regan, Phil	3.00	4.00	8.00	10.00
Reginald, Lionel	10.00	12.00	22.00	28.00
Rehan, Ada	10.00	12.50	30.00	27.00
Reid, Wallace	200.00			550.00
Reiner, Carl	2.00	4.00	8.00	10.00
Renaldo, Duncan	35.00	41.00	76.00	95.00
Revelle, Hamilton	13.00	15.00	28.00	35.00
Revere, Anne	7.00	10.00	15.00	19.00
Reynolds, Gene	5.00	6.00	11.00	14.00

Name	Signature Only	Letter or Document Signed	Autograph Letter Signed	Signed Photograph
Rhea	10.00	12.00	21.00	30.00
Rhodes, Billie	3.00	4.00	8.00	10.00
Rhodes, Erik	7.00	9.00	16.00	20.00
Rice, Florence	6.00	6.00	12.00	15.00
Rich, Irene	10.00	12.00	21.00	30.00
Richardson, Ian	2.00	3.00	6.00	8.00
Richardson, Ralph	15.00	17.00	32.00	40.00
Richman, Charles	10.00	12.00	21.00	25.00
Richman, Harry	4.00	6.00	12.00	15.00
Riefenstahl, Leni				40.00
Riggs, Tommy	5.00	6.00	11.00	14.00
Ritter, Tex	50.00	58.00	108.00	135.00
Ritter, Thelma	46.00	53.00	100.00	125.00
Ritz Brothers (3)	85.00			230.00
Ritz, Jimmy	10.00	12.00	21.00	40.00
Roach, Hal	18.00	21.00	40.00	50.00
Robards, Jason	6.00	11.00	19.00	16.00
Robbins, Gale	9.00	11.00	20.00	25.00
Robeson, Paul	50.00	64.00	119.00	150.00
Robinson, Bill	55.00	64.00	119.00	150.00
Robson, Dame Flora	12.00	14.00	26.00	35.00
Robson, May	10.00	11.00	20.00	25.00
Robson, Stuart	15.00	18.00	33.00	41.00
Rogers, Buddy	11.00	13.00	24.00	30.00
Rogers, Ginger	14.00	28.00	48.00	40.00
Rogers, Jimmy	46.00	53.00	100.00	125.00
Rogers, Will	200.00	214.00	398.00	500.00
Roland, Ruth	17.00	19.00	36.00	45.00
Romanoff, "Prince" Michael	34.00	40.00	75.00	50.00
Rose, Billy	34.00	40.00	75.00	50.00
Ross, Charles J.	3.00	4.00	8.00	10.00
Ross, Lanny	10.00	17.00	21.00	25.00
Roth, Lillian	18.00	26.00	48.00	60.00
Rothafell, S. L.	10.00	12.00	21.00	25.00
Rubens, Alma	46.00	53.00	100.00	125.00
Rubinoff	4.00	6.00	12.00	15.00
Rubinstein, Arthur	50.00	58.00	110.00	125.00
Ruggles, Charles	18.00	21.00	39.00	45.00
Ruggles, Wesley	15.00	18.00	33.00	35.00
Ruick, Barbara	3.00	4.00	8.00	10.00
Russell, Annie	5.00	6.00	11.00	14.00
Russell, Lillian	32.50	38.00	71.00	90.00
Russell, Rosalind	15.00	17.00	32.00	40.00
Russell, Sol Smith	9.00	11.00	20.00	25.00
Rutherford, Ann	9.00	17.00	29.00	32.00
Rutherford, Margaret	37.00	43.00	80.00	100.00
Ryan, Robert	17.00	19.00	36.00	45.00
Saba	28.00			75.00
Sablon, Jean	15.00	18.00	33.00	35.00
Sale, Chic	18.00	21.00	40.00	50.00
Sampson, Will	9.00	11.00	20.00	25.00
Sanders, George	50.00	64.00	119.00	150.00
Sanderson, Julia	4.00	6.00	12.00	15.00
Sauer, Emil	9.00	11.00	20.00	25.00

Name	Signature Only	Letter or Document Signed	Autograph Letter Signed	Signed Photograph
Savage, Ann	4.00	6.00	12.00	15.00
Savales, George	5.00	6.00	11.00	14.00
Sayao, Bidu	5.00	6.00	11.00	21.00
Scheff, Fritzi	20.00	24.00	44.00	55.00
Schell, Maximillian	9.00	11.00	20.00	25.00
Schildkraudt, Joseph	50.00	75.00	139.00	175.00
Schipa, Tito	30.00	35.00	65.00	85.00
Schneider, Romy	13.00	15.00	28.00	35.00
Schumann-Heink, E.	30.00	45.00	75.00	80.00
Scott, Randolph	30.00	35.00	65.00	85.00
Scott, Zachary	35.00	41.00	76.00	85.00
Seberg, Jean	67.50	64.00	119.00	150.00
Seeley, Blossom	22.00	26.00	48.00	60.00
Segovia, Andres	10.00	12.00	21.00	30.00
Sellers, Peter	46.00	53.00	100.00	125.00
Selznick, David O.	75.00	150.00	250.00	150.00
Selznick, Irene	26.00	30.00	56.00	40.00
Sennett, Mack	80.00		240.00	300.00
Serling, Rod	15.00	18.00	33.00	40.00
Sharpe, Karen	5.00	6.00	10.00	13.00
Shaw, Artie	20.00	24.00	44.00	48.00
Shawn, Ted	7.00	13.00	23.00	19.00
Shearer, Moira	20.00	24.00	44.00	45.00
Shearer, Norma	35.00	64.00	119.00	150.00
Sheridan, Ann	15.00	17.00	32.00	40.00
Sherwood, Bobby	5.00	6.00	11.00	15.00
Shirley, Anne	9.00	11.00	20.00	25.00
Shriner, Herb	2.00	4.00	6.00	7.00
Shubert, John	21.00	25.00	46.00	55.00
Sidney, Sylvia	6.00	12.00	20.00	17.00
Signoret, Simone	30.00	35.00	65.00	50.00
Sills, Milton	20.00	24.00	44.00	55.00
Silvers, Phil	11.00	13.00	24.00	30.00
Simon, Simone	6.00	6.00	12.00	15.00
Skelton, Red	12.00	22.00	38.00	32.00
Skinner, Otis	15.00	18.00	33.00	40.00
Skipworth, Alison	10.00	12.00	21.00	25.00
Smith, Buffalo Bob	3.00	4.00	8.00	10.00
Smith, C. Aubrey	23.00	27.00	50.00	60.00
Smith, Joe	3.00	4.00	8.00	10.00
Smith, Kate	25.00	30.00	35.00	45.00
Sondergaard, Gale	20.00	24.00	44.00	55.00
Sothern, Ann	5.00	6.00	11.00	15.00
Sothern, E. A.	20.00	24.00	44.00	55.00
Sparks, Ned	20.00	24.00	44.00	55.00
Spong, Hilda	5.00	6.00	11.00	14.00
Stander, Lionel	7.00	9.00	16.00	20.00
Starrett, Charles	20.00	24.00	44.00	45.00
St. Cyr, Lili	9.00	17.00	29.00	24.00
St. Denis, Ruth	28.00	32.00	60.00	75.00
Steele, Bob	13.00	15.00	28.00	35.00
Sten, Anna	10.00	12.00	21.00	30.00
Stern, Isaac	10.00	12.00	21.00	30.00
Stevens, Inger	60.00	75.00	131.00	165.00

Name	Signature Only	Letter or Document Signed	Autograph Letter Signed	Signed Photograph
Stevens, K. T.	5.00	6.00	11.00	14.00
Stewart, James	16.00	53.00	125.00	30.00
Stokowski, Leopold	15.00	18.00	33.00	40.00
Stone, Fred	10.00	12.00	21.00	27.00
Stone, Lewis S.	25.00	29.00	54.00	68.00
Stone, Paula	11.00	13.00	25.00	30.00
Stoopnagle, Colonel	10.00	12.00	21.00	20.00
Storm, Gale	4.00	5.00	10.00	12.00
Storm, Tempest	9.00	11.00	20.00	25.00
Stratten, Dorothy	9.00	11.00	20.00	25.00
Strauss, Robert	28.00	32.00	60.00	75.00
Stromberg, Hunt	26.00	30.00	56.00	40.00
Stroud Twins	14.00			25.00
Sullavan, Margaret	28.00	32.00	60.00	75.00
Sullivan, Ed	20.00	24.00	44.00	42.50
Summerville, Slim	9.00	11.00	20.00	25.00
Sutton, Grady	6.00	7.00	13.00	16.00
Swanson, Gloria	20.00	21.00	40.00	50.00
Swarthout, Gladys	12.00	14.00	26.00	30.00
Sweet, Blanche	8.00	9.00	18.00	22.00
Taber, Robert	5.00	6.00	11.00	14.00
Talbot, Lyle	9.00	11.00	20.00	25.00
Tallchief, Maria	11.00	13.00	24.00	30.00
Talley, Marion	7.00	9.00	16.00	20.00
Talmadge, Constance	18.00	50.00	30.00	50.00
Tamiroff, Akim	25.00	29.00	54.00	75.00
Tashman, Lilyan	25.00	29.00	54.00	65.00
Taylor, Estelle	15.00	18.00	33.00	35.00
Taylor, Joan	2.00	4.00	10.00	10.00
Taylor, Laurette	20.00	24.00	40.00	55.00
Taylor, Robert	30.00	34.00	64.00	80.00
Teasdale, Veree	15.00	18.00	33.00	35.00
Tempest, Marie	22.00	26.00	48.00	60.00
Templeton, Fay	20.00	24.00	44.00	55.00
Tennant, Veronica	9.00	11.00	20.00	25.00
Terry, Ellen	20.00	24.00	44.00	55.00
Terry, Fred	10.00	12.00	22.00	20.00
Terry, Phillip	3.00	4.00	8.00	10.00
Tetrazzini, Luisa	18.00	32.00	65.00	50.00
Thalberg, Irving	190.00	225.00	420.00	525.00
Thaxter, Celia	15.00	18.00	33.00	35.00
Theiss, Ursula	7.00	8.00	14.00	18.00
Thomas, John Charles	23.00	27.00	50.00	63.00
Thomas, Olive	28.00	32.00	60.00	75.00
Thompson, Marshall	4.00	7.00	12.00	10.00
Thorndike, Sybil	16.00	20.00	35.00	44.00
Thorne, Charles Robert	37.00	43.00	80.00	100.00
Tibbett, Lawrence	15.00	18.00	33.00	40.00
Tobin, Genevieve	5.00	6.00	11.00	14.00
Today Show (early)	25.00			60.00
Todd, Thelma	150.00			375.00
Toler, Sidney	43.00	50.00	93.00	120.00
Tone, Franchot	7.00	9.00	16.00	20.00
Toomey, Regis	7.00	8.00	14.00	18.00

Name	Signature Only	Letter or Document Signed	Autograph Letter Signed	Signed Photograph
Torres, Raquel	4.00	5.00	10.00	12.00
Toscanini, Arturo	195.00			500.00
Totter, Audrey	9.00	11.00	20.00	25.00
Toumanova, Tamara	11.00	13.00	24.00	30.00
Tracy, Spencer	100.00	118.00	219.00	275.00
Travers, Patricia	3.00	4.00	8.00	10.00
Treacher, Arthur	10.00	15.00	28.00	35.00
Truax, Ernest	9.00	11.00	20.00	25.00
Tucker, Sophie	4.00	6.00	10.00	15.00
Tufts, Sonny	12.50	15.00	27.00	35.00
Turner, Lana	7.00	14.00	24.00	20.00
Tuttle, Lurene	3.00	4.00	8.00	10.00
Twelvetrees, Helen	37.00	43.00	80.00	100.00
Ulmar, Geraldine	5.00	6.00	11.00	14.00
Ure, Mary	7.00	8.00	15.00	19.00
Valentino, Rudolph	500.00			1200.00
Vallee, Rudy	6.00	7.00	13.00	20.00
Van, Gloria	3.00	4.00	8.00	10.00
Van Vooren, Monique	2.00	3.00	6.00	8.00
Veidt, Conrad	33.00	38.00	72.00	90.00
Velez, Lupe	46.00	53.00	100.00	125.00
Veloz and Yolanda	9.00	11.00	20.00	25.00
Venable, Evelyn	12.00	14.00	26.00	35.00
Vickers, Martha	5.00	6.00	11.00	10.00
Vidor, Florence	18.00	21.00	40.00	50.00
Vidor, King	15.00	18.00	33.00	35.00
Vinson, Helen	10.00	12.00	22.00	27.50
Vokes, Rosina	5.00	6.00	11.00	10.00
Von Zell, Harry	7.00	9.00	16.00	20.00
Walker, Robert	25.00	29.00	54.00	70.00
Waller, Fats	95.00	106.00	179.00	225.00
Wallis, Ruth	4.00	5.00	9.00	11.00
Walsh, Blanche	5.00	6.00	11.00	14.00
Walsh, Raoul	7.00	9.00	16.00	20.00
Walston, Ray	4.00	6.00	12.00	15.00
Walter, Bruno	13.00	15.00	28.00	35.00
Walthall, Henry B.	18.00	21.00	40.00	50.00
Walton, Gladys	3.00	4.00	8.00	10.00
Walton, Jayne	4.00	5.00	9.00	11.00
Ward, Genevieve	4.00	5.00	10.00	12.00
Ware, Linda	4.00	6.00	12.00	15.00
Warfield, David	20.00	24.00	44.00	55.00
Waring, Fred	9.00	11.00	20.00	25.00
Warner, Harry M.	30.00	35.00	65.00	80.00
Warner, Jack	50.00	58.00	107.00	135.00
Warnow, Mark	4.00	5.00	9.00	11.00
Washburn, Bryant	4.00	6.00	12.00	15.00
Waters, Ethel	15.00	17.00	32.00	40.00
Wayne, Carol	11.00	13.00	24.00	30.00
Wayne, John	175.00	225.00	400.00	375.00
Webb, Clifton	30.00	35.00	65.00	50.00
Webb, Jack	4.00	6.00	12.00	15.00
Weber, Joe	15.00	18.00	33.00	41.00
Weissmuller, Johnny	22.00	26.00	48.00	60.00

Name	Signature Only	Letter or Document Signed	Autograph Letter Signed	Signed Photograph
Welles, Orson	18.00	21.00	40.00	50.00
Wessell, Vivian	3.00	4.00	8.00	10.00
West, Mae	25.00	30.00	56.00	70.00
Westman, Nidia	9.00	11.00	20.00	25.00
Whalen, Michael	9.00	11.00	20.00	25.00
Wheeler, Ellie	7.00	9.00	16.00	20.00
White, Alice	12.00	14.00	26.00	35.00
White, George	40.00	47.00	87.00	75.00
White, Pearl	73.00	86.00	159.00	200.00
Whiteman, Paul	48.00	56.00	103.00	130.00
Whiting, Jack	5.00	6.00	11.00	14.00
Whittle, Josephine	3.00	4.00	8.00	10.00
Whitty, Dame May	24.00	28.00	52.00	65.00
Wieck, Dorothea	9.00	11.00	20.00	25.00
Wiere Brothers	3.00	4.00	8.00	10.00
Willard, Edward	5.00	6.00	11.00	14.00
William, Warren	5.00	6.00	12.00	15.00
Williams, Esther	4.00	5.00	10.00	12.50
Williams, Van	7.00	9.00	16.00	20.00
Wills, Chill	10.00	12.00	21.00	25.00
Wilson, Francis	5.00	6.00	11.00	14.00
Wilson, Lois	10.00	12.00	17.00	16.00
Wilson, Marie	18.00	21.00	40.00	50.00
Winchell, Paul	11.00	13.00	24.00	30.00
Windsor, Claire	11.00	13.00	25.00	31.00
Wing, Toby	7.00	9.00	16.00	20.00
Winkler, Betty	3.00	4.00	8.00	10.00
Winninger, Charles	17.00	20.00	37.00	47.00
Winters, Roland	15.00	18.00	33.00	45.00
Withers, Jane	4.00	6.00	12.00	15.00
Wolff, Amalie	20.00		50.00	
Wong, Anna May	15.00	17.00	32.00	40.00
Wood, Natalie	17.00	19.00	36.00	45.00
Wood, Peggy	4.00	6.00	12.00	15.00
Woods, Donald	12.00	13.00	24.00	30.00
Woodward, Marjorie	3.00	4.00	7.00	9.00
Wray, Fay				42.50
Wright, Cobina, Sr. and Jr.			15.00	19.00
Wyman, Jane	11.00	13.00	24.00	30.00
Wymore, Patrice	4.00	6.00	12.00	15.00
Wyndham, Sir Charles	14.00	16.00	30.00	38.00
Wyndham, Lady Mary	13.00	15.00	28.00	35.00
Wynn, Ed	28.00	32.00	60.00	75.00
Wynyard, Dianna	9.00	11.00	20.00	25.00
Yankovic, Frank	3.00	4.00	7.00	9.00
Young, Alan	5.00	6.00	11.00	12.00
Young, Gig	24.00	28.00	52.00	65.00
Young, Lester	40.00	47.00	88.00	110.00
Young, Roland	28.00	32.00	60.00	75.00
Youngman, Henny	5.00	6.00	11.00	12.00
Ziegfeld, Florenz	200.00	233.00	434.00	545.00
Zimbalist, Efrem, Sr.	10.00	12.00	21.00	27.00
Zorina, Vera	9.00	10.00	19.00	24.00

Football

This section includes both college and pro football players and coaches of superior ability, including Heisman Trophy winners and members of the College or the Professional Football Hall of Fame. These prices are subject to regional premiums (especially in a team or college's hometown), but generally, signatures and signed photographs are currently selling at the guidelines listed below. In sports autographs, collectors are normally interested in only these two categories—hence our exclusion of Letter Signed/Document Signed and Autograph Letter Signed pricing.

Name	Signature	Signed Photograph
Agajanian, Ben	4	10
Akers, Fred	3	7
Albert, Frank	5	15
Allen, George	3	8
Allen, Marcus	4	15
Alworth, Lance	6	15
Alzado, Lyle	4	20
Ameche, Alan	5	12
Anderson, Ken	4	10
Arnett, Jon	4	12
Arnsbarger, Bill	4	8
Atkins, David "Davy"	3	6
Atkins, Doug	5	15
Badgro, Morris "Red"	10	20
Baker, Terry	5	10
Bakken, Jim	4	8
Banks, Carl	5	10
Bartkowski, Steve	4	12
Bass, Dick	4	8
Battles, Cliff	5	25
Baugh, Sammy	15	35
Baughan, Maxie	3	6
Beban, Gary	4	15
Bednarik, Chuck	4	10
Bell, Bobby	4	15
Bell, Ricky	5	25
Bellino, Joe	4	12
Bennett, C. Leeman	4	8
Bergey, Bill	3	5
Berry, Raymond	4	10
Bertelli, Angelo	5	15
Berwanger, Jay	5	25
Bettis, Tom	3	6
Bierman, Bernie	15	45

Name	Signature	Signed Photograph
Biletnikoff, Fred	5	10
Blaik, Earl "Red"	10	20
Blanchard, Doc	10	20
Blanda, George	6	12
Bleier, Rocky	5	10
Booth, Albie	40	80
Bosco, Robbie	4	7
Bowden, Bobby	4	8
Box, Cloyce	8	12
Boydston, Max	4	8
Bradshaw, Terry	5	20
Brennan, Terry	5	10
Breunig, Bob	4	8
Brock, Dieter	4	8
Brockington, John	5	10
Brodie, John	4	9
Brown, Dave	7	12
Brown, Jim	10	25
Brown, Paul E.	15	30
Brown, Roosevelt	6	20
Brown, Willie	15	25
Broyles, Frank	4	8
Bruhm, Milt	4	8
Bryant, Paul "Bear"	15	45
Buoniconti, Nick	4	8
Burk, Adrian	4	8
Burns, Jerry	3	8
Burt, Jim	4	12
Butkus, Dick	6	15
Byars, Keith	5	8
Caddel, Ernie	5	12
Camp, Walter	50	100
Campbell, Earl	6	15
Campbell, Hugh	3	6
Campbell, Marion	4	6
Canadeo, Tony	5	10
Cannon, Billy	10	25
Cappeletti, Gino	5	15
Cappelletti, John	5	12
Carson, Harry	4	12
Carter, Anthony	5	12
Carter, Rubin	4	8
Casanova, Len	5	10
Casey, Bernie	4	8
Cassady, Howard "Hopalong"	5	15
Chappuis, Bob	5	10
Christensen, Todd	6	12
Christiansen, Jack	5	20
Clark, Dwight	6	12
Clark, Earl "Dutch"	10	25
Cogdill, Gail	5	10
Collinsworth, Cris	5	10
Cone, Fred	3	6
Conerly, Charles	5	10

Clifford Branch

John Elway

Dan Marino

Russ Grimm

Bernie Kosar

Walter Payton

Vinny Testaverde

Doug Williams

Name	Signature	Signed Photograph
Connor, George	5	15
Coryell, Don	4	8
Cribbs, Joe	4	8
Crow, John David	7	15
Crow, Lindon	4	8
Crowley, Jim	15	35
Csonka, Larry	5	12
Cunningham, Sam	5	9
Curry, Bill	4	8
Curtice, "Cactus Jack"	5	10
Danowski, Ed	4	8

Name	Signature	Signed Photograph
Daugherty, "Duffy"	10	20
Davis, Glenn	5	15
Davis, Willie	4	8
Davison, Ben	5	15
Dawkins, Pete	5	12
Dawson, Len	4	8
DeBartolo, Ed, Jr.	3	6
DeBerry, Fisher	3	5
Delaney, Joe	10	30
Devaney, Bob	6	12
Dickerson, Eric	5	20
Didier, Clint	4	9
Dil, Steve	4	8
Dillon, Bobby	5	15
Ditka, Mike	5	12
Doll, Don	3	6
Donahue, Terry	3	6
Donovan, Art	6	12
Dooley, Vince	4	8
Dorais, Charles "Gus"	20	40
Dorsett, Tony	5	12
Douglass, Bobby	4	10
Dowler, Boyd	5	10
Drazenovich, Chuck	4	8
Dryer, Fred	5	20
Dudley, Bill	5	10
Dye, Pat	4	10
East, Ron	3	6
Edwards, Lavelle	6	8
Eller, Carl	5	15
Elliott, Pete	3	6
Elway, John	5	15
Elway, John, Sr.	4	8
English, Doug	3	6
Evashevski, Forest	10	20
Everett, Jim	5	10
Ewbank, Weeb	4	12
Farkas, Andy	10	20
Faust, Gerry	3	6
Fazio, "Foge"	3	6
Fears, Tom	5	12
Feathers, Beattie	18	30
Ferguson, Joe	4	8
Fertig, Craig	3	6
Fesler, Wes	4	18
Filchock, Frank	8	20
Finks, Jim	3	6
Flaherty, Ray	4	18
Flatly, Paul	4	8
Flores, Tom	4	8
Flutie, Doug	5	20
Ford, William Clay	5	12
Fortmann, Danny	7	20
Fouts, Dan	5	12
Frank, Clint	5	15

Name	Signature	Signed Photograph
Friedman, Benny	10	25
Fritsch, Ted	5	10
Frontiere, Georgia	4	8
Fry, Hayden	3	7
Fysal, Ellis D.	3	5
Gabriel, Roman	5	12
Garrett, Mike	5	15
Garrison, Walt	4	10
Gastineau, Mark	4	15
Gatski, Frank	4	12
Gehrke, Fred	3	6
George, Bill	20	40
Gifford, Frank	4	12
Gill, Paul	5	12
Gillman, Sid	4	8
Gilmer, Harry	5	10
Goldberg, Marshall	10	25
Goldenberg, Charles "Buckets"	5	15
Goodnight, Clyde	3	6
Graham, Capt. Otto	10	20
Grange, Harold "Red"	10	25
Grant, Bud	4	12
Grayson, Bobby	7	25
Greene, Joe "Mean Joe"	5	10
Gregg, Forrest	4	8
Grier, Roosevelt "Rosie"	5	12
Griese, Bob	5	12
Griffin, Archie	10	20
Grogan, Steve	4	8
Grosscup, Lee	4	8
Groza, Lou	5	10
Haden, Pat	4	12
Hadl, John	4	12
Halas, George	20	50
Ham, Jack	5	18
Hamilton, Tom	4	8
Hanifin, Jim	3	6
Hanratty, Terry	4	8
Harmon, Tom	5	20
Harris, Cliff	4	8
Harris, Franco	4	10
Hart, Jim	4	8
Hart, Leon	5	10
Hatfield, Ken	4	8
Hayes, Bob	7	20
Hayes, Woody	8	25
Hays, Harold	3	6
Healey, Ed	10	20
Heffelfinger, "Pudge"	30	150
Hein, Mel	5	10
Heinrich, Don	4	8
Hendricks, Ted	4	8
Henry, Wilbur "Fats"	25	75
Herber, Arnie	5	15

Name	Signature	Signed Photograph
Hickman, Herman	10	25
Hill, Calvin	5	15
Hill, Harlon	6	12
Hill, Jess	4	8
Hill, King	4	8
Hinkle, Clarke	8	16
Hirsch, Elroy "Crazylegs"	6	15
Hoernschemeyer, Bob "Hunchy"		15
Holland, Terry	4	8
Holtz, Lou	4	8
Hornung, Paul "The Golden Boy"	5	10
Horvath, Les	10	20
Houston, Ken	5	10
Howell, Jim Lee	4	8
Huarte, Johnny	4	8
Hubbard, Cal	25	50
Huff, Sam	5	10
Hunt, Lamar	5	10
Hunter, Scott	3	6
Hutson, Don	10	20
Isbell, Cecil	5	10
Jackson, Bo	8	28
James, Craig	4	8
James, Don	4	8
Janowicz, Vic	4	15
Jauch, Ray	4	8
Jefferson, Roy "Sweet Pea"	4	8
Jenke, Noel C.	3	6
Johnson, Charley	4	8
Johnson, Jimmy	5	10
Johnson, John Henry	10	20
Joiner, Charlie	6	10
Jones, Deacon	5	15
Jordan, Lee Roy	4	8
Josephson, Les	4	8
Jurgensen, "Sonny"	10	25
Justice, Charlie "Choo Choo"	10	25
Kapp, Joe	4	8
Karras, Alex	8	15
Kavanaugh, Ken	15	25
Kazmaier, Dick	5	15
Kelly, Jim	7	10
Kemp, Jack	5	20
Kilmer, Bill	5	10
Kimbrough, Johnny	5	10
Kinard, Frank "Bruiser"	10	20
Knox, Chuck	4	8
Kosar, Bernie	6	12
Kramer, Jerry	6	12
Kramer, Ron	5	10
Krause, Ed "Moose"	5	10
Krause, Paul	3	6
Kush, Frank	4	8

Name	Signature	Signed Photograph
Laird, Bill	3	6
Lambeau, Earl "Curley"	25	50
Lamonica, Daryl	5	12
Landry, Tom	5	10
Lane, Dick "Night Train"	5	15
Langer, Jim	5	10
Lanier, Willie	5	10
Largent, Steve	4	10
Lary, Yale	5	10
Lattner, Johnny	5	10
Lavelli, Dante "Gluefingers"	5	10
Layden, Elmer	20	40
Layne, Bobby	5	20
Leahy, Frank	20	40
LeBaron, Eddie	4	8
Leemans, Alphonse "Tuffy"	15	30
Lewis, Leo	5	10
Lilly, Bob	5	10
Lincoln, Keith	4	8
Lipps, Louis	4	8
Lipscomb, Gene "Big Daddy"	20	40
Liscio, Tony	4	8
Little, Larry	4	8
Lomax, Neil	5	12
Lombardi, Vince	40	100
Long, Howie	6	12
Lothridge, Billy	4	8
Loudd, Rommie	4	8
Luckman, Sid	7	15
Lund, Francis "Pug"	5	12
Lujack, Johnny	5	15
MacAfee, Ken	4	8
Mackey, John	5	10
Mackovic, John	4	8
Madden, John	4	12
Majors, Johnny	4	12
Manders, Dave	5	10
Manning, Archie	4	8
Mara, Wellington T.	4	8
Marchetti, Gino	5	20
Mardall, Jim	5	15
Marino, Dan	5	15
Marshall, George Preston	20	40
Martha, Paul	4	8
Marvin, Mickey	4	8
Mason, Tommy	5	10
Mathys, Charlie	5	10
Matson, Ollie	5	10
Matte, Tom	4	12
Maynard, Don	5	15
McAdoo, Bob	4	8
McAfee, George	5	10
McCallum, Napoleon	8	15
McClain, Dave	4	12
McCormack, Mike	4	10

Name	Signature	Signed Photograph
McElhenney, Hugh	5	12
McGuire, Frank	4	8
McHan, Lamar	4	8
McKay, John	4	8
McMahon, Jim	5	15
McNally, Johnny Blood	40	80
McNeil, Freeman	5	10
Mecklenberg, Karl	7	12
Meredith, Don	5	10
Meyer, Ron	4	8
Michaels, Walt	5	8
Michalske, "Mike"	5	20
Miller, Chris	5	10
Millner, Wayne	5	20
Mitchell, Bobby	4	10
Mix, Ron	4	10
Modell, Art	4	8
Moegle, Dick	5	10
Montana, Joe	5	15
Moomaw, Donn	4	8
Moon, Warren	4	8
Moore, Lenny	5	10
Morris, Joe	5	15
Morrison, Joe	4	8
Morton, Craig	4	8
Moses, Haven	4	8
Moss, Perry	4	8
Motley, Marion	5	12
Munson, Bill	4	8
Musso, George	5	15
Mutscheller, Jim	5	10
Nagurski, Bronko	10	25
Namath, Joe	5	18
Nance, Jim	5	10
Nelson, Darrin	6	12
Nevers, Ernie	25	50
Nitschke, Ray	5	10
Nobis, Tommy	4	8
Nolan, Dick	4	8
Nomellini, Leo	15	25
O'Brien, Davey	25	40
O'Brien, Jim	4	8
O'Brien, Ken	4	8
Olsen, Merlin	5	10
Osmanski, Bill	25	50
Owens, Jim	5	10
Owens, R. C. "Alley Oop"	7	20
Owens, Steve	5	10
Otto, Jim	5	10
Page, Alan	4	12
Parcells, Bill	4	9
Pardee, Jack	4	8
Parker, Clarence "Ace"	4	12
Parker, Jim	6	12
Parker, Raymond "Buddy"	5	20

Name	Signature	Signed Photograph
Parseghian, Ara	5	10
Paterno, Joe	5	10
Paul, Don	4	8
Payton, Walter	10	25
Pearson, Drew	5	10
Perkins, Don	4	8
Perkins, Ray	5	10
Perles, George	4	8
Perry, Joe	5	10
Perry, William "Refrigerator"	4	15
Phillips, Bum	4	8
Phillips, Jim	4	8
Piccolo, Brian	10	20
Pihos, Pete	5	150
Pilney, Andy	4	8
Plank, Doug	4	8
Plum, Milt	4	8
Plunkett, Jim	5	15
Price, Eddie	10	25
Prothro, Tommy	4	8
Ralston, John	4	8
Randle, Sonny	30	50
Ratterman, George	10	25
Reeves, Dan	4	8
Renfro, Mel	5	10
Renfro, Mike	7	20
Rentzel, Lance	5	20
Retzlaff, Pete	5	12
Reynolds, Bob	7	25
Rice, Jerry	5	15
Richter, Les	5	12
Riggins, John	5	15
Ringo, Jim	5	10
Robertson, Isiah	4	8
Robinson, John	4	8
Robinson, Johnny	4	8
Robustelli, Andy	5	10
Rockne, Knute	200	800
Rockne, Mrs. Knute	5	10
Rodgers, Pepper	4	8
Rooney, Art	5	15
Rosenbloom, Caroll	10	30
Ross, Bobby	4	8
Rote, Kyle	5	12
Royal, Darrell	5	9
Rozelle, Pete	5	15
Rozier, Mike	5	12
Rutigliano, Sam	4	8
Ryan, Buddy	5	8
Saban, Lou	4	8
Saimes, George	4	8
Sayers, Gale	10	20
Schembeckler, Bo	4	8
Schmidt, Joe	5	10
Schnellenberger, Howard	4	8

Name	Signature	Signed Photograph
Schnitgen, Dick	4	8
Schottenheimer, Marty	4	8
Schramm, Tex	4	8
Schroeder, Jay	5	10
Shaw, George	4	8
Shofner, Del	5	10
Shula, Don	5	10
Simms, Phil	5	15
Simpson, O. J.	5	15
Sims, Billy	4	15
Sims, Ken	4	8
Singletary, Mike	4	10
Sinkwich, Frankie	20	35
Skoronski, Bob	5	10
Smith, Bubba	5	20
Smith, Dave "Sweetback"	4	8
Soltau, Gordon	4	8
Spears, Ron	4	8
Spurrier, Steve	5	10
Stabler, Ken	10	20
Stagg, Amos Alonzo	30	75
Stanfel, Dick	4	8
Starr, Bart	5	12
Staubach, Roger	5	12
Stautner, Ernie	5	10
Stickles, Monty	4	8
Stonebreaker, Steve	4	8
Strode, Woody	12	25
Strong, Ken	10	25
Stuhldreher, Harry	20	40
Stydahar, Joe	5	20
Sullivan, Pat	5	10
Swain, Bill	4	8
Swann, Lynn	5	10
Switzer, Barry	5	10
Symanski, John	5	10
Tarkenton, Fran	10	20
Tatum, Jack	5	15
Taylor, Charley	5	12
Taylor, Jim	5	10
Taylor, Lawrence	5	18
Taylor, Lionel	5	10
Testaverde, Vinny	9	35
Theismann, Joe	5	10
Thomas, Aurealius	4	8
Thomas, Duane	4	10
Thompson, J. Lee	5	10
Tittle, Y. A.	10	25
Todd, Richard	5	10
Tollner, Ted	4	8
Towler, Dan "Deacon"	10	20
Trimble, Jim	4	8
Trippi, Charley	10	20
Turner, Clyde "Bulldog"	10	20
Tyler, Wendell	5	10

Name	Signature	Signed Photograph
Unitas, Johnny	8	16
Upshaw, Gene	5	12
Van Brocklin, Norm	20	45
Van Buren, Steve	5	15
Vataha, Randy	4	8
Vessels, Billy	15	25
Villapiano, Phil	5	10
Wacker, Jim	4	8
Waldorf, Lynn O.	15	35
Walker, Doak	10	20
Walker, Herschel	10	20
Walker, Wayne	4	8
Walker, Wesley	5	10
Walsh, Bill	5	10
Walston, Bobby	4	10
Warburton, Cotton	25	50
Warfield, Paul	5	15
Warmath, Murray	4	8
Warner, Curt	6	10
Warner, Glenn S. "Pop"	90	180
Washington, Kenny	10	25
Washington, Vic	4	8
Waterfield, Bob	20	45
Waters, Charlie	5	10
Webster, Alex	4	10
Weinmeister, Arnie	5	10
Welsh, George	4	8
White, Byron "Whizzer"	20	40
White, Charles	7	20
White, Danny	5	10
White, Randy	5	10
Widseth, Ed	5	10
Wilder, James	5	9
Wildung, Dick	4	8
Wilkinson, C. B. "Bud"	10	25
Willey, Norman "Wildman"	4	8
Williams, Bob	4	8
Williams, Howard Bennett	4	10
Willis, Bill	6	15
Wilson, Billy G.	5	10
Wistert, Francis "Whitey"	6	20
Wojciechowicz, Alex	5	10
Wood, Dick	4	8
Wright, Elmo	4	8
Wyche, Sam	4	8
Yost, Fielding H.	25	100
Young, Claude "Buddy"	20	35
Young, Jim	4	8
Young, Steve	9	15
Youngblood, Jack	9	15
Younger, Tank	5	12
Zorn, Jim	5	10

General Sports

This section represents all sports except baseball, football, and boxing, which are elsewhere in this book (basketball, hockey, and golf Hall-of-Famers are also listed separately). Collectors are showing great interest in the area of general sports autographs now, and the average price will surely be going up in the next few years.

Name	Sport/ Affiliation	Signature Only	Signed Photograph
Aaron, Tommy	Golf	$ 4	$ 8
Abdul-Jabbar, Kareem	Basketball	20	40
Albright, Tenley	Skating	5	15
Alcott, Amy	Golf	4	8
Allison, Bobby	Auto Racing	4	12
Alsup, Bill	Auto Racing	4	8
Anderson, Dick	Football	4	8
Anderson, Paul	Weightlifting	10	25
Andretti, Mario	Auto Racing	6	15
Andretti, Michael	Auto Racing	4	12
Arcaro, Eddie	Horse Racing	5	12
Archibald, Nate	Basketball	5	10
Arfons, Art	Auto Racing	5	15
Arizin, Paul	Basketball	3	8
Arledge, Roone	Broadcaster	5	10
Armour, Tommy	Golf	5	10
Armstrong, Debbie	Skiing	4	12
Ashe, Arthur	Tennis	4	8
Ashenfelter, Horace	Track	5	15
Ashford, Evelyn	Track	4	15
Atkinson, Ted	Horse Racing	5	15
Austin, Tracy	Tennis	4	15
Babashoff, Shirley	Swimming	5	12
Baker, W. Thane	Track	5	15
Ballard, Greg	Basketball	4	8
Ballesteros, Seve	Golf	5	15
Bannister, Roger	Track	10	25
Barber, Jerry	Golf	4	8
Barber, Tom	Golf	2	4
Barbuti, Ray	Track	4	8
Barnes, Lee	Track	6	25
Barry, Martin "Marty"	Hockey	4	8
Barry, Rick	Basketball	5	15
Bartow, Gene	Basketball	4	8
Baugh, Laura	Golf	6	15
Bayi, Filbert	Track	5	15
Baylor, Elgin	Basketball	5	15

Kareem Abdul-Jabbar

Amy Alcott

Bobby Allison

Mario Andretti

Eddie Arcaro

Tommy Armour

Henry Armstrong

Ted Atkinson

Arthur Ashe

Jerry Barber

Susan Berens

Andy Bean

Patty Berg

Bjorn Borg

Bennie Borgman

Ralph Boston

Jean Borotra

Frank Brimsek

Larry Brown

Dick Button

Mike Bossy

Ann Calvello

Dave Butz

Donald Campbell

Name	Sports Affiliation	Signature Only	Signed Photograph
Beamon, Bob	Track	6	12
Bean, Andy	Golf	4	8
Becker, Bobby and George	Wrestling	5	10
Beliveau, Jean	Hockey	5	15
Bellamy, Walt	Basketball	5	12
Bennett, Bruce	Track	5	10
Benoit, Joan	Track	5	15
Berens, Susan	Skating	2	4
Berg, Patty	Golf	5	15
Berning, Susie Maxwell	Golf	4	8
Bettenhausen, Gary	Auto Racing	5	10
Bibby, Henry	Basketball	4	8
Bird, Larry	Basketball	10	30
Blatnik, Jeff	Wrestling	5	12
Blears, Lord	Wrestling	10	30
Borg, Bjorn	Tennis	5	20
Borgmann, Bernie	Basketball	5	10
Boros, Julius	Golf	4	10
Borotra, Jean	Tennis	6	12
Bossy, Mike	Hockey	6	15
Boston, Ralph	Track	5	15
Boudenant, Bob	Auto Racing	4	8
Bouvia, Gloria	Bowling	4	8
Bowman, Scotty	Hockey	6	12
Brabham, Jack	Auto Racing	10	20
Bradley, Pat	Golf	4	8
Bradley, Sen. Bill	Basketball	5	15
Bragg, Don	Track	5	12
Breedlove, Craig	Auto Racing	5	10
Brimsek, Frank	Hockey	4	15
Brown, Larry	Basketball	4	8
Brundage, Avery	Track and Field	15	40
Budge, Don	Tennis	5	15
Bunn, John	Basketball	4	8
Burghley, Lord	Track	5	10
Buss, Jerry	Basketball	4	8
Button, Dick	Skating	5	15
Callen, Gloria	Swimming	5	10
Calvello, Ann	Roller Derby	4	8
Cameron, Fred L.	Marathon	20	40
Campbell, Donald	Auto Racing	15	30
Campbell, Sir Malcolm	Auto Racing	20	40
Cann, Howard G.	Basketball	5	10
Cannon, Jimmy	Sports Writer	5	15
Caras, Jimmy	Billiards	4	8
Carnesecca, Lou	Basketball	4	8
Carnevale, Bernard L.	Basketball	5	10
Carter, Fred	Basketball	4	8
Casals, Rosemary	Tennis	4	8
Casper, Billy	Golf	5	10
Cauthen, Steve	Horse Racing	7	15
Chadwick, Florence	Swimming	5	10
Chamberlain, Wilt	Basketball	10	30

Howard G. Cann

Jimmy Caras

Billy Casper

Florence Chadwick

M. L. Carr

Wilt Chamberlain

Billy Conn

Bobby Clampett

Lex Connelly

Maureen Connolly

Jimmy Connors

"Lighthorse" Harry Cooper

Angel Cordero, Jr.

Yvan Cournoyer

Bob Cousy

Ben Crenshaw

Glenn Cunningham

Ralph Da Palma

Sincerely yours,
Dwight R. Davis
Secretary of War.

Dwight R. Davis—Founder of the Davis Cup

Everett S. Dean

Swimmingly yours
Gertrude Ederle

Gertrude Ederle

Lefty Driesell

Herb Elliott

Dick Enberg

James Fitzsimmons

341

Name	Sports Affiliation	Signature Only	Signed Photograph
Chataway, Chris	Track	5	10
Ciccarelli, Dino	Hockey	6	10
Clampett, Bobby	Golf	4	8
Clancy, "King" F. M.	Hockey	10	25
Clark, Jim	Auto Racing	25	50
Cleary, Bill	Hockey	4	8
Cochran, Roy	Track	4	8
Colangelo, Jerry	Basketball	4	8
Connelly, Lex	Rodeo	2	4
Conner, Bart	Gymnastics	5	12
Conner, Dennis	Yachting	10	20
Connolly, Harold	Track	4	12
Connolly, Maureen "Little Mo"	Tennis	20	50
Connolly, Olga	Track	5	15
Connors, Jimmy	Tennis	5	15
Conrad, Max	Flying	5	20
Cooke, Jack Kent	Owner	5	10
Cooper, "Lighthorse" Harry	Golf	5	10
Copeland, Lillian	Track	4	8
Cordero, Angel	Horse Racing	5	10
Cosell, Howard	Broadcaster	4	10
Costas, Bob	Broadcaster	4	8
Costello, Larry	Basketball	4	8
Counts, Mel	Basketball	6	12
Cournoyer, Yvan	Hockey	8	12
Cousy, Bob	Basketball	6	12
Cowens, Dave	Basketball	4	12
Crenshaw, Ben	Golf	4	8
Crum, Denny	Basketball	4	8
Culbertson, Ely	Bridge	15	60
Cunningham, Bill	Basketball	4	8
Cunningham, Glenn	Track	10	30
Dancer, Stanley	Harness Racing	5	20
Darden, Tom "Satch"	Basketball	4	8
Davenport, Willie	Track	5	12
Davies, Bob	Basketball	5	10
Davis, Dwight F.	Tennis	15	30
Davis, Glenn	Track	5	15
DeBusschere, Dave	Basketball	5	15
Dean, Everett S.	Basketball	5	12
Dean, "Man Mountain"	Wrestling	20	40
Decker, Mary	Track	6	15
Delahoussaye, Eddie	Horse Racing	5	10
Delany, Ron	Track	7	25
Delvecchio, Alex	Hockey	5	15
Demaret, Jimmy	Golf	5	25
Dent, Jim	Golf	4	8
DePalma, Ralph	Auto Racing	45	90
DePaolo, Peter	Auto Racing	20	45
Devlin, Bruce	Golf	4	8
Dillard, Harrison	Track	6	15
Dionne, Marcel	Hockey	5	15
Dixon, Rod	Track	5	10

Harold E. "Bud" Foster
Harold E. Foster

A. J. Foyt

Dick Francis
Dick Francis

Gretchen Fraser
Gretchen Fraser

Shirley Fry
Shirley Fry

Pancho Gonzales

Althea Gibson

Charles Goren

Ebbie Goodfellow
Ebbie Goodfellow

Wayne Gretzky

Walt Hazzard
Atlanta, Hawks
Walt Hazzard

Walter Hagen
Walter Hagen

Eric Heiden
Eric Heiden

Bill Hartack
Bill Hartack

Sonja Henie
Sonja Henie

Graham Hill
Graham Hill

Sir Edmund Hillary   30 Jan 1962

Ben Hogan
Ben Hogan

Bobby Hull
Bobby Hull

Ted Husing
Ted Husing

Hale Irwin
Hale Irwin

Lew Jenkins
Lew Jenkins

Bruce Jenner
Bruce Jenner

Name	Sports Affiliation	Signature Only	Signed Photograph
Donohue, Mark	Auto Racing	10	30
Dooley, Eddie	Football	4	8
Douglas, Bob	Basketball	4	8
Drake, Bruce	Basketball	4	8
Draves, Vicki	Diving	10	30
Driesell, Charles "Lefty"	Basketball	4	8
Dumas, Charles	Track	5	15
Dutra, Mortie	Golf	4	8
Ederle, Gertrude	Swimming	20	65
Elliot, Win	Broadcaster	4	8
Elliott, Herb	Track	7	25
Enberg, Dick	Broadcaster	4	8
Eruzione, Mike	Hockey	5	10
Erving, Julius	Basketball	10	25
Evert, Chris	Tennis	5	15
Fangio, Juan Manuel	Auto Racing	10	25
Fell, Jeff	Horse Racing	5	20
Firestone, Dennis	Auto Racing	5	15
Fitzsimmons, Jim	Horse Racing	15	30
Fixx, Jim	Track	15	35
Fleming, Peggy	Skating	5	15
Flowers, Richmond	Football	4	8
Floyd, Ray	Golf	5	10
Foster, Harold E. "Bud"	Basketball	5	12
Foust, Larry	Basketball	5	10
Foyt, A. J.	Auto Racing	5	15
Francis, Dick	Horse Racing	10	25
Fraser, Gretchen	Skiing	10	20
Fratiane, Linda	Skating	4	10
Frazier, Walt	Basketball	5	15
Fry, Shirley	Golf	8	12
Furgol, Ed	Golf	4	8
Furlow, Terry	Basketball	4	8
Gabl, Pepi	Skiing	4	8
Gable, Dan	Wrestling	4	8
Gainey, Bob	Hockey	4	8
Gant, Harry	Auto Racing	5	20
Gardner, Randy	Skating	4	8
Garrison, Kelly	Gymnastics	4	8
Gaylord, Mitch	Gymnastics	7	20
Geiberger, Al	Golf	4	8
Geddes, Jane	Golf	4	8
Gervin, George	Basketball	5	15
Gibson, Althea	Tennis	5	12
Gilbert, Gibby	Golf	4	8
Gilder, Bob	Golf	4	8
Gilmore, Artis	Basketball	5	15
Gola, Tom	Basketball	5	15
Gomez, Avelino	Horse Racing	4	8
Gonzales, Pancho	Tennis	5	10
Goodell, Brian	Swimming	4	8
Goodfellow, Ebbie	Hockey	5	10
Goodrich, Gail	Basketball	4	8

Gordon Johncock

Jack Johnson

Parnelli Jones

Billy Kidd

Betsy King

Billie Jean King

Bob Knight

Jack Kramer

Tom Kite

Ivan Lendl

Ed "Strangler" Lewis

Johnny Longden

Nancy Lopez

Angelo "Hank" Luisetti

Alice Marble

Edward C. Macauley

Bob Mathias

Larry Mahan

Sir Stanley Matthews

Jim McKay

Basketball".

George Mikan

345

Name	Sports Affiliation	Signature Only	Signed Photograph
Goolagong, Evonne	Tennis	5	15
Goren, Charles	Bridge	5	10
Gottlieb, Eddie	Basketball	4	8
Gowdy, Curt	Broadcaster	4	8
Graf, Steffi	Tennis	8	30
Graham, David	Golf	4	8
Graham, Lou	Golf	4	8
Granatelli, Andy	Auto Racing	5	10
Green, Hubert	Golf	4	8
Greenleaf, Ralph	Billiards	50	100
Gretzky, Wayne	Hockey	10	25
Guldahl, Ralph	Golf	10	25
Guthrie, Janet	Auto Racing	5	15
Hagen, Walter	Golf	25	75
Hagge, Marlene B.	Golf	4	12
Hall, Joe B.	Basketball	4	8
Hamill, Dorothy	Skating	5	20
Hannum, Alex	Basketball	4	8
Hardin, Glenn	Track	5	10
Harding, Reggie	Basketball	4	8
Harper, Chandler	Golf	5	10
Hartack, Bill	Horse Racing	5	10
Hartung, Jim	Gymnastics	4	12
Havlicek, John	Basketball	5	15
Hayes, Elvin	Basketball	5	15
Hayes, Mark	Track	4	8
Hazzard, Walt	Basketball	4	8
Heiden, Eric	Skating	5	15
Henie, Sonja	Skating	50	100
Hernandez, Ruben	Horse Racing	5	20
Hill, Graham	Auto Racing	10	35
Hill, Phil	Auto Racing	10	25
Hillary, Sir Edmund	Mountain Climbing	20	42
Hinkle, Lon	Golf	4	8
Hoad, Lew	Tennis	5	10
Hobbs, Sir John Berry	Cricket	5	10
Hobson, Howard	Basketball	5	10
Hogan, Ben	Golf	13	35
Hogan, Cliff	Basketball	4	8
Holm, Eleanor	Swimming	10	30
Holman, Nat	Basketball	10	25
Holzman, Red	Basketball	4	8
Hoppe, Willie	Billiards	30	75
Howe, Gordon	Hockey	10	25
Hull, Bobby	Hockey	10	25
Hull, Dennis	Hockey	4	10
Husing, Ted	Broadcaster	15	30
Iba, Henry P.	Basketball	5	10
Imhoff, Darrell	Basketball	4	8
Iness, Sim	Track	5	10
Inkster, Juli	Golf	4	12
Irish, Edward "Ned"	Basketball	25	50

Louis Meyer

Sincerely,

JOHNNY MILLER

JM/11f   Johnny Miller

Stan Mikita

Archie Moore

Stirling Moss

Willie Mosconi

Byron Nelson

Brent Musburger

John Newcombe

Jack Nicklaus

Greg Norman

Paavo Nurmi

Sincerely,

Lawrence F. O'Brien

Barney Oldfield

Francis Ouimet

Arnold Palmer

Jerry Pate

Your friend,

Edson = Pelé

Edson Pelé

Calvin Peete

Fred Perry
1935.

Fred Perry

Bob Pettit

Gary Player

Richard Petty

Art Pollard

Willis Reed

347

Name	Sport/Affiliation	Signature Only	Signed Photograph
Irwin, Hale	Golf	5	10
Jacobs, Helen Hull	Tennis	15	30
Jacobsen, Peter	Golf	4	8
Jacoby, Oswald	Bridge	10	20
Jazy, Michel	Track	10	25
Jenkins, Carol Heiss	Skating	5	15
Jenkins, Dr. Charlie	Track	5	10
Jenkins, Hayes A.	Skating	4	10
Jenner, Bruce	Track	5	10
Johncock, Gordon	Auto Racing	7	15
Johnson, Bill	Skiing	5	12
Johnson, Earvin "Magic"	Basketball	10	20
Johnson, Kathy	Gymnastics	5	10
Johnson, Rafer	Track	10	20
Johnston, Neil	Basketball	4	8
Jones, K. C.	Basketball	5	10
Jones, Parnelli	Auto Racing	15	30
Jones, Robert T. "Bobbie"	Golf	65	175
Jordan, Michael	Basketball	10	25
Kahanamoku, Duke	Swimming	40	100
Kelly, John B., Jr.	Rowing	10	25
Kidd, Billy	Skiing	7	15
Killy, Jean-Claude	Skiing	10	25
King, Betsy	Golf	7	10
King, Billie Jean	Tennis	10	20
Kite, Tom	Golf	5	10
Knievel, Evel	Motorcyclist	7	20
Knight, Bobby	Basketball	5	15
Kramer, Jack	Tennis	10	20
Kratzer, Bill	Golf	4	8
Krushelnyski, Mike	Hockey	5	10
Kurland, Bob	Basketball	10	20
Lacey, Sam	Basketball	5	10
LaLanne, Jack	Body Building	5	10
Lampley, Jim	Broadcaster	5	10
Langer, Bernhard	Golf	10	25
Lavelli, Tony	Basketball	4	8
Laver, Rod	Tennis	5	15
Lee, Clyde	Basketball	4	8
Lee, Jesse E.	Basketball	4	8
Lee, Dr. Sammy	Diving	5	15
Lefleur, Guy	Hockey	5	10
Lema, Tony	Golf	10	25
Lenglen, Suzanne	Tennis	25	50
Levin, Dave	Wrestling	5	10
Lewis, Carl	Track	10	25
Lewis, Ed "Strangler"	Wrestling	10	20
Lewis, Guy	Basketball	4	8
Lietzke, Bruce	Golf	4	10
Lipton, Sir Thomas	Yachting	15	30
Liquori, Marty	Track	10	25
Little, Sally	Golf	5	10
Littler, Gene	Golf	10	25

Chico Resch

Sir Gordon Richards

Polly Riley

Cathy Rigby

Doc Rivers

Oscar Robertson

Knute Rockne

Karen Rogers

Wilma Rudolph

Gene Sarazen

Sandow

Dolph Schayes

Ma Schmeling

Wilbur Shaw

Arnold Schwarzenegger

Jack Sharkey

Willie Shoemaker

Tod Sloan

Dean E. Smith

Sam Snead

Pam Shriver

Jan Stephenson

David Thompson

Danny Sullivan

John L. Sullivan

John A. Thompson

349

Name	Sports Affiliation	Signature Only	Signed Photograph
Londos, Jim	Wrestling	15	30
Longden, Johnny	Horse Racing	10	25
Lopez, Nancy	Golf	5	15
Louganis, Greg	Diving	8	15
Love, Davis, III	Golf	4	8
Luisetti, Angelo "Hank"	Basketball	10	40
Lusch, Ernie	Wrestling	4	8
Macauley, Ed "Easy Ed"	Basketball	5	15
Mahaffey, John	Golf	4	12
Mahan, Larry	Rodeo	6	12
Mahovlich, Frank	Hockey	5	12
Mahre, Phil	Skiing	6	12
Malone, Moses	Basketball	7	20
Mangrum, Lloyd	Golf	10	25
Maple, Eddie	Horse Racing	5	10
Maravich, "Pistol Pete"	Basketball	10	25
Marble, Alice	Tennis	12	25
Marsh, Graham	Golf	4	8
Martens, George	Horse Racing	5	20
Martin, Slater	Basketball	5	10
Mathias, Bob	Track	5	15
Matthews, Sir Stanley	Soccer	10	20
McCormick, Patricia	Diving	5	15
McEnroe, John	Tennis	15	30
McKay, Jim	Broadcaster	4	8
McKenzie, Stan	Basketball	4	8
McKinley, Chuck	Tennis	4	8
McNamee, Graham	Broadcaster	20	40
Meadowes, Earl	Track	6	12
Meagher, Mary T.	Swimming	5	10
Mears, Rick	Auto Racing	10	20
Menandez, Luis	Wrestling	4	8
Meyer, Debbie	Swimming	7	15
Meyer, Lou	Auto Racing	10	20
Meyer, Ray	Basketball	4	8
Middlecoff, Cary	Golf	5	10
Mikan, George	Basketball	10	22
Mikita, Stan	Hockey	7	15
Miller, Dr. Dean D.	Sports Physician	4	8
Miller, Johnny	Golf	5	10
Milton, Tommy	Auto Racing	50	100
Mitchell, Jeff	Track	4	8
"Minnesota Fats"	Billiards	10	30
Moody, Orville	Golf	4	8
Moran, Gussy	Tennis	5	10
Morgan, Gil	Golf	4	8
Mosconi, Willie	Billiards	5	15
Moses, Edwin	Track	7	25
Mosley, Mike	Auto Racing	7	15
Moss, Stirling	Auto Racing	10	20
Murphy, Bob	Golf	4	8
Murphy, Charles "Stretch"	Basketball	5	10
Musburger, Brent	Broadcaster	4	8

Jim Thorpe

Bill Tilden

Lee Trevino

Gene Tunney

Bobby Unser

Jim Valvano

Jersey Joe Walcott

Mickey Walker

Cornelius Warmerdam

Johnny Weissmuller

Spud Webb

Hazel Hotchkiss Wightman

Edward Bennett Williams

Dominique Wilkins

Ike Williams

"Tug" Wilson

Helen Wills

John Wooden

George Yardley

Tony Zale

Name	Sports Affiliation	Signature Only	Signed Photograph
Nastase, Ilie	Tennis	10	20
Navratilova, Martina	Tennis	7	20
Neal, Lloyd	Basketball	4	8
Nelson, Byron	Golf	5	20
Nelson, Cindy	Skiing	4	8
Nelson, Don	Basketball	4	8
Newcombe, John	Tennis	5	10
Niatta, Dick	Basketball	4	8
Nicklaus, Jack	Golf	10	25
Norman, Greg	Golf	5	12
Nurmi, Paavo	Track	25	50
Nuthall, Betty	Tennis	15	30
Nyad, Diana	Swimming	4	8
O'Brien, Lawrence F.	Basketball	5	10
O'Brien, Parry	Track	10	20
Oerter, Al	Track	5	15
Oldfield, Barney	Auto Racing	40	100
Oosterhaus, Peter	Golf	4	8
Orr, Bobby	Hockey	7	15
Orr, Johnny	Basketball	4	8
Ouimet, Francis	Golf	35	75
Owens, Jesse	Track	20	50
Palmer, Arnold	Golf	5	10
Parish, Robert	Basketball	4	12
Parker, Dan	Sportswriter	4	8
Parsons, Johnny	Auto Racing	10	20
Pate, Jerry	Golf	4	8
Patton, Mel	Track	10	20
Paultz, Bill	Basketball	4	8
Pavin, Corey	Golf	5	10
Peete, Calvin	Golf	5	10
Pelé	Soccer	15	30
Perkins, Sam	Basketball	4	8
Perry, Fred	Tennis	10	30
Petrie, Geoff	Basketball	4	8
Peters, Mary	Track	4	8
Pettit, Bob	Basketball	15	40
Petty, Kyle	Auto Racing	4	8
Petty, Richard	Auto Racing	5	10
Pfister, Dan	Basketball	4	8
Phelps, "Digger"	Basketball	5	10
Phillips, "Bunny"	Auto Racing	5	10
Picard, Henry G.	Golf	10	20
Piggott, Lester	Horse Racing	10	20
Pincay, Laffit, Jr.	Horse Racing	10	20
Player, Gary	Golf	5	15
Plimpton, George	Sportswriter	4	8
Pollard, Art	Auto Racing	10	20
Pollard, Jim	Basketball	5	12
Purtzer, Tom	Golf	4	8
Rahal, Bobby	Auto Racing	10	20
Ramsay, Jack	Basketball	4	8
Rathmann, Jim	Auto Racing	10	20

 Elaine Zayak

 Fuzzy Zoeller

Name	Sports Affiliation	Signature Only	Signed Photograph
Rawls, Betsy	Golf	8	15
Reed, Willis	Basketball	5	15
Renner, Jack	Golf	4	8
Retton, Mary Lou	Gymnastics	6	15
Revson, Peter	Auto Racing	45	100
Rice, Grantland	Sportswriter	20	50
Richard, J. H. Maurice "Rocket"	Hockey	10	20
Richards, Alma W.	Track	4	8
Richards, Rev. Bob	Track	5	15
Richards, Sir Gordon	Horse Racing	15	30
Richmond, Tim	Auto Racing	5	10
Rigby, Cathy	Gymnastics	5	15
Riggs, Bobby	Tennis	5	15
Riley, Polly	Golf	10	20
Roberts, Floyd	Auto Racing	25	75
Robertson, Oscar ·	Basketball	10	20
Rodgers, Bill	Marathon	5	15
Rogers, Bill	Golf	4	8
Rogers, Karen	Horse Racing	8	20
Roosma, John S.	Basketball	10	20
Rosewall, Ken	Tennis	5	10
Rote, Kyle, Jr.	Soccer	4	8
Rudolph, Wilma	Track	15	25
Rupp, Adolph	Basketball	5	15
Russell, Bill	Basketball	150	300
Russell, Cazzie	Basketball	4	8
Rutherford, Johnny	Auto Racing	10	20
Ryun, Jim	Track	10	20
Salazar, Alberto	Marathon	7	15
Samourand, M.	International Chairman of Olympics	5	10
Sampson, Ralph	Basketball	10	20
Sande, Earle	Horse Racing	40	80
Sanders, Doug	Golf	4	8
Sandow	Weightlifting	20	50
Santee, Wes	Track	10	20
Sarazen, Gene	Golf	20	40
Savard, Serge	Hockey	5	10
Sawchuck, Terrance	Hockey	5	10
Schayes, Adolph "Dolph"	Basketball	5	10
Schenkel, Chris	Broadcaster	4	8
Schlueter, Dale	Basketball	4	9
Schmidt, Milton	Hockey	5	10
Schollander, Don	Swimming	5	10

Name	Sports Affiliation	Signature Only	Signed Photograph
Schwarzenegger, Arnold	Body Building	10	30
Scully, Vin	Broadcaster	4	8
Seagren, Bob	Track	10	20
Segura, Pancho	Tennis	10	20
Seltzer, Leo	Roller Derby	25	50
Selvy, Frank	Basketball	4	8
Sharman, Bill	Basketball	5	12
Shaw, Wilbur	Auto Racing	45	100
Shoemaker, Willie	Horse Racing	10	25
Shore, Ernie	Hockey	10	20
Shorter, Frank	Marathon	5	10
Simons, Jim	Racing	4	8
Simpson, Scott	Golf	5	10
Sloan, Tod	Horse Racing	150	300
Smith, Dean E.	Basketball	5	10
Smith, Greg	Basketball	4	8
Smith, Horton	Golf	10	20
Smith, Robyn	Horse Racing	5	15
Snead, Sam	Golf	10	20
Snell, Peter	Track	5	10
Sneva, Tom	Auto Racing	5	10
Spitz, Mark	Swimming	10	20
Stadler, Craig	Golf	5	15
Stahley, Skip	Athletic Director	4	8
Starbuck, JoJo	Skating	5	10
Stephens, Woody	Horse Racing	10	20
Stephenson, Jan	Golf	7	15
Stewart, Jackie	Auto Racing	12	25
Stewart, Payne	Golf	5	10
Stockton, Dave	Golf	4	8
Stone, Dwight	Track	4	8
Stranahan, Frank	Golf	10	20
Strange, Curtis	Golf	5	10
Suggs, Louise	Golf	8	20
Sullivan, Danny	Auto Racing	10	20
Sumners, Rosalynn	Skating	4	8
Sutton, Hal	Golf	4	8
Tarkanian, Jerry	Basketball	4	8
Tatum, "Goose"	Basketball	5	10
Tewell, Doug	Golf	4	8
Thomas, John	Track	4	10
Thompson, David	Basketball	4	8
Thompson, John	Basketball	5	10
Thompson, John "Cat"	Basketball	10	20
Thorpe, Jim	Track/Football	250	500
Thurmond, Nate	Basketball	5	12
Tilden, William "Big Bill"	Tennis	25	50
Torres, Enrique	Wrestling	5	10
Trabert, Tony	Tennis	5	10
Travers, Jerome D.	Golf	20	40
Trevino, Lee	Golf	10	20
Turner, Ted	Broadcaster/Owner	5	10

Name	Sports Affiliation	Signature Only	Signed Photograph
Turnesa, Jim	Golf	10	20
Tway, Bob	Golf	6	12
Tyus, Wyomia	Track	10	20
Unser, Al	Auto Racing	5	15
Unser, Bobby	Auto Racing	5	15
Valvano, Jim	Basketball	5	10
Van Arsdale, Dick	Basketball	5	10
Vanderbilt, Harold S.	Yachting	20	40
Vardon, Harry	Golf	25	65
Varipapa, Andy	Bowling	20	40
Velasquez, Jorge	Horse Racing	10	25
Venturi, Ken	Golf	10	20
Vidmar, Peter	Gymnastics	6	12
Vines, Ellsworth, Jr.	Tennis	10	25
Vukovich, Billy	Auto Racing	5	15
Wade, Virginia	Tennis	5	10
Wadkins, Lanny	Golf	5	12
Walker, John	Track	10	20
Walsh, Christy	Sportswriter	12	35
Walton, Bill	Basketball	7	20
Ward, Jimmy	Hockey	5	10
Ward, Rodger	Auto Racing	10	20
Warmerdam, Cornelius	Track	10	20
Watson, Tom	Golf	5	15
Weber, Dick	Bowling	5	12
Weiskopf, Tom	Golf	5	10
Weissmuller, Johnny	Swimming	50	100
Werblin, Sonny	Sportsman	5	10
West, Jerry	Basketball	10	20
Westphal, Paul	Basketball	4	8
Whittaker, James	Mountain Climbing	4	8
Whitworth, Kathy	Golf	5	10
Wicks, Sidney	Basketball	5	10
Wightman, Mrs. Hazel	Tennis	20	40
Wilkens, Lenny	Basketball	5	10
Wilkins, Mac	Track	7	15
Williams, Edward Bennett	Sportsman/Owner	5	10
Wills, Helen	Tennis	25	50
Wood, Gar	Speedboat Racing	25	50
Wooden, John	Basketball	10	20
Worsham, Lew, Jr.	Golf	5	10
Wottle, Dave	Track	6	12
Wright, Mickey	Golf	5	10
Wright, Warren	Horse Racing	20	60
Yarborough, Cale	Auto Racing	10	25
Yardley, George	Basketball	4	8
Zaharias, "Babe" Didrikson	Track/Golf	100	150
Zayak, Elaine	Skating	4	8
Zoeller, Fuzzy	Golf	5	10

Golf Hall of Fame Members

Here are prices for members of the Golf Hall of Fame. One exception is Bing Crosby, who may be found in the Entertainers (Vintage) category.

Name	Signature Only	Signed Photograph
Anderson, Willie	$10	$ 20
Armour, Tommy	10	20
Ball, John, Jr.	10	20
Berg, Patty	6	18
Boros, Julius	5	15
Braid, James	10	20
Casper, Billy	5	12
Corcoran, Fred	10	20
Cotton, Henry	10	20
Dey, Joseph C.	10	20
Evans, Charles "Chick"	20	40
Graffis, Herb	10	20
Guldahl, Ralph	10	25
Hagen, Walter	25	75
Hilton, Harold	10	20
Hogan, Ben	13	35
Howe, Dorothy Campbell	15	30
Jones, Robert T., Jr.	65	175
Little, Lawson	20	40
Locke, Bobby	15	30
Morris, Tom, Jr.	15	30
Morris, Tom, Sr.	15	30
Nelson, Byron	5	20
Nicklaus, Jack	10	25
Ouimet, Francis	35	75
Palmer, Arnold	5	10
Player, Gary	5	15
Roberts, Clifford	12	35
Ross, Donald	10	20
Sarazen, Gene	20	40
Snead, Sam	10	20
Suggs, Louise	8	20
Taylor, John H.	10	20
Travers, Jerome D.	20	40
Travis, Walter J.	10	20
Trevino, Lee	10	20
Varden, Harry	25	65
Vare, Glenna Collett	10	20

Name	Signature Only	Signed Photograph
Wethered, Joyce	10	20
Whitworth, Kathy	5	10
Wright, Mickey	5	10
Zaharias, Babe Didrikson	100	150

Governors

Collecting autographs from governors of the various states is becoming more popular. Below is a cross-section of prices from those currently available. The abreviations used are

- ALS—Autograph Letter Signed (that is, the whole letter handwritten)
- ANS—Autograph Note Signed
- AQS—Autograph Quotation Signed
- DS—Document Signed
- FDC—First Day Cover (stamps)
- SIG—Signature
- SP—Signed Photograph
- TLS—Typed Letter Signed

Governor	State	Type	Amount
Agnew, Spiro	Maryland	TLS	$ 25
Aiken, George D.	Vermont	TLS	20
Aiken, William	South Carolina	SIG	25
Alexander, J. B.	Guam	SIG	5
Alger, Russell A.	Michigan	DS	35
Altgeld, John Peter	Illinois	SIG	25
Ames, Oliver	Massachusetts	DS	25
Anderson, John, Jr.	Kansas	LS	10
Andrew, John A.	Massachusetts	SIG	20
Andrew, John A.	Massachusetts	ALS	40
Ariyoshi, George R.	Hawaii	TLS	15
Askew, Reubin	Florida	SP	12
Austin, Horace	Minnesota	SIG	10
Babcock, Tim	Montana	SP	12
Bacon, Walter W.	Delaware	SP	10
Bailey, Carl E.	Arkansas	TLS	15
Baldwin, Raymond E.	Connecticut	SIG	7
Baldwin, R. S.	Connecticut	ALS	30

Governor	State	Type	Amount
Barnett, Ross R.	Mississippi	TLS	25
Barrows, Lewis O.	Maine	SIG	10
Baxter, Percival P.	Maine	ANS	10
Beaver, James A.	Pennsylvania	DS	25
Benson, Elmer A.	Minnesota	SIG	10
Bissell, William H.	Illinois	DS	25
Blackburn, Luke P.	Kentucky	DS	30
Blanton, Ray	Tennessee	TLS	10
Blood, Robert O.	New Hampshire	TLS	10
Boe, Nils A.	South Dakota	DS	15
Booth, Newton	California	SIG	20
Bottolfsen, C. A.	Idaho	SIG	10
Bouck, William C.	New York	DS	20
Brann, Louis J.	Maine	DS	15
Bricker, John W.	Ohio	TLS	25
Brown, Edmund G. "Jerry"	California	TLS	25
Brown, Edmund G. "Pat"	California	TLS	20
Bryan, Charles W.	Nebraska	TLS	25
Buck, C. Douglass	Delaware	SIG	10
Buckingham, William A.	Connecticut	ALS	35
Bull, William, II	South Carolina	SIG	45
Bumpers, Dale	Arkansas	TLS	12
Burns, John A.	Hawaii	TLS	15
Burroughs, John	New Mexico	TLS	10
Busby, George	Georgia	TLS	10
Byrnes, James F.	South Carolina	SIG	25
Campbell, Jack M.	New Mexico	TLS	10
Campbell, James E.	Ohio	TLS	20
Carey, Hugh L.	New York	TLS	10
Carlson, Frank	Kansas	SIG	6
Carroll, John Lee	Maryland	ALS	25
Carroll, Julian M.	Kentucky	SIG	10
Carroll, William	Tennessee	DS	35
Carvel, Elbert M.	Delaware	TLS	10
Carville, Edward P.	Nevada	SP	12
Case, Norman S.	Rhode Island	DS	20
Castro, Raul H.	Arizona	SP	12
Chandler, A. B. "Happy"	Kentucky	SP	15
Cherry, R. Gregg	North Carolina	TLS	15
Clark, Barzilla W.	Idaho	TLS	12
Clark, Myron H.	New York	ALS	35
Clinton, De Witt	New York	ALS	100
Cochran, Robert L.	Nebraska	SIG	10
Collins, LeRoy	Florida	SP	12
Connally, John	Texas	SP	15
Cooper, Prentice	Tennessee	TLS	15
Dicks, Jacob	New York	TLS	15
Docking, Robert	Kansas	SP	10
Draper, Eben S.	Massachusetts	TLS	12
Dukakis, Michael S.	Massachusetts	SIG	15
Dupont, Pierre S.	Delaware	SIG	12
Earle, George H.	Pennsylvania	SIG	10
Eberhart, Adolph O.	Minnesota	DS	20
Edwar, James B., DS	South Carolina	SIG	10

Governor	State	Type	Amount
Egan, William A.	Alaska	SP	10
Ellington, Buford	Tennessee	TLS	12
Evans, Daniel J.	Washington	TLS	12
Evans, John V.	Idaho	TLS	10
Exon, J. James	Nebraska	TLS	10
Fairbanks, Erastus	Vermont	ALS	30
Faubus, Orval E.	Arkansas	SP	35
Faubus, Orval E.	Arkansas	TLS	35
Ferguson, Miriam A. "Ma"	Texas	DS	50
Fielder, James F.	New Jersey	TLS	12
Findlay, William	Pennsylvania	DS	45
Fisher, John S.	Pennsylvania	SIG	10
Foraker, Joseph B.	Ohio	DS	35
Fort, George F.	New Jersey	DS	30
Fort, John Franklin	New Jersey	TLS	12
Freeman, Orville	Minnesota	DS	12
Fuller, Alvan T.	Massachusetts	TLS	15
Furcolo, Foster	Massachusetts	ALS	25
Furnas, Robert W.	Nebraska	SIG	10
Futrell, J. M.	Arkansas	TLS	12
Garcelon, Alonzo	Maine	SIG	12
Gardner, O. Max	North Carolina	TLS	15
Gibbs, Addison C.	Oregon	DS	35
Green, Dwight H.	Illinois	DS	10
Griffin, S. Marvin	Georgia	FDC	10
Griswold, Matthew	Connecticut	SIG	12
Guild, Curtis, Jr.	Massachusetts	TLS	12
Haines, Daniel	New Jersey	ALS	30
Hall, David	Oklahoma	TLS	12
Hammond, Jay S.	Alaska	SIG	10
Harriman, Averell	New York	SP	20
Harrison, Albertis S., Jr.	Virginia	TLS	10
Harrison, Henry B.	Connecticut	SIG	12
Hartley, Roland H.	Washington	SIG	12
Hartranft, John F.	Pennsylvania	ALS	25
Hastings, Daniel H.	Pennsylvania	TLS	25
Hatfield, Mark O.	Oregon	SP	10
Hawkins, William	North Carolina	DS	70
Hearnes, Warren E.	Missouri	TLS	10
Hickel, Walter J.	Alaska	SIG	12
Hill, John F.	Maine	TLS	12
Hoegh, Leo A.	Iowa	SP	12
Hoey, Clyde R.	North Carolina	TLS	20
Hoff, Philip H.	Vermont	TLS	10
Hoffman, Harold Giles	New Jersey	TLS	30
Hoffman, John Thompson	New York	SIG	10
Hollings, Ernest	South Carolina	FDC	10
Holmes, Robert D.	Oregon	ANS	10
Holshouser, James E.	North Carolina	SP	12
Holton, Linwood	Virginia	SP	12
Horner, Henry	Illinois	SP	20
Hughes, Richard J.	New Jersey	TLS	12
Hunt, George W. P.	Arizona	SIG	10
Hunt, James B., Jr.	North Carolina	SP	10

Governor	State	Type	Amount
Hunt, Washington	New York	ALS	45
Hurley, Charles F.	Massachusetts	SIG	10
Ingersoll, Charles R.	Connecticut	ALS	15
Jacob, John J.	West Virginia	SIG	12
Jewell, Marshall	Connecticut	SIG	10
Johnson, Keen	Kentucky	TLS	10
Keys, Henry W.	New Hampshire	SIG	10
Kirk, Claude R., Jr.	Florida	TLS	12
Kirman, Richard, Sr.	Nevada	SIG	10
Knight, Goodwin J.	California	TLS	12
LaFollette, Philip	Wisconsin	SIG	25
Landon, Alf M.	Kansas	TLS	20
Lane, Joseph	Oregon	SIG	20
Langlie, Arthur	Washington	TLS	12
Lausche, Frank J.	Ohio	SP	12
Lawrence, David L.	Pennsylvania	TLS	15
Lehman, Herbert H.	New York	TLS	15
Leslie, Preston H.	Kentucky	ANS	12
Long, Huey P.	Louisiana	SIG	50
Long, Earl K.	Louisiana	TLS	20
Longley, James B.	Maine	SIG	7
Love, John A.	Colorado	TLS	12
Low, Frederick F.	California	DS	45
Lowry, Robert	Mississippi	DS	25
Maddox, Lester	Georgia	TLS	25
Mandel, Marvin	Maryland	SP	25
Martin, Charles H.	Oregon	DS	20
Martin, Clarence D.	Washington	TLS	15
Maybank, Burnet R.	South Carolina	DS	18
McCall, Tom	Oregon	SP	15
McKeldin, Theodore R.	Maryland	TLS	15
McLean, George P.	Connecticut	AQS	15
McMullen, Richard C.	Delaware	TLS	10
McNair, Robert	South Carolina	FDC	10
McNutt, Paul V.	Indiana	TLS	15
Mechan, E. L.	New Mexico	SP	10
Merriam, Frank F.	California	TLS	15
Miller, Leslie A.	Wyoming	SIG	10
Miller, Nathan L.	New York	SIG	15
Milliken, William G.	Michigan	TLS	15
Moeur, Benjamin B.	Arizona	SIG	10
Moore, Arch A., Jr.	West Virginia	SP	15
Moore, Dan K.	North Carolina	TLS	15
Morehead, John M.	North Carolina	TLS	25
Morrill, Lot N.	Maine	DS	25
Morton, Oliver P.	Indiana	DS	25
Murphy, Franklin	New Jersey	DS	15
Muskie, Edmund S.	Maine	TLS	15
Nall, Philip W.	Indiana	SP	10
Norblad, A. W.	Oregon	FDC	25
Noyes, Edward F.	Ohio	DS	15
O'Callaghan, Mike	Nevada	TLS	15
O'Daniel, W. Lee "Pappy"	Texas	SP	40
Osborne, Sidney P.	Arizona	SIG	10
Osborne, Thomas A.	Kansas	SIG	10

Governor	State	Type	Amount
Parker, Joel	New Jersey	SIG	10
Pastore, John A.	Rhode Island	SP	12
Patterson, John	Alabama	SP	12
Patterson, Paul L.	Oregon	TLS	10
Pattison, Robert T.	Pennsylvania	DS	25
Perpich, Rudolph G.	Minnesota	SIG	10
Perry, Madison S.	Florida	DS	45
Pinchot, Gifford	Pennsylvania	TLS	30
Poindexter, Joseph B.	Hawaii	SIG	10
Ponder, James	Delaware	SIG	10
Porter, James D.	Tennessee	ALS	35
Powers, Ridgely C.	Mississippi	AQS	30
Price, James H.	Virginia	DS	12
Pryor, David	Arkansas	TLS	12
Quinn, Robert E.	Rhode Island	SIG	10
Quinn, William F.	Hawaii	SP	10
Ratner, Payne	Kansas	TLS	12
Ray, Robert D.	Iowa	SP	10
Ray, Dixie Lee	Washington	SP	15
Reagan, Ronald	California	(See "Presidents")	
Ribicoff, Abraham	Connecticut	TLS	20
Rockefeller, John D., IV	West Virginia	SP	12
Rockefeller, Nelson A.	New York	DS	40
Rockefeller, Winthrop	Arkansas	SP	15
Rolph, James	California	SIG	20
Romney, George	Michigan	SP	15
Rosellini, Albert D.	Washington	TLS	15
Ross, Nellie Tayloe	Wyoming	TLS	35
Russell, Charles	Nevada	FDC	10
Saulsbury, Grove	Delaware	AQS	20
Schricker, Henry F.	Indiana	DS	20
Scott, W. Kerr	North Carolina	SP	20
Scranton, Bill	Pennsylvania	SP	15
Seymour, Horatio	New York	ALS	50
Shapp, Milton J.	Pennsylvania	SIG	10
Sibley, Henry H.	Minnesota	ALS	75
Sigler, Kim	Michigan	TLS	15
Smith, Alfred E.	New York	TLS	35
Smith, Charles M.	Vermont	DS	15
Smith, Elmo	Oregon	TLS	20
Smith, James Y.	Rhode Island	ALS	30
Smith, J. Gregory	Vermont	DS	15
Smith, Nels H.	Wyoming	SP	12
Snyder, Simon	Pennsylvania	ALS	35
Sparks, Chuncey	Alabama	DS	20
Sprague, Charles A.	Oregon	DS	20
Stafford, Robert T.	Vermont	TLS	15
Stanford, R. C.	Arizona	TLS	12
Stassen, Harold	Minnesota	SP	15
Stevenson, Adlai	Illinois	SP	35
Stratton, William G.	Illinois	SIG	10
Straub, Robert W.	Oregon	SIG	10
Straw, Ezekiel A.	New Hampshire	SIG	15
Sulzer, William	New York	TLS	35
Swann, Thomas	Maryland	ALS	25

Governor	State	Type	Amount
Talmadge, Eugene	Georgia	SP	75
Talmadge, Eugene	Georgia	TLS	50
Tawes, J. Millard	Maryland	TLS	15
Thompson, Jim	Illinois	SP	15
Thompson, M. E.	Georgia	TLS	15
Thornton, Dan	Colorado	FDC	10
Throop, Enos T.	New York	DS	40
Thurmond, J. Strom	South Carolina	TLS	20
Tingley, Clyde	New Mexico	SIG	10
Tod, David	Ohio	LS	20
Townsend, M. Clifford	Indiana	SIG	10
Trumbull, John	Connecticut	SIG	10
Umstead, William B.	North Carolina	TLS	15
Vance, Zebulon	North Carolina	DS	100
Vanderbilt, William H.	Rhode Island	TLS	20
Van Wagoner, Murray D.	Michigan	TLS	20
Walker, Gilbert C.	Virginia	SIG	10
Wallace, George C.	Alabama	SP	20
Wallace, Lurleen B.	Alabama	SIG	12
Waller, Thomas M.	Connecticut	ALS	30
Wells, James M.	Louisiana	DS	25
White, Hugh	Mississippi	TLS	15
Youngdahl, Luther	Minnesota	FDC	10

Heads of State

The following price list is for foreign (that is, non–U.S.) heads of state, royalty, and other world leaders. If the name of any person has been excluded, it means only that data on a philographic item of his or hers was not accessible at the time of publishing.

* = Data incomplete, estimate only. ** = Last published price.

Name	Signature Only	Letter or Document Signed	Autograph Letter Signed	Signed Photograph
Aberdeen, Lord	$ 20.00	$ 30.00	$ 65.17	
Addington, Henry	15.00	35.00	95.00	
Adenauer, Konrad	20.00	95.00	150.00	$ 63.00
Aga Khan III	10.00	35.00	80.00	15.00

Clement R. Attlee

Louis Napoléon Bonaparte

Menachem Begin

Willy Brandt

King Juan Carlos, Spain

Joe Clark, Canadian Prime Minister

Catherine (II) the Great

Idi Amin Dada

Benjamin Disraeli

Francis Duvalier, Haiti

Sir Anthony Eden

Queen Elizabeth II, England

Indira Gandhi

Mahatma Gandhi

Frederick the Great, Prussia

Guiseppe Garibaldi

Charles de Gaulle

King George I, England

Mikhail S. Gorbachev

Salvador Allende Gossens

Andrei A. Gromyko

Prince Hassam, Morocco

Edward Heath

Keith Holyoake, Prime Minister of New Zealand

Name	Signature Only	Letter or Document Signed	Autograph Letter Signed	Signed Photograph
Aguinaldo, Emilio	75.00	140.00	165.00	140.00
Akihito, Prince	100.00	200.00	454.00	225.00
Albert, Prince (Victoria)	118.33	207.00	272.20	
Albert I (Belgium)	25.00	115.00	195.00	40.00
Albert III (Rainier—Monaco)	75.00	200.00	495.00	120.00
Alexander I (Russia)	225.00	556.00	880.00	
Alexander II (Russia)	175.00	596.67	1,490.00	
Alexander III (Russia)		600.00	150.00	
Alexandra (Edward VII)	20.00	80.00	166.67	512.50
Alexandra (Nicholas II—Russia)	70.00	235.00	581.67	
Alfonso XIII (Spain)	120.00	250.00	625.00	
Allende, Salvador G.	35.00	120.00	270.00	55.00
Amin Dada, Idi	37.00	100.00	190.00	50.00
Anna Ivanova (Russia)	265.00	900.00	2,250.00	
Anne, Queen (England)	285.00	867.50	2,150.00	
Asquith, Herbert H.	25.00	45.00	110.00	
Assad, Hafez Al	10.00	35.00	85.00	60.00
Attlee, Clement	40.00	175.00	330.00	70.00
Auckland, Earl of	10.00	20.00	50.00	
Ayub Khan, Gen.	8.00	12.00	30.00	
Baldwin, Stanley	25.00	75.00	120.00	50.00
Balewa, Sir Arthur	10.00	32.00	80.00	20.00
Balfour, Arthur J.	34.00	60.29	110.00	85.67
Bandaranike, S. W. R. D.	5.00	25.00	45.00	10.00
Banisadr, A.	10.00	30.00	80.00	40.00
Batista, Fulgencio	25.00	70.00	175.00	35.00
Baudouin, King (Belgium)	30.00	100.00	250.00	100.00
Beatrix, Queen (Netherlands)				200.00
Beauharnais, Eugene	30.00	95.00	163.00	
Begin, Menachem	45.00	103.75	210.00	90.00
Belaunde, Fernando T.	10.00	20.00	50.00	15.00
Benes, Eduard	20.00	40.00	65.00	165.00
Ben-Gurion, David	100.00	431.25	709.00	410.00
Bennett, William Andrew	3.00	10.00	20.00	8.00
Ben-Zvi, Itzhak	10.00	75.00	90.00	20.00
Bernadotte, Jean B.	100.00	264.50	450.00	
Bismarck, Otto von	175.00	375.00	725.00	650.00
Blum, Léon (Premier—France)	15.00	40.00	100.00	30.00
Bolivar, Simón	275.00	2,266.67	5,500.00	
Bonaparte, Jérôme	20.00	35.00	50.00	
Bonaparte, Joseph	100.00	247.50	300.00	
Bonaparte, Louis	40.00	200.00	335.00	
Bonaparte, Lucien	20.00	35.00	50.00	
Bordaberry, Juan Maria	7.00	15.00	25.00	10.00
Borghese, Camillo	15.00	50.00	125.00	
Boris III (Bulgaria)	95.00			160.00
Bourguiba, Habib	15.00	40.00	100.00	20.00
Bowen, Sir George F.	5.00	10.00	20.00	
Brandt, Willy	30.00	85.00	210.00	50.00
Brezhnev, Leonid I.	45.00	175.00	430.00	215.00
Buhari, Mohammed	15.00	50.00	130.00	25.00
Bulow, Bernhard von	10.00	35.00	85.00	30.00

Henry III, France—His Early Years

Henry III, France—Old Age

King Hussein, Jordan

Chiang Kai-Shek

King Louis VIII, France

Madam Chiang Kai-Shek

Jomo Kenyatta

Paul Kruger

Trygve Lie

King Louis-Philippe I, France

Ramon Magaysay

N. W. Manley

Sincerely yours,

FERDINAND E. MARCOS

Ferdinand E. Marcos

Y. Nakasone

R.G. MUGABE

R. G. Mugabe

Napoleon

Jawaharlal Nehru (Prime Minister of India)

Olaf Palme

Sir Robert Peel

Lord North

1783.

Lester B. Pearson

Prince Rainier, Monaco

Col. Muammar Al-Qaddafi, Libya

Syngman Rhee, President of Korea

Name	Signature Only	Letter or Document Signed	Autograph Letter Signed	Signed Photograph
Caceres, Andreas A.	10.00	25.00	65.00	15.00
Calderon, Gen. A. W.	5.00	15.00	25.00	10.00
Callaghan, James	37.50	55.00	135.00	38.75
Camargo, Alberto	7.00	15.00	25.00	10.00
Campbell-Bannerman, H.	10.00	25.00	60.00	
Canning, George	35.00	135.00	175.00	
Carlo Alberto (Sardinia)	45.00	150.00	375.00	
Carlotta (Mexico)	285.00	770.00	1,700.00	
Caroline (George II—England)	295.00	400.00	1,000.00	
Caroline (George IV—England)	20.00	75.00	170.00	
Castro, Fidel	275.00	700.00	1,350.00	1,250.00
Catherine de Médicis (France)	210.00	638.50	1,700.00	
Catherine I (Russia)	520.00	2,000.00	4,500.00	
Catherine II (The Great)	275.00	1,085.83	2,800.00	
Chamberlain, Neville	73.33	125.00	280.00	100.00
Charlemagne**		75,000.00		
Charles Edward Stuart	95.00	325.00	815.00	
Charles I (England)	625.00	1,829.75	4,500.00	
Charles II (England)	325.00	863.47	2,700.00	
Charles V (Charles I—Spain)	580.00	2,000.00	5,000.00	
Charles IX (France)	150.00	490.00	1,700.00	
Charles X (France)	125.00	287.50	725.00	
Charles XIV (Sweden)	117.50	350.00	880.00	
Charles XV (Sweden/Norway)	40.00	125.00	320.00	
Charles, Prince of Wales	350.00	540.00	1,350.00	400.00
Charlotte (George III)	45.00	150.00	375.00	
Charlotte, Grand Duchess (Luxembourg)	20.00	65.00	165.00	45.00
Chirac, Jacques	25.00	75.00	185.00	35.00
Chou En-Lai	1,155.00	4,000.00	10,000.00	2,000.00
Christian VII	85.00	250.00	625.00	
Christina (Sweden)	250.00	850.00	2,287.50	
Chun Doo-Hwan				50.00
Churchill, Winston S.	325.00	1,118.18	1,727.78	1,313.18
Clemenceau, Georges	40.00	65.00	86.25	50.00
Clement VIII, Pope		550.00	1,300.00	
Cobham, Gov. Gen. (New Zealand)	3.00	8.00	13.00	5.00
Cromwell, Oliver	1,000.00	3,500.00	11,700.00	
Daladier, Edouard	25.00	75.00	100.00	40.00
Dalai Lama	50.00	100.00	170.00	55.00
de Gaulle, Charles	210.00	420.00	1,025.00	425.00
Debre, Michael	5.00	20.00	50.00	
Denman, Thomas Baron	5.00	8.00	15.00	
Derby, 12th Earl of (Edward Stanley)	10.00	25.00	70.50	
D'Estaing, Valéry Giscard	15.00	40.00	100.00	60.00
Devonshire, 4th Duke of	3.00	10.00	25.00	
Diaz, Porfirio (Mexico)	65.00	135.00	235.00	225.00
Diefenbaker, John	15.00	45.00	110.00	20.00
Disraeli, Benjamin	98.75	240.00	478.33	
Dobrinyin, Anatole	38.00	130.00	325.00	65.00

Margaret Thatcher

Pierre Trudeau, Canadian Prime Minister

Tito, Yugoslavia

Kurt Waldheim

Queen Victoria

Duke of Wellington

Kaiser Wilhelm

William IV, England

Name	Signature Only	Letter or Document Signed	Autograph Letter Signed	Signed Photograph
Du Barry, Marie Jeanne	240.00	716.67	1,033.33	
Dutra, Enrico Gaspar	5.00	20.00	50.00	
Duvalier, François	75.00	50.00		150.00
Eden, Sir Anthony	30.00	75.00	147.50	55.00
Edward, Duke of Windsor	122.00	510.80	641.25	656.00
Edward, Duke of Kent	40.00	135.00	350.00	
Edward IV (England)		25,000.00		
Edward VII (England)	50.00	189.78	221.83	495.00
Edward VIII	122.00	510.00	641.00	656.00
Elizabeth (George VI)	35.00	100.00	255.00	320.00
Elizabeth I	2,200.00	6,333.33	12,700.00	
Elizabeth II	316.67	482.00	675.00	450.00
Erhard, Ludwig	20.00	70.00	170.00	50.00
Eshkol, Levi	65.00	225.00	560.00	110.00
Eugénie, Empress (Napoleon III)	175.00	237.50	300.00	300.00
Faisal (Saudi Arabia)	10.00	34.00	75.00	16.00
Ferdinand II (Spain)	275.00	975.00	2,375.00	
Ferdinand IV (Naples)	35.00	125.00	310.00	
Ferdinand V (Spain)	625.00	2,500.00	8,437.50	
Ferdinand VII (Spain)	25.00	85.00	200.00	
Figueres, José	15.00	45.00	110.00	20.00
Fonseca, Roberto A.	5.00	16.00	40.00	20.00
Francis I (France)	450.00	2,550.00		
Francis II	40.00	195.00	340.00	
Franco, Francisco	150.00	525.00	1,300.00	250.00
Franz Joseph I (Austria)	120.00	281.25	700.00	
Franz Joseph II	25.00	63.00	125.00	40.00
Frederick II (The Great—Prussia)	322.50	425.00	1,750.00	

Name	Signature Only	Letter or Document Signed	Autograph Letter Signed	Signed Photograph
Frederick III (Prussia)	50.00	200.00	425.00	200.00
Frederick IV (Denmark)	75.00	250.00	625.00	
Frederick IX (Denmark)	40.00	145.00	350.00	
Frederick V (Denmark)	60.00	200.00	500.00	
Frederick William I (Prussia)	65.00	225.00	300.00	
Frederick William III (Prussia)	55.00	195.00	475.00	
Frederick William IV (Prussia)	60.00	200.00	475.00	
Freeland, Paul van	5.00	16.00	40.00	20.00
Frondizi, Arturo	10.00	30.00	75.00	50.00
Gambetta, Leon	25.00	75.00	185.00	
Gandhi, Indira	73.00	195.00	363.00	143.33
Gandhi, Mohandas K. (Mahatma)	170.00	475.00	751.25	600.00
Garibaldi, Giuseppe	85.00	125.00	300.00	350.00
Geisel, Ernesto	7.00	15.00	25.00	15.00
George I (England)	166.67	670.83	2,475.00	
George I (Greece)	40.00	70.00	123.00	
George II (England)	150.00	389.17	1,350.00	
George II (Greece)	30.00	65.00	165.00	
George III (England)	185.00	343.04	1,163.33	
George IV (England)	63.00	335.71	450.00	
George V (England)	90.00	244.00	390.00	617.00
George VI (England)	181.33	201.00	302.50	405.00
Gersel Cemal	20.00	65.00	170.00	35.00
Gladstone, William	27.50	65.00	105.71	75.00
Goderich, Frederick John	10.00	35.00	85.00	
Gomes, Francisco	15.00	55.00	135.00	25.00
Grace de Monaco (Grace Kelly)	75.00	210.00	530.00	120.00
Gray, Earl of (2nd)	40.00	55.00	125.00	
Grey, Sir George	5.00	20.00	50.00	
Gromyko, Andrei A.	65.00	110.00	270.00	140.00
Gustavus II (Gustavus Adolphus— Sweden)	350.00	1,000.00	2,300.00	
Gustavus III (Sweden)	115.00	398.00	985.00	
Halifax, Earl of (Charles Wood)	10.00	35.00	45.00	25.00
Hammarskjöld, Dag	70.00	227.00	395.00	225.00
Hannan, al Bakr, Ahmad	10.00	35.00	90.00	18.00
Hardinge, Charles	5.00	10.00	24.00	
Hassam, Crown Prince	5.00	20.00	50.00	20.00
Hassan, Crown Prince	5.00	10.00	50.00	20.00
Hastings, Warren	15.00	90.00	125.00	
Hawke, Robert	15.00	40.00	130.00	25.00
Heath, Edward	25.00	47.50	75.00	35.00
Henry II	280.00	985.00	2,460.00	
Henry III (France)	175.00	546.57	1,325.00	
Henry IV (France)	155.00	532.00	1,325.00	
Henry VI (England)	145.00	400.00	1,000.00	
Henry VII (England)	800.00	1,660.00	10,000.00	
Henry VIII	2,100.00	6,066.67	17,500.00	
Herriot, Edouard	20.00	70.00	175.00	
Herzl, Theodor	150.00	900.00	1,200.00	250.00
Hess, Rudolph	150.00	400.00	793.75	395.00
Hindenburg, Paul von	70.00	225.33	350.00	150.00

Name	Signature Only	Letter or Document Signed	Autograph Letter Signed	Signed Photograph
Hirohito	375.00	650.00	1,500.00	525.00
Hitler, Adolf	1,150.00	1,911.11	17,800.00	1,787.50
Ho Chi Minh	225.00	525.00	1,500.00	600.00
Holyoake, Sir Keith	40.00	55.00	125.00	45.00
Home, Alec Douglas	30.00	60.00	150.00	60.00
Horthy, Adm. Miklos	50.00	170.00	425.00	125.00
Huerta, Victoriano	75.00	250.00	625.00	120.00
Humbert II	25.00	80.00	200.00	40.00
Hussein, King (Jordan)	50.00	125.00	380.50	65.00
Isabel II (Spain)	100.00	275.00	685.00	
Isabella I (Spain)	400.00	1,100.00	6,500.00	
Ivan IV, The Terrible		35,000.00		
James I and VI (England)	780.00	1,630.00	4,475.00	
James II (England)	500.00	928.50	1,700.00	
Jimenez, Enrique A.	8.00	15.00	25.00	10.00
Jimenez, Marcos P.	5.00	20.00	50.00	10.00
Josephine (Napoleon)	425.00	1,013.00	2,400.00	
Joseph II (Germany)	100.00	350.00	875.00	
Juan Carlos, King	45.00	90.00	225.00	100.00
Juarez, Benito	330.00	1,000.00	1,804.50	1,264.50
Juliana (Netherlands)	90.00	250.00	705.50	140.00
Kai-Shek, Chiang	50.00	180.00	440.00	150.00
Kai-Shek, Mme. Chiang	45.00	150.00	375.00	75.00
Kalakaua, David (Hawaii)	75.00	425.00	775.00	400.00
Kasavubu, Joseph	20.00	70.00	175.00	35.00
Kaunda, Kenneth	40.00	140.00	350.00	70.00
Kenyatta, Jomo	125.00	220.00	525.00	150.00
Kerensky, Alexander	130.00	210.00	725.00	300.00
Khalid, King	15.00	55.00	135.00	50.00
Khanh, Gen. Nguyen	20.00	60.00	175.00	35.00
King, MacKenzie	21.67	55.00	90.00	55.00
Kohl, Helmut	15.00	25.00	60.00	25.00
Kossuth, Lajos	25.00	115.00	210.00	40.00
Kosygin, Aleksei	275.00	350.00	875.00	480.00
Kruger, Paul	50.00	125.00	175.00	175.00
Kruschchev, Nikita S.	75.00	250.00	495.00	250.00
Kubitschek, Juscelino	10.00	35.00	90.00	20.00
Ky, Nguyen Cao	30.00	100.00	250.00	75.00
Lange, David	5.00	15.00	30.00	16.00
Law, Andrew Bonar	25.00	68.00	100.00	
Lawrence, 1st Baron of	10.00	30.00	75.00	
Lebrun, Albert	15.00	50.00	125.00	30.00
Lemass, Sean	5.00	10.00	25.00	20.00
Leopold I (Belgium)	25.00	117.50	222.50	
Leopold I (Hungary)	75.00	375.00	625.00	
Leopold II (Belgium)	65.00	325.00	540.00	
Lie, Trygve	30.00	100.00	250.00	62.50
Liliuokalani (Hawaii)	125.00	337.50	775.00	400.00
Liverpool, 2nd Earl of	100.00	103.33	180.00	
Lloyd George, David	60.00	198.33	302.50	216.67
Lorne, Marquis of	5.00	15.00	25.00	
Louis Philippe (France)	35.00	135.00	180.00	

Name	Signature Only	Letter or Document Signed	Autograph Letter Signed	Signed Photograph
Louis XII (France)	800.00	2,250.00	4,200.00	
Louis XIII (France)	850.00		4,750.00	
Louis XIV (France)	220.00	450.00	3,500.00	
Louis XV (France)	440.00	916.67	5,500.00	
Louis XVI (France)	210.00	588.33	2,550.00	
Louis XVIII (France)	170.00	378.67	1,362.50	
Ludwig I (Bavaria)	55.00	250.00	450.00	
Ludwig II (Bavaria)	55.00	287.50	475.00	
Lyautey, Louis	5.00	20.00	50.00	25.00
Macartney, George	10.00	35.00	85.00	
MacDonald, J. Ramsey	25.00	86.33	195.00	110.00
MacMahon, Marie E. P.	30.00	100.00	225.00	
MacMillan, Harold	20.00	63.33	150.00	50.00
Magsaysay, Ramon	20.00	50.00	140.00	30.00
Mahendra Bir Bikram	30.00	45.00	115.00	50.00
Makarios III (Archbishop)	30.00	75.00	185.00	55.00
Malenkov, Georgi M.	175.00	350.00	800.00	250.00
Malik, Charles	5.00	10.00	30.00	5.00
Manley, N. W.	3.00	10.00	25.00	5.00
Marcos, Ferdinand E.	15.00	20.00	125.00	25.00
Maria Theresa	130.00	400.00	980.00	
Marie Antoinette (France)	362.50	1,150.00	5,000.00	
Marie Louise (Napoleon)	190.00	606.33	1,590.67	
Marie of Romania	30.00	95.00	240.00	100.00
Marshall, Sir John	10.00	20.00	35.00	20.00
Mary Adalaide (England)	5.00	25.00	40.00	
Mary I (England)	810.00	3,000.00	7,500.00	
Mary II (William II)	370.00	1,240.00	3,100.00	
Mary of Teck (George V—England)	25.00	90.00	155.00	270.00
Masaryk, Jan	70.00	118.33	170.00	75.00
Masaryk, Thomas G.	150.00	250.00	575.00	
Maurey, Pierre	5.00	15.00	30.00	10.00
Maximilian (Mexico)	55.00	270.00	450.00	
Maximilian II (Roman Empire)	75.00	250.00	600.00	
Medici, Fernando de	370.00	1,250.00	3,125.00	
Medicis, Cosimo de	160.00	862.50	1,350.00	
Medicis, Francesco de	60.00	200.00	500.00	
Meir, Golda	60.00	200.00	510.00	162.50
Melbourne, Lord William L.	32.00	63.75	72.00	
Menzies, Sir Robert G.	15.00	55.00	125.00	25.00
Metternich, Prince	60.00	240.00	343.67	
Millerand, Alexandre	25.00	30.00	35.00	35.00
Mollet, Guy	16.00			
Mubarak, Pres. M. H.	35.00	110.00	275.00	70.00
Mugabe, Robert G.	20.00	55.00	140.00	30.00
Muldoon, Robert	10.00	20.00	30.00	20.00
Mussolini, Benito	250.00	475.00	1,017.50	545.00
Nakasone, Y.	25.00	35.00	85.00	30.00
Napoleon I	375.00	1,047.67	15,000.00	
Napoleon II (Duke Reichstadt)	260.00	800.00	2,200.00	
Napoleon III	60.00	300.00	455.00	

Name	Signature Only	Letter or Document Signed	Autograph Letter Signed	Signed Photograph
Nash, Walter	10.00	40.00	85.00	20.00
Nasser, Gamal Abdel	50.00	150.00	350.00	162.50
Nehru, Jawaharlal	87.50	350.00	710.00	200.00
Nicholas, Prince (Greece)	20.00	50.00	150.00	
Nicholas I (Russia)	125.00	476.25	250.00	
Nkomo, Joshua	55.00	110.00	275.00	80.00
Noor, Queen (Hussein)	15.00	40.00	125.00	25.00
North, Lord Frederick	70.00	325.00	595.00	
Northbrook, Lord (T. Baring)	10.00	20.00	50.00	
Nyerere, Julius	10.00	25.00	65.00	30.00
O'Connell, Daniel	25.00	137.50	235.00	
Orlando, Vittorio E.	50.00	110.00	275.00	
Orléans, Le Duc d'	10.00	20.00	50.00	
Oscar II (Sweden/Norway)	50.00	180.00	425.00	
Otto I (Greece)	70.00	225.00	560.00	
Otto The Great**		170,000.00		
Owen, Rt. Hon. David	5.00	20.00	40.00	10.00
Pahlavi, Riza (Iran)	135.00	200.00	375.00	150.00
Palme, Olaf	30.00	50.00	125.00	25.00
Palmerston, Henry J.	20.00	60.00	80.71	
Paul I (Russia)	195.00	650.00	1,625.00	
Pearson, Lester B.	30.00	70.00	175.00	35.00
Pedro II (Brazil)	65.00	175.00	253.50	
Peel, Sir Robert	35.00	81.67	166.67	
Pelham, Henry	25.00	100.00	195.00	
Perceval, Spencer	45.00	170.00	226.67	
Perez, Mariano	10.00	20.00	85.00	20.00
Peron, Juan Domingo	95.00	175.00	435.00	225.00
Pétain, Henri P.	25.00	80.00	200.00	40.00
Peter I (Serbia/Yugoslavia)				400.00
Peter I, The Great (Russia)	650.00	1,900.00	4,500.00	
Philip (Duke of Edinburgh)	100.00	162.50	325.00	320.00
Philip II (Spain)	160.00	400.00	1,000.00	
Philip IV (Spain)	150.00	500.00	1,250.00	
Ping, Deng Xiao				700.00
Pinochet, Augusto	30.00	105.00	255.00	50.00
Pitt, William (Elder)	80.00	182.50	365.00	
Pitt, William (Younger)	65.00	175.00	100.00	
Pius IX, Pope	30.00	100.00	250.00	
Pius XII, Pope	250.00	845.00	2,115.00	770.00
Poincaré, Raymond	15.00	25.00	50.00	105.00
Pompadour, Mme. J. A.	110.00	365.00	915.00	
Portland, Duke of	25.00	60.00	150.00	
Portsmouth, Duchess of (Charles II)	65.00	250.00	550.00	
Qaddafi, Muammar el-	75.00	200.00	500.00	165.00
Quang, Thich Tri	20.00	45.00	125.00	30.00
Raab, Julius	5.00	10.00	25.00	10.00
Rabin, Yitzhak	15.00	45.00	190.00	50.00
Radhakrishnan, S.	45.00	150.00	380.00	75.00
Rahman, Abdul	7.00	32.00	80.00	10.00
Rainier, Prince, III	50.00	75.00	190.00	100.00

Name	Signature Only	Letter or Document Signed	Autograph Letter Signed	Signed Photograph
Renner, Dr. Karl	25.00	40.00	85.00	35.00
Rhee, Syngman	30.00	125.00	250.00	50.00
Rhodes, Cecil	100.00	170.00	250.00	600.00
Richelieu, Armand			105.00	
Richelieu, Cardinal	200.00	700.00	1,650.00	
Robespierre, Maximilien	900.00	2,175.00	12,500.00	
Roldan, Salvador C.	5.00	20.00	50.00	10.00
Rosebery, 5th Earl of	10.00	36.00	107.50	
Rowling, William E.	10.00	15.00	20.00	20.00
Roxas, Manuel	25.00	75.00	195.00	100.00
Rudolf I of Hapsburg (Austria)			540.00	612.50
Russell, Lord John	24.00	48.00	78.85	
Sadat, Anwar	40.00	130.00	325.00	128.33
Said, Nuri (Prime Minister—Iraq)	5.00	15.00	32.50	10.00
Salisbury, Lord Robert	15.00	35.00	57.22	
San Martin, José de	500.00	1,000.00	2,650.00	
Sato, Eisaku	15.00	50.00	130.00	26.00
Scheidemann, Philippe	10.00	20.00	50.00	40.00
Schuschnigg, R. von	25.00	70.00	175.00	50.00
Seipel, Dr. Ignas	10.00	30.00	80.00	40.00
Selassie, Haile	160.00	377.50	737.50	433.33
Shamir, Yitzhak	20.00	30.00	55.00	25.00
Sihanouk, Prince	15.00	40.00	100.00	40.00
Smith, Ian	10.00	20.00	50.00	20.00
Smuts, Jan Christian	28.00	85.00	225.00	195.00
Soustelle, Jacques	5.00	15.00	40.00	15.00
Spaak, Paul-Henri	5.00	18.00	45.00	20.00
Spencer, John P.	5.00	10.00	20.00	
Stalin, Joseph	1,290.00	4,750.00	8,600.00	2,150.00
Stanislas II (Poland)	70.00	250.00	562.50	
Strauss, Franz Josef	10.00	25.00	70.00	20.00
Suharto, General	10.00	28.00	70.00	30.00
Sun Yat Sen	350.00	480.00	900.00	500.00
Talleyrand, Charles M.	100.00	237.00	480.00	
Thant, U	45.00	130.00	295.00	200.00
Thatcher, Margaret	25.00	85.00	210.00	60.00
Thiers, A.	10.00	35.00	75.00	
Thieu, Nguyen Van	15.00	40.00	110.00	25.00
Tito, Marshal J. Broz	75.00	100.33	235.00	140.00
Trotsky, Leon	375.00	1,412.50	3,125.00	1,100.00
Trudeau, Pierre	25.00	65.00	90.00	78.33
Tshombe, Moise	15.00	50.00	125.00	87.50
Umberto I (Italy)	45.00	150.00	375.00	
Victor Emmanuel II (Italy)	60.00	200.00	475.00	95.00
Victoria, Mary Louisa	40.00	110.00	195.00	
Victoria, Queen	70.00	360.91	708.00	1,975.00
Vishinsky, Andrei	70.00	230.00	580.00	120.00
Vorster, Balthazar J.	20.00	60.00	150.00	50.00
Wallis, Duchess of Windsor	150.00	175.00	225.00	175.00
Walpole, Sir Robert	63.33	223.00	575.00	

Ward, Sir Joseph	10.00	25.00	55.00	
Welensky, Sir Roy	15.00	56.00	112.50	
Wellington, Duke of	100.00	152.50	266.67	
Wilhelm I (Germany)	50.00	185.00	410.00	
Wilhelm II (Kaiser—Germany)	70.00	197.50	417.50	291.67
William III (England)	275.00	887.50	2,433.33	
William IV (England)	80.00	147.92	216.25	
Wilson, Harold	25.00	63.00	88.00	33.67
Witte, Count Serge	10.00	20.00	50.00	
Zuazo, Hernan Siles	8.00	12.00	22.00	10.00

Hockey Hall of Fame Members

This section contains prices for the members of the Hockey Hall of Fame. Prices for other hockey players, including those still active, are in the General Sports section.

Players	Signature Only	Signed Photograph
Abel, Sidney	$ 5	$ 10
Adams, John	10	20
Apps, C. J. "Syl"	10	20
Armstrong, George	7	15
Bailey, I. W. "Ace"	7	15
Bain, Donald	7	15
Baker, Hobart	7	15
Barry, Martin	7	15
Bathgate, Andrew	5	12
Beliveau, Jean	5	15
Benedict, Clinton	7	15
Bentley, Douglas	10	25
Bentley, Maxwell	10	20
Blake, Hector "Toe"	12	30
Boon, Richard	7	15

Players	Signature Only	Signed Photograph
Bouchard, Emile "Butch"	10	20
Boucher, Frank	10	20
Boucher, George "Buck"	10	20
Bower, John	7	15
Bowie, Russell	7	15
Brimsek, Francis	5	15
Broadbent, H. L. "Punch"	10	20
Broda, W. E. "Turk"	6	20
Bucyk, Johnny	5	12
Burch, Billy	10	20
Cameron, Harold	7	15
Cheevers, Gerry	5	12
Clancy, F. M. "King"	10	25
Clapper, Aubrey "Dit"	15	30
Cleghorn, Sprague	10	20
Colville, Neil	10	20
Conacher, Charles	10	20
Connell, Alex	10	20
Cook, William	10	20
Coulter, Arthur	10	20
Cournoyer, Yvan	8	12
Cowley, William	10	20
Crawford, S. R. "Rusty"	10	20
Darragh, John	10	20
Davidson, A. M. "Scotty"	10	20
Day, Clarence "Hap"	10	20
Delvecchio, Alex	5	15
Denneny, Cyril	10	20
Drillon, Gordon	7	15
Drinkwater, Charles	7	15
Dunderdale, Thomas	7	15
Durnan, William	10	20
Dutton, M. A. "Red"	7	15
Dye, C. H. "Babe"	7	20
Esposito, Phil	7	20
Farrell, Arthur	7	15
Foyston, Frank	7	15
Frederickson, Frank	7	15
Gadsby, William	10	20
Gardiner, Charles	10	20
Gardiner, Herbert	7	15
Gardner, James	7	15
Geoffrion, J. A. B. "Boom Boom"	7	15
Gerard, Eddie	10	20
Gilbert, Rod	5	15
Gilmour, H. L. "Billy"	10	20
Goheen, F. X. "Moose"	10	20
Goodfellow, Ebbie	10	20
Grant, Michael	10	20
Green, W. "Shorty"	10	20
Griffis, Silas	10	20
Hainsworth, George	10	20
Hall, Glenn	6	20
Hall, Joseph	10	20

Players	Signature Only	Signed Photograph
Harvey, Douglas	6	20
Hay, George	15	30
Hern, W. M. "Riley"	10	20
Hextall, Bryan	10	20
Holmes, Harry	10	20
Hooper, C. Thomas	10	20
Horner, G. R. "Red"	10	20
Horton, M. G. "Tim"	15	40
Howe, Gordon	10	25
Howe, Sydney	10	20
Howell, Harry	7	15
Hull, Robert Marvin	10	25
Hutton, J. B. "Bouse"	10	20
Hyland, Harry	10	20
Irvin, J. D. "Dick"	10	20
Jackson, H. "Busher"	10	20
Johnson, E. "Moose"	10	20
Johnson, Ivan "Ching"	20	40
Johnson, Thomas	10	20
Joliat, Aurel	10	20
Keats, G. "Duke"	10	20
Kelly, L. P. "Red"	10	20
Kennedy, T. S. "Teeder"	10	20
Lach, Elmer	10	20
Lalonde, E. C. "Newsy"	10	20
Laviolette, Jean	10	20
Lehman, Hugh	10	20
Lemaire, Jacques	7	15
LeSeur, Percy	10	20
Lindsay, Robert "Ted"	6	15
Lumley, Harry	15	30
MacKay, D. "Mickey"	10	20
Mahovlich, Frank	5	15
Malone, Joseph	10	20
Mantha, Sylvio	10	20
Marshall, John	10	20
Maxwell, Fred "Steamer"	15	30
McGee, Frank	10	20
McGimsie, William	10	20
McNamara, George	10	20
Moore, Richard	10	20
Moran, Patrick	10	20
Morenz, Howie	75	200
Mosienko, William	10	20
Nighbor, Frank	10	20
Noble, E. Reginald	10	20
Oliver, Harry	10	20
Olmstead, Bert	7	15
Orr, Bobby	7	15
Parent, Bernie	6	15
Patrick, Lester	15	30
Patrick, Lynn	15	30
Phillips, Tommy	10	20
Pilote, J. A. Pierre	10	20
Pitre, Didier "Pit"	10	20

Players	Signature Only	Signed Photograph
Plante, J. Jacques	10	30
Pratt, Walter "Babe"	20	40
Primeau, A. Joseph	10	20
Pronovost, J. R. Marcel	7	15
Pulford, Harvey	7	15
Quackenbush, H. G. "Bill"	10	20
Rankin, Frank	7	15
Ratelle, Jean	5	12
Rayner, C. E. "Chuck"	7	15
Reardon, Kenneth	10	20
Richard, Henri	5	12
Richard, J. H. Maurice "Rocket"	10	20
Richardson, George	10	20
Roberts, Gordon	10	20
Ross, Arthur	10	20
Russel, Blair	10	20
Ruttan, J. D. "Jack"	10	20
Sawchuk, Terrance	5	10
Scanlan, Fred	10	20
Schmidt, Milton	5	10
Schriner, D. "Sweeney"	10	20
Seibert, Earl	10	20
Seibert, Oliver	10	20
Shore, Edward	10	20
Siebert, A. C. "Babe"	15	30
Simpson, Harold	10	20
Smith, Alfred	10	20
Smith, R. "Hooley"	10	20
Smith, Thomas	10	20
Stanley, Allen	10	20
Stanley, R. "Barney"	10	20
Stewart, John	10	20
Stewart, Nelson	10	20
Stuart, Bruce	10	20
Stuart, Hod	10	20
Taylor, F. "Cyclone"	10	20
Thompson, C. R. "Tiny"	10	20
Trihey, Col. Harry J.	10	20
Ullman, Norm	7	15
Vezina, Georges	40	100
Walker, John	10	20
Walsh, Martin	10	20
Watson, Harry	10	20
Weiland, Ralph "Cooney"	10	20
Westwick, Harry	10	20
Whitcroft, Fred	10	20
Wilson, Gordon	10	20
Worsley, Lorne "Gump"	10	20
Worters, Roy	10	20

Referees	Signature Only	Signed Photograph
Ashley, John	$10	$20
Chadwick, William	10	20
Elliott, Chaucer	10	20
Hewitson, Robert	10	20
Ion, Fred "Mickey"	10	20
Rodden, Michael	10	20
Smeaton, J. Cooper	10	20
Storey, R. A. "Red"	10	20
Udvari, Frank	10	20

Builders	Signature Only	Signed Photograph
Adams, Charles	$15	$30
Adams, Weston	10	20
Ahearn, Thomas "Frank"	10	20
Ahearne, John "Bunny"	10	20
Allen, Sir Montague	10	20
Ashley, John	10	20
Ballard, Harold	10	20
Bickell, John	10	20
Brown, George	10	20
Brown, Walter	10	20
Buckland, Frank	10	20
Butterfield, Jack	10	20
Calder, Frank	10	20
Campbell, Angus	10	20
Campbell, Clarence	20	40
Cattarinich, Joseph	10	20
Dandurand, Joseph "Leo"	10	20
Dilio, Francis	10	20
Dudley, George	10	20
Dunn, James	10	20
Francis, Emile	5	10
Gibson, Dr. John	10	20
Gorman, Thomas	10	20
Hay, Charles	10	20
Hendy, James	10	20
Hewitt, Foster	10	20
Hewitt, William	10	20
Hume, Fred	10	20
Imlach, George "Punch"	15	30
Ivan, Thomas	20	40
Jennings, William	10	20
Kilpatrick, Gen. John	10	20
Leader, George	10	20
LeBel, Robert	10	20
Lockhart, Thomas	10	20
Loicq, Paul	10	20
Mariucci, John	6	18
McLaughlin, Maj. Frederic	10	20
Milford, John C. "Jake"	15	30
Molson, Hon. Hartland	10	20
Nelson, Francis	10	20
Norris, Bruce	20	40

Builders	Signature Only	Signed Photograph
Norris, James, Sr.	40	75
Norris, James D.	30	60
Northey, William	10	20
O'Brien, John	10	20
Patrick, Frank	15	30
Pickard, Allan	10	20
Pilous, Rudy	10	20
Pollock, Samuel	10	20
Raymond, Sen. Donat	10	20
Robertson, John	10	20
Robinson, Claude	10	20
Ross, Philip	10	20
Selke, Frank	10	20
Smith, Frank	10	20
Smythe, Conn	20	40
Stanley, Lord (of Preston)	10	20
Sutherland, Capt. James	10	20
Tarasov, Anatoli	20	40
Turner, Lloyd	10	20
Tutt, William	10	20
Voss, Carl	10	20
Waghorne, Fred	10	20
Wirtz, Arthur	15	30
Wirtz, William	15	30

Little-Known But Collectible Names

For those who enjoy the hobby of collecting autographs, from time to time there is the problem of identifying just who a person is or was, and what that person is famous for. Many a person who is known to the world by what he or she did, not necessarily by name, has been passed over by philographers who simply didn't match that name with the deed.

This often means that the number of available autographs from such little-known names is far lower than it should be. It seems that such people are usually quite affable about providing autographs because they are asked far less often than the really famous names are.

Below are some selections for the *Little-Known Hall of Fame* (and our thanks to Chuck McKeen for suggesting and researching this category). The prices included are for Signatures and Signed Photographs, respectively.

Robert Ballard. Led the team that discovered the *Titanic*. $10.00, $20.00.

Ann E. Bancroft. First woman to reach the North Pole. $10.00, $25.00.

Dewey Beard (Indian name: "Iron Hail"). Last survivor of the Battle of Little Big Horn (died November, 1955). $50.00, $150.00.

Jay Berwanger. First winner of football's Heisman Trophy. $5.00, $25.00.

George Bruns. Wrote the music for many of Walt Disney's movies, including the lyrics for *The Ballad of Davy Crockett*. $15.00, $50.00.

Gen. Marion Carl. WWII fighter ace who held the air speed record until Chuck Yeager broke the sound barrier. $15.00, $40.00.

George Caron. Tail gunner on the *Enola Gay*. $10.00, $20.00.

Suzette Charles. Took over as Miss America when Vanessa Williams was forced to relinquish the crown because of the publication of nude photos. $10.00, $20.00.

Judge Ronald Davies. In 1957, as a federal judge, ordered the integration of Little Rock, Arkansas, schools. $25.00, $50.00.

Melvin Dummar. Claimed he picked up Howard Hughes in the desert, and that Hughes's will named him as beneficiary. $12.00, $25.00.

John P. East. Only U.S. Senator in this century to commit suicide while in office. $20.00, $40.00.

Daniel Ellsberg. Leaked the Pentagon Papers to the *New York Times*. $18.00, $30.00.

Tommy Facenda. His 1959 hit record, "High School U.S.A.," reached number 3 in *Billboard* ratings, and had the most versions ever recorded of any song, as Atlantic Records released 28 different versions with the names of various high schools in different cities. $20.00, $40.00.

Jim Frelle. Track star and longtime standard-bearer, having run the most sub-four-minute miles of any U.S.A. runner. $8.00, $20.00.

Dolores Hart. Movie star of the late 1950s/early 1960s who entered a convent and is now Mother Dolores. $15.00, $75.00.

Bill Hayes. Sang 1955 million-selling record "The Ballad of Davy Crockett." $8.00, $15.00.

Paul Henning. Creator/producer of such hit TV series as "The Beverly Hillbillies," "Green Acres," and "Petticoat Junction." Also wrote the hit "Beverly Hillbillies" theme song. $10.00, $20.00.

Clarence Henry. *Frog Man* had a distinctive singing style, with such 1950s hits as "Ain't Got No Home." $12.00, $30.00.

Frank Kappa. Only U.S. veteran of all the four twentieth-century wars that America fought in. $10.00, $20.00.

L. Bruce Laingen. 1980 hostage in Iran. $10.00, $20.00.

Candy Lightner. Founder of MADD (Mothers Against Drunk Driving). $12.00, $25.00.

Dr. Paul MacCready. Led development of the *MacCready Solar Challenger*, the first solar-powered airplane. $20.00, $40.00.

Al McDonald. Head of Morton-Thiokol solid-rocket motor project for the space shuttle. Blew the whistle on NASA and Thiokol over the *Challenger* disaster. $12.00, $25.00.

Lou Meyer. First driver to win three Indianapolis races. $12.00, $30.00.

Rosa Parks. The woman who refused to give up her seat in Montgomery, Alabama—the catalyst that led to Dr. Martin Luther King's freedom marches and sit-ins. $15.00, $40.00.

Marina Porter. She was married to Lee Harvey Oswald when he assassinated President John F. Kennedy. $20.00, $50.00.

Perez Prado. Cuban-born mambo band leader; his 1955 hit record, "Cherry Pink and Apple Blossom White," was number 1 on the *Billboard* Top 40 for ten weeks. Since the rankings began, only one artist has done better—Elvis Presley's two-sided hit of "Hound Dog" and "Don't Be Cruel." $30.00, $75.00.

Dr. John P. Stapp. Member of the International Space Hall of Fame. $15.00, $20.00.

Howard Stevens. All-time Division I college football leader in career all-purpose running per-game yardage, with 193.7 per game at University of Louisville. $6.00, $12.00.

Carl Stolz. Founded Little League baseball. $12.00, $25.00.

Levi Stubbs. Lead singer for the Four Tops, a group with 22 Top 40 hits. $15.00, $30.00.

Kathryn Sullivan. First U.S. woman astronaut to walk in space. $10.00, $20.00.

Clyde Tombaugh. Discovered the ninth planet, Pluto, in 1930. $11.00, $25.00.

Dr. J. A. Van Allen. Discovered the the radiation belt that encircles the earth and now bears his name. $17.00, $20.00.

Will Vinton. Invented the clay-mation process seen in those raisin ("Heard It Through the Grapevine") TV commercials. $8.00, $20.00.

Rev. Benjamin Weir. Former hostage in Beirut. $12.00, $20.00.

The above examples are only a few from literally thousands of autograph possibilities. In autographs, as in many other hobbies, your collection is limited only by your imagination.

Military Leaders

These prices are for outstanding military leaders of all nations. If the name of any person has been excluded, it means only that data on a philographic item of his or hers was not accessible at the time of publishing.

Name	Signature Only	Letter or Document Signed	Autograph Letter Signed	Signed Photograph
Abrams, Creighton W.	$ 15.00	$ 30.00	$ 45.00	$ 30.00
Acheson, George R.	5.00	10.00	20.00	10.00
Albury, Capt. Charles D.	15.00	45.00	60.00	40.67
Alexander, Harold R. L.	20.00	45.00	75.00	40.00
Allen, Frank A., Jr.	10.00	20.00	45.00	
Allen, Henry T.	10.00	25.00	50.00	
Allen, Roderick R.	10.00	20.00	35.00	
Allenby, Fld. Marshal	20.00	60.00	75.00	40.00
Almond, Edward M.	10.00	20.00	50.00	
Anderson, George W.	10.00	30.00	40.00	20.00
Anderson, John B.	5.00	10.00	20.00	
Anderson, Samuel E.	5.00	10.00	20.00	
Anglesea, Marquis of	10.00	35.00	40.00	
Arnold, Archibald	5.00	10.00	20.00	
Arnold, Henry "Hap"	30.00	60.00	90.00	90.00
Atkinson, Joseph H.	10.00	25.00	30.00	
Auckland, George Eden, Earl	10.00	25.00	50.00	
Aurand, Henry S.	5.00	10.00	20.00	15.00
Baden-Powell, Robert	20.00	50.00	195.00	185.00
Bainbridge, William	50.00	140.00	180.00	
Barrow, Robert H.	10.00	30.00	40.00	10.00
Beatty, Adm. David	30.00	90.00	115.00	100.00
Beresford, Lord Charles	15.00	35.00	60.00	35.00
Berthier, Louis A.	35.00	100.00	150.00	
Bittrich, Wilhelm	27.00	70.00	135.00	60.00
Black, Richard B.	10.00	25.00	40.00	
Bligh, Capt. William	500.00	1,150.00	2,300.00	
Bliss, Tasker H.	10.00	25.00	58.00	20.00
Blücher, Gebhart von	100.00	300.00	500.00	
Bormann, Martin	140.00	350.00	750.00	695.00
Borne, Hermann von Dem.	16.00	45.00	80.00	
Brabazon-Moore, J. T.	15.00	45.00	70.00	
Bradley, John	10.00	30.00	50.00	15.00
Bradley, Omar N.	40.00	69.44	155.00	95.00
Brauchitsch, W. von	60.00	140.00	185.00	115.00
Brefoort, H. B.	10.00	25.00	45.00	
Brennecke, Kurt	12.00	30.00	57.00	25.00
Briggs, James E.	10.00	25.00	50.00	18.50
Brown, Norma	10.00	20.00	30.00	15.00

Name	Signature Only	Letter or Document Signed	Autograph Letter Signed	Signed Photograph
Bucher, Lloyd	15.00	30.00	45.00	35.00
Bullard, Robert Lee	20.00	55.00	95.00	50.00
Buller, Redvers	10.00	25.00	45.60	30.00
Burke, Arleigh	13.00	20.00	40.00	20.00
Buttlar-Brandenfels, F. H.	5.00	12.00	24.00	11.00
Butler, Smedley D.	10.00	30.00	50.00	25.00
Calley, William	20.00	35.00	45.00	40.00
Campbell, Sir Colin	12.00	30.00	43.00	50.00
Campbell, R. L.	5.00	15.00	20.00	10.00
Cannon, John K.	10.00	20.00	50.00	
Cardigan, 7th Earl of	65.00	175.00	250.00	130.00
Carl, Marion	5.00	15.00	25.00	
Carleton, Baron Guy	70.00	175.00	335.00	
Carney, Robert B.	5.00	12.50	16.25	10.00
Caron, George R.	20.00	40.00	61.67	25.00
Carpenter, William S.	10.00	15.00	45.00	
Cates, Clifton B.	10.00	25.00	50.00	18.00
Chaffee, Adna R.	10.00	25.00	48.00	20.00
Chauncey, Isaac	15.00	35.00	70.00	
Cheshire, Leonard	10.00	20.00	25.00	15.00
Clark, Mark W.	20.00	78.33	118.67	31.00
Clark, Mary	5.00	7.50	15.00	15.00
Clarkson, Matthew	10.00	30.00	50.00	
Clary, B. A.	4.00	12.00	20.00	7.00
Clay, Lucius	25.00	75.00	100.00	22.50
Clinton, George	55.00	151.25	312.50	
Clinton, Sir Henry	300.00	860.00	1,800.00	
Clive, Robert	165.00	550.00	1,150.00	
Cochrane, Sir Basil	10.00	20.00	25.00	
Cockburn, Sir George	35.00	100.00	140.00	
Collins, J. Lawton	20.00	50.00	75.00	40.00
Conway, Henry Seymour	20.00	45.00	80.00	
Cornwallis, Charles	95.00	235.00	586.25	
Craig, Malin	6.00	15.00	30.00	
Davis, Benjamin O., Jr.	15.00	40.00	75.00	35.00
Dayan, Moshe	20.00	63.00	100.00	45.00
Dayton, Elias	65.00	164.00	305.00	
Dean, William F.	10.00	25.00	45.00	30.00
Denfeld, Louis M.	10.00	25.00	40.00	20.00
Denton, Jerry	10.00	20.00	30.00	18.00
Devereux, James P. S.	15.00	30.00	75.00	
Devers, Jacob	5.00	15.00	20.00	30.00
Dewey, George	20.00	40.00	92.50	200.00
Diaz, Armando	35.00	100.00	165.00	75.00
Doenitz, Karl	65.33	175.00	295.00	120.00
Doniphan, A. W.	90.00	225.00	440.00	
Donovan, William J.	40.00	100.00	190.00	95.00
Dornberger, Walter	30.00	45.00	88.00	
Dreyfus, Alfred	115.00	275.00	450.00	220.00
Drum, Lt. Gen. Hugh A.	25.00	65.00	120.00	50.00
Dundas, Dean	10.00	30.00	50.00	30.00
Dundas, Henry	15.00	35.00	65.00	

Name	Signature Only	Letter or Document Signed	Autograph Letter Signed	Signed Photograph
Eben, Emael	30.00	85.00	140.00	60.00
Eichmann, Adolf	225.00	450.00	1,400.00	515.00
Eisenhower, John S. D.	10.00	15.00	20.00	10.00
Ellis, Robert H.	8.00	23.00	42.00	
Evans, Robley D.	10.00	20.00	30.00	150.00
Felt, Adm. Harry	10.00	30.00	50.00	25.00
Flagler, D. W.	15.00	20.00	25.00	15.00
Fletcher, Frank Jack	25.00	60.00	120.00	60.00
Foch, Ferdinand	20.00	87.50	162.50	92.50
Franklin, Sir John	50.00	135.00	235.00	
Fritsch, Werner von	55.00	150.00	210.00	175.00
Fuchida, Mitsuo	300.00			
Fuchs, Rutger	40.00	125.00	195.00	95.00
Funston, Frederick	20.00	50.00	85.00	45.00
Gabreski, Frances	20.00	55.00	95.00	40.00
Gambier, James	30.00	50.00	145.00	
Garrison, Vermont	12.00	35.00	60.00	
Gavin, James M.	15.00	35.00	70.00	40.00
George, Harold L.	35.00	90.00	170.00	75.00
Gibson, George	5.00	15.00	25.00	
Gillis, J. H.	5.00	15.00	25.00	
Glubb, Sir John	15.00	30.00	40.00	20.00
Goebbels, Joseph	200.00	650.00	1,250.00	500.00
Goodpaster, Andrew	10.00	20.00	38.00	20.00
Goodwin, Hugh H.	25.00	65.00	125.00	50.00
Gordon, Charles G.	90.00	335.00	390.00	600.00
Göring, Hermann W.	270.00	800.00	1,600.00	450.00
Gourand, Henri-Joseph E.	30.00	75.00	150.00	75.00
Grant, Frederick D.	10.00	25.00	40.00	
Grant, U. S., III	10.00	30.00	50.00	
Greely, Adolphus W.	60.00	165.00	280.00	145.00
Greene, Nathanael	515.00	1,400.00	2,500.00	
Gregory, Frederick D	5.00	15.00	25.00	10.00
Gridley, Charles Vernon	200.00		850.00	
Gridley, Richard	170.00	450.00	790.00	
Grouchy, Marquis Emmanuel de	30.00	70.00	125.00	
Guderian, Hans	20.00	40.00	65.00	35.00
Guderian, Heinz	40.00	105.00	195.00	95.00
Guingand, Francis	10.00	30.00	50.00	
Haig, Alexander M.	15.00	30.00	50.00	40.00
Haig, Earl Douglas	20.00	55.00	95.00	50.00
Halder, Franz	45.00	80.00	160.00	115.00
Halsey, William F. "Bull"	30.00	57.50	105.00	100.00
Hanami, Kohei		250.00		
Harbord, James G.	25.50	138.00	170.00	80.00
Harkins, Paul	10.00	25.00	50.00	25.00
Harris, Sir Arthur T.	40.00	110.00	190.00	100.00
Hartmann, Erich	45.00	120.00	210.00	100.00
Hay, William Henry	5.00	15.00	25.00	
Haywood, Thomas	3.00	5.00	12.00	6.00
Hess, Rudolf	150.00	400.00	750.00	375.00

Name	Signature Only	Letter or Document Signed	Autograph Letter Signed	Signed Photograph
Heydrich, Reinhard	200.00	575.50	1,350.00	600.00
Hill, A. P.	140.00	475.00	1,150.00	550.00
Hill, Gen. Rowland	35.00	80.00	170.00	
Himmler, Heinrich	163.33	537.50	1,000.00	500.00
Hobson, Richmond P.	55.00	145.00	265.00	125.00
Holstrom, E. W. "Brick"	10.00	30.00	50.00	20.00
Homma, Masaharu	60.00	160.00	290.00	150.00
Hood, Sir Alexander	40.00	100.00	190.00	
Hood, John B.	65.00	225.00	365.00	225.00
Hood, Samuel	25.00	55.00	100.00	
Houston, Sam	326.67	850.00	2,677.50	
Howe, Richard Earl	40.00	100.00	385.00	
Howe, William	150.00	275.00	675.00	
Hull, Isaac	80.00	200.00	375.00	
Hull, William	110.00	375.00	450.00	
Huntington, Jedediah	35.00	80.00	165.00	
Hylton, Lord	5.00	15.00	20.00	
Ismay, Hastings Lionel	10.00	25.00	40.00	
Jellicoe, John R.	15.00	40.00	75.00	47.50
Jesup, Thomas S.	10.00	25.00	63.00	
Jesup, William H.	5.00	15.00	25.00	
Jodl, Alfred	95.00	195.00	400.00	230.00
Joffre, Joseph Jacques	60.00	155.00	225.00	210.00
Johnson, Harold K.	10.00	30.00	50.00	25.00
Johnson, Leon W.	9.00	20.00	35.00	
Joyce, Richard	40.00	100.00	175.00	
Kaltenbrunner, Ernst	60.00	150.00	185.00	160.00
Kawato, Mike	45.00	90.00		
Keitel, Wilhelm	250.00	635.00	1,205.00	550.00
Keith, George K. E.	20.00	45.00	80.00	
Kenney, George	20.00	55.00	95.00	50.00
Kesselring, Albert	70.00	195.00	407.00	140.00
Keyes, Roger	15.00	30.00	55.00	25.00
Kimmel, Husband E.	55.00	145.00	255.00	130.00
King, Ernest J.	10.00	35.00	50.00	70.00
Kirby-Smith, Edmund	45.00	115.00	200.00	
Kitchener, Horatio H.	55.00	80.00	175.00	60.00
Kossa, Frank R.	5.00	5.00	6.50	5.00
Kroesen, Fred J.	3.00	10.00	15.00	6.00
Lafayette, Marquis de	235.00	362.50	694.38	
Leahy, William D.	25.00	115.00	155.00	105.00
Lee, Henry	125.00	275.00	455.00	
Lejeune, John Archer	32.00	75.00	140.00	75.00
LeMay, Curtis S.	25.00	45.00	85.00	10.00
Lemnitzer, L. L.	13.00	25.00	50.00	15.00
Lewis, Morgan	40.00	65.00	87.50	
Lincoln, Benjamin	65.00	165.00	310.00	
Luce, Adm. S. B.	10.00	30.00	50.00	25.00
Luckner, Count Felix	31.33	125.00	195.00	73.00
Ludendorff, Erich von	85.00	220.00	335.00	175.00
MacArthur, Arthur	40.00	80.00	110.00	60.00
MacArthur, Douglas	75.00	325.00	420.00	332.50

Name	Signature Only	Letter or Document Signed	Autograph Letter Signed	Signed Photograph
MacArthur, Douglas, II	5.00	10.00	20.00	10.00
MacArthur, Jean	10.00	10.00	15.00	10.00
Macdonogh, P. M. W.	5.00	15.00	20.00	
MacDonough, Thomas	30.00	80.00	150.00	
Mackensen, August von	10.00	20.00	35.00	50.00
Madden, Charles Edward	45.00	120.00	215.00	100.00
Mahan, Alfred Thayer	10.00	25.00	30.00	15.00
Manteuffel, Hasso von	30.00	75.00	145.00	135.00
Marlborough, Duke of (John Churchill)	155.00	355.00	750.00	
Marshall, George C.	52.20	146.00	275.00	135.00
Mayo, Henry T.	15.00	40.00	75.00	40.00
McAuliffe, Anthony	25.00	38.00	68.33	25.00
McColpin, Carroll W.	10.00	30.00	50.00	25.00
McHenry, James	40.00	100.00	175.00	
McKone, John R.	10.00	20.00	35.00	20.00
McNair, Leslie J.	25.00	70.00	120.00	60.00
McNaughton, Kenneth	4.00	9.00	15.00	10.00
Meigs, Return J., Jr.	55.00	140.00	250.00	
Mellnik, Steve	5.00	25.00	35.00	
Melville, George W.	35.00	90.00	170.00	
Merritt, Wesley	25.00	70.00	120.00	65.00
Meyer, E. C.	5.00	10.00	25.00	15.00
Mifflin, Thomas	50.00	195.00	320.00	
Milch, Erhard	80.00	250.00	395.00	
Minh, Gen. Duong Van	15.00	40.00	75.00	40.00
Mitchell, William	125.00	440.00	600.00	325.00
Moltke, Count Helmuth	70.00	175.00	335.00	170.00
Moltke, H. Johann L.	10.00	25.00	45.00	25.00
Montcalm, L. J. de	275.00	680.00	1,600.00	
Montgomery, Bernard	36.67	205.00	337.50	152.00
Moore, Gen. Jeremy	5.00	15.00	25.00	15.00
Moore, Sir John	30.00	75.00	135.00	
Mountbatten, Louis	39.67	168.29	245.00	193.75
Muhlenberg, John P.	15.00	60.00	185.00	
Munster, Earl of	10.00	25.00	40.00	
Murat, Joachim	90.00	180.00	450.00	
Murphy, Audie	50.00	150.00	300.00	300.00
Napier, Sir Charles James	10.00	20.00	60.00	
Napier, Sir Robert C.	12.00	30.00	50.00	
Napier, Sir William F. P.	15.00	35.00	60.00	
Nelson, Horatio	538.00	1,500.00	3,205.00	
Neurath, Constantin von	45.00	80.00	150.00	115.00
Ney, Michel	90.00	225.00	550.00	
Nimitz, Chester	38.75	110.00	195.00	166.67
Norstad, Lauris	5.00	15.00	25.00	25.00
North, Oliver	35.00	90.00	170.00	75.00
North, William	75.00	185.00	350.00	
Ogden, Aaron	15.00	40.00	75.00	
Older, Charles H.	12.00	25.00	40.00	
Olds, Robin	10.00	25.00	40.00	18.00
Otis, Elwell Stephen	10.00	30.00	50.00	25.00

Name	Signature Only	Letter or Document Signed	Autograph Letter Signed	Signed Photograph
Otis, Harrison Gray	70.00	185.00	335.00	
Papen, Franz von	35.00	165.00	190.00	140.00
Parker, David	10.00	25.00	40.00	
Patch, Alexander M.	85.00	225.00	395.00	240.00
Patton, George S.	820.00	1,750.00	3,750.00	2,250.00
Patton, George S., III	10.00	20.00	45.00	15.00
Peary, Robert E.	45.00	195.00	237.50	365.00
Pepperell, William	60.00	165.00	400.00	
Perry, Matthew G.	70.00	238.00	325.00	
Perry, Oliver H.	150.00	540.00	1,250.00	
Pershing, John J.	30.00	114.00	165.00	187.50
Pilsudski, Joseph	115.00	305.00	550.00	275.00
Poniatowski, Jozef	140.00	585.00	2,000.00	
Prien, Guenther	130.00	335.00	635.00	300.00
Putnam, Israel	170.00	425.00	800.00	
Quantrill, William C.	785.00	1,750.00	3,700.00	
Quisling, Vidkun	105.00	190.00	400.00	450.00
Raeder, Erich	45.00	105.00	175.00	80.00
Raglan, Fitzroy (Somerset)	40.00	90.00	150.00	
Rawlings, Edward W.	5.00	10.00	20.00	10.00
Ribbentrop, Joachim von	95.00	175.00	525.00	230.00
Rickover, Hyman G.	75.00	200.00	405.00	185.00
Ridgway, Matthew B.	25.00	80.00	100.00	55.00
Risner, James R.	10.00	25.00	30.00	20.00
Roberts, Frederick S.	15.00	50.00	75.00	40.00
Rochambeau, D. M. J. de	20.00	80.00	145.00	
Rodgers, George Washington	40.00	95.00	195.00	
Rodgers, Comdr. John	50.00	125.00	240.00	
Rogers, Bernard W.	10.00	15.00	50.00	25.00
Rommel, Erwin	615.00	1,575.00	3,000.00	1,415.00
Roosevelt, Theodore, Jr.	20.00	50.00	95.00	40.00
Rosenberg, Alfred	90.00	160.00	300.00	180.00
Rosenthal, Joe	45.00	120.00	215.00	100.00
Rowan, Andrew S.	25.00	70.00	120.00	65.00
Rudel, Hans-Ulrich	20.00	50.00	95.00	50.00
Rundstedt, Gerd von	110.00	150.00	200.00	175.00
Salan, Raoul	20.00	55.00	95.00	50.00
Sampson, William T.	25.00	70.00	120.00	65.00
Santa Anna, A. L. de	300.00	1,050.00	1,400.00	915.00
Santa Rosa, Count	20.00	55.00	100.00	
Scheer, Reinhard	20.00	45.00	80.00	40.00
Schley, Winfield S.	85.00	225.00	405.00	200.00
Schmalz, Wilhelm	15.00	40.00	75.00	30.00
Schuyler, Philip J.	75.00	195.00	350.00	
Sellers, David Foote	20.00	55.00	95.00	50.00
Sellers, Winfield S.	15.00	40.00	75.00	40.00
Sharon, Gen. Ariel	18.00	50.00	85.00	45.00
Sharp, U. S. Grant	10.00	22.00	35.00	15.00
Sherman, Forrest P.	20.00	50.00	95.00	50.00
Sherman, Frederick C.	15.00	30.00	60.00	30.00
Shoup, David M.	15.00	40.00	75.00	35.00
Sigsbee, Charles D.	14.50	40.00	70.00	35.00

Name	Signature Only	Letter or Document Signed	Autograph Letter Signed	Signed Photograph
Sims, Adm. William S.	20.00	42.50	95.00	50.00
Singlaub, John K.	5.00	15.00	25.00	10.00
Skinner, Cortlandt	30.00	70.00	125.00	
Skorzeny, Otto	85.00	230.00	450.00	175.00
Slim, William Joseph	30.00	65.00	110.00	60.00
Smith, Walter B.	30.00	45.00	90.00	45.00
Sparks, William E.	15.00	30.00	50.00	
Speer, Albert	40.00	50.00	160.00	105.00
Speidel, Hans	30.00	80.00	145.00	75.00
Spruance, Raymond A.	25.00	70.00	120.00	60.00
Stanhope, Edward	10.00	20.00	30.00	
Stanley, Capt. Henry	5.00	15.00	25.00	
Stansbury, Howard	20.00	55.00	100.00	
Stapp, Col. John	5.00	15.00	20.00	10.00
Stark, Harold R.	15.00	40.00	75.00	40.00
Starry, Donald A.	3.00	6.00	15.00	5.00
St. Clair, Arthur	95.00	250.00	350.00	
Steuben, Friedrick von	380.00	863.00	4,500.00	
Stilwell, Joseph W.	40.00	115.00	160.00	450.00
Stockton, R. F.	110.00	275.00	480.00	
Strauss, Adolf	6.00	15.00	30.00	13.00
St. Vincent, John J.	10.00	20.00	30.00	
Sweeney, Walter C.	5.00	15.00	25.00	10.00
Tallmadge, Benjamin	75.00	195.00	350.00	
Taufflieb, Gen.	45.00	120.00	215.00	100.00
Taylor, H. C.	7.00	20.00	57.50	15.00
Taylor, Maxwell D.	25.00	35.00	62.00	50.00
Thayer, Silvanus	45.00	115.00	200.00	
Thornhill, F. D.	10.00	20.00	30.00	
Tojo, Hideki	185.00	365.00	825.00	450.00
Townsend, Peter	10.00	30.00	50.00	25.00
Vandenberg, Gen. Hoyt	10.00	20.00	50.00	32.50
Vandergrift, Alexander A.	15.00	35.00	75.00	35.00
Van Fleet, Gen. James	10.00	20.00	65.00	22.50
Varick, Richard	20.00	50.00	95.00	
Villa, Pancho	275.00	635.00	1,800.00	725.00
Von Papen, Franz	95.00	225.00	380.00	175.00
Wainwright, Jonathan	90.00	170.00	300.00	155.00
Walker, Fred L.	10.00	30.00	50.00	
Walker, Walton H.	15.00	30.00	75.00	40.00
Walker, William	125.00	210.00	350.00	580.00
Washington, William	60.00	150.00	290.00	
Wavell, Sir Archibald	20.00	55.00	95.00	50.00
Wayne, Anthony	370.00	800.00	1,500.00	
Wenck, Walter	25.00	60.00	120.00	52.00
Wermuth, Arthur W.	10.00	20.00	35.00	20.00
Wert, Richard L.	5.00	15.00	25.00	15.00
Westmoreland, William C.	14.33	25.00	57.50	33.80
Weygand, Maxime	10.00	25.00	40.00	20.00
Whisner, William T.	12.00	30.00	45.00	
Wilson, Henry	10.00	27.50	46.67	20.00
Wingate, Sir F. R.	30.00	75.00	145.00	75.00

Name	Signature Only	Letter or Document Signed	Autograph Letter Signed	Signed Photograph
Winslow, John A.	15.00	40.00	75.00	
Wolseley, Garnet J.	15.00	32.50	50.00	20.00
Wood, Leonard	17.00	35.00	55.00	30.00
Woodfill, Samuel	10.00	30.00	50.00	
Worth, William	25.00	70.00	125.00	
Yamamoto, Isoroku	125.00	250.00	500.00	420.00
Yamashita, Tomoyuki	105.00	275.00	490.00	255.00
York, Sgt. Alvin	50.00	62.50	190.00	85.00
Zais, Melvin	5.00	15.00	25.00	8.00
Zhukov, Georgi K.	80.00	200.00	500.00	325.00
Zumwalt, Elmo	10.00	30.00	50.00	15.00

Olympic Stars

The Olympic Games are again in the international sports spotlight this year. And for autograph collectors, the problems of obtaining signatures of non–U.S.A. medal-winners continue to escalate. The normal problems of finding celebrities is multiplied when they live outside the U.S.A.; in some cases, autographs of internationally acclaimed athletes are virtually impossible to get.

For instance, two of the most difficult autographs of legitimate superstars of the past 20 years are both from former Olympic stars—gymnasts Nadia Comaneci and Olga Korbut. Neither seems reachable by mail, which means the supply of available autographs is limited to those signed when these athletes were competing in the U.S.

There are many other Olympic stars that are more available, but few foreign Olympic medalists would be termed common. Despite this, there has been rapid growth in the number of collectors who have begun trying to put together complete collections of all Olympic gold medalists.

Name	Sport	Signature	Signed Photograph
Coe, Sebastian	track	$ 8	$20
Comaneci, Nadia	gymnastics	25	65
Curry, John	figure skating	7	18
Dibiasi, Klaus	diving	7	18
Ender, Kornelia	swimming	10	20

Name	Sport	Signature	Signed Photograph
Enke, Karin	speed skating	10	20
Fraser, Dawn	swimming	10	25
Gross, Michael	swimming	10	25
Killy, Jean-Claude	skiing	10	25
Kim, Nelli	gymnastics	15	50
Klammer, Franz	skiing	10	25
Korbut, Olga	gymnastics	30	75
Mittermaier, Rosi	skiing	10	20
Nadig, Marie-Therese	skiing	10	20
Poetsch, Annet	figure skating	8	18
Rose, Murray	swimming	12	25
Sailer, Toni	skiing	12	25
Schenk, Ard	speed skating	10	20
Schneider, Petra	swimming	10	20
Schuba, Beatrix	figure skating	12	25
Stock, Leonhard	skiing	10	22
Theumer, Petra	swimming	12	25
Thompson, Daley	decathlon	15	30
Thoeni, Gustav	skiing	12	22
Thorvill and Dean	figure skating	15	30
Viren, Lasse	track	10	20
Wenzel, Hanni	skiing	10	22
Witt, Katarina	figure skating	12	22
Zatopek, Emil	track	25	50

Revolutionary War

Collecting signatures of notables from the American Revolutionary War era is not the least expensive part of the autograph hobby by any means. Some of these autographs, being a part of this country's history, are worth a great deal indeed. Since this period dates before the invention of the camera, we have included no Signed Photograph prices. (If you do have a photograph of Sam Adams or Paul Revere, we'd certainly like to see it.)

Autograph values included here are for pre- and post–Revolutionary War Colonial personages, those of the French Revolution era, signers of the Declaration of Independence, members of the Continental Congress, pioneers, and other notable people of the period.

Name	Signature Only	Letter or Document Signed	Autograph Letter Signed
Adams, Samuel		$ 532.50	$ 2,875.00
Alexander, Robert		30.00	
Amherst, Jeffrey Baron	$ 240.00	600.00	785.00
André, John	1,200.00	3,500.00	7,500.00
Arnold, Benedict	650.00	1,075.00	2,672.50
Augereau, C. (Castiglione)	90.00	262.50	
Austin, Moses	355.00	975.00	2,233.33
Avery, John, Jr.		35.00	70.00
Barclay, Thomas		20.00	40.00
Barere de Vieuzac, B.	26.00	113.00	150.00
Barras, Paul	85.00	250.00	
Barry, John		2,750.00	
Bartlett, Josiah	165.00	343.67	540.80
Bayard, John	20.00	55.00	105.00
Bedford, Gunning		40.00	
Belcher, Jonathan	107.50	325.00	550.00
Belliard, Count Augustin		48.00	100.00
Benson, Egbert		50.00	
Berlier, Count Theophile	50.00	150.00	295.00
Bernard, Sir Francis		160.00	250.00
Berthier, Alexandre	50.00	145.83	285.00
Bessieres, Bertrand		55.00	100.00
Beugnot, Count J. C.		75.00	145.00
Biddle, Clement		48.00	96.67
Bingham, William	45.00	130.00	250.00
Blennerhassett, Harman		285.00	562.50
Blodget, Samuel, Jr.		750.00	
Boone, Daniel	1,650.00	7,500.00	18,000.00
Boudinot, Elias	190.00		390.00
Bourrienne, L. A. F. de		35.00	50.00
Bradstreet, John		125.00	275.00
Braxton, Carter	75.00	200.00	412.50
Brearly, David		250.00	800.00
Brown, Lt. John	72.00	175.00	400.00
Brune, G. M. A.		120.00	250.00
Burgoyne, John		2,042.50	5,700.00
Butler, John	55.00		310.00
Butler, Pierce	25.00	95.00	200.00
Cambaceres, J. J. R. (Parma)		101.67	125.00
Carnot, Lazare N. M.	55.00	162.67	322.67
Carroll, Charles (Carrollton)	75.00	355.00	425.50
Cathcart, Sir William Schaw		45.00	100.00
Chase, Samuel	261.00	775.00	1,400.00
Chouteau, Auguste	330.00	800.00	1,515.00
Church, Benjamin	195.00		1,095.00
Clark, Abraham	225.00	688.00	
Clark, George Rogers	575.00	1,650.00	4,150.00
Clarke, Thomas	165.00	550.00	
Clayton, Joshua		200.00	395.00
Clymer, George	87.00	241.67	502.50
Colden, Cadwallader		100.00	204.00
Coxe, Tench	25.00	80.00	155.00

Name	Signature Only	Letter or Document Signed	Autograph Letter Signed
Cushing, Thomas		565.00	1,100.00
Cutler, Manasseh		425.00	550.00
Dane, Nathan		40.00	85.00
Danforth, Thomas		387.50	466.00
Danton, Georges-Jacques		1,077.00	
Davenport, Addington	65.00	150.00	300.00
Davies, William	27.00		150.00
Davout, Louis N.	30.00	87.50	175.00
Dayton, Elias		40.00	
Dayton, Jonathan		200.00	1,175.00
Deane, Silas		350.00	687.50
DeHart, John		55.00	110.00
De Lancey, Stephen	50.00		287.50
Dick, Samuel	10.00	35.00	140.00
Dickenson, John	150.00	450.00	
Duane, James		206.67	405.00
Ducos, Jean François		100.00	195.00
Dudley, Joseph	215.00	525.00	985.00
Dudley, Paul	85.00	250.00	
Duroc, Geraud C. M.	15.00	50.00	95.00
Ellery, William	140.00	291.75	625.00
Ellicott, Andrew	52.00	150.00	295.00
Ernouf, (Baron) Manuel L. J.		75.00	145.00
Estaing, Count Charles H. T.	175.00	500.00	
Exelman, Count Remi J. I.			50.00
Fairfax, George William	60.00	190.00	350.00
Fairfax, Lord Thomas	185.00	525.00	
Fiorella, Pascal A.	17.00	50.00	
Fish, Nicholas	10.00	40.00	85.00
Fitzgerald, John	35.00	95.00	203.00
Fitzsimons, Thomas		110.00	238.00
Flahaut, Count A. C. J.		10.00	25.00
Floyd, William	242.00	613.33	1,500.00
Fonda, Jelles		100.00	215.00
Forman, Thomas M.		45.00	100.00
Fouche, Joseph (Duc d'Otrante)	65.00	187.50	395.00
Foy, Count Maximilian S.	8.00	22.00	50.00
Franklin, Benjamin	925.00	3,642.86	8,583.33
Fregeville, Marquis C. L. J.	15.00	35.00	75.00
Freron, Louis M. S.	15.00	35.00	75.00
Friant, Count Louis	27.00		150.00
Gage, Thomas	175.00	511.67	817.50
Galloway, Joseph		260.00	550.00
Ganteaume, Count Honoré	20.00	60.00	125.00
Gardanne, Gaspard A.	40.00	115.00	250.00
Gates, Horatio	170.00	500.00	1,185.00
Gelston, David		80.00	150.00
Genet, Edmond C.	40.00	120.00	225.00
Gerry, Elbridge (V)	162.50	325.00	1,698.18
Giles, William Branch	30.00	79.00	150.00
Glover, John	175.00	500.00	
Gore, Christopher	70.00	192.00	350.00

Name	Signature Only	Letter or Document Signed	Autograph Letter Signed
Gorham, Nathaniel		364.00	688.00
Gratz, Barnard	75.00	212.00	400.00
Grenville, Baron William W.	95.00	270.00	588.00
Griffin, Cyrus	300.00	750.00	
Gudin de la Sablonnière		100.00	212.00
Guyot, Pierre	20.00	50.00	100.00
Gwinnett, Button	135,000.00		
Habersham, Joseph	60.00	173.00	332.50
Hall, Lyman		1,820.00	2,750.00
Hancock, John	666.67	1,851.38	3,125.00
Hand, Edward	120.00	350.00	750.00
Harrison, Benjamin	160.00	462.50	2,200.00
Harrison, Robert Hanson	165.00	400.00	750.00
Hart, John	185.00	375.00	850.00
Heath, William	30.00	100.00	
Hedouville, Count G. M. T. J.		65.50	125.00
Henry, John	25.00		130.00
Henry, Patrick	350.00	713.00	1,625.00
Hewes, Joseph	1,200.00	3,500.00	7,000.00
Heyward, Thomas, Jr.		330.00	1,325.00
Hoban, James		675.00	
Hoche, Lazare		187.00	395.00
Hopkins, Samuel		235.00	500.00
Hopkins, Stephen	145.00	422.50	
Hopkinson, Francis	145.00	487.50	766.67
Huger, Isaac	50.00	150.00	306.50
Humphreys, David	35.00	98.00	200.00
Hunter, Robert		507.50	1,036.00
Huntington, Benjamin	50.00	145.00	
Huntington, Samuel	135.00	280.20	875.00
Ingersoll, Jared	30.00	91.50	188.00
Inskeep, Jonathan		80.00	175.00
Irvine, James		122.00	250.00
Irvine, William	55.00	160.00	300.00
Jackson, William	120.00	350.00	750.00
Jencks, Joseph		250.00	
Jourdan, Count Jean B.	35.00	105.00	180.00
Junot, Jean Andoche		90.00	183.50
Kellerman, F. C., Duke of Valmy		80.00	170.00
Kent, James	35.00	100.00	225.00
Kenton, Simon	225.00	625.00	
King, Rufus	49.50	150.00	301.50
Kléber, Jean Baptiste	145.00	410.00	855.00
Kosciusko, Thaddeus	300.00	740.00	1,500.00
Laine, Viscount J. L. J.	30.00	85.00	
Langdon, John	180.00		1,375.00
Lapoype, Baron J. F. C.	20.00		125.00
La Revellière-Lepaux, L.		60.50	125.00
Larrey, Baron Dominick	45.00	151.50	310.00
Latour-Maubourg, M. V. N. F.			65.00
Lear, Tobias	45.00	126.67	212.50
Lee, Francis Lightfoot	665.00	1,200.00	4,000.00

Name	Signature Only	Letter or Document Signed	Autograph Letter Signed
Lee, Richard Henry	155.00	475.00	1,100.00
Lefebvre, F. J., Duke		160.00	310.00
Leverett, John	50.00		275.00
Lewis, Francis	360.00	1,135.00	2,600.00
Livingston, Philip	325.00	500.00	1,050.00
Livingston, William		1,300.00	1,800.00
Lovell, James	70.00	187.50	430.00
Lynch, Thomas, Jr.	4,200.00		
MacDonald, J. E. J. A.	25.00	75.00	145.00
Maison, Marquis N. J.	27.00	90.00	183.00
Malet, C. François de		118.00	240.00
Malher, J. P. F.	25.00	80.00	150.00
Marat, Hugues B., Duke	35.00	100.00	200.00
Marat, Jean Paul			4,500.00
Marbot, J. B. A. M.	15.00	45.00	80.00
Marescot, Armand S.	30.00	80.00	170.00
Maret, Hugues B., Duke		70.00	150.00
Marmont, A. F. L. V., Duke		41.00	85.00
Massena, André, Duke	93.50	305.00	450.00
Mather, Cotton	375.00	1,875.00	3,100.00
Matlack, Timothy	50.00	149.00	305.00
McDougall, Alexander	90.00	200.00	412.50
McIntosh, Lachlan	115.00	300.00	525.00
McKean, Thomas	85.00	240.00	587.50
Merlin de Douai, P. A.	35.00		185.00
Middleton, Arthur	1,250.00	2,500.00	3,850.00
Miollis, S. A. F.		100.00	212.00
Mirabeau, Gabriel H. R.	95.00	270.00	575.00
Molitor, G. J. J.		75.00	153.50
Moncey, Bon Adrien J. de		100.00	125.00
Montalivet, Count J. P. B.		100.00	
Moreau, Jean Victor	45.00	119.50	245.00
Morris, Gouverneur	65.00		350.00
Morris, Lewis	260.00	640.00	1,150.33
Morris, Robert	225.00	477.50	1,030.00
Mortier, Edouard A. C. J.	30.00	93.33	191.00
Morton, John	300.00	762.50	
Moulton, William	20.00	62.00	
Moutrie, Alexander	35.00		200.00
Munro, Peter Jay	30.00	65.00	140.00
Murat, Joachim		385.00	575.00
Murray, William Vans	15.00	36.00	75.00
Nelson, Thomas, Jr.	300.00	1,200.00	2,600.00
Ney, Michel	90.00	225.00	550.00
Nicholson, John	25.00	73.00	150.00
Otis, James	150.00	323.33	510.00
Oudinot, N. Charles		50.00	65.00
Paca, William	250.00	575.00	1,500.00
Pache, Jean Nicholas	20.00	65.00	
Paine, Robert Treat	135.00	307.00	740.00
Penn, John	542.50	1,666.67	3,383.33
Penn, William	825.00	3,125.00	5,625.00

Name	Signature Only	Letter or Document Signed	Autograph Letter Signed
Perignon, D. C., Marquis de	40.00	125.00	
Peters, Richard, Jr.	15.00	45.00	85.00
Petiet, Claude		125.00	265.00
Pettit, Charles	20.00		125.00
Pichegru, Charles	30.00	105.00	195.00
Pike, Zebulon	15.00	50.00	85.00
Pinkney, Thomas	12.00	35.00	75.00
Pownall, Thomas		250.00	275.00
Putnam, Rufus	120.00	320.00	650.00
Pynchon, John			3,750.00
Randolph, John (Roanoke)	75.00	220.00	450.00
Rawdon-Hastings, Francis	10.00	30.00	65.00
Rawson, Edward	125.00	350.00	685.00
Read, George	95.00	245.00	448.00
Real, Count Pierre F.	12.00	35.00	72.50
Regnaud de Saint-Jean			95.00
Revere, Paul	1,746.67	4,900.00	8,000.00
Robinson, John	60.00	175.00	340.00
Rochambeau, Count J. B. D.	170.00	486.60	896.67
Roederer, Count Pierre C.	15.00	45.00	85.00
Rogers, Robert	335.00	1,195.00	3,300.00
Roland de la Platière, J. W.	30.00	90.00	183.00
Roosevelt, Nicholas J.	18.00		100.00
Ross, George	80.00	200.00	406.67
Rush, Benjamin	895.00	2,000.00	5,000.00
Rutledge, Edward	140.00	395.00	700.00
Saint-Cyr, Gouvion	30.00	85.00	185.00
Saint Hilaire, L. V. Joseph	25.00		139.00
Sargent, Winthrop	25.00	85.00	175.00
Scammell, Alexander			1,500.00
Schuyler, Philip J.	117.50	265.00	840.00
Scott, Gustavus	15.00		85.00
Scott, John Morin	30.00	72.00	136.67
Sewall, David	16.00	42.00	90.00
Shaw, Lemuel	12.00	35.00	62.00
Shelby, Isaac		350.00	525.00
Sherman, Roger	65.00	193.33	416.67
Shirley, William	95.00	257.50	780.00
Sitgreaves, John	25.00	60.00	113.33
Smith, James		175.00	375.00
Smith, John	2,200.00	11,500.00	29,000.00
Smith, Melancton		48.00	95.00
Smith, Richard	40.00	100.00	220.00
Smith, Samuel	27.00	75.00	150.00
Soult, Nicolas Jean		143.50	292.00
Standish, Myles	1,883.00	8,800.00	26,400.00
Stark, John	410.00	650.00	1,565.00
Stephen, Adam		150.00	320.00
Stevens, Ebenezer	26.00	75.00	
Stevens, John			50.00
Stirling, Lord William Alexander		385.00	950.00
Stockton, Richard	250.00	1,135.00	2,750.00

Name	Signature Only	Letter or Document Signed	Autograph Letter Signed
Stone, Thomas	305.50	841.67	1,795.00
Stoughton, William	76.00	188.00	375.00
Strong, Caleb	35.00	100.00	150.00
Suchet, Louis G., Duc d'A—	63.00	150.00	320.00
Sullivan, James	30.00	75.00	200.00
Sullivan, John	63.00	200.00	355.00
Sullivan, William	16.00	37.00	75.00
Symmes, John Cleves	100.00	375.00	500.00
Talcott, Joseph	24.00	70.00	135.00
Talmadge, Benjamin		220.00	465.00
Tarleton, Banastre	99.00	275.00	575.00
Taylor, George	1,400.00	3,850.00	7,050.00
Ten Broeck, Abraham	30.00	65.00	140.00
Thomas, Isaiah	100.50	281.00	575.00
Thomas, John	225.00	612.00	1,250.00
Thompson, Benjamin (Rumford)		275.00	450.00
Thomson, Charles	185.00	532.50	1,025.00
Thornton, Matthew	265.00	675.00	1,500.00
Tilghman, James	18.75	50.00	112.50
Treadwell, John	15.00	38.00	75.00
Treilhard, J. B.	10.00		50.00
Trumbull, Jonathan, Jr.	125.00	275.00	563.00
Trumbull, Jonathan, Sr.		235.00	293.75
Truxton, Thomas	95.00	270.00	575.00
Tryon, William		375.00	
Tucker, Samuel	125.00	323.67	670.50
Turreau de Garambouville	15.00		75.00
Valette, A. J. M.	12.00		75.00
Van Dam, Rip	60.00	175.00	357.00
Vandamme, Dominique René	35.00	100.00	204.00
Van Dike, Nicholas	110.00	305.50	625.00
Van Horne, David	10.00		75.00
Van Ness, Cornelius P.	11.00	35.00	55.00
Vaubois, J. F. G.	5.00	15.00	40.00
Vendôme, Louis Joseph, Duc de	150.00	450.00	
Vernier, Count Theodore	30.00	100.00	
Victor, Claude Perrin	30.00	75.00	140.00
Vivian, Sir Richard H.	45.00	125.00	255.00
Walker, Benjamin	34.33	95.00	175.00
Walton, George	102.50	311.67	504.00
Ward, Artemas		1,300.00	935.00
Warner, Seth			1,200.00
Warren, James	85.00	215.00	398.00
Warren, Joseph		6,875.00	
Wentworth, Benning	80.00	230.00	470.00
Wentworth, John	60.00	175.00	340.00
Wharton, Thomas	105.00	292.50	565.00
Whipple, William	239.50	605.33	1,200.00
White, Anthony Walton	45.00		250.00
White, William		130.00	262.50
Wilkinson, James	90.00	200.00	300.00
Williams, Otho	115.00		645.00

Name	Signature Only	Letter or Document Signed	Autograph Letter Signed
Williams, William	88.33	188.00	310.00
Wilson, James	200.00	480.00	1,200.00
Winslow, Edward	14.00	40.00	81.50
Winslow, John	10.00	25.00	40.00
Winthrop, John	800.00	1,900.00	4,750.00
Winthrop, Thomas L.	15.00	40.00	85.00
Witherspoon, John		350.00	2,326.67
Wolcott, Oliver	120.00	292.50	765.00
Wood, James	28.00		40.00
Wright, Turbutt	15.00	40.00	65.00
Wythe, George	312.00	768.60	1,978.75
Yates, Peter W.	7.00	25.00	40.00
Yeates, Jasper	10.00	20.00	45.00

Rock Music Stars

Here are prices for rock music stars. As in all categories, we will be happy to receive additional pricing data in order to expand this and our other lists in the next edition.

Name	Signature Only	Signed Photograph
Abba	$ 30	$ 75
Aerosmith	35	85
Anderson, Laurie	10	25
Ashford and Simpson	15	40
Bananarama	20	50
The Beach Boys	150	350
The Beatles	600	1,000
Beck, Jeff	15	30
Benatar, Pat	10	25
Benson, George	15	30
Berry, Chuck	30	65
Blood, Sweat and Tears	35	80
Bon Jovi	35	75
Bowie, David	30	65
Branigan, Laura	10	30
Brown, James	40	75

Name	Signature Only	Signed Photograph
Browne, Jackson	8	25
Buffett, Jimmy	6	20
Charles, Ray	25	50
Chicago	35	85
Clapton, Eric	15	35
Cocker, Joe	15	35
Collins, Judy	10	20
Collins, Phil	20	35
Commodores	25	60
Cooke, Sam	175	350
Costello, Elvis	10	30
Cougar, John	10	35
Cream	35	75
Creedence Clearwater Revival	40	90
Cross, Christopher	6	20
Daltry, Roger	12	35
Daniels, Charlie	6	20
Devo	30	60
Dire Straits	30	75
Dolby, Thomas	20	40
The Doobie Brothers	40	80
The Doors	450	900
Duran Duran	60	125
Dylan, Bob	50	115
Eagles	40	80
Easton, Sheena	12	35
Electric Light Orchestra	35	75
Emerson, Lake and Palmer	35	80
Eurythmics	30	60
The Everly Brothers	30	60
Fleetwood Mac	50	100
Fogelberg, Dan	6	20
Fogerty, John	10	30
Four Tops	40	80
Gaye, Marvin	50	100
Genesis	40	80
Grant, Amy	10	25
Grateful Dead	40	85
Green, Al	10	20
Hagar, Sammy	10	20
Haley, Bill	125	250
Hall and Oates	20	40
Harrison, George	75	150
Hart, Corey	15	30
Heart	30	75
Hendrix, Jimi	250	500
Henley, Don	15	35
Holly, Buddy	1,000	2,000
Houston, Whitney	30	75
Ian, Janis	20	45
Jackson, Joe	20	35
Jagger, Mick	25	50
Jefferson Airplane	100	200
Jefferson Starship	40	80

Name	Signature Only	Signed Photograph
Jethro Tull	30	75
Joel, Billy	15	35
John, Elton	20	40
Jones, Quincy	12	30
Jones, Rickie Lee	20	35
Joplin, Janis	250	500
Journey	25	50
Kansas	30	60
Khan, Chaka	15	30
King, Carole	8	25
The Kinks	40	85
Knight, Gladys	15	30
Led Zeppelin	35	70
Lennon, John	175	350
Lennon, Julian	20	40
Lewis, Huey	10	35
Lewis, Jerry Lee	20	40
Little River Band	25	50
Loggins and Messina	25	50
Loggins, Kenny	10	25
Loverboy	35	75
Madonna	50	100
Manchester, Melissa	10	25
Manhattan Transfer	30	65
Manilow, Barry	20	45
Marley, Bob	50	100
Mayall, John	15	30
McCartney, Paul	80	160
Meat Loaf	15	35
Mitchell, Joni	15	35
The Moody Blues	75	150
Morrison, Jim	375	750
Morrison, Van	12	30
Mr. Mister	30	60
Newman, Randy	10	20
Newton-John, Olivia	25	50
Nicks, Stevie	30	60
Nilsson, Harry	50	100
Nugent, Ted	10	30
Oliver, Jane	6	15
Osborne, Ozzy	20	35
Palmer, Robert	20	35
Parker, Graham	20	35
Petty, Tom	20	40
Pink Floyd	75	140
Pointer Sisters	30	60
The Police	40	75
Presley, Elvis	132	300
Prince	75	100
Procol Harum	35	65
Reed, Lou	15	30
Richie, Lionel	12	25
The Righteous Brothers	20	40
Robinson, Smokey	15	30

Name	Signature Only	Signed Photograph
The Rolling Stones	500	1,000
Ronstadt, Linda	20	40
Ross, Diana	30	60
Sade	15	35
Scaggs, Boz	15	35
Seger, Bob	20	40
Simon, Carly	15	30
Simon, Paul	20	35
Simon and Garfunkel	30	60
Springfield, Rick	12	25
Springsteen, Bruce	55	110
Starr, Ringo	50	100
Steely Dan	30	60
Steppenwolf	75	150
Stevens, Cat	20	40
Stewart, Rod	20	40
Stills, Stephen	15	35
Sting	20	40
Styx	25	50
Summer, Donna	15	30
Supertramp	35	75
Talking Heads	30	60
Taylor, James	20	35
Tears for Fears	30	60
The Temptations	40	80
Thompson Twins	25	50
Toto	25	50
Townsend, Pete	20	40
Trower, Robin	15	30
Turner, Tina	20	35
The Turtles	35	75
Tyler, Bonnie	15	30
U2	65	130
Wakeman, Rick	15	30
The Who	50	100
Wilson, Jackie	150	300
Wonder, Stevie	40	80
Yes	40	80
Young, Neil	20	40
ZZ Top	35	70

Science and Technology

The following represents persons of note in the fields of science and technology. If the name of any person has been excluded, it means only that data on a philographic item of his or hers was not accessible at the time of publishing.

* = Data incomplete, estimate only. ** = Last published price.

Name	Signature Only	Letter or Document Signed	Autograph Letter Signed	Signed Photograph
Adler, Alfred	$ 90.00	$ 200.00	$ 450.00	
Adrian, Lord Edgar	15.00	40.00	100.00	
Agassiz, Jean Louis	43.33	60.00	128.33	
Aitken, Robert G.	10.00	20.00	40.00	
Alexanderson, E. F. W.	40.00	100.00	180.00	
Alvarez, Dr. Luis W.	10.00	25.00	50.00	$ 25.00
Ampère, André Marie	135.00	360.00	750.00	
Anfinsen, Dr. Christian	6.00	20.00	40.00	10.00
Armstrong, Dr. William	15.00	35.00	75.00	15.00
Axelrod, Julius	30.00	45.00	95.00	20.00
Bache, Alexander D.	20.00	50.00	110.00	
Baird, John Logie	135.00	270.00	560.00	
Baltimore, David	5.00	15.00	35.00	10.00
Banting, Frederick G.	155.00	350.00	540.00	
Bardeen, John	14.00	45.00	95.00	20.00
Barnard, Dr. Christian	20.00	35.00	85.00	32.00
Beadle, G. Wells	10.00	20.00	45.00	15.00
Beebe, William	15.33	50.00	100.00	20.00
Bell, Alexander Graham	275.00	675.00	1,500.00	
Benacerraf, Baruj	5.00	7.00	12.00	5.00
Berg, Paul	5.00	15.00	35.00	10.00
Berthollet, Count Claude	60.00	150.00	330.00	
Berzelius, Jons Jacob	55.00	165.00	350.00	
Blackett, Dr. Patrick	18.00	25.00	50.00	20.00
Bloch, Dr. Konrad	5.00	10.00	25.00	15.00
Bloembergen, Dr. Nicolaas	10.00	20.00	35.00	20.00
Bohr, Aage Niels	125.00	195.00	375.00	185.00
Borlaug, Dr. Norman	13.00	25.00	70.00	15.00
Bowen, Ira Sprague	5.00	20.00	35.00	10.00
Bragg, William Lawrence	38.00	70.00	140.00	
Brattain, Walter	20.00	35.00	85.00	37.50
Braun, Wernher von	40.00	125.00	280.00	115.00
Brewster, David	20.00	55.00	112.50	

Louis Agassiz

John Bardeen—Nobel Prize Winner

Sir William Armstrong

Dr. Christian Barnard

Patrick M. S. Blackett—Nobel Prize Winner

Alexander Graham Bell

Niels Bohr

Norman E. Borlaug

Wernher von Braun

Norman E. Borlaug

Luther Burbank

Alexis Carrel—Nobel Prize Winner

Melvin Calvin

Vannevar Bush

Denton A. Cooley

George Washington Carver

Jacques Cousteau

Harvey W. Cushing

Sir Humphrey Davy

Dr. Michael DeBakey

Charles Darwin

William C. De Vries

Thomas A. Edison

Dr. Lee de Forest

Albert Einstein

Dr. Paul Ehrlich

Sir Alexander Fleming

Michael Faraday

Richard Gatling

Alexander von Humboldt

Asa Gray

Thomas Henry Huley

401

Name	Signature Only	Letter or Document Signed	Autograph Letter Signed	Signed Photograph
Broglie, Louis Victor de	20.00	55.00	105.00	25.00
Bronk, Detlev W.	5.00	15.00	35.00	10.00
Brown, Herbert C.	10.00	15.00	25.00	10.00
Bunsen, Robert W.	90.00	285.00	595.00	
Burbank, Luther	27.50	187.50	225.00	150.00
Bush, Vannevar	35.00	100.00	235.00	45.00
Bushnell, David	215.00	675.00	1,185.00	
Butenandt, Adolf	10.00	15.00	25.00	10.00
Calvin, Melvin	10.00	25.00	50.00	30.00
Cannon, Dr. Martha H.	20.00	30.00	55.00	25.00
Carrel, Dr. Alexis	45.00	150.00	230.00	50.00
Carver, George Washington	143.00	225.00	430.00	
Cavell, Edith	155.00	560.00	730.00	
Chamberlain, Owen	5.00	15.00	35.00	10.00
Charcot, Jean	65.00	205.00	425.00	
Cheever, Dr. Charles A.	15.00	35.00	75.00	30.00
Cockcroft, John D.	60.00	110.00	220.00	
Colt, Samuel	200.00	504.00	1,212.50	
Compton, Arthur H.	30.00	90.00	200.00	
Congreve, Sir William	45.00	125.00	250.00	
Cooley, Dr. Denton A.	20.00	45.00	95.00	25.00
Coolidge, Dr. William D.	15.00	35.00	60.00	15.00
Cooper, Dr. Leon	6.00	15.00	25.00	23.33
Cori, C. F.	12.00	20.00	42.00	15.00
Corner, George W.	50.00	95.00	195.00	50.00
Cornforth, J. W.	10.00	18.00	38.00	10.00
Cousteau, Jacques	10.00	35.00	70.00	40.00
Crick, Dr. Francis	5.00	15.00	35.00	10.00
Curie, Marie	500.00	1,225.00	2,462.50	
Curie, Pierre	325.00	760.00	1,650.00	
Cushing, Dr. Harvey	140.00	350.00	575.00	
Cuvier, Baron Georges Léopold	25.00	92.50	165.00	
Dafoe, Dr. Allan Roy	20.00	35.00	135.00	35.00
Daguerre, Louis	135.00	450.00	1,200.00	
Darwin, Charles	383.33	1,325.00	1,772.00	800.00
Davy, Sir Humphrey	55.00	145.00	208.00	
DeBakey, Dr. Michael	17.67	28.33	35.00	10.00
de Forest, Dr. Lee	150.00	200.00	325.00	100.00
De Vries, Dr. William	15.00	25.00	40.00	20.00
DuBridge, Dr. Lee	15.00	40.00	85.00	20.00
Dulbecco, Renato	5.00	15.00	30.00	7.00
Duryea, Charles	40.00	235.00	350.00	75.00
DuVigneaud, Vincent	7.50	15.00	35.00	10.00
Edison, Thomas Alva	267.86	513.64	1,575.00	709.17
Ehrlich, Dr. Paul	150.00	275.00	450.00	
Einstein, Albert	340.00	1,518.75	3,426.67	1,500.00
Enders, Dr. John	15.00	50.00	90.00	21.67
Euler, Ulf von	10.00	30.00	55.00	20.00
Faraday, Michael	95.00	275.00	325.00	
Fitch, Dr. Val L.	3.00	5.00	7.00	5.00
Flammarion, Camille	150.00			
Fleming, Sir Alexander	125.00	300.00	425.00	800.00

C. G. Jung

Ernest Lawrence

Alfred C. Kinsey

Mary D. Leakey

Sir Joseph Lister

Dr. Willy Ley

Guglielmo Marconi

Hiram Percy Maxim

William J. Mayo

Margaret Mead

C. W. Mayo, M. D.
Charles W. Mayo

Karl A. Menninger, M. D.

Robert Moog

Samuel F. B. Morse

Hermann Oberth

Robert Oppenheimer

Dr. Albert B. Sabin

Glenn Seaborg

Dr. Jonas Salk

Adolphe Sax

William Shockley

Elmer A. Sperry

W. M. Stanley

Dr. Benjamin Spock

Charles P. Steinmetz

Edward Teller

Nikola Tesla

James Watt

James Van Allen

Orville Wright

Name	Signature Only	Letter or Document Signed	Autograph Letter Signed	Signed Photograph
Flory, Paul J.	16.00	30.00	55.00	18.00
Fowler, Dr. William	7.00	15.00	35.00	16.00
Freud, Sigmund	700.00	2,500.00	3,300.00	
Friedman, Herbert	10.00	30.00	55.00	18.00
Fuller, Buckminster	16.00	45.00	95.00	63.00
Fulton, Robert	120.00	450.00	1,333.33	
Gajdusek, D. Carleton	10.00	15.00	25.00	15.00
Galileo*	4,500.00	14,900.00	26,400.00	
Gatling, Richard J.	125.00	325.00	525.00	
Geiger, Johannes H.	125.00	350.00	750.00	
Glaser, Donald A.	10.00	30.00	60.00	30.00
Glashow, Sheldon Lee	7.00	12.00	20.00	10.00
Goddard, Robert H.	150.00	420.00	920.00	1,150.00
Goethals, George W.	25.00	65.00	160.00	
Gorgas, William C.	30.00	110.00	175.00	
Granit, Ragnar	15.00	40.00	85.00	25.00
Gray, Asa	25.00	42.00	80.00	
Guillemin, Dr. Roger	15.00	45.00	90.00	15.00
Guillotin, Joseph I.	120.00	400.00	700.00	
Hahn, Otto	90.00	245.00	495.00	110.00
Hammond, William A.	45.00	100.00	250.00	
Hartline, Haldan K.	20.00	70.00	135.00	25.00
Harvey, William	750.00	3,750.00	11,000.00	
Hayward, George	5.00	15.00	25.00	5.00
Heisenberg, Werner	20.00	55.00	110.00	40.00
Heller, Dr. John R.	10.00	15.00	20.00	5.00
Hench, Philip S.	15.00	45.00	85.00	20.00
Henry, Joseph	15.00	35.00	70.00	
Hering, Constantine	10.00	25.00	50.00	
Herschel, William	90.00	245.00	475.00	
Hershey, Dr. Alfred	5.00	15.00	30.00	5.00
Herzberg, Gerhard	10.00	20.00	40.00	20.00
Hess, Victor F.	10.00	25.00	50.00	15.00
Hess, Walter R.	10.00	25.00	50.00	20.00
Hewish, Anthony	15.00	40.00	85.00	20.00
Hofstadter, Robert	10.00	20.00	35.00	14.00
Holley, Dr. Robert	5.00	10.00	20.00	15.00
Horsford, Eben N.	5.00	7.00	10.00	5.00
Houssay, Bernando A.	20.00	55.00	110.00	45.00
Howe, Elias	160.00	360.00	795.00	
Huggins, Charles	22.00	60.00	117.00	25.00
Humboldt, Alexander von	60.00	110.00	200.00	
Huxley, Julian	22.00	45.00	65.00	
Huxley, Thomas Henry	30.00	70.00	112.50	
Jackson, Dr. James C.	5.00	10.00	15.00	5.00
Jarvik, Dr. Robert	10.00	30.00	60.00	25.00
Jenner, Edward	267.50	800.00	1,383.33	
Jenner, Sir William	15.00	40.00	85.00	
Jung, Karl Gustav	235.00	726.25	1,760.00	450.00
Kahoutek, Lubos	5.00	13.00	25.00	5.00
Kantrowitz, Dr. Adrian	25.00	68.00	145.00	30.00
Katz, Sir Bernard	5.00	15.00	25.00	5.00

Name	Signature Only	Letter or Document Signed	Autograph Letter Signed	Signed Photograph
Kelly, Howard A.	10.00	27.50	55.00	40.00
Kelvin, Lord William T.	35.00	125.00	200.00	175.00
Kendall, Edward C.	25.00	45.00	90.00	30.00
Keys, Ancel	5.00	15.00	30.00	10.00
Keyserling, Hermann	10.00	25.00	50.00	20.00
Khorana, Dr. Har G.	7.00	15.00	40.00	10.00
Kilby, J. S.	10.00	30.00	52.00	15.00
Kinsey, Dr. Alfred C.	85.00	230.00	350.00	95.00
Koch, Robert			700.00	1,500.00
Krebs, Hans	5.00	25.50	38.00	10.00
Kusch, Poyl K.	5.00	12.00	23.00	5.00
Labouisse, Eve Curie	15.00	45.00	90.00	35.00
Lacepede, Bernhard de	25.00	60.00	120.00	
Lamarck, Jean Baptiste	125.00	355.00	750.00	
Langmuir, Irving	20.00	55.00	110.00	
Larson, Dr. Leonard	5.00	15.00	30.00	10.00
Lavoisier, Antoine L.	255.00	805.00	2,000.00	
Lawrence, Ernest O.	40.00	70.00	140.00	50.00
Leakey, Mary D.	10.00	20.00	55.00	25.00
Lee, Dr. T. D.	5.00	15.00	30.00	5.00
Leloir, Luis	10.00	18.00	35.00	7.00
Lesseps, Ferdinand, Vicomte de	45.00	165.00	264.25	150.00
Ley, Willy	25.00	70.00	135.00	30.00
Libby, W. F.	10.00	30.00	55.00	20.00
Linnaeus, Carl	650.00	975.00		
Lister, Joseph	105.00	275.00	725.00	
Liston, Robert	8.00	23.00	45.00	
Lovell, Dr. Bernard	15.00	25.00	40.00	15.00
Mackenzie, Sir Morell	60.00	165.00	350.00	
Mantell, G. A.	7.00	18.00	35.00	8.00
Marconi, Guglielmo	120.00	240.00	470.00	370.00
Maskelyne, Neville	40.00	115.00	266.67	
Maxim, Sir Hiram S.	50.00	95.00	195.00	
Maxim, Hudson	35.00	73.33	160.00	125.00
Mayo, Dr. Charles H.	50.00	145.00	300.00	300.00
Mayo, Dr. Charles W.	20.00	45.00	115.00	25.00
Mayo, Dr. William J.	55.00	110.00	330.00	300.00
McCormick, Cyrus H.	80.00	212.50	480.00	
Mead, Margaret	35.00	90.00	120.00	55.00
Medawar, Peter B.	11.00	30.00	58.00	12.00
Mendel, Gregor	300.00	700.00	1,875.00	
Menninger, Dr. Karl	20.00	60.00	120.00	40.00
Menninger, Roy	10.00	22.00	55.00	27.00
Menninger, William C.	10.00	25.00	60.00	15.00
Mesmer, F. Anton*	115.00	285.00	535.00	
Miller, Stanley	12.00	34.00	65.00	14.00
Milliken, Robert A.	40.00	126.25	200.00	187.50
Mitchell, Maria	25.00	55.00	120.00	
Mitchell, Silas Weir	10.00	20.00	35.00	15.00
Moog, Bob	50.00	70.00	110.00	45.00
Moore, Dr. Francis D.	10.00	30.00	55.00	10.00
Morse, Samuel F. B.	215.00	450.00	1,012.50	840.00

Name	Signature Only	Letter or Document Signed	Autograph Letter Signed	Signed Photograph
Morton, W. T. G.	150.00	410.00	825.00	
Mossbauer, Rudolph L.	20.00	40.00	85.00	30.00
Mulliken, Robert S.	5.00	15.00	25.00	10.00
Murphy, William P.	20.00	55.00	110.00	25.00
Newcomb, Simon	50.00	176.67	263.33	
Newton, Sir Isaac	525.00	3,500.00	4,200.00	
Nightingale, Florence	170.00	270.00	655.00	
Nirenberg, Marshall W.	10.00	20.00	45.00	15.00
Nobel, Alfred	185.00	375.00	550.00	325.00
Nordau, Max	25.00	70.00	220.00	40.00
Northrup, John H.	6.00	15.00	25.00	10.00
Oberth, Dr. Hermann	20.00	55.00	115.00	25.00
Ochoa, Dr. Severo	10.00	35.00	80.00	23.00
Oersted, H. C.		2,500.00		
Oppenheimer, Dr. Robert	90.00	250.00	467.50	85.00
Osler, William	227.50	825.00	1,200.00	
Pasteur, Louis	325.00	625.00	1,145.00	1,900.00
Pauling, Linus	12.00	25.00	42.00	30.00
Penzias, Dr. Arno	10.00	30.00	65.00	15.00
Perutz, Max	14.00	38.00	75.00	16.00
Piccard, Auguste	25.00	97.50	150.00	87.50
Piccard, Jean	25.00	125.00		125.00
Pickering, Dr. William	10.00	30.00	60.00	25.00
Planck, Max	70.00	190.00	378.33	
Playfair, Lyon	8.00	23.00	45.00	9.00
Porter, George	10.00	30.00	55.00	18.00
Priestley, Joseph	190.00	450.00	1,100.00	
Proctor, Richard Anthony	5.00	10.00	20.00	
Pupin, Dr. Michael	35.00	135.00	200.00	
Purcell, Edward M.	10.00	20.00	45.00	15.00
Ramsay, Sir William	235.00	665.00	900.00	
Rank, Otto	75.00	195.00	415.00	
Reed, Walter	300.00	750.00	975.00	650.00
Reich, Wilhelm	105.00	275.00	605.00	
Reik, Theodor	105.00	285.00	600.00	
Richardson, Sir John	15.00	30.00	40.00	
Richter, Dr. Burton	15.00	40.00	65.00	30.00
Rittenhouse, David		850.00	750.00	
Robbins, Frederick	10.00	25.00	40.00	20.00
Roebling, John A.	75.00	125.00	260.00	
Roebling, Washington A.	50.00	110.00	225.00	
Roentgen, Wilhelm	300.00	1,243.50	1,850.00	
Rous, Dr. Peyton	10.00	25.00	40.00	15.00
Roux, Pierre Paul Emile	15.00	41.00	80.00	20.00
Rutherford, Ernest	65.00	170.00	350.00	90.00
Ryle, Sir Martin	34.00	95.00	185.00	40.00
Sabin, Dr. Albert B.	25.00	35.00	65.00	35.00
Sagan, Dr. Carl	10.00	30.00	50.00	25.00
Salk, Dr. Jonas	37.50	54.00	85.00	40.00
Sax, Adolphe	45.00	120.00	206.25	
Schally, Dr. Andrew	10.00	15.00	25.00	
Schawlow, Arthur L.	10.00	15.00	· 25.00	

Name	Signature Only	Letter or Document Signed	Autograph Letter Signed	Signed Photograph
Schick, Dr. Bela	30.00	50.00	90.00	40.00
Schmidt, Dr. Maarten	10.00	20.00	30.00	15.00
Schrieffer, John R.	5.00	12.00	24.00	5.00
Schweitzer, Dr. Albert	60.00	175.00	400.00	287.50
Schwinger, Dr. Julian	5.00	10.00	15.00	15.00
Seaborg, Glenn	25.00	40.00	75.00	45.00
Segre, Emilio	5.00	10.00	15.00	15.00
Semmelweis, Ignaz	375.00	895.00	2,685.00	
Shockley, William	18.00	55.00	100.00	40.00
Silliman, Benjamin	20.00	30.00	45.00	
Simon, Herbert A.	12.00	20.00	45.00	18.00
Simpson, Sir James Y.	20.00	90.00	187.50	
Smith, Dr. Hamilton	5.00	20.00	30.00	10.00
Snell, Dr. George D.	6.00	15.00	30.00	10.00
Soddy, Frederick	35.00	95.00	195.00	45.00
Spalanzani, Lazzaro	120.00	400.00	700.00	
Sperry, Elmer A.	15.00	50.00	125.00	25.00
Sperry, Roger	5.00	20.00	45.00	10.00
Spock, Dr. Benjamin	15.50	21.00	45.00	15.00
Stanley, Wendell M.	15.00	40.00	85.00	25.00
Steinmetz, Charles P.	60.00	100.00	190.00	
Stephenson, George	150.00	405.00	860.00	
Stephenson, Robert	30.00	80.00	165.00	
Talbot, H. F.			750.00	
Tatum, Edward L.	40.00	60.00	110.00	
Teller, Edward	15.00	50.00	125.00	65.00
Temin, Dr. Howard M.	10.00	32.50	55.00	15.00
Tesla, Nikola	70.00	125.00	263.00	95.00
Ting, Dr. Samuel C. C.	10.00	20.00	45.00	15.00
Tombaugh, Clyde W.	11.00	20.00	30.00	15.00
Townes, Charles H.	8.00	16.00	50.00	
Tyndall, John	20.00	50.00	90.50	
Urey, Harold C.	19.17	35.00	65.00	45.00
Van Allen, James	20.00	45.00	85.00	25.00
Vigneaud, Vincent du	8.00	24.00	46.00	10.00
Volta, Alessandro	165.00	575.00	1,150.00	
Waksman, Selman A.	35.50	55.00	90.00	60.00
Walker, Dr. Mary	150.00	235.00	470.00	400.00
Wassel, Dr. C. M.	40.00	75.00	150.00	50.00
Watson, Dr. James D.	5.00	20.00	50.00	10.00
Watson, Thomas Augustus	45.00	120.00	250.00	500.00
Watt, James	270.00	870.00	1,525.00	
Weizmann, Chaim	365.00	975.00	2,075.00	750.00
Weller, Dr. Thomas H.	5.00	20.00	45.00	10.00
Whipple, George H.	40.00	65.00	130.00	
Whitney, Eli	475.00	848.33	1,475.00	
Wiesel, Dr. Torsten S.	5.00	7.00	12.00	5.00
Wigner, Dr. Eugene P.	3.00	5.00	7.00	5.00
Wilkinson, Geoffrey	7.00	20.00	40.00	9.00
Wilson, Dr. Robert	10.00	15.00	25.00	20.00
Woodward, R. B.	10.00	35.00	85.00	15.00
Yalon, Rosalyn S.	10.00	15.00	25.00	10.00

Name	Signature Only	Letter or Document Signed	Autograph Letter Signed	Signed Photograph
Yang, Dr. C. N.	5.00	15.00	25.00	10.00
Ziegler, Karl	10.00	30.00	58.00	12.00
Zworykin, Vladimir	37.00	100.00	120.00	50.00

U.S. Presidents

Until November of 1988, Presidential autograph collecting will be limited to 40 names. Still, the signatures of these 40 men are widely sought. A signature from *any* president, therefore, is obviously worth considerable money.

Name	Signature Only	Letter or Document Signed	Autograph Letter Signed	Signed Photograph
Adams, John	$1,028.50	$1,375.00	$5,681.25	
Adams, John Quincy	246.20	490.91	956.25	$1,500.00
Arthur, Chester A.	266.67	640.00	1,092.50	
Atchison, David R.	200.00	350.00	975.00	
Buchanan, James	205.00	455.00	1,166.88	
Carter, Jimmy	142.00	245.00	1,125.00	183.89
Cleveland, Grover	125.00	288.57	452.50	387.50
Coolidge, Calvin	133.50	281.11	1,550.00	320.00
Eisenhower, Dwight D.	201.25	350.00	1,310.00	343.33
Fillmore, Millard	195.57	328.75	653.23	6,000.00
Ford, Gerald R.	105.00	177.69	740.00	166.25
Garfield, James A.	163.75	413.33	567.14	1,500.00
Grant, Ulysses S.	182.50	455.71	1,234.33	1,320.00
Harding, Warren G.	175.00	304.60	1,416.67	350.00
Harrison, Benjamin	149.00	401.36	875.00	
Harrison, William Henry	315.00	804.17	2,225.00	
Hayes, Rutherford B.	128.13	373.75	828.33	2,500.00
Hoover, Herbert	78.00	176.94	2,666.67	344.00
Jackson, Andrew	286.67	860.00	3,053.13	
Jefferson, Thomas	1,431.25	4,312.50	6,705.56	
Johnson, Andrew	266.67	441.88	5,166.67	2,250.00
Johnson, Lyndon B.	150.00	250.00	1,060.00	250.00
Kennedy, John F.	592.50	700.00	4,225.00	1,133.33
Lincoln, Abraham	1,787.00	2,723.18	4,067.50	
Madison, James	325.00	1,098.89	2,620.00	

J. Adams
John Adams

J. Q. Adams.
John Quincy Adams

Chester A. Arthur

David R. Atchison
David R. Atchison—
President of the U.S. for One Day

respectfully your friend
James Buchanan
James Buchanan

Jimmy Carter
Jimmy Carter

Dwight Eisenhower
Dwight D. Eisenhower

Grover Cleveland
Grover Cleveland

Calvin Coolidge
Calvin Coolidge

Millard Fillmore
Millard Fillmore

Gerald R. Ford
Gerald R. Ford

J. A. Garfield
James A. Garfield

Charles Guiteau
Charles Guiteau—Assassin of President Garfield

U. S. Grant
U. S. Grant

Warren G. Harding
Defendant
Warren G. Harding

Benj Harrison
Benjamin Harrison

Wm H. Harrison
William Henry Harrison

R B Hayes
Rutherford B. Hayes

Herbert Hoover
Herbert Hoover

Andrew Johnson
Andrew Johnson

Andrew Jackson
Andrew Jackson

Abraham Lincoln
Abraham Lincoln

Lyndon Johnson
Lyndon Johnson

Sincerely yours,
John F. Kennedy

Dolley Madison
Dolley Madison

James Madison
James Madison

William McKinley

James Monroe

Richard Nixon

James K. Polk

Franklin Pierce

Ronald Reagan

Theodore Roosevelt

Franklin D. Roosevelt

William Howard Taft

Zachary Taylor

Harry S. Truman

John Tyler

Martin Van Buren

George Washington

Woodrow Wilson

Name	Signature Only	Letter or Document Signed	Autograph Letter Signed	Signed Photograph
McKinley, William	270.00	378.13	955.00	900.00
Monroe, James	292.00	570.67	2,445.00	
Nixon, Richard M.	130.36	245.31	6,250.00	203.85
Pierce, Franklin	191.43	556.25	1,087.50	
Polk, James K.	325.00	1,137.50	2,875.00	
Reagan, Ronald	123.13	213.00	1,467.86	201.50
Roosevelt, Franklin D.	295.00	354.74	1,013.89	612.08
Roosevelt, Theodore	198.57	350.88	1,060.55	700.00
Taft, William Howard	165.71	258.18	666.88	365.00
Taylor, Zachary	513.00	908.33	4,596.00	
Truman, Harry S.	117.50	268.94	1,850.00	259.09
Tyler, John	247.50	400.00	969.17	
Van Buren, Martin	200.00	506.67	747.14	
Washington, George	2,362.50	9,650.00	18,860.00	
Wilson, Woodrow	190.00	316.82	1,737.50	491.67

U.S. Vice-Presidents and Cabinet Members

Here is the pricing for American vice-presidents and cabinet members. This is a fascinating area of autograph collecting which is only now beginning to come into its real potential.

Name	Signature Only	Letter or Document Signed	Autograph Letter Signed	Signed Photograph
Acheson, Dean	$ 18.00	$ 32.50	$ 107.50	$ 25.00
Adams, Charles Francis	15.00	25.00	45.00	
Adams, Sherman	20.67	30.00	102.33	50.00
Agnew, Spiro (V)	17.50	63.00		38.33
Alexander, Joshua Wallis	18.00	38.00		
Alger, Russell	15.00	25.00		
Anderson, Robert B.	5.00	11.67	35.00	15.00
Andrus, Cecil D.	5.00	10.00	35.00	15.00
Armstrong, John	40.00	88.00	250.00	
Bacon, Robert	15.00	25.00		
Badger, George E.	5.00	15.00	25.00	
Baker, Newton D.	20.00	45.00	55.00	
Baldridge, Malcolm	10.00	15.00		
Ballinger, Richard A.	8.00	25.00	50.00	20.00
Bank, C. D.	10.00			
Barkley, Alben W. (V)	12.50	31.60	80.00	50.00
Barr, Joseph W.	5.00	15.00	27.50	
Bates, Edward	30.00	80.00	179.60	
Bayard, Thomas F.	10.00	20.00	40.00	
Belknap, William W.	15.00	40.00	75.00	
Bell, Griffin	5.00	15.00	35.00	15.00
Bell, John	10.00	25.00	50.00	
Bell, Terrel H.	5.00	12.00	26.00	10.00
Benson, Ezra Taft	16.67	28.33	60.00	25.00
Bergland, Bob	3.00	10.00	20.00	10.00
Berrien, J. Macpherson	10.00	38.00	55.00	
Bibb, George M.	10.00	25.00	45.00	
Biddle, Francis	15.00	26.67	60.00	25.00
Bingham, John Armor	15.00	35.00	80.00	
Blaine, James G.	13.00	25.00	55.00	20.00
Bliss, Cornelius	8.00	25.00	55.00	40.00
Block, John R.	4.00	10.00	15.00	10.00
Blount, Winton M.	4.00	7.50	12.00	5.00
Blumenthal, W. Michael	4.00	9.00	15.00	13.00
Boutwell, George S.	15.00	15.00	33.33	30.00

Name	Signature Only	Letter or Document Signed	Autograph Letter Signed	Signed Photograph
Bowles, Chester	7.00	15.00	35.00	15.00
Bradford, William	115.00	215.00	590.00	
Branch, John	10.00	30.00	60.00	
Breckinridge, John (V)	75.00	250.00		
Bristow, B. H.	15.00	45.00	100.00	
Brownell, Herbert Jr.	10.00	18.00	37.00	16.00
Bryan, William Jennings	15.00	61.25	202.86	187.50
Burleson, Albert S.	10.00			
Burr, Aaron (V)	167.50	321.25	708.00	
Bush, George (V)	35.00	65.00	140.00	55.00
Butler, Benjamin F.	10.00	55.00	125.00	
Butz, Earl L.	5.00	12.50	30.00	25.00
Calhoun, John C. (V)	112.50	274.00	320.00	500.00
Cameron, Simon	45.00	87.50	100.00	
Campbell, George W.	45.00	130.00	290.00	
Carter, Hodding	4.00	8.00	12.00	15.00
Cass, Lewis	20.00	58.00	155.00	
Chandler, William E.	10.00	38.33	33.75	
Chandler, Zachariah	10.00	30.00	70.00	
Chapman, Oscar L.	10.00	15.00	20.00	10.00
Civiletti, Benjamin	5.00	10.00	20.00	10.00
Clay, Henry	88.00	149.17	335.45	245.00
Clifford, Clark M.	4.00	10.00	15.00	15.00
Cohen, Wilbur J.	5.00	7.00	12.00	10.00
Colfax, Schuyler (V)	15.00	63.00	85.83	
Connelly, Matthew J.	7.00	20.00	30.00	15.00
Connor, John T.	6.00	20.00	35.00	15.00
Conrad, Charles Magill	5.00	20.00	40.00	
Conway, Rose A.	2.00	5.00	10.00	4.00
Coolidge, T. Jefferson	4.00	9.00	20.00	
Crawford, William H.	25.00	70.00	150.00	
Creswell, John A. J.	15.00	20.00	27.00	
Crowley, Leo	3.00	5.00	10.00	5.00
Crowninshield, Benjamin W.	25.00	75.00	170.00	
Cummings, Homer	12.50	33.00	75.00	75.00
Curtis, Charles (V)	22.50	67.50	150.00	80.00
Cushing, Caleb	17.00	42.50	75.20	
Dallas, Alexander J.	10.00	25.00	50.00	
Dallas, George M. (V)	25.00	150.00	165.00	
Daniels, Josephus	20.00	60.17	140.00	118.00
Daugherty, Harry M.	20.00	48.00	110.00	45.00
Davis, Dwight F.	16.00	77.50	170.00	65.00
Davis, James J.	15.00	40.75	85.00	35.00
Dawes, Charles G. (V)	13.00	75.00	165.00	65.00
Day, J. Edward	3.00	5.00	11.25	5.00
Dearborn, Henry M.	40.00	65.00	200.00	
Denby, Edwin	10.00	30.00	65.00	30.00
Devens, Charles	5.00	30.00	23.25	10.00
Dickenson, Don M.	15.00	20.00	45.00	20.00
Dickerson, Mahlon	10.00	30.33	65.00	
Dillon, C. Douglas	5.67	15.00	25.00	15.00
Dobbin, James C.	20.00	50.00	110.00	

Name	Signature Only	Letter or Document Signed	Autograph Letter Signed	Signed Photograph
Dodd, William E.	10.00	50.00	50.00	20.00
Dole, Elizabeth	4.00	8.00	20.00	20.00
Donaldson, Jesse M.	10.00	15.00	33.00	10.00
Dulles, John Foster	20.00	86.67	125.00	50.00
Dunlop, John T.	5.00	10.00	15.00	15.00
Eaton, John	5.00	15.00	35.00	
Eaton, John Henry	5.00	25.00	46.36	
Edison, Charles	10.00	20.00	45.00	15.00
Edwards, James	10.00	15.00	35.00	10.00
Eizenstat, Stuart E.	4.00	8.00	12.00	10.00
Elkins, Stephen B.	10.00	25.00	55.00	20.00
Endicott, William C.	15.00	22.00	35.00	15.00
Eustis, William	25.00	67.00	150.00	
Evarts, William M.	16.25	58.00	150.00	20.00
Everett, Edward	10.00	20.00	130.00	
Ewing, Thomas	35.00	105.00	215.00	
Fairbanks, Charles W. (V)	15.00	56.67	83.33	20.00
Fairchild, Charles S.	15.00	30.00	55.00	35.00
Fall, Albert B.	40.00	70.00	150.00	60.00
Farley, James A.	10.00	30.00	70.00	26.25
Fessenden, W. P.	10.00	40.00	88.00	
Finletter, Thomas A.	5.00	12.00	30.00	15.00
Fish, Hamilton	17.50	50.13	105.00	
Floyd, John B.	15.00	25.00	50.00	
Folger, Charles J.	5.00	15.00	30.00	15.00
Forrestal, James	45.00	62.50	125.00	50.00
Forsyth, John	15.00	48.50	95.00	
Foster, Charles	15.00	45.00	85.00	
Foster, John W.	5.00	15.00	30.00	
Fowler, Henry	5.00	20.00	30.00	15.00
Freeman, Orville	5.00	15.00	22.00	10.00
Frelinghuysen, Frederick	15.00	43.00	90.00	40.00
Gage, Lyman J.	10.00	21.67	45.00	30.00
Gallatin, Albert	50.00	151.00	225.00	
Gardner, John W.	5.00	15.00	31.00	10.00
Garfield, James R.	10.00	35.00	70.00	30.00
Garner, John Nance (V)	30.17	41.67	152.50	100.00
Garrison, Lindley M.	5.00	15.00	35.00	15.00
Glass, Carter	10.00	40.00	55.00	20.00
Goldschmidt, Neil	4.00	11.00	28.00	15.00
Good, James W.	15.00	25.00	30.00	15.00
Graham, John	55.00	170.00	350.00	
Graham, William A.	15.00	33.00	72.00	
Granger, Gideon	25.00	65.00	135.00	
Gresham, Walter Q.	12.50	30.00	60.00	
Hamilton, Alexander	295.00	565.63	1,883.75	
Hamlin, Hannibal (V)	33.83	100.00	202.78	
Hardin, Clifford M.	5.00	10.00	18.00	10.00
Harlan, James A.	15.00	35.00	65.00	
Harmon, Judson	5.00	20.00	35.00	15.00
Harriman, W. Averell	10.00	22.50	65.00	20.00

Name	Signature Only	Letter or Document Signed	Autograph Letter Signed	Signed Photograph
Harris, Patricia Roberts	5.00	15.00	26.00	20.00
Hay, John	25.00	93.00	187.50	35.00
Heller, Walter W.	5.00	15.00	30.00	15.00
Hendricks, Thomas A. (V)	23.00	100.00	136.67	
Henshaw, David	5.00	20.00	35.00	
Herbert, Hilary A.	8.00	15.00	35.00	15.00
Hickel, Walter	10.00	15.00	30.00	15.00
Hills, Carla A.	5.00	15.00	35.00	12.00
Hitchcock, Frank H.	10.00	30.00	35.00	20.00
Hobart, Garret A. (V)	15.00	150.00	275.00	75.00
Hobby, Oveta Culp	10.00	20.00	40.00	30.00
Holt, Joseph	50.00	150.00		
House, Edward M.	10.00	25.00	55.00	20.00
Hufstedler, Shirley	5.00	10.00	14.50	5.00
Hughes, Charles Evans	14.00	38.00	80.00	30.00
Hull, Cordell	15.00	37.86	85.00	30.00
Humphrey, Hubert H. (V)	15.00	35.60	75.00	39.50
Hunt, William H.	9.00	30.00	55.00	20.00
Hurley, Patrick	15.00	46.00	60.00	25.00
Hyde, Arthur W.	7.00	15.00	30.00	10.00
Ickes, Harold L.	12.50	30.33	60.00	25.00
Ingham, Samuel	25.00	58.00	105.00	
James, Thomas L.	8.00	20.00	40.00	
Jardine, William	10.00	25.00	55.00	20.00
Jay, John	100.00	485.00	1,212.50	
Jenkins, Thornton Alexander	4.00	20.00	25.00	
Jewell, Marshall	5.00	25.00	25.00	
Johnson, Cave	30.00	78.00	175.00	
Johnson, Hugh S.	10.00	15.00	25.00	10.00
Johnson, Louis	10.00	45.00	55.00	20.00
Johnson, Reverdy	15.00	40.00	75.00	
Johnson, Richard H. (V)	20.00	60.00	125.00	
Jones, Jesse H.	3.00	7.00	12.00	5.00
Jordan, Hamilton	4.00	10.00	13.00	10.00
Kellogg, Frank B.	15.00	46.25	80.00	20.00
Kendall, Amos	15.00	40.00	82.50	
Kennedy, John P.	25.00	30.00	50.00	
Kennedy, Robert F.	113.40	167.50	440.00	241.25
Key, David M.	10.00	12.00	20.00	
King, Horatio	10.00	20.00	40.00	
King, William R. (V)		250.00		
Kirkpatrick, Jean J.	4.00	10.00	25.00	20.00
Kirkwood, Samuel J.	10.00	23.00	48.00	30.00
Kissinger, Henry	10.00	35.00	85.00	35.00
Kleppe, Thomas S.	7.50	20.00	40.00	15.00
Knox, Frank	9.00	125.00	80.00	20.00
Knox, Henry	100.00	475.00	525.00	
Knox, Philander C.	10.00	25.00	65.00	25.00
Kreps, Juanita M.	4.00	9.00	15.00	11.00
Laird, Melvin	6.00	18.00	22.00	10.00
Lamont, Daniel S.	5.00	10.00	20.00	17.50
Lance, Bert	3.00	5.00	15.00	10.00

Name	Signature Only	Letter or Document Signed	Autograph Letter Signed	Signed Photograph
Landrieu, Moon	3.00	5.00	10.00	10.00
Lansing, Robert	12.00	20.00	30.00	15.00
LeHand, M. A. (Missy)	15.00	46.67	85.00	35.00
Lee, Charles	100.00	230.00	612.50	
Levi, Edward H.	7.00	25.00	45.00	10.00
Lincoln, Robert Todd	57.50	125.00	160.20	
Livingston, Edward	20.00	60.00	120.00	
Livingston, Robert R.	170.00	250.00	1,083.33	
Lodge, Henry Cabot	4.00	15.00	25.00	10.00
Long, John D.	5.00	27.00	35.00	15.00
Lovett, Robert	5.00	10.00	20.63	10.00
MacVeagh, Franklin	7.00	24.00	55.00	20.00
Marcy, William L.	20.00	53.33	117.50	
Marshall, Thomas R. (V)	60.00	125.00	385.00	90.00
McAdoo, William G.	20.00	80.50	130.00	50.00
McCulloch, Hugh	24.00	65.00	50.00	
McHenry, James	135.00	205.00	375.00	
McIntyre, Marvin H.	3.00	10.00	15.00	
McLane, Louis	10.00	41.67	50.00	
McNamara, Robert S.	10.00	20.00	45.00	15.33
Meese, Edwin III	5.00	20.00	35.00	15.00
Meredith, Edwin T.	5.00	20.00	30.00	15.00
Meredith, Samuel	30.00	85.00	195.00	
Meyer, George von L.	13.00	20.00	28.00	17.50
Miller, William H. H.	10.00	30.00	50.00	20.00
Mills, Ogden L.	5.00	25.00	30.00	10.00
Mitchell, John	35.00			40.00
Mitchell, William D.	4.00	25.00	30.00	10.00
Mondale, Walter (V)	25.00	83.50	120.00	39.20
Morgenthau, Henry, Jr.	10.00	35.00	50.00	35.00
Morrill, Lot M.	15.00	25.00	50.00	
Morton, J. Sterling	20.00	45.71	125.00	75.00
Morton, Levi P. (V)	28.00	65.00	110.00	237.50
Muskie, Edmund	10.00	16.00	40.00	15.00
Neff, Francine I.	4.00	10.00	23.00	10.00
New, Harry	15.33	20.00	40.00	15.00
Newberry, Truman H.	10.00	17.00	30.00	
Noble, John W.	16.00	50.00	105.00	95.00
O'Brien, Lawrence F.	5.00	12.00	30.00	10.00
Olney, Richard	10.00	25.00	45.00	30.00
Ortega, Katherine D.	3.00	8.00	20.00	8.00
Palmer, A. Mitchell	5.00	25.00	36.00	30.00
Paulding, James Kirke	20.00	55.00	113.00	
Payne, Henry C.	12.00	20.00	28.00	
Payne, T. H. (Acting)	4.00	25.00		
Perkins, Frances	12.00	65.00	135.00	55.00
Persons, Wilton B.	3.00	15.00	20.00	
Phillips, William (Undersecretary)	3.00	15.00	20.00	
Pickering, Timothy	46.00	154.17	304.45	
Pierrepont, Edwards	15.00	45.00	88.00	
Pinkney, William	45.00	130.00	263.00	

Name	Signature Only	Letter or Document Signed	Autograph Letter Signed	Signed Photograph
Poinsett, Joel R.	40.00	118.00	242.00	
Porter, James M.	20.00	65.00	130.00	
Porter, John Addison	10.00	30.00		
Preston, William B.	15.00	40.00	95.00	
Priest, Ivy Baker	10.00	15.00	30.00	18.00
Proctor, Redfield	5.00	20.00	35.00	25.00
Ramsey, Alexander	15.00	40.00	88.00	
Randolph, Edmund J.	60.00	275.00	360.00	
Rawlins, John A.	25.00	75.00	150.00	
Redfield, William C.	10.00	20.00	42.00	15.00
Reedy, George	3.00	15.00	20.00	5.00
Regan, Donald	5.00	10.00	25.00	15.00
Ribicoff, Abraham	5.00	10.00	25.00	15.00
Richards, J. K. (Acting)	3.00	15.00	25.00	
Richardson, Elliot	7.00	25.00	50.00	15.00
Richardson, William A.	15.00	50.00	85.00	
Richey, Lawrence	3.00	10.00		
Robeson, George M.	10.00	50.33	80.00	
Rockefeller, Nelson (V)	14.00	40.86	130.00	37.50
Rodney, Caesar	115.00	500.00	710.00	
Rogers, William P.	12.00	21.50	40.00	24.00
Root, Elihu	15.00	40.25	65.00	40.00
Roper, Daniel	10.00	25.00	35.00	15.00
Rowe, Leo S. (Assistant Secretary)	5.00	20.00	35.00	10.00
Rumsfeld, Donald	10.00	20.00	45.00	15.00
Rush, Richard	30.00	82.50	170.50	
Rusk, Dean	21.67	35.00	80.00	17.50
Rusk, Jeremiah M.	15.00	40.00	85.00	
Salinger, Pierre	5.00	15.00	35.00	12.00
Sargent, John G.	12.00	28.75	60.00	25.00
Sawyer, Charles	5.00	25.00	30.00	10.00
Saxbe, William B.	6.00	10.00	20.00	15.00
Schlesinger, James R.	5.00	10.00	25.00	12.00
Schwellenback, Lewis B.	10.00	32.00	70.00	10.00
Seward, F. W. (Assistant Secretary)	15.00	40.00		
Seward, William H.	30.00	62.00	133.50	235.00
Sherman, James S. (V)	38.00	55.00	135.00	150.00
Sherman, John	12.80	31.00	45.75	
Shriver, Sargent	4.00	10.00	22.00	12.00
Shultz, George P.	10.00	25.00	55.00	20.00
Simon, William E.	5.00	15.00	25.00	20.00
Smith, Caleb	25.00	70.00	140.50	
Smith, Charles Emory	10.00	15.00	25.00	20.00
Smith, Hoke	10.00	31.67	65.00	25.00
Smith, Robert	40.00	150.00	238.00	
Speakes, Larry	4.00	10.00	16.00	10.00
Speed, James	30.00	45.00	85.00	
Spencer, John C.	10.00	30.00	60.00	
Spinner, Francis Elias	15.00	43.00	55.00	675.00

Name	Signature Only	Letter or Document Signed	Autograph Letter Signed	Signed Photograph
Stanbery, Henry	10.00	20.00	40.00	
Stanton, Edwin M.	33.67	152.50	225.00	138.00
Stettinius, Edward R., Jr.	30.00	88.67	190.00	40.00
Stevenson, Adlai	13.00	36.00	287.50	20.00
Stevenson, Adlai E., Sr. (V)	25.00	65.00	118.67	148.00
Stimson, Henry L.	15.00	100.00	205.00	35.00
Stoddert, Benjamin	70.00	300.00	450.00	
Strauss, Robert	4.00	12.00	20.00	10.00
Stuart, Alexander H. H.	15.00	25.00	50.00	
Summerfield, Arthur E.	10.00	20.00	30.00	20.00
Swanson, Claude	10.00	25.00	55.00	20.00
Symington, Stuart	5.00	15.00	32.00	15.00
Teller, Henry M.	15.00	20.00	40.00	15.00
Thompson, Jacob	10.00	30.00	70.00	
Thompson, Richard W.	10.00	30.00	45.00	
Tompkins, Daniel (V)		296.25	166.67	
Toucey, Isaac	10.00	30.00	45.00	
Tracy, Benjamin F.	10.00	30.00	50.00	
Tully, Grace G.	10.00	21.67	46.00	20.00
Tumulty, Joseph P.	5.00	17.00	37.00	15.00
Tyner, James N.	10.00	40.00	75.00	
Upshur, Abel Parker	10.00	40.00	68.00	
Usher, John P.	35.00	95.00	195.00	
Vance, Cyrus	10.00	15.00	35.00	20.00
Volcker, Paul A.	3.00	5.00	7.00	10.00
Walker, Frank C.	3.00	9.00	20.00	10.00
Wallace, Henry A. (V)	17.00	58.75	140.00	60.00
Wallace, Henry C.	7.00	25.00	45.00	20.00
Watt, James	3.00	10.00	20.00	12.00
Weaver, Robert C.	4.00	10.00	20.00	10.00
Webster, Daniel	92.00	237.50	350.00	310.00
Weinberger, Casper	5.00	10.00	25.00	10.00
Welles, Gideon	40.20	120.00	233.75	
Welles, Sumner	25.00	67.50	160.00	60.00
Whitney, William C.	13.00	25.00	57.50	25.00
Wickersham, George W.	15.00	30.00	50.00	
Wilbur, Curtis D.	10.00	25.00	30.00	
Wilbur, Ray Lyman	10.00	25.00	55.00	19.00
Wilson, George Henry	15.00	50.00	95.00	130.00
Wilson, Henry (V)	31.00	90.00	105.00	
Wilson, James	9.00	30.00	57.00	
Windom, William	25.00	25.00	38.00	30.00
Wirt, William	20.00	65.00	130.00	
Wolcott, Oliver, Jr.	25.00	54.67	172.50	
Woodring, Henry H.	10.00	25.00	50.00	20.00
Work, Hubert	20.00	45.00	110.00	30.00
Wright, Luke E.	15.00	45.00	90.00	35.00
Ziegler, Ronald L.	4.00	10.00	25.00	30.00

15
A Final Word on Pricing

Every effort has been made to provide as accurate an accounting of prices as is humanly possible. We have retrieved thousands and thousands of figures, tabulated them, averaged them, and entered them into what has become our permanent database.

These raw numbers have come from every corner of our country as well as from Great Britain, France, Germany, Switzerland, and Scandinavia. We have selectively incorporated the prices of *nonspecialized* material. By that we mean letters, documents, and so forth that do not contain or illustrate important historical content. Letters by composers discussing music, by scientists theorizing about their field of expertise, or by authors, artists, military personnel, aviators, politicians, and so on doing likewise would be some examples of specialized material. We cannot put a price on this type of content. Its importance could double, triple, or quadruple the value of an otherwise moderately priced item.

We have also excluded signed musical quotations, literary quotations, and signed manuscripts because these, too, have special added value. Space does not allow us to include them in this issue of Wallace-Homestead's *Price Guide to Autographs.*

Please note that the presidential entries included here are nonpresidential. Presidentially signed pieces have considerably more value (in most cases) than nonpresidential ones. That even extends to signed White House or Executive Mansion cards.

When possible, the Civil War letters and documents reported are, for the most part, pre- or postwar. Some material is, of course, only available with war dates, and in the case of extreme rarity in any category, we have reported the price(s) available.

We have presented to you "The Market." We have not *created* this market; therefore you may find among these thousands of entries some incongruities, whereby an Autograph Signed Letter is priced lower than a Letter Signed/Document Signed, or Signed Photographs are significantly more valuable in a specific category because of particular group interest.

You will find bargains available where certain autographs in a category are priced far below others of equal importance, rarity, and collectibility.

These numbers have all been recorded to serve as *guides*. They are not cast in cement. They are not constants. Unlike stamps, every autograph is an original work of art. Each one is different, and consequently, the value of each piece varies. There is no *standard* price. These prices comprise an average of many prices and should be referred to accordingly, with the reader taking into account the possible range of a given price to determine the level of value that a particular item warrants. The higher the printed price, the wider the fluctuation (both up and down) you can anticipate. The *relative* value among autographs will also be of interest and help.

These figures are not reflections of a particular autograph personality's ability, talent, intelligence, greatness, or beauty. They represent material—presented to the public from all over the world—that a knowledgeable buyer should be able to purchase from a knowledgeable seller.

Because of the vastness and ad infinitum concept of this book, there may be errors. For these we apologize. Further, we take no responsibility for quoting others' published prices in the compilation of our data. We can, however, sincerely hope that this book will be of assistance to you in either your hobby or your business and that subsequent volumes will keep you in touch with the autograph marketplace as we bring you additional entries and updated quotes.

Appendix
Addresses of Autograph Dealers

Abraham Lincoln Book Shop
Dan Weinberg
18 E. Chestnut St.
Chicago, IL 60611
(312) 944-3085

ADS Autographs
Joseph R. Sakmyster
P.O. Box 8006
Webster, NY 14580
(716) 671-2651

William H. Allen, Bookseller
2031 Walnut St.
Philadelphia, PA 19103
(215) 563-3398

American Museum of
Historical Documents
Todd Axelrod
3601 West Sahara Ave.
Las Vegas, NV 89102
(702) 364-1000

Raleigh DeGeer Amyx
2103 Sheriff Ct.
Vienna, VA 22180

Antebellum Covers
P.O. Box 3494
Gaithersburg, MD 20878-0494
(301) 869-2623

Antique Paper Emporium
Frank Matthews
3798 N. Bern
Flagstaff, AZ 86001
(602) 526-6587

Antiquities Ltd.
Rhodes T. Rumsey
607 State St.
Greensboro, NC 27405
(919) 275-2122

Charles Apfelbaum
39 Flower Rd.
Valley Stream, NY 11581
(516) 791-2801 and (212) 783-4466

W. Graham Arader III
Neale Lanigan, Director
1308 Walnut St.
Philadelphia, PA 19107
(215) 735-8811

Archives
119 Chestnut Hill Rd.
Wilton, CT 06897
(203) 226-3920

Autograph Alcove
Bill Luetge and Jim Twelmeyer
6907 W. North Ave.
Wauwatosa, WI 53213
(414) 771-7844

Autograph House
George and Helen Sanders
P.O. Box 658
Enka, NC 28728
(704) 667-9835

Autographia
Dr. Elizabeth Hazelton-Vincent
P.O. Box 2912
San Rafael, CA 94912-2912
(415) 499-0313

Autograph International
PostBoks 8
Molia 1, N-6200 Stranda
Oslo
Norway
47-71-60-970

Autographs of America
Tim Anderson
P.O. Box 461
Provo, UT 84603
(801) 374-1888

Autos & Autos
B. C. West, Jr.
P.O. Box 280
Elizabeth City, NC 27909
(919) 335-1117

Conway Barker
P.O. Box 670625
Dallas, TX 75367-0625
(214) 358-3786

Catherine Barnes
P.O. Box 30117
Philadelphia, PA 19103

James Barnes Studio
Gary D. Eyler
8056 Pantano Pl.
Alexandria, VA 22302
(703) 799-0448

Robert F. Bachelder
1 West Butler Ave.
Ambler, PA 19002
(215) 643-1430

Leon Becker
7624 El Camino Rd.
Carlsbad, CA 92008
(619) 436-2321

Walter R. Benjamin Autographs
Mary Benjamin
255 Scribner Hollow Rd.
Hunter, NY 12442
(518) 263-4133

Susan and Patrick Bennett
P.O. Box 5
Maggie Valley, NC 28751
(704) 926-0715

Bickerstaff's
William H. Itoh
6020 N. 16th St.
Arlington, VA 22205
(703) 534-5077

B. J. S. Autographs
P.O. Box 886
Forest Hills, NY 11375
(718) 897-7275

Norman Boas
6 Brandon Ln.
Mystic, CT 06355

Edward N. Bomsey
7317 Farr St.
Annandale, VA 22003-2516
(703) 642-2040

Robert S. Brunk Auction Services
Robert S. Brunk
Rt. 2, Box 296
Weaverville, NC 28787
(704) 626-2955

Captain's Bookshelf, Inc.
Chandler Gordon
26½ Battery Park Ave.
Asheville, NC 28801
(704) 253-6631

Cohasco, Inc.
Postal 821
Yonkers, NY 10702

Collectors' Choice Ltd.
Will Paulsen
406 E. Water St.
Charlottesville, VA 22901

Connecticut Historical Center
Alan Levi
P.O. Box 2842
Stamford, CT 06906
(203) 637-0126

Herman Darvick Autograph Auctions
Herman Darvick
P.O. Box 467
Rockville Centre, NY 11571-0467
(516) 766-0093

Roy Deeley
2 Rosemary Crescent
Worplesdon Rd.
Guilford, Surrey
England

Kevin Brian Dooley Autographs
Diamond Rock Hill
Malvern, PA 19355

Sophie Dupre
14 The Green, Calne
Wilts SN11 8DQ
England
(0249) 816-793

East Coast Books (Auction)
Kay and Marv Slotnik
P.O. Box 849
Wells, ME 04090
(207) 646-3584

Gene Elliott
47 Rue de la Fontaine au Roi
75011 Paris
France

Joan Enders
7305 Aztec NE
Albuquerque, NM 87110

Frederick M. Evans
P.O. Box 367
Havre de Grace, MD 21078
(301) 838-1295

Federal Hill Autographs
P.O. Box 6405
Baltimore, MD 21230

Fricelli Associates
Joe Fricelli
P.O. Box 247, Bath Beach Station
Brooklyn, NY 11214

Gifts of Americana
Peter Paul Morgus
105 Oakwood Pl.
Hendersonville, NC 28739

Phillis Goldman
404 E. 75th St.
New York, NY 10021

Jack B. Good
P.O. Box 4462
Ft. Lauderdale, FL 33338
(305) 564-7390

Jerry Granat
1481 Stevenson Rd.
Hewlett, NY 11557
(516) 374-7809

Charles and Diane Hamilton
127 E. 59th St. (Ste. 201)
New York, NY 10022

Harmer-Rooke Autographs
Richard Gordon
3 E. 57th St.
New York, NY 10022
(212) 751-1900

Doris Harris
5410 Wilshire Blvd.
Los Angeles, CA 90036
(213) 939-4500

Paul Hartunian
65 Christopher St.
Montclair, NJ 07042
(201) 746-9132

Jim Hayes, Antiquarian
P.O. Box 12557
James Island, SC
(803) 795-0732

Gary Hendershott
1637 E. 15th St.
Little Rock, AK 72202

Swede Holmberg
175 Supreme Ct.
Lawrenceville, GA 30245

Jeanne Hoyt Autographs
P.O. Box 1517
Rohnert Park, CA 94928-1112
(707) 584-4077

Hudson Rogue Company
255 Main St.
Nelsonville, NY 10516
(914) 265-2211

JFF Autographs Inc.
Joe Fawls
P.O. Box U
Manhasset, NY 11030

Scott G. Kalcik
1533 River Road
Wisconsin Dells, WI 53965
(608) 254-7751 and (312) 788-9022

Christine and Roger Katcham
509 1st St.
Tryon, NC 28782
(704) 859-5055

Brian Kathenes
P.O. Box 77296
West Trenton, NJ 08628
(609) 530-1350

Daniel F. Kelleher Co., Inc.
40 Broad St. (Ste. 830)
Boston, MA 02109
(617) 742-0883

Peter and Susan Kerville
Box 5454, Gold Coast Mail Centre
Queensland 4217, Tre 4217
Australia

Sy Kessler
16 Sleepy Ln.
Hicksville, NY 11801

Stephen Koschal
P.O. Box 201
Verona, NJ 07044

Ann Krafthofer
13101 Serpentine Wy.
Silver Spring, MD 20904

Joe Kraus
P.O. Box 55328
Stockton, CA 95205

La Part du Reve
Jean-Jacques Faure
Librairie-Galérie
Case Postale 397
1211 Genève 11
Switzerland

LaScala Autographs, Inc.
P.O. Box 368
Hopewell, NJ 08525
(609) 466-3071

L'Autographe S.A.
5, Chemin de la Chevillarde
Ch - 1208 Genève
Switzerland
22-48-77-55

Robert A. LeGresley
P.O. Box 1199
Lawrence, KS 66044

Erroll Leslie
224 W. Washington St.
Charleston, WV 25414
(304) 725-7512

Les Neuf Muses
Alain Nicolas
41 Quai des Grands Augustins
750006 Paris
France

Librairie de l'Echiquier
Frederic Castaing
13, Rue Chapon
75003 Paris
France
274-69-09

William Linehan
Box 1203
Concord, NH 03301
(603) 224-7226

Lion Heart
David H. Lowenherz
12 W. 37th St. (Ste. 1212)
New York, NY 10018

Lone Star Autographs
Larry Vrzalik and Michael Minor
P.O. Drawer 500
Kaufman, TX 75142
(214) 563-2115

James Lowe Autographs, Ltd.
30 E. 60th St.
New York, NY 10022
(212) 759-0775

Doug Macleay
6 Glacier Crescent
Sherwood Park, Alberta T8A 2Y5
Canada
(403) 464-2377

Maggs Brothers, Ltd.
Miss Hinda Rose
50, Berkeley Sq.
London W1X 6EL
England
01-493-7160

Magic Lantern Books
Gil Moody
107 Broyles Dr.
Johnson City, TN 37601
(615) 282-6004

Manuscript Co. of Springfield
Terry and Jeanette Alford
P.O. Box 1151
Springfield, VA 22151
(703) 256-6748

Manuscript Investments
85 East Gay St.
Columbus, OH 43215
(614) 224-1442

McBride Stamp Auctions, Inc.
3653 S.E. 34th Ave.
Portland, OR 97202
(503) 239-8808

Charles and Pam McKeen
1840 N.E. 10th Ave.
Hillsboro, OR 97124
(503) 648-4977

George Robert Minkoff
R.F.D. 3, Box 147
Great Barrington, MA 01230

Monetary Investment Ltd.
Chip Muchin and Eugene Muchin
P.O. Box 17246
Milwaukee, WI 53217

Howard S. Mott, Inc.
Sheffield, MA 01257
(413) 229-2019

Winfred A. Myers Ltd.
91 St. Martin's Ln., Ste. 52
London, WC2
England
01-836-1940

National Pastime
Harvey Brandwein
93 Iselin Dr.
New Rochelle, NY 10804
(914) 576-1755

Neal's
192 Mansfield Rd.
Nottingham, NG1 3HV
England
0602-624141

Harold R. Nestler
13 Pennington Ave.
Waldwick, NJ 07463
(201) 444-7413

Dr. F. Don Nidiffer, Inc.
Dr. F. Don Nidiffer
P.O. Box 8184
Charlottesville, VA 22906
(804) 296-2067

Noble Enterprises
Donn Noble
5319 Vale
Greenville, TX 75401
(214) 455-1231

The Nostalgia Factory
Brick Market Pl.
Newport, RI 02840
(401) 849-3441

Oregon State Coin Co.
P.O. Box 89
Umpqua, OR 97486
(503) 459-4730

Ralph Paticchio
P.O. Box 129
Everett, MA 02149

Personalities Plus+
James and Karen Oleson
254 N. Paseo Campo
Anaheim Hills, CA 92807

Philadelphia Rare Books
Cynthia Davis Buffington
P.O. Box 9536
Philadelphia, PN 19124

Phillips Enterprises
Alice Phillips
28 Midwood Rd.
Rockville Centre, NY 11570
(516) 764-7084

Cordelia and Tom Platt
1598 River Rd.
Belle Mead, NJ 08502
(201) 359-7959

Robert L. Polk
4728 N. Lavergne Ave.
Chicago, IL 60630

Profiles in History
Joseph Maddalena
2049 Century Park E., #5080
Los Angeles, CA 90067
(800) 942-8856

Lynn Pruett Autographs
Rt. 3, Box 193
Beeville, TX 78102
(512) 358-2581

R & R Enterprises
Bob Eaton
P.O. Box 52
Newton Center, MA 02159
(617) 969-6040

Diana J. Rendell, Inc.
177 Collins Rd.
Waban, MA 02168
(617) 969-1774

The Kenneth W. Rendell Gallery, Inc.
Kenneth Rendell
The Place des Antiquaires
125 E. 57th St.
New York, NY 10022
(212) 935-6767

Riba Auctions, Inc.
Brian Riba
P.O. Box 53, Main St.
South Glastonbury, CT 06073
(203) 633-3076

Paul C. Richards
High Acres
Templeton, MA 01468
(800) 637-7711

Robbins' Rarities Inc.
2038C Laurens Rd.
Greenville, SC 29607
(803) 297-7948

Cedric L. Robinson
597 Palisado St.
Windsor, CT 06095
(203) 688-2582

Joseph Rubinfine
505 South Flagler Dr., Ste. 1301
West Palm Beach, FL 33401
(305) 659-7077

Rulon-Miller Books
716 N. First St.
Minneapolis, MN 55401

Michael Saks
2 Catalpa
Providence, RI 02906
(401) 272-6318

David Schulson Autographs
Four E. 64th St.
New York, NY 10021
(212) 517-8300

The Scriptorium
427 North Canon Dr.
Beverly Hills, CA 90210

Seaport Autographs
41 Tipping Rock Rd.
Stonington, CT 06378
(203) 535-1224

Searles' Autographs
Pat and Charles Searle
P.O. Box 849
Woodbine, GA 31659

R. M. Smythe & Co., Inc.
Raymond Helsel
26 Broadway
New York, NY 10004
(212) 943-1880

Christophe Stickel
1080 Sullivan Ave., #4
Daly City, CA 94015
(415) 755-4483

Sy Sussman
2962 S. Mann St.
Las Vegas, NV 89102

Swann Galleries, Inc.
George S. Lowrey
104 E. 25th St.
New York, NY 10010
(212) 254-4710

Georgia Terry Autographs
840 N.E. Cochran Ave.
Gresham, OR 97030
(503) 667-0950

Tollet and Harman
175 W. 76th St.
New York, NY 10023
(212) 877-1566

U.A.C.C. Auctions
P.O. Box 6181
Washington, DC 20044-6181

Mark Vardakis Autographs
P.O. Box 408
Coventry, RI 02816
(401) 884-2575

Virginia Stamp Auctions
P.O. Box 29066
Richmond, VA 23229
(804) 740-6214

Waverly Auctions
Dale Sorenson, Ph.D.
4931 Cordell Ave. (Ste. AA)
Bethesda, MD 20814

The Williams
9 Osborne Grove
Sherwood, Nottingham
England

John Wilson
50 Acre End St.
Eynsham, Oxford
England

Scott J. Winslow Associates
P.O. Box 6033
Nashua, NH 03063
(800) 225-6233

Wright's Coin & Stamp Shop
William J. Wright
4 South Tunnel Rd.
Asheville, NC 28805
(704) 298-5402

Garry Zimet
620 Ft. Washington Ave.
New York, NY 10040
(212) 795-6651

Zullo and Van Sickle Books
12137 Darnestown Rd.
Gaithersburg, MD 20878
(301) 963-7878

Index

Cross-Reference Index
of Autograph Values
(By Category)

Aadland, Beverly	Entertainers (Vintage)
Aaron, Henry "Hank"	Baseball
Aaron, Tommy	General Sports
Abba	Rock
Abbado, Claudio	Entertainers (Vintage)
Abbey, Edwin Austin	Artists
Abbott, Bud	Entertainers (Vintage)
Abbott, George	Entertainers (Vintage)
Abbott, Glenn	Baseball
Abbott, Lyman	Authors
Abbott, Senda (Berenson)	Basketball HoF
Abdul-Jabbar, Kareem	General Sports
Abel, Sidney	Hockey HoF
Abel, Walter	Entertainers (Vintage)
Aberdeen, Lord	Heads of State
Abernathy, Ralph	Celebrities
Abraham, F. Murray	Entertainers (Current)
Abrams, Cal	Baseball
Abrams, Creighton W.	Military
Abzug, Bella	Celebrities
Acheson, Dean	U.S. V.P. & Cabinet
Acheson, George R.	Military
Acosta, Bert	Aviation
Acuff, Roy	Country Music Stars
Adamic, Louis	Authors
Adams, Abigail	Celebrities
Adams, Ansel	Artists
Adams, Brooke	Entertainers (Current)
Adams, Charles Francis	U.S. V.P. & Cabinet
Adams, Charles	Hockey HoF
Adams, Don	Entertainers (Current)
Adams, Edie	Entertainers (Current)
Adams, Henry	Authors
Adams, Joey	Entertainers (Vintage)
Adams, John	U.S. Presidents
Adams, John	Hockey HoF
Adams, John Quincy	U.S. Presidents
Adams, Julie	Entertainers (Current)
Adams, Louisa C.	Celebrities
Adams, Maude	Entertainers (Vintage)
Adams, Nick	Entertainers (Vintage)
Adams, Red	Baseball
Adams, Samuel	Revolutionary War
Adams, Sherman	U.S. V.P. & Cabinet
Adams, Weston	Hockey HoF
Adams, William T.	Authors
Adamson, James C.	Astronauts
Adcock, Joe	Baseball
Addams, Charles	Artists
Addams, Jane	Celebrities
Adderley, Herb	Football
Addie, Pauline Betz	Tennis HoF
Addington, Henry	Heads of State
Addinsell, Richard	Composers
Addison, Joseph	Authors
Ade, George	Authors
Adee, George T.	Tennis HoF
Adenauer, Konrad	Heads of State
Adkins, Charles "Chuck"	Boxing
Adler, Alfred	Science
Adler, Luther	Entertainers (Vintage)
Adler, Max	Business
Adler, Richard	Composers
Adler, Stella	Entertainers (Vintage)
Adoree, Renee	Entertainers (Vintage)
Adrian, Iris	Entertainers (Vintage)
Adrian, Lord Edgar	Science
Aerosmith	Rock
Aga Khan III	Heads of State
Agajanian, Ben	Football
Agar, John	Entertainers (Vintage)
Agassiz, Jean Louis	Science
Agnew, Spiro (VP)	U.S. V.P. & Cabinet
Aguinaldo, Emilio	Heads of State
Aguirre, Hank	Baseball
Agutter, Jenny	Entertainers (Current)
Ahearn, Thomas "Frank"	Hockey HoF
Ahearne, John "Bunny"	Hockey HoF
Aherne, Brian	Entertainers (Vintage)
Aiken, Conrad	Authors
Aiken, George D.	Governors
Aiken, William	Governors
Ainge, Dan	Baseball
Aitken, Robert	Artists
Aitken, Robert G.	Science
Akers, Fred	Football
Akihito, Prince	Heads of State
Akin, Susan	Celebrities
Akins, Claude	Entertainers (Current)
Akins, Virgil	Boxing
Albanese, Licia	Entertainers (Vintage)
Albee, Edward	Authors
Alberghetti, Anna M.	Entertainers (Vintage)
Albert I (Belg)	Heads of State
Albert III(Rainier-Monaco	Heads of State
Albert, Eddie	Entertainers (Current)
Albert, Frank	Football
Albert, Prince(Victoria)	Heads of State
Albertson, Jack	Entertainers (Vintage)
Albertson, Joseph A.	Business
Albright, Lola	Entertainers (Vintage)
Albright, Tenley	General Sports
Albritton, Louise	Entertainers (Vintage)
Albury, Capt Chas. D	Military
Alcock, John W.	Aviation
Alcott, A. Bronson	Authors
Alcott, Amy	General Sports
Alcott, Louisa May	Authors
Alda, Alan	Entertainers (Current)
Alda, Robert	Entertainers (Vintage)
Aldrich, Thos Bailey	Authors
Aldrin, Edwin "Buzz"	Astronauts
Alen, James H. Van	Tennis HoF
Alexander I (Rus)	Heads of State
Alexander II (Rus)	Heads of State
Alexander III (Rus)	Heads of State
Alexander, Fred B.	Tennis HoF
Alexander, George	Entertainers (Vintage)
Alexander, Harold R.L.	Military
Alexander, Henry	Business

Name	Category
Alexander, Jane	Entertainers (Current)
Alexander, J. B.	Governors
Alexander, Joshua Wallis	U.S. V.P. & Cabinet
Alexander, Robert	Revolutionary War
Alexanderson, E. F. W.	Science
Alexandra (Edw VII)	Heads of State
Alexandra (Nich.II Rus.)	Heads of State
Alfonso XIII (Sp)	Heads of State
Alger, Horatio	Authors
Alger, Russell	U.S. V.P. & Cabinet
Ali, Muhammad	Boxing
Alicia, Ana	Entertainers (Current)
Allan, Buddy	Country Music Stars
Allen, Bernie	Baseball
Allen, Debbie	Entertainers (Current)
Allen, Elizabeth	Entertainers (Vintage)
Allen, Frank A., Jr.	Military
Allen, Fred	Entertainers (Vintage)
Allen, George	Football
Allen, Gracie	Entertainers (Vintage)
Allen, Grant	Authors
Allen, Henry T.	Military
Allen, Joseph P.	Astronauts
Allen, Karen	Entertainers (Current)
Allen, Marcus	Football
Allen, Mel	Baseball
Allen, Peter	Composers
Allen, Phog	Basketball HoF
Allen, Rex	Entertainers (Current)
Allen, Roderick R.	Military
Allen, Sir Montague	Hockey HoF
Allen, Steve	Entertainers (Current)
Allen, Valerie	Entertainers (Vintage)
Allen, Viola	Entertainers (Vintage)
Allen, William M.	Business
Allen, Woody	Entertainers (Current)
Allenby, Fld Marshal	Military
Allende, Salvador G.	Heads of State
Allison, Bob	Baseball
Allison, Bobby	General Sports
Allison, Wilmer L.	Tennis HoF
Allyn, Kirk	Entertainers (Current)
Allyson, June	Entertainers (Current)
Alma Tadema, Lawrence	Artists
Almond, Edw. M.	Military
Aloma, Luis	Baseball
Alonso, Manuel	Tennis HoF
Alpert, Herb	Entertainers (Current)
Alphand, Nicole H.	Celebrities
Alsop, Joseph	Celebrities
Alsop, Stewart	Celebrities
Alston, Walt	Baseball
Alsup, Bill	General Sports
Alt, Carol	Entertainers (Current)
Altgeld, John Peter	Governors
Altieri, Albert	Celebrities
Altman, Robert	Entertainers (Current)
Alvarez, Dr. Luis W.	Science
Alvarez, Roma	Entertainers (Current)
Alvord, Benjamin	Civil War
Alworth, Lance	Football
Alzado, Lyle	Football
Amalfitano, Joe	Baseball
Amaro, Ruben	Baseball
Ambers, Lou	Boxing
Ameche, Alan	Football
Ameche, Don	Entertainers (Current)
Ames, Leon	Entertainers (Vintage)
Ames, Nancy	Entertainers (Vintage)
Ames, Oliver	Governors
Amherst, Jeffrey Baron	Revolutionary War
Amin Dada, Idi	Heads of State
Amis, Kingsley	Authors
Ammen, Daniel	Civil War
Amos & Andy	Entertainers (Vintage)
Amos, Wally "Famous"	Business
Ampere, Andre Marie	Science
Amundsen, Roald	Celebrities
Ancerl, Karel	Entertainers (Vintage)
Anders, William A.	Astronauts
Andersen, Hans Christian	Authors
Anderson Jr., John	Governors
Anderson, "Bronco"	Entertainers (Vintage)
Anderson, Bill	Country Music Stars
Anderson, Brad	Cartoonists
Anderson, Carl	Cartoonists
Anderson, Dick	General Sports
Anderson, George "Sparky"	Baseball
Anderson, George W.	Military
Anderson, Harry	Entertainers (Current)
Anderson, Harold	Basketball HoF
Anderson, Jack	Authors
Anderson, John B.	Military
Anderson, Judith	Entertainers (Current)
Anderson, Ken	Football
Anderson, Laurie	Rock
Anderson, Les	Country Music Stars
Anderson, Leroy	Composers
Anderson, Lonnie	Entertainers (Current)
Anderson, Lynn	Country Music Stars
Anderson, Marian	Entertainers (Vintage)
Anderson, Maxwell	Authors
Anderson, Mary	Entertainers (Vintage)
Anderson, Paul	General Sports
Anderson, Richard	Entertainers (Current)
Anderson, Robert B.	U.S. V.P. & Cabinet
Anderson, Roy A.	Business
Anderson, Robert	Authors
Anderson, S. R.	Civil War
Anderson, Samuel E.	Military
Anderson, Sherwood	Authors
Anderson, Willie	Golf HoF
Andrade, Cisco	Boxing
Andre, John	Revolutionary War
Andress, Ursula	Entertainers (Current)
Andretti, Mario	General Sports
Andretti, Michael	General Sports
Andrew, John A.	Governors
Andrews Sisters	Entertainers (Vintage)
Andrews, Dana	Entertainers (Current)
Andrews, Julie	Entertainers (Current)
Andrews, Maxine	Entertainers (Vintage)
Andriola, Alfred	Cartoonists
Andrus, Cecil D.	U.S. V.P. & Cabinet
Andujar, Joaquin	Baseball
Anfinsen, Dr. Christ'n	Science
Angel, Heather	Entertainers (Vintage)
Angell, Sir Norman	Authors
Anglesea, Marquis of	Military
Anka, Paul	Composers
Ankers, Evelyn	Entertainers (Vintage)
Ann-Margaret	Entertainers (Current)
Anna Ivanova (Rus)	Heads of State
Annabella	Entertainers (Vintage)
Anne, Queen (Eng)	Heads of State
Annenberg, Walter H.	Business
Anouilh, Jean	Authors
Ansara, Michael	Entertainers (Current)
Anthony, Ray	Entertainers (Vintage)
Anthony, Susan B.	Celebrities
Anton, Susan	Entertainers (Current)
Antonelli, Laura	Entertainers (Current)
Aparicio, Luis	Baseball
Apollo 11 (Pix 3 Astros)	Astronauts
Apostoli, Fred	Boxing
Appleby, Ray	Entertainers (Vintage)
Appling, Luke	Baseball
Appolinaire, Guillaume	Authors
Apps, C. J. "Syl"	Hockey HoF
Apt, Jay	Astronauts
Aquilera, Rick	Baseball
Aragon, Art "Golden Boy"	Boxing
Arbuckle, Maclyn	Entertainers (Vintage)
Arbuckle, Roscoe "Fatty"	Entertainers (Vintage)
Arcaro, Eddie	General Sports
Archer, Anne	Entertainers (Current)
Archibald, Nate	General Sports
Arden, Elizabeth	Business
Arden, Eve	Entertainers (Current)
Arden, Nicke	Entertainers (Vintage)
Arfons, Art	General Sports
Ariyoshi, George R.	Governors

Name	Category
Arizin, Paul	Basketball HoF
Arkell, Bartlett	Business
Arkell, W. J.	Business
Arkin, Alan	Entertainers (Current)
Arledge, Roone	General Sports
Arlen, Harold	Composers
Arlen, Richard	Entertainers (Vintage)
Armas, Tony	Baseball
Armetta, Henry	Entertainers (Vintage)
Armour, Tommy	Golf HoF
Arms, Russ	Entertainers (Current)
Armstead, Henry Hugh	Artists
Armstrong, Dr. William	Science
Armstrong, Debbie	General Sports
Armstrong, George	Hockey HoF
Armstrong, Henry	Boxing
Armstrong, John	U.S. V.P. & Cabinet
Armstrong, Louis	Entertainers (Vintage)
Armstrong, Martin	Authors
Armstrong, Neil A.	Astronauts
Armstrong, Robert	Entertainers (Vintage)
Arnaz, Desi	Entertainers (Vintage)
Arnaz, Lucie	Entertainers (Current)
Arness, James	Entertainers (Current)
Arnett, Jon	Football
Arngrim, Alison	Entertainers (Current)
Arnold, Archibald	Military
Arnold, Benedict	Revolutionary War
Arnold, Eddie	Country Music Stars
Arnold, Edward	Entertainers (Vintage)
Arnold, Henry "Hap"	Military
Arnold, Matthew	Authors
Arnold, Sir Edwin	Authors
Arnsbarger, Bill	Football
Arquette, Cliff	Entertainers (Vintage)
Arquette, Rosanna	Entertainers (Vintage)
Arriola, Gus	Cartoonists
Arsdale, Dick Van	General Sports
Arthur, Beatrice	Entertainers (Current)
Arthur, Chester A.	U.S. Presidents
Arthur, Jean	Entertainers (Vintage)
Arvin, Newton	Authors
Ash, Roy L.	Business
Ashburn, Richie	Baseball
Ashby, Hal	Entertainers (Current)
Ashe, Arthur	Tennis HoF
Ashenfelter, Horace	General Sports
Ashford & Simpson	Rock
Ashford, Evelyn	General Sports
Ashley, Elizabeth	Entertainers (Current)
Ashley, John	Hockey HoF
Ashworth, Ernie	Country Music Stars
Asimov, Isaac	Authors
Askew, Reubin	Governors
Asner, Ed	Entertainers (Current)
Asquith, Herbert H.	Heads of State
Assad, Hafez Al	Heads of State
Assante, Armand	Entertainers (Current)
Astaire, Fred	Entertainers (Vintage)
Asther, Nils	Entertainers (Vintage)
Astin, John	Entertainers (Current)
Astor, John Jacob Jr	Business
Astor, John J. Mrs.	Business
Astor, John Jacob	Business
Astor, Mary	Entertainers (Vintage)
Astor, Nancy(Viscountess)	Celebrities
Astor, Waldorf	Business
Astor, William B.	Business
Asturias, Miquel Angel	Authors
Atchison, David R.	U.S. Presidents
Atherton, Gertrude	Authors
Atkins, Chet	Country Music Stars
Atkins, Christopher	Entertainers (Current)
Atkins, David "Davy"	Football
Atkins, Doug	Football
Atkinson, Joseph H.	Military
Atkinson, Juliette	Tennis HoF
Atkinson, Ted	General Sports
Atlas, Charles	Business
Attell, Abe	Boxing
Attlee, Clement	Heads of State
Auberjonois, Rene	Entertainers (Current)
Auchincloss, Louis	Authors
Auchincloss, Janet L.	Business
Auckland, Baron	Celebrities
Auckland, Earl of	Heads of State
Auckland, Geo. Eden, Earl	Military
Auden, W. H. (Wystan)	Authors
Audubon, John J.	Artists
Auel, Jean M.	Authors
Auer, Mischa	Entertainers (Vintage)
Auerbach, Rick	Baseball
Auerback, Arnold J. (Red)	Basketball HoF
Auger, Christopher C.	Civil War
Augereau, C.(Castiglione)	Revolutionary War
Auker, Elden	Baseball
Auld, Georgie	Entertainers (Vintage)
Aumont, Jean Pierre	Entertainers (Vintage)
Aurand, Henry S.	Military
Auriol, Jacqueline	Aviation
Austen, Jane	Authors
Austin, Bobby	Country Music Stars
Austin, Horace	Governors
Austin, Karen	Entertainers (Current)
Austin, Moses	Revolutionary War
Austin, Stephen F.	Celebrities
Austin, Tracy	General Sports
Autry, Gene	Entertainers (Vintage)
Avalon, Frankie	Entertainers (Current)
Avedon, Richard	Artists
Averill, Earl	Baseball
Avery, John, Jr.	Revolutionary War
Avery, Margaret	Entertainers (Current)
Avery, Sewell	Business
Avery, Tex	Cartoonists
Axelrod, Julius	Science
Axton, Hoyt	Country Music Stars
Aykroyd, Dan	Entertainers (Current)
Ayres, Agnes	Entertainers (Vintage)
Ayres, Lew	Entertainers (Vintage)
Ayres, R. B.	Civil War
Ayub Khan, General	Heads of State
Babashoff, Shirley	General Sports
Babcock, Barbara	Entertainers (Current)
Babcock, Orville	Civil War
Babcock, Tim	Governors
Baby Peggy	Entertainers (Vintage)
Bacall, Lauren	Entertainers (Current)
Bach, Barbara	Entertainers (Current)
Bach, Catherine	Entertainers (Current)
Bach, Johann S.	Composers
Bacharach, Burt	Composers
Bacharach, Fabian	Artists
Bache, Alexander D.	Science
Bache, Harold L.	Business
Back, George Sir	Celebrities
Backman, Wally	Baseball
Backus, Jim	Entertainers (Current)
Bacon, Edmund	Celebrities
Bacon, Francis	Authors
Bacon, Frank	Entertainers (Vintage)
Bacon, Kevin	Entertainers (Current)
Bacon, Robert	U.S. V.P. & Cabinet
Bacon, Walter W.	Governors
Baddeley, Hermione	Entertainers (Vintage)
Badeau, Adam	Civil War
Bader, Douglas	Aviation
Badger, George E.	U.S. V.P. & Cabinet
Badgro, Morris "Red"	Football
Badler, Jane	Entertainers (Current)
Baekeland, L. H. Dr.	Business
Baer, Buddy	Boxing
Baer, George F.	Business
Baer, John	Entertainers (Current)
Baer, Max	Boxing
Baez, Joan	Entertainers (Current)
Bagby Jr., Jim	Baseball
Bagian, James P.	Astronauts
Bailey, Carl E.	Governors
Bailey, F. Lee	Celebrities
Bailey, I. W. "Ace"	Hockey HoF
Bailey, Jack	Entertainers (Vintage)

Bailey, Pearl	Entertainers (Current)	Barber, Jerry	General Sports
Bailey, Temple	Authors	Barber, Red	Baseball
Bailey, Theodorus	Civil War	Barber, Rex T.	Aviation
Baillie, Joanne	Authors	Barber, Samuel	Composers
Bain, Barbara	Entertainers (Current)	Barber, Tom	General Sports
Bain, Donald	Hockey HoF	Barbera, Joe	Entertainers (Current)
Bainbridge, William	Military	Barbier, George	Entertainers (Vintage)
Baio, Scott	Entertainers (Current)	Barbuti, Ray	General Sports
Baird, John Logie	Science	Barclay, Thomas	Revolutionary War
Bairnsfather, Bruce	Celebrities	Bardeen, John	Science
Baker, "Wee" Bonnie	Entertainers (Vintage)	Bardot, Brigitte	Entertainers (Current)
Baker, Alpheus	Civil War	Barere de Vieuzac, B.	Revolutionary War
Baker, Blanche	Entertainers (Current)	Baretti, Giuseppe	Authors
Baker, Carroll	Entertainers (Current)	Barger-Wallach, Maud	Tennis HoF
Baker, Dame Janet	Entertainers (Current)	Bari, Lynn	Entertainers (Vintage)
Baker, Del	Baseball	Baring, Francis Sir	Celebrities
Baker, Diane	Entertainers (Current)	Baring-Gould, Sabine	Authors
Baker, Edward D.	Civil War	Barker, Bob	Entertainers (Current)
Baker, Franklin	Baseball	Barker, Lex	Entertainers (Vintage)
Baker, George	Cartoonists	Barkley, Alben W. (V)	U.S. V.P. & Cabinet
Baker, Hobart	Hockey HoF	Barks, Carl	Cartoonists
Baker, John "Dusty"	Baseball	Barlick, Al	Baseball
Baker, Josephine	Entertainers (Vintage)	Barlow, Francis C.	Civil War
Baker, Kenny	Entertainers (Vintage)	Barlow, Jane	Authors
Baker, Lawrence A.	Tennis HoF	Barlow, Thomas	Basketball HoF
Baker, Newton D.	U.S. V.P. & Cabinet	Barnabee, Henry Clay	Entertainers (Vintage)
Baker, Samuel Sir	Celebrities	Barnard, Dr. Christian	Science
Baker, Terry	Football	Barnard, F.A.P.	Celebrities
Baker, W. Thane	General Sports	Barne, Michael	Celebrities
Bakken, Jim	Football	Barnes, Binnie	Entertainers (Vintage)
Balanchine, George	Entertainers (Vintage)	Barnes, Djuna	Authors
Balbo, Italo	Aviation	Barnes, Joanna	Entertainers (Current)
Balchen, Bernt	Aviation	Barnes, Lee	General Sports
Baldridge, Malcolm	U.S. V.P. & Cabinet	Barnes, Priscilla	Entertainers (Current)
Baldwin, Faith	Authors	Barnett, Ross R.	Governors
Baldwin, Henry (SC)	Celebrities	Barney, Rex	Baseball
Baldwin, James	Authors	Barnum, Phineas T.	Celebrities
Baldwin, Judy	Entertainers (Current)	Barr, Doug	Entertainers (Current)
Baldwin, R.S.	Governors	Barr, Joseph W.	U.S. V.P. & Cabinet
Baldwin, Raymond E.	Governors	Barras, Paul	Revolutionary War
Baldwin, Stanley	Heads of State	Barrett, Marty	Baseball
Balewa, Arthur Sir	Heads of State	Barrett, Rona	Entertainers (Vintage)
Balfour, Arthur J.	Heads of State	Barrie, Barbara	Entertainers (Current)
Ball Jr., John	Golf HoF	Barrie, Mona	Entertainers (Vintage)
Ball, Lucille	Entertainers (Current)	Barrie, Sir James M.	Authors
Ballard, Greg	General Sports	Barrie, Wendy	Entertainers (Vintage)
Ballard, Harold	Hockey HoF	Barrow, Robert H.	Military
Ballard, Kaye	Entertainers (Current)	Barrows, Lewis O.	Governors
Ballard, Robert Dr.	Celebrities	Barry, Don "Red"	Entertainers (Vintage)
Ballenfant, Lee	Baseball	Barry, Gene	Entertainers (Current)
Ballesteros, Seve	General Sports	Barry, John Wolfe, Sir	Celebrities
Ballew, Smith	Entertainers (Vintage)	Barry, John	Revolutionary War
Ballinger, Richard A.	U.S. V.P. & Cabinet	Barry, Marion	Celebrities
Balsam, Martin	Entertainers (Current)	Barry, Martin	Hockey HoF
Baltimore, David	Science	Barry, Marty	General Sports
Balzac, Honore de	Authors	Barry, Rick	General Sports
Bamberger, Hal	Baseball	Barry, Sam	Basketball HoF
Bananarama	Rock	Barry, Wesley	Entertainers (Vintage)
Bancroft, Anne	Entertainers (Current)	Barrymore, Drew	Entertainers (Current)
Bancroft, Dave	Baseball	Barrymore, Diana	Entertainers (Vintage)
Bancroft, George	Authors	Barrymore, Ethel	Entertainers (Vintage)
Bancroft, George	Entertainers (Vintage)	Barrymore, John	Entertainers (Vintage)
Bandaranike, S.W.R.D	Heads of State	Barrymore, Lionel	Entertainers (Vintage)
Bando, Sal	Baseball	Bartell, Dick	Baseball
Banisadr, A.	Heads of State	Barth, John	Authors
Bank, C. D.	U.S. V.P. & Cabinet	Barth, Karl Dr.	Celebrities
Bankhead, Tallulah	Entertainers (Vintage)	Barthelmess, Rich'd	Entertainers (Vintage)
Banks, Carl	Football	Bartholdi, Auguste	Artists
Banks, Ernie	Baseball	Bartholomew, Freddie	Entertainers (Vintage)
Banks, Joseph	Celebrities	Bartkowski, Steve	Football
Banks, Michael A.	Authors	Bartle, Joyce	Entertainers (Current)
Banks, Nathaniel P.	Civil War	Bartlett, Bonnie	Entertainers (Current)
Banky, Vilma	Entertainers (Vintage)	Bartlett, Josiah	Revolutionary War
Banning, Margaret C.	Authors	Bartlett, Paul Wayland	Artists
Bannister, Roger	General Sports	Bartok, Bela	Composers
Banting, Frederick G.	Science	Barton, Bruce	Business
Bara, Theda	Entertainers (Vintage)	Barton, Clara	Celebrities
Baraka, Imanu Amiri	Authors	Bartow, Gene	General Sports
Barbe-Marbois, F.	Celebrities	Barty, Billy	Entertainers (Current)
Barbeau, Adrienne	Entertainers (Current)	Baruch, Bernard M.	Celebrities
Barbejacque, Prince	Entertainers (Vintage)	Baryshnikov, M.	Entertainers (Current)

Barzun, Jacques	Authors
Basehart, Richard	Entertainers (Vintage)
Basie, Count	Entertainers (Vintage)
Basilio, Carmen	Boxing
Basinger, Kim	Entertainers (Current)
Bass, Dick	Football
Bass, Richard "Dick"	Baseball
Bassett, Charles A.	Astronauts
Bateman, Justine	Entertainers (Current)
Bates, Blanche	Entertainers (Vintage)
Bates, Edward	U.S. V.P. & Cabinet
Bates, Katharine Lee	Authors
Bathgate, Andrew	Hockey HoF
Batista, Fulgencio I	Heads of State
Batiuk, Tom	Cartoonists
Battalino, Battling	Boxing
Battles, Cliff	Football
Baucus, Bob	Aviation
Baudouin, King (Belg)	Heads of State
Bauer, Hank	Baseball
Bauer, Jaime Lyn	Entertainers (Current)
Bauer, Steven	Entertainers (Current)
Baugh, Laura	General Sports
Baugh, Sammy	Football
Baughan, Maxie	Football
Baum, L. Frank	Authors
Baumer, Steven	Entertainers (Current)
Baumholtz, Frank	Baseball
Baur, Hans	Aviation
Baxley, Barbara	Entertainers (Current)
Baxter, Anne	Entertainers (Vintage)
Baxter, James P. III	Authors
Baxter, Keith	Entertainers (Current)
Baxter, Percival P.	Governors
Baxter, Warner	Entertainers (Vintage)
Baxter-Birney, M.	Entertainers (Current)
Bayard, John	Revolutionary War
Bayard, Thomas F.	U.S. V.P. & Cabinet
Bayi, Filbert	General Sports
Baylor, Don	Baseball
Baylor, Elgin	Basketball HoF
Bayne, Beverly	Entertainers (Vintage)
Beach Boys	Rock
Beach, Rex	Authors
Beacham, Stephanie	Entertainers (Current)
Beadle, G. Wells	Science
Beal, John	Entertainers (Vintage)
Beals, Jennifer	Entertainers (Current)
Beamon, Bob	General Sports
Bean, Alan L.	Astronauts
Bean, Andy	General Sports
Beane, Hilary	Entertainers (Vintage)
Beardsley, Aubrey	Artists
Beatles	Rock
Beaton, Cecil	Artists
Beatrix, Queen (Neth)	Heads of State
Beatty, Clyde	Entertainers (Vintage)
Beatty, David Adm.	Military
Beatty, Warren	Entertainers (Current)
Beaty, Ned	Entertainers (Current)
Beaudelaire, Charles	Authors
Beauharnais, Eugene	Heads of State
Beauregard, P.G.T.	Civil War
Beaver, James A.	Governors
Beaverbrook, Wm., Lord	Celebrities
Beban, Gary	Football
Beck, Dave	Celebrities
Beck, Jeff	Rock
Beck, John	Entertainers (Current)
Becker, Barbara	Entertainers (Vintage)
Becker, Bobby & George	General Sports
Beckett, Samuel	Authors
Beckman, John	Basketball HoF
Bedelia, Bonnie	Entertainers (Current)
Bedford, Gunning	Revolutionary War
Bednarik, Chuck	Football
Bee, Barnard E.	Civil War
Bee, Clair	Basketball HoF
Bee, Molly	Country Music Stars
Beebe, William	Science
Beecher, Henry Ward	Authors
Beems, Patricia	Entertainers (Vintage)
Beerbohm, Max	Authors
Beery, Noah Jr.	Entertainers (Current)
Beery, Noah	Entertainers (Vintage)
Beery, Wallace	Entertainers (Vintage)
Beethoven, Ludwig van	Composers
Begin, Menachem	Heads of State
Begley, Ed Sr.	Entertainers (Vintage)
Begley, Ed Jr.	Entertainers (Current)
Behan, Brendan F.	Authors
Behr, Karl	Tennis HoF
Behrman, S. N.	Authors
Beith, Ian Hay	Authors
Beke, Chas. Tilstone	Celebrities
Bel Geddes, Norman	Celebrities
Belafonte, Shari	Entertainers (Current)
Belanger, Mark	Baseball
Belasco, David	Entertainers (Vintage)
Belaunde, Fernando T	Heads of State
Belcher, Edward, Sir	Celebrities
Belcher, Jonathan	Revolutionary War
Belita	Entertainers (Vintage)
Beliveau, Jean	Hockey HoF
Belknap, William W.	Civil War
Belknap, William W.	U.S. V.P. & Cabinet
Bell, Alexander Graham	Science
Bell, Bobby	Football
Bell, Buddy	Baseball
Bell, E.T.(See Taine)	Authors
Bell, Griffin	U.S. V.P. & Cabinet
Bell, James "Cool Papa"	Baseball
Bell, John	U.S. V.P. & Cabinet
Bell, Ricky	Football
Bell, Terrel H.	U.S. V.P. & Cabinet
Bellamy, Edward	Authors
Bellamy, Elizabeth W.	Authors
Bellamy, Madge	Entertainers (Vintage)
Bellamy, Ralph	Entertainers (Vintage)
Bellamy, Walt	General Sports
Bellanca, Giuseppe M.	Aviation
Beller, Kathleen	Entertainers (Current)
Belli, Melvin	Celebrities
Belliard, Augustin (Count	Revolutionary War
Bellino, Joe	Football
Belloc, Hilaire	Authors
Belloc-Lowndes, Marie	Authors
Bellonte, Maurice	Aviation
Bellow, Saul	Authors
Bellows, George	Artists
Bellson, Louis	Entertainers (Vintage)
Bellwood, Pamela	Entertainers (Current)
Belmont, August	Business
Belushi, James	Entertainers (Current)
Bemelmans, Ludwig	Authors
Ben-Gurion, David	Heads of State
Ben-Zvi, Itzhak	Heads of State
Benacerraf, Baruj	Science
Benatar, Pat	Rock
Bench, Johnny	Baseball
Benchley, Peter	Authors
Benchley, Robert	Authors
Bender, Chief	Baseball
Bendix, William	Entertainers (Vintage)
Benedict, Bruce	Baseball
Benedict, Clinton	Hockey HoF
Benedict, Dirk	Entertainers (Current)
Benes, Eduard	Heads of State
Benet, Stephen Vinc.	Authors
Benet, William Rose	Authors
Benjamin, Judah P.	Civil War
Bennett, Bruce	General Sports
Bennett, Bruce	Entertainers (Vintage)
Bennett, C. Leeman	Football
Bennett, Constance	Entertainers (Vintage)
Bennett, Floyd	Aviation
Bennett, Joan	Entertainers (Vintage)
Bennett, Julie	Entertainers (Current)
Bennett, Tony	Entertainers (Current)
Bennett, Wm. Andrew	Heads of State
Benning, Henry Lewis	Civil War
Benny, Jack	Entertainers (Vintage)

435

Benoit, Joan	General Sports
Benson, Egbert	Revolutionary War
Benson, Elmer A.	Governors
Benson, Ezra Taft	U.S. V.P. & Cabinet
Benson, Frank Robert	Entertainers (Vintage)
Benson, George	Rock
Benson, Robbie	Entertainers (Current)
Bent, James Theodore	Celebrities
Benteen, F. W.	Civil War
Bentley, Douglas	Hockey HoF
Bentley, Maxwell	Hockey HoF
Benton, Barbi	Entertainers (Current)
Benton, Thomas Hart	Artists
Benton, William	Business
Berardino, Johnny	Baseball
Berens, Susan	General Sports
Berenson, Marisa	Entertainers (Current)
Beresford, Lord Chas.	Military
Berg, Alban	Composers
Berg, Gertrude	Entertainers (Vintage)
Berg, Moe	Baseball
Berg, Patty	Golf HoF
Berg, Paul	Science
Bergen, Candice	Entertainers (Current)
Bergen, Edgar	Entertainers (Vintage)
Bergen, Frances	Entertainers (Vintage)
Bergen, Polly	Entertainers (Current)
Berger, Senta	Entertainers (Vintage)
Bergere, Lee	Entertainers (Current)
Bergey, Bill	Football
Bergland, Bob	U.S. V.P. & Cabinet
Bergman, Ingrid	Entertainers (Vintage)
Bergman, Ingmar	Entertainers (Current)
Bergman, Sandahl	Entertainers (Current)
Bergner, Elizabeth	Entertainers (Vintage)
Bergson, Henri	Authors
Berkeley, Busby	Entertainers (Vintage)
Berkowitz, David	Celebrities
Berle, Milton	Entertainers (Current)
Berlier, Theophile, Count	Revolutionary War
Berlin, Irving	Composers
Berlioz, Hector	Composers
Berman, Shelley	Entertainers (Current)
Bernadotte, Jean B.	Heads of State
Bernard, Francis Sir	Revolutionary War
Berndt, Walter	Cartoonists
Bernhardt, Sarah	Entertainers (Vintage)
Bernie, Ben	Entertainers (Vintage)
Berning, Susie Maxwell	General Sports
Bernstein, Elmer	Composers
Bernstein, Leonard	Composers
Berosini, Josephine	Entertainers (Vintage)
Berra, Yogi	Baseball
Berrien, J. Macpherson	U.S. V.P. & Cabinet
Berrigan, Daniel, Fr.	Celebrities
Berry, Chuck	Rock
Berry, Jim	Celebrities
Berry, Ken	Entertainers (Vintage)
Berry, Raymond	Football
Bersen, Corbin	Entertainers (Current)
Bertelli, Angelo	Football
Berthier, Alexandre	Revolutionary War
Berthier, Louis A.	Military
Berthollet, Count Claude	Science
Bertinelli, Valerie	Entertainers (Current)
Berwanger, Jay	Football
Berzelius, Jons Jacob	Science
Besant, Annie	Authors
Bess, Gordon	Cartoonists
Bessemer, Sir Henry	Business
Besser, Joe	Entertainers (Vintage)
Bessieres, Bertrand	Revolutionary War
Best, Edna	Entertainers (Vintage)
Best, James	Entertainers (Current)
Beswick, Martine	Entertainers (Current)
Betham-Edwards, M.	Authors
Bethune, Mary M., Dr.	Celebrities
Betjeman, Sir John	Authors
Bettenhausen, Gary	General Sports
Bettina, Melio	Boxing
Bettis, Tom	Football

Beugnot, J.C., Count	Revolutionary War
Bevacqua, Kurt	Baseball
Bevans, Bill	Baseball
Bevin, Ernest	Celebrities
Bey, Turhan	Entertainers (Vintage)
Bialik, Chaim	Authors
Bibb, George M.	U.S. V.P. & Cabinet
Bibby, Henry	General Sports
Bibby, Jim	Baseball
Bickell, John	Hockey HoF
Bickford, Charles	Entertainers (Vintage)
Biddle, Clement	Revolutionary War
Biddle, Francis	U.S. V.P. & Cabinet
Biddle, George	Artists
Biddle, Nicholas	Business
Biehn, Micheal	Entertainers (Current)
Bierce, Ambrose	Authors
Bieri, Ramon	Entertainers (Current)
Bierman, Bernie	Football
Bierstadt, Albert	Artists
Bigelow, Erastus B.	Business
Biggers, Earl Derr	Authors
Biittner, Larry	Baseball
Biletnikoff, Fred	Football
Billings, Josh	Authors
Billingsley, Barbara	Entertainers (Current)
Bing, Rudolph	Entertainers (Vintage)
Bingham, Amelia	Entertainers (Vintage)
Bingham, John Armor	U.S. V.P. & Cabinet
Bingham, William	Revolutionary War
Binns, Edward	Entertainers (Current)
Bird, Jerry	Country Music Stars
Bird, Larry	General Sports
Birdseye, Clarence	Business
Birney, David	Entertainers (Current)
Birney, William	Civil War
Bishop, Jim	Authors
Bishop, Joey	Entertainers (Current)
Bishop, Julie	Entertainers (Vintage)
Bishop, Wm. "Billy"	Aviation
Bismark, Otto von	Heads of State
Bissell, William H.	Governors
Bisset, Jacqueline	Entertainers (Current)
Bitter, Karl	Artists
Bittrich, Wilhelm	Military
Bixby, Bill	Entertainers (Current)
Bizet, Georges	Composers
Bjoerling, Jussi	Entertainers (Vintage)
Bjornsen, Bjornstierne	Authors
Black, Alexander	Authors
Black, Eugene R.	Business
Black, Hugo (SC)	Celebrities
Black, Joe	Baseball
Black, Karen	Entertainers (Current)
Black, Richard B.	Military
Blackburn, Luke P.	Governors
Blackett, Dr. Patrick	Science
Blackett, Patrick	Science
Blackman, Honor	Entertainers (Current)
Blackmer, Sidney	Entertainers (Vintage)
Blackmun, Harry A. (SC)	Celebrities
Blackstone, Harry Jr	Entertainers (Current)
Blackwell, Alice Stone	Celebrities
Blackwell, Ewell	Baseball
Blackwell, Otis	Composers
Blaha, John E.	Astronauts
Blaik, Earl "Red"	Football
Blaine, James G.	U.S. V.P. & Cabinet
Blaine, Vivian	Entertainers (Vintage)
Blair, Frank	Entertainers (Current)
Blair, Janet	Entertainers (Vintage)
Blair, John (SC)	Celebrities
Blair, Linda	Entertainers (Current)
Blair, Paul	Baseball
Blake, Bud	Cartoonists
Blake, Eubie	Entertainers (Vintage)
Blake, Eugene Carson	Celebrities
Blake, Hector "Toe"	Hockey HoF
Blake, Robert	Entertainers (Current)
Blakely, Susan	Entertainers (Current)
Blalock, Jim	Baseball

Name	Category		Name	Category
Blanc, Louis	Authors		Bolling, Tiffany	Entertainers (Current)
Blanc, Mel	Entertainers (Vintage)		Bollweg, Don	Baseball
Blanchard, Doc	Football		Bombeck, Erma	Authors
Blanchard, John	Baseball		Bon Jovi	Rock
Blanda, George	Football		Bonaparte, Caroline	Celebrities
Blane, Sally	Entertainers (Vintage)		Bonaparte, Joseph	Heads of State
Blanks, Mary Lynn	Entertainers (Current)		Bonaparte, Jerome	Heads of State
Blanton, Ray	Governors		Bonaparte, Louis	Heads of State
Blasco-Ibanez, Vicente	Authors		Bonaparte, Lucien	Heads of State
Blasingame, Don	Baseball		Bond, Carrie Jacobs	Composers
Blass, Bill	Business		Bond, Johnny	Country Music Stars
Blass, Steve	Baseball		Bond, Julian	Celebrities
Blatchford, Samuel (SC)	Celebrities		Bondi, Beulah	Entertainers (Vintage)
Blatnik, Jeff	General Sports		Bonerz, Peter	Entertainers (Current)
Blatty, William Peter	Authors		Bonham, Bill	Baseball
Blaylock, Gary	Baseball		Bonham, M. L.	Civil War
Blaylock, Marv	Baseball		Bonheur, Rosa	Artists
Blears, Lord	General Sports		Bonura, Zeke	Baseball
Bleier, Rocky	Football		Bonvalot, Gabriel	Celebrities
Blennerhassett, Harman	Revolutionary War		Book, Sorrell	Entertainers (Current)
Bleriot, Louis	Aviation		Boon, Richard	Hockey HoF
Bligh, Capt. Wm.	Military		Boone, Bob	Baseball
Bliss, Cornelius	U.S. V.P. & Cabinet		Boone, Daniel	Revolutionary War
Bliss, George Jr.	Civil War		Boone, Lute "Danny"	Baseball
Bliss, J. S.	Civil War		Boone, Pat	Entertainers (Current)
Bliss, Tasker H.	Military		Boone, Richard	Entertainers (Vintage)
Bliss, Zenas R.	Civil War		Booth, Albie	Football
Bloch, Dr. Konrad	Science		Booth, Ballington	Celebrities
Bloch, Ernst	Celebrities		Booth, Edwin	Entertainers (Vintage)
Bloch, Raymond	Composers		Booth, Evangeline	Celebrities
Bloch, Richard	Business		Booth, John Wilkes	Civil War
Block, Herb	Cartoonists		Booth, Maude	Celebrities
Block, John R.	U.S. V.P. & Cabinet		Booth, Newton	Governors
Block, Joseph L.	Business		Booth, Shirley	Entertainers (Vintage)
Blodget, Samuel Jr.	Revolutionary War		Booth, William	Celebrities
Bloembergen, Nicolaas Dr.	Science		Boothe, Powers	Entertainers (Current)
Blondell, Joan	Entertainers (Vintage)		Boozer, Brenda	Entertainers (Current)
Blood Sweat And Tears	Rock		Boozer, John	Baseball
Blood, Ernest	Basketball HoF		Borchers, Afoll	Aviation
Blood, Robert O.	Governors		Bordaberry, Juan Maria	Heads of State
Bloodworth, Jimmy	Baseball		Borden, Olive	Entertainers (Vintage)
Bloom, Claire	Entertainers (Current)		Bordoni, Irene	Entertainers (Vintage)
Bloom, Lindsay	Entertainers (Current)		Borg, Bjorn	General Sports
Blore, Eric	Entertainers (Vintage)		Borge, Victor	Entertainers (Current)
Blough, Roger	Business		Borghese, Camillo	Heads of State
Blount, Winton M.	U.S. V.P. & Cabinet		Borglum, Gutzon	Artists
Bloustein, Edward J.	Celebrities		Borglum, Lincoln	Artists
Blucher, G. von	Military		Borgmann, Bennie	Basketball HoF
Blue, Ben	Entertainers (Vintage)		Borgmann, Bernie	General Sports
Blue, Monte	Entertainers (Vintage)		Boris III (Bulg)	Heads of State
Blue, Vida	Baseball		Borlaug, Dr. Norman	Science
Bluege, Ossie	Baseball		Borman, F. & Lovell, J.	Astronauts
Bluford, Guion S. Jr.	Astronauts		Borman, Frank	Astronauts
Blum, Leon (Pres FR)	Heads of State		Bormann, Martin	Military
Blumenthal, W. Michael	U.S. V.P. & Cabinet		Borne, Hermann von Dem.	Military
Blyden, Larry	Entertainers (Current)		Borodin, Alexander	Composers
Blyleven, Bert	Baseball		Boros, Julius	Golf HoF
Blyth, Ann	Entertainers (Current)		Borotra, Jean	Tennis HoF
Boardman, Eleanor	Entertainers (Vintage)		Borotra, Jean	General Sports
Boardman, Russell	Aviation		Borowy, Hank	Baseball
Bobko, Karol J.	Astronauts		Bosanquet, Helen D.	Authors
Bochner, Lloyd	Entertainers (Current)		Bosco, Robbie	Football
Boddicker, Mike	Baseball		Boshell, Louise	Entertainers (Vintage)
Bodenschatz, Karl	Aviation		Bosson, Barbara	Entertainers (Current)
Boe, Nils A.	Governors		Bossy, Mike	General Sports
Bogart, Humphrey	Entertainers (Vintage)		Boston, Ralph	General Sports
Bogdonavich, Peter	Entertainers (Current)		Bostwick, Barry	Entertainers (Current)
Boggs, Wade	Baseball		Boswell, Connie	Entertainers (Vintage)
Bohay, Heidi	Entertainers (Current)		Bosworth, Hobart	Entertainers (Vintage)
Bohr, Aage Niels	Science		Bottolfsen, C.A.	Governors
Bok, Edward	Authors		Bottome, Margaret	Authors
Boland, Frederick	Celebrities		Bottoms, Joseph	Entertainers (Current)
Boland, Mary	Entertainers (Vintage)		Bottoms, Sam	Entertainers (Current)
Bolden, Charles F. Jr.	Astronauts		Bouchard, Emile "Butch"	Hockey HoF
Boles, John	Entertainers (Vintage)		Boucher, Frank	Hockey HoF
Bolger, Jim	Baseball		Boucher, George "Buck"	Hockey HoF
Bolger, Ray	Entertainers (Vintage)		Boucicault, Dion	Entertainers (Vintage)
Bolingbroke, Henry	Celebrities		Bouck, William C.	Governors
Bolivar, Simon	Heads of State		Boudenant, Bob	General Sports
Boll, Heinrich	Authors		Boudinot, Elias	Revolutionary War
Bolling, Milt	Baseball		Boudreau, Lou	Baseball

Boulez, Pierre	Composers	Braque, Georges	Artists
Boulle, Pierre	Authors	Brattain, Walter	Science
Bourguiba, Habib	Heads of State	Brauchitsch, W. von	Military
Bourke-White, Margaret	Artists	Braun, Eva	Celebrities
Bourrienne, L.A.F. de	Revolutionary War	Braxton, Carter	Revolutionary War
Bouton, Bill	Baseball	Brazzi, Rossano	Entertainers (Current)
Bouton, Chas. Marie	Artists	Brearly, David	Revolutionary War
Bouton, Jim	Baseball	Breathed, Berke	Celebrities
Boutwell, George S.	U.S. V.P. & Cabinet	Brecheen, Harry	Baseball
Bouvia, Gloria	General Sports	Brecht, Bertolt	Authors
Bow, Clara	Entertainers (Vintage)	Breckinridge, Wm. C.	Civil War
Bowa, Larry	Baseball	Breckinridge, John (V)	U.S. V.P. & Cabinet
Bowden, Bobby	Football	Breeding, Marv	Baseball
Bowden, Doris	Entertainers (Current)	Breedlove, Craig	General Sports
Bowe, Rosemarie	Entertainers (Vintage)	Breen, Bobby	Entertainers (Vintage)
Bowen, Ira Sprague	Science	Brefoort, H. B.	Military
Bowen, John S.	Civil War	Breger, Dave	Celebrities
Bowen, Sir George F.	Heads of State	Breland, Mark	Boxing
Bower, Antoinette	Entertainers (Current)	Brendel, El	Entertainers (Vintage)
Bower, John	Hockey HoF	Breneman, Tom	Entertainers (Vintage)
Bowes, Major Edward	Entertainers (Vintage)	Brennan, Eileen	Entertainers (Current)
Bowie, David	Rock	Brennan, Joseph	Basketball HoF
Bowie, Russell	Hockey HoF	Brennan, Terry	Football
Bowker, Judy	Entertainers (Current)	Brennan, Walter	Entertainers (Vintage)
Bowles, Chester	U.S. V.P. & Cabinet	Brennan, William J. (SC)	Celebrities
Bowman, Lee	Entertainers (Vintage)	Brennecke, Kurt	Military
Bowman, Scotty	General Sports	Brent, Evelyn	Entertainers (Vintage)
Box, Cloyce	Football	Brent, George	Entertainers (Vintage)
Boxleitner, Bruce	Entertainers (Current)	Brent, J. L.	Civil War
Boyd, Belle	Celebrities	Breslin, Jimmy	Celebrities
Boyd, Bill	Entertainers (Vintage)	Bressoud, Ed	Baseball
Boyd, Steven	Entertainers (Vintage)	Breton, Andre	Authors
Boydston, Max	Football	Brett, George	Baseball
Boyer, Charles	Entertainers (Vintage)	Breuer, Marcel	Celebrities
Boyer, Ken	Baseball	Breuer, Marv	Baseball
Boyesen, Hjalmar H.	Authors	Breunig, Bob	Football
Boyington, Greg. "Pappy"	Aviation	Brewer, David J. (SC)	Celebrities
Boyle, John J.	Artists	Brewer, Teresa	Entertainers (Current)
Boyle, Kay	Authors	Brewster, David	Science
Boyle, Peter	Entertainers (Current)	Brewster, Kingman Jr	Celebrities
Brabazon-Moore, J.T.	Military	Brezhnev, Leonid I.	Heads of State
Brabham, Jack	General Sports	Brice, Fannie	Entertainers (Vintage)
Bracken, Eddie	Entertainers (Vintage)	Bricker, John W.	Governors
Bradbury, Ray	Authors	Bridges, Beau	Entertainers (Current)
Braddock, James J.	Boxing	Bridges, Harry	Celebrities
Bradford, William	U.S. V.P. & Cabinet	Bridges, Jeff	Entertainers (Current)
Bradley, Bill	Basketball HoF	Bridges, Lloyd	Entertainers (Current)
Bradley, Ed	Celebrities	Bridges, Rocky	Baseball
Bradley, John	Military	Bridges, Roy D. Jr.	Astronauts
Bradley, Joseph P. (SC)	Celebrities	Bridges, Tommy	Baseball
Bradley, Omar N.	Military	Bridgman, Laura D.	Celebrities
Bradley, Pat	General Sports	Briggs, Claire	Cartoonists
Bradley, Sen. Bill	General Sports	Briggs, James E.	Military
Bradley, Tom	Celebrities	Bright, John	Celebrities
Bradna, Olympe	Entertainers (Vintage)	Briles, Nelson	Baseball
Bradshaw, Terry	Football	Brimsek, Francis	Hockey HoF
Bradstreet, John	Revolutionary War	Brimsek, Frank	General Sports
Brady, "Diamond Jim"	Business	Brinegar, Paul	Entertainers (Current)
Brady, Mathew B.	Artists	Brinker, Maureen Connolly	Tennis HoF
Brady, Scott	Entertainers (Current)	Brinkley, Christie	Entertainers (Current)
Brady, William A.	Entertainers (Vintage)	Brisbane, Arthur	Authors
Braga, Sonia	Entertainers (Current)	Brisebois, Danielle	Entertainers (Current)
Bragan, Bobby	Baseball	Brisson, Carl	Entertainers (Vintage)
Bragg, Braxton	Civil War	Bristow, B. H.	U.S. V.P. & Cabinet
Bragg, Don	General Sports	Brittany, Morgan	Entertainers (Current)
Bragg, Edward S.	Civil War	Britten, Benjamin	Composers
Bragg, Wm. Lawrence	Science	Britton, Barbara	Entertainers (Vintage)
Braggs, Glenn	Baseball	Britton, Sherry	Entertainers (Vintage)
Brahanski, Tom	Baseball	Brix, Herman	Entertainers (Vintage)
Brahms, Johannes	Composers	Broadbent, H. L. "Punch"	Hockey HoF
Braid, James	Golf HoF	Broccli, Cubby	Entertainers (Current)
Braithwaite, Wm. Stanley	Authors	Brock, Dieter	Football
Branca, Ralph	Baseball	Brock, Greg	Baseball
Branch, John	U.S. V.P. & Cabinet	Brock, Lou	Baseball
Branch, Lawrence O.	Civil War	Brock, William G. Sen.	Business
Brand, Vance D.	Astronauts	Brockington, John	Football
Brandeis, Louis D. (SC)	Celebrities	Brocklin, Norm Van	Football
Brandenstein, Daniel	Astronauts	Broda, W. E. "Turk"	Hockey HoF
Brandt, Willy	Heads of State	Broderick, Matthew	Entertainers (Current)
Branigan, Laura	Rock	Brodhead, James E.	Entertainers (Current)
Brann, Louis J.	Governors		

438

Brodie, John	Football	Bruhm, Milt	Football
Broglie, Louis Victor de	Science	Brummel, Geo. B. "Beau"	Celebrities
Brokow, Tom	Celebrities	Brunansky, Tom	Baseball
Brolin, James	Entertainers (Current)	Brundage, Avery	General Sports
Bromfield, John	Entertainers (Current)	Brune, G.M.A.	Revolutionary War
Bromfield, Louis	Authors	Bry, Ellen	Entertainers (Current)
Bronk, Detlev W.	Science	Bryan, Charles W.	Governors
Bronson, Charles	Entertainers (Current)	Bryan, Jane	Entertainers (Vintage)
Brook, Alexander	Artists	Bryan, William Jennings	U.S. V.P. & Cabinet
Brook, Clive	Entertainers (Vintage)	Bryant, Alys McKey	Aviation
Brooke, Hilary	Entertainers (Vintage)	Bryant, Anita	Entertainers (Current)
Brooke, John R.	Civil War	Bryant, Paul "Bear"	Football
Brooke, Rupert	Authors	Bryant, Wm. Cullen	Authors
Brookes, Norman Everard	Tennis HoF	Buber, Martin	Celebrities
Brooks, Foster	Entertainers (Current)	Buchanan, Edgar	Entertainers (Vintage)
Brooks, Gwendolyn	Authors	Buchanan, James	U.S. Presidents
Brooks, Leslie	Entertainers (Vintage)	Bucher, Jim	Baseball
Brooks, Mel	Entertainers (Current)	Bucher, Lloyd	Military
Brooks, Phillips	Authors	Buchli, James F.	Astronauts
Brooks, Rand	Entertainers (Vintage)	Buchwald, Art	Authors
Brooks, Randi	Entertainers (Current)	Buck, C. Douglass	Governors
Brophy, Kevin	Entertainers (Current)	Buck, Frank	Entertainers (Vintage)
Brosnan, Pierce	Entertainers (Current)	Buck, Paul H.	Authors
Brothers, Joyce	Celebrities	Buck, Pearl S.	Authors
Brough, Candi, Randi	Entertainers (Current)	Buckingham, William A.	Governors
Brough, Fanny	Entertainers (Vintage)	Buckland, Frank	Hockey HoF
Brough, Lionel	Entertainers (Vintage)	Buckle, Henry Thomas	Authors
Brougham, Henry	Celebrities	Buckley, William F.	Celebrities
Broun, Heywood	Authors	Buckner, Bill	Baseball
Browder, Earl	Celebrities	Buckner, Simon B.	Civil War
Brown, Authur W.	Aviation	Bucyk, Johnny	Hockey HoF
Brown, Blair	Entertainers (Current)	Budd, Julie	Entertainers (Current)
Brown, Bo	Cartoonists	Budge, Don	General Sports
Brown, Bothwell	Entertainers (Vintage)	Budge, J. Donald	Tennis HoF
Brown, Dave	Football	Buell, Don Carlos	Civil War
Brown, Dick	Baseball	Bueno, Maria	Tennis HoF
Brown, Dr. Bobby	Baseball	Buffett, Jimmy	Rock
Brown, Edmund G. "Jerry"	Governors	Buhari, Mohammed	Heads of State
Brown, Edmund G. "Pat"	Governors	Buick, David D.	Business
Brown, George	Hockey HoF	Bujold, Genevieve	Entertainers (Current)
Brown, Helen Gurley	Authors	Bull, John S.	Astronauts
Brown, Henry B. (SC)	Celebrities	Bullard, Robert Lee	Military
Brown, Herbert C.	Science	Buller, Redvers	Military
Brown, James	Rock	Bullock, Walter	Authors
Brown, Jim	Football	Bulow, Bernhard von	Heads of State
Brown, Jim Ed	Country Music Stars	Bulwer, Henry	Celebrities
Brown, Joe E.	Entertainers (Vintage)	Bumbry, Al	Baseball
Brown, Joe L.	Baseball	Bumbry, Grace	Entertainers (Current)
Brown, John	Civil War	Bumpers, Dale	Governors
Brown, Johnny Mack	Entertainers (Vintage)	Bunche, Ralph	Celebrities
Brown, Larry	General Sports	Bundy, May Sutton	Tennis HoF
Brown, Lt. John	Revolutionary War	Bundy, McGeorge	Celebrities
Brown, Mace	Baseball	Bunn, John	Basketball HoF
Brown, Mark N.	Astronauts	Bunning, Jim	Baseball
Brown, Mordecai	Baseball	Bunny, John	Entertainers (Vintage)
Brown, Moses	Celebrities	Bunsen, C. J. Baron	Celebrities
Brown, Nicholas	Business	Bunsen, Robert W.	Science
Brown, Norma	Military	Bunting, Mary	Celebrities
Brown, Paul E.	Football	Buntline, Ned	Authors
Brown, Roosevelt	Football	Buoniconti, Nick	Football
Brown, Tom	Entertainers (Vintage)	Burbank, Luther	Science
Brown, Walter	Hockey HoF	Burch, Billy	Hockey HoF
Brown, Walter	Basketball HoF	Burda, Bob	Baseball
Brown, Willie	Football	Burdette, Lew	Baseball
Browne, Charles F.	Authors	Burdette, Robert J.	Authors
Browne, Coral	Entertainers (Current)	Buren, Steve Van	Football
Browne, Dik	Cartoonists	Burger, Warren E. (SC)	Celebrities
Browne, Jackson	Rock	Burgess, Smoky	Baseball
Browne, Leslie	Entertainers (Current)	Burghley, Lord	General Sports
Browne, Mary K.	Tennis HoF	Burgoyne, John	Revolutionary War
Brownell, Herbert Jr.	U.S. V.P. & Cabinet	Burk, Adrian	Football
Browning, Eliz. Barrett	Authors	Burke, Arleigh	Military
Browning, Robert	Authors	Burke, Billie	Entertainers (Vintage)
Browning, Tom	Baseball	Burke, Delta	Entertainers (Current)
Broyles, Frank	Football	Burke, Paul	Entertainers (Current)
Brubeck, Dave	Entertainers (Current)	Burke, Selma	Artists
Bruce, Carol	Entertainers (Vintage)	Burkhart, Ken	Baseball
Bruce, Virginia	Entertainers (Vintage)	Burleson, Albert S.	U.S. V.P. & Cabinet
Bruch, Max	Composers	Burleson, Rick	Baseball
Bruckner, Anton	Composers	Burne-Jones, Edward, Sir	Artists
Brugnon, Jacques	Tennis HoF	Burnett, Carol	Entertainers (Current)

Burnett, Frances, H.	Authors	Cadwalader, Lambert	Celebrities
Burnett, Leo	Business	Cadwalader, George	Civil War
Burnette, Smiley	Entertainers (Vintage)	Caesar, Irving	Composers
Burns, Bob	Entertainers (Vintage)	Caesar, Sid	Entertainers (Current)
Burns, George	Entertainers (Current)	Cage, John	Composers
Burns, Jerry	Football	Cage, Nicholas	Entertainers (Current)
Burns, John A.	Governors	Cagney, James	Entertainers (Vintage)
Burns, Robert	Authors	Cahill, Mabel	Tennis HoF
Burns, Tommy	Boxing	Cahn, Sammy	Composers
Burns, W. J.	Business	Cain, Bob	Baseball
Burns, William W.	Civil War	Caine, Michael	Entertainers (Current)
Burnside, Ambrose E.	Civil War	Caine, Sir Thos. Hall	Authors
Burpee, David	Business	Calder, Alexander	Artists
Burpee, Jonathan	Business	Calder, Frank	Hockey HoF
Burr, Aaron (V)	U.S. V.P. & Cabinet	Calderon, A. W. Gen.	Heads of State
Burr, Raymond	Entertainers (Current)	Caldwell, Erskine	Authors
Burroughs, Edgar Rice	Authors	Caldwell, Zoe	Entertainers (Current)
Burroughs, John	Governors	Calhern, Louis	Entertainers (Vintage)
Burroughs, Jeff	Baseball	Calhoun, Alice	Entertainers (Vintage)
Burroughs, John	Authors	Calhoun, Eleanor	Entertainers (Vintage)
Burrows, Abe	Authors	Calhoun, John C. (V)	U.S. V.P. & Cabinet
Burstyn, Ellen	Entertainers (Current)	Calhoun, Rory	Entertainers (Current)
Burt, Jim	Football	Calkin, Dick	Cartoonists
Burton, Charlotte	Entertainers (Vintage)	Callaghan, James	Heads of State
Burton, Harold H. (SC)	Celebrities	Callahan, Laurence K.	Aviation
Burton, Lady Isabel	Authors	Callahan, Mushy	Boxing
Burton, LeVar	Entertainers (Current)	Callas, Charlie	Entertainers (Current)
Burton, Richard	Entertainers (Vintage)	Callas, Maria	Entertainers (Vintage)
Busby, George	Governors	Calleia, Frank	Entertainers (Vintage)
Busby, Jim	Baseball	Callen, Gloria	General Sports
Busby, Steve	Baseball	Calley, William	Military
Busch, August A.	Business	Calloway, Cab	Entertainers (Vintage)
Busey, Gary	Entertainers (Current)	Calloway, Cab	Entertainers (Current)
Bush, George	U.S. V.P. & Cabinet	Calvello, Ann	General Sports
Bush, Guy	Baseball	Calvert, Louis	Entertainers (Vintage)
Bush, Vannevar	Science	Calvet, Corinne	Entertainers (Current)
Bushkin, Joe	Entertainers (Vintage)	Calvin, Melvin	Science
Bushman, Francis X.	Entertainers (Vintage)	Camargo, Alberto	Heads of State
Bushmiller, Ernie	Cartoonists	Cambaceres, J.J.R.(Parma)	Revolutionary War
Bushnell, David	Science	Cameron, Betsy	Authors
Buss, Jerry	General Sports	Cameron, Fred L.	General Sports
Butenandt, Adolf	Science	Cameron, Harold	Hockey HoF
Butkus, Dick	Football	Cameron, Rod	Entertainers (Vintage)
Butler, Benjamin F.	U.S. V.P. & Cabinet	Cameron, Simon	U.S. V.P. & Cabinet
Butler, Carl & Pearl	Country Music Stars	Camilli, Dolph	Baseball
Butler, Daws	Entertainers (Current)	Cammaerts, Emile	Authors
Butler, John	Revolutionary War	Camp, Colleen	Entertainers (Current)
Butler, M. Calbraith	Civil War	Camp, Walter	Football
Butler, Nicholas M.	Celebrities	Campanella, Joseph	Entertainers (Current)
Butler, Pierce (SC)	Celebrities	Campanella, Roy	Baseball
Butler, Pierce	Revolutionary War	Campaneris, Bert	Baseball
Butler, Samuel	Authors	Campanis, Al	Baseball
Butler, Smedley D.	Military	Campbell, Angus	Hockey HoF
Butterfield, Jack	Hockey HoF	Campbell, Archie	Country Music Stars
Butterfield, Daniel	Civil War	Campbell, Beatrice	Entertainers (Vintage)
Buttlar-Brandenfels, F.H.	Military	Campbell, Chas. Thos.	Civil War
Button, Dick	General Sports	Campbell, Clarence	Hockey HoF
Buttram, Pat	Entertainers (Vintage)	Campbell, Douglas	Aviation
Butz, Earl L.	U.S. V.P. & Cabinet	Campbell, Donald	General Sports
Buzzi, Ruth	Entertainers (Current)	Campbell, E. Simms	Cartoonists
Byars, Keith	Football	Campbell, Earl	Football
Byers, Samuel Hawkins	Authors	Campbell, George J. D.	Celebrities
Byner, John	Entertainers (Current)	Campbell, George W.	U.S. V.P. & Cabinet
Byrd, Harry	Baseball	Campbell, Glen	Entertainers (Current)
Byrd, Richard E.	Aviation	Campbell, Hugh	Football
Byrd, Sam	Baseball	Campbell, James E.	Governors
Byrne, Bobby	Entertainers (Vintage)	Campbell, Jack M.	Governors
Byrne, Jane	Celebrities	Campbell, John A. (SC)	Celebrities
Byrne, Tommy	Baseball	Campbell, Marion	Football
Byrnes, James F. (SC)	Celebrities	Campbell, Oliver S.	Tennis HoF
Byron, Arthur	Entertainers (Vintage)	Campbell, R. L.	Military
Byron, Lord Geo. Gordon	Authors	Campbell, Sir Colin	Military
Caan, James	Entertainers (Current)	Campbell, Sir Malcolm	General Sports
Cabana, Robert D.	Astronauts	Campbell-Bannerman, H.	Heads of State
Cable, George	Authors	Camus, Albert	Authors
Cabot, Bruce	Entertainers (Vintage)	Canadeo, Tony	Football
Caceres, Andreas A.	Heads of State	Canby, Edward	Civil War
Cadbury, Richard	Business	Candini, Milo	Baseball
Caddel, Ernie	Football	Candler, Asa Griggs	Business
Cadman, Chas. Wakefield	Composers	Candy, John	Entertainers (Current)
Cadmus, Paul	Artists	Canetti, Elia	Authors

Caniff, Milton	Cartoonists	Carr, Vicki	Entertainers (Current)
Cann, Howard	Basketball HoF	Carradine, Keith	Entertainers (Current)
Canning, George	Heads of State	Carrel, Dr. Alexis	Science
Cannon, Billy	Football	Carrera, Barbara	Entertainers (Current)
Cannon, Dr. Martha H.	Science	Carrillo, Leo	Entertainers (Vintage)
Cannon, Dyan	Entertainers (Current)	Carroll, Chas(Carrollton)	Revolutionary War
Cannon, Jimmy	General Sports	Carroll, Diahann	Entertainers (Current)
Cannon, John K.	Military ·	Carroll, Earl	Entertainers (Vintage)
Canova, Diana	Entertainers (Current)	Carroll, John Lee	Governors
Canova, Judy	Entertainers (Vintage)	Carroll, John	Entertainers (Vintage)
Canseco, Jose	Baseball	Carroll, Julian M.	Governors
Cantinflas	Entertainers (Vintage)	Carroll, Lisa Hart	Entertainers (Current)
Cantor, Eddie	Entertainers (Vintage)	Carroll, Madeleine	Entertainers (Vintage)
Cantrell, Lana	Entertainers (Current)	Carroll, William	Governors
Canutt, Yakima	Entertainers (Vintage)	Carryl, Guy Wetmore	Authors
Canzoneri, Tony	Boxing	Carson, Harry	Football
Capers, Virginia	Entertainers (Current)	Carson, Johnny	Entertainers (Current)
Capka, Carol	Entertainers (Current)	Carson, Rachel	Authors
Caplin, Mortimer	Celebrities	Carson, Sunset	Entertainers (Vintage)
Capote, Truman	Authors	Carter, Anthony	Football
Capp, Al	Cartoonists	Carter, Benny	Entertainers (Vintage)
Cappelletti, Gino	Football	Carter, Billy	Celebrities
Cappelletti, John	Football	Carter, Boake	Celebrities
Capra, Frank	Entertainers (Current)	Carter, Fred	General Sports
Capshaw, Kate	Entertainers (Current)	Carter, Gary	Baseball
Captain & Tennile	Entertainers (Current)	Carter, Helen	Country Music Stars
Capucine	Entertainers (Current)	Carter, Hodding	U.S. V.P. & Cabinet
Caras, Jimmy	General Sports	Carter, Janis	Entertainers (Vintage)
Cardenal, Jose	Baseball	Carter, Jimmy	U.S. Presidents
Cardigan, 7th Earl	Military	Carter, Jimmy	Boxing
Cardozo, Benjamin N. (SC)	Celebrities	Carter, Joe	Baseball
Cardwell, Don	Baseball	Carter, Leslie Mrs.	Entertainers (Vintage)
Carew, Rod	Baseball	Carter, Lillian	Celebrities
Carey, Andy	Baseball	Carter, Lynda	Entertainers (Current)
Carey, Harry Jr.	Entertainers (Current)	Carter, Mother Maybelle	Country Music Stars
Carey, Harry	Entertainers (Vintage)	Carter, Rosalynn	Celebrities
Carey, Hugh L.	Governors	Carter, Rubin	Football
Carey, Macdonald	Entertainers (Current)	Carter, Sonny	Astronauts
Carey, Max	Baseball	Carter, Tony	Entertainers (Current)
Carey, Michele	Entertainers (Current)	Carter, Wilf	Country Music Stars
Carey, Ron	Entertainers (Current)	Cartland, Barbara	Authors
Carl, Marion	Aviation	Cartwright, Angela	Entertainers (Current)
Carleton, Guy (Baron)	Military	Carty, Rico	Baseball
Carleton, Will	Authors	Caruso, Anthony	Entertainers (Vintage)
Carlin, George	Entertainers (Current)	Caruso, Enrico	Entertainers (Vintage)
Carlin, Lynn	Entertainers (Current)	Carvel, Elbert M.	Governors
Carlisle, Earl of	Celebrities	Carver, Geo. Washingtn	Science
Carlisle, Kitty	Entertainers (Vintage)	Carville, Edward P.	Governors
Carlisle, Mary	Entertainers (Vintage)	Casals, Pablo	Composers
Carlo Alberto (Sardinia)	Heads of State	Casals, Rosemary	General Sports
Carlotta (Mex)	Heads of State	Casanova, Len	Football
Carlson, Dr. H. Clifford	Basketball HoF	Casanovo, Giacomo	Authors
Carlson, Frank	Governors	Case, Everett	Basketball HoF
Carlton, Steve	Baseball	Case, Norman S.	Governors
Carlyle, Thomas	Authors	Casella, Alfredo	Composers
Carman, Tex J.	Country Music Stars	Casey, Bernie	Football
Carmen, Jean	Entertainers (Vintage)	Casey, Silas	Civil War
Carmichael, Hoagy	Composers	Cash, Johnny	Country Music Stars
Carnarvon, Henry 4th Earl	Celebrities	Cash, June Carter	Country Music Stars
Carne, Judy	Entertainers (Current)	Cash, Norm	Baseball
Carnegie, Andrew	Business	Cash, Rosanne	Entertainers (Current)
Carnegie, Dale	Business	Cash, Tommy	Country Music Stars
Carnera, Primo	Boxing	Casper, Billy	Golf HoF
Carnesecca, Lou	General Sports	Casper, John H.	Astronauts
Carnevale, Bernard L.	General Sports	Cass, Lewis	U.S. V.P. & Cabinet
Carnevale, Ben	Basketball HoF	Cassady, Howard"Hopalong"	Football
Carney, Robert B.	Military	Cassatt, Mary	Artists
Carnot, Lazare N.M.	Revolutionary War	Cassavetes, John	Entertainers (Current)
Carnovsky, Morris	Entertainers (Vintage)	Cassidy, Joanna	Entertainers (Current)
Carol, Sue (Ladd)	Entertainers (Vintage)	Cassin, Rene	Celebrities
Caroline (Geo. IV-Eng)	Heads of State	Cassini, Oleg	Business
Caroline (Geo. II-Eng)	Heads of State	Castellani, Rocky	Boxing
Caron, George R.	Military	Castle, Irene	Entertainers (Vintage)
Caron, Leslie	Entertainers (Current)	Castle, Lee	Entertainers (Vintage)
Carpenter, Carleton	Entertainers (Vintage)	Castle, Peggy	Entertainers (Current)
Carpenter, Richard	Entertainers (Current)	Castleman, Clydell	Baseball
Carpenter, Scott	Astronauts	Castro, Fidel	Heads of State
Carpenter, William S	Military	Castro, Raul H.	Governors
Carpentier, Georges	Boxing	Cates, Clifton B.	Military
Carr, Darleen	Entertainers (Current)	Cates, Phoebe	Entertainers (Current)
Carr, Gerald P.	Astronauts	Cathcart, Wm. Schaw Sir	Revolutionary War

441

Cather, Willa	Authors
Catherine I (Rus)	Heads of State
Catherine II (The Great)	Heads of State
Catherine de Medicis (Fr)	Heads of State
Catherwood, Mary	Authors
Catlett, Walter	Entertainers (Vintage)
Catt, Carrie Chapman	Celebrities
Cattarinich, Joseph	Hockey HoF
Catton, Bruce	Authors
Caudill, Bill	Baseball
Caulfield, Joan	Entertainers (Vintage)
Cauthen, Steve	General Sports
Cavanaugh, Hobart	Entertainers (Vintage)
Cavaretta, Phil	Baseball
Cavell, Edith	Science
Cayvan, Georgia	Entertainers (Vintage)
Cecil, Algernon Lord	Celebrities
Cedeno, Cesar	Baseball
Cellini, Benvenuto	Artists
Cello, Aldo	Business
Cepeda, Orlando	Baseball
Cerf, Bennett	Authors
Cernan, Eugene A.	Astronauts
Cervantes, Miguel de	Authors
Cervi, Al (Digger)	Basketball HoF
Cey, Ron "Penguin"	Baseball
Cezanne, Paul	Artists
Chabas, Paul Emile	Artists
Chabot, Phillipe (Brion)	Celebrities
Chabrier, Emmanuel	Composers
Chace, Malcolm	Tennis HoF
Chadwick, Florence	General Sports
Chadwick, William	Hockey HoF
Chaffee, Adna R.	Military
Chaffee, Roger	Astronauts
Chagall, Marc	Artists
Chakiris, George	Entertainers (Current)
Chaliapin, Fyodor	Entertainers (Vintage)
Chamberlain, Neville	Heads of State
Chamberlain, Wilt	Basketball HoF
Chamberlain, Austen	Celebrities
Chamberlain, Rich.	Entertainers (Current)
Chamberlain, Joshua	Civil War
Chamberlain, Owen	Science
Chamberlin, Clarence	Aviation
Chambers, Marilyn	Entertainers (Current)
Chambers, Robert Wm.	Authors
Chambers, Whittaker	Celebrities
Chambers,Dorothea Lambert	Tennis HoF
Chambliss, Chris	Baseball
Chaminade, Cecile	Composers
Champion, Marge	Entertainers (Current)
Chance, Dean	Baseball
Chandler, "Spud"	Baseball
Chandler, A.B. "Happy"	Baseball
Chandler, Dorothy "Buff"	Business
Chandler, George	Entertainers (Current)
Chandler, Jeff	Entertainers (Vintage)
Chandler, Norman	Business
Chandler, Otis	Business
Chandler, Raymond	Authors
Chandler, William E.	U.S. V.P. & Cabinet
Chandler, Zachariah	U.S. V.P. & Cabinet
Chanel, Coco	Business
Chang, Franklin R.	Astronauts
Channing, Carol	Entertainers (Current)
Channing, Stockard	Entertainers (Current)
Channing, William E.	Authors
Chaparral, John and Paul	Country Music Stars
Chapin, Harry	Composers
Chaplin, Charles	Entertainers (Vintage)
Chaplin, Geraldine	Entertainers (Current)
Chaplin, Lita Grey	Entertainers (Vintage)
Chaplin, Sydney	Entertainers (Vintage)
Chapman, Ben	Baseball
Chapman, Oscar L.	U.S. V.P. & Cabinet
Chapman, Philip K.	Astronauts
Chapman, Sam	Baseball
Chappuis, Bob	Football
Charcot, Jean	Science
Charisse, Cyd	Entertainers (Vintage)
Charlemagne**	Heads of State
Charles Edw. Stuart	Heads of State
Charles I (Eng)	Heads of State
Charles II (Eng)	Heads of State
Charles IX (Fr)	Heads of State
Charles V (Chas. I {Sp})	Heads of State
Charles X (Fr)	Heads of State
Charles XIV John (Swe)	Heads of State
Charles XV (Swe-Nor)	Heads of State
Charles, Ezzard	Boxing
Charles, Prince of Wales	Heads of State
Charles, Ray	Entertainers (Current)
Charles, Suzette	Entertainers (Current)
Charlotte (George III)	Heads of State
Charlotte, Gr. Duch.(Lux)	Heads of State
Charo	Entertainers (Current)
Charpentier, Gustave	Composers
Charteris, Leslie	Authors
Chase, Chevy	Entertainers (Current)
Chase, Hal	Baseball
Chase, Ilka	Entertainers (Vintage)
Chase, Mary Ellen	Authors
Chase, Salmon P. (SC)	Celebrities
Chase, Samuel	Revolutionary War
Chataway, Chris	General Sports
Chateaubriand, Count F.R.	Authors
Chateaubriand, F. Rene de	Celebrities
Chatterton, Ruth	Entertainers (Vintage)
Chauncey, Isaac	Military
Chavez, Carlos	Composers
Chavez, Cesar E.	Celebrities
Chavez, George A.	Aviation
Chayefsky, Paddy	Authors
Checkers, Chubby	Entertainers (Current)
Cheever, Dr. Charles A.	Science
Cheever, John	Authors
Cheevers, Gerry	Hockey HoF
Chekhov, Anton	Authors
Chenault, Claire L.	Aviation
Chennault, Anna	Celebrities
Cher	Entertainers (Current)
Cherry, R. Gregg	Governors
Cherubini, Luigi	Composers
Cheshire, Leonard	Military
Chesterton, G. K.	Authors
Chevalier, Albert	Composers
Chevalier, Maurice	Entertainers (Vintage)
Chicago	Rock
Chichester, Francis, Sir	Celebrities
Child, Julia	Celebrities
Childs, George Wm.	Celebrities
Chiles, Lois	Entertainers (Vintage)
Chirac, Jacques	Heads of State
Chiti, Harry	Baseball
Choate, Joseph H.	Celebrities
Chopin, Frederic	Composers
Chou En-Lai	Heads of State
Chouteau, Auguste	Revolutionary War
Christensen, Todd	Football
Christian, VII	Heads of State
Christians, Mady	Entertainers (Vintage)
Christiansen, Jack	Football
Christie, Agatha	Authors
Christie, Julie	Entertainers (Current)
Christina (Swe)	Heads of State
Christine, Virginia	Entertainers (Current)
Christopher, Warren	Celebrities
Christopher, Dennis	Entertainers (Current)
Christopher, William	Entertainers (Current)
Christy, Howard Chandler	Artists
Chrysler, Walter P.	Business
Chun Doo-Hwan	Heads of State
Chung, Connie	Celebrities
Church, Benjamin	Revolutionary War
Church, Frederick E.	Artists
Churchill, Clementine S.	Celebrities
Churchill, Jennie(Jerome)	Celebrities
Churchill, Randolph, Lord	Celebrities
Churchill, Sarah	Celebrities
Churchill, Winston	Authors
Churchill, Winston S.	Heads of State

Chuvalo, George	Boxing	Clymer, George	Revolutionary War
Chylak, Nestor	Baseball	Coates, Eric	Composers
Ciccarelli, Dino	General Sports	Coats, Michael L.	Astronauts
Cicotte, Eddie	Baseball	Cobb, Howell	Civil War
Cimino, Michael	Entertainers (Current)	Cobb, Irvin S.	Authors
Citroen, Andre	Business	Cobb, Lee J.	Entertainers (Vintage)
Civiletti, Benjamin	U.S. V.P. & Cabinet	Cobb, Ty	Baseball
Claire, Ina	Entertainers (Vintage)	Cobham, Alan J.	Aviation
Clampett, Bobby	General Sports	Cobham, Gov. Gen. NZ	Heads of State
Clancy, F. M. "King"	Hockey HoF	Cobo, Albert E.	Celebrities
Clancy, King	General Sports	Coburn, James	Entertainers (Current)
Clanton, Jimmy	Entertainers (Vintage)	Coca, Imogene	Entertainers (Vintage)
Clapp, Louise Brough	Tennis HoF	Cochet, Henri	Tennis HoF
Clapper, Aubrey "Dit"	Hockey HoF	Cochran, Jacqueline	Aviation
Clapton, Eric	Rock	Cochran, Robert L.	Governors
Clark, "Cottonseed"	Country Music Stars	Cochran, Roy	General Sports
Clark, Abraham	Revolutionary War	Cochran, Steve	Entertainers (Vintage)
Clark, Barzilla W.	Governors	Cochrane, Basil Sir	Military
Clark, Candy	Entertainers (Current)	Cochrane, Gordon "Mickey"	Baseball
Clark, Charles	Civil War	Cockburn, George Sir	Military
Clark, Dane	Entertainers (Vintage)	Cockcroft, John D.	Science
Clark, Dick	Entertainers (Current)	Cocker, Joe	Rock
Clark, Dwight	Football	Coco, James	Entertainers (Vintage)
Clark, Earl "Dutch"	Football	Cocteau, Jean	Authors
Clark, George Rogers	Revolutionary War	Cody, Buck	Entertainers (Vintage)
Clark, Jack	Baseball	Cody, Iron Eyes	Entertainers (Vintage)
Clark, Jim	General Sports	Cody, John Cardinal	Celebrities
Clark, Joseph S.	Tennis HoF	Cody, Lew	Entertainers (Vintage)
Clark, Marguerite	Entertainers (Vintage)	Cody, William F.	Celebrities
Clark, Mark W.	Military	Cogdill, Gail	Football
Clark, Mary	Military	Cohan, George M.	Composers
Clark, Myron H.	Governors	Cohen, Octavus Roy	Authors
Clark, Petula	Entertainers (Current)	Cohen, Wilbur J.	U.S. V.P. & Cabinet
Clark, Roy	Country Music Stars	Cohn, Roy	Celebrities
Clark, Susan	Entertainers (Current)	Coker, Jack	Entertainers (Current)
Clark, Tom C. (SC)	Celebrities	Colangelo, Jerry	General Sports
Clark, William	Celebrities	Colavito, Rocky	Baseball
Clarke, Annie	Entertainers (Vintage)	Colbert, Claudette	Entertainers (Vintage)
Clarke, Arthur C.	Authors	Colden, Cadwallader	Revolutionary War
Clarke, Fred C.	Baseball	Cole, Edward N.	Business
Clarke, Mae	Entertainers (Vintage)	Cole, Michael	Entertainers (Current)
Clarke, Thomas	Revolutionary War	Cole, Nat King	Entertainers (Vintage)
Clarkson, Matthew	Military	Coleman, Dabney	Entertainers (Current)
Clary, B. A.	Military	Coleman, Gary	Entertainers (Current)
Clary, Robert	Entertainers (Current)	Coleman, Gerry	Baseball
Clavell, James	Authors	Coleman, Gordon	Baseball
Clay, Cassius M.	Boxing	Coleman, Nancy	Entertainers (Vintage)
Clay, Henry	U.S. V.P. & Cabinet	Coleman, Vince	Baseball
Clay, Lucius	Military	Coleridge, John Duke	Celebrities
Clayburgh, Jill	Entertainers (Current)	Coleridge, Sam'l Taylor	Authors
Clayton, Jan	Entertainers (Vintage)	Coleridge-Taylor, Samuel	Composers
Clayton, Joshua	Revolutionary War	Colfax, Schuyler (V)	U.S. V.P. & Cabinet
Cleary, Bill	General Sports	Colgate, James C.	Business
Cleave, Mary	Astronauts	Collette, Sidonie G.	Authors
Cleese, John	Entertainers (Current)	Collier, Peter F.	Business
Cleghorn, Sprague	Hockey HoF	Collinge, Patricia	Entertainers (Vintage)
Clemenceau, Georges	Heads of State	Collins Jr., Eddie	Baseball
Clemens, Roger	Baseball	Collins, "Eddie"	Baseball
Clemens, Sam'l L.(Twain)	Authors	Collins, J. Lawton	Military
Clement VIII, Pope	Heads of State	Collins, Jackie	Authors
Clemente, Roberto	Baseball	Collins, James "Rip"	Baseball
Cleveland, Frances F.	Celebrities	Collins, Jimmy	Baseball
Cleveland, Grover	U.S. Presidents	Collins, Joan	Entertainers (Current)
Cliburn, Van	Entertainers (Current)	Collins, Joe	Baseball
Clifford, Clark M.	U.S. V.P. & Cabinet	Collins, Judy	Rock
Clifford, Nathan (SC)	Celebrities	Collins, Judy	Entertainers (Current)
Clift, Harland	Baseball	Collins, LeRoy	Governors
Clifton, "Flea"	Baseball	Collins, Lottie	Entertainers (Vintage)
Cline, Patsy	Country Music Stars	Collins, Michael	Astronauts
Cline, Ty	Baseball	Collins, Phil	Rock
Clingman, T. L.	Civil War	Collins, Wilkie	Authors
Clinton, De Witt	Revolutionary War	Collinsworth, Cris	Football
Clinton, George	U.S. V.P. & Cabinet	Colman, Ronald	Entertainers (Vintage)
Clinton, Sir Henry	Military	Colonna, Jerry	Entertainers (Vintage)
Clive, Robert	Military	Colosi, Nick	Baseball
Cloggers, Stoney Mtn.	Country Music Stars	Colquitt, Alfred H.	Civil War
Clooney, Rosemary	Entertainers (Current)	Colson, Charles	Celebrities
Close, Glenn	Entertainers (Current)	Colt, Samuel	Science
Clothier, William J.	Tennis HoF	Colton, Joe	Baseball
Clovio, Giorgio Guilio	Artists	Columbo, Russ	Entertainers (Vintage)
Clyde, June	Entertainers (Vintage)	Colville, Neil	Hockey HoF

443

Name	Category
Combs, Earle	Baseball
Combs, Merrill	Baseball
Comden, Betty	Composers
Comiskey, Charles	Baseball
Commodores	Rock
Como, Perry	Entertainers (Current)
Compson, Betty	Entertainers (Vintage)
Compton, Arthur H.	Science
Compton, Joyce	Entertainers (Vintage)
Conacher, Charles	Hockey HoF
Conant, James Bryant	Celebrities
Conatser, Clint	Baseball
Concepcion, Dave	Baseball
Condon, Richard	Authors
Cone, Dave	Baseball
Cone, Fairfax M.	Business
Cone, Fred	Football
Conerly, Charles	Football
Conforti, Gino	Entertainers (Current)
Congreve, William	Science
Conigliaro, Tony	Baseball
Conklin, Chester	Entertainers (Vintage)
Conlan, John B. "Jocko"	Baseball
Conley, Gene	Baseball
Conley, Joe	Entertainers (Current)
Conn, Billy	Boxing
Connally, John	Governors
Connell, Alex	Hockey HoF
Connelly, Lex	General Sports
Connelly, Marc	Authors
Connelly, Matthew J.	U.S. V.P. & Cabinet
Conner, Bart	General Sports
Conner, Dennis	General Sports
Connery, Sean	Entertainers (Current)
Conniff, Ray	Entertainers (Vintage)
Connolly, Harold	General Sports
Connolly, Maureen	General Sports
Connolly, Olga	General Sports
Connolly, Walter	Entertainers (Vintage)
Connor, George	Football
Connor, Harry P.	Aviation
Connor, James	Civil War
Connor, John T.	U.S. V.P. & Cabinet
Connors, Chuck	Entertainers (Vintage)
Connors, Jimmy	General Sports
Connors, Mike	Entertainers (Current)
Connors, Patti Mc.	Entertainers (Current)
Conover, Harry	Business
Conquest, Ida	Entertainers (Vintage)
Conrad, Charles Magill	U.S. V.P. & Cabinet
Conrad, Charles Jr.	Astronauts
Conrad, Gerhard	Aviation
Conrad, Max	General Sports
Conrad, Michael	Entertainers (Vintage)
Conrad, William	Authors
Conrad, William	Entertainers (Current)
Conried, Hans	Entertainers (Vintage)
Conroy, Kevin	Entertainers (Current)
Consolo, Billy	Baseball
Consuegra, Sandy	Baseball
Conte, John	Entertainers (Vintage)
Conte, Richard	Entertainers (Current)
Conti, Bill	Composers
Conway, Henry Seymour	Military
Conway, Rose A.	U.S. V.P. & Cabinet
Conway, Tim	Entertainers (Current)
Coogan, Jackie	Entertainers (Vintage)
Coogan, Richard	Entertainers (Vintage)
Cook, Cliff	Baseball
Cook, Elisha Jr.	Entertainers (Current)
Cook, Frederick A., Dr.	Celebrities
Cook, James Capt.	Celebrities
Cook, Joseph	Celebrities
Cook, Thomas	Celebrities
Cook, William	Hockey HoF
Cooke, Alistair	Authors
Cooke, Jack Kent	General Sports
Cooke, Jay	Business
Cooke, Sam	Rock
Cooke, Terence Cardinal	Celebrities
Cool, Harry	Entertainers (Vintage)
Cooley, Dr. Denton A.	Science
Cooley, Spade	Country Music Stars
Coolidge, Calvin	U.S. Presidents
Coolidge, Dr. William D.	Science
Coolidge, Grace	Celebrities
Coolidge, T. Jefferson	U.S. V.P. & Cabinet
Coolidge, William D.	Celebrities
Coombs, Patricia	Artists
Cooney, Gerry	Boxing
Cooper, Alfred Duff	Celebrities
Cooper, Alice	Entertainers (Current)
Cooper, Cecil	Baseball
Cooper, Charles (Tarzan)	Basketball HoF
Cooper, Dr. Leon	Science
Cooper, Gary	Entertainers (Vintage)
Cooper, Gladys Dame	Entertainers (Vintage)
Cooper, Gordon	Astronauts
Cooper, Harry	General Sports
Cooper, Jackie	Entertainers (Vintage)
Cooper, James Fennimore	Authors
Cooper, Peter	Business
Cooper, Prentice	Governors
Cooper, Samuel	Civil War
Cooper, Thos. Sidney	Artists
Cooper, Walker	Baseball
Cooper, Wilbur	Baseball
Coors, W. K.	Business
Coots, J. Fred	Composers
Copas, Cowboy	Country Music Stars
Copeland, L. du Pont	Business
Copeland, Lillian	General Sports
Copland, Aaron	Composers
Copley, John Singleton	Artists
Copperfield, David	Entertainers (Current)
Coppola, Francis	Entertainers (Current)
Corbett, James J.	Boxing
Corbusier, Le	Celebrities
Corcoran, Fred	Golf HoF
Cordero, Angel	General Sports
Corelli, Marie	Authors
Corey, Wendell	Entertainers (Vintage)
Cori, C. F.	Science
Corio, Ann	Entertainers (Vintage)
Corlett, Irene	Entertainers (Vintage)
Cornell, Ezra	Business
Cornell, Joseph	Artists
Cornell, Katharine	Entertainers (Vintage)
Cornell, Lydia	Entertainers (Current)
Corner, George W.	Science
Cornfeld, Bernard	Business
Cornforth, J. W.	Science
Corning, Erastus	Business
Cornwallis, Charles	Military
Corot, J. B. Camile	Artists
Corrigan, Douglas	Aviation
Corrigan, M. /B. Williams	Celebrities
Corse, John M.	Civil War
Cortez, Ricardo	Entertainers (Vintage)
Coryell, Don	Football
Cosby, Bill	Entertainers (Current)
Cosby, George B.	Civil War
Coscarart, Pete	Baseball
Cosell, Howard	General Sports
Costas, Bob	General Sports
Coste, Dieudonne	Aviation
Costello, Delores	Entertainers (Vintage)
Costello, Elvis	Rock
Costello, Larry	General Sports
Costello, Lou	Entertainers (Vintage)
Cotten, Joseph	Entertainers (Current)
Cotton, Carolina	Country Music Stars
Cotton, Henry	Golf HoF
Couch, Darius Nash	Civil War
Couch, Virgil	Celebrities
Cougar, John	Rock
Coughlin, Charles E.	Celebrities
Coulon, Johnny	Boxing
Coulter, Arthur	Hockey HoF
Coulter, Jessie	Country Music Stars
Coulter, Richard	Civil War
Counts, Mel	General Sports

444

445

D'Oyly Carte	Entertainers (Vintage)
Dafoe, Dr. Allan Roy	Science
Daguerre, Louis	Science
Dahl, Arlene	Entertainers (Current)
Dahl, Roald	Authors
Dahlberg, Edward	Authors
Dahlgren, Babe	Baseball
Dahlgren, John A.	Civil War
Dailey, Dan	Entertainers (Vintage)
Dailey, Peter F.	Entertainers (Vintage)
Daladier, Edouard	Heads of State
Dalai Lama	Heads of State
Daley, Richard J.	Celebrities
Dali, Salvador	Artists
Dallas, Alexander J.	U.S. V.P. & Cabinet
Dallas, George M. (V)	U.S. V.P. & Cabinet
Dallessandro, Dom	Baseball
Dalrymple, Clay	Baseball
Dalton, Abby	Entertainers (Current)
Dalton, Charles	Entertainers (Vintage)
Dalton, Dorothy	Entertainers (Vintage)
Dalton, Emmett	Celebrities
Daltry, Roger	Rock
Daly, James	Entertainers (Current)
Daly, John	Entertainers (Current)
Daly, John Charles	Entertainers (Vintage)
Daly, Tyne	Entertainers (Current)
Damita, Lily	Entertainers (Vintage)
Damon, Cathryn	Entertainers (Current)
Damrosch, Walter	Composers
Dana, Charles A.	Celebrities
Dana, Richard Henry	Authors
Dancer, Stanley	General Sports
Dandurand, Joseph "Leo"	Hockey HoF
Dane, Nathan	Revolutionary War
Danforth, Thomas	Revolutionary War
Dangerfield, Rodney	Entertainers (Current)
Dangerfield, George	Authors
Daniel, Peter Vivian (SC)	Celebrities
Daniels, Bebe	Entertainers (Vintage)
Daniels, Charlie	Rock
Daniels, Josephus	U.S. V.P. & Cabinet
Daniloff, Nick	Celebrities
Danner, Blythe	Entertainers (Current)
Dannihill, Albert	Entertainers (Current)
Danning, Harry	Baseball
Danning, Sybil	Entertainers (Current)
Dano, Royal	Entertainers (Current)
Danova, Cesare	Entertainers (Current)
Danowski, Ed	Football
Danson, Ted	Entertainers (Current)
Danton, Georges-Jacques	Revolutionary War
Danza, Tony	Entertainers (Current)
Danzig, Allison	Tennis HoF
Danzig, Sarah Palfrey	Tennis HoF
Darden, Tom "Satch"	General Sports
Dark, Al	Baseball
Darling, Ron	Baseball
Darnell, Linda	Entertainers (Vintage)
Darragh, John	Hockey HoF
Darrell, Johnny	Country Music Stars
Darro, Frankie	Entertainers (Vintage)
Darrow, Clarence	Celebrities
Dart, Justin	Business
Darwin, Charles	Science
Darwin, Danny	Baseball
Dascoli, Frank	Baseball
Daubigny, Charles F.	Artists
Daugherty, "Duffy"	Football
Daugherty, Harry M.	U.S. V.P. & Cabinet
Daumier, Honore	Artists
Dauvray, Helen	Entertainers (Vintage)
Daval, Danny	Entertainers (Current)
Davalillo, Vic	Baseball
Dave, Red River	Country Music Stars
Davenport, Addington	Revolutionary War
Davenport, Fanny	Entertainers (Vintage)
Davenport, Homer C.	Artists
Davenport, Jim	Baseball
Davenport, Willie	General Sports
Davey, Chuck	Boxing
David, Hal	Composers
David, Jacques Louis	Artists
Davidson, A. M. "Scotty"	Hockey HoF
Davidson, Jo	Artists
Davidson, John	Entertainers (Current)
Davies, Bob	Basketball HoF
Davies, Mandy Rice	Celebrities
Davies, Marion	Entertainers (Vintage)
Davies, Rhys	Authors
Davies, Ronald N.	Celebrities
Davies, William	Revolutionary War
Davis, Alvin	Baseball
Davis, Angela	Celebrities
Davis, Benj. O. Jr.	Military
Davis, Bette	Entertainers (Vintage)
Davis, Brad	Entertainers (Current)
Davis, Charles Henry	Civil War
Davis, Chili	Baseball
Davis, Clifton	Entertainers (Current)
Davis, David (SC)	Celebrities
Davis, Dwight F.	General Sports
Davis, Dwight F.	Tennis HoF
Davis, Dwight F.	U.S. V.P. & Cabinet
Davis, Eric	Baseball
Davis, Fay	Entertainers (Vintage)
Davis, Geena	Entertainers (Current)
Davis, George	Baseball
Davis, Glenn	Football
Davis, Governor Jimmie	Country Music Stars
Davis, James J.	U.S. V.P. & Cabinet
Davis, Jefferson	Civil War
Davis, Jim	Entertainers (Vintage)
Davis, Jim	Cartoonists
Davis, Jo	Entertainers (Vintage)
Davis, Jody	Baseball
Davis, John W.	Celebrities
Davis, Johnny "Scat"	Entertainers (Vintage)
Davis, Mack	Country Music Stars
Davis, Nancy (Reagan)	Celebrities
Davis, Nancy	Entertainers (Vintage)
Davis, Nelson H.	Civil War
Davis, Noah	Celebrities
Davis, Patti	Entertainers (Current)
Davis, Phyllis	Entertainers (Current)
Davis, Rich'd Harding	Authors
Davis, Sammy Jr.	Entertainers (Current)
Davis, Storm	Baseball
Davis, Tommy	Baseball
Davis, Varina	Civil War
Davis, Willie	Baseball
Davis, Willie	Football
Davison, Ben	Football
Davout, Louis N.	Revolutionary War
Davy, Humphrey Sir	Science
Dawber, Pam	Entertainers (Current)
Dawes, Charles G. (V)	U.S. V.P. & Cabinet
Dawkins, Pete	Football
Dawson, Andre	Baseball
Dawson, Len	Football
Day, Chon	Cartoonists
Day, Clarence "Hap"	Hockey HoF
Day, Dennis	Entertainers (Current)
Day, Doris	Entertainers (Current)
Day, J. Edward	U.S. V.P. & Cabinet
Day, Laraine	Entertainers (Vintage)
Day, Linda (George)	Entertainers (Current)
Day, William R. (SC)	Celebrities
Dayan, Moshe	Military
Dayton, Elias	Revolutionary War
Dayton, Jonathan	Revolutionary War
De Acosta, Mercedes	Authors
De Gaulle, Charles	Heads of State
De Havilland, Geoffrey	Aviation
De Kooning, Willem	Artists
De La Mare, Walter	Authors
De La Renta, Oscar	Business
De Lancey, Stephen	Revolutionary War
De Windt, Harry	Celebrities
DeBakey, Dr. Michael	Science
DeBartolo Jr., Ed	Football

DeBernardi, Forrest	Basketball HoF	Denfeld, Louis M.	Military
DeBerry, Fisher	Football	Denkinger, Don	Baseball
DeBusschere, Dave	Basketball HoF	Denman, Thomas Baron	Heads of State
DeCarlo, Yvonne	Entertainers (Current)	Dennehy, Brian	Entertainers (Current)
DeCasseres. Benjamin	Authors	Denneny, Cyril	Hockey HoF
DeCinces, Doug	Baseball	Denning, Richard	Entertainers (Vintage)
DeCordova, Fred	Entertainers (Current)	Dennison, Jo Carroll	Entertainers (Current)
DeForest, Dr. Lee	Science	Dent, Jim	General Sports
DeHart, John	Revolutionary War	Dente, Sam	Baseball
DeHaven, Gloria	Entertainers (Current)	Denton, Jerry	Military
DeHavilland, Olivia	Entertainers (Current)	Denver, Bob	Entertainers (Current)
DeKoven, Reginald	Composers	Denver, James W.	Celebrities
DeLaCroix, Raven	Entertainers (Current)	Denver, John	Entertainers (Current)
DeLaPena, George	Entertainers (Current)	Depew, Chauncey M.	Celebrities
DeLorean, Cristina	Entertainers (Current)	Derby,XIVEarl(ED.Stanley)	Heads of State
DeLuise, Dom	Entertainers (Current)	Derek, Bo	Entertainers (Current)
DeMaestri, Joe	Baseball	Derek, John	Entertainers (Current)
DeMille, Agnes	Entertainers (Vintage)	Dern, Bruce	Entertainers (Current)
DeMille, Cecil B.	Entertainers (Vintage)	Descartes, Rene	Authors
DeMille, Katherine	Entertainers (Vintage)	Deutsch, Patti	Entertainers (Current)
DeMornay, Rebecca	Entertainers (Current)	Devaney, Bob	Football
DeNiro, Robert	Entertainers (Current)	Devens, Charles	U.S. V.P. & Cabinet
DePalma, Ralph	General Sports	Devereux, James P.S.	Military
DePaolo, Peter	General Sports	Devers, Jacob	Military
DeSilva, Howard	Entertainers (Vintage)	Devine, Andy	Entertainers (Vintage)
DeVane, William	Entertainers (Current)	Devlin, Bruce	General Sports
DeVito, Danny	Entertainers (Current)	Devo	Rock
DeVries, Dr. William	Science	Devonshire, 4th Duke	Heads of State
DeWitt, Joyce	Entertainers (Current)	Dewey, George	Military
DeWolf, Billy	Entertainers (Vintage)	Dewey, John	Authors
Dean, "Man Mountain"	General Sports	Dewey, Thomas E.	Celebrities
Dean, Eddie	Country Music Stars	Dey, Joseph C.	Golf HoF
Dean, Everett S.	General Sports	Dey, Susan	Entertainers (Current)
Dean, Everett	Basketball HoF	DiMaggio, Dom	Baseball
Dean, Jay "Dizzy"	Baseball	DiMaggio, Joe	Baseball
Dean, Jimmy	Country Music Stars	DiMaggio, Vince	Baseball
Dean, John	Celebrities	Diamond, Neil	Entertainers (Current)
Dean, Julia	Entertainers (Vintage)	Diamond, Selma	Entertainers (Vintage)
Dean, Paul "Daffy"	Baseball	Diaz, Armando	Military
Dean, William F.	Military	Diaz, Porfirio (Mex)	Heads of State
Deane, Silas	Revolutionary War	Dibrell, G. G.	Civil War
Dearborn, Henry M.	U.S. V.P. & Cabinet	Dick, Samuel	Revolutionary War
Debeck,Billy	Cartoonists	Dickens, Charles	Authors
Debre, Michael	Heads of State	Dickens, Jimmy	Country Music Stars
Debs, Eugene	Celebrities	Dickenson, Angie	Entertainers (Current)
Debussy, Claude	Composers	Dickenson, Don M.	U.S. V.P. & Cabinet
Decker, Joe	Baseball	Dickenson, John	Revolutionary War
Decker, Mary	General Sports	Dickerson, Eric	Football
Dee, Francis	Entertainers (Current)	Dickerson, Mahlon	U.S. V.P. & Cabinet
Dee, Ruby	Entertainers (Current)	Dickey, Bill	Baseball
Dee, Sandra	Entertainers (Current)	Dickey, James	Authors
Deems, Charles Force	Celebrities	Dickinson, Anna Eliz.	Authors
Deering, Olive	Entertainers (Current)	Dickinson, Emily	Authors
Defoe, Daniel	Authors	Dicks, Jacob	Governors
Degas, Edgar	Artists	Diddle, Edgar	Basketball HoF
Dehner, John	Entertainers (Current)	Didier, Clint	Football
Dehnert, H. G. (Dutch)	Basketball HoF	Didier-Pouget, W.	Artists
Del Rio, Delores	Entertainers (Vintage)	Diefenbaker, John	Heads of State
Delacroix, F.V. Eugene	Artists	Dietrich, Marlene	Entertainers (Vintage)
Delafield, Richard	Civil War	Dil, Steve	Football
Delahoussaye, Eddie	General Sports	Dilio, Francis	Hockey HoF
Delaney, Joe	Football	Dilke, Charles W.	Celebrities
Delaney, Kim	Entertainers (Current)	Dillard, Harrison	General Sports
Delany, Ron	General Sports	Diller, Phyllis	Entertainers (Current)
Delibes, Leo	Composers	Dillman, Bradford	Entertainers (Current)
Delius, Frederick	Composers	Dillon, Bobby	Football
Dell, Gabriel	Entertainers (Current)	Dillon, C. Douglas	U.S. V.P. & Cabinet
Dell, Myrna	Entertainers (Vintage)	Dillon, Matt	Entertainers (Current)
Della Chiesa, Vivian	Entertainers (Vintage)	Dinesen, Isak	Authors
Dello Joio, Norman	Composers	Ding, J.N. Darling	Cartoonists
Delsing, Jim	Baseball	Dionne, Marcel	General Sports
Delvecchio, Alex	General Sports	Dire Straits	Rock
Delvecchio, Alex	Hockey HoF	Dirks, Rudolph	Cartoonists
Demarest, William	Entertainers (Vintage)	Disney, Walter E.	Business
Demaret, Jimmy	General Sports	Disney, Walt	Entertainers (Vintage)
Demeter, Don	Baseball	Disney, Walt	Cartoonists
Dempsey, Jack	Boxing	Disraeli, Benjamin	Heads of State
Dempsey, Rick	Baseball	Ditka, Mike	Football
Demslow, W.W.	Cartoonists	Dix, Dorothea	Civil War
Denby, Edwin	U.S. V.P. & Cabinet	Dix, Dorothy	Authors
Deneuve, Catherine	Entertainers (Current)	Dix, John Adams	Civil War

Name	Category	Name	Category
Dix, Richard	Entertainers (Vintage)	Douglas, Donald W. Jr.	Business
Dixey, Henry E.	Entertainers (Vintage)	Douglas, Helen G.	Entertainers (Vintage)
Dixon, Donna	Entertainers (Current)	Douglas, Kirk	Entertainers (Current)
Dixon, George	Boxing	Douglas, Leon	Country Music Stars
Dixon, Rod	General Sports	Douglas, Lloyd C.	Authors
Dixon, Thomas	Authors	Douglas, Melvyn	Entertainers (Vintage)
Dizengoff, Meir	Celebrities	Douglas, Michael	Entertainers (Current)
Dobbin, James C.	U.S. V.P. & Cabinet	Douglas, Mike	Entertainers (Current)
Dobie. Charles Cald.	Authors	Douglas, Paul	Entertainers (Vintage)
Dobrinyin, Anatole	Heads of State	Douglas, Stephen A.	Celebrities
Dobson, Joe	Baseball	Douglas, William O. (SC)	Celebrities
Dobson, Kevin	Entertainers (Current)	Douglass, Bobby	Football
Doby, Larry	Baseball	Douglass, Frederick	Celebrities
Docking, Robert	Governors	Douglass, Robyn	Entertainers (Current)
Doctorow, E. L.	Authors	Dove, Billie	Entertainers (Vintage)
Dodd, Ed	Celebrities	Dow, Neal	Civil War
Dodd, William E.	U.S. V.P. & Cabinet	Dow, Tony	Entertainers (Current)
Dodge, Jerry	Entertainers (Current)	Dowden, Edward	Authors
Dodge, Joseph M.	Business	Dowler, Boyd	Football
Dodge, Mary Mapes	Authors	Dowling, Eddie	Entertainers (Vintage)
Dodge, William Earl	Business	Down, Lesley-Anne	Entertainers (Vintage)
Dodge, William G.	Civil War	Downey, Morton	Entertainers (Vintage)
Dodgson, C.L.(L.Carroll)	Authors	Downing, Al	Baseball
Dodson, Jack	Entertainers (Current)	Downing, Big Al	Entertainers (Current)
Doeg, John H.	Tennis HoF	Downing, Brian	Baseball
Doenitz, Karl	Military	Downs, Hugh	Entertainers (Current)
Doering, Arnold	Aviation	Doyle, Arthur Conan	Authors
Doerr, Bobby	Baseball	Dragonette, Jessica	Entertainers (Vintage)
Doherty, H. Laurence	Tennis HoF	Drake, Bruce	General Sports
Doherty, Reginald	Tennis HoF	Drake, Bruce	Basketball HoF
Dolby, Thomas	Rock	Drake, Frances	Entertainers (Vintage)
Dole, Elizabeth	U.S. V.P. & Cabinet	Drake, Tom	Entertainers (Vintage)
Dole, James D.	Business	Draper, Eben S.	Governors
Dole, Sanford B.	Business	Draper, Rusty	Country Music Stars
Doll, Don	Football	Draper, Ruth	Entertainers (Vintage)
Dollar, Robert	Business	Dravecky, Dave	Baseball
Domingo, Placido	Entertainers (Current)	Draves, Vicki	General Sports
Domino, Fats	Entertainers (Current)	Drayton, Gracie	Cartoonists
Donahue, Elinor	Entertainers (Current)	Drazenovich, Chuck	Football
Donahue, Terry	Football	Dreesen, Tom	Baseball
Donahue, Troy	Entertainers (Current)	Dreiser, Theodore	Authors
Donald, Atley	Baseball	Dressen, Chuck	Baseball
Donaldson, Jesse M.	U.S. V.P. & Cabinet	Dresser, Louise	Entertainers (Vintage)
Donat, Peter	Entertainers (Current)	Drew, Ellen	Entertainers (Vintage)
Donat, Robert	Entertainers (Vintage)	Drew, John	Entertainers (Vintage)
Donatelli, Augie	Baseball	Drexel, J. A.	Aviation
Doniphan, A. W.	Military	Dreyfus, Alfred	Military
Donizetti, Gaetano	Composers	Dreyfus, Richard	Entertainers (Current)
Donnell, Jeff	Entertainers (Current)	Dribrell, George G.	Civil War
Donnelly, Ruth	Entertainers (Vintage)	Driesell, "Lefty"	General Sports
Donohue, Mark	General Sports	Drillon, Gordon	Hockey HoF
Donovan, Art	Football	Drinkwater, Charles	Hockey HoF
Donovan, Hedley	Celebrities	Drinkwater, John	Authors
Donovan, Wm. J.	Military	Driscoll, Bobby	Entertainers (Vintage)
Doobie Brothers	Rock	Dropo, Walt	Baseball
Doohan, James "Scotty"	Entertainers (Current)	Drouet, Robert	Entertainers (Vintage)
Dooley, Eddie	General Sports	Dru, Joanne	Entertainers (Vintage)
Dooley, Paul	Entertainers (Current)	Drum, Hugh A. Lt.Gen	Military
Dooley, Vince	Football	Drum, Richard C.	Civil War
Doolittle, Hilda	Authors	Drury, Allen	Authors
Doolittle, James H.	Aviation	Dryer, Fred	Football
Doors	Rock	Drysdale, Don	Baseball
Dorais, Charles "Gus"	Football	Du Barry, Marie Jeanne	Heads of State
Doran, Ann	Entertainers (Vintage)	Du Chaillu, Paul B.	Authors
Doran, Ann	Entertainers (Current)	Du Maurier, Daphne	Authors
Dore, Paul Gustave	Artists	Du Maurier, George	Authors
Dorish, Harry	Baseball	Du Pont, Elizabeth H	Business
Dornberger, Walter	Military	Du Pont, Pierre S.	Business
Dorr, Julia C. R.	Authors	DuBois, W. E. B.	Celebrities
Dors, Diana	Entertainers (Vintage)	DuBridge, Dr. Lee	Science
Dorsett, Tony	Football	DuVigneaud, Vincent	Science
Dorsey, Jimmie	Entertainers (Vintage)	Duane, James	Revolutionary War
Dorsey, Tommy	Entertainers (Vintage)	Duchin, Eddie	Entertainers (Vintage)
Dos Passos, John	Authors	Duchin, Peter	Entertainers (Current)
Dostoevsky, Fyodor	Authors	Ducos, Jean Francois	Revolutionary War
Doubleday, Abner	Civil War	Dudley, Bill	Football
Doucette, John	Entertainers (Current)	Dudley, Dave	Country Music Stars
Douglas, Bob	General Sports	Dudley, George	Hockey HoF
Douglas, Bob	Basketball HoF	Dudley, Joseph	Revolutionary War
Douglas, Donna	Entertainers (Current)	Dudley, Paul	Revolutionary War
Douglas, Donald W. Sr.	Aviation	Duer, Al O.	Basketball HoF

449

Elliot, Win	General Sports
Elliott, Bob	Entertainers (Current)
Elliott, Carter	Composers
Elliott, Chaucer	Hockey HoF
Elliott, Glenn	Baseball
Elliott, Herb	General Sports
Elliott, Maxine	Entertainers (Vintage)
Elliott, Pete	Football
Elliott, Sam	Entertainers (Current)
Ellis, Havelock	Authors
Ellis, Robert H.	Military
Ellison, James	Entertainers (Vintage)
Ellsberg, Daniel	Celebrities
Ellsworth, Elmer	Civil War
Ellsworth, Oliver (SC)	Celebrities
Elman, Mischa	Entertainers (Current)
Eltinge, Julian	Entertainers (Vintage)
Elvira	Entertainers (Current)
Elway, John Sr.	Football
Elway, John	Football
Ely, Ron	Entertainers (Current)
Emerson, Lake and Palmer	Rock
Emerson, Ralph Waldo	Authors
Emerson, Roy	Tennis HoF
Emmett, Daniel D.	Composers
Emory, W. H.	Civil War
Enberg, Dick	General Sports
Endacott, Paul	Basketball HoF
Enders, Dr. John	Science
Endicott, William C.	U.S. V.P. & Cabinet
Engel, Georgia	Entertainers (Current)
England, Anthony W.	Astronauts
Engle, Joe Henry	Astronauts
English, Doug	Football
Ennis, Del	Baseball
Enright, James	Basketball HoF
Enriquez, Rene	Entertainers (Current)
Epstein, Jacob Sir	Artists
Erhard, Ludwig	Heads of State
Erickson, Leif	Entertainers (Current)
Ericsson, John	Civil War
Ernouf, Manuel L.J(Baron)	Revolutionary War
Ernst, Max	Artists
Erskine, Carl	Baseball
Erskine, John	Authors
Eruzione, Mike	General Sports
Erving, Julius	General Sports
Erwin, Durward	Country Music Stars
Eshkol, Levi	Heads of State
Esposito, Phil	General Sports
Esposito, Phil	Hockey HoF
Estaing, Chas.H.T.Count	Revolutionary War
Estes, Billy Sol	Celebrities
Estevez, Emilio	Entertainers (Current)
Estrada, Erik	Entertainers (Current)
Etchebarren, Andy	Baseball
Etchebaster, Pierre	Tennis HoF
Etten, Nick	Baseball
Eubanks, Bob	Entertainers (Current)
Eugenie, Empress(Nap.III)	Heads of State
Euler, Ulf von	Science
Eurythmics	Rock
Eustis, William	U.S. V.P. & Cabinet
Evans, Charles "Chick"	Golf HoF
Evans, Dale	Entertainers (Current)
Evans, Daniel J.	Governors
Evans, Darrell	Baseball
Evans, Dwight	Baseball
Evans, Gene	Entertainers (Current)
Evans, Joan	Entertainers (Vintage)
Evans, John V.	Governors
Evans, Linda	Entertainers (Current)
Evans, Lt. Col. D. M	Civil War
Evans, Madge	Entertainers (Vintage)
Evans, Ray	Composers
Evans, Robley D.	Military
Evans, Ronald E.	Astronauts
Evarts, William M.	U.S. V.P. & Cabinet
Evashevski, Forest	Football
Everest. F.K. "Pete"	Aviation
Everett, Chad	Entertainers (Current)

Everett, Edward	U.S. V.P. & Cabinet
Everett, Jim	Football
Everett. Edward	Celebrities
Everly Brothers	Rock
Evers, Charles	Celebrities
Evers, Walter "Hoot"	Baseball
Evert, Chris	General Sports
Evigan, Greg	Entertainers (Current)
Ewbank, Weeb	Football
Ewell, Tom	Entertainers (Current)
Ewing, Thomas	U.S. V.P. & Cabinet
Exelman, Remi J.I. Count	Revolutionary War
Exon, J. James	Governors
Eythe, William	Entertainers (Vintage)
Eytinge, Rose	Entertainers (Vintage)
F.Hurley, Charles	Governors
Fabares, Shelley	Entertainers (Current)
Faber, J. Eberhard	Business
Faber, Urban "Red"	Baseball
Fabian, John M.	Astronauts
Fabray, Nanette	Entertainers (Current)
Face, ElRoy	Baseball
Factor, Max Jr.	Business
Fagan, Clifford B.	Basketball HoF
Fain, Ferris	Baseball
Fairbanks Jr., Douglas	Entertainers (Current)
Fairbanks, Charles W. (V)	U.S. V.P. & Cabinet
Fairbanks, Douglas	Entertainers (Vintage)
Fairbanks, Erastus	Governors
Fairchild, Charles S.	U.S. V.P. & Cabinet
Fairchild, David	Authors
Fairchild, Lucius	Civil War
Fairchild, Morgan	Entertainers (Current)
Fairchild, Sherman	Business
Fairfax, George Wm.	Revolutionary War
Fairfax, Thomas Lord	Revolutionary War
Fairless, Benjamin F.	Business
Faisal (Saudi Arabia)	Heads of State
Faithfull, Emily	Celebrities
Falch, Wolfgang	Aviation
Falk, Peter	Entertainers (Current)
Falkenburg, Robert	Tennis HoF
Falkenburg, Jinx	Entertainers (Current)
Fall, Albert B.	U.S. V.P. & Cabinet
Falla, Manuel de	Composers
Falwell, Jerry	Celebrities
Fangio, Juan Manuel	General Sports
Fantin-Latour, Henri	Artists
Fanzone, Carmen	Baseball
Faraday, Michael	Science
Fargo, Donna	Country Music Stars
Fargo, J. C.	Business
Fargo, William G.	Business
Farkas, Andy	Football
Farley, James A.	U.S. V.P. & Cabinet
Farman, Henri	Aviation
Farmer, Frances	Entertainers (Vintage)
Farnsworth, Richard	Entertainers (Current)
Farnum, Dustin	Entertainers (Vintage)
Farr, Jamie	Entertainers (Current)
Farr, Tommy	Boxing
Farragut, David E.	Civil War
Farrar, Geraldine	Entertainers (Vintage)
Farrell, Arthur	Hockey HoF
Farrell, Charles	Entertainers (Vintage)
Farrell, Glenda	Entertainers (Vintage)
Farrell, Mike	Entertainers (Current)
Farrow, Mia	Entertainers (Current)
Fast, Howard	Authors
Faubus, Orval E.	Governors
Faulkner, William	Authors
Faure, Gabriel	Composers
Faust, Gerry	Football
Fawcett, Farrah	Entertainers (Current)
Fawcett, Millicent, Dame	Celebrities
Fay, Frank	Entertainers (Vintage)
Faye, Alice	Entertainers (Vintage)
Faye, Julia	Entertainers (Vintage)
Faylen, Frank	Entertainers (Vintage)
Fazenda, Louise	Entertainers (Vintage)
Fazio, "Foge"	Football

Fonda, Jane	Entertainers (Current)
Fonda, Jelles	Revolutionary War
Fonda, Peter	Entertainers (Current)
Fonseca, Lew	Baseball
Fonseca, Roberto A.	Heads of State
Fontaine, Joan	Entertainers (Vintage)
Fonteyn, Margot	Entertainers (Current)
Foraker, Joseph B.	Governors
Forbes, Bertie Charles	Business
Forbes, Malcolm	Business
Forbes, Ralph	Entertainers (Vintage)
Forbes-Robertson, J.	Entertainers (Vintage)
Ford, Benson	Business
Ford, Edsel	Business
Ford, Edsel B. II	Business
Ford, Gerald R.	U.S. Presidents
Ford, Glenn	Entertainers (Current)
Ford, Harrison	Entertainers (Current)
Ford, Harrison	Entertainers (Vintage)
Ford, Henry II	Business
Ford, Henry	Business
Ford, John	Entertainers (Vintage)
Ford, John Anson	Business
Ford, John T.	Celebrities
Ford, Tennessee Ernie	Country Music Stars
Ford, Walter Clay	Baseball
Ford, Whitey	Baseball
Ford, William Clay	Football
Foreman, George	Boxing
Forester, C. S.	Authors
Forman, Thomas M.	Revolutionary War
Formes, Karl	Entertainers (Vintage)
Forrest, Edwin	Entertainers (Vintage)
Forrest, Nathan Bedfd	Civil War
Forrest, Sally	Entertainers (Vintage)
Forrestal, James	U.S. V.P. & Cabinet
Forslund, Constance	Entertainers (Current)
Forster, Edw. Morgan	Authors
Forster, John	Authors
Forsyth, John	U.S. V.P. & Cabinet
Forsythe, John	Entertainers (Current)
Fort, George F.	Governors
Fort, John Franklin	Governors
Fortas, Abe (SC)	Celebrities
Fortmann, Danny	Football
Fosdick, Harry E.	Celebrities
Foss, Joe	Aviation
Foss, Sam Walter	Authors
Fosse, Bob	Entertainers (Vintage)
Fosse, Ray	Baseball
Foster, Charles	U.S. V.P. & Cabinet
Foster, George	Baseball
Foster, Hal	Cartoonists
Foster, Harold (Bud)	Basketball HoF
Foster, Harold E. "Bud"	General Sports
Foster, Jodie	Entertainers (Current)
Foster, John W.	U.S. V.P. & Cabinet
Foster, John Gray	Civil War
Foster, Myles B.	Artists
Foster, Norman	Entertainers (Vintage)
Foster, Preston	Entertainers (Vintage)
Foster, Stephen	Composers
Foster, Susanna	Entertainers (Vintage)
Fouche, Jos.Duc d'Otrante	Revolutionary War
Fountain, Pete	Entertainers (Current)
Four Tops	Rock
Foust, Larry	General Sports
Fouts, Dan	Football
Fowler, Dr. William	Science
Fowler, Henry	U.S. V.P. & Cabinet
Fowles, John	Authors
Fox, Fontaine	Cartoonists
Fox, Michael J.	Entertainers (Current)
Fox, Nelson	Baseball
Foxworth, P. E.	Celebrities
Foxworth, Robert	Entertainers (Current)
Foxx, Jimmie	Baseball
Foy, Eddie Jr.	Entertainers (Vintage)
Foy, Maximilian S. Count	Revolutionary War
Foyston, Frank	Hockey HoF
Foyt, A.J.	General Sports

Frakes, Jonathan	Entertainers (Current)
France, Anatole	Authors
Franchi, Sergio	Entertainers (Current)
Franciosa, Anthony	Entertainers (Current)
Francis I (Fr)	Heads of State
Francis II	Heads of State
Francis, Anne	Entertainers (Current)
Francis, Arlene	Entertainers (Vintage)
Francis, Connie	Entertainers (Current)
Francis, Dick	General Sports
Francis, Emile "Cat"	General Sports
Francis, Emile	Hockey HoF
Francis, Genie	Entertainers (Current)
Francis, Kay	Entertainers (Vintage)
Franciscus, James	Entertainers (Current)
Franck, Cesar	Composers
Franco, Francisco	Heads of State
Franco, John	Baseball
Frank, Clint	Football
Frankfurter, Felix (SC)	Celebrities
Franklin, Benjamin	Revolutionary War
Franklin, Bonnie	Entertainers (Current)
Franklin, John, Sir	Celebrities
Franklin, Sir John	Military
Franklin, Wm. Buell	Civil War
Frann, Mary	Entertainers (Current)
Franz Joseph I (Aus)	Heads of State
Franz Joseph II	Heads of State
Fraser, Gretchen	General Sports
Fratiane, Linda	General Sports
Frazier, "Smokin" Joe	Boxing
Frazier, Walt	General Sports
Frederick II (Great-Prus)	Heads of State
Frederick III (Prus)	Heads of State
Frederick IV (Den)	Heads of State
Frederick IX (Den)	Heads of State
Frederick V (Den)	Heads of State
Frederick Wm. IV (Prus)	Heads of State
Frederick Wm. III (Prus)	Heads of State
Frederick Wm. I (Prus)	Heads of State
Fredericks, Fred	Cartoonists
Frederickson, Frank	Hockey HoF
Freed, Bert	Entertainers (Current)
Freehan, Bill	Baseball
Freeland, Paul van	Heads of State
Freeman, Mona	Entertainers (Current)
Freeman, Orville	U.S. V.P. & Cabinet
Freeman, Ted	Astronauts
Freese, Gene	Baseball
Freese, George	Baseball
Fregeville, C.L.J.Marquis	Revolutionary War
Freleng, Friz	Entertainers (Current)
Frelinghuysen, Frederick	U.S. V.P. & Cabinet
Fremont, Jessie B.	Civil War
Fremont, John C.	Civil War
French, Daniel Chester	Artists
French, Larry	Baseball
French, Samuel Gibbs	Civil War
French, Victor	Entertainers (Current)
French, William H.	Civil War
Freron, Louis M.S.	Revolutionary War
Freud, Sigmund	Science
Frey, Lonny	Baseball
Friant, Louis. Count	Revolutionary War
Frick, Ford	Baseball
Fricke, Jane	Entertainers (Current)
Friedman, Benny	Football
Friedman, Herbert	Science
Friedman, Max (Marty)	Basketball HoF
Friedman, Milton	Celebrities
Friend, Bob	Baseball
Friganza, Trixie	Entertainers (Vintage)
Friml, Rudolf	Composers
Frisch, Frank	Baseball
Fritchie, Barbara	Celebrities
Frith, William Powell	Authors
Fritsch, Ted	Football
Fritsch, Werner von	Military
Frizzell, Lefty	Country Music Stars
Frohman, Daniel	Entertainers (Vintage)
Froman, Jane	Entertainers (Vintage)

Name	Category
Fromme, Lynette	Celebrities
Frondizi, Arturo	Heads of State
Frontiere, Georgia	Football
Frontiersmen, The	Country Music Stars
Frost, A.B.	Cartoonists
Frost, D. M.	Civil War
Frost, Robert	Authors
Fry, Christopher	Authors
Fry, Elizabeth	Celebrities
Fry, Hayden	Football
Fry, James Barnet	Civil War
Fry, Shirley	General Sports
Fuchida, Mitsuo	Military
Fuchs, Rutger	Military
Fuchs, Vivian E. Sir	Celebrities
Fulks, Joe	Basketball HoF
Fuller, Alvan T.	Governors
Fuller, Buckminster	Science
Fuller, John G.	Celebrities
Fuller, Melville W. (SC)	Celebrities
Fuller, Robert	Entertainers (Current)
Fullerton, Chas. Gordon	Astronauts
Fullmer, Gene	Boxing
Fulton, Fitz	Astronauts
Fulton, Robert	Science
Funicello, Annette	Entertainers (Current)
Funk, Isaac K.	Business
Funston, Frederick	Military
Furcolo, Foster	Governors
Furgol, Ed	General Sports
Furillo, Carl	Baseball
Furlow, Terry	General Sports
Furnas, Robert W.	Governors
Furness, Betty	Entertainers (Vintage)
Furstenberg, Betsy v	Entertainers (Vintage)
Fusari, Charlie	Boxing
Futrell, J.M.	Governors
Fysal, Ellis D.	Football
Gabet, Sharon	Entertainers (Current)
Gabl, Pepi	General Sports
Gable, Clark	Entertainers (Vintage)
Gable, Dan	General Sports
Gable, Kay	Entertainers (Vintage)
Gabor, Zsa Zsa	Entertainers (Current)
Gabreski, Frances	Military
Gabriel, Roman	Football
Gabrielson, Len	Baseball
Gadsby, William	Hockey HoF
Gadski, Johanna	Entertainers (Vintage)
Gaetti, Gary	Baseball
Gaffke, Fabian	Baseball
Gagarin, Yuri	Astronauts
Gage, Lyman J.	U.S. V.P. & Cabinet
Gage, Thomas	Revolutionary War
Gail, Max	Entertainers (Current)
Gaines, Clarence	Basketball HoF
Gaines, Edmund P.	Civil War
Gaines, Joe	Baseball
Gainey, Bob	General Sports
Gainsborough, Thomas	Artists
Gajdusek, D. Carleton	Science
Galan, Augie	Baseball
Galard, Genevieve de	Celebrities
Galbraith, John Ken.	Celebrities
Gale, Lauren, (Laddie)	Basketball HoF
Gale, Zona	Authors
Galileo	Science
Galland, Adolf	Aviation
Gallatin, Albert	U.S. V.P. & Cabinet
Galle, Emile	Artists
Galli-Curci, Amelita	Entertainers (Vintage)
Gallian, Ketti	Entertainers (Vintage)
Gallico, Paul W.	Authors
Gallo, Ernest & Julio	Business
Galloway, Joseph	Revolutionary War
Gallup, George	Business
Galsworthy, John	Authors
Galvin, Robert	Business
Gam, Rita	Entertainers (Vintage)
Gambetta, Leon	Heads of State
Gambier, James	Military
Gandhi, Indira	Heads of State
Gandhi, Mohandas K.	Heads of State
Gannett, Frank E.	Business
Gant, Harry	General Sports
Ganteaume, Honore,Count	Revolutionary War
Garagiola, Joe	Baseball
Garbo, Greta	Entertainers (Vintage)
Garcelon, Alonzo	Governors
Garcia, Ceferino	Boxing
Gardanne, Gaspard A.	Revolutionary War
Garden, Mary	Entertainers (Vintage)
Gardenia, Vince	Entertainers (Current)
Gardiner, Charles	Hockey HoF
Gardiner, Herbert	Hockey HoF
Gardner, Ava	Entertainers (Vintage)
Gardner, Dale A.	Astronauts
Gardner, Erle Stanley	Authors
Gardner, Guy S.	Astronauts
Gardner, Jack	Basketball HoF
Gardner, James	Hockey HoF
Gardner, John W.	U.S. V.P. & Cabinet
Gardner, O. Max	Governors
Gardner, Randy	General Sports
Garfield, James A.	U.S. Presidents
Garfield, James R.	U.S. V.P. & Cabinet
Garfield, John	Entertainers (Vintage)
Garfield, Lucretia R.	Celebrities
Gargan, William	Entertainers (Vintage)
Garibaldi, Giuseppe	Heads of State
Garland, Charles S.	Tennis HoF
Garland, Hamlin	Authors
Garland, Judy	Entertainers (Vintage)
Garner, James	Entertainers (Current)
Garner, John Nance (V)	U.S. V.P. & Cabinet
Garnett, Francis H.	Authors
Garnett, R. B.	Civil War
Garr, Terri	Entertainers (Current)
Garrett, Betty	Entertainers (Current)
Garrett, Mike	Football
Garriott, Owen I.	Astronauts
Garrison, Kelly	General Sports
Garrison, Lindley M.	U.S. V.P. & Cabinet
Garrison, Vermont	Military
Garrison, Walt	Football
Garrison, Wm. Lloyd	Celebrities
Garroway, Dave	Entertainers (Vintage)
Garson, Greer	Entertainers (Current)
Garson, Greer	Entertainers (Vintage)
Garver, Ned	Baseball
Garvey, Steve	Baseball
Gary, Elbert H.	Business
Gaskell, Eliz. Cleghorn	Authors
Gastineau, Mark	Football
Gately, George	Cartoonists
Gates, Horatio	Revolutionary War
Gatlin Brothers	Entertainers (Current)
Gatling, Richard J.	Science
Gatski, Frank	Football
Gatty, Harold	Aviation
Gaugin, Paul	Artists
Gavin, James M.	Military
Gavin, John	Celebrities
Gaxton, William	Entertainers (Vintage)
Gay, Sydney Howard	Authors
Gaye, Marvin	Rock
Gayle, Crystal	Country Music Stars
Gaylord, Mitch	General Sports
Gaynor, Janet	Entertainers (Vintage)
Gaynor, Mitzi	Entertainers (Current)
Gaynor, William J.	Celebrities
Geary, Anthony "Tony"	Entertainers (Current)
Geary, John W.	Civil War
Geddes, Jane	General Sports
Geer, Ellen	Entertainers (Current)
Geezinslaw, Sam & Dewayne	Country Music Stars
Gehrig, Lou	Baseball
Gehringer, Charley	Baseball
Gehrke, Fred	Football
Geiberger, Al	General Sports
Geiger, Johannes H.	Science
Geisel, Ernesto	Heads of State

Gelston, David	Revolutionary War	Gilliland, Richard	Entertainers (Current)
Geneen, Harold S.	Business	Gillis, J. H.	Military
Genesis	Rock	Gillman, Sid	Football
Genet, Edmond C.	Revolutionary War	Gillmore, Quincy A.	Civil War
Genet, Jean	Authors	Gilmer, Harry	Football
Genn, Leo	Entertainers (Vintage)	Gilmore, Artis	General Sports
Gentry, Bobbie	Country Music Stars	Gilmore, Gary	Celebrities
Gentry, Jerauld R.	Astronauts	Gilmore, Virginia	Entertainers (Vintage)
Geoffrion, J. A. B.	Hockey HoF	Gilmour, H. L. "Billy"	Hockey HoF
George I (Eng)	Heads of State	Gilruth, Robert R.	Astronauts
George I (Gr)	Heads of State	Gimbel Brothers	Business
George II (Eng)	Heads of State	Gimbel, Bernard F.	Business
George II (Gr)	Heads of State	Gingold, Hermione	Entertainers (Vintage)
George III (Eng)	Heads of State	Ginsberg, Allen	Authors
George IV (Eng)	Heads of State	Gionfriddo, Al	Baseball
George V (Eng)	Heads of State	Girard, Stephen	Business
George VI (Eng)	Heads of State	Gish, Lillian	Entertainers (Vintage)
George, Bill	Football	Givenchy, Hubert de	Business
George, Christopher	Entertainers (Vintage)	Givens, Edward G. Jr.	Astronauts
George, Gladys	Entertainers (Vintage)	Glad, Gladys	Entertainers (Vintage)
George, Grace	Entertainers (Vintage)	Gladden, Washington	Authors
George, Harold L.	Military	Gladstone, William	Heads of State
George, Henry	Authors	Glaser, Donald A.	Science
George, Phyllis	Entertainers (Current)	Glashow, Sheldon Lee	Science
George, Susan	Entertainers (Current)	Glass, Carter	U.S. V.P. & Cabinet
Gerard, Eddie	Hockey HoF	Glaviano, Tommy	Baseball
Gerard, Gil	Entertainers (Current)	Glazer, Tom Paul	Country Music Stars
Gere, Richard	Entertainers (Current)	Gleason, Jackie	Entertainers (Vintage)
Gerlache, Adrien de	Celebrities	Glenn, John	Astronauts
Gerland, Alfred	Aviation	Gless, Sharon	Entertainers (Current)
German, Sir Edward	Composers	Gloucester,(Wm.Frederick)	Celebrities
Gernreich, Rudi	Business	Glover, Danny	Entertainers (Current)
Gerri, Toni	Entertainers (Vintage)	Glover, John	Revolutionary War
Gerry, Elbridge (V)(Rev)	U.S. V.P. & Cabinet	Glubb, John Sir	Military
Gerry, Elbridge (V)	Revolutionary War	Glueck, Nelson	Celebrities
Gersel Cemal	Heads of State	Glyn, Elinor	Authors
Gershwin, George	Composers	Goard, Nona	Aviation
Gershwin, Ira	Composers	Gobel, George	Entertainers (Current)
Gervin, George	General Sports	Goddard, Paulette	Entertainers (Vintage)
Getty, J. Paul	Business	Goddard, Robert H.	Science
Ghostley, Alice	Entertainers (Current)	Goderich, Fred. John	Heads of State
Giambra, Joey	Boxing	Godfree, Kathleen McKane	Tennis HoF
Giannini, A. P.	Business	Godfrey, A. Earl	Aviation
Giardello, Joey	Boxing	Godfrey, Arthur	Entertainers (Vintage)
Gibb, Cynthia	Entertainers (Current)	Godoy, Manuel de	Celebrities
Gibbon, Edward	Authors	Gody, Louis A.	Celebrities
Gibbons, Floyd	Aviation	Goebbels, Joseph	Military
Gibbs, Addison C.	Governors	Goering, Hermann W.	Military
Gibbs, Marla	Entertainers (Current)	Goethals, George W.	Science
Gibran, Kahlil	Authors	Goethals, Geo.W.(Science)	Celebrities
Gibson, Althea	Tennis HoF	Goethe, Johann W. von	Authors
Gibson, Bob	Baseball	Gofourth, Derrel	Football
Gibson, Charles Dana	Artists	Gogh, Vincent van	Artists
Gibson, Dr. John	Hockey HoF	Gogol, Nicholai	Authors
Gibson, Edward G.	Astronauts	Goheen, F. X. "Moose"	Hockey HoF
Gibson, George	Military	Gola, Tom	General Sports
Gibson, Hoot	Entertainers (Vintage)	Gola, Tom	Basketball HoF
Gibson, Kirk	Baseball	Golan, Menahem	Entertainers (Current)
Gibson, Mel	Entertainers (Current)	Goldberg, Arthur J. (SC)	Celebrities
Gibson, Robert L.	Astronauts	Goldberg, Arth.(SC)(Cele)	U.S. V.P. & Cabinet
Gide, Andre	Authors	Goldberg, Marshall	Football
Giesler, Jerry	Celebrities	Goldberg, Rube	Cartoonists
Gifford, Frank	Football	Goldberg, Whoopi	Entertainers (Current)
Gifford, Walter S.	Business	Goldblum, Jeff	Entertainers (Current)
Gilbert, A. C.	Business	Goldenberg, Charles	Football
Gilbert, Billy	Entertainers (Vintage)	Goldenson, Leonard H.	Business
Gilbert, Cass	Celebrities	Golding, Louis	Authors
Gilbert, Gibby	General Sports	Golding, William	Authors
Gilbert, H. E.	Celebrities	Goldman, Emma	Celebrities
Gilbert, Lynn	Entertainers (Vintage)	Goldman, Michael	Authors
Gilbert, Rod	Hockey HoF	Goldschmidt, Neil	U.S. V.P. & Cabinet
Gilbert, Sir Wm. S.	Composers	Goldsmith, Fred E.	Baseball
Gilder, Bob	General Sports	Goldwyn, Sam	Entertainers (Vintage)
Gilder, Jeannette L.	Authors	Golonka, Arlene	Entertainers (Current)
Giles, Warren C.	Baseball	Gombell, Minna	Entertainers (Vintage)
Giles, William Branch	Revolutionary War	Gomes, Francisco	Heads of State
Gill, Amory (Slats)	Basketball HoF	Gomez, Avelino	General Sports
Gill, Paul	Football	Gomez, Vernon "Lefty"	Baseball
Gillespie, Dizzy	Entertainers (Current)	Gompers, Samuel	Celebrities
Gillette, Anita	Entertainers (Current)	Gonder, Jesse	Baseball
Gillette, William	Entertainers (Vintage)	Gonzales, Pancho	General Sports

Gonzalez, Richard A.	Tennis HoF	Grainger, Percy	Composers
Good, James W.	U.S. V.P. & Cabinet	Granatelli, Andy	General Sports
Goodell, Brian	General Sports	Grandi, Count Dino	Celebrities
Gooden, Dwight	Baseball	Grandy, Fred	Entertainers (Current)
Goodfellow, Ebenezer	Hockey HoF	Grange, E. R.	Aviation
Goodfellow, Ebbie	General Sports	Grange, Harold "Red"	Football
Goodman, Benny	Entertainers (Vintage)	Granger, Gideon	U.S. V.P. & Cabinet
Goodman, Dody	Entertainers (Vintage)	Granger, Stewart	Entertainers (Current)
Goodnight, Clyde	Football	Granit, Ragnar	Science
Goodpaster, Andrew	Military	Grant Jr., Bryan M.	Tennis HoF
Goodrich, Gail	General Sports	Grant, Amy	Entertainers (Current)
Goodson, Mark	Entertainers (Current)	Grant, Bud	Football
Goodwin, E. S.	Aviation	Grant, Cary	Entertainers (Vintage)
Goodwin, Hugh H.	Military	Grant, Frederick D.	Military
Goodwin, Nat	Entertainers (Vintage)	Grant, Gogi	Entertainers (Current)
Goodyear, Charles Jr.	Business	Grant, Jim "Mudcat"	Baseball
Goodyear, Charles	Business	Grant, Julia D.	Celebrities
Goolagong, Evonne	General Sports	Grant, Kirby	Entertainers (Current)
Goosens, Eugene	Composers	Grant, Lee	Entertainers (Current)
Gordon, Charles G.	Military	Grant, Michael	Hockey HoF
Gordon, Gale	Entertainers (Current)	Grant, U. S. III	Military
Gordon, George W.	Civil War	Grant, U. S.	U.S. Presidents
Gordon, George H.	Civil War	Grant, W. T.	Business
Gordon, Huntley	Entertainers (Vintage)	Granville, Bonita	Entertainers (Vintage)
Gordon, Joe	Baseball	Grass, Gunter	Authors
Gordon, John F.	Business	Grasser, Hartmann	Aviation
Gordon, John Brown	Civil War	Grassle, Karen	Entertainers (Current)
Gordon, Mack	Composers	Grateful Dead	Rock
Gordon, Richard F. Jr.	Astronauts	Gratz, Barnard	Revolutionary War
Gordon, Ruth	Entertainers (Vintage)	Graue, Dave	Cartoonists
Gordon, Sid	Baseball	Grauman, Sid	Entertainers (Vintage)
Gore, Artie	Baseball	Gravatte, Marianne	Entertainers (Current)
Gore, Christopher	Revolutionary War	Graveline, Duane E M.D.	Astronauts
Goren, Charles	General Sports	Graves, Peter	Entertainers (Current)
Gorgas, Josiah	Civil War	Graves, Robert	Authors
Gorgas, William C.	Science	Gray, Asa	Science
Gorham, Nathaniel	Revolutionary War	Gray, Bowman	Business
Gorki, Maxim	Authors	Gray, Colleen	Entertainers (Current)
Gorman, Thomas	Hockey HoF	Gray, David	Tennis HoF
Gorme, Eydie	Entertainers (Current)	Gray, Earl of (2nd)	Heads of State
Gorney, Karen Lynn	Entertainers (Current)	Gray, Erin	Entertainers (Current)
Gorshin, Frank	Entertainers (Current)	Gray, Gilda	Entertainers (Vintage)
Goslin, Leon "Goose"	Baseball	Gray, Harold	Cartoonists
Gossage, Rich "Goose"	Baseball	Gray, Horace (SC)	Celebrities
Gosse, Sir Edmund	Authors	Gray, Linda	Entertainers (Current)
Gottfrederson, Floyd	Cartoonists	Gray, Pete	Baseball
Gottlieb, Eddie	General Sports	Gray, Thomas	Authors
Gottlieb, Edward	Basketball HoF	Grayco, Helen	Entertainers (Current)
Goudal, Jetta	Entertainers (Vintage)	Grayson, Bobby	Football
Gough, John B.	Celebrities	Grayson, Kathryn	Entertainers (Current)
Gould, Chester	Cartoonists	Graziano, Rocky	Boxing
Gould, Elliott	Entertainers (Current)	Greco, Bobby Del	Baseball
Gould, George	Business	Greco, Jose	Entertainers (Vintage)
Gould, Harold	Entertainers (Current)	Greco, Jose	Entertainers (Current)
Gould, Jay	Business	Greeley, Horace	Authors
Gould, Morton	Composers	Greely, Adolphus W.	Military
Gould, Samuel B.	Celebrities	Green, Adolph	Composers
Goulding, Ray	Entertainers (Current)	Green, Al	Rock
Gounod, Charles	Composers	Green, Anna Kath.	Authors
Gourand, Henri-Joseph E.	Military	Green, Dick	Baseball
Gowdy, Curt	Baseball	Green, Dorothy	Entertainers (Vintage)
Goya, Francisco	Artists	Green, George "Dallas"	Baseball
Goz, Harry	Entertainers (Current)	Green, Hubert	General Sports
Grabe, Ronald J.	Astronauts	Green, John(ny)	Composers
Grable, Betty	Entertainers (Vintage)	Green, Mitzi	Entertainers (Vintage)
Grace de Monaco (G Kelly)	Heads of State	Green, Thomas	Civil War
Grace, E. G.	Business	Green, W. "Shorty"	Hockey HoF
Graf, Herman	Aviation	Green, William	Celebrities
Graf, Steffi	General Sports	Greenaway, Kate	Artists
Graffis, Herb	Golf HoF	Greenberg, Hank	Baseball
Graham, Billy, Dr.	Celebrities	Greene, Graham	Authors
Graham, Capt. Otto	Football	Greene, Joe "Mean Joe"	Football
Graham, David	General Sports	Greene, Lorne	Entertainers (Vintage)
Graham, Donald	Business	Greene, Nathanael	Military
Graham, John	U.S. V.P. & Cabinet	Greene, Shecky	Entertainers (Current)
Graham, Katherine	Business	Greenleaf, Ralph	General Sports
Graham, Lou	General Sports	Greenwood, Charlotte	Entertainers (Vintage)
Graham, Martha	Entertainers (Current)	Greenwood, G.(Lippincott)	Authors
Graham, William A.	U.S. V.P. & Cabinet	Greer, Hal	Basketball HoF
Grahame, Kenneth	Authors	Greer, Jane	Entertainers (Current)
Grahame-White, Claude	Aviation	Gregg, Forrest	Football

Gregg, Virginia	Entertainers (Vintage)	Guilford, Lord	Celebrities
Gregory, Dick	Entertainers (Current)	Guillaume, Robert	Entertainers (Current)
Gregory, F. H.	Civil War	Guillemin, Dr. Roger	Science
Gregory, Frederick D.	Astronauts	Guillotin, Joseph I.	Science
Gregory, James	Entertainers (Current)	Guinan, Texas	Celebrities
Grenfell, Wilfred Sir	Celebrities	Guingand, Francis	Military
Grenville, Wm. W. Baron	Revolutionary War	Guinness, Alec	Entertainers (Current)
Gresham, Walter Q.	U.S. V.P. & Cabinet	Guinness, Edward C.	Business
Gretzky, Wayne	General Sports	Guisewite, Cathy	Cartoonists
Grey, George Sir	Heads of State	Guitar, Bonnie	Country Music Stars
Grey, Joel	Entertainers (Current)	Guiteau, Charles	Celebrities
Grey, Nan	Entertainers (Vintage)	Gulager, Clu	Entertainers (Current)
Grey, Virginia	Entertainers (Vintage)	Guldahl, Ralph	General Sports
Grey, Zane	Authors	Guldahl, Ralph	Golf HoF
Gridley, Chas. Vernon	Military	Gulick, Dr. Luther H.	Basketball HoF
Gridley, Richard	Military	Gullickson, Bill	Baseball
Grieg, Edvard	Composers	Gumpert, Randy	Baseball
Grier, Pam	Entertainers (Current)	Gurie, Sigrid	Entertainers (Vintage)
Grier, Roosevelt "Rosie"	Football	Gustav V (King of Sweden)	Tennis HoF
Grierson, Benjamin	Civil War	Gustavus II Adolphus(Swe)	Heads of State
Griese, Bob	Football	Gustavus III (Swe)	Heads of State
Griffin, Archie	Football	Gutherie, Arlo	Country Music Stars
Griffin, Clarence	Tennis HoF	Guthrie, Arlo	Entertainers (Current)
Griffin, Cyrus	Revolutionary War	Guthrie, Janet	General Sports
Griffin, S. Marvin	Governors	Gutierrez, Sid	Astronauts
Griffis, Silas	Hockey HoF	Guy, Thomas	Celebrities
Griffith, Andy	Entertainers (Current)	Guyot, Pierre	Revolutionary War
Griffith, Calvin	Baseball	Gwinnett, Button	Revolutionary War
Griffith, Clark C.	Baseball	Gwynn, Chris	Baseball
Griffith, Corinne	Entertainers (Vintage)	Gwynn, Fred	Entertainers (Current)
Griffith, David W.	Entertainers (Vintage)	Gwynn, Tony	Baseball
Griffith, Emile	Boxing	Gwynne, Anne	Entertainers (Vintage)
Griffith, Melanie	Entertainers (Current)	Gye, Albani	Entertainers (Vintage)
Grimes, Burleigh	Baseball	H.Green, Dwight	Governors
Grimes, Tammy	Entertainers (Vintage)	Habberton, John	Authors
Grimm, Charlie	Baseball	Habersham, Joseph	Revolutionary War
Grimm, Jacob	Authors	Hack, Shelley	Entertainers (Current)
Grimm, Wilhelm	Authors	Hack, Stan	Baseball
Grinnell, Moses H.	Business	Hackett, Bobby	Entertainers (Vintage)
Grissom, Virgil I."Gus"	Astronauts	Hackett, Buddy	Entertainers (Current)
Griswold, Matthew	Governors	Hackett, Harold H.	Tennis HoF
Grizzard, George	Entertainers (Current)	Hackett, J. K.	Entertainers (Vintage)
Grodin, Charles	Entertainers (Current)	Hackett, Joan	Entertainers (Vintage)
Grofe, Ferde	Composers	Hackman, Gene	Entertainers (Current)
Grogan, Steve	Football	Haddix, Harvey	Baseball
Gromyko, Andrei A.	Heads of State	Haden, Pat	Football
Gronau, Wolfgang von	Aviation	Hadl, John	Football
Groom, Victor	Aviation	Haenschen, Gus	Entertainers (Vintage)
Gropius, Walter	Celebrities	Hafey, Charles "Chick"	Baseball
Gropper, William	Artists	Hagan, Cliff	Basketball HoF
Gross, Calvin	Celebrities	Hagar, Sammy	Rock
Gross, Chaim	Artists	Hagen, Walter	General Sports
Gross, Courtlandt	Business	Hagen, Walter	Golf HoF
Gross, Milt	Cartoonists	Haggard, Merle	Country Music Stars
Grosscup, Lee	Football	Haggard, Sir H. Rider	Authors
Grossinger, Jennie	Celebrities	Hagge, Marlene B.	General Sports
Grossmith, George	Entertainers (Vintage)	Haggerty, Dan	Entertainers (Current)
Grosvenor, Gilbert H.	Business	Hagler, Marvin	Boxing
Grote, Jerry	Baseball	Hagman, Larry	Entertainers (Current)
Groth, Johnny	Baseball	Hague, Frank	Celebrities
Grouchy, Marquis E. de	Military	Hahn, Otto	Science
Grove, Robert "Lefty"	Baseball	Haig, Alexander M.	Military
Grover, Cuvier	Civil War	Haig, Earl Douglas	Military
Groza, Lou	Football	Hailey, Arthur	Authors
Gruelle, Johnny	Cartoonists	Haines, Daniel	Governors
Gruenig, Robert (Ace)	Basketball HoF	Haines, Jesse	Baseball
Guardino, Harry	Entertainers (Current)	Haines, William	Entertainers (Vintage)
Guderian, Hans	Military	Hainsworth, George	Hockey HoF
Guderian, Heinz	Military	Haise, Fred W. Jr.	Astronauts
Gudin de la Sablonniere	Revolutionary War	Halaby, Najeeb	Celebrities
Gudunov, Alexander	Entertainers (Current)	Halas, George	Football
Guerrero, Pedro	Baseball	Haldeman, George W.	Aviation
Guest, Edgar A.	Authors	Haldeman, H. R.	Celebrities
Guest, Lance	Entertainers (Current)	Halder, Franz	Military
Guest, Winston Mrs.	Business	Hale, Alan Jr.	Entertainers (Current)
Guggenheim, Daniel	Business	Hale, Barbara	Entertainers (Current)
Guggenheim, Peggy	Business	Hale, Edward Everett	Authors
Guidry, Ron	Baseball	Hale, John	Baseball
Guilbert, Yvette	Entertainers (Vintage)	Hale, Monte	Entertainers (Current)
Guild Jr., Curtis	Governors	Hale, Richard	Entertainers (Vintage)
Guild, Nancy	Entertainers (Vintage)		

Halevy, Jacques	Composers	Hanson, Victor	Basketball HoF
Halevy, Ludivic	Authors	Harbord, James G.	Military
Haley, Alex	Authors	Harburg, E. Y. "Yip"	Composers
Haley, Bill	Rock	Hard, Darlene R.	Tennis HoF
Haley, Jack	Entertainers (Vintage)	Hardee, W. L.	Civil War
Halifax,(Chas. Wood) Earl	Heads of State	Hardee, William J.	Civil War
Hall & Oates	Rock	Hardie, Russell	Entertainers (Vintage)
Hall, Abraham O.	Celebrities	Hardin, Clifford M.	U.S. V.P. & Cabinet
Hall, Alvin W.	Celebrities	Hardin, Glenn	General Sports
Hall, David	Governors	Hardin, John Wesley	Celebrities
Hall, Dick	Baseball	Hardin, Ty	Entertainers (Current)
Hall, Glenn	Hockey HoF	Harding, Ann	Entertainers (Vintage)
Hall, Gus	Celebrities	Harding, Florence Kling	Celebrities
Hall, Harry	Entertainers (Current)	Harding, Reggie	General Sports
Hall, Huntz	Entertainers (Vintage)	Harding, Warren G.	U.S. Presidents
Hall, Joe B.	General Sports	Hardinge, Charles	Heads of State
Hall, Jon	Entertainers (Vintage)	Hardwicke, Cedric	Entertainers (Vintage)
Hall, Josephine	Entertainers (Vintage)	Hardy, Carroll	Baseball
Hall, Joseph	Hockey HoF	Hardy, Thomas	Authors
Hall, Joyce C.	Business	Harkins, Paul	Military
Hall, Lyman	Revolutionary War	Harlan, James A.	U.S. V.P. & Cabinet
Hall, Monty	Entertainers (Current)	Harlan, John Marshall(SC)	Celebrities
Hall, Pauline	Entertainers (Vintage)	Harland, Marion	Authors
Hall, Tom T.	Country Music Stars	Harlow, Jean	Entertainers (Vintage)
Halle, Wilhelmine	Entertainers (Vintage)	Harman, Fred	Cartoonists
Halleck, Henry W.	Civil War	Harmon, Chuck	Baseball
Haller, Tom	Baseball	Harmon, Judson	U.S. V.P. & Cabinet
Halliburton, Richard	Celebrities	Harmon, Mark	Entertainers (Current)
Halop, Billy	Entertainers (Vintage)	Harmon, Tom	Football
Halpine, Charles G.	Authors	Harper, Chandler	General Sports
Halsey, Wm. F. "Bull"	Military	Harper, Joseph W.	Celebrities
Ham, Jack	Football	Harper, Tess	Entertainers (Current)
Hamblen, Stewart	Country Music Stars	Harper, Valerie	Entertainers (Current)
Hamel, Veronica	Entertainers (Current)	Harrelson, Bud	Baseball
Hamill, Dorothy	General Sports	Harridge, William	Baseball
Hamill, Mark	Entertainers (Current)	Harriman, Averell	Governors
Hamilton, Alexander	U.S. V.P. & Cabinet	Harriman, Edw. Henry	Business
Hamilton, Alex. Jr.	Celebrities	Harriman, W. Averell	U.S. V.P. & Cabinet
Hamilton, Donald	Authors	Harrington, Pat	Entertainers (Current)
Hamilton, Margaret	Entertainers (Current)	Harris, Arthur T. Sir	Military
Hamilton, Milo	Baseball	Harris, Cliff	Football
Hamilton, Neil	Entertainers (Vintage)	Harris, Ed	Entertainers (Current)
Hamilton, Tom	Football	Harris, Franco	Football
Hamlin, Hannibal (V)	U.S. V.P. & Cabinet	Harris, Jean	Celebrities
Hamlin, Harry	Entertainers (Current)	Harris, Joel Chandler	Authors
Hamlin, Luke	Baseball	Harris, Julie	Entertainers (Current)
Hamlisch, Marvin	Composers	Harris, Patricia Roberts	U.S. V.P. & Cabinet
Hammarskjold, Dag	Heads of State	Harris, Richard	Entertainers (Current)
Hammer, Armand	Business	Harris, Robert H.	Entertainers (Current)
Hammerstein, Oscar	Composers	Harris, Spencer	Baseball
Hammett, Dashiell	Authors	Harris, Stanley "Bucky"	Baseball
Hammond, Jay S.	Governors	Harrison Jr., Albertis S.	Governors
Hammond, L. Blaine	Astronauts	Harrison, Benjamin	U.S. Presidents
Hammond, William A.	Science	Harrison, Benjamin	Revolutionary War
Hampden, Walter	Entertainers (Vintage)	Harrison, George	Rock
Hampton, Hope	Entertainers (Vintage)	Harrison, Gregory	Entertainers (Current)
Hampton, Lionel	Entertainers (Current)	Harrison, Henry B.	Governors
Hampton, Wade	Civil War	Harrison, Jenilee	Entertainers (Current)
Hanami, Kohei	Military	Harrison, Lester	Basketball HoF
Hancock, Fred	Baseball	Harrison, Mary Lord	Celebrities
Hancock, Herbie	Composers	Harrison, Rex	Entertainers (Current)
Hancock, John Jr.	Celebrities	Harrison, Robert Hanson	Revolutionary War
Hancock, John	Revolutionary War	Harrison, William Henry	U.S. Presidents
Hancock, Winfield S.	Civil War	Harrold, Kathryn	Entertainers (Current)
Hand, Edward	Revolutionary War	Harshman, Marv	Basketball HoF
Handel, Geo. F.	Composers	Harstad, Oscar	Baseball
Handelman, Stanley M.	Entertainers (Current)	Hart, Corey	Rock
Hands, Bill	Baseball	Hart, Corey	Entertainers (Current)
Handy, W. C.	Composers	Hart, Dolores	Entertainers (Vintage)
Haney, Fred	Baseball	Hart, Doris	Tennis HoF
Hanifin, Jim	Football	Hart, Dorothy	Entertainers (Vintage)
Hanna and Barbera	Cartoonists	Hart, Jim	Football
Hanna, Marcus A.	Celebrities	Hart, John	Revolutionary War
Hanna-Barbera	Entertainers (Current)	Hart, Johnny	Cartoonists
Hannan, Jim	Baseball	Hart, Leon	Football
Hannan, al Bakr, Ahmad	Heads of State	Hart, Mary	Entertainers (Current)
Hannum, Alex	General Sports	Hart, Moss	Authors
Hanratty, Terry	Football	Hart, Paul	Entertainers (Vintage)
Hansell, Ellen Forde	Tennis HoF	Hart, Terry J.	Astronauts
Hansen, Ron	Baseball	Hart, William S.	Entertainers (Vintage)
Hansen, William	Entertainers (Vintage)	Hartack, Bill	General Sports

Name	Category
Harte, Francis Bret	Authors
Hartford, George L.	Business
Hartford, Huntington	Business
Hartley, Mariette	Entertainers (Current)
Hartley, Roland H.	Governors
Hartline, Haldan K.	Science
Hartman, Bob	Baseball
Hartman, David	Celebrities
Hartman, David	Entertainers (Current)
Hartman, Lisa	Entertainers (Current)
Hartmann, Erich	Military
Hartmann, Erich	Aviation
Hartnett, Leo "Gabby"	Baseball
Hartranft, John F.	Civil War
Hartranft, John F.	Governors
Hartsfield, Henry W. Jr	Astronauts
Hartsuff, George L.	Civil War
Hartung, Clint	Baseball
Hartung, Jim	General Sports
Hartwell, Alfred S.	Civil War
Harvey, Douglas	Hockey HoF
Harvey, Lawrence	Entertainers (Vintage)
Harvey, Lilian	Entertainers (Vintage)
Harvey, Paul	Celebrities
Harvey, Paul	Entertainers (Current)
Harvey, William	Science
Hasen, Irwin	Cartoonists
Haskell, James K.	Entertainers (Vintage)
Hassam, Childe	Artists
Hassan, Crown Prince	Heads of State
Hasselhoff, David	Entertainers (Current)
Hassett, "Bud"	Baseball
Hastings, Daniel H.	Governors
Hastings, Warren	Celebrities
Hastings, Warren	Heads of State
Haswell, Charles H.	Civil War
Hatch, John Porter	Civil War
Hatcher, Richard G.	Celebrities
Hatfield, Fred	Baseball
Hatfield, Hurd	Entertainers (Vintage)
Hatfield, Ken	Football
Hatfield, Mark O.	Governors
Hatlo, Jimmy	Cartoonists
Hatton, Robert	Civil War
Hauck, Frederick H.	Astronauts
Haught, Helmut	Aviation
Hauptmann, Gerhart	Authors
Hauser, Joe	Baseball
Hausner, Jerry	Entertainers (Current)
Haven, Annette	Entertainers (Current)
Havens, Beckwith	Aviation
Haver, June	Entertainers (Vintage)
Havlicek, John	Basketball HoF
Havoc, June	Entertainers (Vintage)
Hawes, Elizabeth	Artists
Hawke, Robert	Heads of State
Hawkins, Anthony Hope	Authors
Hawkins, Jack	Entertainers (Vintage)
Hawkins, William	Governors
Hawks, Frank	Aviation
Hawley, Joseph R.	Civil War
Hawley, Steven A.	Astronauts
Hawn, Goldie	Entertainers (Current)
Haworth, Jill	Entertainers (Current)
Hawple, Stu	Cartoonists
Hawthorn, Alex T.	Civil War
Hawthorne, Nathaniel	Authors
Hay, Charles	Hockey HoF
Hay, George	Hockey HoF
Hay, John	U.S. V.P. & Cabinet
Hay, William Henry	Military
Hayakawa, Sessue	Entertainers (Vintage)
Hayden, Mellisa	Entertainers (Vintage)
Hayden, Tom	Celebrities
Haydn, Joseph	Composers
Hayes, Bob	Football
Hayes, Elvin	General Sports
Hayes, Helen	Entertainers (Vintage)
Hayes, Isaac Israel	Celebrities
Hayes, Isaac	Entertainers (Current)
Hayes, Joseph	Civil War
Hayes, Margaret	Entertainers (Vintage)
Hayes, Mark	General Sports
Hayes, Rutherford B.	U.S. Presidents
Hayes, Von	Baseball
Hayes, Woody	Football
Haynes, Linda	Entertainers (Current)
Hays, Harold	Football
Hays, Robert	Entertainers (Current)
Hays, Will H.	Entertainers (Vintage)
Hayward, George	Science
Hayward, Louis	Entertainers (Vintage)
Hayward, Susan	Entertainers (Vintage)
Haywood, Thomas	Military
Hayworth, Ray	Baseball
Hayworth, Rita	Entertainers (Vintage)
Hazen, Wm. Babcock	Civil War
Hazzard, Walt	General Sports
Healey, Ed	Football
Healey, Robert C.	Authors
Healy, Ted	Entertainers (Vintage)
Hearn, Jim	Baseball
Hearnes, Warren E.	Governors
Hearns, Thomas	Boxing
Hearst, George (Senators)	Celebrities
Hearst, Patricia	Celebrities
Hearst, Phoebe	Business
Hearst, Wm. Rand. Jr	Business
Hearst, Wm. Randolph	Business
Heart	Rock
Heath, Edward	Heads of State
Heath, Tommy	Baseball
Heath, William	Revolutionary War
Heatherton, Joey	Entertainers (Current)
Hebert, Paul O.	Civil War
Heckart, Eileen	Entertainers (Current)
Heckerling, Amy	Entertainers (Current)
Hedin, Sven	Celebrities
Hedison, David	Entertainers (Current)
Hedouville, G.M.T.J,Count	Revolutionary War
Hedren, Tippi	Entertainers (Current)
Heffelfinger, "Pudge"	Football
Heffner, Don	Baseball
Heflin, Van	Entertainers (Vintage)
Hefner, Christie	Business
Hefti, Neal	Composers
Hegan, Jim	Baseball
Heiden, Eric	General Sports
Heidt, Horace	Entertainers (Vintage)
Heifetz, Jascha	Entertainers (Vintage)
Hein, Mel	Football
Heine, Heinrich	Authors
Heinrich, Don	Football
Heintzelman, Sam'l P	Civil War
Heinz, Henry John	Business
Heisenberg, Werner	Science
Helbig, Joachim	Aviation
Held Jr., John	Cartoonists
Held, Anna	Entertainers (Vintage)
Held, Woody	Baseball
Heldman, Gladys	Tennis HoF
Helen, H.R.H. Princess	Celebrities
Helf, "Hank"	Baseball
Heller, Dr. John R.	Science
Heller, Joseph	Authors
Heller, Walter	Celebrities
Heller, Walter W.	U.S. V.P. & Cabinet
Hellinger, Mark	Authors
Hellman, Lillian	Authors
Helmond, Katherine	Entertainers (Current)
Helms, Richard	Celebrities
Helps, Sir Arthur	Authors
Hemingway, Ernest	Authors
Hemingway, Margaux	Entertainers (Current)
Hemingway, Mariel	Entertainers (Current)
Hemingway, Mary	Authors
Hemsley, Sherman	Entertainers (Current)
Hemus, Solly	Baseball
Hench, Philip S.	Science
Henderson, Florence	Entertainers (Current)
Henderson, Ricky	Baseball
Hendricks, Thomas A. (V)	U.S. V.P. & Cabinet

459

Hobaugh, Ed	Baseball	Hood, Thos. (Younger)	Authors
Hobbs, Sir John Berry	General Sports	Hooker, Joseph M.	Civil War
Hobby, Oveta Culp	U.S. V.P. & Cabinet	Hooks, Benjamin L.	Celebrities
Hobson, Howard	Basketball HoF	Hooper, C. Thomas	Hockey HoF
Hobson, Howard	General Sports	Hooper, Harry	Baseball
Hobson, Richmond P.	Military	Hoover, Herbert	U.S. Presidents
Hoche, Lazare	Revolutionary War	Hoover, J. Edgar	Celebrities
Hock, Robt C.(SKYLAB)	Astronauts	Hoover, Lou Henry	Celebrities
Hoderlein, Mel	Baseball	Hope, Bob	Entertainers (Current)
Hodges, Gil	Baseball	Hopkins, Anthony	Entertainers (Current)
Hodiak, John	Entertainers (Vintage)	Hopkins, Bo	Entertainers (Current)
Hoegh, Leo A.	Governors	Hopkins, Mark	Celebrities
Hoerner, Joe	Baseball	Hopkins, Miriam	Entertainers (Vintage)
Hoernschemeyer, Bob	Football	Hopkins, Samuel	Revolutionary War
Hoest, Bill	Cartoonists	Hopkins, Stephen	Revolutionary War
Hoey, Clyde R.	Governors	Hopkinson, Francis	Revolutionary War
Hoff, Philip H.	Governors	Hopman, Harry	Tennis HoF
Hoffa, James A.	Celebrities	Hopp, Johnny	Baseball
Hoffer, Eric	Celebrities	Hoppe, Willie	General Sports
Hoffman, Dustin	Entertainers (Current)	Hopper, DeWolf	Entertainers (Vintage)
Hoffman, Harold Giles	Governors	Hopper, Hedda	Entertainers (Vintage)
Hoffman, Jeffrey A.	Astronauts	Horlen, Joe	Baseball
Hoffman, John Thompson	Governors	Hornberger, Rich. H.	Authors
Hoffman, Maud	Entertainers (Vintage)	Horne, Lena	Entertainers (Current)
Hoffman, Paul G.	Business	Horne, Marilyn	Entertainers (Current)
Hofman, Bobby	Baseball	Horner, Bob	Baseball
Hofmann, Josef	Entertainers (Vintage)	Horner, G. R. "Red"	Hockey HoF
Hofstadter, Robert	Science	Horner, Henry	Governors
Hogan, Ben	Golf HoF	Hornsby, Rogers	Baseball
Hogan, Cliff	General Sports	Hornung, Paul	Football
Hogan, Paul	Entertainers (Current)	Horowitz, David	Celebrities
Hogarth, Burne	Cartoonists	Horowitz, Vladimir	Entertainers (Vintage)
Hogarth, Wm.	Artists	Horsford, Eben N.	Science
Hoiriis, Holger	Aviation	Horsley, Lee	Entertainers (Current)
Hokinson, Helen	Cartoonists	Horthy, Miklos Adm.	Heads of State
Holbrook, Hal	Entertainers (Current)	Horton, Edw. Everett	Entertainers (Vintage)
Holden, William	Entertainers (Vintage)	Horton, M. G. "Tim"	Hockey HoF
Hole, Jonathan	Entertainers (Current)	Horton, Robert	Entertainers (Current)
Holladay, Ben	Business	Horvath, Les	Football
Holland, Josiah Gilb	Authors	Hostak, Al	Boxing
Holland, Terry	Football	Houdini, Harry	Entertainers (Vintage)
Holley, Dr. Robert	Science	Houghton, Katharine	Entertainers (Vintage)
Holley, Marietta	Authors	Houk, Ralph	Baseball
Holliday, Polly	Entertainers (Current)	House, Edw. M."Colonel"	Celebrities
Holliman, Earl	Entertainers (Current)	House, Edward M.	U.S. V.P. & Cabinet
Hollings, Ernest	Governors	House, Frank	Baseball
Hollins, Geo. Nichols	Civil War	House, Tom	Baseball
Holloway, Sterling	Entertainers (Vintage)	Houseman, John	Entertainers (Current)
Holly, Buddy	Rock	Houssay, Bernando A.	Science
Holm, Celeste	Entertainers (Current)	Houston, David	Country Music Stars
Holm, Eleanor	General Sports	Houston, Ken	Football
Holman, Nat	Basketball HoF	Houston, Sam	Military
Holmes, Burton	Authors	Houston, Whitney	Rock
Holmes, D. Brainerd	Celebrities	Hovey, Fred	Tennis HoF
Holmes, Harry	Hockey HoF	Hovis, Larry	Entertainers (Current)
Holmes, Larry	Boxing	Howard, Elston	Baseball
Holmes, Oliver W. (SC)	Celebrities	Howard, John	Entertainers (Vintage)
Holmes, Robert D.	Governors	Howard, Ken	Entertainers (Current)
Holmes, Tommy	Baseball	Howard, Leslie	Entertainers (Vintage)
Holmquest, Donald L.	Astronauts	Howard, Moe	Entertainers (Vintage)
Holshouser, James E.	Governors	Howard, Oliver O.	Civil War
Holst, Gustav	Composers	Howard, Ron	Entertainers (Current)
Holstrom, E.W."Brick	Military	Howard, Sidney	Authors
Holt, Jack	Entertainers (Vintage)	Howard, Willie	Entertainers (Vintage)
Holt, Joseph	U.S. V.P. & Cabinet	Howe, Albion P.	Civil War
Holton, Linwood	Governors	Howe, Art	Baseball
Holtz, Lou	Football	Howe, Dorothy C. Hurd	Golf HoF
Holtzman, Ken	Baseball	Howe, Elias	Science
Holyoake, Keith Sir	Heads of State	Howe, Gordon	Hockey HoF
Holzman, Red	General Sports	Howe, Julia Ward	Authors
Home, Alec Douglas	Heads of State	Howe, Richard Earl	Military
Homer, Winslow	Artists	Howe, Samuel	Celebrities
Homesteaders, The	Country Music Stars	Howe, Steve	Baseball
Homma, Masaharu	Military	Howe, Sydney	Hockey HoF
Homolka, Oscar	Entertainers (Vintage)	Howe, William	Military
Honeycutt, Rick	Baseball	Howell, Harry	Hockey HoF
Honnegger, Arthur	Composers	Howell, Jim Lee	Football
Hood, Alexander Sir	Military	Howell, Millard "Dixie"	Baseball
Hood, John Bell	Civil War	Howell, Thomas C.	Entertainers (Current)
Hood, Samuel	Military	Howes, Barbara	Authors
Hood, Thomas (Elder)	Authors	Howland, Beth	Entertainers (Current)

Name	Category	Name	Category
Howser, Dick	Baseball	Hurdle, Clint	Baseball
Hoyle, Edmund	Authors	Hurley, Patrick	U.S. V.P. & Cabinet
Hoyt, George	Basketball HoF	Hurst, Fannie	Authors
Hoyt, LaMarr	Baseball	Hurt, John	Entertainers (Current)
Hoyt, Waite	Baseball	Hurt, Mary Beth	Entertainers (Current)
Hoz, Mike de la	Baseball	Hurt, William	Entertainers (Current)
Hrbek, Kent	Baseball	Husing, Ted	General Sports
Huarte, Johnny	Football	Husky, Ferlin	Country Music Stars
Hubbard, Cal	Football	Hussein, King (Jord)	Heads of State
Hubbard, Cal	Baseball	Hussey, Olivia	Entertainers (Current)
Hubbard, Elbert	Authors	Hussey, Ruth	Entertainers (Current)
Hubbard, Gardiner	Celebrities	Huston, Anjelica	Entertainers (Current)
Hubbard, Glenn	Baseball	Huston, John	Entertainers (Vintage)
Hubbell, Carl	Baseball	Huston, Walter	Entertainers (Vintage)
Hudson, Rochelle	Entertainers (Vintage)	Hutchins, Will	Entertainers (Vintage)
Hudson, Rock	Entertainers (Vintage)	Hutchinson, Josephin	Entertainers (Vintage)
Huerta, Victoriano	Heads of State	Hutson, Don	Football
Huff, Sam	Football	Hutton, Betty	Entertainers (Vintage)
Huffman, Bennie	Baseball	Hutton, Gunilla	Country Music Stars
Hufstedler, Shirley	U.S. V.P. & Cabinet	Hutton, J. B. "Bouse"	Hockey HoF
Huger, Isaac	Revolutionary War	Hutton, Jim	Entertainers (Vintage)
Huggins, Charles	Science	Hutton, Lauren	Entertainers (Current)
Hughes, Charles Evans	U.S. V.P. & Cabinet	Hutton, Timothy	Entertainers (Current)
Hughes, Charles E. (SC)	Celebrities	Huxley, Aldous	Authors
Hughes, Howard	Business	Huxley, Julian	Science
Hughes, Jim	Baseball	Huxley, Thomas Henry	Science
Hughes, Langston	Authors	Hyams, Leila	Entertainers (Vintage)
Hughes, Mary Beth	Entertainers (Vintage)	Hyatt, Chuck	Basketball HoF
Hughes, Richard J.	Governors	Hyde, Arthur W.	U.S. V.P. & Cabinet
Hughes, Rupert	Authors	Hyde-White, Wilfrid	Entertainers (Vintage)
Hugo, Victor	Authors	Hyer, Martha	Entertainers (Current)
Hull, Bobby	General Sports	Hyland, Harry	Hockey HoF
Hull, Cordell	U.S. V.P. & Cabinet	Hylton, Lord	Military
Hull, Dennis	General Sports	II, William Bull	Governors
Hull, Henry	Entertainers (Vintage)	III, Davis Love	General Sports
Hull, Isaac	Military	IV, John D. Rockerfeller	Governors
Hull, Robert Marvin	Hockey HoF	Iacocca, Lee A.	Business
Hull, Warren	Entertainers (Vintage)	Ian, Janis	Rock
Hull, William	Military	Iba, Hank	Basketball HoF
Hulse, Tom	Entertainers (Current)	Iba, Henry P.	General Sports
Hulshoff, Karl	Aviation	Ibsen, Henrik	Authors
Humbert II	Heads of State	Ickes, Harold L.	U.S. V.P. & Cabinet
Humboldt, Alex. von	Science	Imboden, John Dan'l	Civil War
Hume, Fred	Hockey HoF	Imhoff, Darrell	General Sports
Hume, Joseph	Celebrities	Imlach, George "Punch"	Hockey HoF
Humes, William Y.C.	Civil War	Impellitteri, Vincent	Celebrities
Hummel, Johann Nepomuk	Composers	Incaviglia, Pete	Baseball
Humperdinck,Engelbrt	Composers	Indiana, Robert	Artists
Humphrey, Hubert H. (V)	U.S. V.P. & Cabinet	Iness, Sim	General Sports
Humphreys, A. A.	Civil War	Inge, William	Authors
Humphreys, David	Revolutionary War	Ingersoll, Charles R.	Governors
Hunt Jr., James B.	Governors	Ingersoll, Jared	Revolutionary War
Hunt, E. Howard	Celebrities	Ingersoll, Robert H.	Business
Hunt, George W. P.	Governors	Ingersoll, Robert Green	Celebrities
Hunt, H. L.	Business	Ingham, Samuel	U.S. V.P. & Cabinet
Hunt, Helen	Entertainers (Current)	Ingle, Red	Entertainers (Vintage)
Hunt, James Bunker	Business	Ingres, Jean A. D.	Artists
Hunt, John, Sir	Celebrities	Inkster, Juli	General Sports
Hunt, Joseph R.	Tennis HoF	Inman, Jerry	Country Music Stars
Hunt, Lamar	Football	Inskeep, Jonathan	Revolutionary War
Hunt, Marsha	Entertainers (Vintage)	Insull, Samuel	Business
Hunt, Ron	Baseball	Ion, Fred "Mickey"	Hockey HoF
Hunt, Ward (SC)	Celebrities	Ireland, Jill	Entertainers (Current)
Hunt, Washington	Governors	Irish, Edward "Ned"	General Sports
Hunt, William H.	U.S. V.P. & Cabinet	Irish, Ned	Basketball HoF
Hunt, Wm. Holman	Artists	Irons, Jeremy	Entertainers (Current)
Hunter, Bill	Baseball	Irvin, J. D. "Dick"	Hockey HoF
Hunter, David	Civil War	Irvin, Monte	Baseball
Hunter, Francis T.	Tennis HoF	Irvin, Shirley Fry	Tennis HoF
Hunter, Jeff	Entertainers (Vintage)	Irvine, James	Revolutionary War
Hunter, Jim "Catfish"	Baseball	Irvine, William	Revolutionary War
Hunter, Kim	Entertainers (Current)	Irving, Amy	Entertainers (Current)
Hunter, R. M. T.	Civil War	Irving, Henry Sir	Entertainers (Vintage)
Hunter, Robert	Revolutionary War	Irving, John	Authors
Hunter, Scott	Football	Irving, Washington	Authors
Hunter, Tab	Entertainers (Current)	Irwin, David	Celebrities
Huntington, Samuel	Revolutionary War	Irwin, Hale	General Sports
Huntington, Jedediah	Military	Irwin, James B.	Astronauts
Huntington, Benjamin	Revolutionary War	Irwin, May	Entertainers (Vintage)
Huntington, Henry E.	Business	Isabel II (Sp)	Heads of State
Hurd, Peter	Artists	Isabella I (Sp)	Heads of State

462

Johnson, Lynn	Cartoonists
Johnson, Lyndon B.	U.S. Presidents
Johnson, Lynn-Holly	Entertainers (Current)
Johnson, Oliver	Celebrities
Johnson, Osa	Entertainers (Vintage)
Johnson, Rafer	General Sports
Johnson, Reverdy	U.S. V.P. & Cabinet
Johnson, Richard L.	Aviation
Johnson, Richard H. (V)	U.S. V.P. & Cabinet
Johnson, Russ	Entertainers (Current)
Johnson, Thomas	Hockey HoF
Johnson, Walter	Baseball
Johnson, William	Tennis HoF
Johnson, William	Basketball HoF
Johnston, Albert S.	Civil War
Johnston, Joseph E.	Civil War
Johnston, Neil	General Sports
Johnston, Richard M.	Authors
Johnstone, Jay	Baseball
Joiner, Charlie	Football
Joliat, Aurel	Hockey HoF
Jolson, Al	Entertainers (Vintage)
Jones Jr., Robert T.	Golf HoF
Jones, Allan	Entertainers (Vintage)
Jones, Ann Haydon	Tennis HoF
Jones, Anne	Country Music Stars
Jones, Anson	Celebrities
Jones, Anthony Armstrong	Country Music Stars
Jones, Bob	Celebrities
Jones, Buck	Entertainers (Vintage)
Jones, Carolyn	Entertainers (Vintage)
Jones, Casey	Aviation
Jones, Chuck	Cartoonists
Jones, Davy	Baseball
Jones, Deacon	Football
Jones, Dean	Entertainers (Current)
Jones, Edward F.	Civil War
Jones, George	Country Music Stars
Jones, Grace	Entertainers (Current)
Jones, Grandpa	Country Music Stars
Jones, Isham	Entertainers (Vintage)
Jones, James	Authors
Jones, James Earl	Entertainers (Current)
Jones, Janet	Entertainers (Current)
Jones, Jennifer	Entertainers (Current)
Jones, Jesse H.	U.S. V.P. & Cabinet
Jones, K.C.	General Sports
Jones, LeRoi(Baraka,I.A.)	Authors
Jones, Marcia Mae	Entertainers (Current)
Jones, Mary H. "Mother"	Celebrities
Jones, Parnelli	General Sports
Jones, Perry	Tennis HoF
Jones, Quincy	Composers
Jones, R. W.	Basketball HoF
Jones, Ralph "Tiger"	Boxing
Jones, Randy	Baseball
Jones, Rickie Lee	Rock
Jones, Robert T. "Bobbie"	General Sports
Jones, Sam	Basketball HoF
Jones, Shirley	Entertainers (Current)
Jones, Thomas V.	Business
Jones, Tom	Entertainers (Current)
Jones, Tommy Lee	Entertainers (Current)
Jones, Tracy	Baseball
Jones, William E.	Civil War
Jong, Erica	Authors
Jongkind, Johan	Artists
Joost, Eddie	Baseball
Jope, Berhard	Aviation
Joplin, Janis	Rock
Joplin, Scott	Composers
Jordan, Dorothy	Entertainers (Vintage)
Jordan, Hamilton	U.S. V.P. & Cabinet
Jordan, Jim (Fibber)	Entertainers (Vintage)
Jordan, Lee Roy	Football
Jordan, Michael	General Sports
Jordan, Tom	Baseball
Jordon, Hamilton	Celebrities
Jordon, Richard	Entertainers (Current)
Jorgens, Art	Baseball
Jorgensen, Christine	Celebrities

Jory, Victor	Entertainers (Vintage)
Joseph II (Ger)	Heads of State
Josephine (Nap)	Heads of State
Josephson, Les	Football
Joshua, Von	Baseball
Jourdan, Jean B. Count	Revolutionary War
Jourdan, Louis	Entertainers (Current)
Journey	Rock
Jowett, Benjamin	Celebrities
Joy, Leatrice	Entertainers (Vintage)
Joyce, Alice	Entertainers (Vintage)
Joyce, Elain	Entertainers (Current)
Joyce, Richard	Military
Joyner, Wally	Baseball
Juan Carlos, King	Heads of State
Juarez, Benito	Heads of State
Judge, Arline	Entertainers (Vintage)
Judge, Joe	Baseball
Julian, Alvin F. (Doggie)	Basketball HoF
Juliana (Neth)	Heads of State
Jump, Gordon	Entertainers (Current)
Jung, Karl Gustav	Science
Junot, Jean Andoche	Revolutionary War
Jurgensen, "Sonny"	Football
Justice, Charlie	Football
Kaat, Jim	Baseball
Kafka, Franz	Authors
Kahanamoku, Duke	General Sports
Kahn, Madeline	Entertainers (Current)
Kahn, Otto H.	Business
Kahoutek, Lubos	Science
Kai-Shek, Chiang	Heads of State
Kai-Shek, Mme Chiang	Heads of State
Kaiser, Henry J.	Business
Kalakaua, David (Hawaii)	Heads of State
Kaline, Al	Baseball
Kaltenborn, H. V.	Celebrities
Kaltenbrunner, Ernst	Military
Kamm, "Willie"	Baseball
Kammhuber, Josef	Aviation
Kampouris, Alex	Baseball
Kanaly, Steve	Entertainers (Current)
Kander, John	Composers
Kandinsky, Wassily	Artists
Kane, Carol	Entertainers (Current)
Kane, Thomas L.	Civil War
Kangaroo, Captain	Entertainers (Current)
Kanin, Garson	Authors
Kansas	Rock
Kant, Immanuel	Authors
Kantor, MacKinlay	Authors
Kantrowitz, Dr. Adrian	Science
Kaper, Bronislaw	Composers
Kapp, Joe	Football
Kappel, Frederick R.	Business
Karas, Anton	Composers
Karloff, Boris	Entertainers (Vintage)
Karman, Theodore von	Celebrities
Karpis, Alvin	Celebrities
Karras, Alex	Football
Karras, Alex	Entertainers (Current)
Karsh, Yousuf	Artists
Kasavubu, Joseph	Heads of State
Kasem, Casey	Entertainers (Current)
Kashfi, Anna	Entertainers (Current)
Katz, Alvin S.	Celebrities
Katz, Bernard, Sir	Science
Kaufman, Andy	Entertainers (Vintage)
Kaufman, George S.	Authors
Kaunda, Kenneth	Heads of State
Kavanaugh, Ken	Football
Kawato, Mike	Military
Kay, Beatrice	Entertainers (Vintage)
Kay, Dianne	Entertainers (Current)
Kay, Mary	Business
Kaye, Celia	Entertainers (Current)
Kazan, Elia	Entertainers (Current)
Kazmaier, Dick	Football
Keach, Stacy	Entertainers (Current)
Kean, Jane	Entertainers (Vintage)
Keane, Bil	Cartoonists

Keane, Edward	Entertainers (Vintage)	Kent, Rockwell	Artists
Keaney, Frank	Basketball HoF	Kent, Walter	Composers
Kearns, Jack	Boxing	Kenton, Simon	Revolutionary War
Kearny, Philip	Civil War	Kenton, Stan	Entertainers (Vintage)
Keaton, Buster	Entertainers (Vintage)	Kenworthy, Dick	Baseball
Keaton, Diane	Entertainers (Current)	Kenyatta, Jomo	Heads of State
Keats, G. "Duke"	Hockey HoF	Kenyon, Doris	Entertainers (Vintage)
Keble, John	Celebrities	Keogan, George	Basketball HoF
Keeble, John	Authors	Keppel, Francis	Celebrities
Keel, Howard (gum)	Entertainers (Current)	Kercheval, Ken	Entertainers (Current)
Keeler, Ruby	Entertainers (Vintage)	Kerensky, Alexander	Heads of State
Keely, Bob	Baseball	Kern, Jerome	Composers
Keene, Carolyn	Authors	Kerr, Clark	Celebrities
Keene, Charles S.	Entertainers (Vintage)	Kerr, Deborah	Entertainers (Current)
Keifer, Joseph W.	Civil War	Kerr, Johnny	Baseball
Keillor, Garrison	Authors	Kerwin, Joseph P.	Astronauts
Keitel, Wilhelm	Military	Kesey, Ken	Authors
Keith, Brian	Entertainers (Current)	Kesselring, Albert	Military
Keith, David	Entertainers (Current)	Ketcham, Henry K.	Celebrities
Keith, Geo. K. E.	Military	Ketcham, Hank	Cartoonists
Kelcey, Herbert	Entertainers (Vintage)	Kettering, C. F.	Business
Kell, George	Baseball	Key, David M.	U.S. V.P. & Cabinet
Kelland, C. Buddington	Authors	Key, Francis Scott	Authors
Kellard, Ralph	Entertainers (Vintage)	Key, Ted	Cartoonists
Keller, Charlie	Baseball	Keyes, Erasmus	Civil War
Keller, Helen	Celebrities	Keyes, Evelyn	Entertainers (Vintage)
Kellerman, Annette	Entertainers (Vintage)	Keyes, Roger	Military
Kellerman, Sally	Entertainers (Current)	Keynes, John Maynard	Celebrities
Kellerman,FC,Duke Valmy	Revolutionary War	Keys, Ancel	Science
Kelley, Clarence M.	Celebrities	Keys, Henry W.	Governors
Kelley, Deforest	Entertainers (Current)	Keyserling, Hermann	Science
Kellogg, Frank B.	U.S. V.P. & Cabinet	Khalid, King	Heads of State
Kellogg, John Harvey	Business	Khambatta, Persis	Entertainers (Current)
Kellogg, W. K.	Business	Khan, Chaka	Rock
Kelly, Emmett Sr.	Entertainers (Vintage)	Khanh, Nguyen Gen.	Heads of State
Kelly, Gene	Entertainers (Vintage)	Khchaturian, Aram	Composers
Kelly, George L.	Baseball	Khorana, Dr. Har G.	Science
Kelly, Grace	Entertainers (Vintage)	Kibrick, Sidney	Entertainers (Current)
Kelly, Howard A.	Science	Kidd, Billy	General Sports
Kelly, Jim	Football	Kidder, Margot	Entertainers (Current)
Kelly Jr., John B.	General Sports	Kilban, Bill	Cartoonists
Kelly, John H.	Civil War	Kilby, J. S.	Science
Kelly, L. P. "Red"	Hockey HoF	Kiley, Richard	Entertainers (Current)
Kelly, Nancy	Entertainers (Vintage)	Kilgore, Merle	Country Music Stars
Kelly, Patsy	Entertainers (Vintage)	Kilian, Victor	Entertainers (Vintage)
Kelly, Paul	Entertainers (Vintage)	Killebrew, Harmon	Baseball
Kelly, Paula	Entertainers (Current)	Killy, Jean-Claude	General Sports
Kelly, Walt	Cartoonists	Kilmer, Bill	Football
Kelsey, Linda	Entertainers (Current)	Kilmer, Joyce	Authors
Kelton, Pert	Entertainers (Vintage)	Kilpatrick, Gen. John	Hockey HoF
Kelvin, William T. Lord	Science	Kimberly, Lewis	Civil War
Kemp, Hal	Entertainers (Vintage)	Kimbrough, Emily	Authors
Kemp, Jack	Football	Kimbrough, Johnny	Football
Kemp, Steve	Baseball	Kimmel, Husband E.	Military
Kemper, John M.	Celebrities	Kinard, Frank "Bruiser"	Football
Kendal, Madge	Entertainers (Vintage)	Kindermann, K. B.	Aviation
Kendall, Amos	U.S. V.P. & Cabinet	Kiner, Ralph	Baseball
Kendall, Edward C.	Science	King, Alan	Entertainers (Current)
Kennedy, Arthur	Entertainers (Vintage)	King, Betsy	General Sports
Kennedy, Edgar	Entertainers (Vintage)	King, Billie Jean	General Sports
Kennedy, Edward M.	Celebrities	King, Cammie	Entertainers (Vintage)
Kennedy, Ethel	Celebrities	King, Carole	Rock
Kennedy, George	Entertainers (Current)	King, Coretta Scott	Celebrities
Kennedy, Gerald Bishop	Celebrities	King, Don	Boxing
Kennedy, Jacqueline	Celebrities	King, Ernest J.	Military
Kennedy, Jayne	Entertainers (Current)	King, Frank	Cartoonists
Kennedy, John	Baseball	King, Horatio	U.S. V.P. & Cabinet
Kennedy, John P.	U.S. V.P. & Cabinet	King, MacKenzie	Heads of State
Kennedy, John F.	U.S. Presidents	King, Martin Luther	Celebrities
Kennedy, Joseph P.	Business	King, Pee Wee	Country Music Stars
Kennedy, Matthew	Basketball HoF	King, Perry	Entertainers (Current)
Kennedy, Robert F.	U.S. V.P. & Cabinet	King, Rafiu	Boxing
Kennedy, Rose	Celebrities	King, Rufus	Revolutionary War
Kennedy, T. S. "Teeder"	Hockey HoF	King, Stephen	Authors
Kennedy, Terry	Baseball	King, Walter Woolf	Entertainers (Vintage)
Kennedy, Walter	Basketball HoF	King, Wayne	Entertainers (Vintage)
Kenney, George	Military	King, William R. (V)	U.S. V.P. & Cabinet
Kenny, Elizabeth, Sister	Celebrities	Kingman, Dave	Baseball
Kent, Jack	Cartoonists	Kingman, Dong	Artists
Kent, James	Celebrities	Kingsford-Smith, Chas.	Aviation
Kent, James	Revolutionary War	Kingsley, Charles	Authors

464

Name	Category	Name	Category
Kinks	Rock	Kramer, Ron	Football
Kinsey, Dr. Alfred C.	Science	Kramer, Stanley	Entertainers (Current)
Kinski, Nastassia	Entertainers (Current)	Kratzer, Bill	General Sports
Kinstler, E.R.	Cartoonists	Krause, Ed "Moose"	Football
Kintner, Robert	Business	Krause, Edward (Moose)	Basketball HoF
Kipling, Rudyard	Authors	Krause, Paul	Football
Kirby, Jack	Cartoonists	Krausse, Lew	Baseball
Kirby-Smith, Edmund	Military	Krebs, Hans	Science
Kirk Jr., Claude R.	Governors	Kreevich, Mike	Baseball
Kirk, Eddie	Country Music Stars	Kreisler, Fritz	Composers
Kirk, Phyllis	Entertainers (Vintage)	Kreps, Juanita M.	U.S. V.P. & Cabinet
Kirkconnell	Entertainers (Current)	Kresge, S. S.	Business
Kirkland, Lane	Celebrities	Kress, Ralph "Red"	Baseball
Kirkpatrick, Jean J.	U.S. V.P. & Cabinet	Krige, Alice	Entertainers (Current)
Kirkwood, Joe	Entertainers (Current)	Kristel, Sylvia	Entertainers (Current)
Kirkwood, Samuel J.	U.S. V.P. & Cabinet	Kristofferson, Kris	Entertainers (Current)
Kirman Sr., Richard	Governors	Kroc, Mrs. Ray (Joan)	Business
Kirsten, Dorothy	Entertainers (Current)	Kroc, Ray	Business
Kison, Bruce	Baseball	Krock, Arthur	Authors
Kissinger, Henry	U.S. V.P. & Cabinet	Kroesen, Fred J.	Military
Kitchener, Horatio H	Military	Kropotkin, Peter	Celebrities
Kite, Tom	General Sports	Kruger, Kurt	Entertainers (Vintage)
Kitt, Eartha	Entertainers (Current)	Kruger, Paul	Heads of State
Kittinger, Joe	Celebrities	Krupa, Gene	Entertainers (Vintage)
Kittle, Ron	Baseball	Krupinski, Walter	Aviation
Kleber, Jean-Baptiste	Revolutionary War	Krupp, Alfred	Business
Klein, Calvin	Business	Kruschchev, Nikita S.	Heads of State
Klemperer, Werner	Entertainers (Vintage)	Krushelnyski, Mike	General Sports
Kleppe, Thomas S.	U.S. V.P. & Cabinet	Krylov, Ivan A.	Authors
Kline, Kevin	Entertainers (Current)	Kubek, Tony	Baseball
Kline, Ron	Baseball	Kubelik, Jan	Entertainers (Vintage)
Klugman, Jack	Entertainers (Current)	Kubitschek,Juscelino	Heads of State
Kluszewski, Ted	Baseball	Kuenn, Harvey	Baseball
Knievel, Evel	Celebrities	Kuhn, Bowie	Baseball
Knight, Bobby	General Sports	Kunkel, Bill	Baseball
Knight, Gladys	Entertainers (Current)	Kuralt, Charles	Celebrities
Knight, Goodwin J.	Governors	Kurland, Bob	Basketball HoF
Knight, June	Entertainers (Vintage)	Kusch, Poyl K.	Science
Knight, Phil	Business	Kush, Frank	Football
Knight, Ray	Baseball	Kwan, Nancy	Entertainers (Current)
Knight, Shirley	Entertainers (Current)	Ky, Nguyen Cao	Heads of State
Knight, Ted	Entertainers (Vintage)	Kyne, Peter B.	Authors
Knopf, Alfred A.	Business	Kyser, Kay	Entertainers (Current)
Knott, Jack	Baseball	L'Amour, Louis	Authors
Knotts, Don	Entertainers (Current)	La Revelliere-Lepaux,L.	Revolutionary War
Knowles, James S.	Authors	La Rocque, Rod	Entertainers (Vintage)
Knox, Alexander	Entertainers (Current)	LaBarba, Fidel	Boxing
Knox, Chuck	Football	LaDelle, Jack	Entertainers (Current)
Knox, Elyse	Entertainers (Vintage)	LaFarge, John	Artists
Knox, Frank	U.S. V.P. & Cabinet	LaFayette, Marquis(Mil)	Revolutionary War
Knox, Henry	U.S. V.P. & Cabinet	LaFollette, Philip	Governors
Knox, Philander C.	U.S. V.P. & Cabinet	LaGuardia, Fiorello	Celebrities
Knudsen, William S.	Business	LaLanne, Jack	General Sports
Koch, Edward I.	Celebrities	LaLanne, Jack	Entertainers (Current)
Koch, Robert	Science	LaMotta, Jake	Boxing
Kodaly, Zoltan	Composers	LaMotta, Vikki	Celebrities
Koehler, Armin	Aviation	LaRue, Lash	Entertainers (Vintage)
Koenig, Mark A.	Baseball	LaRussa, Tony	Baseball
Kohl, Helmut	Heads of State	Laabs, Chet	Baseball
Kohner, Susan	Entertainers (Current)	Labine, Clem	Baseball
Koosman, Jerry	Baseball	Labouisse, Eve Curie	Science
Koppel, Ted	Celebrities	Lacepede, Bernhard de	Science
Korda, Alexander	Entertainers (Vintage)	Lacey, Sam	General Sports
Koren, Edward	Cartoonists	Lach, Elmer	Hockey HoF
Korman, Harvey	Entertainers (Current)	Lacoste, Rene	Tennis HoF
Korngold, Erich W.	Composers	Lacy, Lee	Baseball
Korvin, Charles	Entertainers (Vintage)	Ladd, Alan	Entertainers (Vintage)
Kosar, Bernie	Football	Ladd, Cheryl	Entertainers (Current)
Kosciusko, Thaddeus	Revolutionary War	Ladd, Diane	Entertainers (Current)
Kossa, Frank R.	Military	Ladd, Sue Carol	Entertainers (Vintage)
Kossuth, Lajos	Heads of State	Laemmle, Carl	Entertainers (Vintage)
Kosygin, Aleksei	Heads of State	Lafayette, Marquis de	Military
Kotzky, Alex	Cartoonists	Lagerkvist, Par F.	Authors
Koufax, Sanford "Sandy"	Baseball	Lagerlof, Selma	Authors
Kovack, Nance (Mehta)	Entertainers (Current)	Lahm, Frank	Aviation
Kove, Martin	Entertainers (Current)	Lahti, Christine	Entertainers (Current)
Kraft, Chris	Astronauts	Laine, J.L.J.,Viscount	Revolutionary War
Kraft, James L.	Business	Laird, Bill	Football
Kragen, Ken	Business	Laird, Melvin	U.S. V.P. & Cabinet
Kramer, Jack A.	Tennis HoF	Lajoie, Napoleon "Larry"	Baseball
Kramer, Jerry	Football	Lake, Arthur	Entertainers (Vintage)

Lake, Simon	Celebrities
Lake, Veronica	Entertainers (Vintage)
Lalonde, E. C. "Newsy"	Hockey HoF
Lamar, Joseph R. (SC)	Celebrities
Lamar, Lucius Q.C. (SC)	Celebrities
Lamarck, Jean Baptiste	Science
Lamarr, Hedy	Entertainers (Current)
Lamas, Fernando	Entertainers (Vintage)
Lamas, Lorenzo	Entertainers (Current)
Lamb, Charles	Authors
Lambeau, Earl "Curley"	Football
Lambert, Ray	Celebrities
Lambert, Ward	Basketball HoF
Lamonica, Daryl	Football
Lamont, Daniel S.	U.S. V.P. & Cabinet
Lamont, Thomas S.	Business
Lamour, Dorothy	Entertainers (Current)
Lampley, Jim	General Sports
Lancaster, Burt	Entertainers (Current)
Lance, Bert	U.S. V.P. & Cabinet
Lanchester, Elsa	Entertainers (Current)
Land, E. S.	Celebrities
Land, Edwin H.	Business
Landau, Martin	Entertainers (Current)
Lander, Frederick West	Celebrities
Landers, Ann	Celebrities
Landers, Audrey	Entertainers (Current)
Landers, Judy	Entertainers (Current)
Landi, Elissa	Entertainers (Vintage)
Landis, Carole	Entertainers (Vintage)
Landis, John	Entertainers (Current)
Landis, Kenesaw Mountain	Baseball
Landon, Alf M.	Governors
Landon, Michael	Entertainers (Current)
Landreaux, Ken	Baseball
Landrieu, Moon	U.S. V.P. & Cabinet
Landrum, Don	Baseball
Landrum, Joe	Baseball
Landry, Tom	Football
Landseer, Sir Edwin H.	Artists
Lane, Abbe	Entertainers (Current)
Lane, Christy	Entertainers (Current)
Lane, Diane	Entertainers (Current)
Lane, Dick "Night Train"	Football
Lane, Joseph	Governors
Lane, Lola	Entertainers (Vintage)
Lane, Priscilla	Entertainers (Vintage)
Lane, Rosemary	Entertainers (Vintage)
Laney, Al	Tennis HoF
Lang, Anton	Entertainers (Vintage)
Lang, Rosa	Entertainers (Vintage)
Lang, Sebastian	Entertainers (Vintage)
Langan, Glenn	Entertainers (Vintage)
Langdon, Harry	Entertainers (Vintage)
Langdon, John	Revolutionary War
Lange, David	Heads of State
Lange, Hope	Entertainers (Current)
Lange, Jessica	Entertainers (Current)
Langer, Bernhard	General Sports
Langer, Jim	Football
Langford, Frances	Entertainers (Vintage)
Langford, Rick	Baseball
Langley, Samuel P.	Aviation
Langlie, Arthur	Governors
Langmuir, Irving	Science
Langston, Mark	Baseball
Langtry, Lily	Entertainers (Vintage)
Lanier, Sidney	Authors
Lanier, Willie	Football
Lanphier, Jr., Tom	Aviation
Lansbury, Angela	Entertainers (Current)
Lansing, Robert	U.S. V.P. & Cabinet
Lantz, Walter	Cartoonists
Lapchick, Joe	Basketball HoF
Lapoype, J.F.C., Baron	Revolutionary War
Larch, John	Entertainers (Current)
Lardner, James L.	Civil War
Lardner, Ring	Authors
Lardner, Ring Jr.	Authors
Laredo, Ruth	Entertainers (Current)
Largent, Steve	Football

Larker, Norm	Baseball
Larmouth, Kathy	Entertainers (Current)
Larned, William A.	Tennis HoF
Larrey, Dominick Baron	Revolutionary War
Larroquette, John	Entertainers (Current)
Larsen, Arthur D.	Tennis HoF
Larsen, Don	Baseball
Larson, Dr. Leonard	Science
Lary, Frank	Baseball
Lary, Yale	Football
Lasker, Mary	Business
Lasorda, Tommy	Baseball
Latham, Hubert	Aviation
Lathrop, George P.	Authors
Latour-Maubourg,M.V.N.F.	Revolutionary War
Lattimore, Richard	Authors
Lattner, Johnny	Football
Lauder, Harry	Entertainers (Vintage)
Laughton, Charles	Entertainers (Vintage)
Lauper, Cyndi	Entertainers (Current)
Laurel & Hardy	Entertainers (Vintage)
Lauren, Ralph	Business
Laurette, Taylor	Entertainers (Vintage)
Laurie, Piper	Entertainers (Current)
Lausche, Frank J.	Governors
Lavagetto, Cookie	Baseball
Lavelli, Dante	Football
Lavelli, Tony	General Sports
Laver, Rod	Tennis HoF
Lavin, Linda	Entertainers (Current)
Laviolette, Jean	Hockey HoF
Lavoisier, Antoine L.	Science
Law, Andrew Bonar	Heads of State
Law, John Phillip	Entertainers (Current)
Law, Ruth	Aviation
Law, Vernon	Baseball
Lawes, Lewis E.	Celebrities
Lawford, Peter	Entertainers (Vintage)
Lawrence, Barbara	Entertainers (Current)
Lawrence, Carol	Entertainers (Current)
Lawrence, D. H.	Authors
Lawrence, David L.	Governors
Lawrence, Ernest O.	Science
Lawrence, Gertrude	Entertainers (Vintage)
Lawrence, Ist Baron	Heads of State
Lawrence, Marc	Entertainers (Vintage)
Lawrence, Sir Thos.	Artists
Lawrence, Steve	Entertainers (Current)
Lawrence, T. E.	Authors
Lawrence, Vicki	Entertainers (Current)
Lawton, A. R.	Civil War
Lay, Herman W.	Business
Layard, Austin Henry	Celebrities
Layden, Elmer	Football
Layne, Bobby	Football
Layne, Rex	Boxing
Lazarus, Mell	Cartoonists
Lazarus, Ralph	Business
Lazenby, George	Entertainers (Current)
Le Gallienne, Eva	Entertainers (Vintage)
LeBaron, Eddie	Football
LeBel, Robert	Hockey HoF
LeBrock, Kelly	Entertainers (Current)
LeCarre, John	Authors
LeGallienne, Eva	Entertainers (Current)
LeGarde, Tom and Ted	Country Music Stars
LeHand, M. A. (Missy)	U.S. V.P. & Cabinet
LeMay, Curtis S.	Military
LeRoy, Mervyn	Entertainers (Vintage)
LeSeur, Percy	Hockey HoF
Leachman, Cloris	Entertainers (Current)
Leader, George	Hockey HoF
Leahy, Frank	Football
Leahy, William D.	Military
Leakey, Mary D.	Science
Lean, David Sir	Entertainers (Current)
Lear, Norman	Entertainers (Current)
Lear, Tobias	Revolutionary War
Lear, William P. Sr.	Business
Learned, Michael	Entertainers (Current)
Lease, Mary Elizabth	Authors

Lebrun, Albert	Heads of State	Lermontov, Mikhail	Authors
Led Zeppelin	Rock	Lerner, Alan Jay	Composers
Lederer, Francis	Entertainers (Vintage)	Lerner, Max	Authors
Ledoux, Harold	Cartoonists	Leslie, Joan	Entertainers (Vintage)
Lee, Anna	Entertainers (Vintage)	Leslie, Preston H.	Governors
Lee, Brenda	Country Music Stars	Lesnevich, Gus	Boxing
Lee, Charles	U.S. V.P. & Cabinet	Lesseps, Ferd. de, Comte	Science
Lee, Charles (U.S. V.P. & Cabinet)	Revolutionary War	Lester, Buddy	Entertainers (Current)
Lee, Clyde	General Sports	Letterman, David	Entertainers (Current)
Lee, Dixie (Mrs Bing C	Entertainers (Vintage)	Levene, Sam	Entertainers (Vintage)
Lee, Dr. Sammy	General Sports	Lever, Wm. Hesketh	Business
Lee, Dr. T. D.	Science	Leverett, John	Revolutionary War
Lee, E. Hamilton	Aviation	Levi, Edward H.	U.S. V.P. & Cabinet
Lee, Fitzhugh	Civil War	Levin, Dave	General Sports
Lee, Francis Lightfoot	Revolutionary War	Levine, David	Cartoonists
Lee, Geo. Wash. Custis	Civil War	Levine, Irving R.	Celebrities
Lee, Gypsy Rose	Entertainers (Vintage)	Levine, James	Entertainers (Current)
Lee, Harper	Authors	Lewis, Carl	General Sports
Lee, Henry	Military	Lewis, David "Duffy"	Aviation
Lee, Henry (Military)	Revolutionary War	Lewis, Ed "Strangler"	General Sports
Lee, Jesse E.	General Sports	Lewis, Emmanuele	Entertainers (Current)
Lee, Lila	Entertainers (Vintage)	Lewis, Francis	Revolutionary War
Lee, Mark C.	Astronauts	Lewis, Guy	General Sports
Lee, Michele	Entertainers (Current)	Lewis, Gwilym H.	Aviation
Lee, Pinkie	Entertainers (Current)	Lewis, Huey	Entertainers (Current)
Lee, Richard Henry	Revolutionary War	Lewis, Huey	Rock
Lee, Robert E.	Civil War	Lewis, James	Entertainers (Vintage)
Lee, Ruta	Entertainers (Current)	Lewis, Jerry	Entertainers (Current)
Lee, Samuel P.	Civil War	Lewis, Jerry Lee	Rock
Lee, William R.	Civil War	Lewis, Joe E.	Entertainers (Vintage)
Leech, John	Artists	Lewis, John Henry	Boxing
Leeds, Andrea	Entertainers (Vintage)	Lewis, John L.	Celebrities
Leemans, Alphonse "Tuffy"	Football	Lewis, Leo	Football
Leestma, David C.	Astronauts	Lewis, Meriwether	Celebrities
Lefebvre, F.J., Duke	Revolutionary War	Lewis, Morgan	Military
Lefebvre, Jim	Baseball	Lewis, Ramsey	Entertainers (Current)
Lefevre, Edwin	Authors	Lewis, Shari	Entertainers (Current)
Lefleur, Guy	General Sports	Lewis, Sinclair	Authors
Legrand, Michel	Composers	Lewis, Ted	Entertainers (Vintage)
Lehar, Franz	Composers	Lewisohn, Adolph	Business
Lehman, Herbert H.	Governors	Ley, Willy	Science
Lehman, Hugh	Hockey HoF	Libby, W. F.	Science
Lehmann, Lotte	Entertainers (Vintage)	Liberace	Entertainers (Vintage)
Lehr, Lew	Entertainers (Vintage)	Liberace, George	Entertainers (Vintage)
Leibman, Ron	Entertainers (Current)	Liberman, Evsei Prof	Celebrities
Leigh, Janet	Entertainers (Current)	Lichtenstein, Roy	Artists
Leigh, Vivien	Entertainers (Vintage)	Liddle, Don	Baseball
Leighton, Frederic	Artists	Liddy, G. Gordon	Celebrities
Leinsdorf, Erich	Entertainers (Vintage)	Lie, Trygve	Heads of State
Leith, Lloyd	Basketball HoF	Lietzke, Bruce	General Sports
Lejeune, John Archer	Military	Liggett, Louis Kroh	Business
Leland, W. C.	Business	Light, Judith	Entertainers (Current)
Leloir, Luis	Science	Lightner, Winnie	Entertainers (Vintage)
Lelouch, Claude	Entertainers (Current)	Lilienthal, David E.	Celebrities
Lema, Tony	General Sports	Liliuokalani (Hawaii)	Heads of State
Lemaire, Jacques	Hockey HoF	Lillie, Beatrice	Entertainers (Vintage)
Lemass, Sean	Heads of State	Lillie, G.A.(Pawnee Bill)	Celebrities
Lembeck, Michael	Entertainers (Current)	Lilly, Bob	Football
Lemmon, Jack	Entertainers (Current)	Liman, Arthur	Celebrities
Lemnitzer, L. L.	Military	Lincoln, Abraham	U.S. Presidents
Lemon, Bob	Baseball	Lincoln, Benjamin	Military
Lenglen, Suzanne	General Sports	Lincoln, Evelyn	Celebrities
Lenglen, Suzanne	Tennis HoF	Lincoln, Keith	Football
Lennon, John	Rock	Lincoln, Mary Todd	Celebrities
Lennon, Julian	Rock	Lincoln, Robert Todd	U.S. V.P. & Cabinet
Lenoir, William B.	Astronauts	Lind, Dòn L.	Astronauts
Lenske, Rula	Entertainers (Current)	Lind, Jenny	Entertainers (Vintage)
Leonard, "Sugar Ray"	Boxing	Lindbergh, Anne Morrow	Authors
Leonard, Benny	Boxing	Lindbergh, Charles A.	Aviation
Leonard, Emil "Dutch"	Baseball	Lindell, Johnny	Baseball
Leonard, Gloria	Entertainers (Current)	Linden, Hal	Entertainers (Current)
Leonard, Sheldon	Entertainers (Current)	Lindfors, Viveca	Entertainers (Current)
Leonard, Walter "Buck"	Baseball	Lindsay, Howard	Authors
Leoncavallo, Ruggiero	Composers	Lindsay, John	Celebrities
Leonov, Aleksei	Astronauts	Lindsay, Margaret	Entertainers (Vintage)
Leontovich, Eugenie	Entertainers (Vintage)	Lindsay, Robert "Ted"	Hockey HoF
Leopardi, Giacomo	Authors	Lindsey, George	Entertainers (Current)
Leopold I (Belg)	Heads of State	Lindsey, Vachel	Authors
Leopold I (Hung)	Heads of State	Lindstrom, Fred	Baseball
Leopold II (Belg)	Heads of State	Linkletter, Art	Entertainers (Current)
Leopold, Nathan F.	Celebrities	Linnaeus, Carl	Science

Linville, Larry	Entertainers (Current)
Lipchitz, Jacques	Artists
Lippman, Walter	Authors
Lipps, Louis	Football
Lipscomb, Gene	Football
Lipton, Peggy	Entertainers (Current)
Lipton, Sir Thomas	General Sports
Liquori, Marty	General Sports
Lisa, Manuel	Celebrities
Liscio, Tony	Football
Liska, Ad	Baseball
Lister, Joseph	Science
Liston, Emil	Basketball HoF
Liston, Robert	Science
Liston, Sonny	Boxing
Liszt, Franz	Composers
Litel, John	Entertainers (Vintage)
Lithgow, John	Entertainers (Current)
Litjens, Stefan	Aviation
Little Richard	Entertainers (Current)
Little River Band	Rock
Little, Cleavon	Entertainers (Current)
Little, Larry	Football
Little, Lawson	Golf HoF
Little, Sally	General Sports
Littler, Gene	General Sports
Litwack Harry	Basketball HoF
Livermore, Dan'l P.	Celebrities
Livermore, Mary A.	Celebrities
Liverpool, 2nd Earl	Heads of State
Livingston, R.R.(U.S. V.P. & Cabinet)	Revolutionary War
Livingston, Jay	Composers
Livingston, Edward	U.S. V.P. & Cabinet
Livingston, Philip	Revolutionary War
Livingston, Margaret	Entertainers (Vintage)
Livingston, Henry B. (SC)	Celebrities
Livingston, William	Revolutionary War
Livingston, Robert R.	U.S. V.P. & Cabinet
Livingstone, David	Celebrities
Llewellyn, Anthony	Astronauts
Lloyd George, David	Heads of State
Lloyd, Christopher	Entertainers (Current)
Lloyd, Harold	Entertainers (Vintage)
Lloyd, Kathleen	Entertainers (Current)
Lloyd, Norman	Entertainers (Current)
LoBianco, Tony	Entertainers (Current)
Locke, Bobby	Golf HoF
Locke, John	Authors
Locke, Sandra	Entertainers (Current)
Locke, William John	Authors
Lockhart, June	Entertainers (Current)
Lockhart, Thomas	Hockey HoF
Lockheed, Alan	Aviation
Locklear, Heather	Entertainers (Current)
Lockman, Whitey	Baseball
Lockwood, Belva A.	Celebrities
Lockwood, Chas.W Capt	Civil War
Lockwood, Margaret	Entertainers (Vintage)
Lodge, Henry Cabot	U.S. V.P. & Cabinet
Lodge, Henry Cabot, Jr.	Celebrities
Loeffler, Kenneth (Ken)	Basketball HoF
Loew, Marcus	Business
Loewe, Frederick	Composers
Logan, Ella	Entertainers (Vintage)
Logan, John A.	Civil War
Logan, Johnny	Baseball
Logan, Josh	Authors
Logan, Joshua	Entertainers (Vintage)
Loggia, Robert	Entertainers (Current)
Loggins & Messina	Rock
Loggins, Kenny	Rock
Loicq, Paul	Hockey HoF
Lolobrigida, Gina	Entertainers (Current)
Lomax, L. L.	Civil War
Lomax, Neil	Football
Lombardi, Vic	Baseball
Lombardi, Vince	Football
Lombardo, Guy	Entertainers (Vintage)
Lonborg, A. C. (Dutch)	Basketball HoF
Lonborg, Jim	Baseball
London, Jack	Authors

London, Julie	Entertainers (Vintage)
Londos, Jim	General Sports
Long, Earl K.	Governors
Long, Howie	Football
Long, Huey P.	Governors
Long, John D.	U.S. V.P. & Cabinet
Long, Johnny	Entertainers (Vintage)
Long, Shelley	Entertainers (Current)
Longden, Johnny	General Sports
Longet, Claudine	Entertainers (Current)
Longfellow, Henry W.	Authors
Longley, James B.	Governors
Longstreet, James	Civil War
Longworth, Alice Roosev.	Celebrities
Loos, Anita	Authors
Loos, Walter	Aviation
Lopat, Ed	Baseball
Loper, Don	Business
Lopes, Davey	Baseball
Lopez, Al	Baseball
Lopez, Aurelio	Baseball
Lopez, Nancy	General Sports
Lorca, Garcia	Authors
Lord, Jack	Entertainers (Current)
Lord, Walter	Authors
Loren, Sophia	Entertainers (Current)
Lorillard, Peter	Business
Loring, Gloria	Entertainers (Current)
Lorne, Marquis of	Heads of State
Losigkeit, Fritz	Aviation
Lossing, Benson J.	Artists
Lossing, Benson	Celebrities
Lothridge, Billy	Football
Lott Jr., George M.	Tennis HoF
Loudd, Rommie	Football
Louganis, Greg	General Sports
Loughlin, Lori	Entertainers (Current)
Loughran, Tommy	Boxing
Louis Philippe (Fr)	Heads of State
Louis XII (Fr)	Heads of State
Louis XIII (Fr)	Heads of State
Louis XIV (Fr)	Heads of State
Louis XV (Fr)	Heads of State
Louis XVI (Fr)	Heads of State
Louis XVIII (Fr)	Heads of State
Louis, Joe	Boxing
Louise, Anita	Entertainers (Vintage)
Louise, Tina	Entertainers (Current)
Lounge, John M.	Astronauts
Lousma, Jack F.	Astronauts
Love, John A.	Governors
Lovecraft, H. P.	Authors
Lovell, Bernard Dr.	Science
Lovell, James A. Jr.	Astronauts
Lovell, James	Revolutionary War
Loverboy	Rock
Lovett, Robert	U.S. V.P. & Cabinet
Low, Frederick F.	Governors
Low, G. David	Astronauts
Low, Sir David	Authors
Lowe, Edmund	Entertainers (Vintage)
Lowell, Amy	Authors
Lowell, James Russell	Authors
Lowrey, Harry "Peanuts"	Baseball
Lowry, Robert	Governors
Loy, Myrna	Entertainers (Current)
Lubbock, F.R. (CivWar)	Celebrities
Lubitsch, Ernst	Entertainers (Vintage)
Lucas, Edward Verrall	Authors
Lucas, George	Entertainers (Current)
Lucas, Jerry	Basketball HoF
Lucci, Susan	Entertainers (Current)
Luce, Clare Boothe	Celebrities
Luce, Henry R.	Business
Luce, S. B. Adm	Military
Lucid, Shannon W.	Astronauts
Luckman, Sid	Football
Luckner, Felix Count	Military
Ludendorff, Erich von	Military
Ludlum, Robert	Authors
Ludwig I (Bav)	Heads of State

468

Ludwig II (Bavaria)	Heads of State
Ludwig, Emil	Authors
Lugosi, Bela	Entertainers (Vintage)
Luisetti, Angelo "Hank"	General Sports
Luisetti, Hank	Basketball HoF
Lujack, Johnny	Football
Lukas, Paul	Entertainers (Vintage)
Luke, Keye	Entertainers (Vintage)
Lum & Abner	Entertainers (Vintage)
Lumiere, Louis	Entertainers (Vintage)
Lumley, Harry	Hockey HoF
Lumley, Joanna	Entertainers (Current)
Lund, Francis "Pug"	Football
Lund, John	Entertainers (Vintage)
Lunney, G.	Astronauts
Lunt & Fontanne	Entertainers (Vintage)
Lupino, Ida	Entertainers (Vintage)
Lupino, Ida	Entertainers (Current)
Lusch, Ernie	General Sports
Luse, Harley	Country Music Stars
Luther, Martin	Celebrities
Luzinski, Greg	Baseball
Lyautey, Louis	Heads of State
Lyle, "Sparky"	Baseball
Lynch, Thomas Jr.	Revolutionary War
Lynde, Paul	Entertainers (Vintage)
Lynley, Carol	Entertainers (Current)
Lynn, Diana	Entertainers (Vintage)
Lynn, Fred	Baseball
Lynn, Jeffrey	Entertainers (Vintage)
Lynn, Loretta	Country Music Stars
Lyon, Sue	Entertainers (Current)
Lyons, Ted	Baseball
Lyons, William	Business
Lytell, Bert	Entertainers (Vintage)
Lytton, E. George Bulwer	Authors
MacAfee, Ken	Football
MacArthur II, Doug.	Military
MacArthur, Arthur	Military
MacArthur, Charles	Authors
MacArthur, Douglas	Military
MacArthur, James	Entertainers (Current)
MacArthur, Jean	Military
MacChesney, Nathan Wm.	Celebrities
MacDonald, J. Ramsey	Heads of State
MacDonald, J.E.J.A.	Revolutionary War
MacDonald, Jeanette	Entertainers (Vintage)
MacDonough, Thomas	Military
MacDowell, Edward	Composers
MacGraw, Ali	Entertainers (Current)
MacKaill, Dorothy	Entertainers (Vintage)
MacKay, D. "Mickey"	Hockey HoF
MacKenzie, Gisele	Entertainers (Current)
MacLaine, Shirley	Entertainers (Current)
MacLeish, Archibald	Authors
MacLeod, Gavin	Entertainers (Current)
MacMahon, Marie E.P.	Heads of State
MacMillan, Harold	Heads of State
MacMillian, Donald B.	Celebrities
MacMurray, Fred	Entertainers (Current)
MacMurray, Fred	Entertainers (Vintage)
MacNelly, Jeff	Cartoonists
MacPhail, Larry	Baseball
MacPhail, Lee	Baseball
MacRae, Gordon	Entertainers (Current)
MacRae, Sheila	Entertainers (Vintage)
MacVeagh, Franklin	U.S. V.P. & Cabinet
Macartney, George	Heads of State
Macaulay, Ed (Easy Ed)	Basketball HoF
Macaulay, Lord Thos. B.	Authors
Macdonogh, P. M. W.	Military
Macfadden, Bernarr	Business
Machado, Anesia Pinheiro	Aviation
Machiavelli, Niccolo	Authors
Mack, Connie	Baseball
Mack, Marion	Entertainers (Vintage)
Mack, Ted	Entertainers (Vintage)
Mackensen, August von	Military
Mackenzie, Sir Morell	Science
Mackey, John	Football
Mackie, Bob	Business
Mackovic, John	Football
Macy, Bill	Entertainers (Current)
Madden, Charles Edw.	Military
Madden, John	Football
Maddox, Lester	Governors
Madigan, Amy	Entertainers (Current)
Madison, Dolley Payne	Celebrities
Madison, Guy	Entertainers (Current)
Madison, James	U.S. Presidents
Madlock, Bill	Baseball
Madonna	Rock
Madsen, Virginia	Entertainers (Current)
Maeterlinck, Maurice	Authors
Maffett, Debbie Sue	Entertainers (Current)
Magg, Alois	Aviation
Maglie, Sal "The Barber"	Baseball
Magritte, Rene	Artists
Magsaysay, Ramon	Heads of State
Mahaffey, John	General Sports
Mahan, Alfred Thayer	Military
Mahan, Larry	General Sports
Maharis, George	Entertainers (Current)
Mahen, Robert A.	Business
Mahendra Bir Bikram	Heads of State
Mahler, Gustav	Composers
Mahoney, Jock	Entertainers (Vintage)
Mahovlich, Frank	Hockey HoF
Mahre, Phil	General Sports
Maiakovski, Vladimir V.	Authors
Mailer, Norman	Authors
Maillol, Aristide	Artists
Maison, N.J. Marquis	Revolutionary War
Majeski, Hank	Baseball
Majors, Johnny	Football
Majors, Lee	Entertainers (Current)
Makarios III (Archbishop)	Heads of State
Makarova, Natalia	Entertainers (Vintage)
Mako, C. Gene	Tennis HoF
Malamud, Bernard	Authors
Malcom X	Celebrities
Malenkov, Georgi M.	Heads of State
Malet, C. Francois de	Revolutionary War
Malher, J.P.F.	Revolutionary War
Malik, Charles	Heads of State
Mallory, Molla Bjurstedt	Tennis HoF
Malmesbury, 1st Earl	Celebrities
Malo, Gina	Entertainers (Vintage)
Malone, Dorothy	Entertainers (Current)
Malone, Dumas	Authors
Malone, Joseph	Hockey HoF
Malone, Moses	General Sports
Maloney, Jim	Baseball
Malthus, Thomas Robert	Celebrities
Malzone, Frank	Baseball
Mamlin, V.T.	Cartoonists
Manchester, Melissa	Rock
Mancini, Henry	Composers
Mancini, Ray "Boom Boom"	Boxing
Mancuso, Gus	Baseball
Mandel, Howie	Entertainers (Current)
Mandel, John	Entertainers (Vintage)
Mandel, Marvin	Governors
Mandell, Sammy	Boxing
Manders, Dave	Football
Mandrell, Barbara	Country Music Stars
Manet, Edouard	Artists
Mangione, Chuck	Entertainers (Current)
Mangrum, Lloyd	General Sports
Manhatten Transfer	Rock
Manilow, Barry	Composers
Mankiewicz, Joseph	Entertainers (Current)
Manley, N. W.	Heads of State
Mann, Horace	Celebrities
Mann, Thomas	Authors
Mann, Thomas Clifton	Celebrities
Mannering, Mary	Entertainers (Vintage)
Manning, Archie	Football
Manning, Henry E.	Celebrities
Manning, Irene	Entertainers (Current)
Manning, William T.	Celebrities
Mansfield, Jayne	Entertainers (Vintage)

Manson, Charles	Celebrities	Martin, Clarence D.	Governors
Mantell, G. A.	Science	Martin, Dean	Entertainers (Current)
Mantell, Robert B.	Entertainers (Vintage)	Martin, Dean Vincent	Entertainers (Vintage)
Manteuffel, Hasso von	Military	Martin, Dick	Entertainers (Current)
Mantha, Sylvio	Hockey HoF	Martin, Fred	Baseball
Mantilla, Felix	Baseball	Martin, Glenn L.	Aviation
Mantle, Mickey	Baseball	Martin, Mary	Entertainers (Current)
Mantovani	Entertainers (Vintage)	Martin, Pamela Sue	Entertainers (Current)
Manush, Henry "Heinie"	Baseball	Martin, Renie	Baseball
Maphis, Joe and Rose Lee	Country Music Stars	Martin, Ross	Entertainers (Current)
Maple, Eddie	General Sports	Martin, Sir Theodore	Authors
Mara, Adele	Entertainers (Vintage)	Martin, Slater	Basketball HoF
Mara, Wellington T.	Football	Martin, Steve	Entertainers (Current)
Maranville, Walter	Baseball	Martin, William McChesney	Tennis HoF
Marat, Hugues B., Duke	Revolutionary War	Martinez, Carmelo	Baseball
Marat, Jean-Paul	Revolutionary War	Martino, Al	Entertainers (Current)
Maravich, "Pistol Pete"	General Sports	Martiny, Philip	Artists
Marble, Alice	Tennis HoF	Marvin, Mickey	Football
Marbot, J.B.A.M.	Revolutionary War	Marx Brothers	Entertainers (Vintage)
Marceau, Marcel	Entertainers (Current)	Marx, Chico	Entertainers (Vintage)
Marcellino, Muzzy	Entertainers (Vintage)	Marx, Groucho	Entertainers (Vintage)
March, Fredric	Entertainers (Vintage)	Marx, Harpo	Entertainers (Vintage)
Marchetti, Gino	Football	Marx, Karl	Authors
Marciano, Rocky	Boxing	Marx, Zeppo	Entertainers (Vintage)
Marconi, Guglielmo	Science	Mary Adalaide (Eng)	Heads of State
Marcos, Ferdinand E.	Heads of State	Mary I (Eng)	Heads of State
Marcus, Stanley	Business	Mary II (Wm II)	Heads of State
Marcy, William L.	U.S. V.P. & Cabinet	Mary(Teck)(Geo V)(Eng)	Heads of State
Mardall, Jim	Football	Masaryk, Jan	Heads of State
Marescot, Armand S.	Revolutionary War	Masaryk, Thomas G.	Heads of State
Maret, Hugues B., Duke	Revolutionary War	Mascagni, Pietro	Composers
Margie,	Cartoonists	Masefield, John	Authors
Margo (Mrs Ed Albert)	Entertainers (Vintage)	Maskelyne, Neville	Science
Maria Theresa	Heads of State	Mason, Alfred Edw. W.	Authors
Marichal, Juan	Baseball	Mason, James	Entertainers (Vintage)
Marie Antoinette (Fr)	Heads of State	Mason, James M.(Civ-War)	U.S. V.P. & Cabinet
Marie Louise (Nap)	Heads of State	Mason, Marsha	Entertainers (Current)
Marie of Romania	Heads of State	Mason, Sully	Entertainers (Vintage)
Marinaro, Ed	Entertainers (Current)	Mason, Tommy	Football
Marino, Dan	Football	Massen, Osa	Entertainers (Vintage)
Marion, Marty	Baseball	Massena, Andre, Duke	Revolutionary War
Maris, Roger	Baseball	Massenet, Jules	Composers
Maritza, Sari	Entertainers (Vintage)	Massey, Illona	Entertainers (Vintage)
Mariucci, John	Hockey HoF	Massey, Raymond	Entertainers (Vintage)
Markham, Albert H., Sir	Celebrities	Massie, Paul	Entertainers (Current)
Markham, Clements, Sir	Celebrities	Masson, Andre	Artists
Markham, Edwin	Authors	Masters, Edgar Lee	Authors
Marks, Johnny	Composers	Masters. Frankie	Entertainers (Vintage)
Marlborough, J., Duke of	Military	Masterson, Bat	Celebrities
Marley, Bob	Rock	Mastrantonio, Mary	Entertainers (Current)
Marlow, Lucy	Entertainers (Vintage)	Mata Hari (G.M. Zelle)	Celebrities
Marlowe, Julia	Entertainers (Vintage)	Mather, Cotton	Revolutionary War
Marly, Florence	Entertainers (Vintage)	Mathers, Jerry "Beaver"	Entertainers (Current)
Marmont, A.F.L.V., Duke	Revolutionary War	Matheson, Tim	Entertainers (Current)
Marquand, John P.	Authors	Mathews, Ed	Baseball
Marquard, Rube	Baseball	Mathias, Bob	General Sports
Marriott, J.	Business	Mathis, Johnny	Entertainers (Current)
Marryat, Frederick	Authors	Mathys, Charlie	Football
Marsalis, Wynton	Entertainers (Current)	Matisse, Henri	Artists
Marsh, Dame Ngaio	Authors	Matlack, Timothy	Revolutionary War
Marsh, Graham	General Sports	Matlock, Jon	Baseball
Marsh, Joan	Entertainers (Vintage)	Matson, Ollie	Football
Marsh, Mae	Entertainers (Vintage)	Matsushita, Konosuke	Business
Marshall, Catherine	Authors	Matte, Tom	Football
Marshall, George C.	Military	Mattern, Jimmie	Aviation
Marshall, Geo. (Military)	U.S. V.P. & Cabinet	Matthau, Walter	Entertainers (Current)
Marshall, George Preston	Football	Matthews, Gary	Baseball
Marshall, Herbert	Entertainers (Vintage)	Matthews, Sir Stanley	General Sports
Marshall, John Sir	Heads of State	Matthews, Stanley (SC)	Celebrities
Marshall, John	Hockey HoF	Mattingly, Don	Baseball
Marshall, John (SC)	Celebrities	Mattingly, Thos. Ken	Astronauts
Marshall, Mike	Baseball	Mature, Victor	Entertainers (Current)
Marshall, Thomas R. (V)	U.S. V.P. & Cabinet	Mauch, Billy	Entertainers (Vintage)
Marshall, Thurgood (SC)	Celebrities	Mauch, Gene	Baseball
Marshall, Willard	Baseball	Maugham, W. Somerset	Authors
Martens, George	General Sports	Mauldin, Bill	Cartoonists
Martha, Paul	Football	Maupassant, Guy de	Authors
Martin, "Pepper"	Baseball	Maurey, Pierre	Heads of State
Martin, Alastair B.	Tennis HoF	Maurois, Andre	Authors
Martin, Billy	Baseball	Maxim, Hudson	Science
Martin, Charles H.	Governors	Maxim, Sir Hiram S.	Science

470

Maximilian (Mex)	Heads of State
Maximilian II (Roman Emp)	Heads of State
Maxwell, Elsa	Celebrities
Maxwell, Fred "Steamer"	Hockey HoF
Maxwell, Marilyn	Entertainers (Vintage)
May, Edna	Entertainers (Vintage)
May, Lee	Baseball
Mayall, John	Rock
Maybank, Burnet R.	Governors
Maye, Carolyn	Entertainers (Current)
Mayer, Louis B.	Entertainers (Vintage)
Mayfair, Mitzi	Entertainers (Vintage)
Maynard, Don	Football
Maynard, Ken	Entertainers (Vintage)
Mayo, Dr. Charles H.	Science
Mayo, Dr. Charles W.	Science
Mayo, Dr. William J.	Science
Mayo, Henry T.	Military
Mayo, Virginia	Entertainers (Current)
Mays, Carl	Baseball
Mays, Willie	Baseball
Maytag, Frederick L.	Business
Mazeroski, Bill	Baseball
Mazurki, Mike	Entertainers (Vintage)
Mazzilli, Lee	Baseball
Mazzini, Joseph	Celebrities
McAdoo, Bob	Football
McAdoo, William G.	U.S. V.P. & Cabinet
McAfee, George	Football
McArdle, Andrea	Entertainers (Current)
McAuliffe, Anthony	Military
McAuliffe, Christa	Astronauts
McBain, Diane	Entertainers (Current)
McBain, Ed	Authors
McBride, Jon A.	Astronauts
McCall, Tom	Governors
McCallister, Lon	Entertainers (Vintage)
McCallum, David	Entertainers (Current)
McCallum, Napoleon	Football
McCandless, Bruce II	Astronauts
McCarthy, Joe	Baseball
McCarthy, Michael W.	Business
McCartney, Paul	Rock
McCay, Winsor	Cartoonists
McClain, Dave	Football
McClanahan, Rue	Entertainers (Current)
McCloskey, Lee	Entertainers (Current)
McColpin, Carroll W.	Military
McCoo, Marilyn	Entertainers (Current)
McCormack, John	Entertainers (Vintage)
McCormack, Mike	Football
McCormack, Patty	Entertainers (Current)
McCormick, Anne O'Hare	Authors
McCormick, Cyrus H.	Science
McCormick, Mike	Baseball
McCormick, Myron	Entertainers (Vintage)
McCormick, Patricia	General Sports
McCormick, Robert R.	Business
McCoskey, Barney	Baseball
McCovey, Willie	Baseball
McCoy, Clyde	Entertainers (Vintage)
McCoy, Tim	Entertainers (Vintage)
McCracken, Branch	Basketball HoF
McCracken, Jack	Basketball HoF
McCrea, Joel	Entertainers (Vintage)
McCrea, Joel	Entertainers (Current)
McCullers, Carson	Authors
McCulley, Michael J.	Astronauts
McCulloch, Hugh	U.S. V.P. & Cabinet
McCullough, Colleen	Authors
McCutchan, Arad	Basketball HoF
McDaniel, Lindy	Baseball
McDivitt, James A.	Astronauts
McDonald, A. J. (Al)	Astronauts
McDonald, Marie	Entertainers (Vintage)
McDonald, Richard J.	Business
McDonald, Skeets	Country Music Stars
McDonnell, James S.	Business
McDougal, Gil	Baseball
McDougall, Alexander	Revolutionary War
McDowell, "Sudden" Sam	Baseball
McDowell, Malcolm	Entertainers (Current)
McDowell, Roddy	Entertainers (Current)
McElhenney, Hugh	Football
McEnroe, John	General Sports
McGee, Frank	Hockey HoF
McGillis, Kelly	Entertainers (Current)
McGimsie, William	Hockey HoF
McGinley, Phyllis	Authors
McGovern, Elizabeth	Entertainers (Current)
McGovern, Terry	Boxing
McGraw, John J.	Baseball
McGraw, Tug	Baseball
McGregor, Scott	Baseball
McGuffy, William H.	Celebrities
McGuigan, James Cardinal	Celebrities
McGuire, Barry	Entertainers (Current)
McGuire, Dorothy	Entertainers (Current)
McGuire, Frank	Football
McGuire, Frank	Basketball HoF
McGwire, Mark	Baseball
McHan, Lamar	Football
McHenry, James	Military
McHenry, James	U.S. V.P. & Cabinet
McHugh, Frank	Entertainers (Vintage)
McIntosh, Lachlan	Revolutionary War
McIntyre, Marvin H.	U.S. V.P. & Cabinet
McIntyre, O. O.	Authors
McKay, Gardner	Entertainers (Current)
McKay, Jim	General Sports
McKay, John	Football
McKean, Thomas	Revolutionary War
McKechnie, Bill	Baseball
McKeldin, Theodore R.	Governors
McKenna, Joseph (SC)	Celebrities
McKenna, Siobhan	Entertainers (Current)
McKenzie, Fay	Entertainers (Vintage)
McKenzie, Stan	General Sports
McKeon, Nancy	Entertainers (Current)
McKinley, Chuck	General Sports
McKinley, William	U.S. Presidents
McKone, John R.	Military
McKuen, Rod	Authors
McLain, Denny	Baseball
McLains, The	Country Music Stars
McLane, Louis	U.S. V.P. & Cabinet
McLarnin, Jimmy	Boxing
McLaughlin, Maurice	Tennis HoF
McLaughlin, Maj. Frederic	Hockey HoF
McLean, George P.	Governors
McLean, Jim (SC)	Celebrities
McLean, Stewart	Boxing
McLendon, John	Basketball HoF
McLeod, Catherine	Entertainers (Vintage)
McLintock, Francis Sir	Celebrities
McMahon, Ed	Entertainers (Current)
McMahon, Jim	Football
McManus, George	Cartoonists
McMillan, Kenneth	Entertainers (Current)
McMillan, Roy	Baseball
McMullen, Richard C.	Governors
McNair, Leslie J.	Military
McNair, Robert	Governors
McNair, Ronald E.	Astronauts
McNally, Dave	Baseball
McNally, Johnny Blood	Football
McNally, W.	Entertainers (Vintage)
McNamara, George	Hockey HoF
McNamara, John	Baseball
McNamara, Robert S.	U.S. V.P. & Cabinet
McNamee, Graham	General Sports
McNaughton, Kenneth	Military
McNee, Patrick	Entertainers (Current)
McNeil, Freeman	Football
McNeill, Don	Entertainers (Vintage)
McNeill, W. Donald	Tennis HoF
McNichols, Kristy	Entertainers (Current)
McNutt, Paul V.	Governors
McPherson, Aimee S.	Celebrities
McPherson, Craig	Artists
McQueen, Butterfly	Entertainers (Vintage)
McQueen, Steve	Entertainers (Vintage)

McReynolds, James C. (SC)	Celebrities
McReynolds, Kevin	Baseball
McShane, Ian	Entertainers (Current)
McWilliams, Caroline	Entertainers (Current)
Mcaffee, Johnny	Entertainers (Vintage)
Mead, Margaret	Science
Meadowes, Earl	General Sports
Meadowlarks	Entertainers (Vintage)
Meagher, Mary T.	General Sports
Meanwell, Dr. Walter E.	Basketball HoF
Meany, George	Celebrities
Meara, Anne	Entertainers (Current)
Mears, Rick	General Sports
Meat Loaf	Rock
Mechan, E.L.	Governors
Mecklenberg, Karl	Football
Medawar, Peter B.	Science
Medici, Fernando de	Heads of State
Medicis, Cosimo de	Heads of State
Medicis, Francesco de	Heads of State
Medina, Harold R.	Celebrities
Medina, Patricia	Entertainers (Vintage)
Medley, Bill	Country Music Stars
Medwick, Joe "Ducky"	Baseball
Meeker, Ralph	Entertainers (Current)
Meeker, Ralph	Entertainers (Vintage)
Meer, Johnny Vander	Baseball
Meese, Edwin III	U.S. V.P. & Cabinet
Mehta, Zubin	Entertainers (Current)
Meighan, Tom	Entertainers (Vintage)
Meigs, Jr., Return J.	Military
Meir, Golda	Heads of State
Melba, Nellie	Entertainers (Vintage)
Melbourne, Wm. L. Lord	Heads of State
Mellnik, Steve	Military
Mellon, Andrew	Business
Melton, Bill	Baseball
Melton, James	Entertainers (Vintage)
Melville, George W.	Military
Melville, Herman	Authors
Menandez, Luis	General Sports
Mencken, H. L.	Authors
Mendel, Gregor	Science
Mendelssohn-Bartholdy, F.	Composers
Menjou, Adolphe	Entertainers (Vintage)
Menken, Helen	Entertainers (Vintage)
Menninger, Dr. Karl	Science
Menninger, Roy	Science
Menninger, William C.	Science
Menotti, Gian Carlo	Composers
Menuhin, Yehudi	Entertainers (Current)
Menzies, Sir Robert G.	Heads of State
Mercer, Frances	Entertainers (Vintage)
Mercer, Johnny	Composers
Mercer, Marian	Entertainers (Vintage)
Mercouri, Melina	Entertainers (Current)
Meredith, Burgess	Entertainers (Current)
Meredith, Don	Football
Meredith, Edwin T.	U.S. V.P. & Cabinet
Meredith, Samuel	U.S. V.P. & Cabinet
Meriwether, Lee	Entertainers (Current)
Merkel, Una	Entertainers (Vintage)
Merlin de Douai, P.A.	Revolutionary War
Merman, Ethel	Entertainers (Vintage)
Merriam, Frank F.	Governors
Merrick, David	Entertainers (Current)
Merrill, Dina	Entertainers (Current)
Merrill, Gary	Entertainers (Current)
Merrill, Henry T.	Aviation
Merrill, Richard	Aviation
Merrill, Robert	Entertainers (Vintage)
Merritt, Wesley	Military
Merullo, Lennie	Baseball
Mesmer, F. Anton	Science
Messerschmitt, Willy	Aviation
Messersmith, Andy	Baseball
Messick, Dale	Cartoonists
Messmer, Otto	Cartoonists
Mesta, Perle	Business
Metternich, Prince	Heads of State
Meusel, Bob	Baseball
Meusel, Emil	Baseball
Meyer, Debbie	General Sports
Meyer, E. C.	Military
Meyer, George von L.	U.S. V.P. & Cabinet
Meyer, Lou	General Sports
Meyer, Ray	Basketball HoF
Meyer, Ron	Football
Meyerbeer, Giacomo	Composers
Michael, Gene	Baseball
Michaels, Walt	Football
Michalske, "Mike"	Football
Michel, Frank Curtis	Astronauts
Michelangelo Buonarroti	Artists
Michele, Denise	Entertainers (Current)
Michelson, Charles	Celebrities
Michner, James A.	Authors
Middlecoff, Cary	General Sports
Middleton, Arthur	Revolutionary War
Midler, Bette	Entertainers (Current)
Mielziner, Jo	Entertainers (Vintage)
Mifflin, Thomas	Military
Mifflin, Thos. (Military)	Revolutionary War
Mifune, Toshiro	Entertainers (Vintage)
Mikan, George	Basketball HoF
Mikita, Stan	General Sports
Miksis, Eddie	Baseball
Milch, Erhard	Military
Miles, Josephine	Authors
Miles, Sarah	Entertainers (Current)
Miles, Sylvia	Entertainers (Current)
Miles, Vera	Entertainers (Current)
Milestone, Lewis	Entertainers (Vintage)
Milford, John C. "Jake"	Hockey HoF
Milhaud, Darius	Composers
Mill, James	Authors
Mill, John Stuart	Celebrities
Millais, Sir John E.	Artists
Milland, Ray	Entertainers (Vintage)
Millay, Edna St. Vincent	Authors
Miller, Arjay R.	Business
Miller, Arthur	Authors
Miller, Chris	Football
Miller, Denny	Entertainers (Current)
Miller, Dr. Dean D.	General Sports
Miller, Glen	Entertainers (Vintage)
Miller, Henry	Authors
Miller, Joaquin	Authors
Miller, Johnny	General Sports
Miller, Leslie A.	Governors
Miller, Marilyn	Entertainers (Vintage)
Miller, Marvin	Entertainers (Current)
Miller, Marvin	Entertainers (Vintage)
Miller, Mitch	Entertainers (Current)
Miller, Nathan L.	Governors
Miller, Patsy Ruth	Entertainers (Vintage)
Miller, Ralph	Baseball
Miller, Roger	Country Music Stars
Miller, Samuel F. (SC)	Celebrities
Miller, Stanley	Science
Miller, Taylor	Entertainers (Current)
Miller, William H. H.	U.S. V.P. & Cabinet
Millerand, Alexandre	Heads of State
Milles, Carl	Artists
Millet, Francis D.	Artists
Millet, Jean Francois	Artists
Milliken, Robert A.	Science
Milliken, William G.	Governors
Millner, Wayne	Football
Mills, Buster	Baseball
Mills, Donna	Entertainers (Current)
Mills, Freddie	Boxing
Mills, Hayley	Entertainers (Current)
Mills, John	Entertainers (Current)
Mills, Juliette	Entertainers (Current)
Mills, Ogden L.	U.S. V.P. & Cabinet
Milne, A. A.	Authors
Milner, Martin	Entertainers (Current)
Milnes, Richard M.	Celebrities
Milosz, Czeslaw	Authors
Milsap, Ronnie	Entertainers (Current)
Milton, Tommy	General Sports

Mimieux, Yvette	Entertainers (Current)
Miner, Jan	Entertainers (Current)
Minh, Duong Van Gen.	Military
Minnelli, Liza	Entertainers (Current)
Minnelli, Vincent	Entertainers (Vintage)
Minoso, Minnie	Baseball
Minow, Newton N.	Celebrities
Minter, Mary Miles	Entertainers (Vintage)
Minton, Sherman (SC)	Celebrities
Miollis, S.A.F.	Revolutionary War
Mirabeau, Gabriel H.R.	Revolutionary War
Mirabehin (M. Slade)	Celebrities
Miranda, Carmen	Entertainers (Vintage)
Miranda, Willy	Baseball
Mirisch, Walter	Entertainers (Current)
Miro, Joan	Artists
Miroslava	Entertainers (Vintage)
Mistral, Frederic	Authors
Mistral, Gabriela	Authors
Mitchell, Billy	Aviation
Mitchell, Bobby	Football
Mitchell, Charles W.	Boxing
Mitchell, Edgar D.	Astronauts
Mitchell, Jeff	General Sports
Mitchell, John	U.S. V.P. & Cabinet
Mitchell, Joni	Rock
Mitchell, Kevin	Baseball
Mitchell, Margaret	Authors
Mitchell, Maria	Science
Mitchell, Martha	Celebrities
Mitchell, Silas Weir	Science
Mitchell, William	Military
Mitchell, William D.	U.S. V.P. & Cabinet
Mitchelson, Marvin	Celebrities
Mitchum, Robert	Entertainers (Current)
Mitford, Jessica	Authors
Mitropoulos, Dimitri	Entertainers (Vintage)
Mix, Ron	Football
Mix, Tom	Entertainers (Vintage)
Mix, Victoria	Entertainers (Vintage)
Mize, Johnny	Baseball
Mizell, "Vinegar Bend"	Baseball
Mobley, Mary Ann	Entertainers (Current)
Modell, Art	Football
Modigliani, A.	Artists
Modjeske, Helena	Entertainers (Vintage)
Moegle, Dick	Football
Moeur, Benjamin B.	Governors
Moffo, Anna	Entertainers (Current)
Mohler, A. L.	Business
Mojica, Jose	Entertainers (Vintage)
Mokray, Bill	Basketball HoF
Molitor, G.J.J.	Revolutionary War
Molitor, Paul	Baseball
Moll, Richard	Entertainers (Current)
Mollet, Guy	Heads of State
Molnar, Ferenc	Authors
Molson, Hon. Hartland	Hockey HoF
Moltke, Count Helmuth	Military
Moltke, H. Johann L.	Military
Momaday, N. Scott	Authors
Moncey, Bon-Adrien J. de	Revolutionary War
Mondale, Walter (V)	U.S. V.P. & Cabinet
Mondrian, Piet	Artists
Monet, Claude	Artists
Money, Don	Baseball
Monk, Thelonious	Entertainers (Vintage)
Monroe, James	U.S. Presidents
Monroe, Marilyn	Entertainers (Vintage)
Monroe, Vaughn	Entertainers (Vintage)
Montagu, John (Sandwich)	Celebrities
Montalban, Ricardo	Entertainers (Current)
Montalivet, J.P.B. Count	Revolutionary War
Montana, Bob	Cartoonists
Montana, Joe	Football
Montana, Monte	Entertainers (Current)
Montand, Yves	Entertainers (Current)
Montcalm, L.J. de	Military
Montenegro, Conchita	Entertainers (Vintage)
Monteverde, George de	Aviation
Monteverde, Alfred de	Aviation
Montez, Maria	Entertainers (Vintage)
Montgomery, Robert	Entertainers (Vintage)
Montgomery, Elizabeth	Entertainers (Current)
Montgomery, Melba	Country Music Stars
Montgomery, George	Entertainers (Vintage)
Montgomery, Bernard	Military
Montgomery, Douglass	Entertainers (Vintage)
Montgomery, George	Entertainers (Current)
Montoya, Carlos	Entertainers (Vintage)
Moody Blues	Rock
Moody, Orville	General Sports
Moody, William H. (SC)	Celebrities
Moog, Bob	Science
Moomaw, Donn	Football
Moon, Wally	Baseball
Moon, Warren	Football
Mooney, Tom	Celebrities
Moore, Arch A. Jr.	Governors
Moore, Archie	Boxing
Moore, Charlie	Baseball
Moore, Clayton	Entertainers (Current)
Moore, Clement C.	Authors
Moore, Colleen	Entertainers (Vintage)
Moore, Dan K.	Governors
Moore, Dick	Entertainers (Vintage)
Moore, Dr. Francis D.	Science
Moore, Dudley	Entertainers (Current)
Moore, Elizabeth H.	Tennis HoF
Moore, Grace	Entertainers (Vintage)
Moore, Henry	Artists
Moore, Jeremy Gen.	Military
Moore, Joanna	Entertainers (Current)
Moore, Joe	Baseball
Moore, Lenny	Football
Moore, Marianne	Authors
Moore, Mary Tyler	Entertainers (Current)
Moore, Richard	Hockey HoF
Moore, Roger	Entertainers (Current)
Moore, Sara Jane	Celebrities
Moore, Sir John	Military
Moore, Terry	Baseball
Moore, Terry	Entertainers (Current)
Moore, Thomas	Authors
Moore, Victor	Entertainers (Vintage)
Moores, Dick	Cartoonists
Moran, Gussy	General Sports
Moran, Lois	Entertainers (Vintage)
Moran, Patrick	Hockey HoF
Moranis, Rick	Entertainers (Current)
Moreau, Jean-Victor	Revolutionary War
Morehead, John M.	Governors
Moreland, Keith	Baseball
Moreland, Mantan	Entertainers (Vintage)
Moreno, Anthony	Entertainers (Vintage)
Moreno, Rita	Entertainers (Current)
Morenz, Howie	Hockey HoF
Morgan, Charles L.	Authors
Morgan, Dennis	Entertainers (Vintage)
Morgan, Edward J.	Entertainers (Vintage)
Morgan, Frank	Entertainers (Vintage)
Morgan, George	Country Music Stars
Morgan, Gil	General Sports
Morgan, Harry	Entertainers (Current)
Morgan, Helen	Entertainers (Vintage)
Morgan, J. P.,Jr.	Business
Morgan, J. P., Sr.	Business
Morgan, Jaye P.	Entertainers (Current)
Morgan, Joe	Baseball
Morgan, Michele	Entertainers (Vintage)
Morgan, Ralph	Basketball HoF
Morgan, Tom	Baseball
Morgenthau, Henry Jr.	U.S. V.P. & Cabinet
Morgenweck, Frank	Basketball HoF
Moriarty, George	Baseball
Morison, Patricia	Entertainers (Vintage)
Morley, Christopher	Authors
Morrill, Lot M.	U.S. V.P. & Cabinet
Morris, Tom Jr.	Golf HoF
Morris, Tom Sr.	Golf HoF

Morris, Anita	Entertainers (Current)
Morris, Chester	Entertainers (Vintage)
Morris, Gouverneur	Revolutionary War
Morris, Jack	Baseball
Morris, Joe	Football
Morris, Lewis	Revolutionary War
Morris, Robert	Revolutionary War
Morris, Sir Lewis	Authors
Morris, Wayne	Entertainers (Vintage)
Morrison, Harold	Country Music Stars
Morrison, Herb	Aviation
Morrison, Jim	Rock
Morrison, Joe	Football
Morrison, Van	Rock
Morrow, Jeff	Entertainers (Vintage)
Morrow, Vic	Entertainers (Vintage)
Morse, Samuel F. B.	Science
Mortier, Edouard A.C.J.	Revolutionary War
Mortimer, Charles	Business
Morton, Craig	Football
Morton, J. Sterling	U.S. V.P. & Cabinet
Morton, John	Revolutionary War
Morton, Levi P. (V)	U.S. V.P. & Cabinet
Morton, Oliver P.	Governors
Morton, W. T. G.	Science
Moscone, George R.	Celebrities
Mosconi, Willie	General Sports
Mosel, Tad	Authors
Moses, A.M.R. (Grandma)	Artists
Moses, Edwin	General Sports
Moses, Haven	Football
Moses, Robert	Celebrities
Mosienko, William	Hockey HoF
Mosley, Jack	Cartoonists
Mosley, Mike	General Sports
Mosley, Oswald, Sir	Celebrities
Moss, Perry	Football
Moss, Stirling	General Sports
Mossadegh, Muhammad	Celebrities
Mossbauer, Rudolph L.	Science
Mostel, Zero	Entertainers (Vintage)
Mota, Manny	Baseball
Motley, John Lothrop	Authors
Motley, Marion	Football
Mott, Lucretia	Celebrities
Moulton, Louise C.	Authors
Moulton, William	Revolutionary War
Mountbatten, Louis	Military
Mountevens,Baron(E Evans)	Celebrities
Moutrie, Alexander	Revolutionary War
Moyer, Denny	Boxing
Moyer, Phil	Boxing
Moyers, Bill	Celebrities
Moynihan, Pat	Celebrities
Mozart, Wolfgang A.	Composers
Mr. Mister	Rock
Mubarak, M. H. Pres.	Heads of State
Mudd. Roger	Celebrities
Mugabe, Robert G.	Heads of State
Muhammed, Elijah	Celebrities
Muhlenberg, John P.	Military
Muir, Jean	Entertainers (Vintage)
Muldaur, Diana	Entertainers (Current)
Muldaur, Maria	Entertainers (Current)
Muldoon, Robert	Heads of State
Mulgrew, Kate	Entertainers (Current)
Mull, Martin	Entertainers (Current)
Mullane, Richard M.	Astronauts
Mulleavy, Greg	Baseball
Mullican, Moon	Country Music Stars
Mulligan, Richard	Entertainers (Current)
Mulliken, Robert S.	Science
Mullin, Pat	Baseball
Mullin, Willard	Cartoonists
Mullowney, Deborah	Entertainers (Current)
Mulloy, Gardnar	Tennis HoF
Mumy, Bill	Entertainers (Current)
Mungo, Van Lingle	Baseball
Muni, Paul	Entertainers (Vintage)
Muniz, Armando	Boxing
Munro, Caroline	Entertainers (Current)
Munro, Peter Jay	Revolutionary War
Munsel, Patrice	Entertainers (Vintage)
Munson, Bill	Football
Munson, Ona	Entertainers (Vintage)
Munster, Earl of	Military
Muntz, Earl "Madman"	Business
Murat, Joachim	Military
Murchison, Clint, Jr.	Business
Murchison, Clint	Business
Murdock, Rupert	Business
Murphy, Audie	Military
Murphy, Ben	Entertainers (Current)
Murphy, Bob	General Sports
Murphy, Charles (Stretch)	Basketball HoF
Murphy, Dale	Baseball
Murphy, Eddie	Entertainers (Current)
Murphy, Franklin	Governors
Murphy, Frank (SC)	Celebrities
Murphy, George	Entertainers (Vintage)
Murphy, John Cullen	Cartoonists
Murphy, William P.	Science
Murray, Anne	Entertainers (Current)
Murray, Arthur	Business
Murray, Eddie	Baseball
Murray, Jan	Entertainers (Current)
Murray, Jim	Baseball
Murray, John C., S.J.	Celebrities
Murray, Ken	Entertainers (Current)
Murray, Mae	Entertainers (Vintage)
Murray, Philip	Celebrities
Murray, R. Lindley	Tennis HoF
Murray, William Vans	Revolutionary War
Murrow, Edward R.	Celebrities
Murtaugh, Danny	Baseball
Musante, Tony	Entertainers (Current)
Musburger, Brent	General Sports
Musgrave, Story Dr.	Astronauts
Musial, Stan "The Man"	Baseball
Muskie, Edmund	U.S. V.P. & Cabinet
Musso, George	Football
Mussolini, Benito	Heads of State
Mutscheller, Jim	Football
Myers, Russell	Cartoonists
Myerson, Bess	Celebrities
Myrick, Julian S.	Tennis HoF
Nabors, Jim	Entertainers (Current)
Nadar (F. Tournachon)	Artists
Nader, George	Entertainers (Current)
Nagel, Conrad	Entertainers (Vintage)
Nagel, Steven R.	Astronauts
Nagurski, Bronko	Football
Naismith, Dr. James	Basketball HoF
Nakasone, Y.	Heads of State
Naldi, Nita	Entertainers (Vintage)
Nall, Philip W.	Governors
Namath, Joe	Football
Nance, Jim	Football
Nansen, Fridtjof	Celebrities
Nap. II (Duke Reichstadt)	Heads of State
Napier, Alan	Entertainers (Vintage)
Napier, Charles	Entertainers (Current)
Napier, McVey	Celebrities
Napier, Sir Chas. Jas.	Military
Napier, Sir Wm. F.P.	Military
Napier, Sir Robert C.	Military
Napoleon I	Heads of State
Napoleon III	Heads of State
Nasby, Petroleum V.	Authors
Nash, Clarence	Entertainers (Current)
Nash, Ogden	Authors
Nash, Walter	Heads of State
Nasser, Gamal Abdel	Heads of State
Nast, Thomas	Cartoonists
Nast, Thomas	Artists
Nastase, Ilie	General Sports
Nathan, George Jean	Authors
Nation, Carrie	Celebrities
Natwick, Mildred	Entertainers (Current)
Navin, Charles F.	Baseball
Navratilova, Martina	General Sports
Nazimova, Alla	Entertainers (Vintage)

474

Neagle, Anna Dame	Entertainers (Vintage)
Neal, Lloyd	General Sports
Neal, Patricia	Entertainers (Current)
Needham, Hal	Entertainers (Current)
Neff, Francine I.	U.S. V.P. & Cabinet
Negri, Pola	Entertainers (Vintage)
Nehru, Jawaharlal	Heads of State
Neill, Noel	Entertainers (Current)
Neiman, LeRoy	Artists
Nelson, Bryon	Golf HoF
Nelson, Cindy	General Sports
Nelson, Darrin	Football
Nelson, Don	General Sports
Nelson, Francis	Hockey HoF
Nelson, George D.	Astronauts
Nelson, Horatio	Military
Nelson, Jimmy	Entertainers (Current)
Nelson, Lori	Entertainers (Current)
Nelson, Rick	Entertainers (Vintage)
Nelson, Samuel (SC)	Celebrities
Nelson, Thomas Jr.	Revolutionary War
Nelson, Willie	Country Music Stars
Nero, Peter	Entertainers (Current)
Nettles, Graig	Baseball
Nettleton, Lois	Entertainers (Current)
Neumann, Theresa	Celebrities
Neun, Johnny	Baseball
Neurath, Constantin von	Military
Nevelson, Louise	Artists
Nevers, Ernie	Football
Neville, Henry	Entertainers (Vintage)
Nevin, Ethelbert	Composers
New, Harry	U.S. V.P. & Cabinet
Newberry, Truman H.	U.S. V.P. & Cabinet
Newcomb, Simon	Science
Newcombe, Don	Baseball
Newcombe, John	General Sports
Newell, Pete	Basketball HoF
Newhart, Bob	Entertainers (Current)
Newhouse, Samuel	Business
Newhouser, Hal	Baseball
Newley, Anthony	Entertainers (Current)
Newman, Barry	Entertainers (Current)
Newman, Edwin	Celebrities
Newman, John Card'l	Celebrities
Newman, Paul	Entertainers (Current)
Newman, Randy	Rock
Newmar, Julie	Entertainers (Current)
Newsom, Bobo	Baseball
Newton, Sir Isaac	Science
Newton, Wayne	Entertainers (Current)
Newton-John, Olivia	Entertainers (Current)
Ney, Michel	Military
Niarchos, Stavro	Business
Niatta, Dick	General Sports
Nicholas I (Rus)	Heads of State
Nicholas, Denise	Entertainers (Current)
Nicholas, Prince (Gr)	Heads of State
Nichols, Charles A.	Baseball
Nichols, Michelle	Entertainers (Current)
Nicholson, Bill	Baseball
Nicholson, Jack	Entertainers (Current)
Nicholson, John	Revolutionary War
Nicholson, Meredith	Authors
Nicklaus, Jack	Golf HoF
Nicks, Stevie	Rock
Nicolay, John G.	Celebrities
Niebuhr, Reinhold	Authors
Niedenfuer, Tom	Baseball
Niekro, Joe	Baseball
Niekro, Phil	Baseball
Nielsen Sr., Arthur C.	Tennis HoF
Nielsen, Alice	Entertainers (Vintage)
Nielsen, Brigitte	Entertainers (Current)
Nielsen, Carl	Composers
Nielsen, Terry	Entertainers (Vintage)
Nielson, Leslie	Entertainers (Current)
Niemoller, Martin Dr	Celebrities
Nietzsche, Friedrich	Authors
Nighbor, Frank	Hockey HoF
Nightingale, Florence	Science
Nikolayev, Andria	Astronauts
Nilssen, Anna Q.	Entertainers (Vintage)
Nilsson, Harry	Rock
Nimitz, Chester	Military
Nimoy, Leonard	Entertainers (Current)
Nin, Anais	Authors
Nirenberg, Marshall W.	Science
Nitschke, Ray	Football
Niven, David	Entertainers (Vintage)
Nixon, Marion	Entertainers (Current)
Nixon, Patricia	Celebrities
Nixon, Richard M.	U.S. Presidents
Nizer, Louis	Celebrities
Nkomo, Joshua	Heads of State
Nobel, Alfred	Science
Nobile, Umberto	Aviation
Nobis, Tommy	Football
Noble, E. Reginald	Hockey HoF
Noble, James	Entertainers (Current)
Noble, John W.	U.S. V.P. & Cabinet
Noel-Baker, Philip	Celebrities
Noguchi, Thomas T.	Celebrities
Nolan, Dick	Football
Nolan, Jeanette	Entertainers (Current)
Nolan, Kathleen	Entertainers (Vintage)
Nolan, Lloyd	Entertainers (Vintage)
Nolte, Nick	Entertainers (Current)
Nomellini, Leo	Football
Noor, Queen (Hussein)	Heads of State
Norblad, A.W.	Governors
Nordau, Max	Science
Nordenskjold, Adolf E.	Celebrities
Nordenskjold, Otto	Celebrities
Nordhoff, Charles	Authors
Noren, Irv	Baseball
Norgay, Tenzing	Celebrities
Norman, Greg	General Sports
Normand, Mabel	Entertainers (Vintage)
Norris, Bruce	Hockey HoF
Norris, Chuck	Entertainers (Current)
Norris, Frank	Authors
Norris, J. Frank Dr.	Celebrities
Norris, James D.	Hockey HoF
Norris, Kathleen	Authors
Norris, Sr., James	Hockey HoF
Norstad, Lauris	Military
North, John Ringling	Business
North, Lord Frederick	Heads of State
North, Oliver	Military
North, Sheree	Entertainers (Current)
North, William	Military
Northbrook,Lord(T.Baring)	Heads of State
Northey, William	Hockey HoF
Northrup, John K.	Business
Northrup, John H.	Science
Norton, Ken	Boxing
Norton-Taylor, Judy	Entertainers (Current)
Novak, Kim	Entertainers (Current)
Novello, Ivor	Entertainers (Vintage)
Noyes, Alfred	Authors
Noyes, Edward F.	Governors
Nucatola, John	Basketball HoF
Nugent, Elliott	Entertainers (Vintage)
Nugent, Ted	Rock
Nungesser, Charles	Aviation
Nureyev, Rudolf	Entertainers (Current)
Nurmi, Paavo	General Sports
Nuthall, Betty	General Sports
Nutter, Mayf	Country Music Stars
Nuxhall, Joe	Baseball
Nuyen, France	Entertainers (Current)
Nyad, Diana	General Sports
Nye, Bill	Authors
Nyerere, Julius	Heads of State
O'Brian, Hugh	Entertainers (Current)
O'Brien, Cubby	Entertainers (Current)
O'Brien, Davey	Football
O'Brien, Edmond	Entertainers (Vintage)
O'Brien, George	Entertainers (Vintage)
O'Brien, Jim	Football
O'Brien, John	Hockey HoF

O'Brien, John	Basketball HoF	Olsen, Harold	Basketball HoF
O'Brien, Ken	Football	Olsen, Merlin	Football
O'Brien, Lawrence F.	U.S. V.P. & Cabinet	Olson, Carl "BoBo"	Boxing
O'Brien, Margaret	Entertainers (Current)	Olson, Merlin	Entertainers (Current)
O'Brien, Parry	General Sports	Olson, Nancy	Entertainers (Vintage)
O'Brien, Pat	Entertainers (Vintage)	Onassis, Aristotle	Business
O'Callaghan, Mike	Governors	Onizuka, Ellison S.	Astronauts
O'Casey, Sean	Authors	Ono, Yoko	Entertainers (Current)
O'Connell, Charles	Business	Ontkean, Michael	Entertainers (Current)
O'Connell, Daniel	Heads of State	Oosterhaus, Peter	General Sports
O'Connell, Helen	Entertainers (Current)	Opatoshu, David	Entertainers (Current)
O'Connor, Basil	Celebrities	Oppenheimer, Dr. Rob't	Science
O'Connor, Bryan D.	Astronauts	Opper, F.B.	Cartoonists
O'Connor, Carroll	Entertainers (Current)	Orbison, Roy	Country Music Stars
O'Connor, Donald	Entertainers (Vintage)	Orczy, Baroness E.	Authors
O'Connor, Sandra Day (SC)	Celebrities	Orlando, Vittorio E.	Heads of State
O'Connor, Thomas Power	Celebrities	Orleans, Le Duc d'	Heads of State
O'Daniel, W. Lee "Pappy"	Governors	Ormandy, Eugene	Entertainers (Current)
O'Dea, Ken	Baseball	Orosco, Jesse	Baseball
O'Dell, Billy	Baseball	Orr, Bobby	Hockey HoF
O'Donald, Emmett	Aviation	Orr, Johnny	General Sports
O'Doul, Lefty	Baseball	Ortega, Katherine D.	U.S. V.P. & Cabinet
O'Hara, Maureen	Entertainers (Current)	Osborne, Baby Marie	Entertainers (Vintage)
O'Higgins, Harvey	Authors	Osborne, John	Authors
O'Keefe, Dennis	Entertainers (Vintage)	Osborne, Ozzy	Rock
O'Keefe, Georgia	Artists	Osborne, Sidney P.	Governors
O'Laughlin, Gerald S.	Entertainers (Current)	Osborne, Thomas A.	Governors
O'Leary, Brian	Astronauts	Oscar I (Swe-Nor)	Heads of State
O'Malley, Peter	Baseball	Osler, William	Science
O'Malley, Walter	Baseball	Osmanski, Bill	Football
O'Neal, Ryan	Entertainers (Current)	Osmond, Donny	Entertainers (Current)
O'Neal, Tatum	Entertainers (Current)	Osmond, Marie	Entertainers (Current)
O'Neill, Eugene	Authors	Osteen, Claude	Baseball
O'Neill, James	Entertainers (Vintage)	Osterkamp, Theo	Aviation
O'Neill, Jennifer	Entertainers (Current)	Osuna, Rafael	Tennis HoF
O'Neill, Peggy	Entertainers (Vintage)	Oswald, Marina	Celebrities
O'Neill, Steve	Baseball	Oswald, Steve	Astronauts
O'Sullivan, Maureen	Entertainers (Vintage)	Otero, Reggie	Baseball
O'Toole, Peter	Entertainers (Current)	Otis, Amos	Baseball
Oakes, Randi	Entertainers (Current)	Otis, Elita Proctor	Entertainers (Vintage)
Oakes, Rehal	Baseball	Otis, Elwell Stephen	Military
Oakie, Jack	Entertainers (Vintage)	Otis, Harrison Gray	Military
Oakley, Annie	Celebrities	Otis, James	Revolutionary War
Oates, Johnny	Baseball	Ott, Mel	Baseball
Oates, Joyce Carol	Authors	Otto I (Gr) (Othon)	Heads of State
Oberhardt, William	Artists	Otto The Great	Heads of State
Oberon, Merle	Entertainers (Vintage)	Otto, Jim	Football
Oberth, Dr. Hermann	Science	Oudinot, N. Charles	Revolutionary War
Oboler, Arch	Entertainers (Vintage)	Ouida	Authors
Ochoa, Dr. Severo	Science	Ouimet, Francis	Golf HoF
Ochs, Adolph S.	Business	Ouimet, Francis	General Sports
Odets, Clifford	Authors	Ouspenskaya, Maria	Entertainers (Vintage)
Oersted, H. C.	Science	Outcault, Richard	Cartoonists
Oerter, Al	General Sports	Outerbridge, Mary Ewing	Tennis HoF
Oeschger, Joe	Baseball	Overmyer, Robert	Astronauts
Offenbach, Jacques	Composers	Ovington, Earle	Aviation
Ogden, Aaron	Military	Owen, Marvin	Baseball
Ogle, William	Celebrities	Owen, Mickey	Baseball
Oglivie, Ben	Baseball	Owen, Rt. Hon. David	Heads of State
Oh, Sadaharu	Baseball	Owens, Buck	Country Music Stars
Oh, Soon-Teck	Entertainers (Current)	Owens, Jesse	General Sports
Ojeda, Bob	Baseball	Owens, Jim	Football
Oland, Warner	Entertainers (Vintage)	Owens, R.C. "Alley Oop"	Football
Olcott, Chauncey	Composers	Owens, Steve	Football
Older, Charles H.	Military	Owens, Tex	Country Music Stars
Oldfield, Barney	General Sports	Oxenberg, Catherine	Entertainers (Current)
Olds, Robin	Military	Oz, Frank	Entertainers (Current)
Olin, John M.	Business	Paar, Jack	Entertainers (Current)
Oliphant, Laurence	Authors	Paca, William	Revolutionary War
Oliva, Tony	Baseball	Pache, Jean Nicholas	Revolutionary War
Oliver, Al	Baseball	Pacino, Al	Entertainers (Current)
Oliver, Edna May	Entertainers (Vintage)	Paciorek, Tom	Baseball
Oliver, Harry	Hockey HoF	Packard, David	Business
Oliver, Jane	Rock	Packard, Vance	Authors
Olivier, Laurence	Entertainers (Current)	Pacula, Joanna	Entertainers (Current)
Olmo, Luis	Baseball	Paderewski, Ignace J.	Composers
Olmos, Edward James	Entertainers (Current)	Paduca, Duke of	Country Music Stars
Olmstead, Bert	Hockey HoF	Pafko, Andy	Baseball
Olmstead, Frederick Law	Celebrities	Paganini, Nicolo	Composers
Olney, Richard	U.S. V.P. & Cabinet	Page H. O. (Pat)	Basketball HoF
Olsen & Johnson	Entertainers (Vintage)	Page, Alan	Football

Page, Anita	Entertainers (Vintage)
Page, Geraldine	Entertainers (Current)
Page, Joe	Baseball
Page, Thomas Nelson	Authors
Pagliaroni, Jim	Baseball
Pagliarulo, Mike	Baseball
Pahlavi, Riza (Iran)	Heads of State
Paige, Janice	Entertainers (Current)
Paige, Janis	Entertainers (Vintage)
Paige, Leroy "Satchel"	Baseball
Paine, Robert Treat	Revolutionary War
Palance, Jack	Entertainers (Current)
Paley, William S.	Business
Palica, Erv	Baseball
Pallette, Eugene	Entertainers (Vintage)
Palme, Olaf	Heads of State
Palmer, A. Mitchell	U.S. V.P. & Cabinet
Palmer, Arnold	Golf HoF
Palmer, Betsy	Entertainers (Current)
Palmer, Jim	Baseball
Palmer, Lilli	Entertainers (Vintage)
Palmer, Robert	Rock
Palmerston, Henry J.	Heads of State
Pangborn, Clyde	Aviation
Pankhurst, Christabel	Celebrities
Pankhurst, Emmeline	Celebrities
Pankhurst, E. Sylvia	Celebrities
Papen, Franz von	Military
Pappas, Milt	Baseball
Parcells, Bill	Football
Pardee, Jack	Football
Parent, Bernie	Hockey HoF
Parish, Robert	General Sports
Park, Roy H.	Business
Parker, Alton B.	Celebrities
Parker, Clarence "Ace"	Football
Parker, Colonel Tom	Entertainers (Vintage)
Parker, Dan	General Sports
Parker, Dave	Baseball
Parker, David	Military
Parker, Dorothy	Authors
Parker, Eleanor	Entertainers (Vintage)
Parker, Fess	Entertainers (Current)
Parker, Frank A.	Tennis HoF
Parker, Graham	Rock
Parker, Jean	Entertainers (Vintage)
Parker, Jim	Football
Parker, Joel	Governors
Parker, Ray Jr.	Entertainers (Current)
Parker, Raymond "Buddy"	Football
Parker, Robert A.	Astronauts
Parker, Sarah Jessica	Entertainers (Current)
Parker, Suzy	Entertainers (Vintage)
Parker, Wes	Baseball
Parkins, Barbara	Entertainers (Current)
Parkman, Francis	Authors
Parks, Rosa	Celebrities
Parnell, Charles Stewart	Celebrities
Parnell, Mel	Baseball
Parrish, Helen	Entertainers (Vintage)
Parrish, Julie	Entertainers (Current)
Parrish, Lance	Baseball
Parrish, Maxfield	Artists
Parry, William E., Sir	Celebrities
Parseghian, Ara	Football
Parsons, Albert Ross	Composers
Parsons, Estelle	Entertainers (Current)
Parsons, Johnny	General Sports
Parsons, Louella O.	Entertainers (Vintage)
Partee, Roy	Baseball
Parton, Dolly	Country Music Stars
Pascual, Camilo	Baseball
Pasqua, Dan	Baseball
Pasternak, Boris	Authors
Pasternak, Joe	Entertainers (Vintage)
Pasteur, Louis	Science
Pastor, Tony	Entertainers (Vintage)
Pastore, John A.	Governors
Patch, Alexander M.	Military
Pate, Jerry	General Sports
Patek, Fred	Baseball

Paterno, Joe	Football
Patkin, Max	Baseball
Patrick, Frank	Hockey HoF
Patrick, Gail	Entertainers (Vintage)
Patrick, Lester	Hockey HoF
Patrick, Lynn	Hockey HoF
Patten, Gilbert	Authors
Patterson, Floyd	Boxing
Patterson, John	Governors
Patterson, Paul L.	Governors
Patterson, Wm. Allan	Business
Patti, Adelina	Entertainers (Vintage)
Pattison, Robert T.	Governors
Patton, George S.	Military
Patton, III, George S.	Military
Patton, Mel	General Sports
Patty, Budge	Tennis HoF
Paul I (Rus)	Heads of State
Paul, Arthur	Celebrities
Paul, Don	Football
Paul, Gabe	Baseball
Paul, Les	Entertainers (Vintage)
Paulding, James Kirke	U.S. V.P. & Cabinet
Pauley, Jane	Celebrities
Paulham, Louis	Aviation
Pauling, Linus	Science
Paulsson, Pat	Entertainers (Current)
Paulton, Harry	Entertainers (Vintage)
Paultz, Bill	General Sports
Paulucci, Jeno F.	Business
Pavarotti, Luciano	Entertainers (Current)
Pavie, Auguste	Celebrities
Pavin, Corey	General Sports
Pavlova, Anna	Entertainers (Vintage)
Pawnee Bill (Lillie,G.A.)	Celebrities
Paycheck, Johnny	Country Music Stars
Payer, Julius von	Celebrities
Payne, Cril	Celebrities
Payne, Henry C.	U.S. V.P. & Cabinet
Payne, T.H. (Act'g)	U.S. V.P. & Cabinet
Payton, Walter	Football
Peabody, Eddie	Entertainers (Vintage)
Peabody, Francis	Celebrities
Peabody, George F.	Business
Peale, Chas. Willson	Artists
Peale, Norman Vincent	Celebrities
Peale, Rembrandt	Artists
Pearl, Minnie	Country Music Stars
Pearson, Albie	Baseball
Pearson, Drew	Football
Pearson, Lester B.	Heads of State
Pearson, Monte	Baseball
Peary, Robert E.	Military
Peck, Gregory	Entertainers (Current)
Peckham, Rufus W. (SC)	Celebrities
Peckinpah, Sam	Entertainers (Vintage)
Peckinpaugh, Roger	Baseball
Pedro II (Braz)	Heads of State
Peel, Robert Sir	Heads of State
Peerce, Jan	Entertainers (Vintage)
Peete, Calvin	General Sports
Pegler, Westbrook	Authors
Pele	General Sports
Pelham, Henry	Heads of State
Pell, Theodore R.	Tennis HoF
Pena, Tony	Baseball
Pendergast, Thomas J.	Celebrities
Pendleton, Nat	Entertainers (Vintage)
Penn, Arthur	Entertainers (Current)
Penn, John	Revolutionary War
Penn, Sean	Entertainers (Current)
Penn, William	Revolutionary War
Penner, Joe	Entertainers (Vintage)
Penney, J. C.	Business
Pennington, Ann	Entertainers (Vintage)
Pennock, Herb	Baseball
Penzias, Dr. Arno	Science
Pep, Willie	Boxing
Peppard, George	Entertainers (Current)
Pepperell, William	Military
Perceval, Spencer	Heads of State

Pereira, William L.	Celebrities
Perez, Mariano	Heads of State
Perez, Tony	Baseball
Perignon, D.C. Marquis de	Revolutionary War
Perkins, Carl	Country Music Stars
Perkins, Don	Football
Perkins, Frances	U.S. V.P. & Cabinet
Perkins, Millie	Entertainers (Vintage)
Perkins, Osgood	Entertainers (Vintage)
Perkins, Ray	Football
Perkins, Sam	General Sports
Perkins, Tony	Entertainers (Current)
Perles, George	Football
Perlman, Itzhak	Entertainers (Current)
Perlman, Rhea	Entertainers (Current)
Peron, Juan Domingo	Heads of State
Perpich, Rudolph G.	Governors
Perrine, Valerie	Entertainers (Current)
Perry, Fred	General Sports
Perry, Frederick J.	Tennis HoF
Perry, Gaylord	Baseball
Perry, Jim	Baseball
Perry, Joe	Football
Perry, Madison S.	Governors
Perry, Matthew G.	Military
Perry, Oliver H.	Military
Perry, William	Football
Perryman, Lloyd	Country Music Stars
Pershing, John J.	Military
Persoff, Nehemiah	Entertainers (Current)
Persons, Wilton B.	U.S. V.P. & Cabinet
Perutz, Max	Science
Pesky, Johnny	Baseball
Petain, Henry P.	Heads of State
Peter I (Serb-Yugo)	Heads of State
Peter I, The Great (Rus)	Heads of State
Peters, Bernadette	Entertainers (Current)
Peters, Brock	Entertainers (Current)
Peters, Gary	Baseball
Peters, Mary	General Sports
Peters, Mike	Cartoonists
Peters, Richard Jr.	Revolutionary War
Peters, Roberta	Entertainers (Current)
Peters, Susan	Entertainers (Vintage)
Peterson, Bruce A.	Astronauts
Peterson, Donald H.	Astronauts
Peterson, Forrest RADM	Astronauts
Peterson, Rudolph A.	Business
Petiet, Claude	Revolutionary War
Petrie, Flinders(M.Matthe	Celebrities
Petrie, Geoff	General Sports
Pettet, Joanna	Entertainers (Current)
Pettit, Bob	Basketball HoF
Pettit, Charles	Revolutionary War
Pettitt, Tom	Tennis HoF
Petty, Kyle	General Sports
Petty, Richard	General Sports
Petty, Tom	Rock
Peugeot, Eugene	Business
Pfeiffer, Michelle	Entertainers (Current)
Pfister, Dan	General Sports
Pflug, Jo Ann	Entertainers (Current)
Phelps, "Digger"	General Sports
Philbin, Mary	Entertainers (Vintage)
Philbrick, Herbert A.	Celebrities
Philip (Duke Edinburgh)	Heads of State
Philip II (Sp)	Heads of State
Philip IV (Sp)	Heads of State
Phillip, Andy	Basketball HoF
Phillips, "Bunny"	General Sports
Phillips, Bill	Country Music Stars
Phillips, Bum	Football
Phillips, Bubba	Baseball
Phillips, Jim	Football
Phillips, Julianne	Entertainers (Current)
Phillips, Michelle	Entertainers (Current)
Phillips, Tommy	Hockey HoF
Phillips, Wendell	Celebrities
Phillips, Wm(Under Sec'y)	U.S. V.P. & Cabinet
Phillpotts, Eden	Authors
Piaf, Edith	Entertainers (Vintage)
Piatigorsky, Gregor	Entertainers (Vintage)
Picard, Henry G.	General Sports
Picasso, Pablo	Artists
Piccard, A.	Science
Piccard, Jean	Science
Piccolo, Brian	Football
Pichegru, Charles	Revolutionary War
Pickard, Allan	Hockey HoF
Pickens, Slim	Entertainers (Vintage)
Pickering, Dr. William	Science
Pickering, Timothy	U.S. V.P. & Cabinet
Pickett, Cindy	Entertainers (Current)
Pickford, Mary	Entertainers (Vintage)
Picon, Molly	Entertainers (Vintage)
Pidgeon, Walter	Entertainers (Vintage)
Pierce, Billy	Baseball
Pierce, Franklin	U.S. Presidents
Pierce, Jane M.	Celebrities
Pierce, Web	Country Music Stars
Pierrepont, Edwards	U.S. V.P. & Cabinet
Piersall, Jimmy	Baseball
Pierson, Roland	Aviation
Piggott, Lester	General Sports
Pignatano, Joe	Baseball
Pihos, Pete	Football
Pike, James A., Bishop	Celebrities
Pike, Zebulon M.	Celebrities
Pike, Zebulon	Revolutionary War
Pillsbury, John S.	Business
Pilney, Andy	Football
Pilney, Andy	Baseball
Pilote, J. A. Pierre	Hockey HoF
Pilous, Rudy	Hockey HoF
Pilsudski, Joseph	Military
Pincay Jr., Laffit	General Sports
Pinchot, Gifford	Governors
Pincus, Harry	Artists
Pine, Phillip	Entertainers (Current)
Pinelli, Babe	Baseball
Pinero, Arthur Wing	Authors
Ping, Deng Xiao	Heads of State
Pingel, Rolf	Aviation
Piniella, Lou	Baseball
Pink Floyd	Rock
Pinkerton, Allan	Business
Pinkerton, Robert A.	Business
Pinkney, Thomas	Revolutionary War
Pinkney, William	U.S. V.P. & Cabinet
Pinochet, Augusto	Heads of State
Pioneers, Sons of the	Country Music Stars
Pipgrass, George W.	Baseball
Pire, Dominique Geo. Fr.	Celebrities
Pissarro, Camile	Artists
Piston, Walter	Composers
Pitney, Gene	Entertainers (Current)
Pitney, Mahlon (SC)	Celebrities
Pitre, Didier "Pit"	Hockey HoF
Pitt, William (Younger)	Heads of State
Pitt, William (Elder)	Heads of State
Pitts, Zazu	Entertainers (Vintage)
Pius IX, Pope	Heads of State
Pius XII, Pope	Heads of State
Plainsmen, The	Country Music Stars
Planck, Max	Science
Plank, Doug	Football
Plante, J. Jacques	Hockey HoF
Player, Gary	Golf HoF
Playfair, Lyon	Science
Pleasence, Donald	Entertainers (Current)
Plesac, Dan	Baseball
Pleshette, Suzanne	Entertainers (Current)
Plimpton, George	Authors
Plowright, Joan	Entertainers (Current)
Plum, Milt	Football
Plummer, Christopher	Entertainers (Current)
Plunkett, Jim	Football
Podoloff, Maurice	Basketball HoF
Podres, Johnny	Baseball
Poe, Edgar Allen	Authors
Pogue, William R.	Astronauts
Poincare, Raymond	Heads of State

Poindexter, Joseph B.	Governors
Poinsett, Joel R.	U.S. V.P. & Cabinet
Pointer Sisters	Rock
Poitier, Sidney	Entertainers (Current)
Polando, John	Aviation
Police	Rock
Poling, Daniel A.	Celebrities
Polish Actor & Actress	Entertainers (Vintage)
Polk, James K.	U.S. Presidents
Polk, Sarah	Celebrities
Pollack, Sydney	Entertainers (Current)
Pollard, Art	General Sports
Pollard, Jim	Basketball HoF
Pollock, Channing	Authors
Pollock, Samuel	Hockey HoF
Pometti, Vincenzo	Entertainers (Vintage)
Pompadour, Mme J. A.	Heads of State
Ponder, James	Governors
Poniatowski, Jozef	Military
Pons, Lily	Entertainers (Vintage)
Ponti, Carlo	Entertainers (Current)
Ponting, Herbert George	Celebrities
Ponty, Jean-Luc	Entertainers (Vintage)
Pope, Alexander	Authors
Pope, Alexander	Artists
Popovich, Pavel	Astronauts
Porizkova, Paulina	Entertainers (Current)
Portal, Charles	Aviation
Porter, Cole	Composers
Porter, Darrell	Baseball
Porter, Don	Entertainers (Current)
Porter, Gene Stratton	Authors
Porter, George	Science
Porter, H. V.	Basketball HoF
Porter, James M.	U.S. V.P. & Cabinet
Porter, James D.	Governors
Porter, John Addison	U.S. V.P. & Cabinet
Porter, Katherine A.	Authors
Porter, Wm. Syd.(O.Henry)	Authors
Portland, Duke of	Heads of State
Portsmouth,Duch.(Chas II)	Heads of State
Post, Augustus	Aviation
Post, Emily	Authors
Post, Marjorie Meri.	Business
Post, Markie	Entertainers (Current)
Post, Wiley	Aviation
Potter, Beatrix	Authors
Potter, Cora	Entertainers (Vintage)
Pound, Ezra	Authors
Povey, Len	Aviation
Powderly, Terence V.	Celebrities
Powell, Adam Clayton	Celebrities
Powell, Dick	Entertainers (Vintage)
Powell, Eleanor	Entertainers (Vintage)
Powell, Jane	Entertainers (Current)
Powell, Lewis F.Jr. (SC)	Celebrities
Powell, Max	Country Music Stars
Powell, Robert Baden-	Military
Powell, Talmage	Authors
Powell, William	Entertainers (Vintage)
Power, Ted	Baseball
Power, Tyrone	Entertainers (Vintage)
Powers, Bert	Celebrities
Powers, Gary Francis	Aviation
Powers, Hiram	Artists
Powers, John Robert	Business
Powers, Mala	Entertainers (Current)
Powers, Preston	Artists
Powers, Ridgely C.	Governors
Powers, Stephanie	Entertainers (Current)
Pownall, Thomas	Revolutionary War
Poynter, Edw John	Artists
Pran, Dith	Celebrities
Pratt, Walter "Babe"	Hockey HoF
Preddy. George E.	Aviation
Preminger, Otto	Entertainers (Vintage)
Prentiss, Paula	Entertainers (Current)
Presley, Elvis	Entertainers (Vintage)
Presley, Priscilla	Entertainers (Current)
Presser, Jackie	Celebrities
Preston the Magician	Entertainers (Vintage)
Preston, Lord Stanley of	Hockey HoF
Preston, Robert	Entertainers (Vintage)
Preston, William B.	U.S. V.P. & Cabinet
Previn, Andre	Composers
Previn, Dorey	Composers
Prevost, Eugene M.	Authors
Price, Eddie	Football
Price, James H.	Governors
Price, Leontyne	Entertainers (Current)
Price, Vincent	Entertainers (Current)
Pride, Charley	Country Music Stars
Prien, Guenther	Military
Priest, Ivy Baker	U.S. V.P. & Cabinet
Priestley, J. B.	Authors
Priestly, Joseph	Science
Primeau, A. Joseph	Hockey HoF
Prince	Rock
Principal, Victoria	Entertainers (Current)
Pringle, Aileen	Entertainers (Vintage)
Prinz, Rosemary	Entertainers (Current)
Prinze, Freddie	Entertainers (Vintage)
Proctor, Edna Dean	Authors
Proctor, Redfield	U.S. V.P. & Cabinet
Proctor, Richard Anthony	Science
Procul Harum	Rock
Profumo, John	Celebrities
Profumo, Valerie (Hobson)	Celebrities
Prokofieff, Serge	Composers
Pronovost, J. R. Marcel	Hockey HoF
Prosky, Robert	Entertainers (Current)
Prothro, Tommy	Football
Prouse, Juliet	Entertainers (Current)
Proust, Marcel	Authors
Provine, Dorothy	Entertainers (Current)
Pryor, Aaron	Boxing
Pryor, David	Governors
Pryor, Richard	Entertainers (Current)
Pryor, Roger	Entertainers (Vintage)
Puccini, Giacomo	Composers
Puckett, Kirby	Baseball
Puelo, Johnny	Entertainers (Vintage)
Puhl, Terry	Baseball
Pulford, Harvey	Hockey HoF
Pulitzer, Joseph	Business
Pulitzer, Joseph Jr.	Celebrities
Pulitzer, Roxanne	Celebrities
Pullman, George M.	Business
Pupin, Dr. Michael	Science
Purcell, Edward M.	Science
Purcell, Lee	Entertainers (Current)
Purcell, Sarah	Entertainers (Current)
Purl, Linda	Entertainers (Current)
Purtzer, Tom	General Sports
Purvis, Melvin	Celebrities
Pusey, Edward B.	Celebrities
Pusey, Nathan M.	Celebrities
Pushkin, Alexander	Authors
Putnam, George Palmer	Business
Putnam, Israel	Military
Putnam, Rufus	Revolutionary War
Putney, Mahlon	Celebrities
Puzo, Mario	Authors
Pyle, Denver	Entertainers (Current)
Pyle, Ernie	Authors
Pyle, Howard	Artists
Pynchon, John	Revolutionary War
Pypys, Samuel	Authors
Qaddafi, Muammar el-	Heads of State
Quackenbush, H. G. "Bill"	Hockey HoF
Quaid, Dennis	Entertainers (Current)
Quale, Anthony	Entertainers (Current)
Quang, Thich Tri	Heads of State
Quant, Mary	Business
Quantrill, Wm. C.	Military
Quarry, Jerry	Boxing
Queen, Ellery (Dannay)	Authors
Queensberry, Wm. Douglas	Celebrities
Quesada, Elwood R.	Aviation
Quigley, Ernest	Basketball HoF
Quinn, Anthony	Entertainers (Current)
Quinn, Carmel	Entertainers (Current)

Quinn, Robert E.	Governors
Quinn, William F.	Governors
Quisenberry, Dan	Baseball
Quisling, Vidkun	Military
Raab, Julius	Heads of State
Rabin, Yitzhak	Heads of State
Rachmaninoff, Sergei	Composers
Radhakrishnan, S.	Heads of State
Raeder, Erich	Military
Raffin, Deborah	Entertainers (Current)
Raft, George	Entertainers (Vintage)
Raglan, Fitzroy(Somerset)	Military
Ragsland, Rags	Entertainers (Vintage)
Rahal, Bobby	General Sports
Rahman, Abdul	Heads of State
Rainer, Luise	Entertainers (Vintage)
Raines, Ella	Entertainers (Vintage)
Raines, Tim	Baseball
Rainey, Ford	Entertainers (Current)
Rainier, Prince III	Heads of State
Rains, Claude	Entertainers (Vintage)
Rainwater, Marvin	Country Music Stars
Raitt, John	Entertainers (Vintage)
Raleigh, Cecil	Entertainers (Vintage)
Raleigh, Sara	Entertainers (Vintage)
Ralston, Esther	Entertainers (Vintage)
Ralston, Jobyna	Entertainers (Vintage)
Ralston, John	Football
Ralston, Vera Hruba	Entertainers (Vintage)
Rambeau, Marjorie	Entertainers (Vintage)
Rambo, Dack	Entertainers (Current)
Ramirez, Rafael	Baseball
Rampling, Charlotte	Entertainers (Current)
Ramsay, Jack	General Sports
Ramsay, Sir William	Science
Ramsey, Alexander	U.S. V.P. & Cabinet
Ramsey, Arthur Mich.	Celebrities
Ramsey, Frank	Basketball HoF
Rand, Sally	Entertainers (Vintage)
Randall, Tony	Entertainers (Current)
Randle, Sonny	Football
Randolph, Boots	Entertainers (Current)
Randolph, Edmund J.	U.S. V.P. & Cabinet
Randolph, John(Roanoke)	Revolutionary War
Randolph, Joyce	Entertainers (Current)
Randolph, Willie	Baseball
Rank, J. Arthur	Entertainers (Vintage)
Rank, Otto	Science
Rankin, Frank	Hockey HoF
Rapaport, Lester	Artists
Raphael	Artists
Raschi, Vic	Baseball
Rasmussen, Knute	Celebrities
Rasputin, Gregori E.	Celebrities
Ratelle, Jean	Hockey HoF
Rathbone, Basil	Entertainers (Vintage)
Rathbone, Monroe J.	Business
Rathmann, Jim	General Sports
Ratner, Payne	Governors
Ratoff, Gregory	Entertainers (Vintage)
Ratterman, George	Football
Ravel, Maurice	Composers
Rawdon-Hastings, Francis	Revolutionary War
Rawlings, Edward W.	Military
Rawlins, John A.	U.S. V.P. & Cabinet
Rawlinson, Herbert	Entertainers (Vintage)
Rawls, Betsy	General Sports
Rawson, Edward	Revolutionary War
Ray, Aldo	Entertainers (Current)
Ray, Charles	Entertainers (Vintage)
Ray, Dixie Lee	Governors
Ray, James Earl	Celebrities
Ray, Johnny	Baseball
Ray, Leah	Entertainers (Vintage)
Ray, Robert D.	Governors
Ray, Susan	Country Music Stars
Raye, Martha	Entertainers (Vintage)
Raymond, Alex	Cartoonists
Raymond, Gene	Entertainers (Vintage)
Raymond, Henry J.	Celebrities
Raymond, Sen. Donat	Hockey HoF
Rayner, C. E. "Chuck"	Hockey HoF
Read, A. C.	Aviation
Read, Dolly	Entertainers (Current)
Read, George	Revolutionary War
Read, T. Buchanan	Artists
Reagan, Maureen	Celebrities
Reagan, Ronald	U.S. Presidents
Real, Pierre F., Count	Revolutionary War
Reardon, "Beans"	Baseball
Reardon, Jeff	Baseball
Reardon, Kenneth	Hockey HoF
Reasoner, Harry	Celebrities
Reddy, Helen	Entertainers (Current)
Redenbacker, Orville	Business
Redfield, William C.	U.S. V.P. & Cabinet
Redford, Robert	Entertainers (Current)
Redgrave, Lynn	Entertainers (Current)
Redgrave, Michael Sir	Entertainers (Vintage)
Redgrave, Vanessa	Entertainers (Current)
Redmond, John E.	Celebrities
Reed, Donna	Entertainers (Vintage)
Reed, Jerry	Entertainers (Current)
Reed, John	Authors
Reed, Lou	Rock
Reed, Phillip	Entertainers (Vintage)
Reed, Rex	Entertainers (Current)
Reed, Robert	Entertainers (Current)
Reed, Stanley (SC)	Celebrities
Reed, Walter	Science
Reed, Willis	Basketball HoF
Reedy, George	U.S. V.P. & Cabinet
Reese, "Pee Wee"	Baseball
Reese, Della	Entertainers (Current)
Reeve, Christopher	Entertainers (Current)
Reeves, Dan	Football
Reeves, Steve	Entertainers (Current)
Reeves-Smith, Olive	Entertainers (Vintage)
Regan, Donald	U.S. V.P. & Cabinet
Regan, Phil	Entertainers (Vintage)
Reginald, Lionel	Entertainers (Vintage)
Regnaud de Saint-Jean etc	Revolutionary War
Rehan, Ada	Entertainers (Vintage)
Rehnquist, William H.(SC)	Celebrities
Reich, Wilhelm	Science
Reichers, Lou	Aviation
Reid, Tim	Entertainers (Current)
Reid, Wallace	Entertainers (Vintage)
Reid, Whitelaw	Celebrities
Reid, William	Basketball HoF
Reik, Theodor	Science
Reiner, Carl	Entertainers (Vintage)
Reiner, Rob	Entertainers (Current)
Reinking, Ann	Entertainers (Current)
Reischauer, Edwin O.	Celebrities
Reiser, Pete	Baseball
Reitsch, Hanna	Aviation
Remarque, Erich Maria	Authors
Rembrandt van Rijn	Artists
Remick, Lee	Entertainers (Current)
Remington, Frederic	Artists
Renaldo, Duncan	Entertainers (Vintage)
Renfro, Mel	Football
Renfro, Mike	Football
Renner, Dr. Karl	Heads of State
Renner, Jack	General Sports
Renoir, Pierre Aug.	Artists
Rentzel, Lance	Football
Repplier, Agnes	Authors
Repulski, Rip	Baseball
Resnick, Mike	Authors
Resnik, Judith	Astronauts
Respighi, Ottorino	Composers
Reston, John "Scotty"	Authors
Retton, Mary Lou	General Sports
Retzlaff, Pete	Football
Reuschel, Rick	Baseball
Reuss, Jerry	Baseball
Reuther, Walter	Celebrities
Revelle, Hamilton	Entertainers (Vintage)
Revere, Anne	Entertainers (Vintage)
Revere, Paul	Revolutionary War

Revson, Peter	General Sports
Rexroth, Kenneth	Authors
Reynolds, Allie	Baseball
Reynolds, Bob	Football
Reynolds, Burt	Entertainers (Current)
Reynolds, Debbie	Entertainers (Current)
Reynolds, Donn	Country Music Stars
Reynolds, Gene	Entertainers (Vintage)
Reynolds, Richard S.	Business
Reynolds, Sir Joshua	Artists
Rhea	Entertainers (Vintage)
Rhee, Syngman	Heads of State
Rhodes, Billie	Entertainers (Vintage)
Rhodes, Cecil	Heads of State
Rhodes, Dusty	Baseball
Rhodes, Erik	Entertainers (Vintage)
Ribbentrop, Joachim von	Military
Ribicoff, Abraham	U.S. V.P. & Cabinet
Rice, Edgar "Sam"	Baseball
Rice, Elmer	Authors
Rice, Florence	Entertainers (Vintage)
Rice, Grantland	General Sports
Rice, Jerry	Football
Rice, Jim	Baseball
Rice, Tim	Composers
Rice-Davies, Mandy	Celebrities
Rich, Irene	Entertainers (Vintage)
Richard, Henri	Hockey HoF
Richard, J. H. Maurice	Hockey HoF
Richard, J.R.	Baseball
Richards, Alma W.	General Sports
Richards, J.K. (Act'g)	U.S. V.P. & Cabinet
Richards, Paul	Baseball
Richards, Rev. Bob	General Sports
Richards, Richard N.	Astronauts
Richards, Sir Gordon	General Sports
Richards, Vincent	Tennis HoF
Richardson, Bobby	Baseball
Richardson, Ralph	Entertainers (Vintage)
Richardson, John, Sir	Celebrities
Richardson, George	Hockey HoF
Richardson, Elliot	U.S. V.P. & Cabinet
Richardson, William A.	U.S. V.P. & Cabinet
Richardson, Ian	Entertainers (Vintage)
Richardson, Sir John	Science
Richelieu, Armand	Heads of State
Richelieu, Cardinal	Heads of State
Richey, Lawrence	U.S. V.P. & Cabinet
Richie, Lionel	Rock
Richman, Charles	Entertainers (Vintage)
Richman, Harry	Entertainers (Vintage)
Richmond, Tim	General Sports
Richter, Dr. Burton	Science
Richter, Les	Football
Richthofen, Manfred von	Aviation
Rickenbacker, Edward	Aviation
Rickey, Branch	Baseball
Rickles, Don	Entertainers (Current)
Rickover, Hyman G.	Military
Riddle, George	Country Music Stars
Ride, Sally K.	Astronauts
Ridgway, Matthew B.	Military
Riefenstahl, Leni	Entertainers (Vintage)
Riegger, Wallingford	Composers
Rigby, Cathy	General Sports
Rigg, Diana	Entertainers (Current)
Riggins, John	Football
Riggs, Robert L.	Tennis HoF
Riggs, Tommy	Entertainers (Vintage)
Righteous Bros.	Rock
Rigney, Bill	Baseball
Riis, Jacob A.	Authors
Riley, James Whitcomb	Authors
Riley, Jeannie C.	Country Music Stars
Riley, Polly	General Sports
Rilke, Rainer Maria	Authors
Rimsky-Korsakov, N.	Composers
Rinehart, Mary Roberts	Authors
Ringling, Henry	Business
Ringling, John	Business
Ringo, Jim	Football

Ringwald, Molly	Entertainers (Current)
Ripken, Cal Jr.	Baseball
Ripken, Cal Sr.	Baseball
Ripken, Bill	Baseball
Ripley, Elmer	Basketball HoF
Ripley, Robert	Cartoonists
Risko, Eddie "Babe"	Boxing
Risner, James R.	Military
Ritchie, Willie	Boxing
Ritt, Martin	Entertainers (Current)
Rittenhouse, David	Science
Ritter, John	Entertainers (Current)
Ritter, Tex	Entertainers (Vintage)
Ritter, Thelma	Entertainers (Vintage)
Ritz, Jimmy	Entertainers (Vintage)
Rivera, Diego	Artists
Rivera, Geraldo	Entertainers (Current)
Rivers, Joan	Entertainers (Current)
Rivers, Larry	Artists
Rixey, Eppa Jr.	Baseball
Rizzuto, Phil	Baseball
Roach, Hal	Entertainers (Vintage)
Roach, Hal Sr.	Entertainers (Current)
Roark, Helen Wills	Tennis HoF
Roarke, Hayden	Entertainers (Current)
Robards, Jason	Entertainers (Vintage)
Robbins, Frederick	Science
Robbins, Gale	Entertainers (Vintage)
Robbins, Harold	Authors
Robbins, Marty	Country Music Stars
Robero, Cesar	Entertainers (Current)
Roberts, Clifford	Golf HoF
Roberts, Doris	Entertainers (Current)
Roberts, Eric	Entertainers (Current)
Roberts, Floyd	General Sports
Roberts, Frederick S.	Military
Roberts, Gordon	Hockey HoF
Roberts, Jack	Country Music Stars
Roberts, Kenneth	Authors
Roberts, Oral	Celebrities
Roberts, Owen J. (SC)	Celebrities
Roberts, Ralph	Authors
Roberts, Robin	Baseball
Roberts, Roy	Entertainers (Vintage)
Roberts, Tanya	Entertainers (Current)
Roberts, Tony	Entertainers (Current)
Roberts, Xavier	Business
Robertson, Cliff	Entertainers (Current)
Robertson, Isiah	Football
Robertson, John	Hockey HoF
Robertson, Oscar	Basketball HoF
Robertson, Pat	Celebrities
Robeson, George M.	U.S. V.P. & Cabinet
Robeson, Paul	Entertainers (Vintage)
Robespierre, Maximilien	Heads of State
Robidoux, Billie Joe	Baseball
Robinson, Bill	Entertainers (Vintage)
Robinson, Brooks	Baseball
Robinson, C. Roosevelt	Celebrities
Robinson, Claude	Hockey HoF
Robinson, Dwight P.	Business
Robinson, Eddie	Baseball
Robinson, Edward A.	Authors
Robinson, Frank	Baseball
Robinson, Jackie	Baseball
Robinson, John	Revolutionary War
Robinson, John	Football
Robinson, Johnny	Football
Robinson, Smokey	Rock
Robinson, Sugar Ray	Boxing
Robinson, Wilbert	Baseball
Robson, Flora Dame	Entertainers (Vintage)
Robson, May	Entertainers (Vintage)
Robson, Stuart	Entertainers (Vintage)
Robustelli, Andy	Football
Rochambeau, D.M.J. de	Military
Rochambeau, J.B.D.Count	Revolutionary War
Roche, James M.	Business
Rockefeller, Nelson (V)	U.S. V.P. & Cabinet
Rockefeller, David	Business
Rockefeller, John D., Jr.	Business

Rockefeller, Happy	Business
Rockefeller, John D.	Business
Rockefeller, Laurance	Business
Rockefeller, Abby A.	Business
Rockerfeller, Nelson A.	Governors
Rockerfeller, Winthrop	Governors
Rockne, Knute	Football
Rockne, Mrs. Knute	Football
Rockwell, Norman	Artists
Rockwell, Robert	Entertainers (Current)
Rodden, Michael	Hockey HoF
Rodgers, Bill	General Sports
Rodgers, Geo. Washington	Military
Rodgers, John	Aviation
Rodgers, Pepper	Football
Rodgers, Richard	Composers
Rodgrs, John, Comdr.	Military
Rodin, Auguste	Artists
Rodman, Judy	Entertainers (Current)
Rodney, Caesar	U.S. V.P. & Cabinet
Roe, Preacher	Baseball
Roebling, John A.	Science
Roebling, Washington A.	Science
Roederer, Pierre C. Count	Revolutionary War
Roehm, Ernest	Celebrities
Roentgen, Wilhelm	Science
Roethke, Theodore	Authors
Rogell, Billy	Baseball
Rogers, Bernard W.	Military
Rogers, Bill	General Sports
Rogers, Buddy	Entertainers (Vintage)
Rogers, Fred	Entertainers (Current)
Rogers, Ginger	Entertainers (Vintage)
Rogers, Jimmy	Entertainers (Vintage)
Rogers, Joseph W.	Aviation
Rogers, Karen	General Sports
Rogers, Marianne & Kenny	Country Music Stars
Rogers, Robert	Revolutionary War
Rogers, Roy	Entertainers (Current)
Rogers, Samuel	Authors
Rogers, Steve	Baseball
Rogers, Will	Entertainers (Vintage)
Rogers, William P.	U.S. V.P. & Cabinet
Roget, Dr. Peter M.	Authors
Rohmer, Sax (A.S.Ward)	Authors
Rojas, Cookie	Baseball
Roland de La Platiere,J.W	Revolutionary War
Roland, Gilbert	Entertainers (Current)
Roland, Ruth	Entertainers (Vintage)
Roldan, Salvador C.	Heads of State
Rolfe, Red	Baseball
Rolfe, William James	Authors
Rolland, Romain	Authors
Rolle, Esther	Entertainers (Current)
Rolling Stones	Rock
Rolls, Charles S.	Business
Rolph, James	Governors
Roman, Ruth	Entertainers (Current)
Romano, John	Baseball
Romanoff, "Prince" M.	Entertainers (Vintage)
Romanoff, Michael	Business
Romberg, Sigmund	Composers
Rome, Harold	Composers
Rome, Sydney	Entertainers (Current)
Romero, Cesar	Entertainers (Current)
Rommel, Erwin	Military
Romney, George	Governors
Romney, George	Artists
Romulo, Carlos P.	Celebrities
Ronstadt, Linda	Country Music Stars
Rooney, Art	Football
Rooney, Mickey	Entertainers (Current)
Roosa, Stuart R.	Astronauts
Roosevelt, Ellen C.	Tennis HoF
Roosevelt, Eleanor	Celebrities
Roosevelt, Edith K.	Celebrities
Roosevelt, Franklin D.	U.S. Presidents
Roosevelt, James	Celebrities
Roosevelt, Nicholas J.	Revolutionary War
Roosevelt, Sarah D.	Celebrities
Roosevelt, Theodore	U.S. Presidents
Roosevelt, Theo. Jr.	Military
Roosma, John S.	Basketball HoF
Roosma, John	General Sports
Root, Charlie	Baseball
Root, Elihu	U.S. V.P. & Cabinet
Roper, Daniel	U.S. V.P. & Cabinet
Rorke, Hayden	Entertainers (Current)
Rose, Billy	Entertainers (Vintage)
Rose, David	Composers
Rose, Fred	Country Music Stars
Rose, Juanita	Country Music Stars
Rose, Pete	Baseball
Rosebery, 5th Earl	Heads of State
Rosellini, Albert D.	Governors
Rosen, Al	Baseball
Rosenberg, Alfred	Military
Rosenbloom, Slapsie Maxie	Boxing
Rosenbloom, Caroll	Football
Rosendahl, Charles	Aviation
Rosenman, Samuel I.	Celebrities
Rosenthal, Joe	Military
Rosenwald, Julius	Business
Rosewall, Ken	General Sports
Rosewall, Kenneth	Tennis HoF
Ross, Arthur	Hockey HoF
Ross, Barney	Boxing
Ross, Bobby	Football
Ross, Charles J.	Entertainers (Vintage)
Ross, Diana	Rock
Ross, Donald	Golf HoF
Ross, George	Revolutionary War
Ross, Jerry L.	Astronauts
Ross, John [Coowescoowe]	Celebrities
Ross, John, Sir	Celebrities
Ross, Katharine	Entertainers (Current)
Ross, Lanny	Entertainers (Vintage)
Ross, Marion	Entertainers (Current)
Ross, Nellie Tayloe	Governors
Ross, Philip	Hockey HoF
Ross, Robert	Authors
Rossetti, Christina	Authors
Rossetti, Dante Gabriel	Artists
Rossini, Gioachino	Composers
Rossman, Edmond	Aviation
Rote, Kyle	Football
Rote, Kyle Jr.	General Sports
Roth, Lillian	Entertainers (Vintage)
Roth, Philip	Authors
Rothafell, S. L.	Entertainers (Vintage)
Rothschild, Guy de	Business
Rothschild, Alix de	Business
Rothschild, Nathan Meyer	Business
Rothschild, Lionel Walter	Business
Rotia, Rocky	Business
Rouault, Georges	Artists
Rountree, Richard	Entertainers (Current)
Rous, Dr. Peyton	Science
Roush, Edd J.	Baseball
Rousseau, Jean J.	Authors
Rousseau, Theodore	Artists
Roux, Pierre Paul Emile	Science
Rowan, Andrew S.	Military
Rowan, Dan	Entertainers (Current)
Rowe, Leo S.(Ass't Sec)	U.S. V.P. & Cabinet
Rowe, Lynwood "Schoolboy"	Baseball
Rowland, Gena	Entertainers (Current)
Rowlandson, Thomas	Artists
Rowling, William E.	Heads of State
Roxas, Manuel	Heads of State
Royal, Darrell	Football
Roylance, Pamela	Entertainers (Current)
Rozelle, Pete	Football
Rozier, Mike	Football
Rubens, Alma	Entertainers (Vintage)
Rubens, Peter Paul	Artists
Rubin, Jerry	Celebrities
Rubinoff	Entertainers (Vintage)
Rubinstein, Arthur	Entertainers (Vintage)
Rubinstein, Helena	Business
Rubinstein, John	Entertainers (Current)
Rubinstein, Anton	Composers

Ruby, Harry	Composers	Saffell, Tom	Baseball
Ruby, Jack	Celebrities	Sagan, Dr. Carl	Authors
Rudel, Hans Ulrich	Aviation	Sagan, Dr. Carl	Science
Rudolf-Hapsburg (Aus)	Heads of State	Sage, Russell	Business
Rudolph, Wilma	General Sports	Sager, Carole Bayer	Composers
Ruel, Herold "Muddy"	Baseball	Sahl, Mort	Entertainers (Current)
Ruffing, Charles "Red"	Baseball	Said, Nuri (PM Iraq)	Heads of State
Ruggles, Charles	Entertainers (Vintage)	Saimes, George	Football
Ruggles, Wesley	Entertainers (Vintage)	Saint Hilaire, L.V. Jos.	Revolutionary War
Ruick, Barbara	Entertainers (Vintage)	Saint Laurent, Yves	Business
Rukeyser, Louis	Celebrities	Saint, Eva Marie	Entertainers (Current)
Rumpler, Edward	Aviation	Saint-Cyr, Gouvion	Revolutionary War
Rumsfeld, Donald	U.S. V.P. & Cabinet	Saint-Gaudens, Aug.	Artists
Rundstedt, Gerd von	Military	Saint-Saens, Camille	Composers
Runkel, Louis	Business	Salan, Raoul	Military
Runyon, Damon	Authors	Salazar, Alberto	General Sports
Rupp, Adolph	Basketball HoF	Sale, Chic	Entertainers (Vintage)
Ruppert, Col. Jacob	Baseball	Sales, Soupy	Entertainers (Current)
Ruppert, Jacob	Business	Salinger, J. D.	Authors
Rush, Barbara	Entertainers (Current)	Salinger, Pierre	U.S. V.P. & Cabinet
Rush, Benjamin	Revolutionary War	Salisbury, Lord Robert	Heads of State
Rush, Richard	U.S. V.P. & Cabinet	Salk, Dr. Jonas	Science
Rusk, Dean	U.S. V.P. & Cabinet	Salmi, Albert	Entertainers (Current)
Rusk, Jeremiah M.	U.S. V.P. & Cabinet	Salt, Jennifer	Entertainers (Current)
Rusk, Johnny	Country Music Stars	Salt, Titus, Sir	Business
Ruskin, John	Authors	Salten, Felix	Authors
Russel, Blair	Hockey HoF	Samms, Emma	Entertainers (Current)
Russell, Annie	Entertainers (Vintage)	Samourand, M.	General Sports
Russell, Bertrand	Authors	Sampson, Ralph	General Sports
Russell, Bill	Baseball	Sampson, Will	Entertainers (Vintage)
Russell, Bill	Basketball HoF	Sampson, William T.	Military
Russell, Cazzie	General Sports	Samuel, Juan	Baseball
Russell, Charles	Governors	San Martin, Jose De	Heads of State
Russell, Charles M.	Artists	Sanborn, Franklin B.	Authors
Russell, Donald J. M.	Business	Sanborn, Katherine A	Authors
Russell, Harold	Entertainers (Current)	Sand, George	Authors
Russell, Jane	Entertainers (Current)	Sandberg, Ryne	Baseball
Russell, John (Honey)	Basketball HoF	Sandburg, Carl	Authors
Russell, Kurt	Entertainers (Current)	Sande, Earle	General Sports
Russell, Lillian	Entertainers (Vintage)	Sanders, Ben	Baseball
Russell, Lord John	Heads of State	Sanders, Doug	General Sports
Russell, Rosalind	Entertainers (Vintage)	Sanders, George	Entertainers (Vintage)
Russell, Sol Smith	Entertainers (Vintage)	Sanders, Harland	Business
Russell, Theresa	Entertainers (Current)	Sanders, John	Baseball
Rustin, Bayard	Celebrities	Sanders, Ray	Baseball
Rutan, Dick	Aviation	Sanders, Reggie	Baseball
Rutgers, Henry	Business	Sanderson, Julia	Entertainers (Vintage)
Ruth, George Herman"Babe"	Baseball	Sanderson, Scott	Baseball
Ruth, Mrs. "Babe"	Baseball	Sandow	General Sports
Rutherford, Ann	Entertainers (Vintage)	Sandoz, Marie	Authors
Rutherford, Johnny	General Sports	Sandwich, 4th Earl of	Celebrities
Rutherford, Ernest	Science	Sanford, Isabel	Entertainers (Current)
Rutigliano, Sam	Football	Sanford, Jack	Baseball
Rutledge, Edward	Revolutionary War	Sanger, Margaret	Celebrities
Rutledge, John (SC)	Celebrities	Sansom, Art	Cartoonists
Rutledge, Wiley B. (SC)	Celebrities	Santa Anna, A.L. de	Military
Ruttan, J. D. "Jack"	Hockey HoF	Santa Rosa, Count	Military
Ryan, Buddy	Football	Santayana, George	Authors
Ryan, Elizabeth	Tennis HoF	Santee, Wes	General Sports
Ryan, Nolan	Baseball	Santiago, Benito	Baseball
Ryan, Robert	Entertainers (Vintage)	Santo, Ron	Baseball
Ryan, Sheila	Entertainers (Current)	Santos, Joe	Entertainers (Current)
Ryan, T. Claude	Aviation	Santos-Dumont, A.	Aviation
Ryder, Albert P.	Artists	Saperstein, Abe	Basketball HoF
Ryle, Martin, Sir	Science	Sarandon, Susan	Entertainers (Current)
Ryn, John Van	Tennis HoF	Sarazen, Gene	General Sports
Ryun, Jim	General Sports	Sarazen, Gene	Golf HoF
Saarinen, G. Eliel	Celebrities	Sardi, Vincent	Business
Saba	Entertainers (Vintage)	Sargent, Dick	Entertainers (Current)
Saban, Lou	Football	Sargent, John Singer	Artists
Sabatini, Rafael	Authors	Sargent, John G.	U.S. V.P. & Cabinet
Saberhagen, Bret	Baseball	Sargent, Winthrop	Revolutionary War
Sabin, Dr. Albert B.	Science	Sarnoff, David	Business
Sablon, Jean	Entertainers (Vintage)	Saroyan, William	Authors
Sacco, Nicola	Celebrities	Sartain, John	Artists
Sacher-Masoch, Leo. von	Authors	Sartre, Jean-Paul	Authors
Sackler, Howard	Authors	Sassoon, Beverly	Entertainers (Current)
Sacks, Leonard	Basketball HoF	Sassoon, Siegfried	Authors
Sadat, Anwar	Heads of State	Sassoon, Vidal	Business
Sade	Rock	Satie, Erik	Composers
Sade, Marquis de	Authors	Sato, Eisaku	Heads of State

Name	Category
Sauer, Emil	Entertainers (Vintage)
Saulsbury, Grove	Governors
Saunder, Stuart J.	Business
Saunders, Hugh W.	Aviation
Saunders, Lori	Entertainers (Current)
Savage, Ann	Entertainers (Vintage)
Savalas, Telly	Entertainers (Current)
Savales, George	Entertainers (Vintage)
Savard, Serge	General Sports
Savitt, Richard	Tennis HoF
Savoia, Attilio	Artists
Sawchuck, Terry	General Sports
Sawchuk, Terrance	Hockey HoF
Sawyer, Charles	U.S. V.P. & Cabinet
Sawyer, Diane	Celebrities
Sax, Adolphe	Science
Sax, Steve	Baseball
Saxbe, William B.	U.S. V.P. & Cabinet
Saxe, John G.	Authors
Sayao, Bidu	Entertainers (Vintage)
Sayers, Dorothy	Authors
Sayers, Gale	Football
Scaggs, Boz	Rock
Scalia, Jack	Entertainers (Current)
Scammell, Alexander	Revolutionary War
Scanlan, Fred	Hockey HoF
Scarlatti, Alessandro	Composers
Scarwid, Diana	Entertainers (Current)
Schaal, Richard	Entertainers (Current)
Schaal, Wendy	Entertainers (Current)
Schabinger, Arthur	Basketball HoF
Schacht, Al	Baseball
Schacht, Hjalmar	Business
Schaff, Philip	Celebrities
Schalk, Ray	Baseball
Schallert, William	Entertainers (Current)
Schally, Dr. Andrew	Science
Schanberg, Sydney, H.	Authors
Scharwenka, Xaver	Composers
Schary, Dore	Entertainers (Current)
Schary, Emanuel	Artists
Schawlow, Arthur L.	Science
Schayes, Adolph (Dolph)	Basketball HoF
Scheer, Reinhard	Military
Scheff, Fritzi	Entertainers (Vintage)
Scheidemann, Philippe	Heads of State
Scheider, Roy	Entertainers (Current)
Schell, Maximillian	Entertainers (Vintage)
Schembeckler, Bo	Football
Schenkel, Chris	General Sports
Schick, Dr. Bela	Science
Schifrin, Lalo	Composers
Schildkraudt, Joseph	Entertainers (Vintage)
Schirra, Walter M.	Astronauts
Schlafly, Phyllis	Celebrities
Schlesinger, James R.	U.S. V.P. & Cabinet
Schlesinger, Arthur Jr	Authors
Schley, Winfield S.	Military
Schliemann, Heinrich	Authors
Schlueter, Dale	General Sports
Schmalz, Wilhelm	Military
Schmeling, Max	Boxing
Schmidt, Dr. Maarten	Science
Schmidt, Ernest	Basketball HoF
Schmidt, Joe	Football
Schmidt, Mike	Baseball
Schmidt, Milton	Hockey HoF
Schmitt, Harrison H.	Astronauts
Schmitz, Johnny	Baseball
Schmucker, Dick	General Sports
Schneider, John	Entertainers (Current)
Schneider,Wm. C.(SKYLAB)	Astronauts
Schnellenberger, Howard	Football
Schnitgen, Dick	Football
Schoenberg, Arnold	Composers
Schoendienst, "Red"	Baseball
Schoenert, Rudolf	Aviation
Schoepfel, Gerhard	Aviation
Schofield, John	U.S. V.P. & Cabinet
Schollander, Don	General Sports
Schommer, John	Basketball HoF
Schopenhauer, Arthur	Authors
Schottenheimer, Marty	Football
Schram, Emil	Business
Schramm, Tex	Football
Schreiber, Avery	Entertainers (Current)
Schreiber, Paul	Baseball
Schricker, Henry F.	Governors
Schrieffer, John R.	Science
Schriner, D. "Sweeney"	Hockey HoF
Schroeder, Frederick R.	Tennis HoF
Schroeder, Jay	Football
Schubert, Franz	Composers
Schulberg, Budd	Authors
Schulz, Charles	Cartoonists
Schumacher, Hal	Baseball
Schumann, Clara	Celebrities
Schumann, Robert	Composers
Schumann-Heink, E.	Entertainers (Vintage)
Schuschnigg, R. von	Heads of State
Schuyler, Philip J.	Military
Schwab, Charles M.	Business
Schwarzenegger, Arnold	Entertainers (Current)
Schwatka, Frederick	Celebrities
Schweickart, Russell L.	Astronauts
Schweitzer, Dr. Albert	Science
Schwellenback, Lewis B.	U.S. V.P. & Cabinet
Schwinger, Dr. Julian	Science
Scobee, Dick	Astronauts
Scopes, John T.	Celebrities
Score, Herb	Baseball
Scott, C. W. A.	Aviation
Scott, Cyril Meir	Composers
Scott, David R.	Astronauts
Scott, Eric	Entertainers (Current)
Scott, George C.	Entertainers (Current)
Scott, Gustavus	Revolutionary War
Scott, John Morin	Revolutionary War
Scott, Jr., Robert	Aviation
Scott, Lizbeth	Entertainers (Current)
Scott, Randolph	Entertainers (Vintage)
Scott, Raymond	Composers
Scott, Robert Falcon	Celebrities
Scott, Sir Walter	Authors
Scott, W. Kerr	Governors
Scott, Willard	Entertainers (Current)
Scranton, Bill	Governors
Scriabin, Alexander	Composers
Scudder, Horace E.	Authors
Scully, Vin	Baseball
Seaborg, Glenn	Science
Seagren, Bob	General Sports
Searle, Ronald	Artists
Sears, Eleonora	Tennis HoF
Sears, Richard D.	Tennis HoF
Seaver, Tom	Baseball
Seawell, Molly Elliot	Authors
Seawell, William T.	Business
Seberg, Jean	Entertainers (Vintage)
Sedaka, Neil	Composers
Seddon, Margaret R.	Astronauts
Sedgman, Frank	Tennis HoF
Sedgwick, Catherine M.	Authors
Sedran, Barney	Basketball HoF
See, Elliot M. Jr.	Astronauts
Seeger, Pete	Entertainers (Current)
Seeley, Blossom	Entertainers (Vintage)
Seeley, Jeannie	Country Music Stars
Segal, George	Entertainers (Current)
Segar, Elzie C.	Cartoonists
Seger, Bob	Rock
Segovia, Andres	Entertainers (Vintage)
Segre, Emilio	Science
Segura, Pancho	General Sports
Seibert, Earl	Hockey HoF
Seibert, Oliver	Hockey HoF
Seignolle, Claude	Authors
Seipel, Ignas Dr.	Heads of State
Seitz, Edward S.	Basketball HoF
Seitzer, Kevin	Baseball
Seixas Jr., E. Victor	Tennis HoF
Seka	Entertainers (Current)

Selassie, Haile	Heads of State
Selfridge, Harry G.	Business
Selke, Frank	Hockey HoF
Selkirk, George	Baseball
Sellecca, Connie	Entertainers (Current)
Selleck, Tom	Entertainers (Current)
Sellers, David Foote	Military
Sellers, Peter	Entertainers (Vintage)
Sellers, Winfield S.	Military
Seltzer, Leo	General Sports
Selvy, Frank	General Sports
Selznick, David O.	Entertainers (Vintage)
Selznick, Irene	Entertainers (Vintage)
Seminick, Andy	Baseball
Semmelweis, Ignaz	Science
Sennett, Mack	Entertainers (Vintage)
Sergeant, John	Celebrities
Serling, Rod	Authors
Serpico, Frank	Celebrities
Servo, Marty	Boxing
Sessi, Walt	Baseball
Sessions, Roger	Composers
Seton, Ernest Thompson	Authors
Seuss, Dr.	Cartoonists
Severinson, Doc	Entertainers (Current)
Seversky, Alex. de	Aviation
Sewall, David	Revolutionary War
Seward, F.W.(Ass't Sec)	U.S. V.P. & Cabinet
Seward, William H.	U.S. V.P. & Cabinet
Sewell, Joe	Baseball
Seymour, Horatio	Governors
Seymour, Jane	Entertainers (Current)
Shackleton, Ernest	Celebrities
Shaffer, Peter L.	Authors
Shaftesbury (A.A.Cooper)	Celebrities
Shahn, Ben	Artists
Shamir, Yitzhak	Heads of State
Shannon, Del	Country Music Stars
Shantz, Bobby	Baseball
Shapiro, Harry	Artists
Shapiro, Karl	Authors
Shapp, Milton J.	Governors
Sharif, Omar	Entertainers (Current)
Sharkey, Jack	Boxing
Sharman, Bill	Basketball HoF
Sharon, Ariel Gen.	Military
Sharp, U. S. Grant	Military
Sharpe, Karen	Entertainers (Vintage)
Shatner, William	Entertainers (Current)
Shaunessy, Charles	Entertainers (Current)
Shavers, Earnie	Boxing
Shaw, Anna Howard	Celebrities
Shaw, Artie	Entertainers (Vintage)
Shaw, Brewster H.	Astronauts
Shaw, George	Football
Shaw, George Bernard	Authors
Shaw, H.W.(J. Billings)	Authors
Shaw, Irwin	Authors
Shaw, Lemuel	Revolutionary War
Shaw, Wilbur	General Sports
Shawkey, "Bob"	Baseball
Shawn, Ted	Entertainers (Vintage)
Shea, "Spec"	Baseball
Shea, William A.	Business
Shear, Rhonda	Entertainers (Current)
Shearer, Moira	Entertainers (Vintage)
Shearer, Norma	Entertainers (Vintage)
Sheedy, Ally	Entertainers (Current)
Sheen, Charles	Entertainers (Current)
Sheen, Fulton J.	Celebrities
Sheen, Martin	Entertainers (Current)
Sheffer, Chris	Entertainers (Current)
Shelby, Isaac	Revolutionary War
Sheldon, Sidney	Authors
Shelley, Percy Bysshe	Authors
Shelton, Deborah	Entertainers (Current)
Shelton, Everett	Basketball HoF
Shepard, Alan B.	Astronauts
Shepherd, Cybill	Entertainers (Current)
Shepherd, William M.	Astronauts
Shera, Mark	Entertainers (Current)

Sheridan, Ann	Entertainers (Vintage)
Sheridan, Rich. Brinsley	Authors
Sherman, Forrest P.	Military
Sherman, Frederick C.	Military
Sherman, James S. (V)	U.S. V.P. & Cabinet
Sherman, John	U.S. V.P. & Cabinet
Sherman, Roger	Revolutionary War
Sherry, Larry	Baseball
Sherwood, Bobby	Entertainers (Vintage)
Sherwood, Martha	Authors
Sherwood, Robert E.	Authors
Shields, Brooke	Entertainers (Current)
Shields, Francis X.	Tennis HoF
Shigeta, James	Entertainers (Current)
Shiras, George, Jr. (SC)	Celebrities
Shirer, William L.	Authors
Shirley, Anne	Entertainers (Vintage)
Shirley, J. Dallas	Basketball HoF
Shirley, William	Revolutionary War
Shockley, William	Science
Shoemaker, Betty Nuthall	Tennis HoF
Shoemaker, William L.	Authors
Shoemaker, Willie	General Sports
Shoen, Sam	Business
Shofner, Del	Football
Shoop, Pamela Susan	Entertainers (Current)
Shore, "Eddie"	General Sports
Shore, Dinah	Entertainers (Current)
Shore, Edward	Hockey HoF
Shore, Ernie	General Sports
Shorter, Frank	General Sports
Shostakovich, Dmitri	Composers
Shoumatoff, Elizabeth	Artists
Shoup, David M.	Military
Showalter, Max	Entertainers (Current)
Shrimpton, Jean	Entertainers (Current)
Shriner, Herb	Entertainers (Vintage)
Shriver, Loren J.	Astronauts
Shriver, Maria	Celebrities
Shriver, Sargent	Celebrities
Shriver, Sargent	U.S. V.P. & Cabinet
Shuba, George "Shotgun"	Baseball
Shubert, John	Entertainers (Vintage)
Shula, Don	Football
Shulman, Ellen L.	Astronauts
Shultz, George P.	U.S. V.P. & Cabinet
Shuman, Charles B.	Celebrities
Shuster, W. Morgan	Business
Sibelius, Jean	Composers
Sibley, Henry H.	Governors
Sickles, Noel	Cartoonists
Sidney, Sylvia	Entertainers (Vintage)
Siebert, A. C. "Babe"	Hockey HoF
Sieburn, Norm	Baseball
Siegel & Shuster	Cartoonists
Siegmeister, Elie	Composers
Sierra, Gregory	Entertainers (Current)
Sierra, Margarita	Entertainers (Current)
Sierra, Ruben	Baseball
Sievers, Roy	Baseball
Sigler, Kim	Governors
Signac, Paul	Artists
Signoret, Simone	Entertainers (Current)
Signoret, Simone	Entertainers (Vintage)
Sigsbee, Charles D.	Military
Sihanouk, Prince	Heads of State
Sikking, James B.	Entertainers (Current)
Sikorsky, Igor	Aviation
Silliman, Benjamin	Science
Sills, Beverly	Entertainers (Current)
Sills, Milton	Entertainers (Vintage)
Silverman, Fred	Business
Silvers, Phil	Entertainers (Vintage)
Simenon, Georges	Authors
Simmons, Al	Baseball
Simmons, Curt	Baseball
Simmons, Jean	Entertainers (Current)
Simmons, Richard	Entertainers (Current)
Simmons, Ted	Baseball
Simms, Phil	Football
Simms, William G.	Authors

Name	Category
Simon & Garfunkle	Rock
Simon, Carly	Rock
Simon, Carly	Entertainers (Current)
Simon, Herbert A.	Science
Simon, Neil	Authors
Simon, Norton	Business
Simon, Paul	Composers
Simon, Simone	Entertainers (Vintage)
Simon, William E.	U.S. V.P. & Cabinet
Simons, Jim	General Sports
Simpson, Harold	Hockey HoF
Simpson, O.J.	Football
Simpson, Scott	General Sports
Simpson, Sir James Y.	Science
Sims, Adm. Wm. S.	Military
Sims, Billy	Football
Sims, Duke	Baseball
Sims, Ken	Football
Sinatra, Frank	Entertainers (Current)
Sinatra, Nancy	Entertainers (Current)
Sinclair, Harry	Business
Sinclair, Upton	Authors
Sinding, Christian	Composers
Singer, Bill	Baseball
Singer, Isaac B.	Authors
Singlaub, John K.	Military
Singletary, Mike	Football
Singleton, Ken	Baseball
Singleton, Penny	Entertainers (Current)
Sinkwich, Frankie	Football
Sisk, Tom	Baseball
Sisler, Dick	Baseball
Sisler, George	Baseball
Sisley, Alfred	Artists
Sisti, Sibbi	Baseball
Sitgreaves, John	Revolutionary War
Sitwell, Dame Edith	Authors
Sitwell, Osbert Sir	Authors
Sixty Minutes (all)	Entertainers (Current)
Skala, Lilia	Entertainers (Current)
Skelton, Red	Entertainers (Vintage)
Skerrit, Tom	Entertainers (Current)
Skinner, B. F.	Authors
Skinner, Cortlandt	Military
Skinner, Cornelia Otis	Authors
Skinner, Otis	Entertainers (Vintage)
Skinner, Stella	Artists
Skipworth, Alison	Entertainers (Vintage)
Skoronski, Bob	Football
Skorzeny, Otto	Military
Skowron, Bill "Moose"	Baseball
Slaughter, Enos	Baseball
Slaughter, Frank G.	Authors
Slayton, Donald K.	Astronauts
Sledd, Patsy	Country Music Stars
Slim, Wm. Joseph	Military
Sliwa, Lisa	Celebrities
Sloan, Alfred P. Jr.	Business
Sloan, Tod	General Sports
Slocum Jr., Henry W.	Tennis HoF
Smalley, Roy	Baseball
Smeaton, J. Cooper	Hockey HoF
Smedley, Richard	Entertainers (Current)
Smiley, Delores	Country Music Stars
Smirnoff, Yakov	Entertainers (Current)
Smith, Al	Cartoonists
Smith, Alexis	Entertainers (Current)
Smith, Alfred	Hockey HoF
Smith, Alfred E.	Governors
Smith, Bernie	Entertainers (Current)
Smith, Bubba	Football
Smith, Buffalo Bob	Entertainers (Vintage)
Smith, C. Aubrey	Entertainers (Vintage)
Smith, Caleb	U.S. V.P. & Cabinet
Smith, Carl	Country Music Stars
Smith, Charles M.	Governors
Smith, Chas. Emory	U.S. V.P. & Cabinet
Smith, Connie	Country Music Stars
Smith, Dave "Sweetback"	Football
Smith, Dave	Baseball
Smith, Dean	Basketball HoF
Smith, Dr. Hamilton	Science
Smith, Elinor	Aviation
Smith, Elmo	Governors
Smith, F. E.	Celebrities
Smith, Francis Hopkins	Artists
Smith, Frank	Hockey HoF
Smith, Frederick W.	Business
Smith, George & Virginia	Cartoonists
Smith, Gerrit	Celebrities
Smith, Greg	General Sports
Smith, Harsen	Business
Smith, Hoke	U.S. V.P. & Cabinet
Smith, Horton	General Sports
Smith, Ian	Heads of State
Smith, Ida B. Wise	Celebrities
Smith, J. Gregory	Governors
Smith, Jaclyn	Entertainers (Current)
Smith, James	Revolutionary War
Smith, James Y.	Governors
Smith, Joe	Entertainers (Vintage)
Smith, John	Revolutionary War
Smith, Joseph	Celebrities
Smith, Kate	Entertainers (Vintage)
Smith, L. C.	Business
Smith, Maggie	Entertainers (Current)
Smith, Martha	Entertainers (Current)
Smith, Melancton	Revolutionary War
Smith, Michael	Astronauts
Smith, Nels H.	Governors
Smith, R. "Hooley"	Hockey HoF
Smith, Richard	Revolutionary War
Smith, Richard (Rev)	Celebrities
Smith, Robert	U.S. V.P. & Cabinet
Smith, Robyn	General Sports
Smith, Samuel	Revolutionary War
Smith, Samuel Francis	Authors
Smith, Sydney	Cartoonists
Smith, Thomas	Hockey HoF
Smith, Walter B.	Military
Smithers, Jan	Entertainers (Current)
Smothers Bros. (both)	Entertainers (Current)
Smuts, Jan Christian	Heads of State
Smythe, Conn	Hockey HoF
Smythe, Reg	Cartoonists
Snead, Sam	Golf HoF
Snead, Sam	General Sports
Snell, Dr. George D.	Science
Snell, Peter	General Sports
Sneva, Tom	General Sports
Snider, Edwin "Duke"	Baseball
Snow, C. P.	Authors
Snow, Hank	Country Music Stars
Snyder, Cory	Baseball
Snyder, Simon	Governors
Soar, "Hank"	Baseball
Soarez, Alana	Entertainers (Current)
Soddy, Frederick	Science
Soglow, Otto	Cartoonists
Soles, P. J.	Entertainers (Current)
Soltau, Gordon	Football
Solzhenitsyn, Alex.	Authors
Somers, Suzanne	Entertainers (Current)
Sommer, Elke	Entertainers (Current)
Sommers, Joanne	Entertainers (Current)
Sondheim, Stephen	Composers
Sontag, Susan	Authors
Sooter, Rudy	Country Music Stars
Sopwith, Thos. O. M.	Aviation
Sothern, Ann	Entertainers (Vintage)
Sothern, Ann	Entertainers (Current)
Sothern, E. A.	Entertainers (Vintage)
Soto, Mario	Baseball
Souchock, Steve	Baseball
Soul, Richard	Entertainers (Current)
Soult, Nicolas Jean	Revolutionary War
Sousa, John Philip	Composers
Soustelle, Jacques	Heads of State
Southampton, 1st Earl of	Celebrities
Southcott, Joanna	Celebrities

Southey, Robert	Authors
Sovine, Red	Country Music Stars
Soyer, Raphael	Artists
Spaak, Paul-Henri	Heads of State
Spaatz, Carl	Aviation
Spahn, Warren	Baseball
Spalanzani, Lazzaro	Science
Spalding, Albert G.	Baseball
Sparks, Chuncey	Governors
Sparks, Ned	Entertainers (Vintage)
Sparks, William E.	Military
Sparv, Camilla	Entertainers (Current)
Speake, Bob	Baseball
Speaker, Tris	Baseball
Speakes, Larry	U.S. V.P. & Cabinet
Spears, Ron	Football
Speed, James	U.S. V.P. & Cabinet
Speed, John Gilmer	Authors
Speer, Albert	Military
Speidel, Hans	Military
Spelling, Aaron	Entertainers (Current)
Spellman, Francis Card'l	Celebrities
Spencer, John P.	Heads of State
Spencer, John C.	U.S. V.P. & Cabinet
Spender, Stephen	Authors
Spenser, Tim	Country Music Stars
Sperry, Elmer A.	Science
Sperry, Roger	Science
Spielberg, David	Entertainers (Current)
Spielberg, Steven	Entertainers (Current)
Spillane, Mickey	Authors
Spink, J.G. Taylor	Baseball
Spinks, Leon	Boxing
Spinner, Francis Elias	U.S. V.P. & Cabinet
Spitz, Mark	General Sports
Splittorff, Paul	Baseball
Spock, Dr. Benjamin	Science
Spofford, Harriet P.	Authors
Spong, Hilda	Entertainers (Vintage)
Spooner, Karl	Baseball
Sprague, Charles A.	Governors
Spring, Sherwood C.	Astronauts
Springer, Robert C.	Astronauts
Springfield, Rick	Rock
Springsteen, Bruce	Rock
Spruance, Raymond A.	Military
Spurrier, Steve	Football
Squibb, Edward R.	Business
Squier, Emma	Authors
St. Clair, Arthur	Military
St. Cyr, Lili	Entertainers (Vintage)
St. Denis, Ruth	Entertainers (Vintage)
St. Jacques, Ramond	Entertainers (Current)
St. John, Jill	Entertainers (Current)
St. John, Lynn	Basketball HoF
St. Johns, Adela Rogers	Authors
St. Vincent, John J.	Military
Stabler, Ken	Football
Stack, Robert	Entertainers (Current)
Stack, Rose Marie B.	Entertainers (Current)
Stacpoole, Henry	Authors
Stadler, Craig	General Sports
Stadlman, Anthony	Aviation
Stafford, Jo	Entertainers (Current)
Stafford, Robert T.	Governors
Stafford, Thomas P.	Astronauts
Stagg, Amos Alonzo	Football
Stahley, Skip	General Sports
Stainback, George "Tuck"	Baseball
Staley, Gerry	Baseball
Stalin, Joseph	Heads of State
Stalin, Svetlana	Celebrities
Stallone, Sylvester	Entertainers (Current)
Stamp, Terence	Entertainers (Current)
Stanbery, Henry	U.S. V.P. & Cabinet
Stander, Lionel	Entertainers (Vintage)
Standish, Myles	Revolutionary War
Stanfel, Dick	Football
Stanford, Leland	Business
Stanford, R. C.	Governors
Stanhope, Edward	Military

Stanhope, Hester, Lady	Celebrities
Stanhope, Philip H.	Authors
Stanhope, Phil.H.,Earl of	Celebrities
Stanislas II (Pol)	Heads of State
Stanley, Allen	Hockey HoF
Stanley, Gerry	Baseball
Stanley, Henry Morton	Celebrities
Stanley, Henry Capt.	Military
Stanley, R. "Barney"	Hockey HoF
Stanley, Wendell M.	Science
Stansbury, Howard	Military
Stanton, Edwin M.	U.S. V.P. & Cabinet
Stanton, Elizabeth Cady	Celebrities
Stanton, Frank, Dr.	Business
Stanton, Harry Dean	Entertainers (Current)
Stanwyck, Barbara	Entertainers (Current)
Stapleton, Jean	Entertainers (Current)
Stapleton, Maureen	Entertainers (Current)
Stapp, John Col.	Military
Starbuck, JoJo	General Sports
Stargell, Willie	Baseball
Stark, Harold R.	Military
Stark, John	Revolutionary War
Starker, Janos	Entertainers (Current)
Starr, Bart	Football
Starr, Dick	Baseball
Starr, Ringo	Rock
Starrett, Charles	Entertainers (Vintage)
Starry, Donald A.	Military
Stassen, Harold	Governors
Statler, Ellsworth M.	Business
Statlers, The	Country Music Stars
Staubach, Roger	Football
Stautner, Ernie	Football
Stead, Wm. Thomas	Authors
Steele, Bob	Entertainers (Vintage)
Steele, Karen	Entertainers (Current)
Steele, Richard	Authors
Steely Dan	Rock
Steenburgen, Mary	Entertainers (Current)
Stefensson, Vilhjalmur	Celebrities
Steffens, Lincoln	Authors
Steib, Dave	Baseball
Steichen, Edward J.	Artists
Steig, William	Cartoonists
Steiger, Rod	Entertainers (Current)
Stein, Gertrude	Authors
Steinbach, Terry	Baseball
Steinbeck, John	Authors
Steinbrenner, George M.	Baseball
Steinem, Gloria	Celebrities
Steinhoff, J. "Mickey"	Aviation
Steinmetz, Christian	Basketball HoF
Steinmetz, Charles P.	Science
Steinway, Henry	Business
Sten, Anna	Entertainers (Vintage)
Stendhal(Marie H. Beyle)	Authors
Stengel, Casey	Baseball
Stephen, Adam	Revolutionary War
Stephens, Woody	General Sports
Stephenson, George	Science
Stephenson, Robert	Science
Stephenson, Jan	General Sports
Stephenson, Riggs	Baseball
Stepp, Hans	Aviation
Steppenwolf	Rock
Sterling, Andrew B.	Composers
Stern, Isaac	Entertainers (Vintage)
Sterrett, Cliff	Cartoonists
Stettinius, Edward R.Jr.	U.S. V.P. & Cabinet
Steuben, Friedrick von	Military
Stevens, Andrew	Entertainers (Current)
Stevens, Cat	Rock
Stevens, Connie	Entertainers (Current)
Stevens, Craig	Entertainers (Current)
Stevens, Ebenezer	Revolutionary War
Stevens, Inger	Entertainers (Vintage)
Stevens, John	Revolutionary War
Stevens, Johnny	Baseball
Stevens, John Paul (SC)	Celebrities
Stevens, K. T.	Entertainers (Vintage)

Stevens, Ray	Country Music Stars
Stevens, Stella	Entertainers (Current)
Stevens, Warren	Entertainers (Current)
Stevenson, Adlai E.	U.S. V.P. & Cabinet
Stevenson, Rob't L.	Authors
Stewart, Alexander T.	Business
Stewart, Jackie	General Sports
Stewart, James	Entertainers (Vintage)
Stewart, John	Hockey HoF
Stewart, John A.	Business
Stewart, Nelson	Hockey HoF
Stewart, Payne	General Sports
Stewart, Potter (SC)	Celebrities
Stewart, Robert L.	Astronauts
Stewart, Rod	Rock
Stewart, Sammy	Baseball
Stewart, Wynn	Country Music Stars
Stickles, Monty	Football
Stieglitz, Alfred	Artists
Still, Wm. Grant	Composers
Stills, Stephen	Rock
Stilwell, Joseph W.	Military
Stimson, Henry L.	U.S. V.P. & Cabinet
Sting	Rock
Stirling, Wm. Alex. Lord	Revolutionary War
Stockton, Dave	General Sports
Stockton, Frank R.	Authors
Stockton, R. F.	Military
Stockton, Richard	Revolutionary War
Stoddert, Benjamin	U.S. V.P. & Cabinet
Stoker, Bram	Authors
Stokes, Carl Burton	Celebrities
Stokowski, Leopold	Entertainers (Vintage)
Stolle, Bruno	Aviation
Stolle, Fred	Tennis HoF
Stoltz, Eric	Entertainers (Current)
Stone, Dwight	General Sports
Stone, Fred	Entertainers (Vintage)
Stone, Harlan Fiske (SC)	Celebrities
Stone, Irving	Authors
Stone, Lewis S.	Entertainers (Vintage)
Stone, Lucy	Celebrities
Stone, Paula	Entertainers (Vintage)
Stone, Thomas	Revolutionary War
Stonebreaker, Steve	Football
Stoneham, Horace C.	Baseball
Stoopnagle, Colonel	Entertainers (Vintage)
Stoppard, Tom	Authors
Storch, Larry	Entertainers (Current)
Storey, R. A. "Red"	Hockey HoF
Storm, Gale	Entertainers (Vintage)
Storm, Tempest	Entertainers (Vintage)
Story, Joseph (SC)	Celebrities
Stottlemyre, Mel	Baseball
Stoughton, William	Revolutionary War
Stout, Rex	Authors
Stowe,Harriet Beecher	Authors
Straight, Beatrice	Entertainers (Current)
Stranahan, Frank	General Sports
Strange, Curtis	General Sports
Strasberg, Lee	Entertainers (Current)
Strasberg. Susan	Entertainers (Current)
Stratten, Dorothy	Entertainers (Vintage)
Stratton, Monty	Baseball
Stratton, William G.	Governors
Straub, Robert W.	Governors
Straus, Jack	Business
Straus, Oscar	Composers
Strause, Charles	Composers
Strauss, Adolf	Military
Strauss, Franz Josef	Heads of State
Strauss, Franz Josef	Celebrities
Strauss, Johann, Jr.	Composers
Strauss, Johann	Composers
Strauss, Richard	Composers
Strauss, Robert	U.S. V.P. & Cabinet
Strauss, Robert	Entertainers (Vintage)
Stravinsky, Igor	Composers
Straw, Ezekiel A.	Governors
Strawberry, Darryl	Baseball
Streep, Meryl	Entertainers (Current)
Streisand, Barbra	Entertainers (Current)
Stribling, T. S.	Authors
Stritch, Sam'l Card.	Celebrities
Strode, Woody	Football
Stromberg, Hunt	Entertainers (Vintage)
Strong, Caleb	Revolutionary War
Strong, Ken	Football
Strong, William (SC)	Celebrities
Stroud Twins	Entertainers (Vintage)
Struthers, Sally	Entertainers (Current)
Stuart, Alexander H. H.	U.S. V.P. & Cabinet
Stuart, Bruce	Hockey HoF
Stuart, Gilbert	Artists
Stuart, Hod	Hockey HoF
Stuhldreher, Harry	Football
Sturge, Joseph	Business
Sturges, John	Entertainers (Current)
Stydahar, Joe	Football
Styne, Julie	Composers
Styron, William	Authors
Styx	Rock
Suchet, Louis G.,Duc d'A	Revolutionary War
Suggs, Louise	Golf HoF
Suharto, General	Heads of State
Sullavan, Margaret	Entertainers (Vintage)
Sullivan, Barry	Entertainers (Current)
Sullivan, Danny	General Sports
Sullivan, Ed	Entertainers (Vintage)
Sullivan, James	Revolutionary War
Sullivan, John	Revolutionary War
Sullivan, John L.	Boxing
Sullivan, Kathryn D.	Astronauts
Sullivan, Pat	Cartoonists
Sullivan, Pat	Football
Sullivan, Sir Arthur	Composers
Sullivan, Susan	Entertainers (Current)
Sullivan, William	Revolutionary War
Sully, Thomas	Artists
Sulzberger, Art Ochs	Business
Sulzer, William	Governors
Summer, Donna	Rock
Summerfield, Arthur E.	U.S. V.P. & Cabinet
Summerville, Slim	Entertainers (Vintage)
Sumners, Rosalynn	General Sports
Sun Yat Sen	Heads of State
Sunday, Wm. A. "Billy"	Celebrities
Sundberg, Jim	Baseball
Supertramp	Rock
Suppe, Franz von	Composers
Surhoff, B.J.	Baseball
Susann, Jacqueline	Authors
Sutcliffe, Rick	Baseball
Sutherland, George (SC)	Celebrities
Sutherland, Donald	Entertainers (Current)
Sutherland, Capt. James	Hockey HoF
Sutherland, Joan	Entertainers (Current)
Sutro, Adolph H. J.	Celebrities
Sutter, Bruce	Baseball
Sutter, John A.	Celebrities
Sutton, Don	Baseball
Sutton, Grady	Entertainers (Vintage)
Sutton, Hal	General Sports
Svenson, Bo	Entertainers (Current)
Swain, Bill	Football
Swain, Dale	Baseball
Swann, Lynn	Football
Swann, Thomas	Governors
Swanson, Claude	U.S. V.P. & Cabinet
Swanson, Gloria	Entertainers (Vintage)
Swayne, Noah H. (SC)	Celebrities
Swayze, John Cam.	Entertainers (Current)
Swearingen, John	Business
Sweeney, Walter C.	Military
Sweet, Blanche	Entertainers (Vintage)
Swigert, John L. Jr.	Astronauts
Swinburne, Algernon C.	Authors
Swindell, Greg	Baseball
Swinnerton, James	Cartoonists
Swit, Loretta	Entertainers (Current)
Switzer, Barry	Football
Swope, Herbert Bayard	Authors

Sylvia	Entertainers (Current)
Symanski, John	Football
Symington, Stuart	U.S. V.P. & Cabinet
Symmes, John Cleves	Revolutionary War
Szell, George	Entertainers (Current)
Szold, Henrietta	Celebrities
T Hooft, Visser	Celebrities
Taber, Robert	Entertainers (Vintage)
Tabler, Pat	Baseball
Taft, Charles P.	Celebrities
Taft, Helen Manning	Celebrities
Taft, Henry W.	Celebrities
Taft, Lorado	Artists
Taft, Wm. Howard	U.S. Presidents
Tagore, Rabindranath	Authors
Taine, John(Eric T. Bell)	Authors
Talbert, William F.	Tennis HoF
Talbot, H. F.	Science
Talbot, Lyle	Entertainers (Vintage)
Talbot, Nita	Entertainers (Current)
Talcott, Joseph	Revolutionary War
Talking Heads	Rock
Tallchief, Maria	Entertainers (Vintage)
Talley, Marion	Entertainers (Vintage)
Talleyrand, Chas. M.	Heads of State
Tallmadge, Benjamin	Military
Talmadge, Benjamin	Revolutionary War
Talmadge, Constance	Entertainers (Vintage)
Talmadge, Eugene	Governors
Talmadge, Eugene	Governors
Tamblyn, Russ	Entertainers (Current)
Tambor, Jeffrey	Entertainers (Current)
Tamiroff, Akim	Entertainers (Vintage)
Tanana, Frank	Baseball
Tandy, Jessica	Entertainers (Current)
Taney, Roger B. (SC)	Celebrities
Tanner, Chuck	Baseball
Tanner, Henry Ossawa	Artists
Tansman, Alexandre	Composers
Tarasov, Anatoli	Hockey HoF
Tarbell, Ida	Authors
Tarkanian, Jerry	General Sports
Tarkenton, Fran	Football
Tarkington, Booth	Authors
Tarleton, Banastre	Revolutionary War
Tarnower, Dr. Herman	Celebrities
Tashman, Lilyan	Entertainers (Vintage)
Tate, Henry, Sir	Celebrities
Tattersall, Richard	Business
Tatum, "Goose"	General Sports
Tatum, Edward L.	Science
Tatum, Jack	Football
Taufflieb, Gen.	Military
Tawes, J. Millard	Governors
Tayback, Vic	Entertainers (Current)
Taylor, Bayard	Authors
Taylor, Bernard	Boxing
Taylor, Charley	Football
Taylor, Chuck	Basketball HoF
Taylor, Deems	Composers
Taylor, Elizabeth	Entertainers (Current)
Taylor, Estelle	Entertainers (Vintage)
Taylor, F. "Cyclone"	Hockey HoF
Taylor, George	Revolutionary War
Taylor, H. C.	Military
Taylor, James	Rock
Taylor, Jim	Football
Taylor, Joan	Entertainers (Vintage)
Taylor, John H.	Golf HoF
Taylor, Laurette	Entertainers (Vintage)
Taylor, Lawrence	Football
Taylor, Lionel	Football
Taylor, Mary	Country Music Stars
Taylor, Maxwell D.	Military
Taylor, Robert	Entertainers (Vintage)
Taylor, Rod	Entertainers (Current)
Taylor, Tony	Baseball
Taylor, Zachary	U.S. Presidents
Taylor-Young, Leigh	Entertainers (Current)
Tchaikovsky, Piotr I.	Composers
Te Kanawa, Kiri Dame	Entertainers (Current)
Teague, Bertha F.	Basketball HoF
Tears For Fears	Rock
Teasdale, Veree	Entertainers (Vintage)
Tebbetts, "Birdie"	Baseball
Tedrow, Irene	Entertainers (Current)
Teller, Edward	Science
Teller, Henry M.	U.S. V.P. & Cabinet
Temin, Dr. Howard M.	Science
Tempest, Marie	Entertainers (Vintage)
Temple, Shirley	Entertainers (Current)
Templeton, Ben	Cartoonists
Templeton, Fay	Entertainers (Vintage)
Templeton, Garry	Baseball
Temptations	Rock
Ten Broeck, Abraham	Revolutionary War
Tenace, Gene	Baseball
Tennant, Veronica	Entertainers (Vintage)
Tenniel, Sir John	Artists
Tennyson,Alfred Lord	Authors
Teresa, Mother	Celebrities
Terhune, Alfr. Payson	Authors
Terkel, Studs	Authors
Terry, Bill	Baseball
Terry, Dr. Luther	Celebrities
Terry, Ellen	Entertainers (Vintage)
Terry, Fred	Entertainers (Vintage)
Terry, Paul	Cartoonists
Terry, Phillip	Entertainers (Vintage)
Terry, Ralph	Baseball
Terwilliger, Wayne	Baseball
Tesla, Nikola	Science
Testaverde, Vinny	Football
Tetard, J.	Aviation
Tetrazzini, Luisa	Entertainers (Vintage)
Tewell, Doug	General Sports
Tewksbury, Bob	Baseball
Thackery, William M.	Authors
Thagard, Norman E.	Astronauts
Thalberg, Irving	Entertainers (Vintage)
Thant, U	Heads of State
Thatcher, Margaret	Heads of State
Thaves, Bob	Cartoonists
Thaw, Harry K.	Business
Thaxter, Celia	Entertainers (Vintage)
Thayer, Abbott	Artists
Thayer, Silvanus	Military
Theismann, Joe	Football
Thiers, A.	Heads of State
Thiess, Ursula	Entertainers (Vintage)
Thieu, Nguyen Van	Heads of State
Thinnis, Roy	Entertainers (Current)
Thomas, Ambroise	Composers
Thomas, Aurealius	Football
Thomas, Betty	Entertainers (Current)
Thomas, Danny	Entertainers (Current)
Thomas, Duane	Football
Thomas, Dylan	Authors
Thomas, Heather	Entertainers (Current)
Thomas, Isaiah	Revolutionary War
Thomas, John	Revolutionary War
Thomas, John	General Sports
Thomas, John Charles	Entertainers (Vintage)
Thomas, Kurt	Entertainers (Current)
Thomas, Lowell	Celebrities
Thomas, Marlo	Entertainers (Current)
Thomas, Norman	Celebrities
Thomas, Olive	Entertainers (Vintage)
Thomas, Philip Evan	Business
Thomas, Richard	Entertainers (Current)
Thompson Twins	Rock
Thompson, Benj. (Rumford)	Revolutionary War
Thompson, C. R. "Tiny"	Hockey HoF
Thompson, Charles	Celebrities
Thompson, David	General Sports
Thompson, Dorothy	Authors
Thompson, Gordon	Entertainers (Current)
Thompson, Hank	Country Music Stars
Thompson, J. Lee	Football
Thompson, Jason	Baseball
Thompson, Jacob	U.S. V.P. & Cabinet

490

Wright, Richard — Authors
Wright, Theresa — Entertainers (Current)
Wright, Turbutt — Revolutionary War
Wright, Warren — General Sports
Wright, Wilbur — Aviation
Wrigley, William, Jr. — Business
Wriothesley(Southampton) — Celebrities
Wunder, George — Celebrities
Wyatt, Jane — Entertainers (Current)
Wyatt, Whitlow — Baseball
Wyche, Sam — Football
Wyeth, Andrew — Artists
Wyeth, Jamie — Artists
Wyeth, N. C. — Artists
Wyler, Gretchen — Entertainers (Current)
Wylie, Philip — Authors
Wyman, Jane — Entertainers (Vintage)
Wyman, Jane — Entertainers (Current)
Wymore, Patrice — Entertainers (Vintage)
Wyndham, Charles Sir — Entertainers (Vintage)
Wyndham, Mary Lady — Entertainers (Vintage)
Wynette, Tammy — Country Music Stars
Wynn, Early — Baseball
Wynn, Ed — Entertainers (Vintage)
Wynn, Keenan — Entertainers (Current)
Wynter, Dana — Entertainers (Current)
Wynyard, Dianna — Entertainers (Vintage)
Wythe, George — Revolutionary War
Yalon, Rosalyn S. — Science
Yamaer, George — Celebrities
Yamamoto, Isoroku — Military
Yamasaki, Minoru — Celebrities
Yamashita, Tomoyuki — Military
Yang, Dr. C. N. — Science
Yankovic, Frank — Entertainers (Vintage)
Yarborough, Cale — General Sports
Yardley, George — General Sports
Yarnell, Lorine — Entertainers (Current)
Yastrzemski, Carl — Baseball
Yates, Peter W. — Revolutionary War
Yawkey, Mrs. Jean — Baseball
Yawkey, Tom — Baseball
Yeager, Chuck — Aviation
Yeager, Jeana — Aviation
Yeager, Steve — Baseball
Yeates, Jasper — Revolutionary War
Yeats, Jack Butler — Authors
Yeats, Wm. Butler — Authors
Yerby, Frank — Authors
Yes — Rock
Yorgesson, Yogi — Country Music Stars
York, Alvin Sgt. — Military
York, Michael — Entertainers (Current)
York, Rudy — Baseball
York, Susanna — Entertainers (Current)
Yorty, Sam — Celebrities
Yost, Eddie — Baseball
Yost, Fielding H. — Football
Youmans, Floyd — Baseball
Young, Alan — Entertainers (Vintage)
Young, Andrew — Celebrities
Young, Art — Cartoonists
Young, Brigham — Celebrities
Young, Burt — Entertainers (Current)

Young, Chic — Cartoonists
Young, Claude "Buddy" — Football
Young, Coleman — Celebrities
Young, Cy — Baseball
Young, Faron — Country Music Stars
Young, Henry E. — Civil War
Young, Jim — Football
Young, John — Astronauts
Young, Lester — Entertainers (Vintage)
Young, Loretta — Entertainers (Vintage)
Young, Lyman — Cartoonists
Young, Neil — Rock
Young, Owen D. — Business
Young, Robert — Entertainers (Vintage)
Young, Steve — Football
Young, Whitney — Celebrities
Youngblood, Jack — Football
Youngdahl, Luther — Governors
Younger, Bob — Celebrities
Younger, Cole — Celebrities
Younger, Tank — Football
Youngman, Henny — Entertainers (Vintage)
Yount, Robin — Baseball
ZZ Top — Rock
Zabach, Florian — Entertainers (Current)
Zadora, Pia — Entertainers (Current)
Zaharias, "Babe" D. — General Sports
Zaharias, Babe Didrikson — Golf HoF
Zahn, Geoff — Baseball
Zais, Melvin — Military
Zale, Tony — Boxing
Zangwill, Israel — Authors
Zanuck, Richard Darryl — Entertainers (Current)
Zapata, Emiliano — Celebrities
Zarate, Carlos — Boxing
Zayak, Elaine — General Sports
Zellerbach, J. D. — Business
Zeman, Jacklyn — Entertainers (Current)
Zeppelin, Ferdinand von — Aviation
Zerbe, Anthony — Entertainers (Current)
Zernial, Gus — Baseball
Zhukov, Georgi K. — Military
Ziegfeld, Florenz — Entertainers (Vintage)
Ziegler, George M. — Civil War
Ziegler, Karl — Science
Ziegler, Ronald L. — U.S. V.P. & Cabinet
Zimbalist, Efrem Sr. — Entertainers (Vintage)
Zimbalist, Efrem Jr. — Entertainers (Current)
Zimbalist, Stephanie — Entertainers (Current)
Zimmer, Norma — Entertainers (Current)
Ziolkowski, Korczak — Artists
Zisk, Richie — Baseball
Zivic, Fritzie — Boxing
Zmed, Adrian — Entertainers (Current)
Zoeller, Fuzzy — General Sports
Zola, Emile — Authors
Zollicoffer, Felix K. — Civil War
Zorina, Vera — Entertainers (Vintage)
Zorn, Jim — Football
Zuazo, Hernan Siles — Heads of State
Zukor, Adolph — Entertainers (Vintage)
Zumwalt, Elmo — Military
Zweig, Stefan — Authors
Zworykin, Vladimir — Science

493

Notes

Notes

Notes

Notes

Notes

Notes

Notes

Notes

Notes

Notes

Notes